Rural Economy and Society in North-western Europe, 500–2000

Social Relations: Property and Power

Rural Economy and Society in North-western Europe, 500–2000

Social Relations: Property and Power

Edited by
Bas van Bavel and Richard Hoyle

in association with
Stefan Brakensiek, Piet van Cruyningen,
Christopher Dyer, Mats Morell
and Nadine Vivier

BREPOLS

Cover illustrations

Top illustration: the castle of Schelderode, a small village in Flanders near Ghent (Belgium) (photograph E. Thoen, 2007). The castle dates from 1864–5 and is built in neo-gothic style. The site and the castle garden are the direct successor of a large medieval manorial and seigneurial centre called since the thirteenth century the 'Land van Rode', a powerful seigneurie that dates back to the tenth century. In the twentieth century the castle was owned for a long period by the Plissart family who played an important role in the politics of the village as mayors of Schelderode.

Bottom illustration: *(Uns) sires et si hommes*. Illustration in the 'Veil rentier', an inventory of the estates of the lord of Pamele (Oudenaarde, Flanders, Belgium) written around 1275. Royal Library of Brussels, Ms 1175, fo.14v.

ISBN 978-2-503-53050-5
D/2010/0095/126

CONTENTS

LIST OF ILLUSTRATIONS

LIST OF MAPS*

* The majority of the maps are orientation maps. They are necessarily superficial and are only intended to clarify the text. They roughly locate the most important place names mentioned in the text.

LIST OF TABLES AND FIGURES

SERIES INTRODUCTION

A new rural history of north-western Europe

This book is the first of a four-volume series dealing with the long term evolution of rural society in north-western Europe from the early middle ages until the end of the twentieth century. In this series an international team of researchers explains how the people of the countries surrounding the North Sea organised agricultural production and trade, and how the rural economy and society of these countries was repeatedly transformed, through periods of shortfall and plenty, poverty and wealth, over the 1500 years between 500 and 2000. The comparative and long term approach of the series reveals processes of convergence and divergence, stagnation and change.

The impact of rural societies on economic and social development cannot be underestimated. Until the nineteenth century, western European economies remained overwhelmingly agricultural. Wealth and political power were normally measured in land. Elite life in the countryside frequently provided the aspirational cultural norm. The development of the industrial world was in many ways closely related to changes in the countryside. It is therefore all the more surprising that syntheses of the history of European agriculture and rural society are so few and far between. The past few decades have seen an enormous increase in our knowledge and understanding of European rural societies and economies, but most of what has been written in that time has been limited by the borders of a single modern state (as, for example, the multi-volume rural histories of England, France and Sweden). The exception was the pioneering (but now dated) book by B. H. Slicher Van Bath, *The agrarian history of western Europe, A.D. 500–1850,* first published in Dutch in 1960. Van Bath covered more or less the same area as is dealt with in this series, and adopted a similar comparative and long-term approach, although limited to the period before 1850 and focussing mainly on agriculture from a technical and 'traditional' productivist point of view. He was less concerned with such social and structural aspects of the rural society as family structures, property and power relations and the relationships of markets and consumers. Van Bath's synthesis was undoubtedly a brilliant and enduring piece of writing, but today, a single-authored synthesis seems an almost impossible task. For this reason, our series is the result of the pooled effort of more than 70 specialists in the field. Our aim is to bring to a new readership – undergraduates, graduates, researchers, the public and, importantly, policy makers in government and non-governmental organisations – a new and comprehensive narrative reflecting many new scholarly interpretations, showing the slow unfolding of European rural history and the deep historical roots of the rural economies and societies of the present day.

The features of the series

The approach of the four volumes is not a 'classical' chronological one, but is thematic, which enables us to focus on developments in rural areas from four crucial and interrelated perspectives, namely: land use and productivity; production, distribution and consumption; family formation, income and labour; and finally property and power relations.

This thematic structure combines three main features. First, it links important research results revealing the macro-economic trends with studies focussing on the regional and local levels. By doing so, the rural producers themselves come to the fore, and we see their constant struggle with environmental and structural limits to which they responded by adapting their production, family and market strategies. Even within geographical and political boundaries, differences between regions and interregional comparisons are, when and where possible, taken into account.

Secondly, each volume presents a long term view. In order to gain an insight into the origins of the north-western European society of today, it is necessary to go as far back as the early middle ages. It was this period (and not the 'Pirennean' watershed of the year 1000) that marked the start of a new European society, at least and especially in the North Sea area, with the fundamental break with the economic, social and political structures of the Roman period taking place in the early Middle Ages.

Third, the main focus of each volume is on the evolution of the ways in which the inhabitants of the countryside managed to produce food for themselves, for local and distant markets, for different tables and tastes. This is analysed from the four different angles we outlined before. Each volume can be read on its own, as a meaningful narrative from one particular point of view within an all-encompassing rural history.

Four volumes, four themes

The series is structured around the four themes of land use and productivity; production, distribution and consumption; family formation, income and labour; and finally property and power relations.

This volume on *Social Relations: Property and Power* deals with the importance of property structures over land and the question of who controlled and secured the income derived from land and the profits of farming. This is a complex question to pose because the land has been subjected to competing claims, varying from region to region: claims from the peasants themselves, claims from different landowning classes and from the central government. Likewise, landowners, the church and government all struggled to secure their share of the farmer's profits – except now, of course, the state subsidizes agriculture rather than the other way round. This volume also looks at the interaction between society and external changes, such as the rise and fall of the market, trends in population and European integration.

In *Struggling with the Environment: Land Use and Production* we consider how, when, to what degree and within what structural boundaries land was used for agriculture. The book focuses on the evolution of land use: why and how was land reclaimed and used? Which actors played a part in this process? But, what were the environmental and social limits of cultivation, and how did these alter with changes in climate, market demand and technical innovation? Production techniques and production systems are scrutinized especially in the light of alleged 'agricultural' and 'green' revolutions.

The Agro-food Market: Production, Distribution and Consumption aims at unravelling the changing character of the agro-food chain, from the field to the table. The path from a self-supporting way of life to the present complex forms of market integration in the global world was far from uniform and linear. This volume explores how food production, market structures and market mechanisms changed over time and differed between regions and countries within the North Sea area.

The final volume – on *Making a living: Family Income and Labour* – deals with the interaction between production, reproduction and labour in rural societies. It investigates the ways in which resources became available to the rural family and its members, and the strategies which were employed to generate these resources. Its goal is to interpret the regional and chronological diversity of household formation and the economic behaviour of its members in relation to labour organisation.

The extent of 'the North Sea area'

As mentioned, in this book series an international team has collaborated in order to explain how people in the countryside surrounding the North Sea organised rural production. Taking the North Sea area as our research area is easy to defend.

First, the area shows many similar features which run over the borders of nations. Like the Mediterranean, the North Sea can be considered as a unity. The countries and regions surrounding it share several physical geographic characteristics. The whole area enjoys a moderate maritime climate and it mostly consists of lowlands with some low mountain ranges. In most of the area, agriculture is dominated by middling and large holdings.

Secondly, the area is an economic and cultural unity because of the strong commercial relations between the countries bordering on the North Sea, enabled by easy and inexpensive transportation. People, technology and ideas traveled smoothly over the North Sea. Over the past millennium and a half, the countries connected by it have progressed from being a periphery of the Mediterranean world to forming the core of the modern world economy. Parts of the North Sea area have played an key role in European economic history. Flanders and Brabant were among the most developed regions in Europe in the Middle Ages. The Dutch Republic was the leading economic power in Europe in the seventeenth century, Britain from the eighteenth century to the early twentieth century. The industrial revolution began in Britain and was followed by Belgium. From an early date, these areas not only had a highly developed trade and industry, but also a highly developed and commercialized agriculture. It was this which enabled these countries to escape the Malthusian trap of population outrunning food supplies at an early date.

The North Sea area includes a variety of landscapes with different rural histories: from regions with a long tradition of extensive agriculture to areas where intensive husbandry was already established in the Middle Ages; from regions where low labour productivity lasted until the late nineteenth century to areas where it was replaced at an early date by labour efficient production systems. But because of the intense contacts between regions along the North Sea littoral, prosperous regions gradually influenced the development of agriculture in more backward areas. And because of common characteristics in their agriculture and transport facilities, the countries around the North Sea often were competitors (for instance Denmark and the Netherlands, both trying to sell their butter into the British market in the nineteenth century). This makes the North Sea area a very rewarding one to study from a comparative perspective.

Some practical choices had to be made in order to determine the borders of the area under consideration. Included within our scheme are the following regions: the Low Countries (Belgium and the Netherlands); England, Wales and Scotland (Ireland, further away from the North Sea, is only taken into account in particular cases); Denmark and the southern coastal areas of Sweden and Norway; north-west Germany, defined as the states of Schleswig-Holstein, Lower Saxony, Saxony-Anhalt and North Rhine-Westphalia, all belonging to the 'Norddeutsche Tiefebene' and north-western France, defined as the area north of the Loire river, stretching from Brittany in the west to the Vosges in the east, including Berry and a part of Burgundy in the south, the core of which is formed by Brittany, Picardy, Normandy and Ile-de-France.

Structure of each volume

Each volume is structured along a combination of chronological, regional, and comparative lines. Both the introduction and the concluding final chapter of each book, written by the volume editors, offer the comparative perspective. The early middle ages (500–1000), a period that is characterised by the scarcity of source material, is the object of a separate chapter, followed by chapters that deal with the different regions under consideration (north-western France, the Britain, the Low Countries, North-west Germany and Scandinavia) during a specific time span (1000–1750, 1750–2000). These regional chapters were all written according to the same template to make the narratives genuinely comparable.

Acknowledgments

The initiative for this series was taken by a group of specialists in rural history who have now been collaborating for around fifteen years in the research group CORN (Comparative Rural History of the North Sea Area), which is sponsored by FWO, Research Foundation - Flanders.

We can reflect that scientific cooperation is never easy, and certainly not between eight countries, each with its own historiographical traditions and historical preoccupations. But cooperation is particularly challenging intellectually and it opens up so many unexpected new horizons. It has been both exciting and a great pleasure to discover that so many scholars were willing to share the pleasures, and sometimes also the difficulties, of this collective enterprise. Meetings were organised in all parts of the North Sea area, drafts were circulated innumerable times, discussed, rewritten, discussed again. The general editorial board is most grateful to the editors of the each of the four volumes and to all the participating authors for their invaluable individual and collective input into the common project. We wish also to express our gratitude to the FWO Research Foundation - Flanders and to Brepols Publishers, in particular Chris VandenBorre, for their long support of the Rural History of the North Sea Area.

THE MEMBERS OF THE GENERAL EDITORIAL BOARD:
ERIK THOEN (DIRECTOR)
BAS VAN BAVEL
YVES SEGERS
ERIC VANHAUTE
LEEN VAN MOLLE
Gent, Leuven and Utrecht, June 2010

PREFACE

As Erik Thoen and the other members of the general editorial board explain in their general introduction, this, the first to appear of the four volume CORN series, is not a work of original research but of synthesis. The essays it contains try to offer overviews of the state of our knowledge of rural power relationships in the countries surrounding the North Sea. The essays themselves are structured along similar lines to allow cross-country comparisons. The first section of each national chapter treats questions of ownership, power relations and the distribution of property, the second discusses the occupiers of the land and the third the role of government. Within those three sections, the same broad issues are considered in the same order which should allow cross-country comparisons to be made easily. Inevitably, the weight given to each section differs between chapters because the national historiographies on which we have to rely have themselves differed so greatly overtime. Hence we hope that this book will not only inform and encourage a new generation of scholarship, but that it will reveal some of the gaps in our knowledge and direct attention to where new research may profitably be carried out.

A few terms might usefully be explained. In this book, the owner of land whose tenants hold by servile or customary arrangements is called a *lord*. *Lords* usually also have some form of jurisdiction over their tenants, holding courts which their tenants are obliged to attend, and which often served to protect the lord's interests as well as offering a service to the tenants. Lords might also take their tenant's rent in the form of labour which enables them to cultivate their land kept in hand, their *demesnes*. The adjective we use throughout this book to describe this environment is seigneurial. *Landlords*, on the other hand, operate in free markets, taking commercial rents from their tenants who normally hold by tenancies of limited length. These tenants pay, for the most part, rents in cash. Whilst national usages vary, a *peasant* is normally taken to be a small-scale cultivator of the soil who draws on a limited amount of labour in addition to what his household can provide (although hired labour often lives in his household). A *farmer* differs from a *peasant* in terms of scale; but in addition a peasant aims for self-sufficiency with a small market surplus where a farmer is strongly orientated towards the provision of goods for the market. It is not to be denied that the word 'peasant' also has a much looser meaning as any inhabitant of the countryside, and it is possible to find commercially-minded figures who live off very small plots of land (usually referred to here as *smallholders*). A *freeholder* is a figure who owns his own land, but if he farms it himself, he is normally referred to as an owner-occupier. A freeholder does not owe rents or other obligations (other than the purely notional) to a lord or landlord: he therefore has full property rights in his land (although he may well be subject to communal systems of agriculture).

Many of the concepts which underpin this volume are discussed at greater length in the introduction.

In preparing the essays we have had had the willing assistance of many rural historians. We offer our thanks to all of them. In particular we offer our thanks to Chris Wickham for contributing the magisterial overview of a half millennium of north European history The national chapters have been drawn together by the editorial board for this volume, and they have fed drafts and ideas into the introduction and conclusion for the book. We have met in a succession of locations – Gregynog, Rome, Paris, Brussels and Utrecht more than once – often on the back of other conferences where some of us were speaking. The book therefore marks a joint endeavour which, as one might suppose, has had its frustrations but has also been marked by a great deal of personal and intellectual pleasure, not least the enjoyment of discovering what lies over the national fences with which all of us are prone to surround ourselves. At the end, Richard Hoyle drew the typescripts together into a book, prepared the introduction from the pooled drafts and drafted the conclusion.

Finally we offer our thanks to Chris VandenBorre of Brepols and, finally, of course, to Erik Thoen, whose idea this venture was and who will, we hope, enjoy if not entirely agree with this, the first fruits of his labours.

Bas van Bavel

Richard W. Hoyle

May 2010

CONTRIBUTORS

Bas van Bavel is Professor of Economic and Social History of the Middle Ages and coordinator of the university focus area 'Origins and Impacts of Institutions', at Utrecht University, the Netherlands.

Gérard Béaur is Director of Research at the CNRS, Professor at EHESS, Chair of the Centre de Recherches Historiques, France.

Stefan Brakensiek is Professor of Early Modern History at the University of Duisburg-Essen, Germany and editor of *Zeitschrift für Agrargeschichte und Agrarsoziologie*.

Paul Brassley is a Research Fellow in Rural History at the University of Exeter, UK.

Paul Brusse is researcher at the Research Institute of History and Culture at Utrecht University, the Netherlands.

Piet van Cruyningen is researcher at the Rural History Group of Wageningen University, the Netherlands.

Christopher Dyer is Professor of Regional and Local History in the Centre for English Local History at the University of Leicester, UK.

Richard Hoyle is Professor of Rural History at the University of Reading, UK and editor of *Agricultural History Review*.

Jean-Pierre Jessenne is Professor of Modern History at the University of Lille, France.

Gunter Mahlerwein is a freelance historian who works as a part-time lecturer at the University of Mainz, Germany.

François Menant is Professor of Medieval History at the Ecole Normale Supérieure in Paris, France.

Mats Morell is Professor of Economic History at Stockholm University, Sweden and editor of *Scandinavian Economic History Review*.

John Ragnar Myking is Professor of Medieval and Early Modern History at the University of Bergen and Bergen University College, Norway.

Mats Olsson is associate Professor at the Department of Economic History at Lund University, Sweden.

Carsten Porskrog Rasmussen is associate Professor of Early Modern History at the Aarhus University, Denmark.

Anton Schuurman is associate Professor in the Department of Rural History at Wageningen University and Research Centre, the Netherlands and co-chair of the Rural History Network at the European Social Science History Conference.

Erik Thoen is Professor of Economic and Environmental History at Ghent University, Belgium, co-ordinator of the CORN Network and director of the editorial board of the series.

Michael Turner is Professor of Economic History at the University of Hull, UK.

Eric Vanhaute is Professor of Economic History and World History at Ghent University, Belgium.

Leen Van Molle is Professor of Social History in the Department of History at the University of Leuven, Belgium and chairperson of ICAG (Interfaculty Centre for Agrarian History).

Nadine Vivier is Professor of Modern History at the University of Le Mans, France.

Christopher Wickham is Chichele Professor of Medieval History in the University of Oxford and a Fellow of All Souls College Oxford, UK.

1 Introduction: social relations, property and power in the North Sea area, 500–2000

Bas van BAVEL AND Richard HOYLE

in association with Stefan BRAKENSIEK, Piet van CRUYNINGEN, Christopher DYER, Mats MORELL and Nadine VIVIER

This volume focuses on the ownership of land, the exercise of power and the management of the rural societies of the countries facing the North Sea over the last 1500 years. This region is of especial interest because of its precocious development, its early escape from the Malthusian trap and the early eradication of intermittent hunger and starvation. In this volume we explain how these developments shaped – and were shaped – by the ways in which land was possessed and owned, the tenurial relationships between landlords and tenants, the employment relationships between farmers and labourers, and the relationship between rural society and the state, and how these relationships shifted and changed over time.

1.1 The character of the North Sea basin

Many authors have celebrated the innovative and 'progressive' farming of north-east France, Flanders, the Netherlands, Denmark and eastern England. From the eighteenth century onwards, writers have used these areas as exemplars of agricultural production. Historians have also described the advanced agricultural techniques employed, but usually within their own national traditions of historical writing and have generally not noted the similarities between countries. And, as they have usually confined themselves – as historians do – to 'their period', they have often not noted the successive episodes in which the rural inhabitants of this region were especially inventive and productive, from the thirteenth century to the twentieth. The story is not one of geographical uniformity. 'Progressive farming' has always existed alongside sections of the countryside characterised by more extensive, low intensity farming. While some farmers have always been quick to adopt advanced and innovative techniques, many others have clung to traditional methods. Nor are we dealing with a story of continuous development, as even the most 'advanced' parts of the Ile-de-France, Artois, Flanders, the Netherlands and eastern England went through occasional periods of slump and regressive development (including the one which marked the last decades of the twentieth century). The episodes of intensity and novelty, however, help to give the North Sea countries their distinctive character.

The growth of towns and trade in this region is an important aspect of its development, but this does not provide a total explanation. Urbanization and trade do not automatically propel agriculture down a road of growing surpluses or rapid transformation, as is shown by the many parts of the North Sea area where these developments did not take place.

Climate and soil, discussed in another volume of this series, are also important elements, but in this respect the North Sea area was not fundamentally better off than other parts of the world. Whilst acknowledging the influence of environmental factors, in this volume we address an alternative explanation rooted in the organization of rights to land, labour and capital, and the incentives these offered owners and occupiers of the land. The central idea that lies behind this book is that our understanding and assessment of rural economy, production and profit depends not just on the land itself and the environment, but also on the people who worked the land, those who gained a share of the fruits of their labour as lords, money lenders or functionaries of the state, and the state itself. Their relations, and the way societies organized the rights to land, labour and capital, determined to an important extent the efficiency of agriculture, the levels of investment and the surpluses generated.

1.2 The factors influencing farming

Before turning to the main subject of this book, we need to be aware of some of the factors that conditioned the rural world and created the environment within which landlords, peasants and farmers operated in the past and still do in the present.

First, the natural endowment of the land is profoundly unequal. Not only do we have to consider climate, but within the North Sea littoral, there are areas of great natural fertility and others – the Norfolk Breckland, the thin soils of Scotland, the sandy soils of Drenthe and of the *Geest* in Lower Saxony, the southern highlands of Småland in Sweden, the rather mediocre sandy loamy soils of inland Flanders and the poor acid granite soils of Brittany – which are far from congenial for arable agriculture. Poor soils could encourage proto-industrialisation as rural populations sought alternative forms of livelihood, but the competition for nutrients could also lead to oppressive seigneurial regimes, as in the poorer areas of Norfolk where lords developed claims to their tenants' sheep dung (the Foldcourse).

Second, the attraction of these lands varied according to the availability of land which in turn is *potentially* (not invariably) a function of the prevailing level of population. When rural populations were at their highest, people were glad to have land which at other times would have been regarded as unattractive and barely worth cultivating. At moments of land hunger, they were pleased to have opportunity to enclose and improve land from the margins of the sea, from the edges of uplands, from native forest. At times when the countryside was full of people, the normal rules of supply and demand allowed those with land to manage the land market for their own advantage, using the competition between tenants to raise rents, shorten leases, divide holdings and command high rents for marginal land. When population fell, there may have been some abandonment of land on the margins and peripheries: where arable was unprofitable, there may have been a recourse to pastoralism. Rents naturally fell too and the bargaining position of tenants improved. Lords might even be willing to turn a blind eye to customary arrangements in order to maintain the occupation of their land. Alternatively, in order to retain their tenants and a labour force for their own demesnes, lords might attempt to tie their tenants to their land and develop new forms of bondage using their control of national legislatures. In these and other ways, the dynamics of tenancy in a world full of people are entirely different to those in a world lacking occupiers of the land. The locus classicus for this is the comparison between the years of high population before the Black Death and the prolonged depression which followed it. But the same economic logic – if with less drastic implications – could apply over much shorter periods at times of recession in agriculture, when landlords could find it hard to secure adequate tenants or a workforce, or after periods of war, as after the Thirty Years War, or in France after World War I, when many men were dead or disabled, and workers were scarce.

Third, we have to address agriculture at least briefly and understand that it is not an unchanging activity. Farmers can change the balance of their crops to meet their own consumption needs and the demands of markets, switching over time between arable and pasture, within arable from winter grains to spring grains. They have at their disposal a whole range of techniques which they can draw on when demand is high. First and foremost they can simply employ more labour to undertake a range of tasks which might otherwise be skimped on – better ploughing, more thorough weeding, even bird scaring – all of which may make a difference to overall production. They can resort to labour-intensive crops, some suitable for smallholders, including market gardening in the urban fringe, others for farmers who are more distant from towns, including dairying. But if demand was high enough, they could also resort to increasing productivity by the use of more advanced techniques: the employment of legumes in rotations, the use of clover and other artificial grasses and following their appearance in eighteenth-century eastern England, the adoption of rotations which used root crops. To a greater or lesser extent, legumes and 'artificial grasses' removed the need for fallows. They not only put nitrogen into the soil, but they also provided a greater supply of fodder for animals, providing an enhanced supply of dung to be added to the soil. Root crops also enabled more animals to be over-wintered and increased the supply of manure.

In the nineteenth century the demand for nitrogen by farmers led to some unlikely places – not merely urban night soil, but also to South America for guano. The limitation which the supply of nitrogen placed on agriculture was resolved by the invention of the Haber process in 1909 for making synthetic nitrogen fertilizer. From henceforth arable agriculture was freed from its reliance on animal manures and yields grew stupendously (with, as we now appreciate, regrettable side-effects). Other developments in agriculture also improved its productivity: not only in plant and animal breeding, but the development of mechanisation (which brought about major improvements in labour productivity), drainage and the rationalisation of farm and field layouts. The enormous growth in agricultural production (as well as productivity) over the nineteenth and twentieth centuries is well known – as, indeed are its consequences. What is less appreciated is the pre-industrial agrarian economy was not, as we have shown, without its potential for growth. Of course, much of that growth may have ended in the cul-de-sac of falling labour productivity as increasing amounts of labour were used to secure marginal increases in the quantity of food produced. Malthus, famously, contrasted the limited possibilities for the improvement of the food supply with the danger of exponential population increase. An influential school of mid-twentieth century French historians adopted the idea that the pre-industrial economy was limited by ceilings on production, beyond which population could not be supported. Hence in this position, population growth could proceed only so far before being ended by starvation (if not death) or migration.[1] A second, optimistic stance, associated with the name of Esther Boserup, argues that pre-industrial economies had the capacity to produce more in response to population growth, and this view has been confirmed at least in part for Britain (Campbell and Overton, 1994: 95–99). Much of this will be investigated in a further volume in this series, but for the moment we should merely note that agriculture does change over time, and that that both peasants and farmers were both more flexible in their response to circumstances – even before the eighteenth century – than has often been appreciated.

Fourth, in pre-industrial economies the demand for land is also conditioned by the availability of markets, but we need to explain why this is no longer the case today. The littoral of the North Sea is associated with great cities, some of which began to be really influential in the tenth and eleventh centuries, notably Bruges, Ghent and London, and others which became important later, such as Antwerp, Amsterdam and Hamburg. Dozens of other towns and ports stretching to Bergen and Aberdeen made the lands adjacent to the North Sea a highly urbanised economy, associated with advances in commercial techniques, such as banking, and the safe and easy transfer of funds. These cities, and a myriad of smaller towns, had a profound stimulus on their surrounding countryside. They also called on foodstuffs from much further afield: grain shipments from eastern Europe to feed the urban populations of the Low Countries grew in importance from the fifteenth century. Cattle were driven overland from Denmark and further east. Fish came from the Baltic, but above all through the Atlantic contacts with northern Norway, Iceland and, from the late fifteenth century, North America. A great north European trade route connected the North Sea with the Baltic, along which were carried the distinctive products of the forests, mines and ironworks of Scandinavia and eastern Europe, from the luxurious furs to the bulkier and cheaper necessities of timber, tar and wax, iron and copper. Trade from southern Europe flowed into the North Sea ports, from which luxurious and exotic goods (from the sixteenth century including transatlantic imports) were distributed over the whole of northern Europe. Great world empires were centred on this region, and ports such as Amsterdam and London became the hubs of a global economy, long before the phrase was invented.

These cities could not have existed without the food and raw materials produced in the nearby countryside. Here societies developed which were influenced by, and interacted with, the centres. On the land around the towns, crops were grown for the market, capital was accumulated, migrants were recruited, and flows of rent helped to finance trade. Townspeople went out to the villages to buy produce and to lend money.

[1] Neo-Malthusian ideas strongly influenced the work of Le Roy Ladurie and others in the 1960s: see Le Roy Ladurie, 1966 and Duby and Wallon (eds), 1975, pp. 576–91. For critical comments see Dewald and Vardi, 1988, pp. 26–7.

These contacts, even when they were channelled through the market, were sometimes marked by unequal relationships. Not only was access to capital and knowledge unevenly spread, but urban merchants or towns might claim a trading monopoly over their town's hinterland, to compel grain and other foodstuffs to be offered for sale in its markets. Market relations were seldom either free or equal, but were a dimension of the power relationship between town and country. Townspeople also bought rural land which was often a safer investment than urban enterprises. Landed assets could provide the wealthier merchants with a new life as country gentlemen.

In short, cities produced a situation in which the demand for land was often high in their hinterlands, and this forced up rents and made land desirable as an investment. Where access to a town was easy, whether over a short distance by road or over a longer distance by water, then grain was often grown for sale. Those who were more locationally disadvantaged often concentrated on cattle production or butter and cheese production – both valued-added, preserved and so transportable forms of milk.

But much of this pre-industrial locational logic no longer applies. Before the nineteenth century, people were constrained in their forms of transport. Goods could generally move no faster than a horse or coastal freighter could carry them. The growth of towns was accompanied by the spread of carrying services, the enhancement of the road network and later canals, but these too operated at the gentle pace of a team of horses and a wagon. The appearance of the railways from the 1830s came as a shock to this system. For the first time, volume goods could be moved at high speeds and at carriage rates much reduced from anything that animal transport could achieve. Cities could reach further into their hinterlands. It became possible to transport perishable goods – vegetables, raw milk, fresh meat – over long distances and for distant suppliers to enter markets previously closed to them. This was only a beginning though. Political calculation in the mid-nineteenth century, following the Dutch and British precedents, often encouraged the free trade in foodstuffs, but this left European farmers vulnerable to unforeseen improvements in transatlantic shipping, the extension of the American railway system into the mid-West and the ploughing of the Russian steppes. New low-cost producers entered European markets who could take advantage of tumbling freight rates to export their grain half way round the world at prices with which local producers could not match. The development of refrigeration and the refrigerated cargo vessel then allowed European markets to be penetrated by fresh (chilled) meat as opposed to preserved, barrelled or tinned meat from Argentina, New Zealand and elsewhere. It was only a matter of time before European markets were flooded with Canadian cheese and New Zealand butter. The urban working classes welcomed the low prices and improved quality of consumption which this brought.

These technical innovations in transport wrought far-reaching changes in the European countryside and its power dynamics. Most north European countries progressively turned to tariffs to protect their own farming communities although this process was uneven and protracted and far from complete by the beginning of World War II. A further response to these new realities was for European farmers to take refuge in value-added production, notably dairying, and within dairying for them to develop new cooperative institutions which gave farmers access to economies of scale. In the of armies became the responsibility of the state and aristocratic violence was stamped on, this consideration no longer mattered to lords, and it is characteristic of seigneurial societies that personal fealty is no longer important: relationships are monetarised and marked only by the payment of rent.

In the medieval west, feudalism disintegrated from within. Where some see the formation of estates before 1000 as being a way of extending protection to tenants in return for fealty, older interpretations of the classic period of feudalism tended to see it as underpinned by the threat of seigneurial violence and placed a great deal of weight on the castle and the lord's retinue as enforcing his rights over a reluctant, even truculent, tenant population. Feudalism originated at a time when the countryside was relatively empty of people and in part perhaps reflects the need on the part of lords to control tenants to maintain the cultivation of their land. (A similar logic helps explains the emergence of 'neo-serfdom' in eastern Europe.) The emptiness of the countryside may initially have condemned the peasantry to arbitrary overlordship. But those peasants who were willing – and able – to move into unexploited areas and being them into cultivation might also be rewarded by the grant of full property rights and personal freedom as an incentive for their labour.

In northern France and the Low Countries, feudalism dissolved early with the manumission of serfs, the granting of charters of liberties to rural communes and the early abandonment of demesne farming at a time when the countryside was heavily populated and commercialised. In England it endured for much longer, but English feudalism worked best when the countryside was full, and the laws of supply and demand disadvantaged tenants by creating a seller's market. It became impossible to maintain the full oppressive apparatus of feudalism in England when population was falling after the Black Death and lords were desperate to acquire tenants to rent their land. But the rights of the lord were in long term decline even before population decline set in. The arbitrary rights of lords over their tenants were replaced by custom and then the real value of customary rights was diminished by inflation. Prudent lords could avoid this by taking rent in the form of labour services for demesne farming: but this was ultimately a cul-de-sac as it set lords up as competing with the tenants for their labour, and then competing with them a second time if they wanted to sell demesne produce into the open market for cash.

In another way the decline of feudalism was also assisted by government. In northern France and the Low Countries, it was the holders of the higher jurisdictions who undermined the rights of lords by conferring charters of liberties on villages. In England the royal courts withdrew from the hearing of suits between lord and their servile tenants after the late twelfth century; but in the late fifteenth they again interested themselves in the affairs of those descendents of serfs who held by copyhold.

The development of capitalist relationships between landlords and tenants in the countryside may be seen as being a recognition that the structures of feudalism could no longer provide lords with an adequate share of the tenant's profit. Agrarian capitalism was a reformulation of the relationship between the lord and the occupier of his land. It was characterised by the lease: but the lease has a much longer history than this. It may be seen to have evolved in a situation where people – whether freeholders

These contacts, even when they were channelled through the market, were sometimes marked by unequal relationships. Not only was access to capital and knowledge unevenly spread, but urban merchants or towns might claim a trading monopoly over their town's hinterland, to compel grain and other foodstuffs to be offered for sale in its markets. Market relations were seldom either free or equal, but were a dimension of the power relationship between town and country. Townspeople also bought rural land which was often a safer investment than urban enterprises. Landed assets could provide the wealthier merchants with a new life as country gentlemen.

In short, cities produced a situation in which the demand for land was often high in their hinterlands, and this forced up rents and made land desirable as an investment. Where access to a town was easy, whether over a short distance by road or over a longer distance by water, then grain was often grown for sale. Those who were more locationally disadvantaged often concentrated on cattle production or butter and cheese production – both valued-added, preserved and so transportable forms of milk.

But much of this pre-industrial locational logic no longer applies. Before the nineteenth century, people were constrained in their forms of transport. Goods could generally move no faster than a horse or coastal freighter could carry them. The growth of towns was accompanied by the spread of carrying services, the enhancement of the road network and later canals, but these too operated at the gentle pace of a team of horses and a wagon. The appearance of the railways from the 1830s came as a shock to this system. For the first time, volume goods could be moved at high speeds and at carriage rates much reduced from anything that animal transport could achieve. Cities could reach further into their hinterlands. It became possible to transport perishable goods – vegetables, raw milk, fresh meat – over long distances and for distant suppliers to enter markets previously closed to them. This was only a beginning though. Political calculation in the mid-nineteenth century, following the Dutch and British precedents, often encouraged the free trade in foodstuffs, but this left European farmers vulnerable to unforeseen improvements in transatlantic shipping, the extension of the American railway system into the mid-West and the ploughing of the Russian steppes. New low-cost producers entered European markets who could take advantage of tumbling freight rates to export their grain half way round the world at prices with which local producers could not match. The development of refrigeration and the refrigerated cargo vessel then allowed European markets to be penetrated by fresh (chilled) meat as opposed to preserved, barrelled or tinned meat from Argentina, New Zealand and elsewhere. It was only a matter of time before European markets were flooded with Canadian cheese and New Zealand butter. The urban working classes welcomed the low prices and improved quality of consumption which this brought.

These technical innovations in transport wrought far-reaching changes in the European countryside and its power dynamics. Most north European countries progressively turned to tariffs to protect their own farming communities although this process was uneven and protracted and far from complete by the beginning of World War II. A further response to these new realities was for European farmers to take refuge in value-added production, notably dairying, and within dairying for them to develop new cooperative institutions which gave farmers access to economies of scale. In the

1930s some countries adopted state-sponsored marketing boards to coordinate production and sale and to act as a vehicle for the distribution of state subsidies. A delayed reaction came after the Second World War with the introduction of mechanisation and attempts to reorganise the landscape to produce bigger farms. A whole range of superior techniques vastly increased the productivity of the European countryside, but at the cost of taxpayer-funded overproduction. The edifice created after 1945 was financially unsustainable and progressively wound down after 1990. The consequence is that the population of the North Sea area now draws its foodstuffs from all over the globe and the contribution of farmers within the area to feeding its population is, whilst not negligible, hardly crucial either. Indeed, it has been argued from time to time throughout the last hundred years in Britain that farming is unnecessary, and it has been maintained in the recent past that the real purpose of the post-productivist countryside is to serve as a playground for urban populations. The role of the early twentieth-first century farmer is often taken to be that of the custodian of landscape, keeping it in order so that it meets public expectations of how it should look, and public subsidy has been increasingly orientated towards this end. The importance attributed to locally-produced food still varies enormously between countries, and old preferences have not entirely disappeared.

The exercise of power and property has to a large extent been shaped by these underlying realities: but it is different patterns of power and property which have resulted in the same exogenous stimuli to the rural economy working themselves out in different ways in different places.

1.3 Approaches to property and power

The approach adopted by this volume is rooted in two debates which have interested rural historians throughout the twentieth century and will continue to do so into the twenty-first, but which are also continuations of discussions which informed eighteenth-century and earlier approaches to agricultural policy.

The first we term the property rights approach. (For a useful introduction, see Cohen, 1996, and for an overview of a number of approaches to the medieval economy, Hatcher and Bailey, 2001). What rights was it necessary to confer on a cultivator of the land to encourage him (it was, of course, mostly him) to farm the land to its best advantage, not only in terms of maximising its output, but also treating the land in a sustainable fashion so that its fertility was maintained for future generations? Did weak property rights retard economic development – as has often been argued? All peasants or farmers, whatever name we use for whatever type of cultivator, tend to regard the land as their own. They invest their time and energy in it: they may well come to an intimate understanding of how the land might best be used; they wish to secure the efforts of their labour for the next generation. Where they do not have full property in the land, there is a tendency for them to press for such rights. These might emerge out of the developing relationship between lords and tenants as, for instance, in the granting of liberties to villages in northern Europe in the twelfth century, or they could be established as customary rights whose recognition by the law could be less than total but which might be backed by peasant solidarity. Full property rights could also be conferred by government, notably when influenced by Physiocratic ideals in the eighteenth century. Where the position of landholders remained entrenched, debate focussed on the length of the ideal term: but in large parts of northern Europe, the security of the peasant in his property remained slight even in the early twentieth century.

We should also note that what is important here is not merely who possessed the property and exercised the power latent in its possession, but how that property was distributed. We need to recognise that the social distribution of land differs wildly from area to area and its distribution produces vastly different political dynamics within the countryside. If a particular countryside is dominated by a small number of very large landowners, do they choose to farm the land themselves or rent it to farmers – or a mix of the two (the medieval 'bipartite estate')? Are villages marked by a unequal distribution of property with a small number of large farmers and large numbers of smallholders and landless? Or is the possession of land more egalitarian with large numbers of small farmers? And what of the number of smallholders and landless men who might be able to labour for their larger neighbours? There are large numbers of possible permutations: moreover, they are often of great antiquity and are slow to change. Freeholding peasantries and weak seigneurial jurisdictions are often associated with the sort of colonising movement that we have identified as being typical of periods of high population pressure. Smallholding may also be associated with encroachments on commons, rural industry or the urban fringes, all situations in which a living could be made from meagre agricultural resources.

The second approach identifies rural society as being divided between the owners of land and the occupiers of the same land and sees the driving force in society as the competition between them for the profits of farming. This is a central theme of the Marxist approach, most recently revived by the American historian Robert Brenner (Aston and Philpin (eds), 1985, and for its application to the Low Countries, Hoppenbrouwers and van Zanden (eds), 2001). Where there was a relationship of dependency, in which cultivators held land from lords or landlords, rent from could be extracted from them in one of several ways: in the form of labour (especially characteristic of feudalism), in the form of crops, or in money rent (characteristic of agrarian capitalism). Feudalism could also be marked by the personal dependency of the tenant on his lord, enforced by the application of non-economic coercion, certainly by the delegation of state judicial powers to the lords of men. At an extreme, the tenant might be a serf, a form of property. Serfs could certainly have to buy their manumission to be treated as free men. Servile tenancies included the right of the lord to licence and take a fine on life-cycle events, especially the death or marriage of a tenant. The lord might be able restrict the mobility of his tenants. In both high medieval feudal society and in early modern 'neo-feudalism', servile tenants were barred from suing their lords in state courts. In agrarian capitalist relationships, landlords and tenants are placed on an even footing before the law and enter contracts as equals. In feudalism men are often valued as military supporters in war or in civil disputes between lords. As the raising of armies became the responsibility of the state and aristocratic violence was stamped on, this consideration no longer mattered to lords, and it is characteristic of seigneurial societies that personal fealty is no longer important: relationships are monetarised and marked only by the payment of rent.

In the medieval west, feudalism disintegrated from within. Where some see the formation of estates before 1000 as being a way of extending protection to tenants in return for fealty, older interpretations of the classic period of feudalism tended to see it as underpinned by the threat of seigneurial violence and placed a great deal of weight on the castle and the lord's retinue as enforcing his rights over a reluctant, even truculent, tenant population. Feudalism originated at a time when the countryside was relatively empty of people and in part perhaps reflects the need on the part of lords to control tenants to maintain the cultivation of their land. (A similar logic helps explains the emergence of 'neo-serfdom' in eastern Europe.) The emptiness of the countryside may initially have condemned the peasantry to arbitrary overlordship. But those peasants who were willing – and able – to move into unexploited areas and being them into cultivation might also be rewarded by the grant of full property rights and personal freedom as an incentive for their labour.

In northern France and the Low Countries, feudalism dissolved early with the manumission of serfs, the granting of charters of liberties to rural communes and the early abandonment of demesne farming at a time when the countryside was heavily populated and commercialised. In England it endured for much longer, but English feudalism worked best when the countryside was full, and the laws of supply and demand disadvantaged tenants by creating a seller's market. It became impossible to maintain the full oppressive apparatus of feudalism in England when population was falling after the Black Death and lords were desperate to acquire tenants to rent their land. But the rights of the lord were in long term decline even before population decline set in. The arbitrary rights of lords over their tenants were replaced by custom and then the real value of customary rights was diminished by inflation. Prudent lords could avoid this by taking rent in the form of labour services for demesne farming: but this was ultimately a cul-de-sac as it set lords up as competing with the tenants for their labour, and then competing with them a second time if they wanted to sell demesne produce into the open market for cash.

In another way the decline of feudalism was also assisted by government. In northern France and the Low Countries, it was the holders of the higher jurisdictions who undermined the rights of lords by conferring charters of liberties on villages. In England the royal courts withdrew from the hearing of suits between lord and their servile tenants after the late twelfth century; but in the late fifteenth they again interested themselves in the affairs of those descendents of serfs who held by copyhold.

The development of capitalist relationships between landlords and tenants in the countryside may be seen as being a recognition that the structures of feudalism could no longer provide lords with an adequate share of the tenant's profit. Agrarian capitalism was a reformulation of the relationship between the lord and the occupier of his land. It was characterised by the lease: but the lease has a much longer history than this. It may be seen to have evolved in a situation where people – whether freeholders or customary tenants – had land which they did not wish to farm themselves but wished to continue owning, or had perhaps bought as an investment. Hence feudal society knew plenty of leases, but with the disappearance of seigneurial relationships, the lease became the predominant form of tenurial relationship. It allowed for rent (in all its forms) to be periodically renegotiated and so it was its flexibility which appealed to both landlords and tenants. As leases might be competitively sought by tenants, the proportion of the tenant's income paid as rent might change over time according to the demand for land. But as we noted, the length of a lease had also to reflect the need to encourage 'good husbandry', and tenants worked to maintain their long term interest in 'their' farm by renewing leases early or claiming rights of nomination to the farm when their lease ended.

Their success in doing this reflects a further question which we have not yet considered: that of peasant solidarity in the face of lords and landlords. There were intermittent attempts on the parts of peasants to overthrow feudal society and to re-establish by violent means a pure peasant society without landlords. Revolts took place in the coastal Low Countries around 1300 (and especially 1323–28) and lords struggled to control the independent peasantry of Drenthe and Frisia. The only area in which a distinctively peasant territorial state was established was in the marshland along the north German coast around the estuary of the River Elbe. This was the subject of a crusade in 1234 which inflicted a heavy defeat on them, but the peasant confederations of this remote area played a role in the politics of Schleswig-Holstein and Denmark until the mid-sixteenth century. It was in Scandinavia that the most highly developed peasant organisations are found. In Denmark they survived as a real force through to the civil wars of the 1533–6. In Sweden the freeholding peasantry were incorporated into the Swedish legislature as a peasant estate but one which took no interest in the plight of the manorial peasantry. It therefore defined itself according to tenurial status rather than admitting any class interest with other cultivators of the soil.

Resistance to serfdom in thirteenth-century England often took the form of appeals to the courts in attempts to prove that serfs were in fact free men. Within the manor serfs engaged in petty acts of rebellion against their lords. Certainly it appears from the detailed English materials that work services were often not well done and that the older view that serfs resented their lord's call on their time was justified. In England the great outburst against feudalism in all its aspects came after the apogee of feudalism, but perhaps when some lords were still trying to make it work in adverse circumstances. This was the Peasant's Revolt of 1381. In the first instance this was aimed at taxation, and it may be the case that peasantries as a whole found it easier to join together to resist governments than they did to resist landlords. Agrarian capitalism, by placing every peasant in competition with his neighbours for land and forcing them to become petty entrepreneurs trying to secure the best price for their produce, may well have atomised the peasantry and left them vulnerable to their landlords. Individual villages continued to mobilise against landlords especially where the latter queried the existing customary rights of the tenants, or tried to seize commons or other communal assets for their own use. It is perhaps chastening to think that the great improvements in peasant conditions in much of northern Europe in the late eighteenth century came not from the actions of the peasantry themselves but from the action of governments and legislative bodies: the late eighteenth-century belief that the best peasantry was a free peasantry with full property rights in land was as much an intellectual and economic fashion in its time as collectivisation, nationalisation and privatisation were in the twentieth century.

In fact, as the state came to deal directly with peasants or farmers, it became suspicious of their organisations until ways were found in the late nineteenth and early twentieth century to integrate them into government as pressure groups. There is a much longer history of government taking the side of the peasantry in at least a general sense because the state was, in effect, a further competitor for peasant income and profit, but through tax rather than rent. It was therefore a common tactic in the nineteenth and twentieth centuries for government to undermine lords or landlords by conferring rights on the peasantry, for instance security of tenure or rights of succession to farms; rights which met peasant demands and could, in addition, be justified by the belief that they would encourage agricultural productivity. The taxation regimes established in some countries also encouraged the breaking up of states and the sale of land by landlords to its occupiers. Ultimately, as we will explain, the government switched from mediating in the relationship between landlord and tenant to protect its share of agricultural income to controlling agricultural income through the regulation of the price of agricultural commodities and the management of markets and subsidy.

For all that the tenurial relationship may seem unimportant today, we would maintain that it was the key relationship in pre-industrial rural societies. It was dynamic and changed over time in exactly the same way as the employment relationship changes over time in modern industrial and post-industrial society: at some moments workers' rights can be generous: at others, such as the time at which we write, they become much less so. The ability of the seigneurial or landlord classes to extract rent from their tenants conditioned how well they lived in ways which we can see today through their remaining houses and the results of their sponsorship of the arts and crafts which fill those houses and public museums. But it was also the labour of the peasant or farmer which ultimately made state building possible, which allowed states to fight wars at home and abroad or provide for its people at home until the taxation of mercantile or industrial society came to dominate state revenues.

1.4 Power

Power, in the sense we employ it here, is the relationship between those with authority, and those who lack that standing. Power is the capacity to make people bend to another's political, economic and social priorities. Power relationships even existed in the household: between husband and wife, parents and children, the family heads and their servants. They are found in the relationship of landowner and tenant, employer and employee, creditor and debtor. In fact people without power are rarely entirely lacking in influence or the ability to bargain. They have recourse to argument and ridicule, obstruction, acts of revenge and insubordination: they maintain their own solidarities. Ultimately they have the power of flight within the countryside, to towns, increasingly to an extra-European colony.

We can identify a number of power relationships in the countryside, each of whose importance varies over time. The first is the relationship between landlord and tenant, between owner and occupier. As we have seen, this relationship took different forms at different times. The second is the relationship of the occupiers, the people who actually farmed the land, with those who undertook the day-to-day tasks of farming. Of course, this relationship could be a dimension of the larger tenurial relationship, where occupiers undertook work for their lords or landlords as a part of their rent, or labour could be proletarianised, without any alternative to wages for its support. The labour relationship has been much less explored than the tenurial relationship and so the weight given it in this volume reflects the relative disinterest in it on the part of previous historians. The third relationship is the dual one between the owners of land and occupiers of the land and the government. If some care is needed in defining who the occupiers are, then it must be recognised that government could distinguish between owners and occupiers and could adopt policies which acted against the interests of one to the advantage of the other. Government could be jealous of the authority which ownership gave in the countryside and could seek to replace it with a direct relationship between itself and the occupiers. Moreover, it could see itself as a rival to the lord or landlord for a share of the profits of farming.

A further power relationship which concerns us here is that between town and country. Even in the middle ages, the larger cities of the Low Countries exhibited ambitions to control their rural hinterlands after the fashion of the Italian city states. The adequacy of urban food supplies was a concern of government from the late middle ages at the latest, particularly in years of high prices. What tipped the balance overwhelmingly in favour of towns was their great expansion in the nineteenth century and the extension of the franchise to the urban working class. Increasingly the countryside could be outvoted and rural or farmers' political parties had to jostle for influence with urban, often socialist, parties. Urban preferences, including that for cheap food, came to predominate and the needs of the countryside, when they were in tension with urban needs, came to be a secondary consideration. That said, there remained, in some nations, a nationalist rhetoric which stressed the foundations of the nation in its countryside and peasantry, and in the inter-war years this could slip into eugenics and racialist ideology.

The slow decline of the electoral influence of the farming community is the context in which governments switched between cheap-food/free trade policies (in the late nineteenth century), to increasingly protectionist policies in the early twentieth and markedly productivist policies within the EC after 1945. Since the great sea change of around 1990, there has been a renewed recourse to free trade policies which have produced extremely low farm gate prices for farmers, and so have returned agriculture to conditions of relative depression. Throughout the period, farmers have never been the masters of their own destiny, but their fortunes have been increasingly determined by government rather than lords or landowners.

1.5 Possession

Before turning to each of the relationships we have identified, we need to be clear about the character of that of which we speak. A fundamental question concerns the possession of land, the word 'possession' being chosen with care because 'ownership' is too direct and absolute a concept to be applied easily. Ownership today is normally a relatively simple concept. Property belongs to an owner who normally has exclusive or 'freehold' rights in it, subject of course to the interests of mortgagors with whose help the land is being purchased. Historically property was a much more confused matter. Land was subject to many superimposed layers of tenancy, lordship, management and sovereignty which often overlapped. Exclusive ownership, in a modern sense, was unknown. A single parcel of land might be in the possession of the man or woman who farmed it, but the possessor paid the lord a rent and, on his death or his sale of the land, a transaction tax. The possession of a particular parcel might bring unwelcome obligations with it: the requirement to attend particular courts for instance, but also rights which might be sought after: access to village officeholding, and, in the case of larger estates, the entitlement to nobility and participation in government. The possessor's right to sell might be compromised by the right of kin to secure it from him at an advantageous price should he wish to sell (rights which survived surprisingly late in some European countries); his possession of family land might come with obligations to provide for retired members of the family or siblings. At other times and places he might be forbidden to sell parcels of his land but was obliged to keep it as an integral unit. He might not be allowed to raise money on the security of his land without seeking permission from a manorial or even state authority. His interest in his land might be formally limited to a term of years or lives even though the right to retain land within the family was a preoccupation of peasant life. At certain times of the agrarian calendar his land might be laid open to allow his fellow villagers to graze with their animals. The implication here is that the occupier was locked into a communally decided (or customary) rotation which made it impossible for him to exploit the land according to his assessment of his best interests. Deviations from communal decisions over land might be prosecuted in a village or seigneurial court.

The long term tendency was for the simplification of property rights to the point where they arrived at the exclusive right that ownership is held to confer today. Exactly how this was done, the timescale on which it was achieved, indeed, the importance given to it, varied from place to place. So too the mechanisms which achieved it. In England enclosure served to make the communal rights over land obsolete but did nothing to alter the tenurial relationships by which it was held. In France simplification of property rights was achieved by fiat of the Revolution and enclosure followed over the following half century. In much of Germany and Scandinavia, the sale of state domains to their farmers and the abolition of corvée was an objective of the late eighteenth and early nineteenth century. This line of liberal thought was completed by the manumission of serfs in late eighteenth-century Denmark and areas of Germany in the mid-nineteenth century.

The appearance of simple forms of possession has been undermined by the growth of government power over land in the nineteenth and twentieth centuries. In the nineteenth century these might be the power to force through enclosure or to improve land for the public benefit where local initiatives had failed to do so. In the twentieth century they became rights of compulsory acquisition and the power to determine how land is used through planning law. Particularly in the third quarter of the century, governments took powers to consolidate farms to achieve economies of scale and reorganise the countryside into larger, more regular, units, to make it more accessible for machinery. The choice of what is grown on the land has come to be increasingly determined by the state through the combination of subsidy, price-fixing and quotas.

1.6 Tenure

The power relationship which concerns us most in this volume is the tenurial relationship between those who own property – and particularly the most important form of property, land – and those who cultivate the same property. This relationship is normally marked by the payment of rent from the tenant to the landowner but it may also be marked by symbolic acts of recognition, compulsory attendance at the lord's courts and the need for the tenant to buy his lord's licence for permission to marry his children, sue outside the village, sub-let parts of his tenement and so on.

Landowners need tenants for a variety of reasons. They often have far more land than they can farm themselves; they may lack the capital and perhaps the expertise to farm their land effectively. In one influential analysis, tenants are seen as a way of removing landlords from the risk of farming with its variable yields and fluctuating prices. Landlords usually required payment in cash or labour at levels fixed for at least the medium term. Labour rent disappeared at an early date in northern France and the Low Countries and in England it has almost entirely gone by 1450. There was a renewed recourse to it in the sixteenth and seventeenth centuries in eastern Europe and it survived to a late date in Denmark, Schleswig and Sweden – particularly in Scania where corvée labour gained importance even in the nineteenth century, at the very time it was disappearing in Denmark. At some times and in some places, for instance seventeenth-century Scotland, eighteenth-century Germany and Scandinavia, landlords received rents in produce and had to involve themselves in the market. In inflationary periods this could be advantageous for them. There was also recourse to sharecropping arrangements by which landlords would receive a fixed proportion of the produce. Overall these are not important in the North Sea area except in western France. Generally speaking, though, at least in the core North Sea littoral area, landlords preferred fixed rents in cash rather than tangling with the uncertainties of production or having to take responsibility for its sale.

Landowners also wished to have tenants for social reasons. The ability to command men in war was valued in pre-modern societies: at a later date landowners enjoyed the respect of tenants and behaved towards them in a paternalistic and philanthropic fashion. The relationship was obviously a profoundly unequal one but also in a way which is often overlooked. While landlords needed tenants to cultivate their land and pay rent, tenants did not need landlords save for the fact that they controlled access to land (although in high medieval Europe, they may also have offered protection to their tenants). Naturally, tenants do not like paying rent for what they tend to regard as their own.

The relationship of landowner and tenant is therefore invariably under tension. Whilst a legal relationship, defined by law, it is often the case that the details of the tenancy contract obscure the economic and social realties which characterise it. Four major categories of tenancy relationship can be identified: full property or freehold; customary tenancy; leasehold; and tenancy by the year. Each is treated in turn.

Freehold

A freeholder is a peasant or farmer who owns their own land in something close to full property, although ownership in the past was rarely exclusive. (Allodial freeholds are found in medieval Scandinavia and sometimes elsewhere.) Freeholders, it may be suggested, can be created in one of three ways. First of all, lords seeking to attract tenants to improve and cultivate unexploited land might well make absolute grants of land to encourage the first generation of colonists. Freeholders of this sort are especially important in parts of the Low Countries and Germany where they originate in grants made to encourage the drainage of peat areas (as in Holland in the eleventh to the thirteenth centuries) and fen areas. Over time though, the character of the freeholder often changes as he ceases to be a figure who both owns and cultivates the land, but through sale, often to a bourgeois or donation to a monastic a house, the freeholder – the person who has 'full' property – becomes a non-resident landlord who sublets the land for profit to a tenant. Second, in ways explained below, customary tenancies may evolve into freeholds. Third, the tendency in modern Europe has been for estates to disappear and the absolute ownership of their land to be transferred to the occupiers. This was *de facto* the case in eighteenth-century France and it was recognised *de jure* in 1789. Again, this may only be a transitory moment as this land may be sold onto investors who install a tenant and take a rent, so creating a new tenurial arrangement.

Customary tenancy

There were also tenants who held land by customary arrangements. Here the tenants claimed a right to buy, sell, and inherit their tenancies. In effect these tenancies were perpetual. In some cases customary tenants were permitted (or claimed the right to) sublet their tenancies. Rents are normally fixed although one-off payments (fines) are often taken on the change of the tenant.

Custom is a dimension of tenant solidarity and a reflection of the strength of the village community. It is a set of expectations amongst tenants about how they should be treated by their landlords. Custom is therefore backward-looking. It upholds the supremacy of the tenants' right of possession over the lords' right of ownership. Hence, once customary regimes have developed, lords find it impossible either to recover the land to exploit themselves, or to secure realistic market rents from their tenants.

Especially after periods of inflation, an increasing proportion of the profits of farming come to rest with the tenant. These types of tenancy tend to evolve into forms of freehold paying fixed free rents to a lord, whilst the customary tenants often have tenants of their own paying market rents. In this situation, most of the profits of tenancy come to rest with the customary tenant and not the legal 'owner'.

Leasehold

Landlords therefore often wish to define and limit the rights of tenants and often do so through a lease, a contract for a fixed period of time. The ideal length of the lease varies over time: but it needed to be sufficiently long to encourage the tenant to invest in the landlord's property but not so long as to prevent the landowner from taking advantage of any change in the value of the leased lands. At the end of the lease, both parties have no further obligation to each other. A landlord might choose a new tenant, a tenant might choose to move. But a new lease can be negotiated, sometimes before the old one has ended, which might allow the landlord to increase the rent but also ensure the continued possession of the tenant (or his family) over consecutive leasehold terms. Because leases allow for the negotiation of new terms at intervals, they assume a market in tenants, that is, that a landlord whose tenant will not meet his terms can look for someone who will, whilst a tenant who finds his landlord's new terms unacceptable might reject them in the knowledge that he can find better terms elsewhere. There is a tendency for landlords in rising markets to offer shorter leases so that rents can be renegotiated more often, and for tenants to demand longer leases at times of depression. Although leases are contracted voluntarily and with mutual agreement, in fact they mark a profoundly unequal relationship. Whilst they define and so limit the tenants' rights, leaseholders also have a degree of power over their lords. At times of agricultural depression, they can run up arrears which landlords have either to tolerate and even write off, or risk losing a tenant at a time when suitable tenants might be in short supply. Thus, apparently fixed terms coexist, as they do in all contracts, with a degree of necessary flexibility in changed conditions. Likewise, the habit of giving tenants finite terms does not preclude the inheritance of tenancies over extended periods of time. Hence leasehold tenancies are often more 'customary' in character than at first sight might appear.[2]

Tenancy at will

Finally we have tenurial arrangements in which the landlord gives no contract to his tenant. In the Low Countries, France and Germany such arrangements were rarely used, but they were familiar in England, especially in the nineteenth century where they were called tenancies at will. But, again, the term often conceals the long-term possession of land by tenants or their families. Even if they had only an annual term, they were

[2] It might also be noticed that 'perpetual leases' are sometimes encountered, normally where the lessor wishes to sell the property but is forbidden from doing so: in this situation a perpetual lease serves their needs.

not expected to move annually. In law, as opposed to custom or practice, tenants at will had no rights other than to receive a period of notice before their eviction. The same applied to tenants on noble land in Sweden. In addition, there is, in most rural societies, a pool of land available for short lets and sometimes seasonal grazing rights.

It has already been shown how individual properties can shift between these four categories over time and this must be emphasised. Tenancies for short terms could become transmuted into customary tenancies if tenants came to exercise the right to sell, bequeath or sub-let their interests. Leasehold or customary tenancies could be transformed into freeholds by the sale of the lord's interest to the occupier. Conversely customary or leasehold land could be added to seigneurial demesnes by purchase, eviction or even after abandonment. Moreover, different rights can exist in the same property at the same time, so, for instance, a tenant in a customary relationship with a freeholder or seigneurial lord (and so paying a rent which did not reflect the real value of the property) could have a sub-tenant paying a commercial rent. One man's freehold may be another's customary holding.

The tendency over the very long term was for forms of tenancy to disappear and for land to be held by owner-occupiers. This was perhaps first achieved first in a broad belt stretching through north-east France into Flanders by 1300, but remains incomplete today in Britain and Sweden. (And yet we will see signs that leasehold – particularly in the leasing of partial farms – has not disappeared but might even have reappeared in new guises.) Even where the tenurial relationship survived, the power of the landowner was progressively eroded over the nineteenth and twentieth centuries. There are a number of ways in which this happened. The first is the very long term decay of manorial jurisdictions – the lord's courts simply ceased to be central to rural society – and were replaced as the practical centres of administration by the commune which was the local branch of the state. Hence there was so much interest in controlling and supervising mayors or village officers by the apparatus of the state. Second, the state tended to confer security of tenure on the tenant so that the landlord's right to choose his tenant, or to take land in hand to farm directly, was much diminished. By the late twentieth century tenants might even have limited succession rights conferred on them by the state. The balance of power in the tenurial relationship was gradually shifted against the owner. Third there was, from early in the nineteenth century, the almost universal appearance of agricultural societies, some based on confessional lines, which allowed the institutionalisation of the sort of conversations – about landlords as well as agriculture – which had doubtless taken place in marketplace inns from time immemorial. But these societies also took advantage of the new spirit of the age provided by the circulation of newspapers and agricultural literature. They were looked on with some anxiety by both landowners and state authorities, and again they show how the landowner had ceased to be the focal point within society. A fourth factor in their decline was the progressive enlargement of the (male) franchise in the nineteenth century. This made rural electorates too big to control, and placed the vote in the hands of men who were probably instinctively anti-landowner. It was no longer possible for the landowner to exercise power through the ballot by organising his tenants to vote for him, nor to play the leading role in the selection of village officers. Moreover, the enlarged franchise inevitably shifted the centre of balance within the state and its legislatures from the countryside to the towns and cities and so contributed to the pursuit of free trade, cheap food polices which helped provoke depression in the countryside. Fifthly, this should remind us that in the later nineteenth and twentieth century, those landowners – whether rentiers or farmers – who remained were no longer necessarily wealthy. Rents were low and the taxation of agrarian incomes was often at high rates. Increasingly over the twentieth century the possession of land no longer carried great cachet. At the same time there was a general tendency for local government to be carried out by local authorities based in regional towns and cities rather than amateurs and volunteers in the village.

1.7 Labour

At the end of the twentieth century landowners remained in the countryside but they were largely invisible. If this marks a break with the past, then so too does the disappearance of the labourer.

Before the progressive mechanisation of the nineteenth and twentieth centuries, agriculture was demanding of labour. Managing a farm's labour requirements was never easy though. At its simplest we might see the peasant household as being reliant on family labour, but as has long been appreciated, the family's ability to provide labour changes over time where the labour required to run a set acreage remains fixed. Hence it was always necessary to extend the labour of the family with additional non-family labour of one sort or another. For this reason the notion of a rural society completely lacking a labour market is hard to envisage.[3] Two other factors need to be born in mind. The labour requirements of arable and pastoral districts differ. Arable has long slack periods, especially in the winter, but also heavy demands for labour in the harvest. Dairying requires a more constant labour input to milk cattle and prepare butter and cheese, and until mechanisation late in the nineteenth century, these last tasks were distinctively female. Finally, where rent was still paid in corvée, the occupiers needed to employ labour which was extra to their own needs to supply their obligations to their lord.

We can see labour being made available in four ways. The area under discussion in this book falls within the area of the Western European Marriage Pattern, marked by a late age at marriage for both men and women and the creation of independent households on marriage (Hajnal, 1983).[4] As a corollary, the system was also marked by an interlude in which the young no longer lived with their natal household but moved to the households of others who could offer them employment as servants (women undertaking domestic tasks or dairying and men farm work). 'Life-cycle service' is therefore our first form of labour. The second is day labouring in which men (and sometimes women) were paid by the task or the day. Normally they would be married with their own households. From the farmer's point of view, they were a pool of labour

[3] The alternative was the reallocation of land within the village to match land to households. This is rarely, if ever, found in the North Sea area.

[4] The co-habitation of generations is found in some parts of Scandinavia.

which could be called on as needed over the year without having to pay for their labour at the slack times. In southern England, where this logic was perhaps taken furthest, the result was that labourers' families were reliant on public welfare assistance for some of the year. By the twentieth century, in England at least, it was perhaps more usual to employ labourers throughout the year. Third, there is the practice found in Scotland and parts of Scandinavia of employing whole families by the year, the farmer offering them cottage accommodation, potato ground (and the manure needed to dung it) and possibly some food. In return for this, the entire family was viewed as available to the farmer as and when he required. Fourth, we should not overlook the continued importance of itinerant seasonal labour, whether Irish labour in England, workmen from Belgium or the Auvergne in northern France or the annual movement from highland to lowland Scandinavia and back again.

Where ever we see them, the position of the agricultural labourer is weak. Labourers generally lacked political power. They found it very hard to organise (assuming, of course, that rural trades unionism was legal). Their dependence on the individual farmer made them either vulnerable to eviction or, if they angered him, ostracisation by other farmers when their term of service ended. They were not without weapons to show their disapproval of the way they were treated – arson, animal maiming, anonymous threatening letters – but ultimately their only real sanction against their employers was migration to towns where higher wages could be coupled with the possibility of an independent, rather than subordinate, lifestyle. The relationship of farmer and labourer could therefore be a very charged and bitter one. Farmers could not control the price their commodities brought them nor the rents they paid; but they could attempt to manage their costs by employing both less labour and cutting its rate of pay. Hence the attraction of mechanisation which labourers plainly feared and which was finally their nemesis. Machinery has gone a long way to make the farmer self-sufficient in labour at most times of the year. In a sense, mechanisation has almost allowed a return to the farming of the middle ages in which the peasant relied on his own labour and that of his household. The seasonal workforce has now been replaced by the agricultural contractor.

1.8 Government

Government has grown enormously in complexity and cost over the last two hundred years. Medieval government had limited objectives: its own survival against both internal and external enemies (including its own peasantries), the preservation of the property rights of the aristocracy (including their rights over men), the supply of legal systems and sound currency. By the eighteenth century there were much higher expectations that government would also involve itself with the welfare of its subjects, and with the development of democracy and universal adult suffrage, this has perhaps become one of the major purposes of the state.

There is something to be said for characterising the medieval state as a 'domain state', living mostly off rents from its land and having recourse to taxation only at times of war. The early modern state was increasingly a 'taxation state' although arguably France and England in the seventeenth century were doing no more than following the path trodden by the Low Countries several centuries earlier. The shift to taxation as the chief source of government income, perhaps coupled with a belief that government should serve the needs of all its subjects rather than the sectional interests of property owners, compelled it to take an interest in all forms of economic activity which might be taxable, as well as expressing concern about aspects of economic activity (depopulating enclosure, the manipulation of markets for profit) which were self-serving, and contrary to the larger needs of the commonwealth. Hence government needed to put in place mechanisms which would allow agricultural and commercial activity to expand (for instance by licensing reclamation from the sea or by authorising markets), which would allow institutional restraints to be overcome (for instance, through enclosure) and which would increase the taxable economic activity within the country. In agriculture, there were, throughout the later eighteenth century and after, debates over how best to achieve this. Some countries saw the British path as the one to follow, believing that the future was one of large farms and capitalist tenants. Others saw the large landowner as a brake on progress and placed a greater premium on the owner-occupier and wished – for reasons of social stability if nothing else – to move the peasant or farmer directly from a position of feudal subordination to one of independence. Outside Britain, the eighteenth century saw a whole series of government initiatives to create owner-occupying farmers, from the sale of church and émigré lands in France in the early 1790s, the sale of state land in Sweden intermittently throughout the century and the emancipation of serfs in Germany and Schleswig-Holstein in the last years of the eighteenth century and early years of the nineteenth. In Britain however, land became even more concentrated in the hands of the aristocracy until the very end of the nineteenth century.

The late eighteenth and early nineteenth century were also marked in Europe by government initiatives to achieve what had largely been undertaken in Britain by landowner and occupier initiatives: enclosure of open field and wastes, and the rationalisation of the countryside into ring-fenced farming units.

This modernising might be associated with ideals of personal freedom, certainly with a new approach to property. It was, by the late eighteenth century, also associated with the belief that owner-occupiers were economically more productive. They were therefore better able to generate taxation income (although in fact the countryside tended to be lightly taxed) and supply growing urban markets. Hence pre-modern governments may be described as being broadly productivist. They valued production and encouraged increases in production, with a particular emphasis on the supply of bread grains. This was the chosen way to ensure the food security of urban populations and so of maintaining urban peace. This long phase in government thinking came to an end in the mid-nineteenth century as the opening of the Russian Steppes and the American mid-West offered new supplies of bread grains at prices below those which domestic producers could match. For an extended period European governments adopted a calculation which saw urban food security as being prominently a matter of *price* rather than *supply*. This ensured the quiescence of the towns, to whom the governments were increasingly beholden as enlarged franchises came to include a progressively larger proportion of urban population. But this all came at the cost of a simmering anger in the countryside which worked itself out in a proliferation of agricultural societies, lobby groups and agrarian parties, often organised along confessional lines. Whilst they all sought to catch government's ear, they were singularly unsuccessful, for protectionism could all too readily be read as an attack on urban living standards for the benefit of landowners and farmers. Nonetheless, some countries did adopt broadly protectionist stances to protect their agricultural sectors (France, Germany, Sweden) whilst for others free trade remained uncontradicted until well into the twentieth century.

The first half of the twentieth-century though was, generally speaking, protectionist, the second half even more so. The forty years after the Second World War combined protectionist and productivist policies, first within individual nation states and then within the progressively enlarged European [Economic] Community. By 1990 the degree of overproduction which it had generated and its costs made it unsustainable, and there was, in any case, a return to the mid-nineteenth century ideology of free trade.

This story is worth telling in somewhat greater detail given its importance in explaining the situation that European farmers and consumers face in the second decade of this still young century. A number of countries introduced tariffs and created marketing boards in the 1930s. The Second World War was a major shock to farming and particularly to an import-led food economy like Britain's. Throughout northern Europe, the reputation of farmers may have received something of a boost. After World War II, the western European countries all felt the need for cooperation. The Organisation for European Economic Co-operation (OEEC) was created in April 1948 to help administer the Marshall Plan which itself aimed to encourage economic co-operation. The European Community for Coal and Steel was created in 1951, but the initiative for a collaboration in agriculture failed.

The Treaty of Rome, signed on 25 March 1957 by the six founding member states (Belgium, France, Germany, Italy, Luxemburg and the Netherlands), established the Common Market. Amongst other objectives, it aimed at encouraging productivity in agriculture so that consumers had a stable supply of food and the Common Market had a viable agricultural sector. Its basic objective was to increase productivity by promoting technical progress and ensuring the optimum use of the factors of production, in particular labour; to ensure a fair standard of living for farmers; to stabilise markets; to secure availability of supplies; and to provide consumers with food at reasonable prices. The principles of the Common Agricultural Policy (CAP) were set out in 1958. The agricultural markets within the six countries were organized, with the free trade of agricultural products, the unity of prices, community preference and financial solidarity being guiding principles. Policy was strongly influenced by the umbrella organization of the national farmers' unions of the member states, COPA (*Comité des organizations professionnelles agricoles de la CEE*), founded in 1958.

From 1962 to 1968, as the CAP developed, there was a hesitation between two kinds of market organisation. Either farmers could sell their products at a price level lower than their production costs and receive a direct grant from the state, the deficiency payment, or products could be sold at a price which would assure a fair return for the farmer but might be artificially high. Both coexisted, but mainly it was the latter strategy which was adopted. In 1973 three new countries were integrated into the CAP: the United Kingdom, Ireland and Denmark. Production increased, the CAP was very successful in meeting its objective of moving the EU towards self-sufficiency and the living standards of farmers notably increased. Nonetheless, its policies were questioned. In December 1968, Sicco Mansholt, European Commissioner for Agriculture and a former Dutch Minister of Agriculture, presented a long term plan that showed the limits of a policy of price and market support. He suggested a reform of structures: in particular small farmers were to be encouraged to give up farming, in order to increase the size of the remaining family farms. This was to go hand in hand with welfare programmes to cover early retirement and vocational training measures; they aimed at a better integration of agriculture in the global economy. At the same moment, a similar plan was proposed in France by Georges Vedel. Both were received with anger by the agricultural community and the reform proposals were temporarily abandoned.

Production surpluses gradually increased and increasing quantities of European funds were used to support the community's agricultural policy: from less than 2 billion ECU in 1970 to 4 billion in 1975, 10 in 1980, 20 in 1985. Measures were adopted in order to reduce surpluses (milk quotas, 1983; fallow fields ('set-aside'), 1984). From 1986, in a context of concurrence with American agriculture, and in order to follow the GATT requirements for free trade, prices were reduced to the point where they no longer covered the cost of production. After the MacSharry reforms of 1992, farmers have had to manage on international market prices while receiving direct income aid for farming in environmentally sound ways.

Hence we can see all too clearly how government has moved from being largely passive in agricultural matters in the Middle Ages to determining the pattern of production in increasing detail. Twenty-first century government *knows* what is being grown, field by field, parcel by parcel. Through the development of planning and zoning laws, government has, in some ways, it has come to occupy the place of landlords in the management of landscapes but not even in Britain, where the practice of designating land as 'green belt' was developed to its furthest, has it been able to stop the suburbanisation of the countryside, the appearance of industrial developments in a rural context and the destruction – often financed by government – of environmentally important landscapes. The countryside in the twentieth century was indeed a diminishing asset: whether in the future agriculture will once again be valued and food production seen as a vital part of national economies must, for the moment, be a matter of speculation. In an age of globalisation, the North Sea basin may in the future be seen as too small an area to have its own distinctive future, but we can savour the achievements of its past and attempt to understand them.

Fibula from Dorestad discovered in 1969, dating from about 800 (Source: National Museum of Antiquities, Leiden)

From 1962 to 1968, as the CAP developed, there was a hesitation between two kinds of market organisation. Either farmers could sell their products at a price level lower than their production costs and receive a direct grant from the state, the deficiency payment, or products could be sold at a price which would assure a fair return for the farmer but might be artificially high. Both coexisted, but mainly it was the latter strategy which was adopted. In 1973 three new countries were integrated into the CAP: the United Kingdom, Ireland and Denmark. Production increased, the CAP was very successful in meeting its objective of moving the EU towards self-sufficiency and the living standards of farmers notably increased. Nonetheless, its policies were questioned. In December 1968, Sicco Mansholt, European Commissioner for Agriculture and a former Dutch Minister of Agriculture, presented a long term plan that showed the limits of a policy of price and market support. He suggested a reform of structures: in particular small farmers were to be encouraged to give up farming, in order to increase the size of the remaining family farms. This was to go hand in hand with welfare programmes to cover early retirement and vocational training measures; they aimed at a better integration of agriculture in the global economy. At the same moment, a similar plan was proposed in France by Georges Vedel. Both were received with anger by the agricultural community and the reform proposals were temporarily abandoned.

Production surpluses gradually increased and increasing quantities of European funds were used to support the community's agricultural policy: from less than 2 billion ECU in 1970 to 4 billion in 1975, 10 in 1980, 20 in 1985. Measures were adopted in order to reduce surpluses (milk quotas, 1983; fallow fields ('set-aside'), 1984). From 1986, in a context of concurrence with American agriculture, and in order to follow the GATT requirements for free trade, prices were reduced to the point where they no longer covered the cost of production. After the MacSharry reforms of 1992, farmers have had to manage on international market prices while receiving direct income aid for farming in environmentally sound ways.

Hence we can see all too clearly how government has moved from being largely passive in agricultural matters in the Middle Ages to determining the pattern of production in increasing detail. Twenty-first century government *knows* what is being grown, field by field, parcel by parcel. Through the development of planning and zoning laws, government has, in some ways, it has come to occupy the place of landlords in the management of landscapes but not even in Britain, where the practice of designating land as 'green belt' was developed to its furthest, has it been able to stop the suburbanisation of the countryside, the appearance of industrial developments in a rural context and the destruction – often financed by government – of environmentally important landscapes. The countryside in the twentieth century was indeed a diminishing asset: whether in the future agriculture will once again be valued and food production seen as a vital part of national economies must, for the moment, be a matter of speculation. In an age of globalisation, the North Sea basin may in the future be seen as too small an area to have its own distinctive future, but we can savour the achievements of its past and attempt to understand them.

Fibula from Dorestad discovered in 1969, dating from about 800 (Source: National Museum of Antiquities, Leiden)

From 1962 to 1968, as the CAP developed, there was a hesitation between two kinds of market organisation. Either farmers could sell their products at a price level lower than their production costs and receive a direct grant from the state, the deficiency payment, or products could be sold at a price which would assure a fair return for the farmer but might be artificially high. Both coexisted, but mainly it was the latter strategy which was adopted. In 1973 three new countries were integrated into the CAP: the United Kingdom, Ireland and Denmark. Production increased, the CAP was very successful in meeting its objective of moving the EU towards self-sufficiency and the living standards of farmers notably increased. Nonetheless, its policies were questioned. In December 1968, Sicco Mansholt, European Commissioner for Agriculture and a former Dutch Minister of Agriculture, presented a long term plan that showed the limits of a policy of price and market support. He suggested a reform of structures: in particular small farmers were to be encouraged to give up farming, in order to increase the size of the remaining family farms. This was to go hand in hand with welfare programmes to cover early retirement and vocational training measures; they aimed at a better integration of agriculture in the global economy. At the same moment, a similar plan was proposed in France by Georges Vedel. Both were received with anger by the agricultural community and the reform proposals were temporarily abandoned.

Production surpluses gradually increased and increasing quantities of European funds were used to support the community's agricultural policy: from less than 2 billion ECU in 1970 to 4 billion in 1975, 10 in 1980, 20 in 1985. Measures were adopted in order to reduce surpluses (milk quotas, 1983; fallow fields ('set-aside'), 1984). From 1986, in a context of concurrence with American agriculture, and in order to follow the GATT requirements for free trade, prices were reduced to the point where they no longer covered the cost of production. After the MacSharry reforms of 1992, farmers have had to manage on international market prices while receiving direct income aid for farming in environmentally sound ways.

Hence we can see all too clearly how government has moved from being largely passive in agricultural matters in the Middle Ages to determining the pattern of production in increasing detail. Twenty-first century government *knows* what is being grown, field by field, parcel by parcel. Through the development of planning and zoning laws, government has, in some ways, it has come to occupy the place of landlords in the management of landscapes but not even in Britain, where the practice of designating land as 'green belt' was developed to its furthest, has it been able to stop the suburbanisation of the countryside, the appearance of industrial developments in a rural context and the destruction – often financed by government – of environmentally important landscapes. The countryside in the twentieth century was indeed a diminishing asset: whether in the future agriculture will once again be valued and food production seen as a vital part of national economies must, for the moment, be a matter of speculation. In an age of globalisation, the North Sea basin may in the future be seen as too small an area to have its own distinctive future, but we can savour the achievements of its past and attempt to understand them.

1.9 Conclusion

Before the nineteenth century, rural history is the study of human society as whole. Cities and towns certainly have their own distinctive experiences, but they were never far removed from the countryside, not only its rhythms and seasons but also its smells. Many people living in towns had been born in the countryside. Their relatives remained there, they perhaps returned for harvests, perhaps harboured ambitions to return there themselves. Something as simple as the size of the loaf told the urban proletariat about how good (or bad) the previous harvest had been and how expectations of the following harvest looked. Much of this has been lost. Most people – even those living in the countryside – cannot tell standing wheat from standing barley. Few could milk a cow, either by hand or using machinery, and virtually none could make cheese any more than they could repair a computer. But we all eat, and food remains a matter of political debate, even anxiety. The problem of how far Europe should be self-sufficient in foodstuffs, and the question of what the appropriate level of return for the farmer should be for his skill, labour and capital is no less an issue for being so much a perennial one.

Moreover, the countryside remains important for its recreational value. Many choose to live in the countryside for its quality of life. This creeping suburbanisation has often brought newcomers, with their urban assumptions about the countryside, into conflict with those for whom the countryside both provides both a livelihood and their place of work. Many others use the countryside for holiday recreation and relish its isolation, its fresh air, its slow pace, and the sports it offers, whether walking, sailing, climbing or shooting. They too can find themselves in conflict with those for whom the countryside is an industrial premises. Rural recreation is mostly free and its costs borne out of general taxation revenues, but the equation has increasingly been made in recent years that subsidies to farmers are actually for their role as custodians of the countryside. This in turn raises questions about the public's right of access to privately-owned property, a matter of contention in England throughout the later twentieth century. An old-fashioned, perhaps even obsolete view of the countryside and its bucolic inhabitants remains etched into the collective psyche of most north European nations, an image which in the late twentieth century became increasingly at odds with the realities of farming.

In these and other respects, the issues discussed in this book are by no means dead. Agricultural or rural history encompasses an enormous subject. The approach taken here is not the only one possible – after all, this is one of four studies of the history of the North Sea area being written concurrently – but we would argue that the approach we adopt, looking at ownership and power in the countryside, not only helps us understand the past, but tells us a great deal about where we are in the present, for we are the beneficiaries of much more than a millennium of development and change. Much is shaped for us: there is little that any generation shapes for itself. The challenges we face are as much the challenges of the past as those of the future.

Bibliography

Aston, T. H. and Philpin, C. H. E. (eds) (1985) *The Brenner Debate. Agrarian class structure and economic development in pre-industrial Europe,* Cambridge.

Cohen, J. (1996) 'Institutions and economic analysis', in T. G. Rawski *et al., Economics and the historian,* Berkeley.

Campbell, B. M. S. and Overton, M. (1993) 'A new perspective on medieval and early modern agriculture: six centuries of Norfolk farming', *Past and Present,* 141, pp. 38–105.

Dewald, J, and Vardi, L. (1998) 'The peasantries of France, 1400–1789', in T. Scott (ed), *The peasantries of Europe from the fourteenth to the eighteenth centuries,* Harlow.

Duby, G. and Armand W. (eds) (1985) *Histoire de la France rurale,* II, *1340–1789,* Paris.

Hajnal, J. (1983) 'Two kinds of pre-industrial household formation system', in R. Wall *et al* (eds), *Family forms in historical Europe*, Cambridge, pp. 65–104.

Hatcher, J. and Bailey, M. (2001) *Modelling the Middle Ages. The history and theory of England's economic development,* Oxford.

Hoppenbrouwers, P. and van Zanden, J. L. (eds) (2001) *Peasants into farmers? The transformation of rural economy and society in the Low Countries (middle ages-19th century) in light of the Brenner debate* (CORN Publication Series 4), Turnhout.

Le Roy Ladurie, E. (1996*) Les paysans de Languedoc,* Paris, pb edn 1969; trans. (1976) *The peasants of Languedoc,* Urbana.

Fibula from Dorestad discovered in 1969, dating from about 800 (Source: National Museum of Antiquities, Leiden)

2 Social relations, property and power around the North Sea, 500–1000

Chris Wickham

At the start of the middle ages, north-western Europe was divided in economic and social terms into two large, sharply contrasted, regions: the former Roman empire in the lands south of the Rhine, and a wide though less clearly defined territory to its north, inhabited by Germanic-speaking groups as far north as central-northern Norway and, in the northern British Isles, Celtic-speaking groups, unified only by the fact that the Romans had never conquered them. This division is a particularly crucial one for a volume focussed on property and political relations.

In the Roman world, landownership was the basis of wealth, and the ownership of numerous estates was the basis of political power. The Roman empire was a tax-based state, so it also had salaried officials, both military and civilian; but only a minority of military leaders, and almost no civilian leaders, were not rich landowners to start with. In the fifth century, however, the empire was replaced in the West by several separate kingdoms as a result of the Germanic invasions, which changed the balance of power between state and aristocracy. (A demographic decline seems to have characterised the fifth century in our area too.) By the sixth century, when this book begins, the political dominance of major landowners was even greater, for by then in the heartland of the Frankish kingdom – the main successor-state to the Roman empire in the North Sea area – the Roman fiscal system was weakening fast. It is only well-documented (up to the eighth century) in the Loire valley, and it seems to have produced much less tax than under the empire even there (Lot, 1928: 83–107; Goffart, 1989: 213–31; Wickham, 2005: 105–15). Henceforth, large-scale landowning was the only secure path to wealth and political power, and it would remain so in the Frankish lands to 1000 and well beyond.

North of the Roman world, we can be much less certain about this equation. Our evidence is poor, both elliptic and late, but what data we have indicate to us that power did not derive from large-scale landowning in any simple way. In some parts of the region (notably Britain), this is because the Roman concept of exclusive land tenure had been abandoned or was never present, leaving royal and aristocratic and peasant landholders with different levels of rights in the same territories. In other regions, versions of exclusive tenure may well have existed, but social hierarchies were relatively flat, and concentrations of wealth very few. In both cases, political power was largely constructed out of different building blocks from those attached to landownership: mainly from the accumulation of armed clients, and the forcible extraction of tribute from those who could not resist. These patterns will be explored in greater detail in the next section, but for now they need to be set out to mark a contrast. And, north of the former Roman world, it is above all the case that even the richest and most powerful people controlled far less wealth than Roman emperors and senators – or than the Frankish kings and aristocrats who succeeded them. The richest élites throughout our

Map 2.1 The North Sea area, 500–1000

period were invariably in the far south of the North Sea area, making the Frankish heartland, what is now northern France, Belgium and western Germany, the political hub of the whole of north-western Europe. Only at the very end of our period, in the middle tenth century, did real concentrations of wealth appear anywhere else: in southern and eastern England and in inland (south-eastern) Saxony.

Up to *c*.400, the northern boundary of the Roman empire, and of Roman-style property-owning and political hierarchies, had been not only the Rhine, but also Hadrian's Wall in what is now the far north of England. The fifth century, however, saw a systemic crisis in Britain, and, by the time good evidence returns (archaeological in the sixth century, documentary in the seventh in both Wales and England), the Anglo-Saxons had settled in numerous small kingdoms and Roman economic structures had vanished. The Roman world had thus retreated from Britain before this book begins. But from the eighth century onwards, Roman/Frankish presuppositions about the nature of landowning power began slowly to move northwards again. This was partly because of conquest: Charles Martel established a form of hegemony over Frisia (roughly the modern Netherlands) at the beginning of the century, and Charlemagne conquered Saxony in a series of bloody campaigns starting in the 770s. By 800 or so, direct Frankish rule extended north to the Danish frontier. Ecclesiastical landowning followed, and secular aristocracies – both Saxon and Frankish – gained in wealth in these northern lands too. Simple conversion to Christianity could reinforce large landowning as well; the conversion of Anglo-Saxon England in the seventh century saw the slow implantation of a church which wished to own land by Roman property law, and which, by the early tenth century, did so, acting as a model for secular élites too. The Danish church by the eleventh century (a century after Danish Christianisation) was in a similar position. For a variety of reasons, then, the possibilities for landowning wealth and power became ever greater, and the possibilities for peasant autonomy became ever smaller. These developments will underpin this entire chapter.

There was always a spectrum of opportunities for political élites. These were greatest by far, even in 1000, in the Frankish heartland, but by then, lowland England and eastern Saxony as well. They then dropped off the further away from that heartland one went: rapidly as one moved into Wales and Scotland, where the power of rulers was incomplete for centuries; more slowly and steadily as one crossed the Rhine into Frisia and western Saxony, went north into Denmark, and then into Norway and Sweden, in the last of which political leaders were even more restricted in their power than in Wales and Scotland. Each of these separate regions thus showed a different relationship between property and power in the early middle ages, and they will have to be discussed separately as a result. This will be the theme of the first main section of this chapter, on property ownership, which will be divided regionally, before some general conclusions are reached. The other main section, on the occupiers of the land, the peasantry, will be less regional, however, for the overall patterns of peasant society across the whole of the North Sea area were rather more uniform. The weakness of the state in this period means that there will not be a separate section on public policies; the actions of kings and other hegemonic political powers will be treated briefly in both section 2.1 and at the end of section 2.2.

The evidence for property and power, and for village society, is very badly distributed in the period 500–1000. There is good documentary evidence only for the Frankish heartland (after *c.*650) and for Wales and England (beginning in the same period, but becoming dense only for certain parts of the region). For England, too, we have the *Domesday Book*, shortly after the end of our period, which gives us some clear indicators for the tenth century. North of the Rhine, however, only a handful of churches and monasteries with substantial lands in Frisia and Saxony – notably Utrecht, Werden and Corvey – preserve documents from our period; Danish (and also Scottish) evidence does not begin until around 1100; and Norwegian/Swedish documentary evidence much later. The further north we go, the more we have to rely on narrative histories, which were of course not focussed on land tenure at all, and which were also either sketchy or late – the fullest, the Norwegian narratives, are twelfth- or thirteenth-century, and their reliability has increasingly been questioned. There is a severe imbalance here, which furthermore means that the regions with Roman/Frankish tenurial patterns are far better documented than the lands without them; and that, in the northern regions, the best-documented types of tenure are also those most similar to Roman/Frankish landowning. In recent decades, a reaction in England, the Netherlands, Germany and Scandinavia against a romantic privileging of 'Germanic freedom', as with the *Gemeinfreie* imagery of nineteenth-century German scholarship, has led to a stress on early medieval aristocratic and royal hierarchies, and to an emphasis on landowning power, including in the North. This is justified: but only as long as one does not go too far. There were sharp differences in the *scale* of wealth and power across the whole North Sea area, as archaeology makes clear, and land documents only illuminate part of that. As a result, I shall argue from documentary absence as well as documentary presence in what follows.

2.1 Ownership, power relations and the distribution of property

This section will be divided into five regional treatments: the Frankish heartland, south of the Rhine; Frisia and Saxony, and the steady impact on them of Frankish hierarchies after 800; England, which arguably saw the greatest social changes of any part of the North Sea area in the early middle ages; Wales and Scotland (treated most briefly), which did not; and western Scandinavia, where stable hierarchies appeared heterogeneously, and not until the very end of our period.

The richest landowners in the post-Roman world lived in northern Francia, between the Loire and the Rhine. The richest by far were the Merovingian kings, after 751 the Carolingian king-emperors, with their huge concentrations of estates in the Île-de-France around Paris; the territory between Metz and Frankfurt; and around Aachen and, in general, in the middle Meuse/Maas valley, the latter of which were mostly the old aristocratic lands of the Pippinid ancestors of the Carolingians (Metz, 1960; Werner, 1980; Barbier, 1990). The greatest Frankish aristocrats also owned dozens of estates, as are shown by wills from the Merovingian and, occasionally, the Carolingian period (Wickham, 2005: 186–93; Kasten, 1990). Aristocratic wealth was further added to in most cases by royal gifts, permanent or temporary (the Carolingians preferred temporary cessions, *beneficia*), gifts which of course above all benefited the politically loyal. Landowning conveyed status directly, along with noble birth and royal office-holding (Goetz, 2007: 173–205). And these secular landed powers were matched by ecclesiastical landowners, of which the best-documented are the great monastic foundations, themselves founded and endowed with royal and aristocratic wealth. David Herlihy calculated convincingly that a third of the land-area of Francia was owned by churches and monasteries by the late ninth century (Herlihy, 1961). We know about the extent of their lands not only because of the survival of gifts of land to them, beginning with the original documents of St-Denis outside Paris in the seventh century, but also because in the ninth century, with royal encouragement, monasteries made and preserved inventories of their estates, called polyptychs, which characteristically listed details of the land, the names of the tenants (and often of all members of tenant families), and the full extent of all rents and services due from each to the church. These are the most detailed sources for the exploitation of land for the whole of early medieval Europe, and have been much studied (see most recently Rösener, 1989; Verhulst, 1992; 2002; Devroey, 2003; 2006; Toubert, 2004; Morimoto, 2008). The society of the bipartite estates, or manors, of northern Francia, on the lands of St-Germain-des-Prés (Paris), or St-Rémi-de-Reims, or St-Bertin (modern St-Omer), or St. Baafs in Gent, or Prüm in the Eifel (Kuchenbuch, 1978), is as a result very well-known, in great detail.

Until the 1960s, the economy and society of the polyptychs was regarded as typical of most of post-Roman Europe. In particular all estates were thought to be bipartite, blocks of land divided into a demesne and peasant tenures, with tenants doing labour service on the demesne, and artisanal production an added obligation; this allowed landlords to be supplied with all their needs without going through the market, although such an estate economy was also criticised as inefficient (see e.g. Latouche, 1956: 204–42, still a good analysis; Duby, 1973: 97–113). The recent work cited above has, by contrast, shown that only a minority of estates (largely in the Loire-Rhine heartland) were organised as tightly as St-Germain's; that such organisation only developed on a large scale after the mid-eighth century; and that, far from inefficient, the manorial economy was the most effective means of extracting surplus from tenants then available, with production largely focussed on sale. Other systems of tenure seem to have relied on more standardised and traditional (and sometimes lower) rents, from both free and unfree tenants, and less intense supervision. But, on the other hand, there has been no contestation of the argument that Frankish estates could be very large, and that great landowners were very rich; this is taken for granted in all accounts. (There is only disagreement about the level of continuity between the major Frankish landowners visible from the late sixth century onwards, and the Roman landowning tradition which may have hit crisis a little over a century before: see Wickham, 2005: 178–86 for continuity and Halsall, 2007: 348–57 for discontinuity.) The Frankish kings hardly taxed after the mid seventh-century, as we have seen; although the Carolingians did expect army service from the richer strata of the free, and took dues from others in lieu of military service when they wished, this did not develop into a stable fiscal system (see e.g. Devroey, 1989: 456–60; Innes, 2000: 153–6). The Carolingians did, however, institute regular tithes, for the benefit of the cathedral churches of each diocese; the existence of tithe from this time on is a clear proof of the institutional wealth of bishoprics as well, which are otherwise less well-documented than monasteries.

This was a world in which landowning peasants were very much on the defensive. Indeed, in parts of Neustria (modern northern France) there may have been few of them, for royal/aristocratic/church estates were often large interlocking blocks of land, leaving little space for more independent owners (Wickham, 2005: 398–406). But, in northern Francia as a whole, and particularly in Austrasia (modern eastern Belgium, Lorraine, and Germany west of the Rhine), great estates were much more fragmented, and there was more space for village-level *rentiers* ('medium owners') and owner-cultivators to exist; the latter are particularly clearly documented in the middle Rhineland around Mainz, thanks to the records of the monastery of Lorsch in the late eighth century and early ninth (see e.g. Staab, 1975; Innes, 2000; Kohl, 2005). There are signs that village-level owners there gained a certain solidarity out of a need to avoid being absorbed by the great landowners around them, although many certainly also entered aristocratic and ecclesiastical clientèles. Carolingian kings made laws to protect them from oppression (Müller-Mertens, 1963), for early medieval kingship was regarded as connected legally to the entire free (male) community, rich and poor, and the Carolingians had a particularly high opinion of their own roles as founts of justice (and, indeed, of religious salvation, at least in principle). Of course, royal legislation was not likely to have been more than intermittently effective, given the fact that in the localities public power was represented by the very aristocrats against whose oppressive acts kings legislated (see e.g. Nelson, 1986); all the same, a landowning peasantry survived in most areas into the tenth century. It was always outnumbered by free and unfree tenants, all the same, who owed heavy obligations to landlords. Unfree tenants were not yet subject to all the obligations of 'serfdom', but their rents and services were higher, and they had no legal protection.

The break-up of Carolingian unity after the late ninth century led to extremes of political fragmentation in Francia by 1000, with between ten and twenty effectively autonomous powers between the Loire and the Rhine – the western half not at all subject to the surviving West Frankish king, who only controlled the Île-de-France; the eastern half nominally part of East Francia, whose Ottonian kings controlled eastern Saxony and some of the Rhineland quite tightly, but had a rather looser hegemony elsewhere. That fragmentation reduced the geographical scale of aristocratic landed power, for few people had lands outside a few counties (the instability of the period often led to the loss by monasteries of their outlying lands, too). But it did not reduce the level of aristocratic dominance inside local areas; on the contrary, it allowed its further intensification, for kings and counts acted less and less as protectors of the peasantry. The smaller-scale strata of the aristocracy that crystallised in the tenth century around the expanding network of private castles were even more intent on local dominance than had been the greater lords of the Merovingian-Carolingian period, for without direct control over their neighbours they might be distinguishable only with difficulty from them. There has recently been an extensive debate between historians who argue that this local 'feudal' dominance was new and revolutionary, and those who argue that it shows considerable continuities with the

Carolingian world (Bournazel and Poly (eds), 1998 and Bisson, 2009 sum up the former position, Barthélemy, 1997 and Barton, 2004 the latter). Whatever position one takes, however, it cannot be denied that after 1000, local lords had coercive resources, called seigneurial or banal lordship (the French *seigneurie banale*) by historians, which were less common, and also less formalised, before: they controlled their own courts and the profits of justice; they demanded castle-guard, or money in lieu of it; they received dues for access to woodland or mills. Peasant owners – where they survived, for they were fewer in number by now (Feller, 1997) – often had to pay these dues along with their tenant neighbours; as for tenants, a more generalised seigneurial subjection would after 1000 increasingly replace older differences between freedom and unfreedom.

The bulk of the early documentation for the whole North Sea area comes from the area south of the Rhine, just discussed, but this does not mean that we should see it as a general model. Frisia and Saxony were very different. Before the Frankish take-over of each in the eighth century, all our evidence is that hierarchies there were relatively restricted. Frisia had a ruler, whose power-base seems to have been in the south, around Utrecht, but archaeology has so far shown no major concentrations of wealth there, although individual Frisians could prosper as merchants (Lebecq, 1983; Heidinga, 1997). Saxony had no centralised rule, and operated as a network of small communities (*pagi*), each with aristocrats, lesser free families, half-free (*liti* or *lazzi*) and unfree (*servi*, *mancipia*) – a hierarchy also found in Frisia. We cannot tell what sort of economic relationship the free and half-free had to the Saxon aristocracy – what sort of estates the latter had, in particular – but again the scale of wealth cannot have been huge. Both the free and the half-free had a voice in the assembly (*concilium*, *conventus*) of each *pagus* (see in general Lintzel, 1961: I, 115–27).

This pattern changed faster in Saxony than in Frisia. It is hard to track networks of estates in ninth- and tenth-century Frisia, except in the concentrations of royal and episcopal land around Utrecht (including the major ports of Dorestad and Tiel) and Nijmegen (Rothoff, 1953; Henderikx, 1987: 115–23). The Frankish monasteries of Werden and Fulda did have cloth-producing estates in the north (Lebecq, 1983: I, 131–8; II, 383–6), and Groningen was a royal *villa*, later ceded to the cathedral of Utrecht (Rothoff, 1953: 86), but along the coast, a mercantile and cloth-making focus, the century of the Viking attacks was not perhaps the best period for the affirmation of landlordly power, and the east Frisian islands remained areas of relative autonomy for at least peasant élites into the later middle ages, as also did the Drenthe south of Groningen. Saxony suffered much more from the violence of Charlemagne's conquest, and the latter implanted by force a Frankish Christian church structure and many new Frankish families, alongside a Saxon aristocracy increasing in power. Rapid social change ensued, including in particular a sharpening of socio-economic hierarchies. The Saxon free and half-free peasantry responded by taking their chance to revolt during the Frankish civil war of the 840s, in the Stellinga uprising of 841–2, by a long way the largest-scale peasants' revolt of early medieval Europe (Epperlein, 1969: 50–68; Müller-Mertens, 1972; Goldberg, 1995). When this failed, the steady extension of tenurial subjection, first to the half-free and soon to the free, could continue without respite.

Even this, however, did not make Saxony like Francia (see in general Reuter, 2006: 300–24). It is true that we find some large-scale bipartite estates in the land documentation for the monasteries of Werden and Corvey, particularly on better agricultural land and in the south of the region; but most estates were more simply structured, with little demesne and on a smaller scale (Rösener, 1985). The tenth-century monastic surveys also show that many estates were fragmented into sets of isolated tenant houses, not all owing labour services. The growth in political importance of the Slav frontier led by the tenth century to a concentration of political and landholding power in the east of Saxony, the heartland of Ottonian power, and increasingly also the main source of silver for western Europe, which kings would fight for long to hold onto. Here, kings, churchmen and aristocrats did their best to behave like élites in Francia. An aristocrat with seven tenants could be described by Adam of Bremen in the late eleventh century as a *pauper*: rich men evidently owned considerably more (Adam of Bremen, 1917: II, 9). But our evidence for large-scale landowning does not cover the whole of Saxony, and in the north, in particular, and towards Frisia, the major political powers (such as the archbishops of Hamburg-Bremen) may have been more isolated. Nor did the private banal lordship of West Francia develop very far here. The lesser free of Saxony retained a greater political status than elsewhere; they were used for military defence by Henry I in the early tenth century, for example (although these were perhaps not always peasants). They were also at least subordinate – sometimes troublesome – players as late as the aristocratic-led Saxon revolt of 1073–5 (see, for a source, Lampert of Hersfeld, 1894: cc. 148, 179, 183–4, 216, 228, 236–8).

Anglo-Saxon England was not conquered by the Franks, but its élites developed in a Frankish direction, probably encouraged by the Frankish example. When our documentary and narrative evidence begins, in the century after 670, we find reference to very large land units, even though Anglo-Saxon kingdoms were then relatively small (equivalent in size for the most part to one or two modern counties). The *tributum* or *pastum* ('tribute', 'feeding') due to kings, and to the churches and monasteries to whom kings gave lands in our documents, also seems to have been relatively small scale. It is most likely that kings, local notables/small scale aristocrats, and peasants all held rights to surplus at different levels inside these land units, and probably all regarded themselves as possessors there (see for a recent survey Wickham, 2005: 314–26). This also fits the absence in the archaeology of striking concentrations of wealth before 750 or so, except for royal prestige-burials like Sutton Hoo and Prittlewell (*Prittlewell,* 2004), both on or near the east coast of England. Wealth seems to have derived from small quantities of surplus funnelled to kings from wide land areas, rather than from the ownership and systematic exploitation of specific estates. This wealth was also used to maintain armed entourages, who were the basis of local political power: successful wars against royal rivals also produced tribute from defeated kingdoms, and a wider – but often temporary – political hegemony (see, among many, Campbell, 1982: 53–68). This model for the relationship between wealth and power, its details clearly visible in Anglo-Saxon narratives such as Bede's *Ecclesiastical history*, has parallels in Wales and Ireland, and probably Scotland; it seems to fit early Scandinavia too. In England, it continued through the eighth century at least.

In that century, however, patterns were already changing. In eastern England, archaeology shows greater concentrations of wealth and artisanal activity in ports like London, Ipswich and York (Scull, 1997), and in estate-centres such as Flixborough in Lincolnshire (Loveluck *et al.*, 2007). In East Anglia, in particular, both standardised Ipswich-ware ceramics and coins are found on most sites by this time (Blinkhorn, 1999; Metcalf, 1994: 483–523), archaeological patterns which for the first time resemble those long normal in Francia. In the Midlands, although the archaeology does not yet change, three generations of Mercian kings created a political hegemony over most of southern England which was durable and increasingly elaborate, even if not fully stable. And the church, recipient of so many land grants, was interested in trying to turn its hegemony over land units into a more stable ownership, an interest that was plausibly shared also by secular aristocrats, who were both clients of steadily stronger kings and tenants of church lands on three-generation leases. Slowly, in a very poorly documented process, the control of the powerful over land and its cultivators increased: first, over sections of land units where cultivators were unfree, and then, steadily, over other central areas, and then outlying areas. This process of increasing control seems to have been particularly important in the ninth century. We can say this because the first documented signs of systematic exploitation date to the first half of the tenth, in the accounts of heavy rents and services paid by free peasants at Hurstborne in Hampshire and Tidenham in Gloucestershire; Hurstborne was indeed a bipartite manor of a type previously only known in Francia and Italy (see for all this Faith, 1997: 56–88, 153–77). The late ninth and early tenth centuries are also the period in which, in much of England, nucleated villages begin to appear, which have been linked to growing aristocratic dominance (e.g. Lewis *et al.*, 1997). Land units were increasingly often subdivided into village-sized blocks, too, perhaps indicating that a new world of estate ownership, and heavier rents, allowed for a smaller landowning units to be profitable.

By the tenth century in England, in the 920s unified under a single king except its northern third, in most areas (even if not necessarily everywhere), a network of landed estates resembling those in Francia thus becomes visible in our evidence. We have an estate-management manual from *c.*1000, the *Rectitudines singularum personarum*, from somewhere in or near the Severn valley, which shows tight manorial control and high rents (Harvey, 1993). *Domesday Book* in 1086 shows high rents and a manorial structure across nearly the whole of the country. Archaeology shows a much more elaborate production and exchange system, and a greater number of rich aristocratic sites (Richards, 2000: 78–108, 139–77). By the end of the tenth century, rural wealth was also exploited directly by kings when they instituted a taxation system, the first in the post-Roman world, initially to pay off Danish raiders, but by the eleventh century (after England's conquest by Danish kings, between 1013 and 1042) directed to kings in the country (Lawson, 1984). All of this means that in the tenth century, in most of England, we can presume that a pattern of landownership and estate management, and a relationship between wealth in land and political power, similar to that we have already seen in Francia, had crystallised – whether by imitation or independent development, but, probably, because of elements of both.

The land gifts by kings to churches and aristocrats in the tenth century, backed up by several lay wills and, a century later, by *Domesday Book,* allow us to say with certainty that secular aristocrats, bishops and monasteries could by now be very rich. Some of the greatest tenth-century aristocrats, all also royal officials, owned dozens of estates, to which the lands attached to the local office of *ealdorman* (the English equivalent of count) could be added; the wills of lesser aristocrats often show large collections of land as well (Stafford, 1989: 38–9, 45–50, 150–61; Whitelock, 1930 for wills). These lands were widely scattered across southern England, which probably implies royal gift-giving; the former West Saxon, now English kings, recent conquerors of Mercia and eastern England, were rich enough to establish new aristocratic élites and still be hegemonic in landowning terms. In the eleventh century, even though the aristocracy documented in the pre-1066 sections of *Domesday Book* by now included two enormously powerful aristocratic families as well as rich lesser aristocrats (Fleming, 1991; Clarke, 1994), the king remained tenurially dominant (Baxter, 2007). This wide-ranging royal, aristocratic and ecclesiastical wealth by now matched that of the wealthiest parts of Francia. It virtually excluded peasant landowning, except in small sections of the East Midlands (though *Domesday Book* does not cover four northern counties, where there may have been more). At most, it may be that some peasants in outlying portions of estates, or on some royal lands, may have been more independent, survivors of older tenurial patterns (Faith, 1997: 89–125, for a maximum view). England had thus moved in three centuries from being one of the least hierarchical regions of the North Sea area to being the most hierarchical, with the lowest level of peasant autonomy. All that England lacked in this respect was seigneurial rights, for kings maintained most powers over justice for the free (Wormald, 1995).

Wales, and probably also Scotland, began with a tenurial pattern very similar to that described here for early eighth-century England. This is above all visible in the seventh-century documents for south-west Wales (Davies, 1978a; 1978b). The difference here is that neither kingship nor aristocratic power increased greatly in intensity for the rest of our period in Wales. Kings did develop wider judicial powers, and perhaps took more tribute, but the small scale of royal power and the instability of wider hegemonies remained in the eleventh century, and signs of greater local organisation only appear in the twelfth (Davies, 1990; Davies, 1987: 56–82). In Scotland, our evidence for landowning and local power is vestigial into the twelfth century, but there are parallels to Wales. Scotland had one large kingdom at its centre, the kingdom of the Picts of the period up to the ninth century, the Alba or Scotia of the tenth and onwards, which had absorbed all the other kingdoms of Scotland's present land area by the early eleventh century with the exception of the Norse earldoms of Orkney and the Western Isles. Alba was thus far larger than any Welsh kingdom (or Irish kingdom – a relevant comparison, for post-900 Alba was dominated by the language and culture of the Irish colonies in western Scotland). But this does not seem to have resulted in an intense control over the land by anyone. By the twelfth and thirteenth centuries, we find estates of a Frankish/English type, particularly in eastern and southern Scotland (though manors were relatively rare and not highly organised); but also constant signs of patterns of tribute which resemble eighth-century England, called by Geoffrey Barrow 'extensive lordship', surviving between the estates described in monastic land surveys (Barrow, 1973: 7–56; Duncan, 1975: 326–48, 392–9). In the Highlands, this form of extensive lordship partially survived in some areas well into the modern period. It was probably not until after 1050 that anyone other than the kings and a handful of churches and aristocrats in Scotland could accumulate wealth from exploiting the free peasantry, and it is likely that not even these had more than a generalised supremacy over the rural population during the period of this chapter. In both Wales and Scotland, then, rapid social change would have to await the twelfth century.

Denmark shows some parallels to Scotland. Like Frisia and Scotland, but unlike Wales and Saxony, it was a single kingdom by 800, and perhaps even by the 720s; like Scotland, it was not conquered by its more powerful southern neighbour. When its documents begin in the late eleventh century and (in particular) the twelfth, the king, aristocrats and churches had large estates. Conversely, it is clear that an independent peasantry also survived, for royal and church estates were often fragmented, small owners existed in their interstices, and peasant communities sometimes contested church tenurial control. The peasantry also maintained some political autonomy, for local assemblies or *thingar* kept a certain importance in Denmark (*Kulturhistorisk leksikon,* 1975: XVIII, cc. 359–66). The church in Denmark did not predate the late tenth-century conversion of the kingdom (newly reunited after a century of political fragmentation), and we could also wonder if a large-scale landowning aristocracy predated that period (Jørgensen, 1995). But Denmark's archaeology also shows greater concentrations of wealth, going back into the fifth century, than any other region north of Francia (Hedeager, 1992: 246–53; Nielsen *et al.* (eds), 1994; Näsman, 2000), so someone, at least political leaders, was already by 500 gaining substantial surplus from a surrounding territory. It is likely that kings had rights of tribute from all the lands they controlled politically, which could make them, at least, rich. There is no sign in Denmark of the sort of complex multi-level possession inside land units visible in England and Wales, and probable in Scotland. All the same, judging by our twelfth-century documents, we might postulate that communities of small owners (grouped into villages throughout our period in Denmark, and for long apparently autonomous and prosperous: see e.g. Hvass, 1988; Nissen-Jaubert, 1996) had increasingly found in the previous two centuries that they were losing ground. Local leaders (called *kuthi* or *thiakn* on standing-stones cut with runes in the ninth century: Randsborg, 1980: 25–33) were perhaps growing in power, from being medium owners and *coqs de village* to claiming lordship over their neighbours; and kings after 950 were very probably granting tribute rights over the heads of the peasantry to newly-founded churches and monasteries, which the latter could sometimes turn into full ownership. These would have been similar to the ways hierarchies developed in England and, later, Scotland, and indeed, more rapidly and violently, in Saxony; outside the North Sea area, they also have close parallels in northern Spain (Pastor, 1980). But such developments remain as speculative as in Scotland, for they had once again taken place before our documentary evidence begins.

The process by which kings established political power over autonomous peasantries is most clearly visible in Norway, a region notionally subject to a single ruler by the tenth century. (In Sweden, this process had barely begun by 1000, and is also less clearly characterised in our texts, so Sweden will be set aside here.) Our evidence for Norway consists mostly of detailed but late narratives, dating to the century after 1150 and mostly written by Icelanders, who idealised the non-royal political system of their own country; we cannot accept the detail of their accounts of tenth- and early eleventh-century politics (see esp. Bagge, 1991), and before *c.*950 we can say very little at all. But these accounts at least take for granted a fairly consistent social structure, which both differed from that in Iceland, and is reflected in two other types of sources: the earliest law codes for two of the Norwegian *thingar*, the Frostathing of the Trondheim area and the Gulathing of the western Norwegian fjords, both probably twelfth-century in their current form with earlier elements (Keyser and Munch (eds), 1846); and the praise poems, often contemporary to the events described, embedded in the histories, particularly in the longest Icelandic-Norwegian narrative, Snorri Sturluson's *Heimskringla*. This social structure was (unlike that of Denmark) based on isolated farms, each controlled by a peasant farmer or *bóndi*, and most of them held in full ownership: indeed, a third or more of Norwegian land was peasant-owned as late as the sixteenth century (Karras, 1988: 77). Aristocrats also existed, who controlled wider lands, often cultivated by unfree tenants, but sometimes also by free *bændr*, as the law codes show (manors, however, are wholly undocumented in Norway as yet). It would be reasonable to suppose that these aristocrats dominated their free neighbours politically, as the law codes also imply; but those neighbours certainly had access to the local *thingar*, even if in the entourage of lords, and decision-making in the *thingar* was fairly broadly-based and autonomous (more than in Denmark). The late Norwegian evidence is, in fact, the most detailed documentation we have (outside Iceland) of the sort of social structure postulated above on other grounds for whole regions of the North Sea area north of Francia, before the growth of aristocratic and church estates in tenth-century England and Saxony, and twelfth-century Denmark and Scotland. (For all this, see Sandvik, 1955; Lunden, 1977; Bagge, 1991: 111–40.)

The sections of the Norwegian histories covering the late tenth- and early eleventh-century rule of Ólafr Tryggvason (d. 1000) and Ólafr Haraldsson (d. 1028) are the most detailed, because they relate to the period of the forcible Christianisation of the country. The histories see this as being accomplished by the kings *thing* by *thing*, against the resistance or with the sullen acquiescence of the local *bændr*, 'free and unfree' (e.g. Snorri, 1941–51: IV, 17; VII, 55, 65–9; VIII, 40, 121). It is clear that the histories see local aristocrats as hegemonic, but the *bændr*, both richer and poorer, are protagonists throughout, and the army that killed Ólafr Haraldsson, though called up by aristocrats, was called the '*bændr* army' (VIII, 216, 225, 235, the latter being a contemporary poem). This sort of peasant protagonism depended on independent landowning, by what the texts call *óðal* right. Aristocrats could not claim any economic dues from landowning peasants. The king took tribute from free men, and could sometimes assign it to aristocrats acting as his local officials, but, conversely, angry or rebellious peasant communities could withhold tribute, and kings had to negotiate with them if they did so.

I base these statements on Snorri's *Heimskringla*, which is the fullest narrative for the period. To repeat, the details of the text must be treated with great caution. But the imagery of *bóndi* protagonism clearly made sense to a thirteenth-century Norwegian audience, and it has no parallels in any text written further south. Given a landowning peasantry in Norway, the relationship between power and the distribution of property led directly to a relatively diffuse power structure, and to kings having to negotiate, not just with aristocrats, but with peasant leaders. That the peasantry was also hierarchically organised, and commonly aristocrat-led, does not subtract from its protagonism. If aristocrats had begun to gain ground at the expense of the peasantry, it is hardly visible to the authors of our twelfth- and thirteenth-century sources.

The history, and the tenurial history, of each region in the North Sea area before 1000 was very different, but some common patterns nonetheless recur. We can clearly see the existence of two basic models for the relationship between property and power. In one, the Roman/Frankish model, kings and aristocrats (both secular and ecclesiastical) owned land on a large scale; status and political power were linked directly to landed wealth; and peasant owners were marginalised politically – indeed, in some areas, like the Paris basin, and southern England by the end of our period, they hardly existed. The areas covered by this tenurial-political model expanded northwards beyond the English Channel and the Rhine after 800, to cover much of England and Saxony as well, though perhaps nowhere else yet by 1000. The second, the northern model, covering the Celtic- and the northern part of the Germanic-speaking lands (and indeed eastwards into the Slavic-speaking world, not part of this book) was one in which most free peasants had much greater autonomy and, often, full ownership over their lands; aristocrats were less wealthy, although they often had strong patronage rights over their peasant neighbours; and the only really rich people were rulers, who accumulated (not necessarily very heavy) tributes from landowners both rich and poor. A tendency for aristocratic and royal power to increase in this second model at the expense of peasant autonomy is not to be doubted, but it was incomplete by 1000, and in some areas (such as Norway) had hardly started. By 1500, the second model was vestigial except in Sweden, inland Norway, the north coast of Frisia and Highland Scotland, but in 1000 it was still powerful, and accepted as normal even by kings. Power relations could be very diffuse as a result, and assembly politics remained influential for a long time.

The economic value of different ways of exploiting agricultural land before 1000 does not often seem to have been an issue for major landowners. This is not because population was low by later standards, leading to less pressure on the land; all our evidence suggests that cultivated areas were the location of at least some competition for resources. It is rather that such a competition mattered most in political and cultural terms; anyone aiming at any form of social prestige needed to control land, everywhere. Land also brought power more directly, particularly in the south, for the powerful used land to reward and support armed entourages. These powerful also included kings, though kings everywhere could also expect armed levies from the free population under their rule, which made them far more powerful than ordinary aristocrats (only in the politically fragmented world of tenth-century West Francia did this process not work). Kings in the regions of the northern model supplemented this by tribute; this put them further ahead of neighbouring aristocrats. Perhaps paradoxically, Frankish kings after 650 or so did not exact generalised tribute; but the scale of their wealth from royal landowning was so huge that it far outweighed the incomings gained by any northern king.

We can identify different levels of the intensity of economic exploitation of the land. Peasant owners cultivated with an eye to subsistence, above all. Aristocrats in much of northern Europe had dependants who owed them relatively low rents (in, for example, pre-ninth-century England), and/or inflexible customary rents. Unfree tenants owed more, which was, as far as we can see, a reflection both of their status and of their inability to negotiate effectively; but they too were mostly part of a customary regime. Both peasants and aristocrats used surpluses to exchange for goods they did not produce; there was always commerce in all these societies, and the richer aristocrats were, the more demand, so the more exchange, there was. But in most of Europe the organisation of production was not, before 1000, related to exchange opportunities. The exception was probably the intense exploitation of land and people associated with the bipartite estate, or manor, which began to be generalised in eighth-century northern Francia and extended northwards by 1000 to much of England and parts of Frisia and Saxony, where it was however more vestigial. The recent argument (see above) that the manor was directed towards exchange opportunities is a strong one. It was not the only possible form of agricultural régime which could be so directed (tenants paying high rents are as effective a resource, and were an increasingly common choice by the twelfth century); but exploitation based on coerced labour seems in empirical terms to have been the first way out of a lowish customary-rent regime that was tried by North Sea area landowners. The areas where manors existed before 1000 were also areas dominated by the Roman/Frankish property model, but this does not mean that all landowners there adopted a manorial structure; for a long time, church estates – and, in Francia, some royal estates – were the main proponents of the régime. Even landowners who adopted the manorial system need not however always have been thinking about economic value, rather than about the political advantages of coercive control over dependants which it brought. Some probably did; but an economic, rather than a social-cultural and political, valuation of land was restricted to a minority of landowners in the early middle ages.

2.2 The occupiers of the land

Peasant autonomy did not by any means mean egalitarianism. There were important differences, in every one of our regions, between free and unfree, landowner and tenant, and rich and poor. Such hierarchical distinctions existed in every village, or (in regions of dispersed settlement, such as Norway) in every territory. Unfree strata existed everywhere. Even in regions where peasant landowning was negligible, such as the Paris basin, or late tenth-century southern England, communities were nevertheless sharply split between free and unfree. The levelling of tenant status to a generic 'serfdom' had not begun yet by 1000, and unfree status was perhaps in retreat at the end of our period only in north-west Francia (see e.g. Bonnassie, 1985, although, unlike him, I avoid the terminology of 'slavery' as potentially misleading; unfree workers were mostly peasant families subsisting on their own plots of land in our period).

All the same, unfree status did not have the same importance everywhere. It was probably most important in the regions of Europe where the northern property model was dominant, those where a free peasantry was relatively influential, for there unfree men and women had a sharply distinctive economic role: they were unpaid and powerless farm workers. Even free peasants had servile labourers in Scandinavia (Karras, 1988: 78–80; aristocrats also had them, though usually as tenants). In England, too, the unfree were often assigned distinctive and menial tasks (Pelteret, 1995; Faith, 1997: 59–70), which seems to mark the survival of the presupposition that free peasants were to an extent autonomous, and only the unfree could be imposed upon; Saxony before the Carolingian conquests, as we have seen, was probably similar. The free-unfree divide was differently structured in eastern Francia (for example the Rhineland), where customary tenants of the great estates were normally unfree (*mancipia*), although living alongside free landowning peasants in Rhineland villages. We can assume that free tenants in such villages (for example ex-owners who had given land to the church and rented it back) were a social category which seriously risked losing status; perhaps they kept their freedom only if they kept at least some land in full property. The societies where the free-unfree division mattered least were those where both groups of peasants had long been tenants, such as on the great north-west Frankish estates documented in the ninth-century polyptychs. Here, intermarriage between free and unfree was common, which was one of the causes of the slow decline of unfree status already mentioned; and, although unfreedom was marked by higher rents and services in general, a greater cross-over of obligations is already visible (particularly where, for example, free tenants took unfree tenures in lease). There was certainly still a sharp status distinction here, but the gap was not as unbreachable as in Scandinavia. Having stressed that status divide, it must also be recognised that manumission, the freeing of unfree dependants, was common everywhere; but freedmen normally remained dependants of their former masters.

The next crucial division, partly but not entirely overlapping with that legal divide, was between landowners and tenants. This was simply a distinction between aristocrats and peasants in regions like the Paris basin and tenth-century southern England; but elsewhere it also marked a division between peasants inside villages, some of whom owned their own land, some of whom were tenants for all their land, and many of whom owned some land parcels and took others in lease (either from aristocrats, or from their peasant neighbours). Landless labourers, who hired out their services, are almost undocumented before 1000, although it is likely that peasants with too little land, or too many children of working age, hired out themselves or their children at high-points of the year such as the harvest, or maybe for longer periods if, for example, lords needed extra labour on demesnes (there is little evidence for this, but some hints exist: see e.g. Levillain, 1900: 361).

The third important distinction was between rich and poor peasants: those with easily enough land to cultivate themselves, and maybe enough to lease out to their neighbours, and those without. The detailed social dynamic between these two social strata is hardly documented in our period; but some points can be stated with relative certainty. There was no sharp legal distinction between peasant and aristocrat in any of our regions, even though the existence of aristocrats as a distinct social stratum (called *nobilis*, *eorl*, *thegn*, *edhilingus*, *hauldr*, and many other terms) can be identified everywhere; as successful peasant and medium owners got richer, they could therefore be recognised as aristocrats, at least in principle – if they were lucky, or good at fighting, or came to the attention of rulers in one way or another. Ex-peasants could, in particular, come to dominate their own villages tenurially in some cases if they accumulated enough land and used it cleverly enough. This did not yet, of course, develop in the direction of agrarian capitalism, but it could sometimes develop towards formal local lordship. Some of the new seigneurial lords of post-'feudal revolution' France may have been of peasant or at least medium-owner origin. But, whether or not this happened, the richest peasants dominated their villages politically. Village leaders in early medieval Europe were universally, as far as we can see, the most prosperous local inhabitants (see Davies, 1988: 100–2, 175–83 for Brittany, and Staab, 1975: 262–78 for the Rhineland, the only two areas bordering on the North Sea area with firm data here; cf. Wickham, 2005: 387–441 for generalisations).

Villages varied in their economic coherence. Common land was not yet very frequently divided up geographically. Estates did include sections of woodland and meadow, and in *Domesday Book* some Kentish estates had specified woodland outliers some distance away in the Weald (Witney, 1976: 104–27); but much of the extensive woodland, open pasture, and coastal salt marsh of the North Sea area was as yet unassigned, and communities had virtually unrestrained access to it. This was partly because populations were still low, for the huge demographic growth of the central middle ages had hardly begun by 1000; a need to exploit woodland or sheep pasture systematically, and thus to argue over who had rights to do so in a given area, had not begun in most regions (see, for example, Wickham, 1994: 121–99). It was also because non-agricultural land was in most regions seen as a public resource, rather than a private one. If kings were powerful they could often claim that public resource to be royal; they could then sometimes grant it away to others, in particular to churches, who would then try to exert private control over it. In tenth-century West Francia, the break-up of royal power also meant that seigneurial lords characteristically claimed their own banal rights over woodland, and both divided it up (against other lords) and charged peasants for their use. Overall, although the trend was only beginning in 1000, a tendency was already visible for much common land to be controlled from above, especially in the southern half of the North Sea area.

Peasant communities also, of course, had a great interest in common land, including in its protection and/or clearance. But we do not have clear evidence of peasant societies focussed on its organised exploitation before 1000. Further south in Europe, in the Alps, Pyrenees and Appennines, peasants sometimes already resisted the privatisation of non-agricultural land (Wickham, 2003), but we do not yet have documentation for this in the North Sea area. We cannot assume that, for example, the Danish villages which controlled the detailed exploitation of their commons collectively in the late middle ages did so already before 1000. In part, again, this was because populations were still too low for it to be essential; but in part it is because we have very little evidence at all for active village communities before 1000. The best-documented local communities in the early middle ages, the *thing* assemblies of Scandinavia, were for rather larger areas than single villages as far as we can see, and village commons were not obviously part of their remit. The Norwegian laws on commons, *almenningr*, are highly generic, and do not envisage much threat to them – which is not surprising given the dominance of non-agricultural land in Norway – although they betray their late date by recognising a superiority in the commons to the king (Keyser and Munch (eds), 1846: *Gulathings-Lov,* cc. 145, 150, *Frostathings-Lov,* XIV, 7–9).

Villages, in the sense of wholly or partly nucleated settlements, or at least settlements with a defined territory even if the houses in them were scattered, were crystallising in most parts of Europe in the early middle ages. In Denmark and Frisia, they existed before the Christian era; in Francia we can find them from the late sixth century, arguably, though they gained in coherence in the eighth, as recent archaeology shows; in England they may have begun in the ninth, though there were some concentrated settlements already in the seventh; only in Norway did they not exist at all. (For all this see Hamerow, 2002; Peytremann, 2003: esp. 319–30, 354–9; Wickham, 2005: 495–514; 2008.) So we can talk with confidence about village society in our period. But village communities with an active internal organisation and political or economic roles are not as yet visible, almost anywhere, in the North Sea area. Only the Breton *plebes*, which had a village-level court system, constitute an exception, in any documented region, and we have no information that they concerned themselves with collective economic decisions (Davies, 1988: 63–7 and passim). It would be the *encellulement* of the eleventh century and onwards (Fossier, 1982), a need to resist local seigneurial power, to run the newly-created church parish, to organise newly-created open fields in some areas, and, indeed, to police the commons in a time of demographic growth, that would require organised village communities. In our period, these needs had not yet developed, and we cannot assume that villages were more than very informally organised, with a local leader dominating his neighbours, as already stated, but in a very ad hoc way – by persuading them to support him in court cases, for example. Village-level power was thus personal in this early period; formal institutions (let alone wider organisations) did not exist.

Peasants did resist lords and kings. I have already mentioned the Stellinga revolt in Saxony in 841–2, focussed on the restoration of 'ancient customs' (which included political representation and, probably, economic autonomy). The *bœndr* army of 1028 in Norway, although led by lords, was also clearly itself seeking to oppose a royal authority which was seen as arbitrary. The peasant *coniuratio* from the land between the Loire and the Seine which fought the Vikings in 859 was seen as subversive, and was destroyed by the local aristocracy; so was the Norman protest of the late 990s, apparently opposed to some of the constraints of the *seigneurie banale* (Wickham, 2003: 571–2). These were exceptional acts, all the same, and local peasant resistance to landlords was doubtless rarely openly violent. In the Carolingian period it could result in peasant pleas against lords in public courts (Nelson, 1986). Individual violence was too dangerous for peasants, unless it was covert, which could not establish legal rights. Large-scale resistance would await the very different environment of the fourteenth century, as we will see later in this book.

Nothing that could be defined as 'governmental' policy towards the peasantry, or indeed the agricultural world, existed in the early middle ages. The closest might be the concern shown by Charlemagne and his successors to try to safeguard the legal rights of the poor free in Carolingian legislation, as already noted, although this did not extend very far (Müller-Mertens, 1963). But all the rulers of the North Sea area were like Charlemagne here, in that they regarded their legitimacy as being associated with their leadership of the free people in arms, which extended to the free peasantry. The *thingar* of Scandinavia were only one example of an assembly politics that extended across every region. The Franks made great use of the *placitum* assembly, for political deliberation at the highest level – the highly aristocratic *placitum generale*, called twice a year by the king in the ninth century – and for hearing court cases in every county. In late Anglo-Saxon England, there were courts not only for the county but also for its subdivisions, the hundreds, which certainly required peasant attendance, and these had parallels at a still smaller scale in the Breton *plebs*. I have doubted that this latter had many parallels elsewhere at the village level. But peasant participation in judicial assemblies, and their theoretical obligation (if they were free and male) to fight, or at least to do public works such as road-building or the maintenance of fortifications, justified a minimum protagonism and political responsibility, at least. All the revolts and acts of resistance mentioned in the previous paragraph were to safeguard that right of involvement. They all failed; and after 1000 peasants steadily lost any rights to be seen as political protagonists anywhere, again with the exception of Norway (and also Sweden), and the northern fringe of Frisia. But in the early middle ages the free community, both peasant and aristocratic, was theoretically united as part of the 'public' world, however little this counted in practice.

We cannot estimate the prosperity of the peasantry in this period. It is only common sense to suppose that peasants who paid little to kings and lords, as many peasants – and perhaps most legally free peasants – did in the northern model, were better off than the burdened dependants of manors and other estates in the Frankish model. This must have outweighed the greater security that the latter supposedly had, given that slaving expeditions, for example, were predominantly carried out at the expense of peoples with weak political systems, less able to resist, like the Slavs (McCormick, 2001: 760–8) or the Irish – although in the ninth and tenth centuries Scandinavian Vikings did this to everyone, strong or weak political systems alike, so even here the Frankish heartland did not have much of an advantage. Conversely, however, archaeology shows that regions with relatively autonomous peasantries did not have much access to exchange in any systematic way; that depended on the existence of hierarchies, and élites with buying power. The subject peasantries of Francia had, in fact, more access to professionally-made artisanal goods than did the more independent peasantries of the northern regions (Wickham, 2005: 794–819). Whatever autonomous peasant communities did with the surplus they did not have to give to others, it was not exchange. I would guess they ate better, and worked less hard, but the latter is not capable of documentation, and the former could only be tested by a systematic comparative analysis of human skeletons in cemeteries, of a type that archaeologists so far have barely contemplated.

The early middle ages are ill-documented by later standards, and the early medieval peasantry is even less documented. As noted earlier, what evidence we have tends to stress Roman/Frankish-style tenure, because it mostly derives from Roman/Frankish landlords, those who were most interested in written documentation as a guide to rights and local control; the more autonomous peasants were, the harder they are to pin down in our evidence. But early medieval realities can be reconstructed, all the same, and it is important to do so in their own terms, not in the terms of succeeding centuries. The early middle ages was not simply the 'prehistory' of later developments; it had its own economic logic, which needs to be studied separately, as it has been here. Only when that logic is understood can we understand how it changed, as other economic systems with their separate logics took over in the central and later middle ages. These new systems were closer to the Roman/Frankish model described here, but they had a different dynamism, for the population was rising fast after 1000, and commercial exchange, including in agricultural products, had a much wider and more complex patterning from now on. These developments, which link closely to changes analysed in the other volumes of this series, will be described and analysed in the next chapters.

Bibliography

Adam of Bremen (1917) *Gesta Hammaburgensis ecclesiae pontificum*, ed. B. Schmeidler, Hanover.

Bagge, S. (1991) *Society and politics in Snorri Sturluson's Heimskringla*, Berkeley.

Barbier, J. (1990) 'Le système palatial franc', *Bibliothèque de l'École de chartes*, 148, pp. 245–99.

Barrow, G. W. S. (1973) *The kingdom of the Scots*, London.

Barthélemy, D. (1997) *La mutation de l'an mil a-t-elle eu lieu?*, Paris.

Barton, R. E. (2004) *Lordship in the county of Maine, c.890–1160,* Woodbridge.

Baxter, S. (2007) *The earls of Mercia*, Oxford.

Bisson, T. N. (2009) *The crisis of the twelfth century*, Princeton.

Blinkhorn, P. (1999) 'Of cabbages and kings', in M. Anderton (ed.), *Anglo-Saxon trading centres: beyond the emporia*, Glasgow, pp. 4–23.

Bonnassie, P. (1985) 'Survie et extinction du régime esclavagiste dans l'Occident du haut moyen âge (IVe-XIe siècle)', *Cahiers de civilisation médiévale*, 28, pp. 307–43.

Bournazel, E. and J.-P. Poly (eds) (1999) *Les féodalités,* Paris.

Campbell, J. (ed.) (1982) *The Anglo-Saxons,* Oxford.

Clarke, P. A. (1994) *The English nobility under Edward the Confessor,* Oxford.

Davies, R. R. (1987) *Conquest, coexistence and change. Wales, 1063–1415,* Oxford.

Davies, W. (1978a) *An early Welsh microcosm*, London.

Davies, W. (1978b) 'Land and power in early medieval Wales', *Past and Present*, 81, pp. 3–23.

Davies, W. (1988) *Small worlds*, London.

Davies, W. (1990) *Patterns of power in early Wales,* Oxford.

Devroey, J.-P. (2003) *Économie rurale et société dans l'Europe franque (VI*^{e}*-IX*^{e} *siècles)*, Paris.

Devroey, J.-P. (1989) 'Problèmes de critique autour du polyptyque de l'abbaye de Saint-Germain-des-Prés', in H. Atsma (ed.), *La Neustrie,* 2 vols, Sigmaringen, I, pp. 441–65.

Devroey, J.-P. (2006) *Puissants et misérables*, Brussels.

Duby, G. (1973) *Guerriers et paysans,* Paris.

Duncan, A. A. M. (1975) *Scotland: the making of the kingdom*, Edinburgh.

Epperlein, S. (1969) *Herrschaft und Volk im karolingischen Imperium,* Berlin.

Faith, R. (1997) *The English peasantry and the growth of lordship,* Leicester.

Feller, L. (2007) *Paysans et seigneurs au Moyen Âge, VIII*^{e}-XVe siècles, Paris.

Feller, L. (1997) 'Statut de la terre et statut des personnes', *Études rurales*, 145–6, pp. 147–64.

Fleming, R. (1991) *Kings and lords in conquest England,* Cambridge.

Fossier, R. (1982) *Enfance de l'Europe,* Paris.

Goetz, H.-W. (2007) *Vorstellungsgeschichte,* Bochum.

Goffart, W. (1989) *Rome's fall and after,* London.

Goldberg, E. J. (1995) 'Popular revolt, dynastic politics and aristocratic factionalism in the early middle ages: the Saxon *Stellinga* reconsidered', *Speculum*, 70, pp. 467–501.

Halsall, G. (2007) *Barbarian migrations and the Roman West, 376–568,* Cambridge.

Hamerow, H. (2002) *Early medieval settlements,* Oxford.

Harvey, P. D. A. (1993) '*Rectitudines singularum personarum* and *gerefa*', *English Historical Rev.*, 108, pp. 1–22.

Hedeager, L. (1992) *Iron-Age societies,* Oxford.

Heidinga, H. A. (1997) *Frisia in the first millennium*, Utrecht.

Henderikx, P. A. (1987) *De beneden-delta van Rijn en Maas,* Hilversum.

Herlihy, D. (1961) 'Church property on the European continent, 701–1200', *Speculum*, 36, pp. 81–105.

Hvass, S. (1988) 'Jernalderens bebyggelse', in P. Mortensen and B. Rasmussen (eds), *Fra stamme til stat i Danmark*, 2 vols, 1988–91, Højbjerg, I, pp. 53–91.

Innes, M. (2000) *State and society in the early middle ages*, Cambridge.

Jørgensen, L. (1995) 'The warrior aristocracy of Gudme', in H. G. Resi (ed), *Produksjon og samfunn,* Oslo, pp. 205–20.

Karras, R. M. (1988) *Slavery and society in medieval Scandinavia,* New Haven.

Kasten, B. (1990) 'Erbrechtliche Verfügungen des 8. und 9. Jahrhunderts', *Zeitschrift der Savigny-Stiftung für Rechtsgeschichte, Germanistische Abteilung*, 105, pp. 236–338.

Keyser, R. and P. A. Munch (eds) (1846) *Norges gamle love indtil 1387*, 5 vols, 1846–95, I, Christiania.

Kohl, T. (2005) 'Gemeinde vor der Gemeinde?', in A. Greule and J. Meier (eds), *Die ländliche Gemeinde im Spätmittelalter,* Berlin, pp. 185–204.

Kuchenbuch, L. (1978) *Bäuerliche Gesellschaft und Klosterherrschaft im 9. Jahrhundert,* Wiesbaden.

Kulturhistorisk leksikon for nordisk middelalder, 18, Copenhagen, 1975.

Lampert of Hersfeld (1894) *Annales*, ed. O. Holder-Egger, *Lamperti monachi Hersfeldensis opera,* Hannover, pp. 1–304.

Latouche, R. (1956) *Les origines de l'économie occidentale (IVe-XIe siècle),* Paris.

Lawson, M. K. (1984) 'The collection of Danegeld and Heregeld in the reigns of Æthelred II and Cnut', *English Historical Rev.*, 99, pp. 373–84.

Lebecq, S. (1983) *Marchands et navigateurs frisons du haut moyen âge*, 2 vols, Lille.

Levillain, L. (1990) 'Les statuts d'Adalhard', *Le moyen âge*, 4, pp. 333–86.

Lewis, C., Mitchell-Fox, P., and Dyer, C. (1997) *Village, hamlet and field,* Manchester.

Lintzel, M. (1961) *Ausgewählte Schriften*, 2 vols., Berlin.

Loveluck, C., *et al.* (2007) *Excavations at Flixborough*, 4 vols, Oxford.

Lot, F., (1928) *L'impôt foncier et la capitation personnelle sous le bas-empire et à l'époque franque*, Paris.

Lunden, K. (1977) *Norge under Sverreætten*, Oslo.

McCormick, M. (2001) *Origins of the European economy*, Cambridge.

Metcalf, D. M. (1994) *Thrymsas and sceattas in the Ashmolean Museum Oxford*, III, London.

Metz, W. (1960) *Das Karolingische Reichsgut*, Berlin.

Morimoto, Y. (2008) *Études sur l'économie rurale du haut moyen âge*, Paris.

Müller-Mertens, E. (1972) 'Der Stellingaaufstand', *Zeitschrift für Geschichtswissenschaft*, 20, pp. 818–42.

Müller-Mertens, E. (1963) *Karl der Grosse, Ludwig der Fromme, und die Freien*, Berlin.

Näsman, U. (2000) 'Exchange and politics: the eighth – early ninth century in Denmark', in I. L. Hansen and C. Wickham (eds), *The long eighth century,* Leiden, pp. 35–68.

Nelson, J. L. (1986) 'Dispute settlement in Carolingian West Francia', in W. Davies and P. Fouracre (eds), *The settlement of disputes in early medieval Europe*, Cambridge, pp. 45–64.

Nielsen, P. O. *et al.* (eds) (1994) *The archaeology of Gudme and Lundeborg*, Copenhagen.

Nissen-Jaubert, A. (1996) *Peuplement et structures d'habitat au Danemark durant les IIIe-XIIe siècles dans leur contexte nord-ouest européen,* Thèse de doctorat, École des Hautes Etudes en Sciences Sociales, Paris.

Pastor, R. (1980) *Resistencias y luchas campesinas en la época del crecimiento y consolidación de la formación feudal Castilla y León, siglos X-XIII*, Madrid.

Pelteret, D. A. E. (1995) *Slavery in early medieval England,* Woodbridge.

Peytremann, E. (2003) *Archéologie de l'habitat rural dans le nord de la France du IVe au XIIe siècle,* 2 vols, Saint-Germain-en-Laye.

Prittlewell prince, The, (2004) London.

Randsborg, K. (1980) *The Viking age in Denmark*, London.

Reuter, T. (2006) *Medieval polities and modern mentalities*, Cambridge.

Richards, J. D. (2000) *Viking age England,* Stroud.

Rösener, W. (1985) 'Zur Struktur und Entwicklung der Grundherrschaft in Sachsen in karolingischer und ottonischer Zeit', in A. Verhulst (ed.), *Le grand domaine aux époques mérovingienne et carolingienne*, Gent, pp. 173–207.

Rösener, W. (ed.) (1989) *Strukturen der Grundherrschaft im frühen Mittelalter*, Göttingen.

Rotthoff, G. (1953) *Studien zur Geschichte des Reichsguts in Niederlothringen und Friesland während der sachsich-salischen Kaiserzeit,* Bonn.

Sandvik, G. (1955) *Hovding og konge i Heimskringla,* Oslo.

Scull, C. (1997) 'Urban centres in pre-Viking England?', in J. Hines (ed.), *The Anglo-Saxons from the migration period to the eighth century*, Woodbridge, pp. 269–310.

Snorri Sturluson (1941–51) *Heimskringla*, ed. B. Aðalbjarnarson, Reykjavik.

Staab, F. (1975) *Untersuchungen zur Gesellschaft am Mittelrhein in der Karolingerzeit,* Wiesbaden.

Stafford, P. (1989) *Unification and conquest*, London.

Taylor, C. (1983) *Village and farmstead*, London.

Toubert, P. (2004) *L'Europe dans sa première croissance*, Paris.

Verhulst, A. (1992) *Rural and urban aspects of early medieval north-west Europe,* Aldershot.

Verhulst, A. (2002) *The Carolingian economy*, Cambridge.

Werner, M. (1980) *Der Lütticher Raum in frühkarolingischer Zeit*, Göttingen.

Whitelock, D. (ed.) (1930) *Anglo-Saxon wills*, Cambridge.

Wickham, C. (2005) *Framing the early middle ages*, Oxford.

Wickham, C. (2008) 'La cristalización de la aldea en la Europa Occidental (800–1100), in *Movimentos migratorios, asentamentos y expansión (siglos VIII-XI)*, Pamplona, pp. 33–51.

Wickham, C. (1994) *Land and power*, London, 1994.

Wickham, C. (2003) 'Space and society in early medieval peasant conflicts', *Settimane di studio*, 50, pp. 551–87.

Witney, K. P. (1976) *The Jutish forest*, London.

Wormald, P. (1995) 'Lordship and justice in the early English kingdom', in W. Davies and P. Fouracre (eds), *Property and power in the early middle ages*, Cambridge, pp. 114–36.

BRITAIN

Map 3.1 Britain, 1000–2000

point of view of the peasants or tenants, the least oppressive lord was the king, as he was a remote lord, for whom details of estate management came low on the agenda. Income from the sixteenth-century crown lands failed to increase in line with inflation, and there was also a strong disinclination to raise rents in the mid-sixteenth century amongst older and long established families (Hoyle, 1992, 76–77). The closest managers of lands were often the gentry. Residence on their lands allowed – and financial exigency forced – them to be attentive and sometimes innovative estate managers who in many cases dealt with their tenants personally and also maintained demesne or 'home' farms (Heal and Holmes, 1994: ch. 3) Freeholding owner-occupying peasants were relatively common in some parts of the country (and notably Eastern England) by the time of Domesday Book. Whilst they were always liable to fall prey to larger landowners, it has been argued that the land market acted to increase the numbers of owner-occupying yeomen between 1540 and 1640, but they then diminished in the very different conditions after 1660 (Hoyle, 1990). As we will see, a fall in the number of smaller owners ('bonnet lairds') in Scotland is visible from the mid-seventeenth century onwards.

Changing social property distribution

1000–1500

The distribution of landed wealth in the late eleventh century is more fully recorded in England than in any other part of Europe because of the survival of Domesday Book, based on a royal inquiry in 1086. It shows that 24 per cent of the land by value was held by the king or members of the royal family (Corbett, 1926: 508). This figure had been pushed to such a high level because William I added estates to those he inherited from his Anglo-Saxon predecessors. The proportion of the landed resources in the hands of the crown had been considerably smaller, perhaps no more than 10 per cent, before 1066. It diminished over the twelfth century as successive rulers granted land to win allies and practise piety. The church's share of landed income in 1086 has been calculated at 26 per cent, which indicates the wealth of bishops and religious houses. The church's lands had probably been of similar extent before 1066, as gains from new foundations after the Conquest were countered by seizures by predatory laymen. The landholdings of the lesser clergy, who served the numerous parish churches, are recorded inconsistently by Domesday, but we can be certain that these individually small properties added one or two percentage points to the proportion of church land.

Domesday has been used to show that the lands of the secular aristocracy, which in total accounted for a half of the national wealth, had been concentrated into the hands of about 200 magnates. Many of the estates of major Anglo-Saxon lords were granted to their Norman successors as working units (Sawyer, 1985). Below the magnates, Domesday records a second tier of 5,000 minor lords, but tenants and supporters of the magnates (they are often described as *thegn* or *cniht*) had existed before 1066, so it can be concluded that throughout the eleventh century, as in subsequent centuries, a large amount of land lay within the estates or honours of great lords, but effective lordship of thousands of manors was exercised by a lesser aristocracy (Palmer, 1999).

An abundance of documentation around 1300 allows a calculation to be made of the distribution of land in England at that time, again based on the annual incomes that high status landholders could expect to obtain from their manors, woods, pastures, mills and other agrarian assets (Mayhew, 1995: 58). The crown's share had diminished to four per cent. The church's endowment had increased to 34 per cent, mainly because of the great wave of new monastic foundations in the twelfth century. The secular aristocracy in England received more than a half of the income from land, but now, with the proliferation of the gentry, the earls and barons of the higher aristocracy lived on 10 per cent, and the knights and gentry 52 per cent. Over the next two centuries, the balance between different types of landholder remained much the same.

In Wales and Scotland precise calculations of the distribution of land cannot be made. The church probably held a smaller proportion than in England as both countries lacked rich bishoprics and large Benedictine monasteries. The new monastic orders arrived in the twelfth century, but attracted limited endowments. Most land was held by the laity, with a cumulatively high proportion in the hands of the lesser aristocracy. It is estimated that late medieval Scotland had about 50 landed magnates and 2,000 lesser families (Whyte, 1995: 78). Much of the landed wealth of parts of both countries, such as the highlands of Scotland, came from tributes, often gathered in kind, rather than the possession of acres of land.

1500–1750

Older discussions of the distribution of property between social groups in England between 1500 and 1640 have tended to concentrate on the changing balance of property between crown, peerage and gentry. Discussions of the land market after 1660 have been more preoccupied with the disappearance of the small landowner (Hoyle, forthcoming a).

The fifteenth-century monarchy had tended to accumulate land. Henry VIII (1509–47) inherited the largest landed endowment of any late medieval English monarch to which was added, between 1536 and 1540, the lands of the monasteries. These were quickly dispersed, mostly by sale to fund war, so that by the accession of Elizabeth in 1558, an estimated two-thirds of the monastic lands had been sold. The crown continued to sell land in wartime to balance its budgets, especially in the 1590s, and the rump of the estates were transferred to the city of London in 1628 in settlement of debt. Thereafter the crown was not a significant landowner. In the seven counties studied by Tawney, the crown held 9.5 per cent of manors in 1561 but only 2.0 per cent in 1640. In these same counties the church consistently held around 7.0 per cent of manors after 1561.

The operation of the sixteenth- and early seventeenth-century land market generated large numbers of gentry who held one or two manors. The challenge for such gentry was to convert the copyhold on their estates into leasehold because manorial incomes tended to decline in real terms. Only leasehold or demesne farming allowed these gentry the prospect of economic survival. The failure in each generation of many smaller gentry allowed for a constant turnover of larger properties in the land market and the possibility of mercantile wealth acquiring land.

The disappearance of the owner-occupier (sometimes equated with the peasant but who might hold several hundred hectares) has also been a constant preoccupation of the English historiography. The number of owner-occupiers or freeholders probably increased in the later sixteenth and early seventeenth centuries as land was sold to tenants. As the security of tenure of copyholders increased, there was a tendency to treat them too as freeholders. Taking these categories together, it seems likely that the number of owner-occupiers in England (and the area they controlled) peaked in the years before 1640 (Hoyle, 1990). Thereafter their numbers fell through a process of attrition which was especially marked in periods of low farm-gate prices. Nonetheless, owner-occupiers survived into the eighteenth century in large numbers. Gregory King's calculations of the ownership of land in England *c.*1690 estimated the total number of freeholders at 180,000, of which 140,000 held lands worth between £5 and £50 per annum, and who together held a little over 40 per cent of the total landed area. A later calculation of 1750–1 by Massie placed the number of freeholders at 210,000 and the number of farmers (i.e. tenants) at 155,000.

The Scottish valuation rolls allows the fate of the smaller landowners or 'bonnet lairds' to be traced in greater detail. They were most numerous in the early seventeenth century and the reduction in the numbers was already underway when the valuation rolls (which are the records of a form of land tax) started to be kept in the mid-seventeenth century. In Aberdeenshire Callander found that the class of large landowners held 27.5 per cent of property by value in 1667 but 49.6 per cent in 1771; the medium landowners held 35.5 per cent in 1667 but 32.9 per cent in 1771; and the smaller landowners 35.5 per cent in 1667 but only 12.3 per cent in 1771. In terms of the number of taxpayers per parish, he offers average numbers of 9.7 in 1667, 8.9 in 1674, 7.0 in 1696, 7.3 in 1715, 6.5 in 1741 and 5.5 in 1771, suggesting that the biggest fall may well have come in the last thirty years of the seventeenth century, between 1667 and 1696 (Callander, 1987).

Systems of tenure

'Tenure' in the English context has two meanings. It is both the legal relationship between crown and landowner (which we discuss first) and the relationship between landlord and the occupier of the land (see here the account in Overton, 1996, 30–35).

First, all land in England was held of the crown: there was no allodial land so every landholder was a tenant of either the king directly or a superior lord, normally in return for military service. Each lord would in turn have subtenants (mesne tenants) who had obligations such as military service, but part of the land was held as demesne, that is land kept under the direct control of the lord for the generation of income.

Knight service became the usual form of feudal tenancy. Such land carried the disadvantage that when the owner was a child and could not undertake military service in person, the land reverted to the superior lord for the duration of a child's minority (wardship). Whilst other feudal dues might be demanded, including relief on inheritance, land held by knight service could be bought, sold and bequeathed by its tenants, sometimes using collusive devices to avoid the full rigour of the law. These were also used to avoid wardship but the crown deliberately set out to revive its feudal claims after 1500 ('fiscal feudalism') so that wardship again became a significant part of crown income. The Court of Wards, which managed the crown's interest in wards' estates, fell into abeyance in 1643–4 and military tenancy was formally abolished by statute in 1660.

Grants in knight service was also widely made in Scotland, especially where English and Flemish adventurers accepted grants of the Scottish crown in the twelfth century. Again, this gave the Scottish monarchs the right to claim feudal incidents, notably wardship (Whyte, 1995: 21–9). Knight service survived longer here, only being abolished after the 1745 rebellion. But Scottish landholding remained essentially feudal in conception. The creation of new feu duties was only forbidden by a statute of 1974: and feudal tenancy as a whole was abolished by the Abolition of Feudal Tenure etc (Scotland) Act of 2000 which vested the ownership of property solely in the hands of the *dominium utile*.

Second, historians distinguish between systems of tenancy which were customary and so heritable, and in which the tenant had the right to sell his interest in the property, and systems which used leases for years or lives, in which a finite term was conferred on the tenant without future obligation. In fact the distinction is much less clear in practice, and tenants by lease often developed the means – with the connivance of their landlords – to establish *de facto* heritable tenancies.

1000–1500

Medieval landed property consisted mainly of holdings with tenants, many of them customary or servile. Eleventh-century charters, still in the age of slavery, granted an estate 'with men'; in the thirteenth century villeins and their families could be conveyed like mills and fisheries. Servile tenants provided rents and services, and in addition tallage, marriage fines and other valuable dues. The benefits of receiving such profits from numerous customary tenants tended to be enjoyed by the lords of larger estates, such as those of the rich and long-established Benedictine monasteries. Around 1300 customary tenure prevailed in the Midlands and south-west, and free tenants clustered in Kent, parts of East Anglia and Lincolnshire, in the far western English counties, and Wales (Campbell and Bartley, 2006: 252–68). Serfdom decayed before 1400 in Scotland, and in England numbers of serfs were reduced in the late fourteenth century. By 1500 they were few in number and their burdens had almost disappeared.

Free tenants, who probably represented a majority of the peasantry, paid a cash rent, a relief, and owed at most a few days of labour service annually. Some were expected to pay a heriot (death duty). Both heriots and labour services had often lapsed by 1500. Free rents were fixed, which gave the tenants an advantage as rents agreed before *c.*1180 were reduced in value by the ensuing inflation, so we find in the later middle ages holdings owing 1*d*. or 2*d*. per acre when the market rate for arable land was 4*d*., 6*d*. or more. Free rents fixed in the thirteenth century at or near to the market rate, of which a large sample are recorded in the Hundred Rolls, could range above *6d.* per acre (Kanzaka, 2002). Freehold land could be divided, inherited, sold, mortgaged and generally used as the tenant wished, and if disputes arose they would be settled before the kings' courts.

Customary tenure, previously ill-defined, was clarified by the introduction *c.*1200 of tests which enabled the courts to decide whether a tenant was free, and therefore eligible for the protection of the royal courts, or servile and therefore subject to the lord's court. Tests included payment of tallage, marriage fines or heavy weekly labour service: each was enough to define a villein, a customary or unfree tenant (Hilton, 1965). Not all of the new category of villeins or customary tenants owed regular weekly labour services or indeed a great burden of rent. An increasingly high proportion of all obligations were being converted into money, in Wales as well as England.

If the annual cost of a heavily burdened customary tenement (typically a yardland of about 30 acres (12 ha) in the Midlands and south, or an oxgang of 15 acres (6 ha) in the North) in the late thirteenth century are calculated, adding to the annual cash rent the value in money of labour services or rent in kind, together with special money rents such as woodhen and hundred penny, the total could rise near to an equivalent of *6d.-8d.* per acre. The rate of marriage fines or of entry fines (that were levied instead of reliefs) were not fixed, while lords claimed that tallages were uncertain in the sum owed and the time at which they were demanded (Dyer, 2007). Recognitions paid when a new lord took over the estate came at unpredictable times. Lords valued variable dues, as they felt empowered by them, just as they enjoyed controlling the succession to customary land in the manor court. Holdings could not be subdivided, inadequate tenants could be set aside, and widows ordered to marry. The most arbitrary powers were possessed by the Welsh marcher lordships, where the lords' courts could impose heavy collective fines (Davies, 1987: 400).

The burdens of customary tenure, and the advantages that it conferred on lords, all diminished in the late fourteenth and fifteenth centuries. Labour services were permanently converted to cash, the overall level of annual rent was reduced, and extra payments like tallage were abolished. Entry fines were often reduced to token payments. Lords lost much of their ability to choose their tenants. By 1500 customary tenure, called copyhold because title was proved by possession of a copy of the relevant entry in the roll of the manor court, was coming to resemble freehold.

Throughout the period leasehold gave tenants either a life interest or a term of years in exchange for a rent in cash, or more rarely in kind. In the thirteenth-century conventionary grants (found in south-west England) gave the tenant a seven-year term in the land for a modest rent, but with a fine which reflected the ups and downs in the demand for land (Hatcher, 1970: 52–58). In other parts of England individual customary tenants in the late thirteenth century who wished to negotiate an escape from their obligations, could replace villein tenure with leasehold by paying a fine to the lord (Hilton, 1953).

In England leasehold was often introduced at times of change, when neither lord nor tenant wished to make a long-term commitment. Hence, it was often adopted as a replacement for customary tenure after the Black Death, and was used to put the demesnes into the hands of tenants. Leasehold rents – in theory – reflected the fluctuating demand for land, and could be adjusted every time a term ended, but in general rents tended to fossilise, and there was a propensity to make leases for long periods (40, 60, even 99 years) in the early sixteenth century (Dyer, 2005: 194–210). In Scotland the late medieval practice was for tenants to hold by either a tack – a lease which might be for life or for a number of years – or as a rentaller, a form of copyhold. Despite contemporary comment on the insecurity of Scottish tenants, these forms of tenancy seem to have been normally treated as hereditary tenancies in the sixteenth century (Whyte, 1995: 88–91; Sanderson, 1982: 41–55).

By the end of the middle ages, rents in England were invariably taken as cash, often due in half-yearly payments. Labour rents in the form of boon days or carrying services are still encountered as late as the seventeenth century, but as an adjunct to money rent payments. Tithes were often taken in kind, but there was a tendency for them to be farmed so that the landowner received a rent, and the tithe payers often preferred to make a customary payment (a modus) in cash. In Scotland, the collection of rent in kind – in arable areas grain, usually oats or oatmeal but in more fertile districts wheat, in pastoral areas cattle, sometimes butter or cheese – remained normal throughout the seventeenth and well into the eighteenth century. This allowed Scottish lords to provision their houses without recourse to the market, but by the end of the seventeenth century, some were also active in the grain export trade. Tenants might also pay small money sums and undertake some harvest works on the lord's demesne farm or 'Mains' or carrying services, often transporting their own grain rents to the house or a port (Whyte, 1979: 33–36, 222–28).

1500–1750

English historians have been especially interested in customary tenants because the loss of customary rights has been regarded as a stage in the dispossession of the peasantry. It has been assumed that the period 1540–1640 saw the transfer of a substantial area of land from the customary to the leasehold sectors. (For what follows, Hoyle, forthcoming, b).

The evolution of customary estates in the century after 1450 has to be seen against the background of changing demand for land. In some places, sixteenth-century copyhold *of inheritance* was the direct descendent of fourteenth-century servile tenure, but elsewhere the history of customary tenure is more complicated and copyhold of inheritance can be seen to have developed out of systems of copyhold *for lives*. As the demand for land increased, tenants sought to add additional lives to leases and they established customs that made the tenant's heir automatically the next life.

This system came under pressure when lords realized that it constrained their freedom of manoeuvre. By the beginning of the sixteenth century, the law recognized a tenant's claim to the estate conferred by a copy for life: by the third quarter of the century Chancery would recognise the tenant's hereditary claim to the estate, but would also hold that the entry fine levied on a tenant could not be so large as to make a tenant's inheritance impossible. As an example of this, we need only look at the emergence of a new system of inheritable tenancy, tenant right, in northern England in the later sixteenth century, the evolution of which is similar to that of copyhold. Son normally followed father in the parental tenement which the tenants regarded as amounting to a hereditary right. Lords, on the other hand, saw family succession as primarily a matter of convenience but when it was challenged, the courts normally accepted the tenant's claims of a customary estate (Hoyle, 1987).

Copyhold of inheritance is mostly found in south-east England. Where it is found outside this zone, it is associated with manors held by low pressure landlords in the later sixteenth century, either the crown or the church. Within the south-east, copyhold seems to have been well-established as an hereditary tenure by the mid-sixteenth century. In turn, this evolution may be connected to the penetration of customary land markets by external investors. In the first instance lords may have welcomed this as it ensured their rents were paid but in order for this to happen, they needed to concede the right for their tenants to sublet. Moreover, investors in manorial land may also have wished to be assured that they were purchasing a perpetual interest and not a lifehold one. None of this mattered when tenants were in short supply, but the concession of rights of inheritance and subletting deprived lords of the possibility of increasing their income when the demand for land increased. The agrarian violence of 1549 may also have deterred them from pressing their case against their tenants. These arrangements achieved the status of 'custom' and secured the protection of the courts. Where hereditary copyhold estates had emerged by 1550, landlords were normally unable to change them unless they could persuade the tenants to surrender them for leases. (There are some examples of landlords doing this.) In a few cases landlords did manage to disprove the tenants' claims of hereditary right by law and that again left the way open for them to substitute leases at market rents. Generally though, late sixteenth-century judicial opinion was sympathetic to tenant claims of an inheritable tenure.

From the landlord's point of view, leasehold, usually for 21 years, was the preferred form of tenancy. In western England, copyhold for lives remained the predominant system of tenure even in the early nineteenth century.

Where copyhold of inheritance was established by 1550, and where manorial lords did not have the energy or guile to extirpate it over the following half century, landlords were locked into a system of customary rents and customary fines. Over the following three centuries, as rents and fines diminished in value, they were, in effect, reduced to the level of annuitants drawing a fixed income from property which, in most ordinary senses, was no longer theirs. Where leasehold was already established, or where leases could be introduced in place of customary arrangements, the lord could demand market rents and fines without any obligation to the sitting tenants and their families. Of course, leasehold arrangements often conceal the possession of land in the same family over several generations. In areas of copyhold for lives, it was normal to buy additional lives as the existing lives 'dropped', i.e. as the named individuals died: but it was always possible for a non-family member to out-bid the family and buy a life in reversion even if they might have to wait for the other lives in being to die before they could enter the property. Outside western England, where three-life leases remained common into the late eighteenth century, terms were normally of 21 years, but shorter terms were found.

Earlier historians have seen customary tenure as disappearing from England in the sixteenth century but custom remained far more important in England, if only regionally, than in Scotland. The Scots possessed their own form of customary tenure, 'kindly tenure', the expectation that next of kin would inherit. This was also a right which could be bequeathed by will and bought and sold. It was therefore a separate matter from the exact terms on which the property was held but as a peasant property right it has a broad similarity to copyhold and tenant right in England. All the signs are that it withered away in the last decades of the sixteenth century (Sanderson, 1982: 56–63). The old view that Scottish tenants in the seventeenth century were mostly tenants at will can no longer be sustained. Whyte has shown that there were many more written leases than once assumed and that they became commoner over the seventeenth century. Nineteen-year leases became the Scottish norm and by the beginning of the eighteenth century, some landlords were making leases with improving covenants (Whyte, 1979: 152–62).

The economic value of land

1000–1500

Medieval lords expected that their landed estates would produce food for their household and a sufficient cash income to buy those goods and services not available from their manors. Domesday gives figures for annual values, that is annual income, which suggest that a minor landlord could hope to gain £5 per annum, and a magnate £100 or more, presumably including cash valuations of revenues in kind. These revenues came both from demesnes and rents. Incomes at least doubled in the next two centuries, allowing a member of the lesser gentry to enjoy an income of £10-£20, and a handful of upper aristocrats more than £1000 per annum. The general economic growth had however also allowed an expansion in wealth among those below the aristocracy. Between 1350 and 1500 all factors – falling population, decreased demand for land, low prices for agricultural produce – diminished landed incomes, though lords were skilful enough to avoid disaster, and most estates lost no more than a quarter of their revenues (Dyer, 1998: 27–48).

About a fifth or a quarter of the total area of arable land consisted of demesnes, which were directly managed by lords and their officials. It was once assumed that demesnes were farmed conservatively and without enterprise. But they were taken in hand around 1200 because lords were sensitive to the growth of the market and rising prices from which they expected to profit (Campbell, 2000). Estates had a strong central administration which collected money, audited accounts and decided on policy, and which also could make regular calculations of profit. Local officials were allowed to take initiatives, because they knew local conditions, and could increase returns by their choice of crops and methods of cultivation (Stone, 2005). In the Midlands, where choices were limited by market opportunities and availability of labour, demesnes tended to follow well-tried routines. In parts of eastern England, such as north-east Norfolk, the land was cultivated intensively, with repeated ploughing, weeding and manuring, which reduced the number of fallows and raised productivity.

Values of demesne land were frequently calculated in the period after *c.*1270, and we can use the figures recorded in the *Inquisitions post mortem* to gain a national picture (Campbell and Bartley, 2006: 178–79). These show that in the first half of the fourteenth century, very high values of 12*d.* per annum for each acre of arable were recorded in small parts of eastern England. A general level of value above 4*d.* is recorded in a large section of the country to the east of a line between south Lancashire and London. The highest values are generally not found in those districts which followed a standard two- or three-field system, but those with more flexible methods of husbandry.

Investment by lords can be calculated from manorial accounts. Around 1300 expenditure on such items as equipment, building, livestock and improvements (drainage or fencing) often fell below five per cent of income. These were once thought to be very low, and reflected a fundamental weakness of the feudal economy, but it is now argued that this level of expenditure was sufficient to keep the demesne working. There were variations between different types of lord, as gentry landlords spent a higher proportion of their income, not because they were more farsighted or enterprising, but simply reflecting the small size of the estate (Britnell, 1980). Lords' awareness of demesne profits is further shown by their withdrawal from direct cultivation in the half-century after 1350 and by 1450 most demesnes were in the hands of rent-paying tenants.

1500–1750

The early modern gentry did not withdraw entirely from farming. Some landlords retained extensive sheep pastures through to the decline in wool prices in the 1620s (although these were often the rising families of the fifteenth and sixteenth centuries whose fortunes were based on wool). At all periods the parks that surrounded major houses were kept in hand, and these may have been used for sport, for feeding cattle for the household or let as grazing (agistment). Thirsk has suggested that there was a revival of interest in farming ('new style demesne farming') in the later sixteenth century and has connected this to an intellectual revival of interest in farming: but it seems equally likely that farming was a necessary fact of life for gentry whose income was squeezed between static rents and rising prices (Thirsk, 1990).

Whilst some land might be leased 'at will' (annual tenancies) for market rents, the normal contractual arrangements between landlords and tenants were designed to minimize the landlord's investment costs. Leases were judged to be sufficiently long for a tenant making an investment in land or buildings to secure a return from it. Early modern landlords therefore spent little on repairs of tenant property except at times of falling rents when investment might be needed to attract or retain tenants.

Rent indices are difficult to calculate before *c.*1650 because landlords often let land by 'beneficial leases' where a tenant paid an entry fine at the beginning of a lease and a low, often customary, annual rent. Steep increases in fines can be seen over the sixteenth century, but the signs are that rents, however measured, sagged in the 1620s and had not returned to their peak by 1640 (Clark, 2002). Thereafter it is broadly true to say that rents stagnated for most of a hundred years and in some decades – the 1680s, 1730s and 1740s – fell significantly. At these periods landlords needed to support their tenants by permitting arrears to accumulate, providing buildings and even capital in the form of animals (Clay, 1985, Bowden, 1985, 62–83; Turner, Beckett and Afton, 1997; Clark, 2002). In a few locations, instances of sharecropping have been found, but this was an extreme measure to avoid taking land in hand whilst allowing tenants to accumulate capital (Griffiths and Overton, 2009).

Cultural value of land

Land was valued in pre-modern societies because it alone could provide a secure and stable income. Leasehold land did not rate so highly as 'freehold' land held by knight service because it could not be inherited beyond its fixed term of years or lives. Land, however, was not just valued as a safe investment and as a source of ready income. The possession of land remained at the heart of British aristocracies into the twentieth century, and today their houses are coveted by the *nouveaux riche*. At all times, the possession of a country estate promised privacy, the possibilities of exercising a paternalist concern for a rural community (which might include holding courts and enforcing moral discipline), the chance to mould the landscape, and access to field sports. At an earlier date, land offered the prestige of leading soldiers to war. In fact landlords interested in status, in all periods, tended to reduce the value of their estates, whether by the creation of parks and the withdrawal of land from intensive agriculture, or, in the eighteenth century, the planting of woodland for aesthetic and sporting reasons. Rich men who desired land for sport might not have to buy it but, by the later seventeenth century, could take advantage of a market in leases for smaller estates and houses, particularly in the Home Counties around London.

Peasants lacked the means to behave in this way. There has been much debate over whether they saw their land simply as a source of income, or whether they invested emotional capital in the holding which they had inherited and expected to pass to the next generation. Certainly peasants in East Anglia seem to have bought and sold land without much sign of sentiment. Peasant families were more likely to keep land through the generations, especially a larger holding, outside the eastern counties, and in the period before 1430 (Razi, 1981). Peasants also seem to have had little regard for the continuities of landholding in the mid-fifteenth century when land was readily available; but at other times the inheritance of land was the only way most people could expect to secure a holding, and the sense of familial attachment to land may have been so much greater. The most recent study of long-term continuities in early modern landholding has found that the motives for holding land were mixed. Some people bought land as an investment and sold it relatively quickly; some land descended in the same family for extended periods although this does not necessarily imply that they regarded it as a special family asset (French and Hoyle, 2003).

3.2 The occupiers of the land

Peasant ownership

1000–1500

Our earliest records depict a stratified peasantry. Around 1000 the *gebur* (with a holding of about 30 acres) can be contrasted with the *cotsetla* with about five acres. In 1086 those villeins with 15–30 acres accounted for 40 per cent of the rural population and another 30 per cent consisted of smallholding bordars and cottars (Darby, 1977: 61–71). The rest of the lower ranks of rural society was made up from freemen and sokemen, who held a varying quantity of land, and slaves who were either landless or smallholders. In the next two centuries the proportion of smallholders tended to increase to almost a half in the Midlands, and to a considerable majority in parts of eastern England. This tendency towards smaller holdings was caused by a growth in population, clearance and drainage of new land, commercial opportunities which gave smallholders employment in crafts and trades, and more intensive cultivation.

A scatter of tenants with 50 acres of land or more can always be identified. They included the *radmen* (riding men) of the eleventh century, and the franklins of the thirteenth and fourteenth centuries. This type of 'rich' peasant grew in numbers after 1350 when land became easily available as the population fell and tenants either died or moved, and it became profitable to manage large holdings with a high proportion of pasture. The decline in numbers also produced a severe rural depopulation and a marked pattern of village desertion. By *c.*1500 perhaps 12 per cent of the tenants held at least 50 acres, and many of them would be called yeomen (Dyer, 1996: 74). They would include the farmers of manorial demesnes (100–400 acres) who were mostly recruited from the better-off peasantry. Theories of differentiation would expect that the growth in holding size at one end of peasant society would be matched by an increase in cottage holders who could provide labour, but smallholders often shrank in numbers. Some of those with large landholdings took over cottages and rented them out to labourers who worked for them (Fox, 1995), or they hired servants who received bed and board as well as a wage.

Yeomen and farmers can in many ways be defined as rural capitalists: they ran large enterprises, produced for the market, innovated to increase profits, and employed labour. Rural society as a whole is more difficult to categorise as capitalist, as the institutions of lordship persisted, even if weakened, and there was no rural proletariat.

1500–1750

By the early sixteenth century population was growing again, and, indeed, English population about doubled over the century. But renewed population growth was not marked by any reversal of the tendencies of the fifteenth century towards bigger holdings and depopulation continued as at least a regional phenomenon. The English countryside in the sixteenth and early seventeenth century was therefore marked by a continuation of existing trends. In the villages of southern England in particular, the rising population was accommodated in sub-divided tenements, in new housing built within villages, in cottages erected on manorial wastes, the edges of woods, moors and marshes. Villages increasingly divided between a small number of farmers and a much larger body of men and women who had no hope of acquiring land, even on lease, and whose entitlement to run a cow on a common might become restricted with the passage of time (Wrightson, 1977).

Peasants, in the sense of subsistence farmers who relied on family labour, had certainly disappeared from England by the middle of the seventeenth century. If they survived at all in the British mainland, it was in the northern uplands and Wales and in the Highlands of Scotland. They had been replaced by labour-employing capitalist farmers, a good number of whom owned their own land either as freehold or on comfortable customary terms. But, and as we saw, the numbers of these owner-occupiers fell after 1650 as hard trading conditions forced a progressive increase in farm size. Thus, there was a transition from peasant to farmer, but the definition of a farmer differed from generation to generation. The classic tripartite configuration of English rural society, of landlords, tenant farmers and labourers, had certainly been established in much of southern England by 1750, but in a few locations in the Midlands, and more so in the North, pockets of owner-occupying yeomen hung on until later in the century.

Communal land use

1000–1500

Throughout the period 1000–1500 open field arable, meadow and pasture were usually held in common, though this was most highly developed in villages following the 'Midland system' in a belt stretching from south-east Scotland and the north-east of England, through the east Midlands to central southern England. The area held communally declined over time as land was taken out of communal regimes and converted to land held in severalty, according to modern ideas of landholding, in which a sole landowner had the exclusive right to its use. Enclosure implied not only the reorganisation of landscapes so that dispersed holdings became concentrated, but also the abolition of common rights over land.

In some areas these rights were not strongly entrenched and enclosure came early. In the south-east and the west lay the countries of 'old enclosure', in which, as early as 1050, much land lay in hedged crofts. Closes increased in number in the twelfth and thirteenth centuries, as most assarts from woodland or intakes from heath and moor were surrounded with hedges and fences. Occasional records show that a group of assarts could have been subdivided into strips as holdings were split by inheritance and sale, leading to the development of a new open field (Thirsk, 1964). In general, however, the proportion of enclosed land increased between 1100 and 1348 with the assarting movement and the fencing of parcels of former common pastures.

Between 1349 and 1500 the proportion continued to increase, but patchily. In areas of old enclosure, tenants asserted their control over closes by excluding rights of common pasture. In landscapes with large wastes, such as woodlands and moorlands, new closes were made, not to plough like the earlier assarts, but to create separate (private) grazing land. Tenants with land in open fields modified their holdings by exchanging strips to consolidate their land into blocks for enclosure. In a more radical move, neighbours might agree to rearrange and enclose their land in a number of furlongs. Such moves were intended to give the tenants more flexibility in the use of land, allowing them to convert arable to pasture, or to vary the rotation of crops to meet their individual needs. A much more radical and controversial move to enclose led to the conversion to pasture of a whole village territory (Dyer, 2005: 72–75). This might have been begun by the activities of an engrossing tenant who took over the holdings of a number of neighbours and converted them to pasture, or the initiative may have come from a demesne farmer. Often the final move would come from the lord who would buy out the remaining tenants or force them to leave. This process of depopulating enclosure was experienced by hundreds of villages, mainly in the Midland belt (Beresford and Hurst, 1971: 39, 66).

1500–1750

Wordie has estimated that 47 per cent of land in England was enclosed by 1600, of which about 10 per cent was former open field land in the Midlands enclosed between 1350 and 1500. The enclosure continued throughout the early modern period although at variable rates and at a much faster pace in some areas than others. Wordie estimated that a further 26 per cent was enclosed between 1500 and 1699 (Wordie, 1983). Much of this was in the same Midland counties which had suffered large-scale depopulation before 1517 (Thirsk, 1967: 213–38). Depopulating enclosure was perceived to be a social problem and the subject of periodic government enquiries. The enclosure of waste land was regarded as an 'improvement' and therefore desirable, and for that reason is poorly recorded in government records.

All enclosure reduced the amount of land under communal regulation. It may be suggested that the land which remained to be enclosed by parliamentary statute after 1750, the classic period of enclosure, was merely the residue of communal assets where a consensus to enclose had proved impossible to achieve earlier, or where the land was worth so little (as in the case of hill-pastures) that the advantages of enclosure were only evident at a period of high land prices. But where open fields remained in 1750, the rights of communal usage had often been already reduced in ways which obviated the need for enclosure. It has been shown, for instance, that open fields might be reorganised from within so that fallows could be replaced with sown grass leys, and, at a later date, turnips. As for commons in the sense of waste, some villages continued to regulate them. But opinion hostile to commons always stressed their poor management, the impossibility of keeping interlopers' animals off them, the tendency towards overgrazing and the desirability of improvement by enclosure.

Power in the village

1000–1500

Village self-government grew in importance in the half-millennium after 1000 without achieving the institutional forms found in northern France or parts of the Low Counties. In the English village, petty misdemeanours were punished in a royal court, the court leet, whilst the economic and legal interests of the lord were protected in the court baron. Both were presided over by the lord's steward and the role of tenants limited to serving as the lord's officers (who exercised a great deal of authority) or sitting on the courts' juries. The leading peasants who served the lord as reeves, rent collectors, haywards, jurors and chief pledges were also expected by the state and church to act as constables, churchwardens and tax collectors. Where a village was divided between two or more manors, villagers might meet to make decisions for the whole community (Dyer, 1994). Manorial courts also offered a forum for dispute resolution, including the prosecution of debts and breaches of contract (Briggs, 2009).

Did the better-off leaders of the community who exercised most influence and authority pursue their sectional interests to the disadvantage of the cottagers, wage earners and poor? Indications that they did so include the harvest regulations which were adopted in many villages from the late thirteenth century, which sought to limit the wages of harvest workers and to restrict the gleaning of corn after the harvest to those who could not work. After the Black Death some wealthier peasants cooperated with the king's justices to enforce the labour laws which attempted to force workers to accept employment at pre-plague wage rates. In the fifteenth century, in the interest of good order and hard work, villagers used the lord's court to prohibit illicit games, to order people to their beds at a reasonable hour, and to prevent bad behaviour such as eavesdropping and gossiping (Ault, 1972). Charity was dispensed by the leading villagers, who kept a common poor box, and relief was channelled in the direction of the deserving poor.

Village society, however, may not have been polarised as much as in the early modern period. Many of the by-laws and ordinances issued by the manor court, about such important matters as the overburdening of the common pasture with livestock, illicit enclosures, and failure to observe the correct crop rotations, were directed not against the poor but were aimed at curbing the self-serving activities of leading tenants. A broad oligarchy ruled the village, which included many middling peasants. The wage earners, who included the younger sons of the leading villagers, and the poor who might include the widows and orphans of once prosperous peasants, did not form a separate class (Hilton, 1975: 20–36).

1500–1750

The tendency for land to be concentrated in fewer hands, and for villages to fill up with the landless, accentuated already existing tendencies to oligarchy. But the addition, the land market generated large numbers of resident gentry in the sixteenth century who might choose to involve themselves in village government. The key was to establish control over housing. Where ownership in a village was limited to one or two landowners, this was easily achieved and these estate-dominated 'closed villages' tended in the long term to depopulation. 'Open villages', marked by larger numbers of property owners, were inclined to grow in population, become occupationally diverse, even industrial, and to harbour religious non-conformists. Inevitably they had larger numbers of poor people and so higher poor rates.

Village self-government by the manorial court invariably declined. By the sixteenth century these were a poor imitation of their medieval predecessors. The majority of manorial courts ceased to be held or were only held intermittently by the early seventeenth century, possibly as a deliberate landlord strategy, and where they continued to be held, there were problems in securing both attendance and compliance with their orders. Where copyhold land transactions needed to be registered, the courts continued to be held even into the twentieth century. Of those courts which remained, few if any dealt with criminal or civil business by the time of the English Civil War (Harrison, 1997). Practical authority in the village passed to the ratepayers' meeting or vestry.

Where was the business of the manorial court transacted after the courts themselves went into abeyance? It is possible that with enclosure, some types of business, for instance the management of drains and fences, disappeared completely. The prosecution of petty crime and inter-personal violence may have been transferred to quarter or petty sessions. The selection of individuals to be prosecuted there conferred a great deal of power on the village's officers. Their power was further enhanced by the creation of the poor law (Hindle, 2000: ch. 8).

Arrangements in Scotland were perhaps more similar to those in England than differences in nomenclature might lead one to suppose. The lord's baron courts remained a vital force for longer than their English equivalents (they were abolished in 1747), protecting the lord's fiscal interests, prosecuting petty crimes and offering a forum for debt litigation. They seem to have been a feature of the Lowlands for the most part and not to have had much force in the Highlands. The particular character of the Scottish Reformation saw the emergence of kirk sessions, presided over by the parochial minister and elected elders, the latter the oligarchic equivalent of the vestry, which acted to enforce moral discipline over the poor and the sexually incontinent. It also provided the little poor relief which was available (Whyte, 1985: ch. 12).

Peasant organisations and resistance

Peasant or farmers' organisations before the nineteenth century remained rudimentary at best: they were also probably illegal. How far ideas and solidarities were shared at markets and fairs cannot now be established, and it is for the most part only extreme forms of resistance which have found their way into the records.

1000–1500

The village community, used by the lord for his administration, could also enable peasants to negotiate contentious matters and if necessary offer resistance. The end product of bargaining between lord and peasants can be seen in declarations of custom such as the announcement of new inheritance arrangements, or general commutations of labour services. When bargaining failed, we see protest and collective non-cooperation, the failure to do labour services, rent strikes, or concealment of seigneurial dues, such as servile women marrying without permission and without paying the marriage fine. Matters could be taken further by collective direct action, like the 'riots' when large crowds removed enclosures which were blocking access to common pasture (recorded on a number of occasions in 1220–1350) (Dyer, 2006). Peasant communities revealed their capacity to organise and to understand the complexities of the law when they claimed privileges as former tenants of the crown before the royal courts. Behind the rather practical aim of preventing lords from levying higher rents, peasants were seeking the king's protection and looking back to an age of freedom. The same idea motivated the rebels in the great rising of 1381, for whom the village served as the basis for organising the revolt, and in which the demand for freedom was linked with the implementation of self-government (Hilton, 1973: 214–32). For a century after 1381 communities continued to negotiate with lords to reduce rents and remove oppressive dues, but whereas the demands before 1381 were rarely achieved, lords were increasingly ready to make concessions as peasants were scarce, and they had perhaps learnt lessons from 1381.

1500–1750

In some respects the late sixteenth and seventeenth centuries seem to mark a retreat from the later Middle Ages when peasants showed themselves to be capable of organising over whole regions. The last instance of widespread peasant solidarity comes from the middle years of the sixteenth century and its bloody repression perhaps persuaded the peasantry that mass action did not pay. How far farmers lay behind the sometimes violent opposition to disafforestation in the 1620s and 1630s and fen drainage in the 1630s has been extensively but inconclusively debated, but the latter was serious enough to see the deployment of troops. The agrarian violence in the Midlands in 1607 seems to have been largely the work of urban crowds prompted by high prices. The breakdown in civil order in 1640–42 saw a great deal of violence directed at new enclosures and parks, but again, it is far from clear who was behind this. The last outbreak of large scale agrarian violence in Britain (as opposed to Ireland) was in Galloway, south-west Scotland in 1724, when disturbances aimed at enclosing landlords were repressed by troops.

English peasants seem to have had little interest in influencing government policy. The nearest we have to an agrarian programme directed at government comes from the articles of 1549 and in a later petition tentatively dated to 1553, both from East Anglia: their complaints include landlords raising rents, their tendency to out-compete tenants in grazing and their exploitation of the fold course (the right of lords to have their tenants fold their sheep on the landlord's own land). From this time forwards, rural communities had few opportunities to generalise their grievances.

Those gentry who lived through 1549 seem to have been cautious about alienating the peasantry, and it was the next generation which set about raising rents or enclosing. They were aided by the new techniques of land surveying (Harvey, 1996). Hence, from the mid-1570s, many individual village communities came under pressure from landlords who wished to recover some of the income lost to inflation and to access the profits of newly buoyant farming. These landlords operated, and their ambitions were contested, manor by manor. There are occasional references to peasant solidarities between manors, but these are few and far between, and it seems likely that the atomisation of the peasantry left them vulnerable to landlord revanchism. The commercialisation of the market in leasehold meant that if tenants failed to come to an agreement with their landlord when new leases were offered, their farm – which the tenants may have regarded as an hereditary possession – would be lost to them. For many pre-civil war landlords, tenants were essentially footloose individuals who were not to be trusted. The relationship of landlord and tenant might be transitory and lack obligation on both sides.

With time, the balance gradually turned against landlords. Particularly where high fines or improved rents were demanded, the need was for skilled, well-capitalised tenants who could maximise their profits to meet the landlord's expected rents. Such people were not readily found even before the Civil War. They became even scarcer in the downturn in agricultural profitability in the 1670s and 1680s. This made for a common identity of purpose between landlords and tenants on the burning agricultural issues of the day such as the banning of Irish cattle imports (finally achieved in 1666) or establishment of the corn bounty. There is no sign of an independent farmers' movement, and if farmers reminded landlords of where their interests lay, it was done informally. Little is known about how far landlords assumed their tenants would vote for them at parliamentary elections. The management of rural electorates is known from the early seventeenth century but probably remained rudimentary for most of that century. By 1715 Robert Walpole, Norfolk landowner and future Prime Minister, was organising 'his' freeholders to travel 'like a regiment' to the county election, with a wagon to carry the infirm, all led by trumpeter. A dialogue published in 1734 juxtaposes the landlord's assumption that his tenant will vote for his candidate with the tenant's claim to independence (and the fear of the tenant's wife that they would be evicted).[1]

Peasant prosperity

In view of their subordinate social and political position, the revival of serfdom around 1200, the many smallholdings and the erosion of common pastures, did the English medieval peasantry live in miserable poverty? There can be no doubt about the problems facing smallholders in the decades around 1300, as with inadequate amounts of land the tenants and their families relied on their earnings, yet work was scarce, wages low and the prices of foodstuffs high (Bailey, 1998). For the more substantial villagers, the thirteenth century presented opportunities in the market, which are apparent if we calculate peasant budgets. More direct evidence comes from the relatively high quality houses that peasants built and the material possessions, such as furnishings and clothing, that they bought. They could evidently afford to pay rents and still have cash to spare for their consumption needs.

---

1 Reproduced in Chipping Local History Society (ed.), *The diary of the Reverend Peter Walkden for 1733–34* (Otley, 2000), pp. 411–14.

After 1350 the less numerous smallholders no longer suffered the disadvantages of low real wages and limited opportunities for earning. Their diet improved with a higher content of meat and fish, and they were more likely than their predecessors to eat white wheat bread and to drink ale regularly (Dyer, 1998: 151–87). Peasants with larger holdings gained less than their forebears from the sale of produce, and especially grain, but they adapted to new circumstances.

Certainly the English believed from the mid-fifteenth century onwards that they had a high standard of living compared to their continental neighbours. Bishop John Aylmer, writing in 1559, compared the English yeoman's freedom from arbitrary taxation and his much higher standard of living with his equivalent in France, Germany or Italy. 'Thou livest like a lord and they like dogs ... we live in paradise'.[2] An observer of the Cheshire yeomanry in 1621 believed that 'though they be but farmers, they live better than many of higher estate in other nations'.[3] Of course, it is hardly unexpected that the English were dismissive of living standards in Scotland which they found squalid and backward.

More than this, there is much late sixteenth and early seventeenth century comment on the rising wealth of yeomen seen in their possession of ready money, the quality of their houses and household furnishings, their aspirations for their children and even their assimilation into the gentry. Inventories demonstrate rising standards of living, but the North and western periphery followed a generation or more behind the south-east. This prosperity was far from universal. Accounts of Leicestershire in the 1650s and the West Midlands in the 1690s draw pictures of acute rural poverty amongst farmers who skimped to survive, and there is little reason to suppose that the increasing prosperity of successful farmers 'trickled down' to improve the standard of housing for their labourers and the poor.

3.3 Government and public policies

State policies and government attitudes

1000–1500

Medieval states had no agrarian policies as such, but they had an agenda to assert their own authority, to maintain public order, and to collect revenue. The English state always coexisted with a wealthy and powerful aristocracy, which had limited local control but which exercised state powers in particular places, especially on the Welsh marches and in parts of the North. Usually king and aristocrats worked together in a mutually supportive relationship, as, for example, when at the end of the twelfth century the king's courts extended their protection of freemen, but left the servile population to

---

2 John Aylmer, *An harborowe for faithfull and true subjects* (1559).

3 Cited in M. E. Campbell, *The English yeoman under Elizabeth I and the early Stuarts* (New Haven, 1942), p. 63.

seigneurial jurisdiction. A typical example of co-operation between crown and aristocracy was the Statute of Merton's provisions on the enclosure of wastes in 1236. The magnates were complaining that it was too easy for free tenants to use the royal courts to prevent enclosures by claiming the loss of common pasture. The new law did not allow lords to ride roughshod over the peasants or the king's courts, but stated that if it could be shown that the free tenants had sufficient grazing, then the enclosure was allowed (Dyer, 2006). In the late thirteenth century the royal courts invariably found against peasants seeking protection from increases in their rents and dues as former tenants of royal demesne, but at the same time lords were prevented by royal enquiries of *quo warranto* from exercising judicial power over their tenants for which they had no provable claim.

The alliance between state and the aristocracy came dangerously close in the period 1350–81, when state legislation sought to defend employers from the effects of the scarcity of labour after the Black Death by attempting to fix wages. In the succeeding century the state asserted greater independence, and in 1488 legislation aimed at curbing depopulating enclosure by landlords. 'Political society' bound together the government and the landed interest, but the state also valued the support of the peasantry, who, from 1334, organised their own assessment and collection of the main direct tax, the lay subsidy.

1500–1750

Where late medieval governments seem to have taken little interest in landscape change and its impact on the inhabitants of the countryside, a new activism took concrete form after 1516. It may have been prompted by concerns over the taxation, military recruitment, or a realisation that the medieval process of village desertion was not reversible. The discouragement of depopulating enclosure then lay at the heart of government policy for 120 years (Thirsk, 1966).

After legislation in 1488 and 1515, Cardinal Wolsey launched an enquiry into depopulating enclosure in 1517. He brought suits against enclosers, and attempted to compel offenders to restore land to tillage and rebuild farms. Further abortive enquiries were held in 1548 and 1565. By the beginning of the 1590s, enclosure was no longer a source of government anxiety and much of the anti-enclosure legislation was repealed in 1593. A succession of poor harvests caused high prices and much distress, and this, coupled with the discovery of a plot to overthrow enclosures in Oxfordshire, threw government into panic. The legislation was reinstated in 1597–8 despite the objections of better-informed commentators. Riots took place in the eastern Midland counties against enclosures in 1607, another year of high prices, and these were followed by renewed enquiries and prosecutions of enclosing landowners. There were further enquiries and prosecutions in the mid-1630s. Despite its attempts, government could neither inhibit long term economic change nor police the countryside efficiently.

The association of enclosure enquiries with years of high prices is clear. Government had to be seen to be active in these years. Its policy, as encapsulated in the Book of Dearth Orders, first issued in 1586 but drawing together established practice, was that the local magistrates should manage markets, undertake searches to prevent hoarding and suppress wasteful activities (notably brewing but also starch making) (Slack, 1980; Walter, 1989: 116–20). Government was anxious to maintain the supply of food to London lest the capital became unmanageable in famine conditions. What it did not do was buy grain on the international market or organise strategic stockpiles. The dearth orders were last issued in 1630 but their memory lingered in the minds of people. They inspired the popular searches for corn in years of high prices which the late E. P. Thompson read as an aspect of the 'moral economy'.

After the Restoration (1660), the government took no interest in enclosure, leaving it to private initiatives which might be registered by decree in the court of Chancery or confirmed by private act of parliament. Scotland, on the other hand, had a general enclosure procedure laid down by law from 1695 (Whyte, 1985: 100–06). By this time the problem faced by English government was one of persisting low corn prices. The policy of forbidding exports except in years of low prices was maintained until the mid-1650s when a more permissive regime was introduced. In 1673 previous policy was reversed and a bounty (subsidy) paid in exports and a duty charged on imports. These arrangements were expressly intended to help support the price of corn so the husbandman could better pay his rent and the landlord his taxes. But the bounty system was allowed to lapse after 1681. It was then reinstated in 1689 as an informal *quid pro quo* for the introduction of a land tax. For the first half of the eighteenth century, farm incomes (and rents) were supported by a system of publicly-funded cereal export subsidies. One observer argued in 1734 that wheat prices were maintained at 4*s*. a bushel because of export demand when their price in a closed market would have been about half that (Thirsk, 1985: 305–9; Chartres: 1985, 448–54). There was a similar reversal of policy in Scotland where exports of grain and other produce were encouraged by statute of 1663.

This was a major success for the landlords' lobby. Their other triumph had come a generation earlier in 1662 when the import of live cattle from Ireland, which was held to be depressing domestic suppliers in the North of England and Wales, was banned (although demands for a ban went back to the early 1620s). It was in this period that government, in a sense, aligned itself with the landowning and farming communities and offered policies to their advantage rather than simply hindering inevitable change. A rather different government intervention in agriculture came with the banning of domestic production of tobacco, first in 1619 at the behest of the Virginia company. Soldiers were used to destroy the standing crop in the 1660s and 1670s but it was finally the low price of Virginian tobacco rather than government action which ended domestic tobacco growing (Thirsk, 1985, 346–56, 342–3).

The English government failed to establish institutions which might have eased agricultural progress. In only four counties were land registries established, the first of 1704, which compares unfavourably with Scotland where, after an abortive initiative of 1599, the Register of Sasines was maintained from 1619. English government did not offer any streamlined process to achieve enclosure before the general enclosure acts of 1836, 1840 and 1845: rather, like the creation of turnpike roads in the eighteenth century and railways in the nineteenth, enclosure proceeded on an *ad hoc* basis, each parish making its own arrangements. There was little uniformity in weights and measures.

The two great initiatives that government did take were to regulate employment (by statute of 1563) and establish a system of publicly-funded poor relief (by statute of 1597, re-enacted in 1601, and which codified earlier statutes). The 1563 statute gave Justices of the Peace the power to force men and women of labouring age to accept work unless they possessed minimum levels of wealth. Wage rates were also to be laid down by the Justices annually, and provision was made to enforce these rates both against labourers who asked too much and employers who offered too much. This may have been a response to labour shortages following the epidemic of 1557–8. Whilst wage rates continued to be issued into the eighteenth century, the oversupply of labour which population growth produced made for falling real wages until after the mid-seventeenth century so the sanctions against labour appear to have been little employed. Similar wage rates were issued – at least occasionally – in Scotland after 1614.

If population growth made much of the 1563 legislation unnecessary, the 1597/1601 statute was in part an answer to un- and underemployment. Begging was forbidden: the poor were to be either set on work or given a weekly relief payment to be funded from a poor rate. The underlying principle was that each person had a home parish in which they had a 'settlement'. The definition of a 'settlement' was progressively defined, but it might be acquired by birth, serving an apprenticeship, renting property or paying poor rates. It reduced the need of the poor to migrate to towns for charity whilst licensing the migration of the able-bodied for work. The poor law was organised at the parish level, with parish officials (the overseers of the poor) being directed by the vestry which selected the poor who deserved support. The overseers levied rates to cover their costs. Rudimentary versions of this provision can be found in south-east English villages as early as the 1580s, but not all parishes were levying poor rates as late as 1640. Increasing costs encouraged some early eighteenth century parishes to house their poor in workhouses – but the majority remained committed to the poor being supported in a domestic context.

The poor law has momentous implications as it created new power structures in the countryside. By making every community responsible for the cost of its poor, it gave them the incentive to reduce their numbers. Some landowners deliberately demolished housing: there are occasional instances of the poor being refused leave to marry, and a pattern emerged of landowners evading the cost of their farm labourers by having them live in 'open villages' from which they walked to work in 'closed villages'.

There was no real equivalent to the English poor law in Scotland. Poor years were met with increased charitable donation and a reliance on kin: hence Scotland continued to be troubled by a problem of vagrancy.

The regulation of the countryside

The chief form of regulation of land use in England was the attempt to maintain tillage by preventing depopulating enclosure between the late fifteenth century and 1640. Other than that, from an early date English and Scottish kings had a policy of preserving woods and wastes for hunting. Pre-Norman kings had hunting reserves, but the Norman and later rulers applied a continental forest law which prevented landowners within the huge areas designated as forests from hunting and clearing land – except at a price (Gilbert, 1979: 5–13). The forests were regarded as a nuisance, especially by the English kings' subjects, and throughout the thirteenth century and especially around 1300 their boundaries were redrawn and areas were disafforested. Nonetheless there were about 300 forests and chases remaining in England and Wales in the sixteenth century, only a minority of which saw any royal hunting. Whilst the royal interest in them focussed on the game, they also served as valuable reserves of wood and timber, and local communities welcomed the pasture, fuel, nuts and industrial raw materials. The crown reduced the number of forests it possessed by disafforestation in the early seventeenth century, felling the timber and enclosing the forest area. A surprising number survived into the eighteenth century, not all of which retained any real woodland cover.

Markets

The English and Scottish crowns exercised the power to license markets and fairs, both to raise revenue from the fees for the charters, but also to maintain order. A network of chartered markets was established, nearly 2000 of them in England by 1300 (Letters *et al.*, 2003: 28) so by this date the great majority of rural producers could gain access to a market within 12 km (seven miles). English markets were not supposed to encroach on one another and were therefore well spaced, and neighbouring markets were not usually held on the same day of the week. In Scotland and Wales towns claimed monopolies on trade in their vicinity, and country traders could be punished.

New markets continued to be created in the sixteenth and seventeenth centuries throughout Britain, where promoters thought that demand could sustain a market and repay their investment. At least 84 new market centres were authorised in Scotland between 1600 and 1630, but 346 between 1660 and 1707, a large proportion of which were in the Highlands and Islands, areas in which markets had previously been scarce (Whyte, 1985: 178–92).

Medieval foreign trade was always regulated for diplomatic and fiscal reasons, with the establishment of staples, notably that fixed at Calais, for English wool exports to the continent. A trade in grain over the North Sea existed in the later Middle Ages but was prohibited in bad harvest years. The problem that early modern England increasingly faced was not one of occasional failures of supply (which were blamed on enclosures), but overproduction and low farm gate prices. As we saw, exports of cereal came to be subsidised: imports of live animals were banned. On the other hand, the export of wool was also banned from 1647. Agriculture was a strategic industry and so free markets, with their unpredictable consequences, could not be allowed to operate until there was total confidence in supply. This had been achieved in England and Scotland by the mid-seventeenth century. It was the very end of the eighteenth century, in renewed conditions of domestic hardship, before government took much notice of agriculture again.

Peasants' political and social standing

Peasants were always perceived as an ambiguous social group by those in authority. On the one hand they were idealised as hard-working contributors to the well being of society, full of common sense and informed by a simple morality. But they could also be portrayed as malevolent, idle, cunning, avaricious and rebellious. In the rising of 1381 the English peasants thought of themselves as the king's true friends, acting against the traitors who had misled him, and demanding that nobles and lawyers be removed. They expected to receive their freedom and a political role as the governors of their villages under the king. Their political education in the following seventy years led them to abandon these millennial fantasies, and to adopt the language of their superiors. In the rebellion of 1450 they claimed a place in the political process, demanding reforms of government just like those who attended parliament. The rebellion was suppressed of course, and peasants, whatever their imaginings, remained excluded from the higher levels of political power (Harvey, 1991).

After the last major risings in 1549, there seems to have been something of a realignment in rural politics as farmers identified their interests as coinciding with those of landlords, with an emphasis on the maintenance of order amongst the growing numbers of landless and poor in the village (Hindle, 2000). The insurrectionary tradition became the possession of rural labourers and urban artisans. Although politically marginal, they had force of numbers, and medieval insurrections were remembered in early seventeenth-century political discourse as the outcome of incautious policies.

The same political discourse saw the husbandman or farmer as one of the fundamental building blocks on which society was based. One speaker in the House of Commons in 1601 referred to 'the husbandman as 'the staple man of the kingdom'. In the same debate Sir Robert Cecil observed that 'whosever doth not maintain the plough destroys this kingdom' and pointed out that the greater proportion of the troops levied were ploughmen.[4] The power of this image diminished over time, but the independence of the freeholder from political fashion, his commitment to traditional notions of freedom and liberty and his role in the maintenance of law and order continued to be valued. But, in common with all economically active trades, farmers were from time to time excoriated for their avarice and profiteering. High prices were blamed on greed, hoarding and profiteering rather than random movements of the weather. By the mid- and later eighteenth century the farmer could be seen as a hard-faced individual, sometimes with only a temporary commitment to the village in which he lived, over-eager to cut his costs by forcing down the poor rate.

4 T. E. Hartley, *Proceedings in the parliaments of Elizabeth I* (3 vols, Leicester, 1981–95), III, pp. 451–2.

Bibliography

Ault, W. O. (1972) *Open-field farming in medieval England*, London.

Bailey, M. (1998) 'Peasant welfare in England, 1290–1348', *Economic History Rev.*, 51, pp. 223–51.

Beresford, M. and Hurst, J. (1971) *Deserted medieval villages: studies*, London.

Bowden, P. J. (1985) 'Agricultural prices, wages, farm profits and rents', in J. Thirsk (ed.), *Agrarian History* V (ii), pp. 1–118.

Briggs, C. (2009) *Credit and village society in fourteenth-century England*, Oxford.

Britnell, R. H. (1980) 'Minor landlords in England and medieval agrarian capitalism',

Past and Present, 89, pp. 3–22.

Callander, R. F. (1987) *A pattern of landownership in Scotland*, Finzean.

Campbell, B. M. S. (2000) *English seigniorial agriculture, 1250–1450*, Cambridge.

Campbell, B. M. S. and Bartley, K. (2006) *England on the eve of the Black Death. An atlas of lay lordship, land and wealth, 1300–49*, Manchester.

Chartres, J. A. (1985) 'The marketing of agricultural produce', in J. Thirsk (ed.), *Agrarian History* V (ii), pp. 406–502.

Clark, G. (2002) 'Farmland rental values and agrarian history: England and Wales, 1500–1912', *European Review of Economic History*, 6, pp. 281–309.

Clay, C. (1985) 'Landlords and estate management in England', in J. Thirsk (ed.), *Agrarian History* V (ii), pp. 119–251.

Corbett, W. J. (1926) 'The development of the Duchy of Normandy and the Norman Conquest of England', *Cambridge Medieval History*, V, pp. 505–13.

Coss, P. (1991) *Lordship, knighthood and locality. A study in English society,* c.*1180*–c.*1280*, Cambridge.

Coss, P. (1989) 'Bastard Feudalism revised', *Past and Present*, 125, pp. 27–64, and 'Debate: Bastard Feudalism revised', 131 (1991), pp. 165–203.

Darby, H. C. (1977) *Domesday England*, Cambridge.

Davies, R. R. (1987) *Conquest, coexistence and change. Wales, 1063–1415*, Oxford.

Dyer, C. (1994) 'The English medieval village community and its decline', *J. British Studies*, 33, pp. 407–29.

Dyer, C. (1997) 'Peasants and farmers: rural settlement in an age of transition', in D. Gaimster and P. Stamper (eds), *The age of transition. The archaeology of English culture, 1400–1600*, Society for Medieval Archaeology monograph, 15, pp. 61–76.

Dyer, C. (1998) *Standards of living in the later middle ages* Cambridge, revised edn.

Dyer, C. (2005) *An age of transition? Economy and society in late medieval England*, Oxford.

Dyer, C. (2005) 'Seigniorial profits on the land market in late medieval England', in L. Feller and C. Wickham (eds), *Le marché de la terre au moyen age*, Rome, pp. 219–36.

Dyer, C. (2006) 'Conflict in the landscape: the enclosure movement in England, 1220–1349', *Landscape Hist.*, 29, pp. 21–33.

Dyer, C. (2007) 'The ineffectiveness of lordship in England, 1200–1400', in C. Dyer *et al.* (eds), *Rodney Hilton's Middle Ages: an exploration of historical themes* (Past and Present Supplement 2), Oxford, pp. 69–86.

Fox, H. S. A. (1995) 'Servants, cottages and tied cottages during the later Middle Ages', *Rural Hist.*, 6, pp. 125–54.

French, H., and Hoyle, R. W. (2003) 'English individualism refuted - and reasserted: the land market of Earls Colne (Essex), 1550–1750', *Economic History Rev.*, 56, pp. 595–622.

Gilbert, J. M. (1979) *Hunting and hunting reserves in medieval Scotland,* Edinburgh.

Griffiths, E. and Overton, M. (2009) *Farming to halves. The hidden history of sharefarming in England from medieval to modern times,* Houndmills.

Harrison, C. (1997) 'Manor courts and the governance of Tudor England', in C. Brooks and M. Lobban (eds.), *Communities and courts in Britain, 1150–1900,* London, pp. 43–59.

Harvey, I. (1991) *Jack Cade's rebellion of 1450,* Oxford.

Harvey, P. D. A. (1996) 'English estate maps: their early history and their use as historical evidence', in D. Buisseret (ed.), *Rural images. Estate maps in the Old and New Worlds,* Chicago, pp. 27–61.

Hatcher, J. (1970) *Rural economy and society in the Duchy of Cornwall, 1300–1500,* Cambridge.

Heal, F. and Holmes, C. (1993) *The gentry in England and Wales, 1500–1700,* Houndmills.

Hilton, R. H. (1953) 'Gloucester Abbey leases of the late thirteenth century', *University of Birmingham Historical J.*, 4, pp. 1–17.

Hilton, R. H. (1965) 'Freedom and villeinage in England', *Past and Present*, 31, pp. 3–19.

Hilton, R. H. (1973) *Bondmen made free. Medieval peasant movements and the English Rising of 1381*, London.

Hilton, R. H. (1975) *The English peasantry in the later middle ages*, Oxford.

Hindle, S. (2000) *The state and social change in early modern England, 1550–1640* Houndmills.

Hoyle, R. W. (1987) '"An Ancient and Laudable Custom"? The development and definition of Tenant Right in the north-west in the sixteenth century', *Past and Present,* 116, pp. 24–55.

Hoyle, R. W. (1990) 'Tenure and the land market in early modern England: or a late contribution to the Brenner Debate', *Economic History Rev.*, 43, pp. 1 20.

Hoyle, R. W. (ed.) (1992) *The estates of the English crown, 1558–1640,* Cambridge.

Hoyle, R. W. (forthcoming, a) *Idleness, Improvement and Industry. The Oxford economic and social history of Britain and Ireland, 1500–1750,* Oxford.

Hoyle, R. W. (forthcoming, b) *Landlords and tenants in Tawney's century; tenurial change in England, 1540–1640,* Oxford.

Kanzaka, J. (2002) 'Villein rents in thirteenth-century England: an analysis of the Hundred Rolls of 1279–80', *Economic History Rev.*, 55, pp. 593–618.

Letters, S. *et al.* (2003) *Markets and fairs in England and Wales to 1516,* List and Index Society, Special Ser., 32 and 33.

Mayhew, N. J. (1995) 'Modelling medieval monetisation', in R. H. Britnell and B. M. S. Campbell (eds), *A commercialising economy. England 1086 to* c.*1300,* Manchester, pp. 55–78.

Mileson, S. (2005) 'The importance of parks in fifteenth-century society', *The Fifteenth Century*, 5, pp. 19–37.

Overton, M. (1996) *Agricultural revolution in England. The transformation of the agrarian economy, 1500–1850,* Cambridge.

Palmer, J. J. N. (1999) 'The wealth of the secular aristocracy in 1086', *Anglo-Norman Studies*, 22, pp. 279–92.

Razi, Z. (1981) 'Family, land and the village community in late medieval England', *Past and Present*, 100, pp. 3–36.

Sanderson, M. H. B. (1982) *Scottish rural society in the sixteenth century*, Edinburgh.

Sawyer, P. H. (1985) '1066–1086: a tenurial revolution?', in P. Sawyer (ed.), *Domesday Book: a reassessment*, London, pp. 71–85.

Slack, P. (1980) 'Books of Orders: the making of English social policy, 1577–1631', *Trans. Royal Historical Society*, fifth ser., 30, pp. 1–22.

Stone, D. (2005) *Decision-making in medieval agriculture*, Oxford.

Thirsk, J. (1964) 'The common fields', *Past and Present*, 29, pp. 3–25.

Thirsk, J. (1967) 'Enclosing and engrossing' in J. Thirsk (ed.), *The Agrarian History of England and Wales*, IV, *1500–1640*, Cambridge, pp. 200–55.

Thirsk J. (1985) 'Agricultural policy: public debate and legislation', in J. Thirsk (ed.), *Agrarian History* V (ii), pp. 298–388.

Thirsk J. (1985) *The agrarian history of England and Wales*, V, *1640–1750,* 2 vols: Cambridge.

Thirsk, J. (1990) 'The fashioning of the Tudor-Stuart gentry', *Bull. John Rylands University Library of Manchester*, 72, pp. 69–85.

Turner, M. E., Beckett, J. V. and Afton, B. (1997) *Agricultural rent in England, 1690–1914,* Cambridge.

Walter, J. (1989) 'The social economy of dearth in early modern England', in J. Walter and R. Schofield (eds), *Famine, disease and the social order in early modern England,* Cambridge, pp. 78–128.

Whyte, I. (1979) *Agriculture and society in seventeenth-century Scotland,* Edinburgh.

Whyte, I. (1995) *Scotland before the industrial revolution. An economic and social history,* c.*1050*-c.*1550,* London.

Wordie, J. R. (1983) 'The chronology of English enclosure, 1500–1914', *Economic History Rev.*, 36, pp. 483–505.

Wrightson, K. (1977) 'Aspects of social differentiation in rural England, *c.*1580–1660', *J. Peasant Studies*, 5, pp. 33–47.

LANDLORD AND TENANT; OR, W'S SAUCE FOR THE GOOSE, &c.

DIZZY.—WELL, MR. FARMER, WE'LL DO WHAT WE CAN FOR YOU: EXPECT YOU TO DO THE SAME FOR HODGE AND HIS FAMILY.

The British Prime Minister Isaac Disraeli (centre) reminds the farmer (left) of his obligations to the farm labourer ('Hodge', right).
Source: *Judy*, 23 April 1873. At the time, a private members' Landlord and Tenant Bill was before the House of Commons.

4 Britain, 1750–2000

Paul BRASSLEY, Richard HOYLE and Michael TURNER

4.1 Ownership, power relations and the distribution of property

Landowners and changing social property distribution

Landholding in nineteenth-century England and Scotland was dominated by a small elite of landowners, whose landholdings were often protected by settlements and entails. These had developed as a device to ensure that landowners could determine the descent of their land and protect it from alienation by feckless successors. The security of settled land made it ideal for lending on mortgage and allowed landowners to carry large amounts of debt, often contracted to finance conspicuous consumption, less often for investment in agricultural improvement. It is true that there were, in every generation, a few spectacular landed failures, but it was often argued that the inflexibility of the settled estates system made for a shortage of land for purchase or building (Habakkuk, 1994).

The scale of aristocratic landholding and the privileges it conferred was a leading political question in England from the 1840s to the 1920s (Cragoe and Readman (eds), 2010). Exactly how much was held by how few people was a matter of debate in the middle years of the century, and it was to spike what he believed were exaggerated claims that the Earl of Derby established an investigation into the possession of land in 1871. The figures, digested and made ready accessible by John Bateman, revealed the essential truth of the radical critique: one quarter of the land or England and Wales was held by a mere 710 individuals, and 5,000 people held three-quarters of the landed area of the British Isles (Beckett, 2000).

Late nineteenth-century government took positive steps to create a landholding peasantry in Ireland, and conceded property rights to the Crofters in the Scottish Highlands and Islands in 1886. But this was to buy social peace. A movement to introduce land legislation on Irish lines into Wales failed, partly because the Welsh made no recourse to violence or rent strikes (Douglas, 1976). There was a government-sponsored movement to create smallholdings in England after a statute of 1892, but overall, there was little positive action against English landowners. Nonetheless, the economic context within which they lived was subtly changed against them, most especially after the institution of Death Duties in 1894. Inheritance taxes became burdensome in the twentieth century and served to force estates into sales of land (and often their libraries and works of art). The 1910 Finance Act introduced a new, comprehensive system of land taxation although it was never implemented because of the First World War and was abandoned afterwards. The rate of taxes on income remained high and it was only in the final quarter of the twentieth century that some of the burden on landowners was lifted. The nationalisation of land was advocated by many on the left from the 1880s through to the 1940s: but there was a realisation by the Labour Party during the Second World War that in post-war conditions it would be unable to raise the money needed to compensate landowners and it settled for the state direction of farming as an alternative means of achieving its objectives (Beckett, 2000; Cannadine, 1990; Tichelar, 2003).

The English approach has therefore been to leave land in the hands of its owners whilst using inheritance taxes to encourage its sale and qualifying the rights of its owners by statute. But what destroyed the landholding elite in England was not taxation or the extension of statutory rights to their tenants so much as the downturn in agricultural rent after 1880 which made it hard for them to service their mortgage debts. The immediate response of many was to economise, including shutting up their houses and reducing their domestic staff, or letting the house for the sporting season. The Settled Lands Acts of 1882 and 1890 allowed the life tenants of settled estates to sell land and invest its proceeds in better-yielding assets. This concession certainly engendered sales, as did the establishment of Death Duties. Hence the land market seems to have busy in the early 1890s. The real rush to sell started with the Finance Act of 1910 which destroyed aristocratic confidence in the future. It was accentuated by the First World War where the mortality amongst aristocrats on active service left many families liable for death duties. But in addition, the loss of so many compounded a sense that the pleasure had gone out of country living. There was an appreciation that the old order was rapidly dissolving in the 1920s, but sales never really ceased throughout the half century after 1920 (Beckett and Turner, 2007; Cannadine, 1990).

Despite everything, a proportion of the aristocracy managed to hold on to their houses and at least some of their estates. A survey conducted by Clemenson in the late 1970s found that out of a sample of 500 English landowners established in the 1870s, 259 were still holding some of the land of their ancestors a hundred years later. If we look at the core of the estates, including the great house, 310 had been sold from the family owning it in *c.*1880. Of the 276 remaining in private hands, 190 had never been sold and 86 sold more than once. When it is considered that there was always a turnover of families through demographic failure, this is impressive evidence for the tenacity with which the aristocracy has held on (Clemenson, 1982, 122–7; Thompson, 1990–93).

Sales allowed the aristocracy to be refreshed by men bringing new wealth into the countryside, but after 1910 the supply of estates far exceeded demand, and a good proportion of landowners had little alternative but to break up their estates, selling the land to their tenants, sometimes demolishing their mansion house. A more relaxed taxation regime from the 1980s fuelled a roaring trade in country houses with their attached estates amongst industrialists, entertainers and pop stars and rich foreigners who wished to buy into the English sporting lifestyle. There was some political debate about the foreign acquisition of farmland in the late 1970s: but a Royal Commission (the Northfield enquiry) which reported in 1979 found that it was relatively unimportant. The purchase of Highland sporting estates by outsiders has a long history though and remains a contentious subject in Scotland. Legislation of 2003 gave both Scottish tenants and communities a right of pre-emption to their land if a landowner indicated his intention of selling: there is nothing equivalent in England.

The National Trust was founded in 1894 to preserve landscapes of great beauty from development and, along with the National Trust for Scotland (founded 1931), became one of the nation's biggest landowners. One consequence of the dissolution of the estates system was after 1945 the Trust became the owner of last resort of architecturally-significant country houses. (In this context we might also notice the acquisition of extensive acreages of environmentally-sensitive land by wildlife charities in the late twentieth century.) The state itself emerged as a major landowner in the twentieth century. Of course, it had the rump of the old crown estates (to be distinguished from the estates which monarchs themselves bought in the nineteenth century), but the state also acquired land on a prodigious scale in wartime for military purposes and for state-sponsored forestry. Local authorities also emerged as substantial landowners, first in the rather special sense of water companies acquiring 'gathering grounds', especially in the Pennines, but also land for recreational purposes. Hence, according to an estimate of 2001, the Forestry Commission was the largest landowner in the UK with 2.4m acres (0.971m ha), the Ministry of Defence second with 0.75m acres (0.3m ha) and the two National Trusts between them had 0.726m acres (0.294m ha) (Cahill, 2001, Table 1.7). A high proportion of this land was of limited agricultural value.

There was some concern in the 1970s about the acquisition of land by financial institutions, sometimes as an investment, sometimes with the intention that they would farm it through managers rather than tenants. Again, Northfield collected data, finding that by the end of 1978 the institutions had acquired about 1.2 per cent of the stock of agricultural land and 1.9 per cent of the area under crops of grass. British supermarket retailers generally avoided buying land, preferring to deal with independent farmers. The exception was the Cooperative Wholesale Society which in 2009 farmed 70,000 acres (28,000 ha), 20,200 (8,200 ha) of which it owned.

It is therefore not too difficult to describe the overall trends in British landholding from the mid-nineteenth century. The *quantification* of these changes in a *dynamic* fashion is much more difficult. The only systematic attempt to establish the dimensions of ownership was the *Return of owners of land in England, Scotland, Ireland and Wales*, published between 1874 and 1876. The fullest data after the 1874 return comes from the agricultural census data for owner-occupation.

The English agricultural census only gathered details on tenancy for short periods and then employed incompatible definitions over time. The data does show that over 82.1 per cent of holdings were entirely tenanted in 1887–91 and surprisingly somewhat more (87.8 per cent) in 1908–14. This had fallen by a couple of per cent by 1919–22. When systematic data was next collected, for 1950, the proportion had fallen to 48.7 per cent. Sturmey estimated the proportion of the cultivated area held by owner-occupiers as 10.9 per cent in 1914, but 36.0 per cent in 1927. Figures for holdings over 5 acres were derived from the National Farm Survey of 1941–3 and this gave 33 per cent of the land in owner occupation. When figures were next collected in 1950 the proportion owned by occupiers stood at 38 per cent: by 1960 it had reached 49 per cent. The direction of change in the 1970s is confused by the growth in the number of mixed holdings – part rented, part freehold – some of which may be explained by younger farmers renting land from retired parents rather than orthodox tenant relationships. The implication is that by mid-century, around 50 per cent of farmers owned some or all of their land: by 1975–7 this had increased to 75 per cent (Sturmey, 1955; MAFF, 1968: 24–5).

Scotland collected data from 1887 to 1960 (with a gap from 1891 to 1908) of the proportion of *cultivated* land rented or mostly rented or owned or mostly owned. At the end of the nineteenth century and in the years immediately before the First World War this stood at about 92 per cent. It then declined over the 1920s (and precipitately between 1926 and 1927, from 86.4 per cent to 83.0 per cent): by 1930 it stood at 79 per cent, declining to 75.8 per cent by 1949. It then again fell abruptly over the next decade so that by the early 1960s it stood at about 59 per cent. By the end of the century, about two thirds of Scottish farmers owned, or mostly owned, their holdings, a third rented or mostly rented. But again rented farms were larger than owner-occupied ones, and again, when allowance is made for land farmed by estates, a figure of 40 per cent for estate ownership seems about right (Anthony, 1997: 26–28; MAFF, 1968: 28–30).

Systems of tenancy

The agronomist Arthur Young (1741–1820) liked to maintain that the success of English agriculture was based on the practice of giving tenants medium term leases (often for 21 years) which encouraged tenant investment and innovation. In 1774 he wrote how

> the improvements which have been wrought in England have been almost totally owing to the custom of granting leases: in those countries where it is unusual to give them, agriculture yet continues much inferior to what we find it where they are usual, nor can it flourish until this custom is adopted. If the mode and progress of country improvements is well considered, they will be found utterly inconsistent with an occupation without a lease.[1]

Yet Young admitted that the lease was by no means universal in England in his day and there is some evidence that the proportion of farmers holding by lease probably diminished over his lifetime. Landlords saw leases as restricting their ability to access agricultural profit during the boom years of the Napoleonic wars: in the post-war depression farmers were reluctant to be tied to long-term commitments. By 1851 Caird could write that

> the great[er] proportion of English farms are held on yearly tenure, which may be terminated at any time by a six months' notice on either side. It is a system preferred by the landlord, as enabling him to retain a greater control over the land, and acquiesced in by the tenants, in consideration of easy rents.

But it had not impeded progress because of the tenants' confidence in their relationship with their landlord.[2]

1 A. Young, *Political arithmetic, containing observations on the present state of Great Britain and the principles of her policy in the encouragement of agriculture* (1774), pp. 15–16.

2 James Caird, *English agriculture in 1850–1* (1852, repr. 1967), p. 504.

The exact chronology of the switch from leases for years to yearly tenancies (tenancies at will) has never been ascertained. By the First World War the lease had virtually disappeared, neither landlord nor tenant being willing to enter into long term contracts at a time of agricultural depression. In Scotland, leases for 19 years seem to have been usual for larger holdings by the end of the seventeenth century (Devine, 1994: 21–22): Caird, writing in 1878, found that 19-year leases at a fixed rent were still standard there, although there were also restraints on the disposal of a lease by a tenant during his term (Caird, 1878: 306). This may have remained the case until the 1930s.

The disappearance of the lease in England led to the practical problem of giving the tenant compensation for the investment he had made in his landlord's property. Whilst this could be achieved by the 'honourable' relationship of lord and tenant, the disappearance of the lease was marked by the establishment of customs of tenant right in which an outgoing tenant received compensation from his landlord (or incoming tenant) for 'unexpired improvements', not only buildings or fences, but also less tangible assets such as crops planted or manure in the soil. Tenant right customs appeared regionally and were initially gentleman's agreements. The first attempt to give them statutory backing came in 1848. A statute of 1875 gave tenant right the sanction of law but allowed landlords to contract out: this right was removed in both England and Scotland in 1883. Thereafter, landlords were exposed to heavy costs when a tenant gave up a farm and claimed compensation for improvements (Mingay, 2000: 793–99). The Agriculture Act of 1920 and a number of later statutes gave the tenant security of tenure except for bad husbandry: landlords who wished to give a tenant notice to quit were obliged to pay the tenant two years' rent for disturbance unless poor husbandry could be proved. So whilst tenants held by annual tenancies with a notice period of a year on either side, 'The system of tenancy … in practice gave farmers as much security as owner-occupiers without the legal cost of buying and selling land; death, a rare bankruptcy, or a decision made by the tenant were the usual means of ending a tenancy' (Whetham, 1979: 318).

Post-war developments continued to tie the landowners' hands. The 1947 Agriculture Act formally introduced security of tenure and a system of tribunals to adjudicate in disputes. Then in 1976 a right of succession was conferred on tenants which allowed close relatives, if they could prove themselves to be suitable persons, to inherit a tenancy. It was a matter of comment by this time that landowners were reluctant to lease land because they could not recover it should they wish to. Moreover, the high level of owner-occupation and the lack of land available for lease was making it difficult for new entrants to enter agriculture. Such land as came available was either being taken in hand to be farmed, or let on short-term Gladstone v. Bower tenancies (named after a judicial decision of 1960) which fell outside the terms of the 1947 act. The Royal Commission under Lord Northfield looked at this problem and subsequent legislation shifted the balance back towards the landlord in an attempt to encourage the leasing of land. Further legislation of 1995 created a new form of tenancy, 'the farm business tenancy', which retained some features which favoured the tenant – two years' notice to quit, arbitration on compensation for disturbance and rent – whilst offering a new freedom of contract and without the danger of a landlord conferring a succession right on his tenant (Rodgers, 1998: ch. 1). Continued agricultural depression forced the development of new forms of landholding at the end of the century. Some landowners adopted sharecropping systems: others abandoned farming and put their property in the hands of management companies.

The economic value of land

Ruminating on the prospects for the Irish landowners in 1881, the Earl of Derby, who had prompted the return of landowners in the previous decade, outlined what he saw as the five benefits of owning land.

> The objects which men aim at when they become possessed of land in the British Isles may, I think, be enumerated as follows: (1) political influence; (2) social importance founded on territorial possession, the most visible and unmistakable form of wealth; (3) power exercised over tenantry; the pleasure of managing, directing and improving an estate itself; (4) residential enjoyment, including what is called sport: (5), the money return or the rent.[3]

Only an aristocrat of long lineage and great wealth could have placed rent last, but what Derby says is essentially true: land was valued in the nineteenth-century not only for its revenue-earning capacities but for a range of non-economic and cultural benefits. The result was that land fetched a premium over its economic price. It needs to be remembered too that the pursuit of the some of the non-economic benefits served to reduce the overall yield of land.

This mindset survived the First World War but not the second. A good number of newly-moneyed men purchased land in the 1920s and 1930s, some with sporting purposes in mind, others out of the conviction that modern technologies and accounting would allow them to return a profit. When land values began to pick up after the Second World War, it was partly because farming had a new buoyancy, so, in the early 1980s it was claimed that most land changing hands was purchased by existing farmers enlarging their businesses. But investment in land and farming was a way of accessing a range of tax reliefs and government grants as well as 'residential enjoyment' and was always a safe investment. For the forty years after the mid-1950s, the price of land in England leapt forwards (Donaldson, 1969: ch. 10).

The best opinion of what the farmer's return should be differed over time. Marshall in 1818 recalled how in the late eighteenth century it was felt that a farm's turnover should be divided three equal ways: one for the landlord, one to cover the expenses of cultivation and the third for the farmer's profit. But by the time he wrote, he thought that land should generate a turnover of five times the rent, of which one rent – 20 per cent – should remain with the farmer. Later commentators thought that rent should be what was left after the tenant had been rewarded with a return – usually

[3] Earl of Derby, 'Ireland and the Land Act', *Nineteenth Century*, Oct. 1881, p. 474, cited by A. Offer, 'Farm tenure and land values in England, c.1750–1950', *Economic History Rev.*, 44 (1991), p. 2.

10 per cent – on his capital and had been remunerated for his farming costs. This, the Ricardian surplus, had the effect of transferring some of the risks inherent in farming to landlords. On the other hand Adam Smith had already argued that leasing was a device for transferring the risk to the tenant by ensuring a fixed income for the landlord no matter how good the harvest or fluctuations in other costs. Whilst this may be seen to have stabilised landlord's income in the short term (at the cost of them missing out in bonanza years), they could not evade the risks of farming, for tenants with falling incomes took a Ricardian approach and ran up arrears or, in the longer term, attempted to renegotiate rents downwards. This may be seen happening in mid nineteenth-century outbreaks of cattle plague, where a proportion of the costs falling on farmers were transferred back to their landlords, or after the onset of agricultural depression in the 1880s when landlords were forced to accept that rents had to fall to retain tenants (the tenant's concern being to protect his own capital, and so future livelihood) (Turner, Beckett and Afton, 1997: ch.1).

Donaldson, writing in 1969, could recall a situation in the 1930s when land was worth £30–40 an acre: the rent was about £2 an acre and the tenant's profits about the same. From the war onwards, farmers' profits rose substantially and rents followed behind. Poor rental returns encouraged landlords to farm their own land: a shortage of land for rent forced rents up, as did the practice of asking for tenders for leases. By the late 1960s a farmer could be paying as much as £10 an acre on new lets but receiving only £5 or £6 an acre to cover his costs as well as his profit. What may have made a great deal of difference was the character of the estate from whom the tenant held: many older estates were seen to be traditional in their approach to rent, if only because of the very high level of marginal tax to which rent increases were liable. Other landlords, especially those using commercial land agents, were interested purely in maximising rent to the farmer's disadvantage (Donaldson, 1969: ch. 10).

The cultural value of land

We have already quoted the Earl of Derby on the five benefits of land and have also seen how some commentators felt that these were much diminished by the time of the First World War. The political influence of the landowner was diminished as a consequence of the progressive extension of the male franchise (1867 and 1884), the removal of plural voting for landowners (1894) and the introduction of the secret ballot in 1872. Both political parties saw the farmer as a constituency to be cultivated and successive governments introduced legislation designed to meet their aspirations. The 'power exercised over tenantry' declined as the law conferred on them rights over compensation for improvements (1875, 1883) and permitted them to take small game on their lands (1881) (Fisher, 2000). In Scotland the landlord's right of hypothec, where he could seize a tenant's goods for arrears of rent, was removed from larger holdings in 1867 and abolished in 1880. In all of these ways, the balance of the tenurial relationship had been considerably altered in favour of the tenant by 1914. To this needs to be added a more antagonistic attitude seen in the emergence of farmer's associations we will discuss later. The administrative powers of the magistrates passed to the county councils after 1892. Sport remained a powerful pull for the landowner, but the truth was that many landowners no longer had enough disposable income to support the lifestyle, and particularly when confronted with the loss of heirs in wartime and death duties, preferred to sell up and turn what could be rescued into more liquid forms of asset.

If there were complaints of a shortage of land for purchase in the nineteenth century, there was a ready supply available to men of industrial and commercial wealth in the early twentieth. There has been much debate about how debilitating the aspiration to own land was to English industrial performance, and how much money was invested in land, and by whom. These have proved to be intractable questions. (For a recent discussion, see Thompson, 2001.) It may be suggested that the majority of successful men bought only smallish estates, and satisfied any greater taste for the rural lifestyle by renting houses or shoots – often in Scotland – for periods of years or even by the season until the cost grew too great or the pleasure of sports palled. This pattern continues into at least the 1930s. Post-war, the middle classes too have penetrated the countryside, aided by improved roads, both to live, but also to acquire weekend homes or houses bought for their letting potential to tourists. This has, in effect, produced a new form of depopulation.

The cultural value of land though came to take other forms: in a sense it was proletarianised. From the end of the nineteenth century, there was a great interest in both bicycling and walking in the countryside. This took more concrete form with the establishment of the Youth Hostels Association (1930) and the Rambler's Association (1935), the latter very much a pressure group for rural access. The need to save landscapes from unwelcome development can be traced through the agitations in favour of the remaining London commons and Epping Forest at the end of the nineteenth century and the campaign against Manchester's exploitation of the Lake District for water (which led to the foundation of the National Trust in 1895). A committee to lobby for the creation of national parks was established in 1936 and their establishment authorised by a statute of 1948. (National Parks were not created in Scotland though.) The spread of the car as a private means of transport allowed yet greater access to the countryside: and from the 1950s onwards it permitted some of the remaining private landowners to develop their houses as tourist attractions, some of whom began talk of their estates as a trust for the future, held privately but for public benefit and pleasure. Many estates continued to offer shooting (or, in Scotland, stalking) by the day, but discretely as public opinion hardened against all types of field sports. The rights of landowners were first qualified by the National Parks Act of 1948 and later by the Countryside and Rights of Way Act of 2000, the latter conferring on the public a 'right to roam' over uncultivated, open land (Burchardt, 2002, Hoyle, 2010).

4.2. The occupiers of the land

Peasant ownership

It is often maintained that by the nineteenth century there was no peasantry in England or lowland Scotland although pockets of small farmers remained, for instance, in Cumberland and Westmorland, or in the Weald of Kent and Sussex where extensive commons allowed opportunities for secondary employments. Remnants of copyhold and other forms of archaic tenancy permitted the survival of 'yeomen' farmers elsewhere in England (Turner, 2009). From the 1870s an interest developed in how and when the English peasant had disappeared and the lifestyle of the remaining 'peasant' societies in Celtic Britain – close to the soil and nature – became a matter of sentimental appreciation. There was a fear that the peasant agitation against landlords might spread from Ireland to the British mainland. Disturbances in the Highland and Islands of Scotland were quickly answered by a Royal Commission and the Crofter's Holding Act (1886) which gave the crofter a security of tenure and right of inheritance as long as he paid his rent. Within England an agitation for smallholdings emerged in the late 1880s as a response to the lack of land for rent, and rural depopulation, but also had marked ideological overtones, because the smallholder was seen as a man of property and both the bulwark against revolution and the opponent of the great landowner. The Smallholdings Act of 1892 gave local authorities the power to make compulsory purchases of land. Some did so on a relatively large scale. By 1946 Norfolk County Council had 1896 tenants on 31,928 acres. (There were also a handful of privately-sponsored smallholding initiatives where estates were bought and divided up.) By the early 1950s Norfolk was amalgamating smallholdings to make more commercially practical units, and many councils disposed of their smallholding estates in the 1980s or later. Smallholding certainly enabled large numbers of families to make a living from the land, but it was a cul-de-sac pursued for a mixture of ideological and sentimental reasons (Wade Martins, 2006).

By the 1950s the small farmer was recognised as a problem. It was easier for estates to amalgamate farms than it was for under-capitalised owner-occupiers to buy out their neighbours. A scheme of 1958 sought to help their efficiency through grant aid, but by 1965 government recognised that their position was hopeless and established a new scheme to bring about farm amalgamation, and offer exit-payments to farmers who wished to leave the industry. Hence large numbers of farm households continued to rely on non-agricultural earnings. Small upland farms presented problems of their own, recognised by the introduction of subsidies and grants for capital improvements from 1946. Despite subsidy, incomes remained extraordinary low on these farms throughout the late twentieth century (Donaldson, 1969: chs. 11–12, 232–36).

Communal land use systems, their adaption and disappearance

Enclosure has been defined as a

> land reform which transformed a traditional method of agriculture under systems of co-operation and communality in communally administered holdings, usually in large fields which were devoid of physical territorial boundaries, into a system of agricultural holding in severalty by separating with physical boundaries one person's land from that of his neighbour (Turner, 1984: 11).

We have already noted that enclosure was a continuing process and that much of England was already enclosed by the beginning of the eighteenth century. Historians have always placed a particular emphasis on the period of parliamentary enclosure, from about 1740 to the mid-nineteenth century, in which enclosure was undertaken with the sanction of a private act of parliament. This was not a government-sponsored movement.

While the movement began in the 1740s and continued through to the early twentieth century, it was concentrated in two defined periods of more or less equal duration, in the 1760s and 1770s, and then in the French Revolutionary and Napoleonic Wars. In entirety, it involved something like 6.8 million acres (21 per cent) of England, of which about two thirds was mainly open field and one third mainly common and waste (Turner: 1984, 21, but see Kain, Chapman and Oliver, 2004: 26–9). The period of the French wars was marginally more important in this process. There were different motivational forces at work over time. The enclosures of the 1760s and 1770s were motivated more by a desire to break with communal husbandry practices although these were actually less inflexible than the traditional historiography believed (Havinden, 1961; Turner, 1980: ch. 6; Turner, Beckett and Afton, 2003). Those of the 1790s and later were more concerned with the reclamation of wastes and commons, stimulated by wartime high prices and a food supply crisis which encouraged the extension of the cultivated area over marginal lands.

The choice between staying in communal husbandry or enclosure hinged on what the Hammonds characterised as a fake piece of democracy in which 'the suffrages were not counted but weighed' (Hammonds, 1927: 25). To secure an act, it was necessary to have the consent of those landowners who it total controlled between two-thirds and four-fifths of the land. Hence, even a single landowner could force through an enclosure. The people who worked the land, the tenants of the large landowners certainly and the owner-occupying yeomen, all counted for little if they could not collectively or individually muster enough ownership to block that controlling interest.

Enclosure often also involved the commutation of tithes. This was considered to be a great point gained because the payment of tithe was often resented (Evans, 1976), but commutation at enclosure was also very expensive. It usually involved a deduction of one fifth of the open fields and perhaps one ninth of the common and waste from the common pool of lands to make an allotment for the tithe owner. To that extent it was a cost in kind but it made the family holding of 30–50 unenclosed acres unviable in its enclosed state. In addition, in order to meet the cost of the parliamentary process, the costs of the commissioners, as well as the cost of new hedges, fences and roads, proprietors were forced to make recourse to savings, mortgaging, or worse, the sale of land. This further reduced the viability of smaller holdings. Add to this the loss of communal places where animals could be tethered, berries could be picked and turves and timber for the fire might be found, and the cost to the smaller yeoman proprietors increased yet further.

The result was that there was still a clear perception amongst some contemporaries – even in the third quarter of the eighteenth century – that enclosure led to rural depopulation and so the decline of the yeomanry, and that it was undesirable for those reasons. This seems to be the case, as recent work by a number of historians has pointed to the demographic decline of parts of the eighteenth-century countryside at a time when, overall, national population was increasing. It was only in the 1790s, with a new wave of enclosure associated with a succession of wartime harvest failures and trade blockades, that the English became fully reconciled to enclosure, whilst the pessimistic scenarios of the opponents of enclosure were exploded by the clearer sense of recent population increase revealed by the 1801 census (Thompson, 2008).

English historians who regard the enclosure movement in England as naked class brigandage generally pay little attention to Scotland where the treatment of the tenant was, if anything, worse. From the mid-eighteenth century, Scottish estates were transformed in both tenure and landscape, and this was associated with a marked reduction in the number of tenants. The lack of freeholders in Scotland, coupled with permissive Scottish statutes of 1695, meant that landowners did not need to make recourse to a higher authority to license the remodelling of their estates. In an institutional sense, there is no parallel to the English parliamentary movement in Scotland, but the contemporaneous Scottish enclosure movement was, if anything, even more drastic.

At the end of the seventeenth century, Scottish lowland estates were characterised by holdings held in multiple tenancy in which a single lease was made to two or more tenants, sometimes even all the tenants of a hamlet or *toun*. Multiple tenancy had never been universal and was probably already in decline, but in the 1690s, around 30 per cent of tenancies were multiple in four counties for which evidence survives, and in a fifth county, 52 per cent (Devine, 1994: Table 1.1). There were also large numbers of sub-tenants and cottagers. This system sustained a high rural population but at a low level of subsistence. Rents were normally paid in fixed renders of foodstuffs in the late seventeenth century, but landlords increasingly preferred cash, and money rents were almost universal by mid-century. A massive reorganisation of the landscape began in the 1750s. In that decade most farms remained unenclosed, with a mixture of lands held in run-rig (openfield), with the use of both infield and outfield, and shared common land. Enclosure began in earnest in the 1760s and 1770s and was associated with the introduction of new rotations, extensive liming and a rapid increase in farm size. Estates adopted leases with improving covenants. Rents increased very quickly over the remainder of the century and there is some evidence that landlords were ruthless about removing tenants who fell into arrears or who lacked the skill to make a success of the new farms. The new enclosed farms had different labour requirements. The cottars who had provided casual labour were replaced by a class of full-time wage labourers. Commonities (commons) were also enclosed, the period of maximum activity here falling between 1760 and 1815. The human cost was great, with what amounts to a clearance of smaller tenants to create large farms. Depopulation was exacerbated by the switch in some districts from arable to stock farming which further reduced the demand for labour. Rural society in Lowland Scotland was therefore transformed by landlord action in an even more severe fashion than in England, but with little outcry or popular opposition (Devine, 1989, 1994).

The exercise of power within the village

The governance of the English village was relatively settled from 1598 to 1834. Manorial jurisdictions were in decline by the end of the sixteenth century and manorial courts had often ceased to be held by 1640 unless they were needed to mark the transfer of land. Villages which retained open fields or commons sometimes continued to hold manorial courts or managed these lands through village meetings. The parish, or in northern England, the township, had four officers in the sixteenth century: churchwardens, responsible for the fabric of the church but also charged with making presentments of infringements of ecclesiastical law to the church courts; constables, responsible for the maintenance of the peace; overseers of the highways, who, like the constables, reported to the Quarter Sessions; and the overseers of the poor who were also supervised by the magistrates. In theory, the poor were to be provided with work: in fact, the overseer levied rates on the parish, and made a mixture of weekly and *ad hoc* payments to the poor according to need. Power in the village came to reside with a meeting of ratepayers, the Vestry. Vestries might be 'open', but most were strongly oligarchic ('select vestries'). As meetings of landowners but particularly farmers, 'vestrymen' selected and supervised the parish officers and it was they, rather than the overseer, who determined who should receive poor relief. The officers themselves could be elected, or appointed by rotation; but there was an increased reliance on salaried parish officers in the eighteenth and early nineteenth century. (From amongst an extensive literature, see Broad, 1999 and Hindle, 2004.)

Parishes also had varying amounts of charitable endowment and might own property used to house the poor. Those making bequests intended their legacy to be a supplement to the parish rate, especially when their charity was to maintain a school or almshouses. But the trustees of charities were often the same as the vestrymen and increasingly over the eighteenth century, charity income was deployed to reduce the poor rate.

Some authors have characterised the eighteenth-century parish as a semi-autonomous republic. Perhaps the clearest example of the latitude which this permitted was the choice of whether or not to house the poor in a workhouse; but the parish operated under the supervision of the county magistracy. As the parish was not a participatory or even a ratepayers' democracy, the vestry's guiding principle was often a desire to cut costs and hence the charge of the poor on the rates. One way of achieving this was by having rural labourers who worked in 'closed' parishes (marked by unity of possession, tight controls over housing and so low poor rates) live in 'open parishes' (with divided landownership, easy access to housing, occupational diversity, religious nonconformity and, inevitably, high rates). The costs of labour was therefore shifted from one parish to the next (Banks, 1988).

The Scots initially copied the sixteenth-century English poor statutes, but the Scottish poor law remained underdeveloped, reliant on charitable donations administered by the kirk sessions, with a distaste for assessment and a refusal to offer relief to the able bodied poor. By the end of the eighteenth century the Scots recognised that their poor law was inadequate, but also praised it for its economy (Mitchison, 1973). The improvement of lowland Scotland also meant, however, that farmers were able to control rural housing, and match rural population to the supply of labour. There was no pool of un- or underemployed labourers in the Scottish countryside, for the labourer without work had no housing either and was forced into migration (Anthony, 1997, 56–8).

Concern over the costs of poor relief led to a new poor law statute in 1834. This removed control from the individual parishes and placed in it the hands of Poor Law Unions spanning a number of parishes. Whilst the Unions had elected Boards of Guardians, they were supervised by a national Poor Law Commission whose purpose was to stop outdoor relief, and, in the name of economy and deterrence, to force the poor into workhouses. This was never fully achieved. Where it was ruthlessly administered, it was sorely hated by the poor for it placed economy over their quality of life. It made it inevitable that labourers who could no longer work would finish their lives in the workhouse unless their family could support them. The Guardians who managed each Union were elected on a ratepayer's vote, but one in which landowners were given supplementary votes. The administration of the Poor Law was therefore subject to a considerable democratic deficit until changes in the franchise in 1894, after which the Boards of Guardians came to represent a much wider range of opinion.

Legislation of 1894 created a three-tier system of government in the countryside which lasted, essentially unchanged, to 1974. Major administrative functions were undertaken by county councils who, even in the years before their abolition, were often dominated by landowners. The tier below, the rural district councils, tended to be led by farmers. Finally there were parish councils which had little practical authority. Rural local government often favoured low rates over expenditure to improve the rural quality of life: one consequence of this was that the quality (and quantity) of housing and rural sanitation, continued to be lamentably poor even in the 1930s. In 1974 rural authorities were swept away, to be replaced by local authorities based on country towns, and urban priorities have since tended to come to the fore.

Peasant organisations: agricultural and farmer's societies

The most noteworthy of the early societies was the Board of Agriculture (founded 1793), which, despite its name, was not a government department but a voluntary lobby group on behalf of agriculture and agricultural improvement. Farmer's societies were both slow to develop and viewed with some suspicion by landlords. The earliest societies were avowedly non-political and were intended to spread good practice amongst farmers by disseminating the latest innovations and ideas. This was the case of the Bath and West of England Society (founded 1777) and the Royal Agricultural Society of England (1838), both of which included landlords and farmers amongst their members though pictures of the early annual meetings of 'The Royal' show a strict segregation of the two. By 1820 there were over 50 regional societies holding shows, offering prizes for skilled workers and advocating improvement through their publications and the example of their members.

The third quarter of the century saw the politicisation of agriculture. The failure of 'the Royal' to take a lead on cattle plague in 1865–6 (because it felt itself to be a non-political organisation) led directly to the establishment of the Central Chamber of Agriculture, but this came to be seen as landowner's front. The Farmer's Alliance, founded in 1879, concerned itself with the tenant farmers' agenda. The 1870s and 1880s saw the emergence of local farmers' societies which no longer accepted the compact between landlord and tenant. Some landlords attempted to maintain discipline on their estates by the eviction of tenants who became too independent minded or outspoken, and others refused to deal with the tenant farmers' clubs but only with their tenants individually (Fisher, 2000: Mutch, 1988). The conflict was particularly bitter in Aberdeenshire where the Scottish Farmer's Alliance campaigned vigorously for improvements in the tenant's position and scored some notable successes after 1881. It became the Scottish Land Reform Alliance and campaigned – unsuccessfully – for the extension of the crofting legislation of 1886 to Scotland as a whole (Callander, 1987: 75–76).

After 1908 it was the (English) National Farmers' Union (NFU), rather than an agrarian party, which emerged as the farmer's representative to government. Whilst the NFU tried to build parliamentary connections in the 1920s and 1930s, its success was based on its utility to government as a means of addressing and mobilising farmers in the Second World War, and it soon discovered that it was far easier to influence policy from inside than from without government. From 1943 it took part in the annual price-setting review (although the union sometimes dissented from the prices set) and remained a powerful lobby as wartime arrangements continued into the post-war years. Hence its power was based on the post-war identification of the farmer's interest with the national interest and government's deference to its opinions. Whilst the NFU always attempted to act as the sole voice of the farmer, and in the 1950s around three-quarters of farmers were members, it was often criticised for being excessively concerned with the interests of the big arable farmers of eastern England: an independent Welsh union was formed in 1955 out of the conviction that the NFU was not interested in the problems of small, upland, sheep farmers. Such currents of dissent notwithstanding, the NFU insinuated itself into the corporate state like no other lobby group: the Country Landowners Association (founded 1907) never achieved a fraction of the same standing or influence (Self and Storing, 1962). Nor did the Scottish National Farmer's Union, founded in 1913, and mirroring the Scottish Board of Agriculture (1912). Agricultural policy was determined on a British basis and the Scottish union (based in Glasgow until 1935) was isolated from policymakers in London. It failed to be the farmers' single voice until it merged with the Scottish Chamber of Agriculture in 1938.

Peasant organisations: mutualism and co-operation

Cooperation has always been weak amongst British farmers. For example, no moves were made to establish farmer's banks or credit unions. Whilst there was some interest in the Danish and Irish cooperatives at the beginning of the twentieth century, farmers' cooperatives remained few and small scale. Indeed, the establishment of the government-sponsored Milk Marketing Board in 1931 led to the disbandment of the existing milk distribution societies. Cooperative companies were prominent in egg distribution in the 1960s and there were a number of farmers' purchasing companies. The 1967 Agriculture Act included funding for the encouragement of cooperatives. But in 1987 the minister of agriculture was asked how many farming cooperatives there were in England and Wales. In reply he admitted that the ministry did not collect statistics – itself revealing – but that an Oxford University study had estimated that there were 540 trading agricultural and horticultural farming cooperatives in England and Wales as well as machinery sharing syndicates.[4] In short, there was probably more mutualism than is sometimes supposed, but it was far from characteristic of British farming.

Forms of peasant resistance to landlord demands

We have already seen how the emergence of societies pressing the farmers' economic viewpoint was viewed with some trepidation in the later nineteenth century. It was a farmers' rather than a landlords' organisation, the NFU, which came to speak on behalf of agriculture.

The major fault line in rural society lay not between landlord and tenant but between farmer and labourer. The English preference was to pay labourers in cash rather than provide them with land and housing for their subsistence on the lowland Scottish or Irish model. Farmers feared that labourers who were to a degree self-sufficient would be less committed to their employer. Exactly how bitter this fault line was in the eighteenth century is not really known. The partial mechanisation of the harvest in southern England prompted disturbances in the early 1830s which took their name from their fictitious leader, Captain Swing. If the threshing machines were not broken by mobs, then the threat to break them in the name of Captain Swing was sufficient for the farmers to leave them in their barns, albeit in the short term (Hobsbawm and Rude, 1969).

Rural dissatisfaction was also expressed through acts of arson, animal maiming and poaching (Hobsbaum and Rude, 1969: Archer, 1990). For a relatively brief time rural class war was endemic, but it was crushed ruthlessly by law, through the threat of transportation to the Antipodes, the New Poor Law of 1834 (which made unemployment so much more unbearable than it had been), the Game Laws of 1831, and finally new anti-poaching legislation in 1862. There was a rash of fires on farms in 1874 after the farmers' campaign against the Labourers' Union: incendiarism was the weapon of the powerless. The gradual spread of allotments in southern England from the 1830s may be seen as a palliative to improve the labourers' condition.

Farmers were fearful of their labourers combining for better wages. An attempt by six labourers to combine at Tolpuddle in Dorset in 1833–4 was answered by their trial and transportation on charges of sedition and oath taking. There was some union activity in the 1850s and 1860s but it was 1872 before the National Agricultural Labourer's Union was formed. This rapidly secured a large membership, but the farmers responded by sacking and blacklisting union members. Union members were locked out in 1874 and a protracted strike followed which the farmers broke by using blackleg labour. The union ran out of funds for strike pay and its members were starved back to work on the

[4] *Hansard, House of Commons*, 25 Mar. 1987.

employers' terms. This setback defeated the union for a generation: in 1874 it had about 116,000 members, but in 1891 only 37,000 and it was wound up in 1896 (Howkins, 1985; Armstrong, 1989; Dewey, 2000). Early attempts to establish labourers' unions in Scotland came to little until the foundation of the Scottish Farm Servants' Union in 1912. Union membership increased rapidly in both England and Scotland during the First World War. Wages boards were established, which were then continued into peacetime. But agricultural wages drifted downwards after the war: attempts to stop further reductions led to a strike in Norfolk in 1923 which almost bankrupted the union and persuaded it that effective strike action was impossible. Strikes in Ross-shire in May 1922 and in East Lothian in May 1923 were more successful. Falling membership forced the Scottish union to merge with the larger Transport and General Workers' Union after 1932.

Whilst the agricultural wages boards gave the unions some standing, wages never kept pace with those of industrial workers and the workforce remained weakly unionised even in the 1970s. A great bitterness between farmer and labourer remained, especially over the use of 'tied cottages', where the labourer had no security of tenancy in his house. In 1976 53 per cent of English farm workers still lived in tied housing. Easier access to the countryside persuaded many farmers to take advantage of a strong market for rural properties by selling their cottages: as a result, the few remaining farm labourers were, by the end of the century, likely to be living in a town and driving to work. Tensions between farmer and labourer was only resolved by the disappearance of the labourer in the face of mechanisation. In general, however, agricultural workers in both the nineteenth and twentieth centuries were not a powerful political force, nor could they be when they worked closely with the employers, often lived in their household, or were dependent on them for their housing. Indeed, twentieth-century farm workers were famously described as 'deferential', and political violence was rare or absent (Newby, 1977).

4.3 Government and public policies

State policies towards landlords, farmers and peasants

Government intervention in economic activity is by no means inevitable. In theory, the invisible hand of the market could serve the needs of the population quite efficiently. In reality the state has regulated markets and protected property rights, and indeed has often gone further to define property rights and create markets (Harris, 2004), but in different ways at different times.

The British state had decided well before 1750 that popular welfare, or the national interest, would best be served by intervening in the markets for farm products. The justifications for such intervention have varied over time, and sometimes have simply reflected the political power and influence of landlords or farmers or both, but they have also often included the strategic desirability of national self-sufficiency, the perceived value of rural life in an industrial country, and, latterly, a desire to protect particular habitats and landscapes.

The first question is to decide whether or not an agricultural policy existed at a particular time. Having discovered that it did, several other questions then follow: what form did the policy take; where were the boundaries between agricultural policy and other policies; and in whose interests did the policies operate? What often emerges is that all the various questions become intertwined. Thus, from the viewpoint of agricultural trade, the period between 1846 and 1939 might appear to be one in which, except for a few years between 1917 and 1921, there was no UK agricultural policy, in the sense that there was no intervention in international markets. But in the same period there was considerable activity to protect animal health, which in practice led to intervention in agricultural trade. There were also measures to protect farmers as consumers, which led to the imposition of trading standards for feedstuffs and fertilizers, and to promote the retention of labour on the land, which led to the promotion of both smallholdings and rural industries. Similarly, the question of the boundary of agricultural policy leads to the problem of food riots. Their suppression in the short run was usually a matter for the Home Office; the promotion of long run agricultural improvement so that food shortages did not occur was not. Likewise, in recent years the question of whether agricultural and rural policy were and should be identical has arisen. In the 1940s, '50s and '60s, in the face of food shortages, agriculture clearly took precedence over other policy claims on rural areas. From the 1970s, as surpluses replaced shortages and environmental concerns increased, this position was challenged, and by the beginning of the present century, reversed. Recently the debate has turned again, as global warming has focused attention on the environmental costs of transport and the advantages of local production. Most agricultural policy questions, therefore, are not purely agricultural, but are linked with a range of other policy objectives from national security to social stability and the environment, and that has been the case throughout the last half millennium.

There was a great deal of anxiety about enclosure, conversion of arable to pasture and depopulation before 1640: but thereafter government took little interest in land use, whilst supporting arable farmers by encouraging exports. Corn export bounties and import duties were introduced in 1667 and 1673 and subsequently lifted and re-imposed as prices rose and fell. Parliamentary bills to encourage the growth of alternative crops, such as hemp, flax, and madder, were introduced in the 1660s and '70s, and the growing of tobacco was restricted at the same time. There were measures to prevent the import of Irish cattle and the export of English wool, to promote land drainage, regulate enclosure, tithes, and markets, and control animal disease, especially the cattle plague (Thirsk, 1985; Evans, 1985; Chartres, 1985). By 1750, Dr Thirsk concluded, agricultural policy 'ranged over a much broader territory' than it had in 1600 (Thirsk, 1985: 301). As the foregoing list reveals, it was concerned with the interests of both landowners and farmers, for prosperous farmers were able to pay higher rents than those afflicted by agricultural depression. Farmers became the focus of state support, and legislation which favoured owner-occupiers over landlords could be enacted, most obviously the 1948 tax regulations which treated owner-occupied land more leniently than tenanted land (Grigg, 1989: 104).

Changing government attitudes towards consolidation and enclosure

As we have already seen, the mechanisms of enclosure and consolidation differed between England and Scotland. In England, where an agreement could not be achieved, parliament offered a solution through a private act which bound all landowners, present and future whether or not they consented, provided that certain criteria were met. These, of course, were privately sponsored acts, rather than instruments of government policy. The Board of Agriculture unsuccessfully promoted a general enclosure bill to avoid the necessity of individual acts in 1796. It was not until the 1830s and '40s that general acts were passed for the enclosure of open field arable and commons and wastes (Mitchison, 1962: 157; Turner, 1980: 26). Similarly, extensive drainage schemes in the Somerset Levels and the fens of eastern England were also private ventures (Prince, 1989: 58–65). Government therefore did little to encourage enclosure, but nothing to hinder it. In fact, by the end of the century, it was advocating the development of a smallholding sector. In Scotland, even more than England, enclosure and consolidation was left to the discretion of the landowner.

Public regulation of the countryside

The public regulation of the countryside, as opposed to public policies relating to agriculture, is, at first sight, a twentieth-century phenomenon. However, it should be remembered that farmers themselves, especially tenant farmers, were affected by legislation relating to field sports, such as the Game Laws, which affected their ability to destroy animals that they perceived as pests, from foxes to pigeons, but which the hunting interest saw as their quarry. Until the twentieth century, government legislative activity in relation to field sports was largely devoted to protecting the interests of owners of sporting rights against poachers, but in 1949 there was an unsuccessful attempt to get a foxhunting ban onto the statute books, followed, in 2004, by a successful but ineffectual ban (Hoyle, 2007: 8, 26–30).

Public policy towards the countryside as a whole, however, emerged from the rise of rural preservationism in the late nineteenth century. As urban people acquired more income and more leisure, and changes in transport technology made the countryside more accessible, so interest in the preservation of landscape, wildlife and rural buildings increased. From the 1860s to the beginning of the First World War numerous preservationist organisations were established. One of the first, the Commons Preservation Society (established 1865), was concerned with access to the countryside, as was the National Footpaths Preservation Society (1884). Others were concerned with the preservation of ancient buildings, with wildlife protection, or with protecting the landscape from visual intrusion. They had little legislative impact before the twentieth century, when the Housing and Town Planning Acts of 1909 and 1919 permitted (but did not require) local authorities to exercise some control over development in rural areas (Burchardt, 2002: 93, 109). Also in 1909, the Development and Road Improvement Funds Act created the Development Commission which, in addition to providing funds for agricultural research and education, also provided grants for a variety of means of improving the rural economy, from the encouragement of rural industries to forestry, land drainage, rural transport, and inland navigation (Rogers, 1999: 10, 19).

In the 1920s and '30s the idealization of the countryside increased in parallel with rising pressures of suburbanization and demand for rural leisure. There were some pieces of legislation directed at specific problems, such as those concerned with the siting of petrol stations (1923), roadside advertising (1925) and the establishment of the London green belt, an area protected from urban development (1938), but the most influential measure was the 1932 Town and Country Planning Act. Although, like the earlier planning Acts, it was only a permissive measure, and did not compel local authorities to use its powers, it did allow them to protect valuable landscapes from inappropriate developments. Nevertheless, the influential Scott Committee report of 1942 took the view that rural land should primarily be devoted to traditional rural activities, most especially agriculture, and this was the principle enshrined in the 1947 Town and Country Planning Act, which still forms the basis of all subsequent rural planning policies (Burchardt, 2002: 161–2). In the same year the National Parks and Access to the Countryside Act established the principle of designating areas of national significance in England and Wales as National Parks, or as Areas of Outstanding National Beauty. This established new tensions within the countryside, but the special status of National Parks did not stop visual disfigurements like quarrying, the erection of electricity pylons, the proliferation of caravan parks, or the building of nuclear power stations within their bounds.

Government encouragement of trade and markets

In the eighteenth century the principal government instrument for market protection and regulation, and the subsidisation of production, was the series of import and export regulations collectively known as the Corn Laws, introduced in 1667 and again in 1673, and subsequently lifted and re-imposed as prices rose and fell (Thirsk, 1985; Chartres, 1985). The general principle behind these was to provide a minimum domestic market price by imposing an import duty on foreign grain, the size of which diminished as market price rose. In low price periods a bounty might also be paid on exports, but in the crisis years of 1795/6, for the first time, a bounty was granted on imports until 1.4 million quarters of wheat and flour had been imported. The specific provisions of the corn laws therefore varied according to the exigencies of the market, and there were at least ten changes in the laws between 1774 and 1843 (Prothero, 1917: 443–7; see also Barnes, 1930 and Sharp, 2010). For the next few years, and indeed for a hundred years thereafter, the central questions of British agricultural policy revolved around Corn Law repeal and its effects.

The debate had been going on, intermittently, since the end of the war of 1812–14 between Britain and the United States when some farmers began to worry about the potential impact of imports from America on the grain market. This anxiety had passed by the mid-1820s. In the following two decades, farmers, newspapers that attracted an agricultural readership, and agricultural societies all supported the protectionist members of the Tory party in parliament. If the Corn Laws were problematic, it was because they were insufficiently effective (Wordie, 2000: 51).

Nevertheless, in the 1830s there were both Whigs and Tories who took the view that the rapidly increasing population would soon outstrip the country's ability to feed itself (Howe, 1997: 8–12; Wordie, 2000: 54). By 1842 the Tory prime minister, Peel, was arguing for fair trade rather than protection in the face of industrial depression, and his 1845 budget reduced protection for many non-agricultural products (Crosby, 1977: 120, 135). Then in 1846 came the potato blight in Ireland. Simply suspending the Corn Laws until the crisis was over would vindicate the argument that they produced scarcity. Hence the corn laws became part of a wider debate about social stability, and given the decreasing proportion of the agricultural population in society as a whole, political logic determined their repeal.

In fact, although 1846 is always remembered as the year of the repeal of the Corn Laws, nominal duties (1*s.* 0*d.* per quarter on grains, and 4*d.* per quarter on flour and meal) remained in force until 1869, when they were totally removed (Prothero, 1917: 447). In the same period a wide range of duties on other food imports, such as meat, dairy products, fruit, vegetables and sugar, were also repealed (Collins, 2000: 46–7). By then, thanks to increased urban demand and the expansion of the rail network that reduced the cost of getting their products to market, farmers were enjoying a period of prosperity. Moreover, the predicted influx of foreign corn failed to materialise for a time, due to a series of accidents: the Crimean war interrupted supplies from Russia, and the American Civil War delayed the appearance of grain from the mid-west until the 1870s. As early as the 1850s protectionism was 'dead in parliament … [and] … dying in the constituencies' (Crosby, 1977: 187–8). Many agricultural opinion leaders were free traders, although the extent to which their followers went with them is debatable (Collins, 2000: 49–54). Prosperity dampened discontent; poverty resurrected it. Increasing grain imports from North America and decreasing prices in the 1880s and '90s produced depression, the extent of which has been a matter of controversy among rural historians for many years (Perren, 1995). At first sight, the establishment of the Board of Agriculture in 1889 might appear to be an attempt to improve the performance of the agricultural industries, but this would be mistaken. The Board was simply an administrative convenience to bring together the Land Commission, previously under Home Office control, with the veterinary and statistics branches of the Privy Council (Foreman, 1989: 3–4). It was, for example, reluctant to fund agricultural education and research, and the Board maintained the laissez-faire views which dominated agricultural policies from 1846 to the outbreak of the First World War. The first attack on this consensus came in 1903 when Joseph Chamberlain's tariff reform policies created a protectionist wing of the Conservative party. It was identified as a 'dear food' movement, and suffered heavy defeat in the 1906 election. As things turned out, the most effectively protectionist measures of this period were those concerned with animal health, following the 1866 outbreak of cattle plague. They culminated in the 1894 and 1896 Diseases of Animals Acts, which either prevented the entry of foreign livestock or required their slaughter at ports of entry (Collins, 2000: 57).

The quarter century after the beginning of the depression (1879) was marked by government torpor. In some respects, we see successive governments of landowners who were unwilling to advance their own sectional interest by the introduction of tariffs because of the likely protests of urban consumers. The political dangers of advocating Protectionism were indeed great, as Chamberlain showed all too well in 1903–6. Until his campaign, the commitment to free trade and cheap food remained more or less unshaken: it was, in a modern phrase, a bipartisan policy. Government, however, was not adverse to investigating conditions. It launched Royal Commissions in 1879–82 and again in 1894–7, but these, like the establishment of the Board of Agriculture in 1889, were widely seen as substitutes for action rather than as material aids to agriculture. There were a few concessions – changes to the system of local rates in 1896 for instance – and a great interest in developing smallholding, but no concerted action to help the agricultural sector.

The 1890s did however see the rapid development of both agricultural education and the appearance of a rudimentary advisory service. The only real centre for agricultural education in England until this time had been the privately-funded college at Cirencester, founded in 1845, and called the Royal Agricultural College from 1880. One or two other colleges followed in the later 1870s. The Royal Agricultural Society of England established its education committee in 1864. But as late as the mid-1880s, there was only one agricultural college of standing – Cirencester – although few of its graduates became farmers. There was only one chair of agriculture in an English university. However, the new County Councils were allowed to spend a penny rate on instruction, including in agriculture, from 1889 and the Board of Agriculture was given a small fund for agricultural education when it was founded the same year. More money was made available the following year. This led to a rapid expansion in the number of university departments of agriculture in the early 1890s. The 1890s also saw the appearance of dairy colleges and agricultural schools in some counties. Counties also employed county agricultural advisors whose role was to improve standards at farm level: in some counties the preoccupation was with the quality of farm-made butter and cheese, both of which were losing market share to creamery-produced products from Denmark and Canada. By 1908 the Reay committee could document 'remarkable progress' in agricultural education, but could still point to the need for vocational technical schools for 13–15 year olds. As Brassley has pointed out, this expansion was really unintended, but followed on from government anxiety over the superior quality of German technical education (Brassley, 2000, 2008).

The security of British food supplies in the event of war was a matter of debate from at least the last years of the 1890s, but whilst a protectionist element argued for contingency measures and the establishment of granaries, the preference was to maintain the flow of foodstuff by the naval protection of supply lines (Collins, 2000: 66–8). The reliance on imports remained through the first two years of the war and it was only the possibility of a poor harvest in 1916 that stimulated the case for intervention in British agricultural markets, and the arrival of a government that was prepared to consider price support that brought it into effect. In wartime conditions, faced with the threat of imports being disrupted by submarine attack, security of supply became the principal objective of agricultural policy, and home production the most certain means of ensuring it. In 1916 the Selborne Committee had recommended minimum prices for wheat and oats, coupled with measures – minimum wages and encouragement of rural industries – to ensure that the labour necessary to produce and harvest increased outputs was retained in agriculture (Dewey, 1989). A debate then followed about whether or not these measures should be continued in peacetime. The 1919 Royal Commission on Agriculture concluded that such support should be applied in wartime only, for it would be 'detrimental to the best interests of agriculture were it to be obliged to conduct its operations on the uncertain basis provided by guaranteed prices'. In the light of its conclusions, the discontinuation of support after 1922, characterised by some contemporaries and subsequent historians as 'the Great Betrayal' of British agriculture, seems less surprising (Whetham, 1974; Moore, 1993; Penning-Rowsell, 1997).

But even in the absence of support, agricultural policy remained politically controversial. While the Conservative government's agricultural White Paper of 1926 explained why there should be no policies of a 'drastic and revolutionary character' that would re-introduce price subsidies or import controls, the Labour Party, then emerging as the alternative party of government, felt differently. Its 1926 policy document not only called for the public ownership of land, but also proposed price subsidies and import controls for cereals (Griffiths, 2007). These arguments continued throughout the inter-war period, but despite some moves towards protectionism in the wake of the 1932 Ottawa Conference, the British market continued to be dominated by food imports.

The Agricultural Marketing Act 1931 had permitted the establishment of marketing boards but conferred no power on them to restrict imports. However, the 1933 Act of the same name did enable such restrictions. Marketing Boards for pigs, potatoes and milk (the MMB) began operations in 1933 after a majority of producers had voted for them. The pig board lasted only until 1937 (Whetham, 1978: 241, 246). The others remained in operation until 1994 and the Wool Marketing Board, founded in 1950, continues to operate. By the 1960s the MMB was not only controlling wholesale milk sales, but also operating its own processing plants, commissioning scientific and economic research, and running a large breed improvement and artificial insemination programme. Marketing Boards were not uncontroversial. Some saw them as a producers' monopoly acting to the detriment of food producers and consumers. Conversely, they did at least afford some countervailing market power to producers in markets which would otherwise have been dominated by oligopsonistic buyers, as was demonstrated by the rapid decrease in the farm gate milk price following the abolition of the MMB.

Despite a continued reluctance until the mid-1930s to create an environment in which domestic agriculture could flourish, there was a continued elaboration of the agricultural advisory services and agricultural education, much of it centrally funded but administered by the county councils. In 1914, 32 of the 60 English councils had an agricultural organiser and their agricultural departments employed 166 staff. By 1939 there were 55 organisers and 468 staff. The record of the county agricultural services before 1939 is judged to be mixed, with many farmers never having contact with them, and the county advisory services were unquestionably underfunded and unequal to the task of reviving agriculture in a hostile climate.

These county administrations were to form the basis of the secretariats of the County War Agricultural Executive Committees which were called into existence on the outbreak of war and which, in turn, were based on the county committees which were created in the second half of the First World War. The extent to which British farming responded to demands for increased output in the Second World War remains a matter of controversy, but what cannot be disputed is the impact of the war on government involvement in agriculture (Short, Watkins and Martin (eds), 2007). Prices, marketing and production, the provision of labour, even the supply of fertilisers and feedstuffs, all were controlled by government. In the long run, the significance of this lies in its demonstration that state control could be used to persuade or cajole an industry to produce what national policies required. This was equally significant in the immediate post-war period, when, although the military barriers to food imports were removed, financial constraints became even more important. Although food may have been more readily available on the world market, the means to pay for it were lacking. Thus home production of food remained as vital in the years after the war, when food rationing continued, and became – if anything – even more severe than it had been in wartime.

This was the immediate economic background to the 1947 Agriculture Act, which is widely accepted as the most significant piece of legislation underpinning what has been called 'the long boom' (Holderness, 1996) in British agriculture between the end of the war and the early 1980s. It was a masterpiece of parliamentary draughtsmanship, in that it allowed the consumer access to food at world market prices when the country could afford the imports, while at the same time stimulating home production by paying farmers higher than world prices, and allowing succeeding governments freedom to interpret the Act as current needs dictated. Such was its flexibility that, despite much subsequent detailed legislation, and not a little criticism of its effects, the principles of support that it introduced lasted until Britain's access to what was then the European Economic Community (EEC) in 1973.

So, for the 40 years after the war agriculture in Britain was very much a state-directed industry. The government eschewed ownership of the means of production: it disciplined farmers through a mixture of price incentives, grants for improvement and through contact with the government advisory services, first NAAS (National Agricultural and Advisory Service) and from 1971 ADAS (Agricultural Development and Advisory Service). Until 1958 government retained wartime reserve powers which allowed it to evict farmers whose husbandry fell short of what was expected. It also invested heavily in agricultural education to secure a better-trained class of farmer. Where about 500 students a year had studied for agricultural decrees in the mid-1930s, by the 1950s the number exceeded 3,000 and by the beginning of the 1990s it had reached 6,000 per annum. (It then fell precipitately: by 2001 it stood at 3,000 again.) In fact the majority of farmers continued to have little or no formal training, learning by apprenticeship from their fathers and taking advice from feed, fertilizer and pesticide salesmen, their bank managers, exhibitors at agricultural shows, the farming press and radio, their neighbours and, of course, their own observation of what did, and did not, work (Brassley, 2008). Moreover, there was the discipline of prices: dairy farmers in particular had to meet the expectations of the Milk Marketing Board with its stringent system of payments according to milk quality.

Until about 1985 the main effect of the Common Agricultural Policy of the EEC was to stimulate production, largely by maintaining domestic European prices above world prices. Thereafter, in response to the high cost of the policy, pressure from other countries, largely applied through the World Trade Organisation, and the eastward expansion of the European Union, the policy changed. Prices came more in line with world prices and farm income support was increasingly targeted towards environmental objectives. But the presupposition remained that the agricultural sector in Europe had an important role in society, and should continue to be supported in ways that many sectors of the economy were not (Brassley and Lobley, 2005).

The social standing of the farmer

Enough has already been said to show that attitudes to the farmer have changed considerably over the past two centuries. For long periods he has been viewed with some indifference, perhaps even regarded as an irrelevance at moments when food was cheap and substantially sourced from overseas. In the Second World War and perhaps for a generation afterwards, the farmer was a hero who through selfless devotion saved the country from wartime starvation. But the great expansion in post-war productivity brought its own reaction. Widespread public doubts appeared over factory farming, especially the keeping of hens in battery cages; the use of pesticides on arable crops and antibiotics as growth promoters in cattle; about the trade in calves for veal (Howkins and Merricks, 1998), the possible spread of an animal disease, BSE, into human populations, which shed an unattractive light on animal feeding practices. There was also hostility to landscape change, whether the removal of hedges or the proliferation of unfamiliar 'unenglish' crops (notably oil seed rape), to field sports and a rising conviction that farmers lived excessively well from public subsidies.

The collapse in farm incomes in the last years of the old century and the first years of the new was widely discussed: but farmers had, by this time, no well of public sympathy on which to call, their political capital was exhausted and they received little public sympathy during the foot and mouth crisis of 2001. They were the victims of an intellectual fashion for globalisation and a political calculation that food could be secured out of international markets at a lower price than it could be produced at home. In one sense matters had come full circle in 60 years: but some public subsidy to the farming sector remained, even if this was orientated towards rewarding farmers not for production, but the maintenance of the countryside.

Bibliography

Anthony, R. (1998) *Herds and hinds. Farm labour in Lowland Scotland, 1900–1939*, East Linton.

Archer, J. E. (1990) *By a Flash and a Scare: Incendiarism, animal maiming and poaching in East Anglia, 1815–1870*, Oxford.

Armstrong, W. A. (1989) 'The position of the labourer in rural society', in Mingay (ed.), *Agrarian history*, VI, pp. 810–35.

Banks, S. (1988) 'Nineteenth-century scandal or twentieth-century model? A new look at open and close parishes', *Economic History Rev.*, 41, pp. 51–73.

Barnes, D. G. (1930) *A history of the English corn laws from 1600–1846,* London.

Beckett, J. V. (2000) 'Agrarian landownership and estate management' in E. J. T. Collins (ed.), *Agrarian History,* VI, pp. 693–758.

Beckett, J. V. and Turner, M. E. (2007) 'End of the old order? F. M. L. Thompson, the land question, and the burden of ownership in England, *c.*1880-*c.*1925', *Agricultural History Rev.*, 55, pp. 265–84.

Broad, J. (1999) 'Parish economies of welfare, 1650–1834' *Historical J.*, 42, pp. 985–1006.

Brassley, P. (2000) 'Agricultural science and education', in E. J. T. Collins (ed.), *Agrarian History*, VII (ii), pp. 594–649.

Brassley P. (2008) 'Agricultural education, training and advice in the UK, 1850–2000', in N. Vivier (ed.), *The state and rural societies. Policy and education in Europe, 1750–2000,* Turnhout.

Brassley, P. and Lobley, M. (2005) 'The Common Agricultural Policy of the European Union', in R. J. Soffe (ed.), *The countryside notebook*, Oxford.

Burchardt, J. (2002) *Paradise Lost: rural idyll and social change since 1800*, London.

Cahill, K. (2001), *Who owns Britain? The hidden facts behind landownership in the UK and Ireland*, Edinburgh.

Caird, J. (1852) *English agriculture in 1850–1*, London (repr. 1968).

Caird, J. (1878) *The landed interest and the supply of food* (4th edn., London, repr. 1967).

Callander, R. F. (1987) *A pattern of landownership in Scotland, with particular reference to Aberdeenshire,* Finzean.

Cannadine, D. (1990) *The decline and fall of the British aristocracy,* London.

Chartres, J. (1985) 'The marketing of agricultural produce', in J. Thirsk (ed.), *Agrarian History*, V (ii), pp. 406–502.

Clemenson, H. (1982) *English country houses and landed estates,* London.

Collins, E. J. T. (2000) 'Food supplies and food policy' in E. J. T. Collins (ed.), *Agrarian History*, VII, pp. 33–71.

Collins, E. J. T. (ed.) (2000) *The agrarian history of England and Wales*, VII, *1850–1914*, Cambridge.

Cooper, A. F. (1989) *British agricultural policy, 1912–36. A study in Conservative politics,* Manchester.

Cragoe, M. and P. Readman (eds) (2010), *The land question in Britain, 1750–1950,* Houndmills.

Crosby, T. L. (1977) *English farmers and the politics of protection, 1815–52,* Hassocks.

Devine, T. M. (1989) 'Social responses to agrarian "improvement": the Highland and Lowland clearances in Scotland', in R. A. Houston and I. D. Whyte (eds), *Scottish Society, 1500–1800,* Cambridge.

Devine, T. M. (1994) *The transformation of rural Scotland. Social change and the agrarian economy, 1660–1815*, Edinburgh.

Dewey, P. (1989) *British agriculture in the First World War*, London.

Dewey, P. (2000) 'Farm labour' in E. J. T. Collins (ed.), *Agrarian History,* VII, pp. 810–62.

Donaldson, J. G. S and Francis (1969) *Farming in Britain today,* Harmondsworth.

Douglas, R. (1976) *Land, people and politics: a history of the land question in the United Kingdom, 1878–1952,* London.

Evans, E. (1976) *The contentious tithe: The tithe problem and English agriculture, 1750–1850*, London.

Fisher, J. R. (2000) 'Agrarian politics', in E. J. T. Collins (ed.), *Agrarian History* VII, pp. 321–57.

Foreman, S. (1989) *Loaves and fishes: an illustrated history of the Ministry of Agriculture, Fisheries and Food, 1889–1989*, London.

Grigg, D. (1989) *English Agriculture: an historical perspective*, Oxford.

Griffiths, C. V. J. (2007) *Labour and the countryside: the politics of rural Britain, 1918–1939*, Oxford.

Habakkuk, H. J. (1994) *Marriage, debt and the estates system: English landownership, 1650–1950,* Oxford.

Hammond, J. L. and B. (1927) *The village labourer, 1760–1832,* 4th edn, London.

Harris, R. (2004) 'Government and the economy, 1688–1850', in R. Floud and P. Johnson (eds), *The Cambridge economic history of modern Britain*, Cambridge, pp. 204–37.

Havinden, M. (1961) 'Agricultural progress in open-field Oxfordshire,' *Agricultural History Rev.*, 9, pp. 73–83.

Hindle, Steve (2004) *On the parish. The micro-politics of poor relief in rural England,* c.*1550–1750,* Oxford.

Hobsbawm, E. J. E. and Rude, G. (1969) *Captain Swing*, London.

Holderness, B. A. (1996) 'Apropos the third agricultural revolution: how productive was British agriculture in the long boom, 1954–73', in P. Mathias and J. Davies (eds), *Agriculture and industrialisation from the eighteenth century to the present day*, London.

Howe, A. (1997) *Free Trade and Liberal England*, Oxford.

Howkins, Alun (1985) *Poor labouring men. Rural radicalism in Norfolk, 1872–1923,* London.

Howkins, A. and L. Merricks (1998), '"Dewy-eyed veal calves": live animals exports and middle-class opinion, 1980–95', *Agricultural History Rev.,* 48, pp. 85–103.

Hoyle, R. W. (ed.) (2007) *Our Hunting Fathers: field sports in England after 1850,* Lancaster.

Hoyle, R. W. (2010) 'Securing access to England's uplands: or how the 1945 revolution petered out', in R. Santos and R. Congost (eds), *Contexts of property: The social embeddedness of property rights to land in Europe*, Turnhout.

Kain, R. J. P., Chapman, J. and Oliver, R. R. (2004) *The enclosure maps of England and Wales, 1595–1918*, Cambridge.

Ministry of Agriculture, Fisheries and Food (1966) *A century of agricultural statistics,* London.

Mingay, G. E. (ed.) (1989) *The agrarian history of England and Wales*, VI, *1750–1850*, Cambridge.

Mingay, G. E. (2000) 'The farmer', in E. J. T. Collins (ed.), *Agrarian History,* VII, pp. 759–809.

Mitchison, R. (1962) *Agricultural Sir John: the life of Sir John Sinclair of Ulbster, 1754–1835*, London.

Mitchison, R. (1973) 'The making of the Old Scottish Poor Law', *Past and Present*, 63 (1974), pp. 58–93.

Moore, S. (1993) 'The real "Great Betrayal"? Britain and the Canadian Cattle Crisis of 1922', *Agricultural History Rev.*, 41, pp. 155–68.

Mutch, A. (1988) *Rural life in south-west Lancashire, 1840–1914*, Lancaster.

Newby, H. (1977) *The deferential worker*, Harmondsworth.

Penning-Rowsell, E. C. (1997) 'Who betrayed whom? Power and politics in the 1920/21 agricultural crisis', *Agricultural History Rev.*, 45, pp. 176–94.

Perren, R. (1995) *Agriculture in depression, 1870–1940*, Cambridge.

Prince, H. C. (1989) 'The changing rural landscape, 1750–1850', in Mingay (ed.) *Agrarian History*, VI, pp. 7–83.

Prothero, R. E. [Lord Ernle] (1917) *English farming past and present*, sec. edn, London.

Rogers, A. (1999) *The most revolutionary measure: a history of the Rural Development Commission, 1909–99*, Salisbury.

Rodgers, C. P. (1998) *Agricultural law,* sec. edn, London.

Self, P., and Storing, H. J. (1962) *The state and the farmer*, London.

Sharp, P. (2010) '1846 and All That: The rise and fall of British wheat protection in the nineteenth century', *Agricultural History Rev.,* 58, pp. 76–94.

Short, B., C. Watkins, and J. Martin (eds) (2007) *The front line of freedom: British farming in the Second World War*, Exeter.

Sturmey, S. G. (1955) 'Owner-farming in England and Wales, 1900–1950', *Manchester School*, 23, pp. 245–68, repr. in W. E. Minchinton (ed.), *Essays in agrarian history* (2 vols, 1968), II, pp. 281–306.

Thompson, F. M. L. (1990–3) 'English landed society in the twentieth century', *Trans. Royal Historical Society*, fifth ser., 40, pp. 1–24; sixth ser., 1, pp. 1–20; 2, pp. 1–23 and 3, pp. 1–22.

Thompson, F. M. L. (2001) *Gentrification and the enterprise culture: Britain, 1780–1980,* Oxford.

Thirsk, J. (1985) 'Agricultural policy: public debate and legislation', in J. Thirsk (ed.), *Agrarian History*, V (ii), pp. 298–388.

Thirsk, J. (ed.) (1985) *The agrarian history of England and Wales*, V, *1640–1750*, 2 vols, Cambridge.

Thompson, S. J. (2008) 'Parliamentary enclosure, property, population and the decline of classical republicanism in eighteenth-century Britain', *Historical J.,* 51, pp. 621–42.

Tichelar, M. (2003) 'The Labour Party, agricultural policy and the retreat from rural land nationalisation during the Second World War', *Agricultural History Rev.*, 51, pp. 209–25.

Turner, M. E. (1980) *English parliamentary enclosure: Its historical geography and economic history*, Folkestone.

Turner, M. E. (1984) *Enclosures in Britain, 1750–1830,* London.

Turner, M. E. (2009) 'The demise of the yeoman, *c.*1750–1940', in J. Broad (ed.), *A common agricultural heritage? Revising French and British rural divergence*, Exeter, pp. 83–103.

Turner, M. E., Beckett, J. V. and Afton, B. (1997) *Agricultural rent in England, 1690–1914,* Cambridge.

Turner, M. E., Beckett, J. V. and Afton, B. (2003) 'Agricultural sustainability and open-field farming in England, *c.*1650–1830', *International J. Sustainable Agriculture*, 1, pp. 124–40.

Wade Martins, S. (2006) 'Smallholdings in Norfolk, 1890–1950: a social and farming experiment', *Agricultural History Rev.*, 54, pp. 304–30.

Whetham, E. H. (1974) 'The Agriculture Act, 1920 and its repeal – the Great Betrayal', *Agricultural History Rev.*, 22, pp. 36–49.

Whetham, E. H. (1978) *The agrarian history of England and Wales,* VIII, *1914–39,* Cambridge.

Winter, M. (1996) *Rural politics: policies for agriculture, forestry, and the environment,* London.

Wordie, J. R. (2000) 'Perceptions and reality: the effects of the Corn Laws and their repeal in England, 1815–1906', in J. R. Wordie (ed.) *Agriculture and politics in England, 1815–1939,* Houndmills, pp. 33–69.

NORTHERN FRANCE

Les très riches heures du duc de Berry, a book of hours illuminated with miniatures: the calendar, June, hay harvest.
The miniatures were painted by Pol, Janneken and Herman von Limbourg between 1410 and 1415 for Jean de France, Duke of Berry (1340–1416), brother of the King Charles (Source: Museum Condé in Chantilly, France)

5 Northern France, 1000–1750

Gérard Béaur, Jean-Pierre Jessenne, François Menant and Nadine Vivier

5.1 Ownership, power relations and the distribution of property

Types of landowners and lords

Peasant freeholding was of declining importance in northern France throughout the half millennium after 1000: the main landowners were the church and the lay aristocracy, whilst rich bourgeois acquired a growing proportion of the land, especially in the vicinity of towns. The church, as a whole, was certainly the main landowner throughout the Middle Ages. Its property included very old and large estates, such as those of Saint-Denis, Saint-Germain-des-Prés, and Notre-Dame of Paris in the Ile-de-France. These had suffered losses over time but still formed huge territorial complexes originating in Carolingian times. Most of these estates consisted of a combination of land farmed directly in arable fields called *coutures* (Latin *culturae*), of peasant holdings, and of manorial rights. Other monastic estates were formed later with the foundation of new monasteries and churches, especially in the eleventh and twelfth centuries. The most remarkable among these new estates were those of the Cistercians and the other monastic orders which managed their own lands and built large farms or granges. Chaalis, founded in 1136 not far from Paris, offers a good example of the endowment of the Cistercian abbeys, with its seven granges in 1151 and twelve in 1204. Most large estates were divided into farms corresponding roughly to an optimal area (like the Cistercian granges): this was about 150 ha in Ile-de-France at the end of the thirteenth century. The famous Cistercian grange of Vaulerent, in Ile-de-France, had 350 ha of ploughed fields in the 1260s; 200 years later, it had been divided into one farm of 200 ha and three smaller ones. The reorganization of the resources of Cluny (1132) assigned to the daily needs of the monks 18 granges. Ecclesiastical property continued expanding in extent in the last centuries of the Middle Ages, for the Church never sold (it might however grant perpetual leases), it still received gifts, and continued to buy land. At the end of the thirteenth century, a large abbey such as Saint-Denis spent several hundred pounds a year on the acquisition of land.

The rural aristocracy also owned an important part of the land, but many estates were threatened by the biological fragility of the families and by the disparity between their income and expenditure. Indebtedness was a recurrent problem for nobles, and it often drove them to sell their estates. During the fourteenth and fifteenth centuries, many aristocratic estates were transferred to newcomers enriched by trade, the king's service or careers in the law: most of these new families of landowners were sooner or later accepted into the nobility.

Throughout the period before the French Revolution, there was no complete or 'full' ownership, but rather a great variety of property rights on the land. In northern

Map 5.1 Northern France, 1000–1750

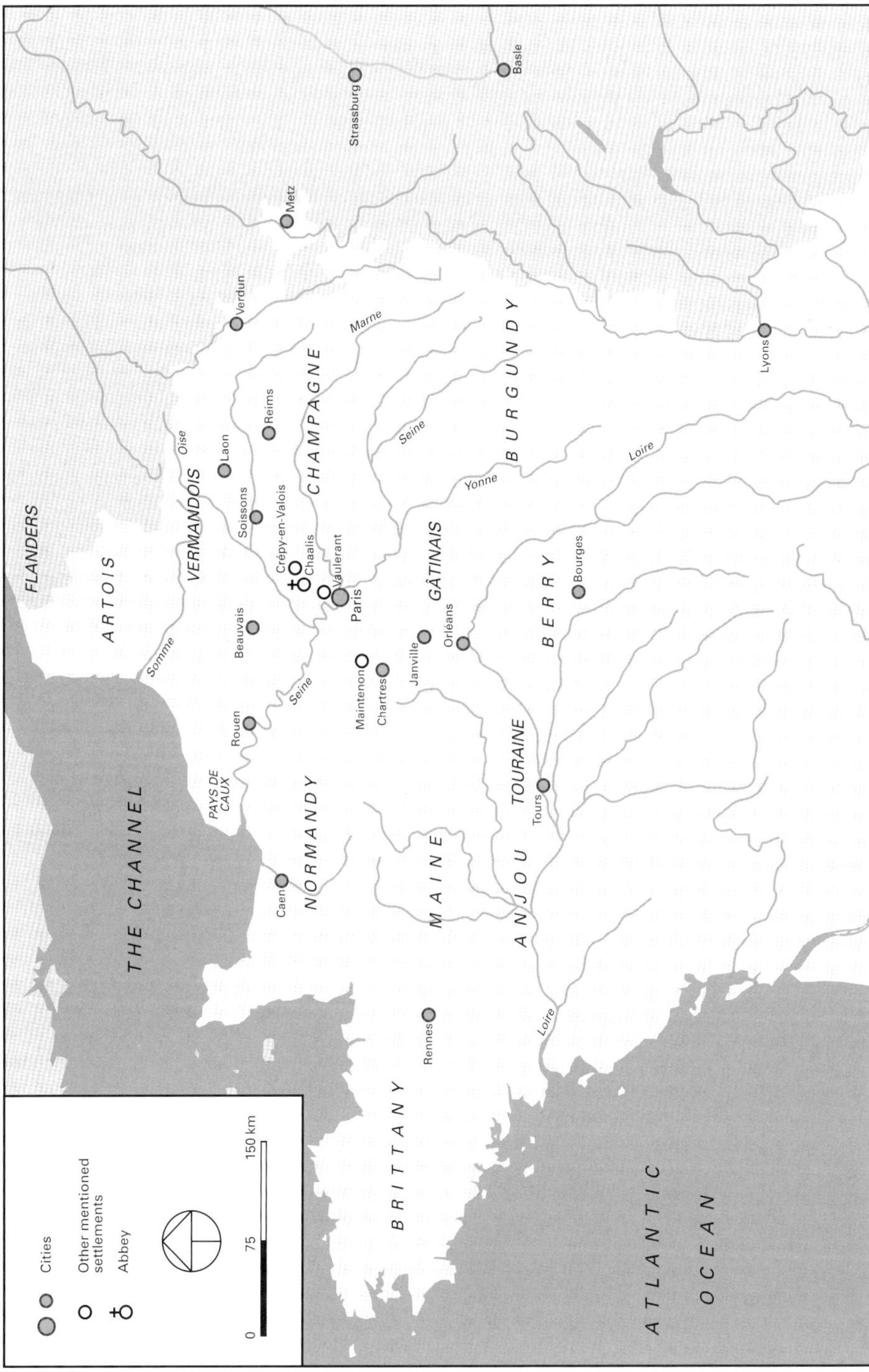

France there were very few *alleux* (plots free from all seigneurial rights) because the rule was one of 'no land without a lord'. There were several individuals with an ownership interest in every plot of land. First, the lord held the *dominium directum* and was therefore entitled to various dues, including *corvées*. Secondly, the tenant or vassal held his land as the lord's dependent, and exercised either *dominium utile* or the fief. But, third, other persons or institutions might have some rights in the land as well. For instance, if land was leased in perpetuity, the leaseholder received a perpetual rent that could be sold separately; if the land was sold, the descendents (*lignage*) had the right to redeem it, particularly in Normandy, unless they sold that right too. In Brittany property rights were extremely complicated under the *bail à domaine congéable,* a system that attributed ownership of buildings and trees to the leaseholder of the domain (Sée, 1906, Le Goff, 1989).

Sometime during the seventeenth or eighteenth centuries, a big change took place in the relative importance of *dominium directum* and *dominium utile*. From a juridical point of view nothing altered: the true owner was the possessor of the *dominium directum*, the landlord. The tenant only had the usufruct: he was forever a tenant. This did not trouble jurists in the sixteenth and seventeenth centuries. For the eminent jurists Dumoulin (1500–66) or Cujas (1522–90), tenants were not the true owners of the land. But slowly, and it is not exactly clear when, *dominium utile* became more important than *dominium directum*. In fact, for a long time the tenants, who were not always peasants, had been accustomed to sell, lease, mortgage and inherit plots without consulting the landlord, since the new owner paid a transfer tax (*lods et ventes*) and continued to pay the annual rents and dues. The tenants considered themselves to be the free owners of the land and behaved as though they were. As an illustration of their conviction, when during the Revolution, the Constituent Assembly decided that seigneurial dues could be redeemed, the tenants refused to purchase the seigneurial rights over land which they believed they already owned (Béaur, 2000).

At the end of the eighteenth century, the geographical distribution of *dominium utile* is fairly clear. According to the records of confiscated property (*biens nationaux*) sold during the Revolution, church property made up about 6 per cent of land in France as a whole, probably rather more in the north (possibly as much as 8 per cent). This proportion varied considerably. It could be very small: 1 or 2 per cent near Domfront, but it could reach 20 per cent in other parts of Normandy, 22.6 per cent in the District of Soissons, 25 per cent near Crépy-en-Valois (in the Ile-de-France), and even 40 per cent near Cambrai in the north (Bodinier and Tessier, 2000). Abbeys and chapters could own large estates: the cathedral chapter of Chartres had 8,500 ha (Vovelle, 1980). Nobles also had large estates, especially in the Beauce plains of the central Paris basin, in Champagne or Burgundy, more in some western areas, less in coastal Flanders (Farcy, 1989; Clère, 1988; Saint Jacob, 1960). A large proportion of these estates was kept as demesne (land not permanently ceded by the lord), such as the vast farms held on lease in the fertile plains of the Paris basin (100 ha. and more), or the smaller *métairies* (20 to 40 ha.) held under sharecropping in the west of France. There was an enormous gulf between the duc de Bourbon-Penthièvre, who had the third greatest fortune in France in the eighteenth century and owned several thousand ha, and the poorer landlords who had only several hundred hectares or sometimes less, even though that was far more than was in the hands of the richest tenant farmers.

The bourgeoisie (merchants, lawyers and rentiers) tended to acquire land around the towns in which they were resident. The distance from a town that their estates extended varied according to its size. At Rennes, with 40,000 inhabitants, the land of wealthy townspeople fell within a radius of 20 km, at Chartres with 10,000 inhabitants within 10 km, at Fougères with 5,000 inhabitants, 5 km (Jarnoux, 1996; Farcy, 1989). It can be assumed that peasants held about 40 to 45 per cent of French soil on the eve of the Revolution, but less in some regions, so under 20 per cent around Paris, in Coastal Flanders and in Champagne, round 30 per cent in Beauce, Picardy, Cambrésis, Burgundy and 40 per cent in Artois. And, of course, there was a wide divergence among peasants, although it can be assumed that even the rich tenant farmers of the Paris basin (*laboureurs*), who took out leases on vast farms of over 100 ha. owned no more than a few hectares themselves (Goubert, 1960, Moriceau, 1994).

Changing social property distribution

1000–1500

Peasants were the main losers in the land market throughout the Middle Ages. Peasant property, which seems initially to have been quite extensive, began to decrease as early as the Carolingian period. Its loss continued throughout the last centuries of the Middle Ages with the transfer from small and medium-sized owners to the bourgeoisie and religious institutions. Regional monographs focusing on the twelfth and thirteenth centuries (on Picardy by Fossier (1968), Chartrain by Chédeville (1973) and so on) include extensive analyses of this trend, stressing the role of the demographic growth which fragmented peasant holdings. Many former freeholders became tenants or day labourers, or sought work in the cities. Some peasants were able to take advantage of economic change in farming, credit and trade, and they acquired large estates and revenues. In the vicinity of Paris at the end of the fifteenth century, one could meet many well-off peasants who were resisting the growing hold of the bourgeoisie, and in Berry (as probably in other regions) the rebuilding after the Hundred Years War allowed the emergence of a prosperous peasantry.

Adalbero, Bishop of Laon (d. 1030–31), in his famous description of the society of his time (*Poem to king Robert*, 1025–27), gave a striking picture of the submissiveness of the peasants, who worked hard to provide warriors and clerics with food and luxuries. Most peasants were subordinate to a lord, to whom they owed duties and charges: some were serfs, tied to the lord by a personal bond, while others, *manants* or *vilains*, were subordinated to him only because of their tenure or of their residence on the seigneurie. The peasant was tried by the manor court, he was required to fulfil his corvée to maintain the castle. The lord also exerted many customary prerogatives: he might requisition food and other products, the tenants had to serve at the feasts at the castle, they supplied carts to transport the lord's crops to the town market, and so on. From the end of the eleventh century, they were also obliged to pay taxes in money, called *taille* (tallage) or *queste*, and they had to use – and to pay to use – the lord's mill, oven and wine press (the set of rights which would be later called *banal*). Many lords, for instance the Parisian monasteries, continued to take a large part of the harvest, often a quarter, as they did in Carolingian times. The peasants also paid the tithe, which was in principle due to the parish church, but was in fact often diverted into the lords' hands.

The manor was therefore both the key to social domination – symbolized by 'gifts' and rituals of submission, which expressed together the ideology of protection and the violence latent in the relationship between lord and tenants – and a first-rate tool to transfer the profits of agriculture from tenant to lord, and to generate a surplus for the market (Bourin and Martìnez Sopena (eds), 2004, 2007). The seigneurial levies were originally conceived as the means by which the lords and their knights could live at the expense of the peasants, but they later stimulated some peasants to produce for the market and take advantage of the commercialisation which was transforming the western economy (Duby, 1962).

From the twelfth century onwards, the manorial system became increasingly formal: it was now ruled by custom, which was increasingly recorded in writing. The demands it made of its peasant tenants were becoming lighter and it was increasingly possible to convert them into cash payments or even redeem them in all or part. Most of the lords were henceforth allowed to govern their tenants and to seize their surpluses only within defined limits, and they were more and more controlled by the king's courts, to which the peasants were allowed to appeal.

The northern part of the kingdom was one of the main regions in Europe for the *chartes de franchise* (charters of liberties) or *chartes de coutume* (custom charters), agreements between lords and their peasant communities which transformed the manorial system during the twelfth and thirteenth centuries (Bourin and Martìnez Sopena (eds), 2004). Between 600 and 700 charters made between 1120 and 1270 have been identified. Most followed a few precedent models such as the charter of Lorris-en-Gâtinais (drafted some years before 1155), which was copied by 80 other communities, the charter of Prisches (1158), or that of Beaumont-en-Argonne (1182), adopted by over by 500 villages. The main result of the charters was that the arbitrary power of the lord over the collection of taxes and justice was restricted.

By fixing the dates and the amounts of the manorial dues payable to the lords, tenants were enabled to plan and accumulate surpluses. Another common concession made by the charters was exemption from or the reduction of tolls and market duties. Henceforth the peasants were able to focus their production on the rapidly-growing market. Many charters also regulated the use of commons at a time when they were being reduced by enclosure. They also allowed for the autonomous management of the community. Some villages, as those around Laon and Soissons, even became communes with a high degree of self-government.

As for the serfs, they were tied hereditarily to a lord; they were therefore called *hommes de corps*, *hommes propres*, *hommes de poté* (Latin, *potestate*, power), and the old word *servus* itself was used again. The revival of the vocabulary of servitude in the thirteenth century reflected the revival of the notion itself. Peasants who had not been included in a charter of liberties were, in future, considered to be unfree, and the revival of Roman law strengthened that opinion, suggesting that they were *serfs de la glèbe*, bound to the place where they were born. The serf was identified by special duties: *chevage* (a head tax in money); *mainmorte* (the lord's right to seize a serf's goods on his death, usually reduced to a heriot); *formariage* (a fine for the serf who married a woman belonging to another lord). From the thirteenth century, all peasants who had not been able to redeem their tallage, and still paid it *à merci*, at the lord's liking, were now considered to be serfs (Bourin and Freedman, 2005). Therefore in the fourteenth century large numbers of peasants were classified as serfs in Champagne, Vermandois (north of Paris) and Burgundy. On the other hand, many serfs took the opportunity to redeem themselves in the years from the mid-thirteenth century to the early fourteenth, especially in the Ile-de-France which became a land of general freedom as the king, the great Parisian abbeys and the chapter of Notre-Dame manumitted thousands.

1500–1750

Throughout the *ancien régime*, lords exercised power over their dependents and exacted charges from them, whether light or burdensome. Seigneurial demands were rigorous in two well-documented regions, Brittany and Burgundy (Sée, 1906; Saint-Jacob, 1960); they were more limited in areas of large-scale intensive farming (such as the clay plains of the Paris basin) where the lord was often an absentee. Peasants were however free, since serfdom had disappeared except in the east of the Paris basin, and survived in attenuated forms from Lorraine to Berry (where manorial restraints on marriage remained stronger) (Bressan, 1997).

Historians used to argue that the seigneurie was an economic structure which made profits out of the peasants by confiscating their surplus. This is not completely wrong, but contrary to this widespread and still valid opinion, a new conception of the seigneurie has recently emerged which considers it to be a legal structure for public utility. It was not opposed to royal administrative authority: it offered useful services to the rural community by, for example, providing local justice and organising communal farming (Antoine, 1994).

It has been widely assumed that the extent of peasant property was reduced under the assaults of the landowners: clergy, nobility and bourgeoisie. But there is no real evidence of a *massive* decline in peasant landowning, although they did lose some land during the sixteenth and seventeenth centuries. The examples of the Hurepoix and the Beauvaisis near Paris support this conclusion (Goubert, 1960; Jacquart, 1974). Historians have shown that both the bourgeoisie and the aristocracy sought to consolidate their landholdings whenever they could, taking advantage of peasant indebtedness, whether due to war or bad harvests, or by the inheritance and division of peasant estates. They bought up land sold by smallholders, many of whom became day labourers with tiny cottages or no land at all. Engrossers, *Rassembleurs de terre*, people who slowly, plot by plot, built up an estate that was leased and handed down for generations, are found in all regions. Around Paris and other cities (Beauvais for example) the amount of peasant-owned land decreased greatly.

There is however evidence to support an argument that peasants maintained the possession of their property with greater resilience during the eighteenth century, and that peasant property may even have increased. The losses caused by recurring crises ought to have been counterbalanced by the gains registered as soon as prosperity returned, as is apparent around Maintenon or Janville in the Beauce (Béaur, 1984). This is the impression gained, for instance, by measuring the cumulative effects of land sales round Lille and Chartres. It bears witness to the land hunger of the peasants, who

Table 5.1: Land gains and losses by the peasantry in the land market in Flanders (near Lille), 1751–2 and in Beauce (near Maintenon and Janville), 1781–90

	Flanders	Maintenon	Janville
	Thousands florins	Thousands of livres	Thousands of livres
Farmers, *Laboureurs* and *Meuniers*	+ 194	+ 57	+ 170
Winegrowers	no	+ 9	no
Journaliers	− 5	− 11	− 1
Others peasants	+ 43		
Rural bourgeoisie	+ 229		
Merchants and Artisans	+ 75[a]	0	0

[a]artisans only.

Source: Vigneron, 2007: 276 and Béaur, 1984: 104.

strove to recover the land they had lost as soon as circumstances became favourable again (Table 5.1) (Béaur, 1984). Whenever peasant proprietors' losses and gains during the eighteenth century have been set against each other, the results have been shown to cancel each other or even to have led to an increase in peasant landholding.

Though day labourers were more or less excluded from the land market because they had nothing to sell and no money to spend, some smallholders, such as winegrowers, achieved a kind of equilibrium, while yeomen (*laboureurs*) found ways of acquiring all the plots that came on the market. These were not big estates, which were rarely offered for sale before 1750 or after, but small plots. Yeomen bought land sold by the bourgeois (for example, around Janville) except when the middle classes of nearby small towns (such as Maintenon) were competing with them (Béaur, 1984).

Systems of tenure

1000–1500

In the eighth and ninth centuries, northern France had been the cradle of the 'bipartite estate', characterised by a combination of land in direct cultivation and land farmed by peasant tenants. The tenants performed heavy corvées (one to three days a week) to cultivate the lord's land, and in addition paid him a part of their harvest as rent. Three centuries later, the system survived only in isolated places like Lorraine (on the margins of Germany, where it remained far more widespread). In most regions the notion of *mansus* was disappearing, corvées were often reduced to only a few days a year, and the system was generally no longer functional. However, on the large estates of the twelfth-fourteenth centuries, peasant obligations still reflected those of Carolingian times. They included a rent for the peasant's arable, consisting of a share of the harvest (*terrage*, *champart*), or a fixed amount of grain, or more rarely a sum of money. The peasants also paid a rent in cash for their house, for the meadows and sometimes for their vineyards, and small 'gifts' of poultry, eggs, or livestock.

The main tendencies from the tenth century onwards were the fragmentation of holdings (more and more fields were rented separately) and the replacement of perpetual or long leasehold contracts (often of three generations) by short and medium-length leases, lasting from a few years to 29. Historians have long believed that another major feature of this evolution was the replacement of rents in kind by rents in cash. Recent research, however, challenges the idea that this last trend was general (Feller, 2009). Indeed, the most prudent ecclesiastical landowners, including the monks of Saint-Denis, tried to increase their rents taken in kind.

Some owners gave up direct cultivation and leased out whole estates for an annual rent in cash, usually for a few years at a time, but renewable. The best-known cases are those of the great monasteries and cathedral chapters, which granted their estates for short term leases as early as the second half of the thirteenth century. The accounts of Saint-Denis show that the new system could be profitable. Many Cistercian monasteries did the same with their granges when it became difficult to continue with direct cultivation. A good many farmers were well-off peasants; some of them were able to incorporate the leased estates into their own familial patrimony, and transmit them to their heirs. Some of these dynasties of big farmers continued for many generations, and became the backbone of rural society in the Ile-de-France, Artois and Picardy.

Other landowners chose to run their estates themselves, with the help of wage-earning workers, on a model inspired by the Cistercian granges that were cultivated by lay brothers. Many of the wage earners were small cottagers of the neighbourhood. Another option for the property owner was *métayage*, sharecropping, which involved his financial commitment to provide animals, seed, tools and the like in return for the division of the harvest and the increase of the livestock equally with the tenant. The owner contributed capital: the tenant his skill and labour, and he also maintained the owner's property. The tenant might also keep some lesser sources of profit such as poultry. *Métayage* spread throughout the western parts of France, where it became a major form of tenancy, and it changed the social structure because it led to the dependence of the tenant on his landlord. The *métairie* was the right size to support one family, which was able to live on its own produce, but it did not permit the accumulation of either land or capital by the tenant.

Landlords were concerned to manage their estates to increase their profitability. As early as the middle of the twelfth century two well-known abbots, Peter the Venerable of Cluny and Suger of Saint-Denis, were trying to adapt the productive system of their estates to changing economic conditions. A classical example of the interest of some lay owners in their estates, and of their rational management, was Thierry de Hireçon (d. 1328), a rich cleric and landowner in Artois. He lived in a region and at a time especially favourable to market agriculture. The accounts of his two estates, which he managed himself with hired workers, show highly profitable corn crops, complemented by sheep-breeding.

1500–1750

When, after the disasters of the fourteenth and fifteenth centuries, the reconstruction of the countryside began at the very end of the fifteenth century, long-term leases of up to 99 years or three lives were used to settle farmers and encourage them to invest. During the seventeenth and eighteenth centuries leases of this length become very rare even if they never quite disappear.

It was much more usual for a landowner who was not farming himself to make either short term leases of his property, or enter into sharecropping contracts with his tenants. Generally, the short-term lease with rent was widespread in the north and in the plains of the Paris basin, from Flanders to the Loire Valley, from Lorraine to Perche. In this area, sharecropping was unknown. By contrast, in the west of France, and in Berry, the *métairie* predominated in association with little farms or plots rented for money. In Burgundy, the '*granger*' cultivated vines by sharecropping, like the '*closier*' in a district of the Loire Valley (Touraine) (Saint Jacob, 1960; Maillard, 1998). Leases were generally made for three, six or nine years, sharecropping contracts for four, six or eight years. During the eighteenth century, the duration of leases tended to lengthen under pressure from farmers and sharecroppers: leases for rent became commoner and sharecropping contracts rarer (Antoine, 1994, 2009; Maillard, 1998).

After the Middle Ages, the surviving *corvée* (labour services) declined everywhere, and sometimes even disappeared totally, while rents in kind were often converted into cash. In some areas however, rents in the form of *champart* (where a part of the harvest was paid) continued to be collected and remained a heavy charge on peasant income. In some parts of Burgundy and in Lorrain, *corvées* were still demanded. By contrast, in the centre of the Paris basin, the seigneurie was less onerous. The *cens*, when taken as a cash rent specified in money, was undermined by inflation and became a token payment. Its actual payment depended on the rigour with which the seigneurie was managed. The '*Assises de fiefs*' of the Bas-Maine were special sessions of the seigneurial court, which the tenants were obliged to attend, acknowledge their subordinate condition and allow the lord to verify that they had paid their correct rents. But the smallest carelessness in record-keeping or collection could be fatal for seigneurial income (Antoine, 1994). The *cens* were less lucrative when they were calculated in money, but they proved the superior power of the lord and therefore gave him the right to claim other rights, such as the tax on land transactions, *lods et ventes* (usually a twelfth or an eighth of the sale price), or the dues for use of the wind or water mills, the bread oven or the wine press (*banalités*).

Peasants tended to evade these charges whenever they were not effectively policed. That is why throughout the eighteenth century many lords attempted to recover forgotten rights and dues which had lapsed. This has been called a feudal reaction: its reality has been much debated by historians. It is not difficult to find seigneurs who tried to restore archaic obligations, who made new *terriers* to discover exactly who owned what, employed *feudists* to study ancient records and map tenant holdings, all ways of getting more land or more duties. This behaviour was not universal. What is certain is that attempts to reorganize the seigneurie were considered oppressive by the tenants because they were not prepared to recommence the payment of lapsed taxes and dues. Their refusal led to numerous conflicts.

Of course, no tenant had to pay all the numerous dues listed by historians. The range of taxes varied according to the seigneurie; in the same seigneurie each holding or family had different obligations. The peasant who did not go to law did not need to pay for a licence to do so, and the one who had no vines would not be charged for using the seigneurial wine press. But, taken all together, these duties represented a heavy burden, to which was added to the church's tithe, charged at widely varying rates. When we take into account the produce – grain, cattle and wine – that landlords received as rent and tithe, we can appreciate just how far they could monopolize trade and the provisioning of towns.

The economic and social value of land

1000–1500

It is extremely difficult to estimate the value of land with enough precision to allow geographical or chronological comparisons. Land could be sold, whatever its status, the main exceptions to this rule being the lands of the church, and also the fiefs, that is land held by the aristocracy that was regarded as conferring nobility. Not only owners, but also customary leaseholders, were allowed to sell their tenure. The landlord received a transaction tax, the *lods et ventes*, normally 8.33 per cent of the price. The registration of the *lods et ventes*, which became usual from the twelfth century, provides price series covering large areas of northern France including the regions of Chartres, Verdun, Reims, Picardy, Burgundy, Anjou and Normandy. It has been suggested recently that land prices cannot be studied without taking into account social and familial factors, and the personal bonds that the transaction was creating or enforcing. In this way, the economy of the land sales and of the creation of rents was not completely separate from the economy of the gift and from the creation of social bonds (Feller and Wickham (eds), 2005). A study of the land market in central France, from Brittany to Burgundy (Beck, 2005: 114), reveals features of general application. Sales, in a modern sense, were very rare up to the thirteenth century and did not form the majority of the transactions in the fifteenth. The seller always kept some interest in the land that he had sold, whether a church service, a fief, a rent, or some form of credit. These arrangements were shown by regional types of contracts such as the Burgundian *gageria*, the Chartrain *hostise*, or the *domaine congéable* of Brittany.

Although it is very difficult to put a figure on the evolution of the value of land, we may say that it seems to have grown until about 1260. It is usually held that the main factor driving growth in this period was demographic pressure, which also caused an increase in the number of transactions. After 1260 most land prices stagnated or dropped. They were badly affected by the slowing of population growth, and also by the appearance of other investment opportunities elsewhere in the economy, whether in credit, trade, or craft industries. Thereafter land prices no longer mirrored the

movement of corn prices or wages, except on the outskirts of the cities: for instance, a fiscal account of Reims (1328) shows that suburban land was valued at two or three times the rate of rural property.

The economic value of the land was extremely variable: good land, especially if it was located near a city and a busy market like Paris (Fourquin, 1964), remained a very attractive investment throughout the fourteenth and fifteenth centuries. Its return was inferior to that of international trade or even of usury, but it was more or less steady and without risk. Other desirable investments were vineyards in regions able to export, such as the Seine valley, from Ile-de-France to Burgundy. On the other hand, the church had granted a great deal of land for perpetual rents which no longer brought any significant income; some land which had been abandoned after the Black Death and during the Hundred Years War, was used for more extensive agriculture, especially pasture.

1500–1750

Land continued to be not only a secure, but also a rewarding investment. However land rent underwent many fluctuations during the three centuries before the Revolution. It rose sharply during the sixteenth century, was then stagnant, and then declined throughout the seventeenth century, before starting to rise again from around 1730 or 1740 (Table 5.3). It was at the end of the seventeenth century that rent hit its lowest point. It collapsed suddenly. When the big farmers faltered, landowners were either forced to agree to allow arrears to accumulate or to reduce the rent for the current and future years. These measures did not succeed in preventing some resounding failures amongst farmers. Only the strongest survived and they were able to take advantage of adverse conditions to increase their holdings, leading to a concentration of land in fewer hands (Moriceau, 1994).

After those troubles, rent probably doubled or even tripled between about 1740 and 1790 (Labrousse, 1933; Béaur, 1984). The rise was gradual until 1768, but strengthened in the 1770s, roughly doubling in 10 years (Table 5.3). The slowdown before the Revolution was clearly a symptom of economic malaise; however, it also demonstrated a misplaced optimism amongst farmers in the 1770s. After benefiting from lagging rents between 1740 and 1770, they agreed to pay higher rents because of the prosperity of the 1770s, but then had to confront the difficulties of the 1780s while paying these high rents. The price of land had kept pace with this movement. It had even anticipated it; so much so that it seems probable that the return from landed capital had declined. What was the rate of profit during the eighteenth century? It may have been between three and five per cent, with sharp local variations; it had probably been higher before that time (Béaur, 1984).

The price of land continued to vary from region to region. It was very expensive in Normandy and in the fertile plains of the Paris basin, but elsewhere rather cheap. It was higher near the towns where the demand for land was strong. Generally speaking meadows were more valuable than vineyards and vineyards more than arable land. Finally small plots commanded a higher price by unit of surface area than big farms. For social reasons, rent paid by small peasants (the so-called Rent II) was higher than

TABLE 5.2: Illustrative land rents in northern France in the sixteenth-early eighteenth centuries

(a) Land rent in Pays de Caux (sous/acre)

1530	1550	1570	1590	1610
43	73	170	214	202

Source: Bottin, 1983: 375, annexe C.

(b) Land rent in Ile-de-France (price in wheat and money (livres) per ha)

	1550	1600	1650	1700	1730
Wheat (hl)	3	2.6	3.6	3.3	3.3
Money (livres)	7.6	15.4	43.9	27	32

Source: Moriceau, 1994: 906–07

(c) Land rent in Ile-de-France : the crisis of the end of the seventeenth century (livres/ha)

1660	1670	1680	1690	1700	1710	1720	1730
42	29	28	40	27	37	46	32

Source: Moriceau, 1994: 906–07.

TABLE 5.3: Land rent in Beauce before the French Revolution (livres/ha)

	1760–61	1765–66	1770–71	1775–76	1780–81	1785–86	1789–90
Maintenon	20	20	25	33	33	32	27
Janville	12	10	15	20	20	30	20

Source: Béaur, 1984: 270.

rent paid by big farmers (the so-called Rent I) (Postel-Vinay, 1974). Farmers were able to resist the landowners' demand for higher rent, but the small peasants could not.

The cultural value of land

1000–1500

Landownership had a high symbolic and social value throughout the Middle Ages. Anyone who rose in social status purchased an estate; the lawyer, the petty merchant or the king's officer bought one or two farms, whereas the banker could afford a manor with a castle, forests for hunting and hundreds of serfs. The rural élites followed the same path at a lower level. The possession of the land allowed them to afford symbols of distinction such as living in a *manoir* or *maison forte* (an aristocratic-style house with a tower, surrounded by a ditch), bearing a sword or other weapons or riding a horse. Paintings and manuscript illuminations show well-to-do peasants in comfortable houses, eating and drinking immoderately.

1500–1750

The struggle for land remained acute throughout the early modern period. Land provided income and social prestige, especially for the upper class. One of the best ways to enter the nobility was by purchasing a seigneurie, living exclusively from rents, and then usurping a title. There were few with money who failed to buy land, even if they drew their fortunes from trade or manufacture. On the other hand, rich or poor peasants did the best they could to increase their estates, although they faced a stagnant market, since much of the land (as we saw) was owned by the church, which never sold it, or by rich landowners.

5.2 The occupiers of the land

Peasant ownership of land

1000–1500

The general trends which transformed the peasant holding, between 1000 and the Black Death, were the erosion of peasant property rights and their claim to 'full' property and a reduction in the average size of their farms and their morcellisation into numerous plots scattered throughout the territory of the village. The estate surveys of the fourteenth century usually show a majority of peasants with very small holdings – often one ha or less – divided in several plots, which they cultivated with spade labour. In a typical village north of Paris in about 1300, 70 peasant families out of the 97 living there had less than half a hectare, and in a neighbouring village, 75 ha were divided into 271 plots, farmed by 171 people. By about 1350, most of the peasants had ceased to be landowners, as their ancestors had been at the beginning of the millenium: they were now tenants, often on a short lease, or they made a living from a small freehold property to which they added additional leased plots and wage labour. Holdings were larger on the poorer lands, where cattle-breeding predominated, so in many regions of western France. Holdings also tended to be larger in the less fertile parts of the village territories. Moreover, the size of a farm had a different meaning where intensive farming was practised, such as in wine-growing districts or the areas of market gardening which surrounded the larger cities.

The direction of change became much more confused after the plague and the damage caused by the Hundred Years War. The post-war reconstruction allowed many peasants to take over abandoned holdings on advantageous terms, and even buy land themselves. Monographs on regions like Berry, Ile-de-France, Anjou or the Bourbonnais provide detailed assessments of this phase of agrarian evolution. It was part of the general, century-long differentiation of the peasantry, which saw the emergence of a proletariat of smallholders and wage labourers and an élite of well-to-do farmers – the division being between those who had, and those who had not, a plough and its team.

1500–1750

In the early modern period there were three main models of land concentration.

Throughout most of northern France, on the fertile plateau of the Paris basin, there was a progressive concentration of property, most of which came into in the hands of rich landowners (the church, nobility, and increasingly the inhabitants of the cities and small towns). Some large scale farmers in the Île de France, Beauce, Brie, Soissonais, Valois, and Cambrésis managed to secure leases on parts of these vast estates because they owned the farm equipment (horses, ploughs, etc.) needed to run such farms (Jacquart, 1974; Moriceau, 1994). The biggest farmers also leased the right to collect tithes and seigneurial dues and therefore could dispose of huge quantities of grain, which they stored and marketed, and on which they could speculate.

On the other hand the vast majority of villagers had only tiny plots of land, which were not usually big enough to feed their own family and had little opportunity to extend their holding except by leasing tiny additional plots. These *journaliers* or *manouevriers* were hired by farmers as day labourers, especially when a large workforce had to be gathered, as at harvest time. Most of them struggled to find enough to live on (Goubert, 1960).

Peasant holdings were plentiful in valleys, around towns, or even in the towns, even though they covered only a very small portion of the land. There were market gardeners (*maraichers*) and nurserymen (*marchands d'abres*) at Vitry, near Paris and winegrowers – such as those of Argenteuil near Paris – all of whom could make an adequate living from very small extents of land by selling their produce into nearby markets.

In other regions, particularly in western France, there were more medium-sized holdings. In Touraine and Anjou we find the *borderies*, holdings of five or six ha owned by peasants, which combined ploughland, vineyards and meadows (Maillard, 1998). In Maine and Poitou there were also *borderies* or *bordages* of similar size, but without vineyards, and in Anjou and Touraine there were *closeries*, tiny holdings specialising in wine growing. However the *métairie* was the most typical holding in the west of France: a holding of 20 to 40 hectares held on a sharecropping lease, combining the cultivation of arable with stockbreeding (Antoine, 1994, 2009).

This did not mean that there were no small peasants in these areas; there were many small landowners surviving on small plots and with a few cattle. They earned wages working on *métairies* or in proto-industrial activities such as linen- or hemp-weaving in Brittany.

Communal land use systems

1000–1500

The northern part of the kingdom of France lacked the vast mountain pastures and forests that backed the economy of many rural communities in the south. However, the eastern regions, Champagne, Bourgogne, Lorraine, had a relatively high proportion of communal lands – about 10 per cent according to modern land surveys – which reveals a situation probably not very different to that of the later Middle Ages. In the central part (Ile-de-France, Picardy, Touraine, Anjou), all the land was private property, and most of it was cultivated. In the west, there were large uncultivated spaces, most of them moors, but they were not communal: a pattern of scattered settlements and communities which lacked internal cohesion and solidarity, made for a situation in which waste land was attached to individual farms rather than being held by the village in common.

The eleventh-thirteenth centuries were a period in which the extent of wasteland was reduced everywhere. The peasants of the high Middle Ages had used woods and moors for hunting and gathering, for cattle grazing, timber and firewood gathering, and for semi-itinerant cultivation. The picture was very different by the end of the thirteenth century: except in poor regions as the west, most land had been brought into cultivation, and the remaining commons were strictly delimited. The right to use them, especially for the grazing of cattle, provoked disputes between neighbouring communities or with the lords. The use of common land was generally granted by the lord to the inhabitants (or only to the property owners) for a rent; cutting wood, hunting, or letting sheep graze was severely restricted or forbidden. The grazing of less destructive cattle, the gathering of firewood and the picking of wild plants was allowed, which was greatly to the benefit of the poorer inhabitants.

A special kind of communal use of the land was *vaine pâture,* which spread from the thirteenth century onwards throughout every region of open field. After the harvest, cattle were allowed to graze on the open fields, a practice defined by custom which required strong community regulation.

1500–1750

Over a large part of the fertile openfield area around Paris, stretching from Flanders to the Beauce and from the Caen plain to western Champagne, communal land had almost disappeared by the thirteenth century. Some extensive pastures were created as response to depopulation caused by war, but this too had all gone by the sixteenth century. All that remained were scraps of communal ground although these might still be contested (Vivier, 1998). Where commons survived however, their use remained a matter of contention between adjoining communities or between commoners and seigneurs. Peasants were always trying to extend their land by encroachment onto common land whilst seigneurs attempted to seize it for their own profit. Rural communities generally argued that they were the true owners of these lands, to which the seigneurs invariably replied that the peasants only had the right of use. Lawsuits over these disputes were frequent and long-lasting; copious evidence of these is presented in Clère's work on the Haute-Marne (eastern Champagne). Rural communities often went into debt to uphold claims against their lords (Clère, 1988).

The main problem in the openfield regions was the survival of collective rights. Private property rights there were restricted by *vaine pâture*. This required there to be no barriers between fields, the opposite to the situation in the west of France. It also required a rotation of wheat → oats → fallow. There were often conflicts with seigneurs and some of the big farmers who tried to avoid the obligation to open their fields to the cattle of the entire community, but who wanted to keep the grass for their own cattle or sheep and the manure for their own fields. The situation differed from one village to another, but it seems clear that in Lorraine, and probably in Champagne, the problem was acute as there was a great deal of communal land and the practice of common grazing on the fallow lands of the villages was general. It has, however, been argued that there was a tendency to restrict these practices in the eighteenth century in the name of the 'fight for agrarian individualism' (Bloch, 1931), and indeed, some members of the village community did want to enclose fields to introduce new crops and protect them from livestock.

The exercise of power within the village

1000–1500

The exercise of power within the village went through important transformations during the Middle Ages. In a first stage (the eleventh to the first part of the twelfth century), a heavy seigneurial domination was exerted by the knights who were garrisoned in the castle and by the officers (*ministeriales*) recruited from amongst the peasant élite, in the Carolingian tradition: a mayor, steward, foresters. This system of domination is found throughout France and has been especially well-studied for the provinces of Picardy (Fossier, 1968), Vendômois (Barthélemy, 1993), Chartrain (Chédeville, 1973), Soissonnais and Valois (Brunel, 1995). In a second stage (in the twelfth and thirteenth centuries), more and more sophisticated and autonomous institutions were established in the village and custom was recorded in writing (Brunel, 1995). Numerous autonomous communities developed, especially in Picardy and the Ile-de-France, where large numbers of charters of liberties were granted. As the charters assigned a part of the administration to the community itself, they allowed the development of a peasant élite, which began to manage the community in collaboration with the seigneurial officers. These charters are the best source in which to observe the formalization of the village institutions, including the assembly of the heads of the households, an executive composed of a few notables, a treasurer, a clerk, and special representatives, *procurators,* for difficult causes.

Religious affairs had a place in the village's organization: one of the major tasks of the community was to maintain the church. It was often the only large building in the village, and served as a gathering place, and, if necessary, as a fortress. The vicar was, of course, one of the notables, and sometimes the only educated person. Tithe, no matter who received it, was an heavy charge on the peasant: one tenth of all crops and cattle. From the thirteenth century onwards, we also observe fraternities (*confréries*), voluntary associations that practised forms of devotion to such or such a saint, and often played a charitable role within the village: the relief of the poor, burial of the destitute, and the even foundation of hospitals.

1500–1750

The wars of the fourteenth and fifteenth centuries strengthened rural communities as self-help was their only protection against soldiers' depredations. The monarchy was weak and the seigneurs unable to intervene. The communities became used to taking more and more decisions on their own, except when the seigneur was able to enforce his authority. In any event, the community of *manants et habitants* took decisions and carried out many functions on behalf of the village, but the seigneur generally had to give his authorisation for a meeting to be held and he either attended it in person or sent a representative (a *procureur fiscal, lieutenant* or *prévot de bailliage*). The assembly elected a syndic as a representative, sometimes a *maire*, a *procureur* to administer local justice, and wardens to protect vines and corn just before the harvest (*messiers*); but generally the seigneur had to approve their nominations. Finally the community had to collect and deliver the royal taxes, the *taille*, and two *asséeurs-collecteurs* were elected from its members (Jacquart, 1974).

The parish council (*assemblée paroissiale*) had to look after the church buildings, the priest's house, the liturgical objects and even the books used in worship. In northern France the *assemblée paroissiale* was the same as the *assemblée des habitants. Marguilliers* were the representatives of the *assemblée* on the vestry council (*fabrique*), which actually managed matters relating to the church. They could come into conflict with the parish priest over a large range of practical, but also religious, matters (Jacquart, 1974).

From the mid-seventeenth century, the village was increasingly supervised by the provincial government. The monarchy created a strong local administration headed by the intendant of each region which increasingly supervised village government. So although village communities had a considerable amount of freedom from about 1480 to 1630, they had less and less autonomy from the mid-seventeenth century onwards. In particular the state intervened in village finances, establishing a system for the reduction of village debt (whilst prohibiting the sale of any property), forcing the community to seek authorization for any decisions it took and excluding the poor from the *assemblées.* It tried to replace the elected syndic by a perpetual syndic, who was expected to purchase the office. From the time of Louis XIV the communities were *sous tutelle* (in a state of tutelage), as Toqueville observed over a century ago.

Peasant organizations

1000–1500

Throughout the Middle Ages, cooperation amongst peasants mainly took the form of the community of the village. Again, northern France differs from the south. The village communities of the north and north-eastern regions of the kingdom were not so wealthy as those of the southern mountains, but they normally possessed a charter of liberties, and, as we saw, they managed local administration. The role of the community was reinforced by the adoption of triennal rotations of crops in openfield regions in the thirteenth century. By contrast, collective solidarities were generally very weak in the west, except for the forms of organization associated with the construction of water defences, such as those of the Loire valley and of the polders of the Aiguillon Bay, on the Atlantic coast.

1500–1750

There was little change before the eighteenth century. The village maintained its supervision of agrarian and communitarian practices: the management of collective land, allocation of access to wood, the appointment of guards to protect against crop thefts and religious associations as fraternities.

There were also sporadic anti-authority movements which may be considered as the first steps towards a specifically peasant organisation. The peasant code from the Breton *Bonnets Rouges* rebellion of 1675 reveals an attempt to regulate collective relationships within the peasantry (Bercé, 1973; Nicolas, 2002). In the eighteenth century, the rise of popular opposition to seigneurial and ecclesiastical impositions, encouraged the formation of landowners' *syndicates* to defend their interests; but these are better known from the south-west than the north of France. Here peasant defiance often took the form of *mauvais gré*, foot-dragging and non-cooperation by farmers, but it was not always collective or organized.

Forms of peasant resistance

1000–1500

Peasant resistance to the lord's demands was certainly not unusual in the Middle Ages, but little is known of the forms it took in France, which lacks documentation comparable to the English manorial court rolls. We can catch a glimpse, here and there, in literary, legal, or administrative texts, of foot-dragging in the fulfilment of corvées, acts of insubordination when faced with the lord's orders, and fraud in the payment of taxes. The main expression of peasant rejection of seigneurial authority in the French case, is the charters of liberties, which show both a willingness to contest but also accept the seigneurial system provided that the seigneur's demands were moderate and in accordance with customary rules.

1500–1750

In the early modern period, even though seigneurial domination was on the whole accepted, there were recurring protests, either latent or open, against dues and tithes. The peasants did not understand why they had to pay for lords or priests who did not live in the village and no longer provided them with protection. However the main revolts did not take place in northern France, apart from a few instances like the *Nu-Pieds* (Bare Feet) in Normandy in 1639 or the *Bonnets Rouges* (Red-Caps) in Brittany in 1675. These disturbances were not really anti-seigneurial but aimed at state taxation after it sharply increased in the 1630s. The *Bonnets Rouges* was the last big rebellion and after 1675 there were only local riots, which mostly coincided with subsistence crises. In these disturbances communities would use force to prevent grain from leaving a region during a shortage. In the name of what is now termed the 'moral economy', those buying bread claimed the right to impose limits on prices and attacked the speculators and monopolists, the *agioteurs*, who hoarded the grain, profited from price increases and were held to starve the people. This is the reason why farmers like Chartier, in the Ile-de France in the mid-eighteenth century, preferred to deliver grain to the market all year round instead of withholding his stock to maximize his profits (Moriceau and Postel-Vinay, 1992).

Resistance to the demands of the seigneurs usually took the form of sporadic violence against his agents, the judge, gamekeeper, estate manager, even the lord himself, who might be confronted by members of the community. It was mostly by fraud, inertia or passive resistance on the one hand or through judicial action on the other that peasants usually opposed his rights. They omitted to declare land purchases to evade paying transfer taxes (*lods et vente*), they neglected to pay annual dues which led to the accumulation of arrears and they avoided using the seigneurial mill or oven. In the eighteenth century at least, peasant communities launched many lawsuits in order to retain or recover their common lands. They disputed the rights of the clergy to levy tithes on types of crop where it had not been the custom to do so. They engaged in petty acts of deceit and insubordination to tithe collectors, often offering them the smallest sheaves.

5.3 Government and public policies

State policies

1000–1500

The state began to play an important part in the economic and social life of the peasantry in the fourteenth century through taxes and war. In other areas of rural society, state intervention remained rather limited: the king and his officers could arbitrate between lords and tenants, and they were also able to intervene in the rural economy when they fixed the price of wheat in years of scarcity. But the main influence of the state upon rural society was in its demand for taxation, which began to be levied around 1300, and increased quickly from the mid-fourteenth century. Taxes weighed heavily upon the peasantry: in Normandy, direct taxes for the year 1347 can be estimated at nearly one month's wages of a day labourer (Bois, 1976: 259). The beginnings of the royal state brought about another blight for the country: the Hundred Years War reduced whole regions to ruins. Its direct and indirect impact upon economic structures and society is incalculable.

1500–1750

The fiscal demands placed by the state on the countryside continued to grow. The village community was the fundamental unit for the collection of the main royal tax, the *taille,* the major part of which was paid by peasants. In much of northern France, it was a direct tax on individuals, divided first between parishes, and then between homesteads by local collectors, so that its allocation within the village was an important collective undertaking. Some provinces, only recently integrated into the French kingdom – like Brittany or Artois – retained their provincial assembly (*Etats*) which organized levies, according to local practice, for example the *centième* in Artois, a land tax inherited from Charles V. Indirect taxes were also numerous and varied from province to province, like the salt tax (the *gabelle*) which was heavy around Paris but unknown in Brittany.

Taxes provoked the most frequent rural rebellions and marked out boundaries inside France, especially between territories of the 'Five big fiscal farms' – which became the General Farm in 1680 – and outlying provinces (Nicolas, 2002).

After a period of very heavy taxation from 1560 to 1590, there was a relative lull under Henry IV and then something like a doubling of the tax burden between 1620 and 1650. By the end of seventeenth century, new levels of taxation were reached and there were attempts to create more universal taxes, like the *dixième*, a land tax, or capitation that everybody should have paid according to a scale of 22 categories of wealth (Bercé, 1991). But these new taxes soon ceased to be inclusive as the nobility and clergy secured their exemption, so that any improvement in the peasants' situation after 1710–20 was due to peace and the buoyancy of the economy as a whole.

Military burdens were not negligible either and could be crushing in times of war and in border regions. During the reign of Louis XIV, changes were introduced which had contradictory effects on rural life. The building of barracks reduced that burden of billeting, but the institution of the militia, in 1688, led to the hated systematic recruitment of soldiers in villages. The establishment of the royal corvée for road building was a further unwelcome burden placed on the village.

Changing government attitudes towards consolidation and enclosure

The monarchy did not have any policy towards consolidation and enclosure before 1750, but it was concerned by the disappearance of commons. The troubles of the sixteenth and seventeenth centuries, wars, dearth and increasing taxes, had led to the communities of north-western France carrying a high burden of debt. In consequence, large parts of their commons passed into the hands of creditors. Successive *ordonnance* claimed the necessity to preserve them in order to ensure the payment of royal taxes (1579, 1629, 1659 and 1683). But on the other hand, the king seized some commons and *ordonnance* of 1677 and 1702 confirmed previous illegal sales on condition that the purchasers paid a fine to the Treasury of one-eighth of the value of the land. These contradictory policies show that ultimately the monarchy was more concerned to generate revenue than it was to maintain commons. Brittany differed from the remainder of the north since here all waste lands were the lords' property.

Public regulation of the countryside

The monarchy was only concerned with the forests: trees were considered to be very precious. As early as the twelfth century, the French kings appointed foresters. The Forest administration was gradually elaborated until the important royal edict of *Eaux et Forêts* in August 1669 established it in its mature form. Whilst the state aimed at maintaining forests of mature trees to provide the Navy with timber, hunting was also a coveted privilege of king and aristocrats.

Government encouragement of trade

By the end of the thirteenth century, royal officers and town councillors had begun to control the production and sale of the foodstuffs, especially corn, needed to feed the cities and to avoid dearth in bad years. A king of the early modern era, who claimed to be a lieutenant of God on earth, was obliged to be interested in the prosperity of his people, and so had to be concerned with agricultural problems and the food supplies of his subjects, if only to avoid public disorder. Three forms of intervention were used, the first of which was the mercantilist encouragement to production by land improvement (the draining of marshes for example) or support for agricultural innovation, of which the best known example is probably Sully's promotion of silkworm breeding. In fact state encouragement of improvement was of little significance in northern France. Second, monarchy could also regulate foreign trade, but before 1750, this had little impact on rural activities. The most frequent and influential intervention was the third, the regulation of the domestic grain market. The idea that the king was the father of his people was widespread and, added to the fear of revolt, led to the regulation of the market, the fixing of the price of flour and the management of bread or stocks of flour in bakeries. In fact, provincial and local authorities took responsibility for the implementation of this policy, apart from some distributions of foodstuffs organized by the king himself, for example by Louis XIV in 1661. Following the economist Pierre de Boisguilbert (1646–1714) and the rise of the idea that 'good prices' were the precondition for agricultural progress, these policies became a key element in debates on political economy.

Peasants as a political force

1000–1500

Revolts against the lords were infrequent before the fourteenth century, the exceptions being the rising of Norman peasants in 997 which was severely suppressed by the aristocracy, and the war fought (and lost) against their lords in 1177 by the militias of the villages around Laon. On the other hand, we are well-informed about the revolts that broke out throughout north-western Europe in the fourteenth century. In France it was the Jacquerie, a brief and violent movement which spread in May-June 1358 throughout the Ile-de-France, Picardy and Champagne. The context was a very peculiar one. The plague of 1348 had undermined social structure, the defeat at Poitiers (1356) and the king's captivity and ransom by the English had launched a period of uncertain authority. Currency fluctuated, Paris was rebellious; above all, the nobility, defeated by English archers, had lost its prestige and seemed useless: so why should the tenants maintain such nobility with their rents? The upheaval was directed against the lords, and led by members of the peasant elite who we are able to identify from the royal letters of pardon (*lettres de rémission*) granted during the suppression of the Jacques. Their leaders were simple workers (*hommes de labour*), but also rural craftsmen, priests, petty royal officers and well-off property owners. As elsewhere in Europe, the insurgent regions were mainly the richer ones. It was not a revolt born out of misery and despair, but out of anger: the rebels rejected the system of domination and taxation, which looked resolutely obsolete; the addition of royal taxes – then rising sharply – to seigneurial taxes seemed to threaten the financial well-being of the rural elites. After some initial successes, the upheaval was quashed by the knights with great bloodshed: it was said that some 20,000 peasants were slaughtered.

Episodes of unrest continued to occur in the French countryside until the middle of the fifteenth century, but it is not always easy to be precise about what part a specifically peasant dissatisfaction played in it. The 5,000 or 6,000 serfs of the Laon cathedral chapter that refused to pay the tallage in 1337 were clearly rebelling against the manorial system. In the guerrilla warfare of the Norman 'partisans' against the English (1419–35), 'patriotic' motives were combined with anti-seigneurial demands, and this is probably why the rebels were abandoned to their fate by French troops (Bois, 1976: 295–308). The companies of discharged soldiers and mercenaries (*routier*) that plundered and terrorized the countryside throughout the kingdom doubtless included amongst their numbers dispossessed peasants who had been driven off the land; but the 'true' peasants were on the other side, in the village militias that fought against the *routiers* (and sometimes regular troops too) to defend their families and their possessions.

1500–1750

The fact that before the eighteenth century public affairs were mainly managed locally, by village communities, suggests we should be careful in using the word 'politics' to describe the collective behaviour of peasants. It does not mean that the peasantry did not have expectations of how the state should behave (Neveux, 2000). These, which are especially revealed during revolts, mixed three main components: the rejection of state interference in rural communities; the claim of the king's protection; and a deep mistrust of the agents of the monarchy, specially fiscal ones.

Indeed, taxation crystallized these expectations: the loss, actual or feared, of fiscal privileges legitimated by tradition, was the most common cause of revolt. In Normandy in 1639, the *Nu-Pieds* were protesting against the threat of abolition of *quart bouillon* which reduced the salt tax, or in Boulonnais, *Lustucrus* stood up for *taille* exemptions. Men who personified the collection of tax were the first target of riots; the *gabelous*, salt-tax collectors, were depicted as monsters who devoured the people of the country. At the same time, the king's person and power were above criticism; he was called upon by his people to aid them. The conviction that the king was on the side of his peasantry was a key justification for the 'moral economy'.

The social standing of the peasant

1000–1500

Through the Middle Ages, peasants, who formed the great majority of the population, remained an inferior social class, held in contempt by both nobles and town-dwellers. Some authors admitted, following Adalbero of Laon, that the exploitation of the peasants' work was the basis of social organization. A few intellectuals of the fourteenth and fifteenth centuries, Nicolas de Clamanges, Gerson, Jean Petit, Alain Chartier, stressed – mainly from a Christian point of view – the injustice which lay at the basis of the social balance.

The cultural inferiority of the peasants also played an important part in their representation. However, the countryside seems to have largely benefited from the spread of elementary education in reading, accounting, and even writing which is characteristic of the fourteenth and fifteenth centuries. Women's literacy was less general, but did exist: Gerson's mother, a Champenois peasant, taught him the rudiments, and later she sent him didactic letters. Among the sons of the well-to-do peasants, some may have continued their studies in the colleges or grammar schools found in many small towns. The best pupils, such as Gerson, may afterwards have gone to university.

1500–1750

In the sixteenth and the seventeenth centuries the visions of peasantry split between three more or less contradictory perspectives. Henry IV's reign was marked by Sully's initiatives to develop agriculture as the foundation of the kingdom's wealth and the publication of the first great agricultural work, *Le théâtre d'agriculture et mesnage des champs* by Olivier de Serres (1600) which established the vision which associated happiness in the fields with general prosperity. The king himself is supposed to have said that every family should enjoy a 'boiled chicken' on Sundays. The bucolic vision is regularly found in art, from Jacques Stella's woodcuts glorifying work in the field to La Fontaine's tales. On the other hand, the misfortunes of the wars of religion stimulated the opposite vision of the peasantry, in which they were portrayed as animals struggling for survival, fearful of death. Jacques Callot's pictures showing the disasters of the Thirty Years' War or the pitiful peasants in La Bruyère's works are similar in character. However, in the seventeenth century, peasant destitution could take a more sacred meaning. The poor peasant became Christ incarnate and thus the subject of charitable care; Le Nain's pictures – especially his famous 'Peasant's Meal' (1643) – can be interpreted as an allegory of the sharing of the Eucharist.

To these symbolic visions, the end of the seventeenth century added a dimension that the mercantilism of Sully (1559–1641) and the economist Laffemas (1545–1612) had foreshadowed: state concern for agriculture and a concern for its improvement. Two attitudes can be distinguished. The first, embodied by Fenelon (1651–1715) or Vauban (1633–1707), was supportive of the peasantry and wished to improve peasant conditions; the other, associated with Boisguilbert (1646–1714), sought to increase agricultural product through the development of the market and farmers' incomes.

In the eighteenth century, many more authors wrote about countryside. A strong tradition associated peasants with rusticity and rudeness. The second edition of the *Dictionnaire de l'Académie* (1718) offered the definition '… We say about a man who is despicable and rude that he is a peasant'. Religious works, looking back to Eden, underlined the holiness found in peasant simplicity and the Enlightment celebrated nature and the countryside in opposition to the corruption of towns. The Marquis of Mirabeau summed up this enthusiasm for the pastoral: 'What places would be better sojourns for innocence and happiness than the fields dedicated to peace and natural fertility?'.[1]

[1] *Mémoire sur l'agriculture envoyé à la très-louable société d'agriculture de Berne* (1760), p. 12.

Bibliography

Antoine, A. (1994) *Fiefs et villages du Bas-Maine au XVIIIe siècle,* Mayenne.

Antoine, A. (2009) 'Metayage, farm productivity and the money economy: lessons from farm account analysis', in J. Broad (ed.), *A common agricultural heritage? Revising French and British rural divergence*, Exeter.

Barthélemy, D. (1993) *La société dans le comté de Vendôme de l'an mil au XIVe siècle*, Paris.

Béaur, G. (2000) *Histoire agraire de la France au XVIIIe siècle. Inerties et changements dans les campagnes françaises à la fin de l'époque moderne (jusqu'en 1815),* Paris.

Béaur, G. (1984) *Le marché foncier à la veille de la Révolution. Les mouvements de propriété beaucerons dans les régions de Maintenon et de Janville de 1761 à 1790*, Paris.

Beck, P. (2005) 'L'historiographie du marché de la terre au Moyen Âge en France médiane (Lyonnais, Bourgogne, Orléanais, Vendômois, Maine, Anjou, Bretagne)' in L. Feller and C. Wickham (eds), *Le marché de la terre au Moyen Âge,* pp. 113–29.

Bercé, Y.-M. (1991) *Croquants et nu-pieds: les soulèvements paysans en France du XVIe au XIXe siècle*, Paris (first edn, 1974).

Bloch, M. (1931) *Les Caractères originaux de l'histoire rurale française*, Oslo, trans. (1966), *French rural society. An essay on its basic characteristics*, Berkeley.

Bodinier, B. and Teyssier, E. (2000) *L'événement le plus important de la Révolution. La vente des biens nationaux en France et dans les territoires annexés, 1789–1867*, Paris.

Bois, G. (1976) *Crise du féodalisme. Economie rurale et démographie en Normandie du début du XIVe siècle au milieu du XVIe siècle*, Paris; trans. (1984) *The crisis of feudalism: economy and society in eastern Normandy, c.1300–1550*, Cambridge.

Bourin, M. and P. Freedman (eds) (2005) *Forms of servitude in northern and central Europe. Decline, resistance and expansion*, Turnhout.

Bourin, M. and S. P. Martìnez (eds) (2004) *Pour une anthropologie du prélèvement seigneurial dans les campagnes médiévales (XIe–XIVe siècles*), I, *Réalités et représentations paysannes*, Paris.

Bourin, M. and S. P. Martìnez (eds) (2007) *Pour une anthropologie du prélèvement seigneurial dans les campagnes médiévales (XIe–XIVe siècles*), II, *Les mots, les temps, les lieux*, Paris.

Bressan, T. (2007) *Serfs et mainmortables en France au XVIIIe siècle. La fin d'un archaïsme seigneurial,* Paris.

Brunel, G. (1995) 'Seigneurs et paysans en Soissonnais et Valois aux XIe–XIIIe siècles', in *Seigneurs et seigneurie au Moyen Âge. Actes du 117e congrès national des sociétés savantes,* Paris, pp. 181–98.

Chédeville, A. (1973) *Chartres et ses campagnes (XIe–XIIIe siècle),* Paris.

Clère, J.-J. (1988) *Les paysans de la Haute-Marne et la Révolution française. Recherches sur les structures foncières de la communauté villageoise*, Paris.

Duby, G. (1962) *L'économie rurale et la vie des campagnes dans l'Occident médiéval*, Paris.

Farcy, J.-C. (1989) *Les Paysans beaucerons au XIXe siècle*, Chartres.

Feller, L. (ed.) (2009) *Calculs et rationalité dans la seigneurie médiévale: les conversions de redevances entre XIe et XVe siècles*, Paris,

Feller, L. and C. Wickham (eds) (2005) *Le marché de la terre au Moyen Âge*, Rome.

Fossier, R. (1968) *La terre et les hommes en Picardie jusqu'à la fin du XIIIe siècle*, Louvain and Paris.

Fourquin, G. (1964) *Les campagnes de la région parisienne à la fin du Moyen Âge (du milieu du XIIIe siècle au début du XVIe siècle)*, Paris.

Goubert, P. (1960) *Beauvais et le Beauvaisis de 1600 à 1730. Contribution à l'histoire sociale de la France du XVIIe siècle*, Paris.

Jacquart, J. (1974) *La crise rurale en Ile-de-France, 1550–1670*, Paris.

Jarnoux, P. (1996) *Les Bourgeois et la Terre. Fortunes et stratégies foncières à Rennes au XVIII siècle,* Rennes.

Labrousse, E. (1933) *Esquisse du mouvement des prix et des revenus en France au XVIII siècle*, Paris.

Lachiver, M. (1982) *Vin, vigne et vignerons en region parisienne du XVIIe au XIXe siècles*, Pontoise.

Le Goff, T. J. A. (1989) *Vannes et sa région. Ville et campagne dans la France du XVIIIe siècle*, Loudéac; previously published as (1981) *Vannes and its region. A study of town and country in eighteenth-century France*, Oxford.

Maillard, B. (1998) *Les campagnes de Touraine au XVIIe siècle. Structures agraires et économie rurale*, Rennes.

Moriceau, J.-M. (1994) *Les Fermiers de l'Ile-de-France. Ascension d'un patronat agricole (XVe–XVIIIe siècles)*, Paris.

Moriceau, J.-M. and Postel-Vinay, G. (1992) *Ferme entreprise famille: grande exploitation et changements agricoles : les Chartier, XVIIe–XIXe siècles*, Paris.

Neveux, H. (1997) *Les révoltes paysannes en Europe: XIVe–XVIIe siècle*, Paris

Nicolas, J. (2002) *La rébellion française: mouvements populaires et conscience sociale, 1661–1789*, Paris.

Postel-Vinay, G. (1974) *La rente foncière dans le capitalisme agricole. Analyse de la voie 'classique' du développement du capitalisme dans l'agriculture à partir de l'exemple du Soissonnais*, Paris.

Saint Jacob, P. de (1960) *Les Paysans de la Bourgogne du nord au dernier siècle de l'Ancien Régime,* Paris.

Sée, H. (1906) *Les classes rurales en Bretagne du XVIe siècle à la Révolution*, Paris.

Vigneron, S. (2007) *La pierre et la terre: le marché foncier et immobilier dans les dynamiques sociales du Nord de la France aux XVIIe et XVIIIe siècles,* Villeneuve-d'Ascq.

Vivier, N. (1998) *Propriété collective et identité communale: les Biens communaux en France (1750–1914),* Paris.

Vovelle, M. (1980) *Ville et campagne au XVIIIe siècle (Chartres et la Beauce)*, Paris.

La Semeuse.

Drawn by Oscar Roty (1846–1911), the Sower was engraved on French coins from 1898 onwards and on stamps from 1903. It became a key symbol of the French Republic throughout twentieth century, represented in common use on stamps in the periods 1903–1941 and 1960–63, and on the one Franc coin between 1899–1927, then 1960–2001, and on the centimes of euros in 2001.

Illustrations:

- the stamp: drawing Oscar Roty, engraving Eugène Mouchon, issued in 1922
- the coin: minted in 1972

6 Northern France, 1750–2000

Jean-Pierre JESSENNE and Nadine VIVIER

6.1 Ownership, power relations and the distribution of property

Landowners and property distribution

The most striking feature of landed property in nineteenth-century France was its wide distribution between many owners. This remained the case throughout the century and was matter of regret on the part of many writers, economists and politicians, both French and foreign. It was commonly held by the end of the century that the extensive peasant ownership originated in the confiscations of the Revolution and was then further increased by the inheritance laws established by the Code Napoleon. Twentieth-century historians still emphasised this explanation even when discussing northern France although this had always been an area of partible inheritance which the Code left unaltered. It has often not been appreciated how much peasant property existed before the Revolution although, as Table 6.1 shows, the social distribution of property varied markedly between regions.

It is certainly true that the French Revolution completely altered property rights. The Declaration of the Rights of Man and of Citizen, enacted by the Assembly on 27 August 1789, sanctified private property. 'Property is inviolable and sacred' (art. 17). Property was defined in a new way: it was considered to be a basic foundation of the new social order. It became a private matter, free from feudal rights, free from the community's intervention and from collective use-rights.

Feudal dues were abolished when the nobility renounced their privileges on the night of 4 August 1789. However the seigneurial rights (linked with the former *propriété éminente*) were declared redeemable. In fact, peasants never accepted their obligation to purchase and no redemption took place. Tithe was abolished in the following year as part of a general reform of taxation and was replaced by a state tax.

The Assembly wanted to suppress collective rights, but the Rural Code enacted on 28 September 1791 was a compromise. Whilst no owner could in future be prevented from enclosing his land for his private use, the code also acknowledged the continued existence of collective practices (for instance, *vaine pâture*, the grazing of livestock on fallow land). It envisaged only two kinds of property: state and private. Collective property, whether of inhabitants or institutions, was viewed as an archaic form of ownership that would disappear. After long debates and two drafts, a bill on the partition of commons was passed on 10 June 1793. In fact the area of commons divided under its authority remained limited and at a rough estimate, the area of common land was reduced by only about one third between 1760 and 1800. In order to restore social concord, Napoleon forbad *de facto* partitioning and ordered municipal property to be protected. And this principle was respected so long as the commons remained under

Map 6.1 Northern France, 1750–2000

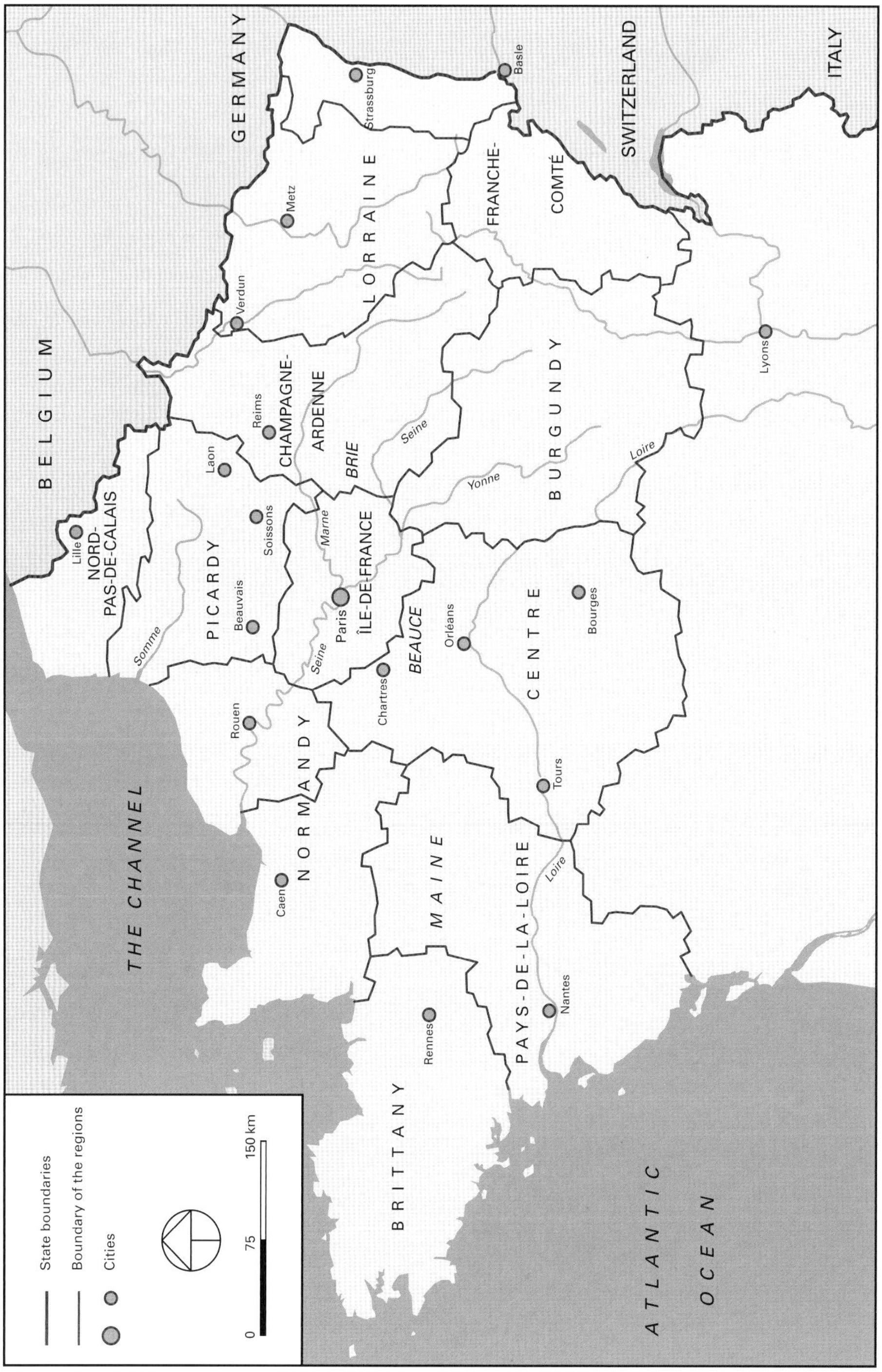

Table 6.1: Estimates of the distribution of landownership in northern France, 1789

	Clergy	Nobility	Bourgeoisie	peasants	commons
Beauce	9.5	30.0	26.5	33.5	0.0
Maritime Flanders	14.0	7.0	44.0	35.0	0.0
Domfrontais (Normandy)	1.5	18.5	53.5	25.0	1.2

Source: Béaur, 2000: 22

threat (that is, until the 1860s). The leasing of commons was encouraged however in order to provide revenue for local councils (Vivier, 1998).

The second major change in ownership due to the Revolution was the sale of the *biens nationaux* (Church property after 1790 and the properties confiscated from the émigrés after 1792). The taking into public ownership of church property affected northern France very unevenly. It was uncommon in Brittany, but very important on fertile soils, the areas of large-scale cereal cultivation. It accounted for around 10 per cent of the land around Paris, to the west (Maine) and north-east. It was much more extensive in the north where it reached 25 per cent of the land in Crépy en Valois and 40 per cent in Cambrai. (The average figure for France as a whole was 6 per cent for church possessions and 3 to 4 per cent for émigré lands.) Nearly all was sold between 1791 and 1797. The buyers were mainly bourgeois living in towns such as Paris or Rouen. Peasants purchased only a small part, though large farmers in the Ile-de-France took the opportunity to acquire land. It was mainly in the north (around Lille, Valenciennes) and in Burgundy that peasants were able to buy small plots, such as glebe land which had belonged to the parish clergy (Bodinier, 2000).

So who possessed the land after the upheavals in the land market of the Revolution? The cadastre, which was both a map and a written survey, made municipality by municipality between 1807 and 1844, gives a precise view of ownership at that time. From it, the number of assessments on landed property in each municipality is known. In all, France had 10 million individual assessments in 1842 but 13.5 million in 1882. As one person might own land in several municipalities, 100 assessments were held to correspond to 60 owners (*Statistique de la France,* 1882).

The increase in the number of owners was notable during the 1850s. Demographic pressure in the countryside peaked at that time, and a higher standard of living increased both the demand for food and raised the price of land. Another factor encouraging ownership was the stability in the level of land taxes in the nineteenth century. In spite of the desire expressed in 1791 to make the land tax the most important source of government income, it was never burdensome. After the restoration of the monarchy in 1815, its rate was reduced by the Chamber of Deputies which was dominated by large and conservative landowners. As industry and its taxes developed, the yield of the land tax remained fixed even though the value of land increased. Some large landowners took advantage of the high price of land and sold parcels in order to invest in industry; and this offered small cultivators the possibility of buying land. In turn, this increased the fragmentation of landholding (Braudel and Labrousse (eds), III: 632). Parcellisation affected predominantly areas around Paris and the other big towns, where land was in demand for building and the development of market gardening.

After 1871 the rate at which land was subdivided slowed down because of the acceleration of rural depopulation and the decline in rent due to the agricultural crisis caused by the low price of wheat and grain, and destruction of vineyards by phylloxera. The declining value of land damaged investors and the smaller owners. This encouraged a tendency for the concentration of landownership. In the period 1871–1901, the number of rural landowners diminished by around 4 per cent, but proportion of the total population who owned land is nonetheless estimated at 13 per cent, a very considerable figure.

The nobility's possessions were most numerous in the west, Brittany and Maine: their numbers gradually decreased. In turn, the amount of land held by the bourgeoisie slowly increased. They formed over 40 per cent of owners in northern France, locally sometimes up to 60 per cent. For the bourgeoisie, the purchase of an estate was an economic investment, but it also met a social need as it gave prestige and allowed them to emulate the noble lifestyle. Their estate had to contain a prestigious residence, offer opportunities for field sports but also be conveniently near to the town. For economic purposes, bourgeois purchasers preferred land providing a good rent, especially in Flanders or the Paris basin. Aristocratic and bourgeois landowners looked to spread the risk in their investments, mixing land, stocks and shares. In the second half of the century, their enthusiasm for landed estates waned. Possession of the land was the peasant's dream: it was the precondition for his independence. Peasant property holding increased from 1850 onwards. High agricultural prices and a declining interest in acquiring land by the upper classes allowed cultivators to buy land, and to expand small farms into middle-sized farms (for example in the Pas-de-Calais, Hubscher, 1979).

In 1881, around 10 per cent of the total area of the land was owned as micro-properties, gardens or buildings of less than 1 ha. Properties from 1 to 10 ha, when added to the previous category, covered 25 per cent of the area. These smaller holdings were especially numerous in Normandy and in the more urbanized areas of the Paris Basin and the north (where they formed 40 to 50 per cent of the area). Middle-size properties of six to 20 ha were numerous in the East, notably Champagne (forming around 30 per cent of the total area) and in Brittany (44 per cent), Normandy and Mayenne. Larger properties covered more than 40 per cent of the total around Rouen, in the Loire valley and in the southern part of Paris basin (Beauce, Brie).

So deep-rooted was the idea of France as a country of small farms that the 1882 enquiry expressed its surprise that this was not entirely so: 'All in all, France is neither a country of small farms nor one of small properties. Large size farms have an important place and they keep, along with large ownership, a leading position' (*Statistique*, 1882).

In the years after the First World War, the land market went through a period of intense activity. 1.3 million men had died, a third of the active male population. Agriculture suffered disproportionately. Nearly half of the dead were employed in agriculture and peasants suffered a high level of attrition because they were often infantry stationed in the front line. During the war, agricultural prices were high. Farmers often had little opportunity to spend their income because of the lack of industrial products, machines and fertilizers, available for purchase. In 1919 families that had lost men might be forced to sell their farm; but on the other side families whose men did return often had savings to invest. And land became relatively cheap. The nominal value of a hectare of land had doubled compared to 1914, but taking inflation into account, it was half the price of 1914. Inflation also devalued rents to the advantage of tenants. In western Normandy during the inter-war period, rents decreased by 40 per cent in terms of their purchasing power. This lightened the burden on cultivators but encouraged landowners to sell and invest in better yielding assets, and made land unattractive to investors, especially in the 1930s. Owner-occupiers took this opportunity to concentrate land into their hands. Some wage earners also bought land and established themselves as small tenant owners (Lévy-Leboyer, 1972).

This explains the major changes which took place in agricultural employment. There were 5.2 million men working in agriculture in 1911 and 4.9 million in 1921. Amongst them, wage earners declined in numbers in the same period from 3.3 million to 2.3 million. The slight overall reduction was due to the increase of the numbers of middle-sized owner-occupiers. The number of labourers shrank as some of them secured land and became established as smallholders, but the number of labourers was also reduced by the introduction of labour-saving machinery. And so the years 1919–45 witnessed the triumph of the family farm.

After the Second World War land continued to lose its attraction to investors who found shares in industrial reconstruction much more rewarding. The prestige value of an estate diminished and tenants could again buy land throughout the 1950s. But then the State intervened in the land market. The *loi d'orientation agricole* of 1960 sought to achieve a modernised agriculture based on middle-sized farms. It created the *Sociétés d'aménagement foncier et d'établissement rural* (SAFER) which were non-profit making semi-public limited companies, with the power to acquire parcels or farms, which they would then reshape into viable farms which were sold to selected agriculturists. The activities of SAFER remained modest, involving less than 75,000 ha each year (15 per cent of the land market) because they were faced with the opposition of landowners.

The price of land climbed during a period of good returns for farmers which lasted to 1980. Afterwards, in the years 1980–98, the market value stagnated, and decreased in real terms because of inflation. Today, the price of land is highest in urbanized areas and in fertile cereal growing districts. In Brittany or Lorraine, one hectare is worth around €3000 while it reaches €7500 in the north of the Paris basin (Agreste).

Table 6.2: Numbers of owners, tenants and sharecroppers in France, various dates, 1852–2000

	Owner-occupiers	%	Farmers	%	Sharecroppers	%	Total
1852	2,072,433	66.4	695,865	22.3	352,307	11.3	3,120,605
1892	4,190,795	74.6	1,078,184	19.2	349,338	6.2	5,618,317
1929	1,771,200	70.6	590,400	23.5	147,600	5.9	2,509,200
2000	329,327	48.5	324,107	47.8	25,046	3.7	678,480

Source: Demonet, 1990: 42; Barral, 1968: 28; Agreste.

Systems of tenure in the nineteenth century

From 1852 onwards, the decennial agricultural enquiries give accurate statistics for the forms of tenancy (Table 6.2). Owner-occupiers were in the majority nearly everywhere. In north-eastern France, they formed over 85 per cent of the number of occupiers and held 60 per cent of the cultivated area. Leasehold farms remained important in the north-western quarter of France where upper class ownership was most entrenched. Here, they normally formed at least 30 per cent of the holdings, with an average of between 20 and 50 per cent of the land. Sharecropping was found only in Mayenne and south Britanny (Demonet, 1990, Barral, 1993) (Map 6.1).

Owner-occupying cultivators owning sufficient land to support their family were considered to be the ideal at the end of the nineteenth century: their land gave them both security and independence. But these independent farmers were rarely in the majority. They were mainly active either in specialized or intensive polyculture: market gardening or mixed farming. In the north-east where they were most numerous (85 per cent), they cultivated about 60 per cent of the soil because they often added leaseholds to their holdings.

The independence of the owner-occupier stood in contrast to the lack of security possessed by the tenant. The nineteenth-century system of leases for six to nine years remained normal well into the twentieth century. The idea that tenants should have a wider, state-conferred, security of tenure beyond their leases was extensively debated. Bills moved by Georges Monnet in 1936 and Louis Salleron in 1941 (when ministers of agriculture) both failed, but a similar proposal was finally enacted in September 1943 and confirmed by the *Statut du fermage* of April 1946. It contained three main provisions. The first was that at the end of a lease, the landlord had to give his tenant the first option on a new lease. Second, if the landowner received an offer more than 30 per cent higher than his tenant's offer, and if the higher bid was honest, it could be used as the basis on which to set a new rent. If

Map 6.2: Ownership of land in northern France, 1882

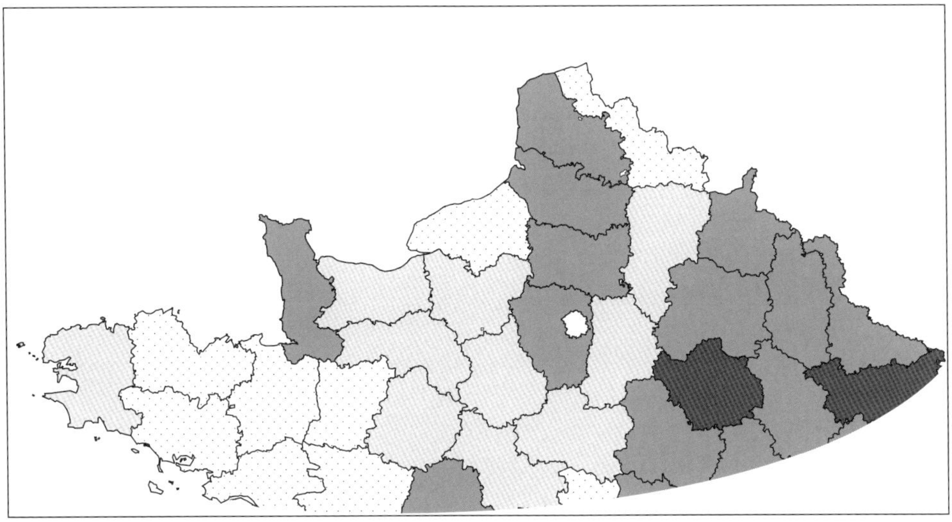

Sources : Enquête agricole de 1882

- over 80 % of cultivator-owners, 13 to 20 % of tenants
- 60 to 79 % of cultivator-owners, 20 to 40 % of tenants
- 30 to 59 % of cultivator-owners, 40 to 50 % of tenants
- over 50 % of tenants, under 30 % of cultivator-owners

the tenant declined to pay this increased rent, he was entitled to compensation for his eviction as well as for any improvements he had made to the farm. Third, if the owner wished to sell some or all of a tenant's land, the tenant was granted a right of pre-emptive purchase. In these ways, the *Statut du fermage* gave farmers a new security of tenure. Its provisions were included in the 1955 Rural Code and periodically restated: they were then incorporated into the legislative framework of the European Community.

During the 1950s, the government helped to create viable holdings through two major means, the regrouping of parcels, and providing a proper legal framework for tenancy. The regrouping of the parcels (*remembrement*) accelerated despite some opposition: 40 per cent of the cultivated areas for the whole of France, but mainly in northern France, were reshaped between 1950 and 2000 (Bonnamour, 1984).

6.2 The occupiers of land

In 1882, the average size of a farm in France as a whole was only 2.3 ha, or 10 ha if gardens of under 0.4 ha are not taken into account. But in northern France there were far fewer smaller holdings. In both Flanders and Brittany small and middle-sized farms of up to 40 ha co-existed. In Finistère, medium-size specialized farms covered more than half of the land area. In the Paris basin and the east, regions of cereals and stock

Map 6.3: Percentage of the total area held by holdings of over 40 ha in northern France, 1882.

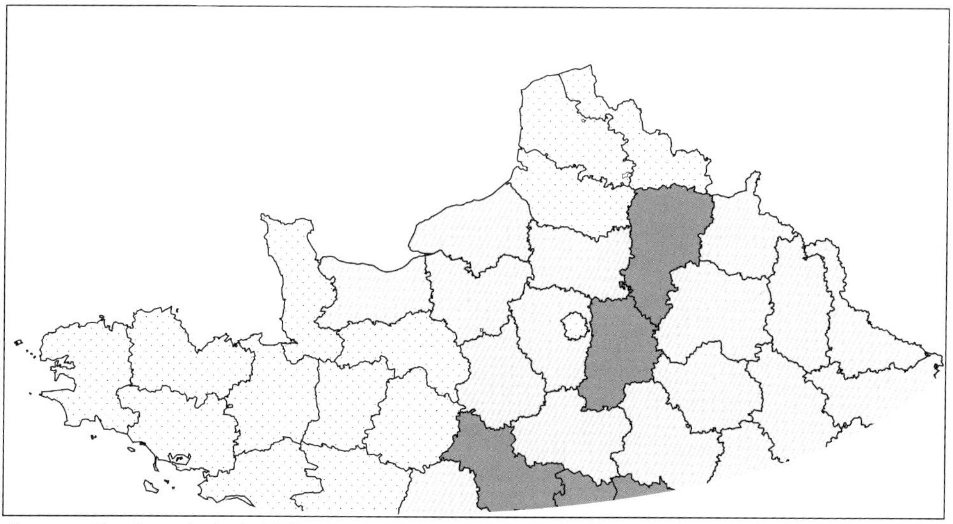

Sources : Enquête agricole de 1882

over 60

45–60

under 45

National average : 45 %

raising (or sheep farming), farms of over 40 ha (reaching 100 to 300 ha) were in the majority (Map 6.2).

Farm size can be related to three distinctive forms of village societies. Where small or medium-sized owner-occupiers prevailed, the society can be characterised as democratic (western Brittany, Basse-Normandie and Flanders, eastern France). Where medium-sized leasehold farms predominated, rural society was strongly hierarchical and the traditional dependency of tenant on landlord survived (Brittany). Large farms on the Ile-de-France and the Picardy plateau required substantial numbers of wage labourers, some of whom were smallholders drawn from within the village, but others were seasonal migrants from elsewhere in France or Belgium. This is the 'capitalist hierarchy' identified by Barral (1968: 42). This structure remained substantially unaltered through to the 1950s, after which it changed quickly and decisively.

The average size of farms in France as a whole increased substantially between 1955 (14 ha) and 1997 (42 ha). This was assisted by the 1962 law which created a new legal framework based on the *Groupement agricole d'exploitation en commun* (*GAEC*). Provision was made for two or more farmers to pool their farms into a single holding so they could manage it like an industrial enterprise. The average size of a GAEC in 1969 was 115 ha. Later it fell to 60 ha, as they were mainly partnerships of father and son or brothers. In 1984 the *Exploitation agricole à responsibilité limitée* (*EARL*) was

Table 6.3: Distribution of the cultivated area according to farm size (ha), various dates, (per cent)

	1–5	5–10	10–40	> 40	Total	Total hectares ('000)
1852	10.5	11.3	45.9	32.2		34,447
1892	13.8	14.2	33.7	38.3		34,720
1929	9.5	14.0	53.1	23.4		33,080
1986	1.7	2.8	43.4	52.1		28,270
		<20	2–50	>50		
2000		2.95	15.7	81.3		25,502

Source: *Statistique de la France*, Agreste.

Table 6.4: Average size of farms in the North Sea area of France, 2000

	Number of farms	Total acreage ('000 ha)	Average size (ha)
Britanny	34.921	1584	45.3
Normandy	25,603	1868	72.9
Ile-de-France	4834	548	113.3
Nord Pas de Calais	13,180	794	60.2
Picardy	11,891	1283	107.8

Source: Agreste, Recensement agricole, 2000.

created in which several members (including non-farmers so long as they did not hold more than half of the shares) could come together in partnership. It acknowledged partnership enterprises owned by couples, allowing wives to be treated as full-time workers. Today, around half of the farms are run by a single farmer and the other half by partnerships: 22.5 per cent are in GAEC arrangements (mainly in cattle breeding and cultivation with a family workforce), and 23.2 per cent in EARL, mainly farms involved in grain production, poultry farming or horticulture (data from Agreste).

Small farms, except for those devoted to specialist crops, progressively disappeared (Table 6.3). Middle-sized farms (20–50 ha) in the western part of France mostly had dynamic tenants and they took the opportunity of the CAP and the modernized credit system to develop their holdings. They passed through difficult conditions after 1970 and the area they cultivated decreased. In the centre and east of the Paris basin, farms of over 50 ha – usually owner-occupied – came to cover three-quarters of the cultivated area. Having adopted machines, their need for labourer declined sharply. Their low costs made them profitable when they had guaranteed prices under the CAP but they now struggle with EC policies, falling commodity prices and rising costs. The situation in 2000 is shown in Table 6.4. Substantial differences in farm size still exist between regions, and those which were historically the 'big-farm regions' remain so to this day.

Communal land use systems

Common arable lands covered only one to five per cent of the area of northern France, but in Brittany common wastes could cover as much as 30 per cent of the land area. Three systems of communal land use can be identified in the mid-eighteenth century (Vivier, 1998).

(a) The traditional collective use of common lands survived – as in Brittany – on land belonging in common to the former vassals of a lord. *Communs* were used for grazing, for gathering heather and the cutting of sods used for the preparation of manure. They progressively disappeared during the second half of nineteenth century as they were divided between the individual commoners. Common grazing survived on very small areas of land, for example the wetlands of the Somme valley.

(b) Communal woodlands, huge areas in the north-east, were managed by the local councils. They provided firewood, timber, grazing (including acorns or beech mast and beechnuts). The 1827 Forest Law handed the management over to the Forestry administration (*Eaux et Forêts*), and the exercise of common grazing and gathering rights forbidden. The profits of the exploitation of timber, exclusively managed by the *Eaux et Forêts*, came to the municipality. In some parts of the north-east of France (Champagne, Lorraine) these revenues were sufficiently large for municipalities owning full-grown forest trees (*futaies*) to avoid levying local taxes.

(c) The small areas of common land surviving in Flanders and Lorraine were administered by local councils. Individual use of this land was encouraged by the state and from the 1770s they were often let as small parcels of land, suitable for a family garden or small scale specialized production on the urban fringe.

Power in the villages from the first municipalities to district communities, 1760–2000

By the 1750s, there were signs that the village institutions of *ancien régime* France were no longer fully functional. Even before the Revolution, there had been attempts at reform. There were several reform proposals after 1760 (L'Averdy in 1764, Turgot in 1776, Loménie de Brienne in 1787) which advocated the establishment of village assemblies to be conducted by the village *sanior pars* and landlords. These proposals, if implemented, would have answered village demands for greater authority. The parish assembly of Rospez (Tregor, Brittany) in 1788 complained of 'the lack of representative people in the states to ask for their right causes, the overloading of poll taxes, ordinary and extraordinary fouages'.[1] The system of oligarchic and hierarchical authority was undermined in a number of ways: by conflicts between village communities and their lords, tithe strikes and the truculence of the villagers, one dimension of which was a growing number of court actions (Nicolas, 2002). Moreover, the worsening of the economic situation after 1786 weakened collective institutions, like those providing welfare. It is not surprising that the older structures showed little resistance to the revolutionary wave of 1789, and that the new structure established after 1790 commanded general support.

The Constituent Assembly decided, on the 25 November 1789, that 'there will be municipalities in each town or village'. This decision was key for the future territorial organization of France, characterized by a great number of 'communes', which usually coincided with traditional communities. For the first municipal elections in January 1790, about two-thirds of the men aged over 25 years were eligible to vote. Even if about a third were excluded, the broad franchise founded the new nation on a very wide participatory base in the countryside, from which only the property-less (and women) were excluded. So we observe straightaway a selective renewing of village administrators. Many independent peasants were elected to local offices in the initial elections, but the electoral system also often acted to preserve the hegemony of the rural oligarchy. Where big farmers were powerful (as in Artois, Beauce, Cambresis, the Ile de France, Picardy, the plains of Caen or Rennes) they often maintained their local power; in more 'democratic' districts, where small or independent peasants were important (as in Brittany, Flanders, Lorraine or the main part of Normandy, but also valleys around Paris), the new municipal offices were more contested between peasants, craftsmen or 'bourgeois'. Contrary to the thesis of anti-revolutionary or village passivity, these results show that villagers were well aware of national changes and used them to take charge of their own affairs.

Nevertheless, signs of conservatism quickly appeared. From 1791, turnout at the polls declines. Religious divisions appeared, the implementation of the purchase of seigneurial rights and the liberalisation of the corn market proved to be more difficult to achieve than was expected. Conflicts emerged over communal land; and after 1792, there was hostility to military enlistment. But there was rarely a breakdown between municipality and government until the revolt of Vendée, in the spring of 1793.

After various experiments, in 1800 the Consulate adopted a territorial organization based on communes, with mayors appointed by the prefects of each department. In practice mayors were chosen with great care by the prefect: their standing in their community and the networks they controlled turned out to be as important as their political loyalties. Lesser officials were also appointed by the state and included many farmers (Jessenne, 2006).

Local government went through small modifications but no major changes between 1800 and 1830. In 1831, the law concerning municipalities conferred the right to vote

[1] C. Kermoal, *Les notables du Trégor, 1770–1850* (2003), p. 178. Fouages are local taxes.

on 10 per cent of the male inhabitants, the leading taxpayers, but required villages to have a minimum of 50 voters. While in towns only wealthy people could vote, in small villages a large proportion of adult males were enfranchised and could be elected to a municipal council; this was a factor in increased public sociability. Historians have recently modified the traditional view of village inactivity during this period: notables acted more as brokers on behalf of their fellow-citizens than as potentates. Road works, church maintenance and schools became the responsibility of local councils and this notably increased their importance in public life. In spite of the adoption of male universal suffrage in 1848, the main change in the power of the municipality occurred under the Third Republic.

A law of 1881 strengthened the mayor's power by providing for his election by the local council. That the Waldeck-Rousseau government invited the 36,000 French mayors to a banquet in Paris on the 22 September 1889 showed the republican interest in rural affairs; the fact that more than 20,000 mayors attended proved that national integration was already well-advanced. Of course, this did not eliminate rivalries between the parties of left and right about local elections, or over policies such as the provision of schooling, or the split between church and state in 1905. But the filling of municipal offices by farmers was genuine, as in Beauce where 50 per cent of mayors were farmers in 1848, and 68 per cent in 1912 (Farcy, 1989). It was the mayors and rural municipalities of the north and east of France, which suffered massive destruction in war, who had to undertake their rebuilding and the repair of the landscape. Between the two World Wars, rural municipalities acquired additional responsibilities for infrastructure: the provision of water-supply and the extension of the electrical grid for example (Duby and Wallon (eds), 1976, IV: 275).

Although the suffrage was extended to women in 1945, the rural municipal system did not change much before the 1980s. There were new problems, however: the drift from the land, then the 'rurbanisation' of some districts, the appearance of second homes in the countryside, agricultural changes, the increase in car ownership, all served to alter access to power. Municipal elections were marked, after 1960, by frequent rivalries between 'natives' – most of them farmers – and the new residents of the countryside. The working out of these conflicts differed from one village or one election to another: and we should not exaggerate the decline in the political importance of the farmers for they remained mayors out of proportion to their numbers in the population. For example, in the Pas-de-Calais, an urbanized department, they provided 40 per cent of mayors in 1960, and 20 per cent in 2007. Whilst the municipalities controlled key aspects of rural life, including schools and the provision of leisure facilities, planning and housing development, reforms from the 1990s have favoured the creation of '*communautés de communes*' responsible for different functions. This was the beginning of integration of local power into national and even European structures.

Peasant organizations

Can we accept that agricultural societies were the first forms of peasant organisation? Yes and no. Undoubtedly, they existed. There were 26 regional societies in the country in 1780, about ten of them in northern France, which held regular meetings, published dissertations and correspondence on rural issues, farming techniques and so on. Monarchy played a central role in the organisation of this network. In 1761, a seven-member agricultural committee was established, with Henri-Léonard Bertin, contrôleur général des finances, as its main instigator. Its links with the Paris agricultural society were strong although not always peaceful. But the membership of these societies and their management was far from peasant. The leading role was taken by agronomists and regional notables; only a minority of farmers could aspire to be members. Moreover, the economic ideas of these societies (which favoured free trade and large commercial farms) did not hold much attraction for the peasant majority.

Under the Constituent Assembly in 1789–91, the Paris agricultural society emerged as an influential lobby which campaigned for a free trade in grain and the abolition of collective rights. It may be argued that the political societies, which became popular and grew in numbers after August 1792, may be interpreted as a new form of rural organisation which articulated the grievances of the small peasant although the number of peasants joining these societies, and their influence within them, is unclear (Jones, 1989). All of them, including the Paris society, were suppressed in 1795.

During the Directory, in 1798, François de Neufchâteau, Minister of the Interior, advocated the re-establishment of agricultural societies like the *Société libre d'agriculture du département de la Seine*, with 36 founder members, 60 associated residents and 150 correspondents. The Imperial government encouraged the creation of one society per department, but their numbers increased substantially in the decade after 1830 when many more were created by private initiatives. In particular, societies named *comices,* which organised agricultural shows, flourished. They brought together three main types of members: farmers, landowners and the liberal or entrepreneurial professions.

The range of agricultural organizations increased yet further at the end of the nineteenth century. Men involved in agricultural training played a major role in the birth of new forms of professional organisation. The intervention of the state in agricultural education began with a bill of October 1848 that structured it on three levels: farm schools which trained workers, regional schools which educated managers, and the national agronomic institute which undertook research. Eventually 78 school farms were established but their numbers decreased after 1860. Three regional schools were located in Grignon near Paris, Grand-Jouan (which moved to Rennes in 1895) and La Saulsaie (which moved to Montpellier in 1870). From the 1860s professors of agriculture were appointed in each district. All those men aimed at encouraging farmers to introduce improvements. They were key figures in the foundation of farmers' cooperatives, established to sell production or to buy fertilizers. Those cooperatives were often the seeds of the syndicates (Vivier, 2008: 247–58).

The emergence of national organisations is linked to the political rivalries at the end of Second Empire and after. In 1867, a number of right-wing Catholic landowners founded the *Société des Agriculteurs de France*. They established a trade union in 1886, the *Union centrale des syndicats agricoles* (nick-named rue d'Athènes after the location of its offices). To counterbalance these initiatives by the Catholic right, Gambetta, aided by prominent republicans, founded a *Fédération nationale de la mutualité et de la coopération agricole* (and called after its offices in Saint-Germain Boulevard) (Barral, 1968). The local syndicates and organisations belonging to these rival networks provided cultivators with varied products and services (including the collection and processing of agricultural produce, insurance and mutual societies for credit). In Brittany, the desire for autonomy (from state, landowners and clergy) led to the creation of a powerful cooperative, the *Office central de Landerneau,* controlled by the larger landowners such as the earl of Guébriant. These organisations did not succeed in overcoming the crisis of agriculture at the end of the century, but there were only a few protest movements in the north of France – unlike the south, centre or south-west. Agricultural workers, though numerous in some regions, struggled to form effective organisations.

From 1920, a number of laws confirmed the close cooperation which existed between the government and the national agricultural organisations, especially with the foundation of a national fund for credit, the *Caise nationale de crédit agricole* (1926). New associations of specialist producers emerged, such as the beetroot producers (*Producteurs de betteraves*) in 1921 and wheat cultivators (*Producteurs de blé*) in 1924; they were dominated by the big farmers of the Parisian Basin, already experienced lobbyists. Agricultural workers' unions, which were weakly developed in the north of France, suffered from the divisions between socialists and communists. During the crisis of the 1930s, financial difficulties and the rise of the anti-authority groups on the fringe of the agrarian system (which we will discuss later) compelled trade unions to reorganize; in 1937 the conservative *Union nationale des syndicats agricoles* of rue d'Athènes had had about 1.2 million members, against one million for the republican Boulevard Saint-Germain Federation.

After the Liberation of France, Pierre Tanguy-Prigent, a socialist minister, attempted but failed to create a General Confederation of Agriculture (*Confédération générale de l'agriculture*) to gather all the agricultural organisations and the State into one body to advance the modernization of the French countryside. Instead, the local syndicates were re-founded, often under managers from the pre-war organisations; in 1947 they established the *Fédération nationale des syndicats d'exploitants agricoles.* FNSEA defended peasant concepts of unity and singularity, especially in their relations with the state, and it excluded departmental federations which did not share its conservative views. It played an important role in the emergence of a new form of farmer's organisation, the *Chambres d'agriculture* founded in 1948 which were charged with managing government funds for agricultural development. FNSEA claimed to be voice of the rural world, but it was always dominated by large farmers from the north Paris basin. Anti-establishment or anti-capitalist syndicates, such as the *comité de Guéret* and then the *Mouvement de Coordination et de Défense des Exploitations Agricoles Familiales* (*MODEF*), created in 1959 and close to the Communist Party, were more deeply rooted in the Midi (Gavignaud, 1996).

The policies and strategies of the existing agricultural organisations had to be rethought with the rise of the *Jeunesse Agricole Chrétienne* or JAC (Agricultural Christian Youth). Although founded as early as 1929, this emerged as a powerful force after the war and by 1960 claimed more than 400,000 members. It urged FNSEA to campaign not only in defence of agricultural prices, but also to encourage agricultural change. In the 1960s its leaders played a decisive role in promoting both family farms and the need for technical modernisation in the context of 'Green Europe'. The evolution of FNSEA from a conservative peasant organisation to a more forward-looking one was not done at once, nor was it without conflicts. Michel Debatisse, secretary of the JAC from 1956, became secretary of the FNSEA in 1966 and then its president (1971–78). The shared management of agriculture by FNSEA and government continued throughout the phase of major changes from the 1960s. Significantly, whilst FNSEA has adapted and survived, other agricultural organisations – the agricultural credit unions, farm product cooperatives – have either disappeared or have been transformed like the remainder of the capitalist economy. The primacy of FNSEA though is still contested by organisations which defend a 'peasant economy'.

6.3 Government and public policies

State policies after 1750

The burden of direct taxation differed greatly from region to region: but it rose in line with prices. Hence, it was viewed with growing hostility by the rural element within the Third Estate. In the second half of the eighteenth century, there were a succession of attempts to reform the tax system. In 1749 Controller-General Machault d'Arnouville introduced the *vingtième*, which taxed all land, including that of the nobility and clergy, at one-twentieth of its rental value. However, the resistance of the nobility and clergy rapidly undermined his initiative. As early as 1751 the clergy secured an exemption; in the meantime the inequitably distributed *taille* continued to supply more than three quarters of all direct tax receipts.

Nevertheless, the combination of physiocratic influence and the rapid deterioration of state finances from the time of the Seven Years' War resulted in episodes of more rigorous tax investigation (notably under Terray in 1771), as well as repeated proposals for land tax reform. For example, the intendant Bertier de Sauvigny launched the making of a cadastre in the *généralité* of Paris in order to establish how burdensome the *taille* was as a proportion of the actual resources of farmers. In 1786–87 Controller-General Calonne returned to the idea of a general land tax (named *subvention territoriale*) in the reforms he presented to the Assembly of Notables. However, opposition from the nobility and clergy led to its rejection.

The weight of taxation was not the only burden placed on the peasantry. Militia service and the *corvée royale,* replaced in 1776 by a money tax, were two further pressures which were both effective and vexatious. Both would be denounced in the *cahiers de doléances* of 1789.

The abolition of fiscal privilege and the introduction of uniform and proportional taxation remains one of the fundamental achievements of the Revolution. The peasant dream of a tax-free society rapidly proved to be an illusion. Confronted with a fiscal emergency, at the end of 1791 the Constituent Assembly introduced a territorial tax assessed at one sixth of the net yield of the land. Two other new taxes, the *mobilière* on housing and the *patente* on industrial activities, were much lighter. However, in the absence of up-to-date tax rolls, the distribution of the burden that had prevailed during the *ancien régime* was perpetuated. Over the next two decades there were many short-term levies, forced loans and requisitions, even the seizure of bell metal for the manufacture of weapons (1793). Sometimes such initiatives fostered a patriotic response, sometimes a deep resistance. From the time of the Directory and more especially under the Empire, indirect taxation provided the mainstay of state revenue just as under the *ancien régime*.

The ambition of the Constituent Assembly to carry out a cadastral survey so that taxation could be placed on an equitable basis was finally implemented. Experiments began in the 1790s and accelerated from 1800 under Martin-Michel-Charles Gaudin, Minister of Finance, 1799–1814. The definitive form of the survey was decided in 1807; around a quarter of communes had been surveyed by 1814 and it was complete by 1850. There were many defects, particularly in the maps executed in the 1820s, but those surveyed in the 1830s and '40s were reliable. The cadastre aimed at being the means by which the tax burden could be equitably redistributed within a municipality; moreover it improved the knowledge of property holdings although it had no value as legal evidence of landownership. People praised the cadastre because it was reliable and led to a fair distribution of tax. Studies confirm that the valuations of land were equitable, but they show also that they were higher in some municipalities than others as a result of the rejection, in the 1820s, of the provisions for equalization which were laid down in 1807.

It has long been held that the fiscal burden was lighter under the revolutionary regime; but more recent research, by Le Goff and Sutherland (1999) amongst others, maintains that the state simply diverted to itself the revenue formerly paid to seigneurs or the church. In reality, how the burden of taxation changed varied greatly according to the social group, the locality and the period. After an undoubted reduction of the fiscal burden at the beginning of the Revolution, the load rose once more from 1798, and would return to the level of 1788 around 1806. Overall, however, when the burden is converted into constant money values, it is clear that the big farmers emerged as winners from the reform of the tax system (Béaur, 2000).

On the other hand, the burden imposed by military service increased considerably. Many young men had to undertake military service, whether as volunteers (1789–92), as quota soldiers following the levy of the 300,000 men in February 1793, or as a consequence of the *levée en masse* (mass mobilization of the whole nation) in August 1793. The biggest contingents were drawn from peasants and craftsmen, partly because of the practice of paying substitutes. In the Vendée, conscription triggered the rebellion of March 1793, and there was also resistance elsewhere. Nevertheless, successive governments succeeded in recruiting, one way or another, the men required for a considerably enlarged military establishment. The *Loi Jourdan* of 1798 is often held to have introduced compulsory military service for all Frenchmen of the age of 20 to 25, although the practice of purchasing a substitute persisted. Napoleon would increase hugely the burden of military conscription, from 60,000 recruits in 1804 to 120,000 in 1812. This 'blood tax' would become henceforth a part of the obligations laid upon the peasants, with all its inequalities.

For the next century and a half, the notion of a nation-in-arms became one of the founding principles of modern France. But the question of military service gave rise to constant debates and many laws. The 1889 law imposing three years military service on all adult males aimed at creating a unified nation state by ensuring that all men went through a shared, common experience. The idea that they should be welded together through a period of national service would persist at least until the 1960s, when the colonial wars came to an end.

Yet the price paid was heavy. The two world wars hit the countryside very badly indeed. The human cost was severe in both wars, indeed of an unprecedented brutality in the case of the First World War (between 500,000 and 700,000 peasants dead and almost as many wounded). Together with increasing migration to towns, the war of 1914–18 brought to an end the overpopulation of the countryside. The Second World War, it is true, was less devastating in terms of military losses, but the civilian population was more severely affected. And, with some 500,000 men taken as prisoners to Germany, the economic dislocation of the war was coupled with a deep trauma. The two world wars severely destabilised the village and henceforward the landscape would be etched with monuments to the dead.

On the other hand, the state treated the peasantry tactfully. The level of the land tax remained fixed and rarely surpassed 10 per cent of rental value throughout the nineteenth century, meaning that it remained moderate when compared with other taxes and particularly those levied on urban property. In fact its contribution to the state's income gradually decreased. The establishment of an income tax in 1913 did not radically alter this situation since the tax was adjusted over the years to help small farmers. Yet this never prevented anti-fiscal campaigns from disturbing relations between country dwellers and the state, particularly when tax increases were perceived as an abuse (for example, the 45 per cent increase in taxes in 1848; or the imposition on farmers of an accounting system by André Tardieu when Prime Minister in 1931). However, considerations of prices and rural credit still carried weight in the formulation of government policy during the twentieth century.

Changing government attitudes towards consolidation and enclosure

In the mid-eighteenth century, French government was anxious that agricultural production should increase. Most of the Physiocrats admired the English model of consolidation and enclosure. French diplomats were asked to enquire into foreign experiments: the British model was investigated with special interest and a well-balanced report of 1763 highlighted the advantages of enclosures leading to larger estates with better production and productivity. It also described the social costs of enclosure, notably the eviction of smaller farmers as a result of enclosures and their migration to towns in large numbers. From 1750 to 1940, French opinion was divided over the merits of enclosure. On the one hand, large properties and large-scale exploitation were praised as more efficient; they possessed capital and were able to modernize. But on the other hand, the social consequences of enclosures were feared; and insofar as urban unrest was a major concern, governments tried to encourage rural people to stay in their village. Changing social context and the evolution of the legal concept of property helps explain the development of government policy. Three periods can be roughly defined (Vivier, 1998).

In the years 1760–80, royal edicts were issued which urged the partitioning of common lands and authorised the enclosure of private properties. Edicts of this sort were issued for Trois évêchés in 1769, Flanders in 1777 and Artois in 1779. In order to avoid the dispossession of poor, it was recommended that commons should be allocated equally between all households. The land was to be privately cultivated but the community would retain ownership. In this way, every household would have the use of a plot of land and the poor would not risk the danger of losing it to creditors.

After 1789, the aims changed. Communal farming was now considered to be the main obstacle to economic progress, and to the modernization of the law by jurists. Moreover, in 1793, social concerns led to the desire of sharing out the commons for the benefit of the landless. The bill of 10 June 1793 fixed the rules of division: an equal plot was to be allotted to every inhabitant, male or female, who thereby received the absolute ownership and not merely the use of the land as had previously been the case. After the revolutionary decade, Napoleon Bonaparte aimed at restoring social peace and partly returned to the previous policy, holding that the ownership of the municipality ought to be preserved. The partitioning of commons was forbidden and local councils were encouraged to lease them in small plots through public auctions.

The Second Empire was every bit as convinced of the necessity of individual farming. The 1850 law for Brittany was enforced; it simplified the enclosure process and resulted in the cultivation of wastes. But Napoleon III also introduced the notion of public utility of land. This led to a new formulation of property rights in woodland and wetland.

Public regulation of the countryside

Public regulation of the landscape became more efficient after the Revolution's reform of property rights. National forests were the oldest concern of the State. The important royal edict, *Eaux et Forêts*, was passed in 1669, and restated by the 'reformation' of Louis XV in 1763. After the extensive damage done to forests in the revolutionary decade, the forestry administration tried to reorganize under the first Empire. Its power was strengthened by the forestry law of 1827 which aimed at restoring forest and encouraging the growth of standing timber instead of brushwood. All grazing rights were suppressed in both national and communal woodlands.

From 1850, public regulation of the countryside intensified. Napoleon III introduced the right of the state to intervene in communal properties for reasons of public utility. By the 1852 law for drainage in Sologne, the state paid for infrastructure works which were then undertaken by local councils. This method was extended by the two laws of 28 July 1860, one for drainage of wastes and wet lands, and the other concerned with soil restoration and afforestation. In both cases, public funds and the state's engineers could be drawn on by local authorities wishing to improve the countryside. A local council could decide to do the work and receive public assistance, or, conversely, if it declined to act, the state was given the power to undertake the works alone, funding them by assuming the ownership of the improved land. In fact most of the work authorised by this law was undertaken in southern France, but wastes in Champagne, wet lands in Normandy and in the Somme valley were drained and forests restored in the Ardennes and Champagne. The 1860 forest law was taken by neighbouring countries to be an exemplary model and was copied by them: within France, it was reinforced by a further law of 1882.

A new afforestation policy was set in motion after the Second World War which aimed at planting some of the lands abandoned by agriculture. Those works received a legal grounding in the *loi d'orientation agricole* ('agricultural orientation law') of 1960: the *zonage agriculture-forêts* ('zoning [between] agriculture [and] forest') divided each municipality's area between that cultivated by farmers and the forest supervised by foresters. This regional land planning was completed by the 1985 law which laid down the relationship between of agriculture and forestry.

In the same period, public intervention contributed to modify the countryside by encouraging the regrouping of farm holdings which was a necessary precondition for mechanisation. The average cultivated plot was increased in size by the removal of hedges. Two main landscape types are now to be found. In Brittany and its fringes (Normandy and Maine), the bocage came to occupy nearly 90 per cent of the land area, while on the alluvial plains of the Paris Basin, a landscape of large unfenced fields came to prevail over 85 per cent of the area.

Government and markets from the eighteenth to the twentieth century

From the 1760s, the Physiocrats succeeded in placing agricultural issues among the major preoccupations of the monarchy. Quesnay himself described the desired outcome: 'Let the land used for the cultivation of grain be consolidated as much as possible in large farms operated by wealthy cultivators, because they have fewer expenses and a higher net product in large agricultural enterprises than in small ones'.[2] But an alternative view of development, based on smallholdings, advocated by Mably, Levassor and others, continued to be influential. In the end, the monarchy's agricultural initiatives remained limited.

In contrast, attempts to establish the free trade in grain intensified with Bertin and Laverdy (1763–64), Turgot (1774) and Necker (1787). Each time, poor harvests, differences in regional supplies, and speculation served to trigger inflation and disturbances. State interventions in the market to build up reserves revived rumours of a famine plot: people suspected officials of speculation and starving the king's subjects. Recurrent crises led local authorities to impose more regulatory measures and the government to restrict freedom of trade, especially grain exports. Thus, the debate on the type of agricultural development was framed in very contradictory terms: large farms v. small ones, subsistence v. market.

On August 29, 1789, a decree of the National Constituent Assembly freed the grain trade from controls, but urban riots made the implementation of a free market

---

2 F. Quesnay, 'Maximes générales du gouvernement économique d'un royaume agricole,' in J. Cartelier (ed.), *Physiocratie* (1991), p. 298.

problematic. Unrest and debates about subsistence did not cease, especially with the depreciation of the *assignat*, the new paper money that was the forced currency. In the autumn of 1792, the assertion of the right to life, and thus the legitimacy of the regulation of food prices, was made in the Convention by some of the Montagnards headed by Robespierre. This was in opposition to the majority view of the Girondin, expressed in the Law of 8 December 1792, which reaffirmed freedom of trade. This was a crucial dividing line throughout the Revolution. In reality, after a partial ceiling on bread prices was adopted in May 1793, the Montagnards (now the dominant party) had the Convention approve agrarian measures promoting small property. In the *Maximum général* of September 1793, the prices of all products were set at a third above their 1790 level, with wages 50 per cent higher. Despite the war, no major subsistence crisis occurred in 1793–94 and the armies were more or less adequately supplied. However the peasants were increasingly recalcitrant and harvest labour went on strike against the ceiling on wages.

Finally, the Thermidorian Convention voted to abrogate the *Maximum* on 24 December 1794. This allowed the price of bread to find its market price and produced the most serious subsistence crisis since the early eighteenth century. From 1795 onwards, the Directory and the Consulate, particularly during the crisis of 1801, conducted a moderate policy in which liberalism was officially declared, but this did not prevent the Consulate from intervening in the market through the formation of a Company of Suppliers responsible for managing grain stocks. This policy of moderate management of the grain market was applied until the 1870s, by which time periodic shortages had disappeared.

Without exaggerating the isolation of rural areas before the mid-nineteenth century, it is nevertheless clear that the years 1830–80 witnessed the integration of domestic commodity markets. The building of a communications network, railways and especially departmental and local roads, was encouraged by the state; a law of 1836 required every local council to improve its roads. The network of fairs and markets reached its maximum density; the movement of goods within the domestic market resulted in a decline in the difference between agricultural prices in different regions. Interdepartmental price differences still exceeded 70 per cent in the first half of the nineteenth century, but they amounted to less than 30 per cent by 1870 (Duby and Wallon (eds), 1976, III: 234). In addition, the circulation of money in the form of either cash or credit increased. Traditional practices persisted and intensified, including lending between individuals on mortgages. Notaries continued to play a vital role as brokers; but after 1830, investors increasingly turned to local or regional banks (Postel-Vinay, 1998). In the regions involved in the industrialization of agriculture such as Brie or Artois, the larger farmers invested in sugar refineries, breweries, and so on.

The official return to free trade in 1860 confirmed the integration of markets. 'Free trade' was the suppression of prohibitions. A fixed and moderate tariff replaced a complex sliding scale of tariffs; bilateral treaties were signed with many countries beginning with the Anglo-French treaty of 1860. Growth in exports of agricultural products was evident throughout the 1860s. Free trade could not endure however. In the dual context of the 'peasant republic', which was the slogan of the Third Republic, and the desperate agricultural depression of the last quarter of the nineteenth century, state intervention intensified again after 1880. The measures taken began as a simple combination of initiatives: the creation of local and regional banks by the agricultural credit laws of 1894 and 1899, and the defence of farmers by protection. In spite of a generally received idea, tariffs for agricultural products came second after those for industrial products. The 'Méline Tariff'(named after Jules Méline, then Minister of Agriculture) of 1890 provided tariffs of 5 to 20 per cent depending on the nature of the product. Agrarian protectionism was justified by saying: '... Only one field of activity and expansion is capable of absorbing all the unemployed ... it is the fruitful and eternal land that feeds humanity, mother of all industries'.[3]

After 1918, the system of co-regulation by government and agricultural organizations, assisted by the creation of a National Bank of Agricultural Credit, benefited in the short term from the liquidity of the countryside. The crisis of the 1930s, marked by the decline in prices and bankruptcies, weakened this system. Whilst in those sectors such as sugar, agreements with the producers limited price fluctuations, grain prices remained very low, and right-wing governments refused to guarantee a minimum price. In spite of the hostility of the major agricultural organizations to 'nationalization', the Popular Front and its socialist minister of agriculture, Georges Monnet, created the *Office National Interprofessionnel du Ble* (*ONIB*) in 1936. The office was given complete authority over French foreign trade: it also supervised domestic trade through cooperatives that purchased grain and set prices. Thereafter, price increases were promoted and farmers' income from grain grew by over 50 per cent between 1935 and 1938. The ONIB met the challenge to supplies posed by the Second World War and the occupation. It responsibilities were enlarged to cover all cereals in 1945 and the office renamed the *Office National Interprofessionnel des Céréales* (*ONIC*).

France in the 1950s, despite rapid innovation in agriculture, did little to alter the organization of markets, which were partly regulated by the big farmers' lobby groups. The other sectors (meat, wine, vegetable and so on) were less regulated and subject to periodic crises. The idea of a common agricultural market emerged, but although the Treaty of Rome was signed in 1957, French forms of regulation still prevailed as agricultural prices remained indexed against costs (as urged by FNSEA). This corporatist approach to markets diminished after the 1960s. Markets were now on a different scale. European regulation and its 'intervention price' prevailed. The Common Agricultural Policy proceeded side-by-side with the national policy of transforming agricultural structures. This was the prelude to the globalization of trade.

Peasants as a political force

Many works on local power and popular politics (Pécout, 1994) have shown the ways in which villages participated in public life as early as the eighteenth century. This has been an important correction to the picture of a delayed integration drawn by Weber

3 Pierre Barral, *Les agrariens français de Méline à Pisani* (Paris, 1968), p. 133.

in his *Peasants into Frenchmen* (1976) which was based mainly on examples from the poorest and least integrated south-western region of France.

From the 1760s, the problem of subsistence created a form of politicization expressed in the demand for government intervention, especially to uphold the 'fair price' by price controls. These demands were not new, but the questioning of monarchical government became more virulent and strengthened the desire of country people to secure political representation. The meetings preparatory to the Estates-General in 1789 and drafting of lists of grievances were an opportunity for the villagers to articulate their views. The most common elements of rural grievance were the privileges of the feudal-manorial complex, village inequality and the tax burden, and the exploitation of the village by the seigneurial interest. Thus, peasant and rural political aspirations converged in the desire of the village communities to secure an equal right to vote for the members of all three estates and their continued loyalty to the king, who was seen as both paternal and national. It was, therefore, logical that the villagers trusted, in 1790–91, the new institutions, particularly the municipalities, and supported the movement for the abolition of the *ancien régime*. Then the execution of Louis XVI and a mixture of agrarian issues, the proliferation of popular societies in the countryside, the conscription of 300,000 men into the army and the Vendee revolt radicalized the countryside. Contrary to many accepted ideas, rural France in 1793 was neither massively revolutionary nor generally counter-revolutionary. A wide variety of political situations had been superimposed upon social diversity (Jessenne, 2006).

This remained the case under the Directory (1795–99). Peasant responses to national events ranged between a withdrawal from local affairs in some places and a strong politicization elsewhere, sometimes electoral abstention but also mass participation. The Consulate (1799–1804) restored a sort of concordat with the villages, marked by the continued hegemony of the village elite and notables, the confirmation of the revolutionary gains, and thereafter there was a relative rural indifference to changing regimes. However, the revival of local interest in national politics was obvious from the period of the July Monarchy (1830–48) onwards. The Second Republic (1848–52) saw the reappearance of political activism in rural areas, although episodes of insurrection were rare in northern France in both 1848 and 1851. The establishment of universal male suffrage by the Second Republic was an important but equivocal step: it led to a high level of participation in the elections of April 1848 (80 per cent of those eligible voted) but then there is Tocqueville's familiar story of how 'his' Norman peasant 'sheep' went in a procession to vote for him. Peasants though became increasingly independent of the local traditional elites over the period of the Second Empire. Support for Louis Napoleon Bonaparte (Napoleon III) prevailed from the presidential election in 1851 until 1870 in northern France because it was based on the fame of his name. This seemed to guarantee the rural status quo, the continuance of the benefits conferred by the Revolution, economic prosperity and anti-Republican repression. This support might have been encouraged by the Emperor's social measures. Their liking for Napoleon III did not prevent the villagers from coming over to the Republic soon after 1871.

It was after this date that the Republicans managed gain acceptance for the idea that they alone knew how to guarantee a France which would be both rural and urban, industrial and agricultural, centralized but respectful of the village's authority, egalitarian but based on property. With great skill, Gambetta expressed this synthesis in his speech at Chateau-Chinon on 26 October 1877:

> The republic that we want is a republic of order, progress, thinking, general interest.... I do not want to flatter you, nor diminish you, but in a country as old as ours, and which has eight million farmers out of over ten million voters, it is certain that the destiny of the motherland and your own destinies will be in your hands.[4]

In fact, this 'rural-Republican' model resulted in a majority vote in favour of the regime, but it did not result in political uniformity. In 1968, Barral distinguished between 'republican democracies' (Lorraine, western Champagne), 'clerical democracies' (Léon, Flanders), 'neutral democracies' (Pays d'Auge, Loire Valley, etc), 'accepted hierarchies' (most of the west, from the Vendée to the inland Brittany), 'capitalist hierarchies' (the plains of the Paris Basin). 'Anti-clerical democracies' and 'contested hierarchies' were uncommon north of the Loire (except in some valleys or perhaps the urban fringes) (Barral, 1968). Rural France remained, therefore, pluralistic, so that a unified Republic was by no means incompatible with the continued persistence of 'small nations' (Chanet, 1996).

Organizations and opinions did not change much after 1918, although returning war veterans became rural personalities, but the various shocks fostered the emergence of conservative forces that in the 1930s seemed about to overwhelm the established parties. The *Parti agrarien* and *Paysan Français* led by Fleurant Agricola and the *Comités de Défense Paysanne* or *Chemise vertes* (green shirts) of Henri D'Halluin, nicknamed 'Dorgères', condemned the sacrifice of the farmers' interests and their leaders' collusion with politicians. They organized spectacular and populist demonstrations against taxes, land seizures, and so on, and operated at the crossroads between the awakening of popular emotions and a modernized populism (Paxton, 1997). Some socialist or communist organizations were reconstituted too, with, for example, the founding in 1933 of the *Confédération Générale des Paysans Travailleurs* which was influential in departments such as Finistère. A rural vote for the Popular Front emerged. But it was agrarian corporatism that placed its imprint upon rural northern France in the late 1930s.

The Vichy regime was the consequence of the defeat of 1940; but it also represented the corporatist view of the countryside. The *Union Nationale des Syndicats Agricoles* and its leader, Louis Salleron, proclaimed their support for Pétain. He extolled the French peasantry. The draft constitution summarized his approach: 'Integrated in the system of continental production and trade, France will become again, much to its advantage, agricultural and primarily peasant'. The Vichy law, 'On the corporate organization of agriculture' was promulgated on 2 December 1940. In 1942–43, the Peasant Corporation was officially established. Although there were numerous examples of peasant and rural support for the Resistance, the empathy of conservative leaders with 'corporatism' and 'peasantism' was undeniable (Boussard, 1980).

---

4 J. Reinach (ed.), *Discours et plaidoyers politiques de M. Gambetta* (11 vols, 1880–85), VII, pp. 320–37.

After 1945, this agrarian tradition promoted the restoration of unions, the creation of a *Parti Paysan* and powerful lobbying of government. When tariffs seemed an inadequate protection for agriculture, as in 1956, FNSEA organized demonstrations to protest against the decline in agricultural prices and in 1957 secured their pegging to an industrial prices index. Once again, the strength of the peasants was enough to secure their protection by the State.

But the restructuring of the 1960s changed the character of the co-management of agriculture by the state and agricultural organization. The promotion of 'family farms' and peasant unity was accompanied by a radical transformation of the structures of farms and markets. Although they were criticised by left-wing organizations opposed to the capitalist influence over agriculture, the majority of agricultural organizations remained a political force whose influence over government exceeded the numerical power of the peasants, not least through the ability of their leaders to play the role of brokers between France's countryside and the decision makers.

The social and political standing of the peasantry

Two opposed views of the character of the peasantry emerged in the preliminary assemblies of the Estates-General in 1789. A large part of enlightened opinion, including the Third Estate, considered the peasants to be incapable of political activity because of their lack of education: '*rustica progenies*' ('rustic race'), in the words of a sub-delegate from Hainaut. But, moderates such as Jacques Guillaume Thouret, a barrister from Rouen, disagreed: 'Be careful, above all, that the class of farmers who populate and fertilize the countryside are effectively represented. They are the foundation and the sinews of the nation'.[5] The first votes proved that they were right. But the revolutionary debates, above all after 1792, formulated contradictory and politicized points of view that we can sum as the contest between a Jacobin-Republican ideal of a peasant France to the physiocratic model of big owners and farmers. In fact, this duality is over simplistic, but its assimilation into historical writing, as much as its place in the political debates of the nineteenth century, have kept it alive (Jessenne, 2006).

This social vocabulary underwent a significant evolution after the Revolution, The terms *paysans* and *cultivateurs* – with their specific senses in French of a man who is living off agriculture for the first and an independent farmer, big or small, owner or leaseholder for the second – became widely employed and replaced the varied vocabulary from the *ancien régime*; and this helped the developing tendency to consider the peasantry as a unified whole although there were deep differences in farmers' conditions.

However, contemporaries had divergent and contradictory views of the peasantry. This may be seen in the writings of Honoré de Balzac and George Sand. Balzac's *The Peasants* (1844–55) were characterized by their amoral greed for land, increased by the French Revolution. In *La mare au diable* (1846) Sand stressed their natural innate

[5] 'Le fonds et le nerf de la nation': J. G. Touret, *Avis des bons Normands à leurs frères tous les bons Francais…* (1789), p. 55.

purity. During the Revolution of 1848 and the Second Republic, such contrary visions of the countryside were common. For some the countryside was a refuge, far from the threatening town, and a guarantee of the traditional order (for instance Vigny, Tocqueville); for others, rural people were the future of the French nation and Republic (Dupont, Michelet).

By about 1870 term 'rural' had taken on negative connotations when used in the press. It was largely due to the fact that the rural population supported Napoleon III and so by the end of the 1860s, they were considered backwards by town dwellers. Zola summarised up the changes that occurred afterwards: he successively described in *La Terre* (1887) the peasant driven by the passion of landownership and in *La Débâcle* (*The Collapse*) (1892) he drew the soldier-peasant as the last hope of France after the 1870 defeat. During the second half of the nineteenth century, there was also a new interest in painting the countryside. Painters were attracted to traditional scenes but also reflected the harsh realities of daily life: so Jules Breton, or Léon L'hermitte.

The Republicans were the main advocates of this reversal. They developed the notion that if the peasants had supported monarchs and emperors, it was out of ignorance; and so it was the Republic's duty to bring about change in the countryside. To this end, they established the Ministry of Agriculture in 1884 and introduced communal schools. Agricultural trade unions, in spite of their divisions and rivalries and the negative connotations of the term 'peasant', had, by the First World War, come to celebrate the peasant as the model Frenchman; thus, in 1913, the president of the Central Union of Agricultural Organisations (*l'Union centrale des syndicats des agriculteurs de France*) could be quoted as saying: 'What a marvellous race, these peasants from France, so full of endurance, courage and good sense! [Whether] under the soldier's tunic or behind the plough, nothing stops him'.[6]

Of course, the First World War was fought by a peasant army, and it was they who bore the brunt of the slaughter. Hence it is not surprising that the glorification of the peasant came to a head between the two world wars, with themes like the land as a guarantee of essential national values and morals, or peasant unity as bastion against the class struggle and the disorder generated by the towns and socialism. The corporatism under the Vichy government was the high point of this vision of the peasantry.

Strangely, the 'ideal' that the interest of the nation and its peasants were one and the same, has, despite the misadventures of the Vichy government, strongly influenced the representation of the countryside in public opinion. So, we have to be careful to take note of its contradictions: on one hand, the united peasantry is a myth, for it has never been homogeneous; and on the other, despite claims of unity, the peasantry has always been divided.

The image of the peasant *cul terreux* ('bumpkin'), struggling to cope with the modern world, is both simple and full of complexity. It did not easily disappear, as Michel Debatisse showed in his book *The Silent Revolution, peasants' struggle* (1963). However

[6] Barral, *Agrariens français*, p. 11.

in a France which was less and less 'peasant', negative representations of the peasantry decreased, while, the accent, the artisan products, the simplicity of the costume, were more and more seen as signs of authenticity. Above all, there was an anxiety and sense of regret arising from the realisation that the peasant world was disappearing. The songs, the novels and the cinema articulated, with varying degrees of idealization, that sense of loss. It may be observed that these nostalgic representations of the countryside show mountains and sun and feature the small scale farming from the south of the Loire much more than the large scale farming of the north.

These idealised visions have willingly been adopted by the French ruling classes. Jacques Chirac (President of the Republic, 1995–2006) in particular, cultivated this tradition and maintained his links with agricultural circles. His decision to do so can be partly explained by the lack of alternatives. The parties of the French left have wavered between analyses of peasant conditions in terms of class struggle, and drawing on a vision of a France fortified by her rural roots. It was Mitterrand, the socialist candidate, who in 1981 placed a village and its church steeple in the background of his posters for his presidential campaign.

In the end, the clichés persist. In their work, with the provocative title *L'archipel paysan, la fin de la république agricole* (*The peasant archipelago,* 2001), in which they question contemporary 'rurality', the sociologists Bertrand Hervieu and Jean Viard very clearly warn us: 'Let's accept that perhaps more than in other cultures, we grasp the question of the countryside through a thick veil of symbolic investments, imaginary or political, in which history prevails over nature as such'.[7]

[7] Bertrand Hervieu and Jean Viard, *L'archipel paysan, la fin de la république agricole* (2001), p. 12.

Bibliography:

Statistique de la France (1838–48), vols 3 and 4; (1867) *Résultats de l'enquête décennale de 1862*; (1887) *Résultats de l'enquête décennale de 1882.*

Agreste, Ministère de l'alimentation, de l'agriculture et de la pêche, la statistique Agreste; http://agreste.agriculture.gouv.fr.

Barral, P. (1993) 'Le secteur agricole dans la France industrialisée, 1950–74', in F. Braudel and E. Labrousse (eds), *Histoire économique et sociale de la France*, IV (3), pp. 1427–66, Paris.

Barral, P. (1968) *Les agrariens français de Méline à Pisani,* Paris.

Béaur, G. (2000) *Histoire agraire de la France au XVIIIe siecle,* Paris.

Bodinier, B. and Teyssier, E. (2000) *L'événement le plus important de la Révolution: la vente des biens nationaux en France et dans les territoires annexés, 1789–1867*, Paris.

Bonnamour, J. (1984) *Paysages agraires et sociétés,* Paris.

Boussard, Isabel (1980) *Vichy et la corporation paysanne,* Paris.

Braudel, F. and E. Labrousse (eds), *Histoire économique et sociale de la France* (4 vols in eight, 1970–92), III, *1789–1880* (1976); IV (1–2), *1880–1950* (1979, new edn, 1993); IV (3), *1950–80* (1982).

Chanet, J.-F. (1996) *L'Ecole républicaine et les petites patries,* Paris.

Demonet, M. (1990) *Tableau de l'agriculture française au milieu du 19*[e] siècle. *L'enquête agricole de 1852*, Paris.

Duby, G. and A. Wallon (eds) *Histoire de la France rurale* (Paris, 4 vols, 1975–6, new edn. 1992).

Farcy, J.-C. (1989) *Les Paysans beaucerons au XIX*[e] *siècle,* Chartres.

Follain, A. (2007) *Le village sous l'Ancien Régime,* Paris.

Gavignaud, G. (1996) *La révolution rurale dans la France contemporaine, 18*[e]*-20*[e] *siecle*, Paris.

Hervieu, B. and Viard J. (2001) *L'archipel paysan, la fin de la république agricole,* La Tour d'Aigues.

Hubscher, R. (1979) *L'agriculture et la société rurale dans le Pas-de-Calais, du milieu du XIX*[e] *siècle à 1914*, Arras.

Jessenne, J.-P. (2006) *Les campagnes françaises entre mythe et histoire,* Paris.

Jones, P. (1989) *The peasantry and the French Revolution*, Cambridge.

Le Goff, T. J. A. and Sutherland, D. M. G. (1999) 'La révolution française et l'économie rurale', *Histoire et Mesure*, 14, pp. 79–120.

Lévy-Leboyer, M. and Désert G. (1972) *Le revenu agricole et la rente foncière en Basse-Normandie*, Paris.

Moulin, A. (1988), *Les paysans dans la société française de la Révolution à nos jours,* Paris; trans. (1991) *Peasantry and society in France since 1789*, Cambridge.

Nicolas, J. (2002) *La rébellion française,* Paris.

Paxton, R.O. (1997) *French Peasant Fascism, Henri Dorgères, Greenshirts and the crisis of French agriculture, 1929-39,* New York.

Pécout, G. (1994) 'La politisation des paysans au XIXe siècle', *Histoire et Sociétés Rurales* 2, pp. 279–92.

Postel-Vinay, G. (1998) *La terre et l'argent, L'agriculture et l'argent en France du XVIII*[e] *au début du XX*[e] *siècle*, Paris.

Vivier, N. (1998) *Propriété collective et identité communale. Les biens communaux en France, 1750–1914,* Paris.

Vivier, N. (ed.) (2009) *State and rural societies. Policy and education in Europe, 1750–2000,* Turnhout.

THE LOW COUNTRIES

(Belgium and the Netherlands)

Barn of the Cistercian abbey of Ter Doest in Lissewege (Flanders), *c.* 1300
(Photograph: E. Thoen, 2010)

7 The Low Countries, 1000–1750*

Bas VAN BAVEL, Piet VAN CRUYNINGEN and Erik THOEN

7.1 Ownership, power relations and the distribution of property

Types of landowners and lords

Within the Low Countries, landownership and lordship was structured quite differently in the north and south from the early Middle Ages onwards. The south of the Low Countries was part of, or proximate to, the core area of the Merovingian and Carolingian Empires. Here, in some of the most densely populated parts of early medieval Europe, great estates were relatively common. Kings held extensive areas out of which many members of the upper nobility, as well as newly created religious institutions, were granted large domains. The post-Carolingian period, broadly the tenth to twelfth centuries, saw the atrophy of central authority and the appearance of new structures of relatively strong lordship and manorial control. In these centuries, lords appropriated the *bannum* and created a patchwork of seigneuries, sometimes partly based on the old power structures and landownership but also on new sources of local power, acting as protectors of ecclesiastical domains (*advocati, villici*) for instance. This does not mean that freeholders did not survive the early Middle Ages, but they were reduced in numbers. In the southern Low Countries most land became a tenure and had to pay rent to its local lords.

As everywhere else, when central power weakened after the year 1000, lordship based on judicial power became more dispersed. It was in the areas where lords had previously held the largest estates that powerful seigneuries, exercising all levels of judicial power, tended to appear. Over the course of the Middle Ages, the emerging overlords (the count of Flanders, the duke of Brabant, the count of Hainault, etc.) could only slowly reduce the power of the local seigneuries.

However, one of the earliest but most powerful principalities emerged in the second half of the ninth century, namely the county of Flanders. Its heartland lay in the coastal area. From an early period the counts created local territorial units (*ambachten*) administered by local officers. In this way they could avoid the emergence of powerful local seigneuries. Similar structures were found also in the coastal area of the northern Low Countries.

Later, largely independent principalities emerged everywhere in the Low Countries. As in many areas of Europe, over the course of the twelfth and thirteenth centuries, most of the local lords had to surrender much of their power to the princely overlords who gradually centralised judicial power, sometimes by using military force. This

* We would like to thank Tim Soens for some data and Richard Paping and Christopher Dyer for their comments on an earlier version of this chapter.

Map 7.1 The Low Countries, 1000–1750

process proceeded fastest and earliest in the most urbanised areas, such as the county of Flanders and a little later the duchy of Brabant, due to the political alliance between the overlord and the cities which had emerged as a power in their own right and saw benefits in the elimination of the influence of the local lordly class (Thoen, 1988). At the end of the thirteenth century, after a period of inflation, many local lords experienced serious difficulties with their incomes due to the inefficient structure of their estates, and only the largest survived. Those lords who accepted offices in service of the overlords formed the basis of the centralised administration of the Burgundian state.

The northern Low Countries (including the northernmost part of Flanders) were characterised by free peasant landownership, especially in the coastal areas, but also in the inland sandy regions, wherever the extension of settlement and cultivation had been undertaken bit by bit by peasants. As a consequence, in these areas peasants paid no rents or at most symbolic rents as a recognition of the judicial power of the overlords, while local lordship was also weak.

There were, however, exceptions to this situation in the northern parts of the Low Countries. Manorial lords had large estates in the fertile Guelders river area and the adjacent river clay districts. From the seventh century, there had been a powerful aristocratic elite here, whose members held manors and serfs. Large church estates, often administered in, or organised as manors, were also found (Dekker; van Bavel, 1993). Later, local lords with noble titles appeared in the northern Low Countries as well, but they were never as significant, nor did they have such an effect on the freedom or possession of the peasants, as lords in many areas of the southern Low Countries. More important was the emergence of territorial principalities. One of these, and one of the most-developed, was the county of Holland.

Other factors help explain why there was such a big difference between the north and the south of the Low Countries in the importance of local seigneurial power. First, many areas in the north were integrated into the Merovingian-Carolingian empire at a late stage, and as a result, the central government remained weaker and the number of royal estates smaller. Some areas along the river Rhine form an exception (van Bavel, 2010a: 52–63). To the north, the Frisians were long able to resist the authority of the Merovingian and Carolingian dynasties. Second, the plunderings of the Vikings in this area between the ninth and eleventh centuries, and especially the first wave of attacks, which started *c.* 800 but dramatically increased around *c.* 830, may have caused a retreat of the local lords towards the area south of the Scheldt and the river Meuse. Their absence allowed the local population to develop a relatively high degree of self-government. As early as 820 there was a *conjuratio* (a sworn association) of peasants, established without the consent of the local lords, in the administrative unit called *Mempiscus* in coastal Flanders. Third, from the eighth century, but at an accelerated pace from the eleventh, a number of regions were opened up, occupied and reclaimed, notably the vast peatlands in Holland and the adjacent area in the prince-bishopric of Utrecht. This process strengthened the position of peasants as landowners. The nobility and church played only a minor role in this expansion. Rather, it was the territorial lords and princes (as holders of the regalian rights over the wastes) and the peasants (as colonisers) who played the key roles. In order to attract people to reclaim these inhospitable lands, the princes offered the peasant-colonisers personal freedom and full property rights over their holdings (Van der Linden, 1956). These were family holdings of an equal size, of 13 ha, giving society here an egalitarian character.

Changing social property distribution

As elsewhere in Europe, the High Middle Ages (the eleventh to thirteenth centuries) were characterised by fundamental changes in property structures. First, in general terms, peasant property was expanding through reclamation. This was especially widespread in Flanders and Holland from the tenth century, but according to recent archaeological results, areas in the northern parts of the Low Countries were also taken under the plough at this time. These reclamations stopped in the thirteenth century in the most populated areas but continued in some northern parts of the Low Countries throughout the later Middle Ages. As a result of this extensive colonisation, large estates increased in an absolute sense, but peasant property by much more. Even where lords succeeded in establishing customary rents, as was the case in many areas of the southern Low Countries during the twelfth–fourteenth centuries, there was a tendency towards the establishment of stronger peasant property rights. At the same time, the area of demesne directly cultivated by large landowners was reduced in size. Almost everywhere demesnes were divided and given in hereditary tenure to peasants (*accensement* or *arrentement*).

This process is connected with another important change in social property structures: the dissolution of manorialism. In those regions where manorialism had existed, most corvées were progressively abolished over the twelfth, thirteenth and fourteenth centuries. In most of the county of Flanders labour services had ceased by the twelfth century. In some parts of the southern, Walloon provinces, where the bipartite manorial system had developed most fully, they survived longer but declined in importance. This development happened long before the Black Death so it cannot be attributed to demographic catastrophe. Rather, the growing opportunities offered by urban and local markets and market exchange encouraged manorial lords to dissolve their manors. Their increased desire for cash to buy luxury products persuaded them to agree to the abolition of corvées and the conversion of rents in kind into money rents. Peasants equally profited from the change to money rents since rural markets, becoming very common in the twelfth century, could function better with a greater circulation of money. Due to inflation – which continued into the late fourteenth century – customary rents lost value to the peasants' advantage. In those regions where territorial lords also took over judicial and banal rights from local lords, there was a clear diminishing influence of the lordly class in the thirteenth and fourteenth centuries. Peasants considered the land – although it was charged with rents – more and more as exclusively their property. This was especially true in those principalities where the power of the manorial lords was counterbalanced by strong territorial lords. Where the territorial lord was able to ally with an emerging urban bourgeoisie (as was most pronounced in the county of Flanders), this evolution took place even faster.

The erosion of the power of the lords did not happen everywhere. In some areas with strong manorial structures and serfdom, most of the former holdings of the serfs became the full property of the former manorial lords, while the people living on those holdings gained their personal freedom but lost their property rights in their land. Here, the dissolution of manorialism did not mean a fundamental break in social property systems, but rather a renegotiation of relations between social groups, while the balance between these groups remained the same. In a region such as the Guelders river area, formerly characterised by strong manorialism, for instance, noblemen, princes and monasteries, the former manorial lords, emerged in the later fourteenth century as the owners of some 85 per cent of the land. We can identify some possible causes of this development: its relatively late, weaker urbanization, the absence of a powerful bourgeoisie and the fact that noblemen retained jurisdictional rights over the countryside. Where local noblemen lost judicial power to the princes due to a power struggle within the lordly class itself, large landownership itself generally diminished in importance. Most princes were not focussed on building up new landed estates so much as concerned to acquire new revenues such as tolls and taxes.

These developments could reverse the social hierarchy of the early and high Middle Ages. However, there were also regions in the Low Countries where manorialism did not disappear so quickly. It lingered in the easternmost parts, such as the Achterhoek, where its weight had never been heavy, but some of its elements remained until the late eighteenth century. Here, lords here retained jurisdictional and other seigneurial/banal rights and even some corvées. The same is true of several Walloon areas in the south-east of the Low Countries, where some traditional customs survived, but, as in many areas of France, these were often no more than a faint echo of the high medieval situation.

Next to the growing property rights of the peasants, another feature of the High Middle Ages was the increased property of ecclesiastical institutions. New orders such as the Cistercians and the Premonstratensians, for instance, received large estates as pious donations. Nevertheless, their role in changing property structures must not be exaggerated for two reasons: first, these orders were not as numerous in the Low Countries as in many other western European countries, and second, they were much less active in reclamation activities than has often been suggested by historians. Exceptions are the Frisian clay areas and the Guelders river area, where monastic houses owned up to a quarter of the land. But elsewhere, and especially in the more urbanized areas, much more weight should be assigned to the influence of religious institutions founded as an aspect of the growth of the towns from the thirteenth century onwards. Many hospitals, urban religious institutions such as churches and mendicant orders, and poor relief institutions acquired estates and rents in the countryside.

In the later Middle Ages, changes in property systems continued, but these were fundamental only in a few regions, such as the coastal area of Flanders and some areas of Holland. In Holland peasant property was diminishing due to growing environmental problems and difficulties with subsistence farming. The combination of these difficulties allowed large landowners to acquire peasant land which they subsequently leased (Thoen and Soens, 2008). One dimension of this, especially from the late thirteenth century, was the growth of landownership by townspeople. Towns grew and the urbanisation rate in the Low Countries reached some 30 to 40 per cent by 1500. The growing wealth of townspeople led to massive investments in rural landownership, partly for prestige, partly as a source of direct provisioning of urban households, but also as an investment.

The purchase of landed property by merchants is no longer seen as a 'betrayal' of trade and manufacturing. On the contrary, it was a necessary part of the financial policy of merchants, reducing risks and making investment possible since the land could be used as security for loans. Over the whole of the Low Countries, with the exception of the Ardennes, townspeople owned perhaps one-fifth of the land in the mid-sixteenth century, but in highly urban areas such as central Holland, the proportion was nearer to two-fifths (van Bavel, 2009). Peasant landownership still persisted. Even in Holland around 1500, about half of the land was still owned by smallholding peasants. In the inland, sandy regions, their share was substantially higher.

At the end of the middle ages, the Low Countries show a wide diversity in social property structures. This is summarised in Table 7.1. There were regions where 80–90 per cent of the cultivated land was owned by peasants, for example in Drenthe and in the peat areas of Holland, or in sandy Flanders, Limbourg and the adjacent parts of Liège, but also regions where half or even three-quarters of the land was owned by sovereign lords, noblemen and ecclesiastical institutions, such as Salland, the Guelders river area and the northern part of the Walloon districts (Hesbaye, Condroz, north of the Ardennes). The table also shows a general association between lordly property and church property. This was clearly an inheritance from the period when great lords made grants from their estates to the church. On the other hand, where peasant property had once been dominant, townsmen had, by the end of the Middle Ages, acquired a large proportion of the land: the growth of urban landownership occurred at the expense of the peasants.

In the early modern period, land ownership by townspeople continued to expand. This happened in sandy soil areas such as the area near Ghent and Antwerp, but the growth of urban ownership of rural land was particularly prevalent in the polders created in sixteenth- and seventeenth-century Holland. Around 1620, 50 per cent or more of the 'old' land in Holland was owned by urban landowners, but their share of the newly-created polders was nearer 80–90 per cent. Particularly in the southern part of Holland, where urbanisation was strongest, wealthy bourgeois continued to buy numerous plots of land from peasants, thus turning small-scale peasant property into large-scale absentee-owned property. This process was accelerated by the civil disturbances and warfare at the end of the sixteenth century. The peasantry, who lacked capital reserves, were especially hard hit by the devastation of the countryside. Perhaps also contributing to this process was the socio-economic polarisation inherent in the rise of proto-industrial activities, in which large parts of the rural population in Holland were engaged (van Zanden, 1993: 11–39; van Bavel, 2003). This, however, should be linked to the capital-intensive character of proto-industries in Holland and the growing dominance of urban investors. In inland Flanders, the labour-intensive types of proto-industries, such as spinning, allowed the peasants to cling on to their diminishing holdings by offering them some additional income.

Table 7.1 Some regions in the Low Countries for which a quantitative reconstruction of the social distribution of land ownership before 1750 has been made (per cent)

Region	Year	Territorial princes and Nobility	Eccclesi-astical houses	Burghers	Non-noble rural population
Netherlands					
Drenthe	*c.* 1630	6	7	0	87
Holland	*c.* 1550	10	10	25	55
Central part of Holland	*c.* 1620	10	8	55	27
Land van Culemborg West (Holland)	*c.* 1550	15	16	16	53
Land van Heusden (Holland)	*c.* 1550	9	21	18	51
Tielerwaard/Waal (Guelders)	*c.* 1550	29	27	14	30
Salland (Overijssel)	1520	32	18	25	25
Land van Buren (Guelders)	*c.* 1550	37	34	8	21
Beesd and Rhenoy +Tielerwaard/Linge (Guelders)	*c.* 1550	36	43	5	16
West Zeeuws-Vlaanderen	1665	3	14	73	12
Land van Culemborg Oost (Guelders)	*c.* 1550	44	30	24	2
Belgium					
Tournaisis	*c.* 1591	21	30	28	21
Oost-Vlaanderen	*c.* 1570	11	9	20	60
West-Vlaanderen (sandy area)	1699	22	9	11	58

Table 7.1 (*Continued*)

Region	Year	Territorial princes and Nobility	Eccclesi-astical houses	Burghers	Non-noble rural population
Coastal area Flanders	*c.* 1390	6	21	15	57
Coastal area Flanders	*c.* 1550	?	33	33	34
Polder area West-Vlaanderen	1569–78	19	20	12	49
Area of Antwerp (Brabant)	*c.* 1570	14	38	25	15
Polder area near Antwerp	1732	42[a]	8		50
Campine Liégoise	18th C.	4	4	17	76
Herve (Liège)	1686	11	3	0	76
Hesbaye Liégioise/ Hutoise	18th C	18	31	12	39
Fagne-Famenne Liégoise	18th C	33	3	12	52
Ardennes e. Sambre-Meuse	18th C	35	2	2	56
Condroz Liégoise	18th C	57	7	10	27
Ardennes (Durbuy)	18th C	44	15	0	42

Note: the area of common is not taken into account.

[a] includes bourgeois

Sources : Drenthe, Bieleman, 1987: 256; Holland, *c.*1550, De Vries, 1974; Holland, *c.*1620, estimate Van Bavel, 2009: 182–84; Land van Culemborg West (Holland), Van Bavel, 1999: 392; Land van Heusden (Holland), Hoppenbrowers, 1992: 819–833; Tielerwaal (Guelders), Van Bavel, 1999: 392; Salland (Overijssel), Slicher van Bath, 1957: 618; Land van Buren (Guelders), Van Bavel, 1999: 392; Beesd and Rhenoy +Tielerwaard/Linge (Guelders), Van Bavel, 1999: 392; W. Zeeuws-Vlaaanderen, Van Cruyningen, 2000: 104; Land van Culoost (Guelders),Van Bavel, 1999: 392; Tournaisis, Billen, 1983; Oost-Vlaanderen, *c.*1570, Van Den Abbeele, 1985; West-Vlaanderen, 1699, De Kezel, 1988: 102; Coastal area of Flanders, c.*1390, c.1550*, Soens, 2009: 97–99; Polder area West-Vlaanderen, 1569–78, Vandewalle, 1986: 123–34; Area around Antwerp (Brabant), Limberger, 2008: 200–06 (this line includes 15 per cent unknown); Polder area near Antwerp, De Kezel, 1988: 102; Campine Liégoise, Delatte, 1945; Herve (Liège), 1686, Ruwet, 1943; Hesbaye Liégioise/Hutoise, Delatte, 1945; Fagne-Famenne Liégoise, Delatte, 1945; Ardennes and Sambre-Meuse, Delatte, 1945; Condroz Liégoise, Delatte, 1945; Ardennes (Durbuy), Pirotte, 1974.

As a result of these developments, the medieval pattern of landownership in these parts of Holland was transformed from one of peasant ownership into medium and large-scale landholding. The same happened in Zeeland Flanders, although here peasant ownership had already diminished in the previous centuries. On average, the share of urban landownership in the seventeenth century was probably close to 60 per cent in Holland and over 70 per cent in Western Zeeland Flanders, similar to the high percentages found in north and central Italy. However, Holland and Zeeland were exceptions within the Low Countries, for in most other districts, no more than a quarter of the total area was owned by townspeople. Only the areas around Antwerp, the Belgian coastal plain and the area near Tournais surpassed this share. Elsewhere, during the early modern period, urban landownership increased more slowly. Plots of land were not restructured into new large holdings but continued to be cultivated by the smallholding peasants, who often retained the ownership of their farmsteads, but now had to lease additional land, which increased their costs. Around the middle of the eighteenth century, certain areas witnessed a slight increase in peasant landownership, as in Zeeland, where some large tenant farmers became substantial property owners (van Cruyningen, 2000: 245, 305; Priester, 1998: 150). However, this reversal of long-standing tendencies did not fundamentally change the existing property structures.

The characteristic feature of property relations in the Low Countries is that in most areas – but not universally – the peasantry acquired freehold property rights at an early date. But in the most urbanised regions this proved to be a Trojan Horse by which urban investors could enter rural land markets and, in effect, dispossess the peasantry by purchase. Urban possession became even more entrenched by the mechanisms of wasteland enclosure. Whereas this had been driven by peasants acting under the authority of the territorial overlords in the eleventh and twelfth centuries, in the sixteenth and seventeenth it was undertaken by consortia of investors and little of the reclaimed land came to be held in owner-occupation.

Systems of tenure and their efficiency as the means of surplus extraction

The main trend in systems of tenure was that property rights to land became more absolute and exclusive over time. This was a slow process, involving the dissolution of manorialism, the enclosure of commons, the atrophy of village systems of agriculture and the reduction of the rights of kin over property (van Bavel, 2010a: 164–72). As elsewhere in Europe, many different forms of tenure existed in the High Middle Ages. Some of them originated in the manorial system, others were the result of new lettings (sometimes due to reclamations), and others had a seigneurial origin (with the growth of the *banal seigneurie*). However, quite early, in the course of the twelfth century in most parts of the Low Countries, the origin of these tenures ceased to matter and the difference between them was mainly in the level of rent. Even the distinction between conventional tenures and *métayage* – a form of tenure found especially in the south – diminished, since these sharecropping rents often became fixed.

In most parts of the southern Low Countries, almost every plot was subject to a rent and can therefore be seen as a tenure. Allods were scarce, except for small areas within the seigneurie, mostly the village centres, which were called *libertates* (free areas). (This is mainly found in southern Flanders, Hainault and Brabant.) From the High Middle Ages, most forms of peasant tenure could be split up, sold and inherited as if freehold, and most non-allodial land owed the payment of a fine on its transfer. However these were never as high as in England. From the thirteenth century in Flanders, Hainault and Namur, tenures could also be sublet, and this allowed non-resident landowners an entry into these land markets. So, in the Low Countries, and especially the northern Netherlands and the coastal areas where a great deal of freehold peasant property was created during the colonisation and reclamation processes, property rights developed which were especially favourable to the peasantry.

At the same time, a new type of tenure started to emerge in the thirteenth century. The rise of short term leasing, of ten or twelve years' duration, was facilitated by the emergence of more sharply delineated, exclusive, property rights to land. However, the peasant idea that tenants should be considered owners of the land they worked died only slowly. It was disappearing in the late thirteenth century from (especially coastal) Flanders, in the fourteenth/fifteenth centuries from the Guelders river area, but only over the course of the sixteenth century in Holland, with its strong peasant tradition (van Bavel, 2009). In parts of the Low Countries, the lease was adopted quickly and on a large scale, especially in the decades around 1300. Partly this happened as a reaction of the lords against the decline of their real incomes from fixed (often cash) rents. However some resistance against this evolution can be found. Long term and even hereditary leases were frequently used at the beginning of this process, especially in the southern Low Countries. In fact, leasehold may conceal continued peasant claims to hereditary property rights. In Holland, peasants as late as the fifteenth century still claimed the customary right to silent re-letting (*tacita reconductio*), the continuation of leases on the same terms without the consent of the landowner. In some cases, tenants even sold the right to take a new term to third parties or granted it away as part of marriage or inheritance settlements. A similar situation can be found elsewhere in the north of the Low Countries, as in parts of Overijssel, Friesland and Groningen (Formsma, 1981). In the latter region, tenants had strong rights over the land they leased, rents were almost frozen and leases were normally either renewed or transmitted by inheritance, even though in theory the lease was only granted for a limited term. In practice, this system of leasing led to a kind of hereditary lease or even outright ownership for the tenant.

Still, by the sixteenth century the only distinction that mattered was between property (*eygendom*) and short-term leasehold (*huer*), even if the older categories of land tenure survived in a legal sense. The early predominance of this new dichotomy was, in a general sense, the result of the swift pace of the fundamental change in society and economy in most parts of the Low Countries, and the early commoditization of land. This evolution was to a large extent a consequence of the early change of labour rents into money rents which were devalued in the twelfth and thirteenth centuries. In many principalities, the power structure played a part as well. The struggle between the territorial lords, the towns, the nobility and the church favoured the peasant until leaseholding made its appearance. The gradual reception of Roman law also had some influence. But more important still was increasing state taxation. When direct taxation on land and/or other real property was put on a regular annual footing – in the principalities constituting the present-day Low Countries this happened from the late fourteenth century onwards – the state as tax collector had to decide who it should assess: the 'owner' of the land or the occupier who cultivated it? The need to identify who was liable promoted the idea that all kinds of hereditary and feudal tenure were really a single type of property.

These changes in property rights had serious consequences for the owners of land. The evolution towards stronger property rights and lower real rents for the peasant tenant, especially in periods of inflation such as the thirteenth century, caused income losses for many large landowners. The old nobility and the church suffered from this, especially in areas where commercialisation proceeded quickly (such as Flanders and Brabant). They could not launch a seigneurial reaction to recover ground because they faced the opposition of the territorial lords. It is no coincidence that many lords went bankrupt from the thirteenth century. The inadequacy of their landed income propelled the nobility towards becoming a service nobility. Only in the southern and easternmost parts of the Low Countries could the nobility could retain at least some of its earlier power, because here developments evolved more slowly. The only non-peasant classes that maintained their position were those who adapted the new forms of leasehold tenancy: the substantial (tenant) farmers but especially, from the late thirteenth century, the new class of bourgeois owners.

Two systems of tenure remained at the end of the Middle Ages. One was where the peasants had a full property or freehold in their land. In this case, extraction of the peasant surplus was by owners of tithes and by the state in the form of taxes. The other type of tenure was where the owners of the freehold, whether large estates or people resident in towns, gave their tenants short-term leases for cash rents. Here too tithes and taxes were levied (although their burden was often shared between owners and tenants). In the Guelders river area, but even more in the polders created in sixteenth and seventeenth-century Holland, Zeeland and coastal Flanders, this resulted in the appearance of agrarian capitalism, with a tripartite hierarchy of large landowners, big tenant farmers and wage labourers and a high surplus extraction level. In both cases, there were also princely taxes, growing in importance and sometimes taking several per cent of the gross yield.

The economic and social value of land

The disappearance of those landowners who could not maintain their real incomes, and the adoption of peasant leasehold tenancies by landowners who successfully navigated the inflation of the late Middle Ages brought about important changes in peasant society and the way the land was managed. In the High Middle ages, the subsistence needs of the family and the rent (and tax) burden directly influenced production. Commons still played their role in this process, although there were areas such as Flanders and Holland where the common fields were rapidly reduced in scale in the twelfth and thirteenth centuries. Rural markets already existed in the twelfth century but probably only served a local trade in agricultural products and foodstuffs for subsistence. With the growing population, and partly due to the changing property structures, a bustling land market emerged in which the peasants were especially active. On the other hand there were the large holdings and demesnes. Demesne production was partly geared to supply the needs of the lords' households, as can be shown for the estates of the count of Flanders in the eleventh and twelfth centuries, and partly aimed at supplying the emerging formal and informal commodity markets. In the period 1100–1400, as trade grew, the lords increasingly retreated from the management of their demesnes, first reducing them in size and finally leasing them in their entirety to farmers. This was especially the case in Flanders. Production and investment decisions were now increasingly made by farmers, while surplus extraction and inheritance possibilities influenced their production strategies. Relations between lords and farmers developed in new ways.

In some regions, the decreasing importance of traditional rents and the growing importance of leaseholding played a large part in the transition of social agro-systems in the later middle ages. In regions like coastal Flanders and the Guelders river area, the structure of rural economy and society underwent an early and profound transition, mainly as the result of the rise of large tenant farms. In coastal Flanders, this process was propelled by environmental stress, to a large extent caused by the erection of dikes, high water management costs and the damaging consequences of over-drainage. These elements contributed to the expulsion of the small peasant owners from their lands from the late thirteenth century onwards. This process was intensified by the prevailing power structures. The territorial lords had full seigneurial power in the region which allowed them to expropriate the peasants after storm surges and regrant their land to large investors, often ecclesiastical institutions, and later urban investors and state officers.

These environmental elements were not necessary for this process to take place, as the example of the Guelders river area shows. Here, tenant farmers took the opportunities offered by the ready availability of land for lease to increase their holding size and ultimately dominate the leasehold land market. Large capitalist farms, worked by wage labour, gradually pushed to one side medium-size and small holdings, worked by the family's own labour. In the course of this process, which went hand in hand with sharp social polarisation, a highly specialised and commercialised agriculture emerged, being at the same time capital-intensive and labour-extensive. This resulted in relatively low physical yields, but also in high labour productivity and large surpluses. The rise of large tenant farms in the Guelders river area and in regions such as coastal Flanders resulted in a halving in the number of farms over a century or more. Thousands of families lost their leasehold land and hence the possibility of operating a farm independently. They became reliant on wage labour for their livelihood, the value of which was itself in decline (van Bavel, 2010a: 246–8).

Another region where social relations changed was Holland. Here, in the later Middle Ages, peasants on their smallholdings combined a labour-intensive agriculture, probably with a rather low labour productivity, with proto-industrial activities.

The land was mostly owned by smallholding peasants with some additional leasing of small plots of land. The proto-industrial sector displayed a strong dynamism here in the fourteenth and fifteenth centuries, with the emergence of highly capital-intensive industries and wage labour. But a second stage of the process, from the middle of the sixteenth century onwards, saw the transformation of the rural economy with the rise of large landownership, and the emergence of large-scale agriculture, capitalist farming and agricultural specialisation (de Vries, 1974; van Bavel, 2003).

In inland Flanders change was much less radical. This district, as well as large parts of Hainault, had evolved a system of social relations similar to Holland, with a predominance of small landowners. However, they co-existed in a kind of symbiosis - via wage earning - with larger holdings owned by the absentee upper classes, often held by lessees. The fragmentation of holdings as a result of population growth especially in the late fifteenth and sixteenth centuries, which was further intensified by the development of proto-industrial activities, forced the smaller peasant-owners to participate in a mixed farming system with very high yields per hectare, high labour inputs but low levels of labour productivity. In contrast to Holland though, this structure remained stable until the nineteenth century, although the polarisation between larger (leased) holdings and ever-smaller (owned) holdings increased over time. The smallholders were forced to become increasingly active in the land market as well as in the commodity and credit markets in order to survive. Over the course of the early modern period, the production per unit area further increased, with the progressive disappearance of fallow land and the adoption of 'up and down husbandry' in the crop rotation and field systems, the famous 'Flemish Husbandry'.

A further form of social relations is found in the sandy inland districts such as Drenthe, in the north-eastern part of the Low Countries. Here, the peasant structure with extensive common fields remained intact over the centuries; there was no structural transformation of rural economy and society. Yields – despite slight tendencies towards intensification – remained low. On their small and medium-sized farms, peasant families concentrated on the cultivation of bread grains and some small-scale livestock farming, mainly for their own subsistence, although in the seventeenth century the middling farmers also raised horses and oxen for sale on the urban markets in Holland. In the sandy Campine area, developments were more akin to those in inland Flanders, although here common fields survived much longer. The result in both Drenthe and Campine was that the yields per hectare in the infields were almost as high as in Flanders, but the total output was much lower due to the much larger size and infertility of the outfields.

A final type of agrarian regime is found in some parts of the Walloon provinces. In regions such as the Condroz, the Hesbaye and the Ardennes, very large farms are found, often originating in the early medieval manorial system. However, these were mostly surrounded by a mass of small peasant property holders, sometimes active in proto-industry (cloth, iron). The large farms, which often specialised in dairy and meat production, were worked with a mix of temporary workers and full-time wage labourers. The big distinction between these areas and others such as Flanders and Holland was the survival of large common woods and temporary cultivated areas (*assartage*).

We know very little about the productivity of farms in these areas in the Middle Ages and the early modern period, but the system had evolved towards one with high productivity of both land and labour by the end of the *ancien régime*.

The cultural value of land

Tenancy cannot be separated from the fundamental role land played in the strategies of both lords and peasants. For the latter, the possession of land was a cornerstone in a variety of survival strategies aimed at securing household control over vital resources, although in most parts of the highly commercialized Low Countries, this consideration weighed less than in other parts of Europe. Recent research shows that the peasant societies of the Low Countries were always active in the land market. However, as in large parts of Flanders, the plots of lands on which the farmstead was situated were rarely sold: peasants were very attached to their houses. As we shall see below, the ownership of land and designated tenements also offered access to office in the village community.

For the lords, landownership and ownership of banal rights were the keys to lordship itself as well as to high social status. Even if the income of the banal rights had been eroded in many areas since the thirteenth century, the ownership of land and titles remained an important source of social prestige. From the later Middle Ages, noblemen were often 'collectors of seigneurial titles', even if many seigneuries no longer had a castle or seigneurial centre. Only in areas like Holland, where the nobility was traditionally weak, did this prestige diminish in the course of the early modern period (Dewald, 1996: 65–67 and 76–77). Moreover, many lords and large landowners, even though they had preferred to live in the towns from an early date, kept a link with their rural estates via the reservation of rooms in their farms or by building country seats, especially after 1500 and notably in the area around Antwerp and in Holland along the river Vecht. Until the seventeenth century, rural holdings retained some importance for the provisioning of both the nobility and the rich bourgeoisie in periods of shortage and high prices. However, after 1700, aristocrats, bourgeois and large landowners increasingly broke the link with their rural estates, leaving their administration to stewards.

7.2 The occupiers of the land

Farm sizes

Smallholdings predominated over the whole of the Low Countries. This fragmentation was due to population pressure, early erosion of demesne farming and manorialism, the precocious development of a market system and urban sector, and the peasant-led expansion into the coastal wastes.

There were large variations however in the size of holdings, and these increased with the development of rural capitalism in certain areas in the later Middle Ages and after. Generally speaking, small peasant farming developed furthest on the sandy soils in the east and south, while commercial farms of more than twenty hectares apiece appeared especially on the clay soils along the coast and in the central river area. However, even within these areas, there were considerable differences. Unfortunately, holding size at an early date is poorly documented and we are forced to draw on data from the sixteenth and the first half of the seventeenth century to illuminate much earlier conditions. Having done so, we will then try to explain the regional variations by going back in time. Finally, the development of holding size until the middle of the eighteenth century will be explored.

In the seventeenth century large farms were dominant in the south-western arable region of the Netherlands, the Flemish and Antwerp Scheldt polders, in the river clay area with mixed farming, in the Frisian dairy districts and probably in the dairying part of Salland in Overijssel. Less good data suggests that this was also true (to at least some extent) in the Condroz and the Ardennes. The origins of the shift towards capitalist farming has been described for Zeeland Flanders, Belgian coastal Flanders and for the Dutch river clay area. Van Bavel (2001) documented the rise of large holdings in the river clay area from the fifteenth century. The average size of tenancies of the abbey of Mariënweerd increased from 6.9 ha in 1442 to 13.7 ha in 1580. In the first year, no tenant had more than 40 ha, but in 1580 eight did, while the number of tenants with less than 17 ha had considerably decreased (Van Bavel, 2001: 186, 188). Although the nearby Land van Heusden had a similar soil and was subject to the same market influences, this development did not take place and holdings remained small (Hoppenbrouwers, 1992).

This divergent development can be explained as a consequence of the distribution of property (van Bavel, 2001). In the Land van Heusden, more than half the land was owned by peasants, while in Mariënweerd and the surrounding area, large landowners were dominant, and this caused the emergence of a lively market for leaseholds and presented opportunities for the accumulation of land. The same phenomena can be demonstrated for demesnes in Zeeland Flanders owned by the abbey of St Peters Ghent from the late thirteenth century.

These processes of accumulation were not initiated by large landowners, but by the farmers themselves, by way of the accumulation of separate parcels of land or leasehold tenancies (van Bavel, 2001: 197; Thoen and Soens, 2001). From the seventeenth century, this evolution was sometimes indirectly advanced by the larger landowners in the southern Low Countries where land abandoned during the religious wars was released in larger units, or when newly reclaimed polders were divided into large, consolidated farms, as in Holland.

Similar tendencies can be seen in other areas as well. In regions that were dominated by large holdings, most land – often more than 80 per cent – was possessed by large landowners. While in Flanders, Friesland and the central river area, the development of large farms began in the later Middle Ages, in Holland the trend towards the formation of larger holdings generally started later. Even around 1560, farms of more than 20 ha were scarce (De Vries, 1974: 63, 66). However, change was on its way and farms grew in size. Changing property relations seem to have caused this development. Wealthy city dwellers bought land in the Holland countryside and leased it to enterprising peasants. Where polders or lakes were reclaimed with urban capital, this trend was at its strongest. Again extensive landed estates and large farms went hand in hand.

Property relations are an important factor in explaining the changes in holding size, but they influence this process in combination with other factors like soil fertility, market conditions, power, and environmental problems (which were mostly caused by human action). On the island of Walcheren, for instance, farms were much smaller than elsewhere in Zeeland because of the poor quality of much of the land, which made it less suitable for arable farming, and because of the proximity of the large city of Middelburg. Small farms could thrive here by producing fresh milk, vegetables and fruit for the Middelburg market. In Zeeland Flanders it is clear that the agency of the count of Flanders had played its part in the evolution towards larger holdings, since – contrary to inland Flanders – his banal power allowed him to confiscate the land of impoverished peasants who were not able to meet the rising costs of the maintenance of water management systems. The confiscated lands were regranted to the person or institution who offered most, a procedure which increased both absentee ownership and lease holding.

The trend towards larger holding sizes continued until the second half of the eighteenth century. In West Zeeland Flanders, around 1750, 93 per cent was held in units of over 20 ha (van Cruyningen, 2000: 99). Despite the depressed economic conditions between 1650 and 1750, large commercial farmers were able to enlarge their holdings because they had a large marketable surplus which secured high prices in years of scarcity, especially in the 1690s.

The predominance of large landownership did not automatically lead to the emergence of large holdings, as can be observed in the eastern part of the Netherlands. In regions like the arable part of Salland, Twente or Achterhoek, holdings remained relatively small in spite of the fact that most land belonged to institutions or large noble estates (Slicher van Bath, 1957). This can be explained by the absence of active land and lease markets. Unlike the coastal areas, no public auctions of leases were held here, farms were leased to members of the same family from generation to generation and leasing of single parcels of land was uncommon. This made the accumulation of land by farmers difficult.

The small landholders in the sandy areas in the east, or those in the Holland area of the Land van Heusden, were not completely detached from commodity markets. Authors like Bieleman (1987) have shown that they were at least to some extent market-orientated. At the same time, *morcellement*, the division of holdings into ever smaller units, was absent in the eastern provinces. This can probably be ascribed in at least part to the aversion of noble landlords towards the fragmentation of holdings. But the farmers themselves also tried to prevent fragmentation. Land-owning farmers in the east bequeathed their whole farm to a single child, usually the oldest son, to prevent its division. This can partly be explained by the continued use of common fields, since in areas where commons were strictly protected and formed an essential part of the farm economy, fragmentation as well as accumulation was slowed down and stability promoted. The infield-outfield system, which remained general in the sandy areas in the east and south of the Netherlands until the nineteenth century, had something of the same effect. Holdings here tended to remain intact until the nineteenth century. One consequence was the emergence of an underclass of cottagers descended from those younger sons who did not remain celibate.

These regions can be compared to some degree with the sandy and sandy-loamy areas in inland Flanders, where another type of 'peasant' was active. Here commons had largely disappeared before the thirteenth century, which forced the peasants to be inventive in order to survive. The smallholders were driven to produce value-added commercial products (wool, flax, yarn, linen, dyes) which in turn prompted population growth, and an ever greater fragmentation of peasant holdings. This evolution was further stimulated by increasing taxes and growing needs of the peasants for cash. But, although this evolution took place over several centuries and only reached its apogee in the sixteenth century, the essence of these 'commercial survival' structures was already present in the thirteenth century (Thoen, 2001).

Communal land use systems

From an early stage in history, common land was unimportant in the marine clay and peat areas of the northern Netherlands. Uncultivated peatlands and marshes were initially common land but by the end of the Middle Ages, all cultivable land had been reclaimed and common had almost entirely disappeared. In Flanders, the early and rapid cultivation of the peatlands and their use for peat digging was made possible because the count of Flanders was able to use his regalian rights to make grants of these wastes for his own profit. In the central Dutch river clay area most commons were already divided by 1300 (van Bavel, 1999: 363), as a response to population pressure and the configuration of large landowners and big, leaseholding farmers.

In the sandy areas in the east and south, the situation was different. Strips within the arable fields were worked by individual farmers, but part of the meadows, and almost all of the uncultivated land and woodlands, were used communally. In many areas these commons survived the middle ages. In the sandy soil areas of Drenthe, Overijssel, Gelderland, the Campine area, the Land van Loon in Limburg, as well as many parts of the Walloon area, villages with their meadows and fields were tiny islands amidst much larger areas of heath and woodland, which even in the early nineteenth century could cover as much as 80 per cent of the village territory. Woodland provided firewood and building materials. The heathlands were used for pasture, to gather fuel, and from the later Middle Ages to fertilize the arable, and so formed a vital component of the agricultural system.

From the thirteenth century, in Drenthe, Overijssel and Gelderland, these areas of heath and woods were administered by associations of villagers called *marken*. The *marken* were mainly founded in the thirteenth century during a period of population growth, when pressure on the commons was heavy. Landlords and farmers formed these organizations to prevent the depletion of vital resources (van Zanden, 1999). The *marke* was considered to be the owner of the commons. At their yearly assembly, the members of the *marke* would make by-laws regarding the maximum number of cattle or sheep that were allowed to graze, the maximum quantity of sods that could be taken from the heath and the amount of fuel that might be gathered. Prevention of overexploitation remained their main goal until the nineteenth century. In the case of the woods, they failed. Most of the eastern Netherlands was completely deforested by the end of the Middle Ages, and only in the area of Veluwe did some woods remain.

Not all villagers had the right to vote at the annual meeting of the *marke*. This right was tied to the farmsteads that existed at the moment when the *marke* had been founded, whose owners had a full share or *waardeel* in the *marke*. When a farm was divided into two, both units had a half share. Cottages which were erected at a later date had no vote and at most only limited rights to use the commons. So there was a clear social distinction within the village between the farmers with full rights and cottagers who had no voting rights and only limited access. But even the influence of farmers with full rights on the decisions of the *marke* was limited. Only in Drenthe did they control the association; in Gelderland and Overijssel the yearly meeting was often dominated by ecclesiastical or noble landowners who owned most of the farmsteads with voting rights.

In Brabant and Limburg the uncultivated lands belonging to villages were called *gemeynten* (commons). The rights to these *gemeynten* were exercised in a different way to that found in the north-eastern *marken*. Especially during the thirteenth and fourteenth centuries, the dukes of Brabant had transferred most of the uncultivated land to village communities in return for an annual rent payment. Whilst the duke remained the nominal owner of the land, the villagers received the right to use the soil for activities like grazing cattle, gathering fuel or digging turf. Often, all villagers had access to the *gemeynte* and the village community as a whole made by-laws for its use.

Whereas in the east, most of the *marken* stayed intact until the nineteenth century, from the fifteenth century onwards parts of the *gemeynten* were sold for reclamation, often because the village needed money, for example, to build or repair the church. Villages could sell part of their commons, but permission from the duke, as the legal owner of the soil, was required. The payment the village received from the sale was considered to be compensation for the loss of the use of part of the *gemeynte*. In this way large areas of common land were sold and reclaimed. In the county of Flanders, although largely situated in the sandy soil area, most commons disappeared in the course of the twelfth-thirteenth centuries and only two or three per cent of the land was still organized as commons in the late Middle Ages (De Moor, 2002). The reasons for their early disappearance include the needs of the local lords for cash, the competition between them to increase the number of inhabitants for short term profit, as well as the impulse of the peasants to develop their 'commercial survival economy' (Thoen, 2001).

The exercise of power within the village

The main distinction to be made here is between areas in the south-eastern part of the Low Countries where local seigneurial power was strongly developed, and the areas where seigneurial power either did not develop or was very weak, mainly in the north-west. These latter areas included maritime regions such as coastal Flanders, Holland and Friesland, but also a sandy area such as Drenthe. Local seigneuries had hardly developed there, and village communities were fairly strong and well-organised. They were formed in the ninth to twelfth centuries and had many functions. They acted as a corporate body when making agreements, buying, selling, contracting debts and undertaking litigation. Often, the village community owned some property, such as land, a mill, oven, market or even a village hall, and received revenues from the rent of common properties, from fines and local taxes. In some regions, as in Holland, the community also assumed a role in collecting taxes, organizing military duties and maintaining internal order. In the coastal areas, the village community, at the same time a jurisdictional, fiscal, military and ecclesiastical unit, often overlapped with the institutions for water management (van der Linden, 1972). The latter were formed as *coniurationes* – associations of colonists – as may be seen most clearly in peatland Holland and the adjacent parts of the prince-bishopric of Utrecht. Here, already in the twelfth century, or perhaps even before, free confederations were responsible for water management, stimulated by the constant threat of flooding, necessitating co-operation and communal organization.

In many cases, village communities were not characterized by equality or homogeneity, let alone any kind of participant democracy. Not all villagers were members of the village community. Often, the landless were excluded and only those owning or holding land were admitted to it (Hoppenbrouwers, 1996: 232–36). The ownership of land was often required to exercise voting rights or to fill local public offices. Landownership also brought duties, especially military service and the payment of land taxes.

In the Holland peat lands this meant broad participation in village government, since virtually all peasant households possessed their own holding and social polarisation was (at least initially) very limited, but in the Guelders river area this was not the case at all, creating a sharp divide in political authority. A growing polarization in social-property structures and proletarianization of large parts of the population, as in fourteenth-century coastal Flanders or sixteenth-century Holland, thus had momentous effects. Loss of landownership could mean exclusion from the making of village decisions. This can be seen in the management of water in coastal Flanders, where the participation of peasants in general meetings was increasingly limited, and decision-making came to rest in the hands of a dwindling group of landowners, who were often absentees (Soens, 2006). It is likely that some of the areas where village communities practiced the widest participation in the Middle Ages had become narrowly-based oligarchies by the seventeenth century.

In other parts of the Low Countries, local lords had been able to establish important lordships in the tenth and eleventh centuries. This was the case in the south-eastern part, including the Campine area (Steurs, 1993), and possibly the Guelders river area. In all of these areas, and throughout the south-east generally, the village community was organised under the direction of its lords. Tenurial courts (*laathoven*) and fiefcourts (*leenhoven*) regulated the village jurisdiction. Banal dues, such as the obligation to use seigneurial mills or breweries, the entitlement to corvées, the rights to demand a heriot on the death of a tenant, as well as to levy taxes (*tallia*), were the most obvious signs of seigneurial power. As demonstrated for Hainault – but still applicable for many of these areas – the really 'unfree' had become a minority during the High Middle Ages and had mostly disappeared by the sixteenth century, but these dues were levied on all the inhabitants of the seigneurie. Their importance and weight differed from area to area, but it is likely that they were more burdensome in the Walloon part of the Low Countries than elsewhere.

Even in these areas, the power of the local lords diminished from the twelfth century. They were probably undermined by economic growth, which produced a new balance of power between lords and peasants, one aspect of which was the creation of new franchises and reduction of feudal dues. To this end, charters were often granted by the territorial lords or princes (as in Brabant, Namur, Hainault and Liège) to entire villages and seigneuries, or parts of them, in emulation of the privileges conferred on towns. The countrymen benefiting from these franchises were sometimes even called 'bourgeois'. As long as they were accompanied by economic and demographic growth and the income of the lords was maintained, these franchises did not undermine the local balance of power.

In some areas, other factors were undermining the position of the local lords. From the thirteenth century, a power struggle developed between them and the princely overlords (counts, dukes, bishops). This had the most dramatic effects in areas where the princes had a strong political and military position, and where they could strike alliances with the bourgeoisie and benefit from their growing economic and political power. One of the instruments used by them to undermine the power of the local lords was the promotion of personal freedom, the support they gave to the establishment of new towns and free areas where people were independent of lordship. This strategy forced lesser lords to grant more freedom to the inhabitants of their own seigneuries (Steurs, 1993; Thoen, 1988). It is telling that in areas where the urban sector was least developed, seigneurial power endured longest, as in parts of Wallonia. An additional instrument used by the princes, especially in Flanders and Brabant, was the institution of the *bourgeoisie forain*. By granting countrymen the status of outburgher of a town, not only was the power of the local lords undermined, but also the solidarity of the village community, since only the richest villagers could become *bourgeois forain*. The comital government profited from this by increasing the taxation of these weakened communities.

A further factor in the decline of the power of local lords was the erosion of the economic basis of the seigneuries. Especially in urbanized areas, many rents in kind as well as services were in the high Middle Ages converted into money rents, because the lords needed cash for the purchase of luxuries. Due to inflation, the real value of these rents in cash declined. This was combined with the erosion of the judicial power of the local lords, in Flanders especially, but also in large parts of Brabant, Hainault, and Loon, already in train about 1300. A process of engrossment of seigneuries in the course of the twelfth and thirteenth centuries could disguise this for a time, but the older nobility almost completely disappeared. At the same time, there was the rise of a new nobility of officials, working in the service of the princes and mostly distanced from rural society. The process of unification of the principalities into one 'state', first under the Dukes of Burgundy and then their Habsburg descendants, did not change this evolution. It may even intensified this divergence within the nobility.

The increasing freedom in the villages also brought new village institutions into existence, such as the aldermen courts (*schepenbanken*) of free countrymen. From the thirteenth century, more and more villages developed these independent courts, which became responsible for voluntary and lower jurisdiction. The higher jurisdiction remained in the hands of the princes. However, the role of local lords did not completely disappear, especially in the south of the Low Countries. In certain periods, lords tried to re-establish local seigneurial power. We have no evidence that this happened in the twelfth century, as was the case in some areas of France, but it did occur in the late thirteenth in Flanders and, much later and only to a limited extent, in Brabant in the second half of the eighteenth century (Scheelings, 1990). But in general there was an institutional continuity from the thirteenth to the eighteenth century (e.g. Genicot, 1982). These feudal reactions were of limited importance and never succeeded in reversing the tendencies already visible during the High Middle Ages.

Social aspects of labour markets

These shifts in power balances, and the disintegration of the demesnes, also affected labour relations. However, these changes were probably was not as profound as once thought, as the manorial system overall showed all kinds of variations, and in many parts of the Low Countries had never existed in its classic, bipartite form.

In the twelfth and thirteenth centuries, the urban elite came into the picture, as townspeople started to buy up land and create large farms. By doing so, they built up relations with the smaller peasants through wage labour and the exchange of capital. In those regions which underwent an evolution towards more capitalist structures in the later Middle Ages, such as coastal Flanders and the Guelders river area, similar relations developed between large farmers and other countrymen, but now on a much bigger scale. The large farms, either directly exploited by lords or by large tenant farmers, had a big impact on the local labour market, with the farmers employing fellow villagers as labourers, particularly at moments of peak seasonal demand. These relations were often personal in character in that servants and maids were recruited locally and lived with their employer's family. On the other hand, labourers were hired on a more casual basis, often through an impersonal labour market via contracts for days or weeks or by the task. Social relations were perhaps weakest with seasonal labourers, who came from other regions with surpluses of workers.

Social aspects of credit markets

In most of the Low Countries, countrymen and even smallholding peasants could rely on the well-functioning credit markets which had emerged in the countryside by the later Middle Ages. The most important instruments for securing credit were perpetual rents and life rents, which were secured on real property, mainly land. These rents (*renten,* 'rent constitutions') emerged in Flanders and Brabant in the thirteenth century, and were created in massive numbers from that period onwards in both town and countryside. From *c.*1300, the sale of rents also started to emerge in the northern parts of the Low Countries. This made long-term credit available at relatively low interest rates for large groups of society, including farmers and peasant smallholders, while at the same time offering ample security to the purchaser who advanced the money. This credit system became even more attractive with the decline of interest rates, especially from the sixteenth century (Thoen and Soens, 2003; Zuijderduijn, 2009: 242–47). In Flanders, the interest rate for perpetual rents sold by private parties and secured on land was about 10 per cent in 1275–81, 8 per cent in 1429–31 (redeemable, thus even more favourable to the rent-payer) and 6.3 per cent in 1569–71. The decline of interest rates was even more pronounced in Holland, and credit was easier to obtain here, even for the peasants with smallholdings. Credit was often the *conditio sine qua non* to start a new peasant holding or tenant farm. In other words, credit became a characteristic of both peasant societies and capitalist farming regions.

In some parts of the Low Countries, it even became possible to sell rents without land as collateral. This innovation was of greater importance to tenant farmers than peasants.

Tenants often did not own any land which they could offer as collateral and hence might become dependent on their landlord for credit. This allowed landlords to link operations in the markets for goods, capital, labour and land in order to create opportunities for rent-seeking. Tenant farmers could avoid this risk if they could gain access to the capital market. Their ability to do so offered them more economic possibilities, but also more equality in their relations with other social groups, most notably their landlords. Nonetheless, from the seventeenth century, credit to farmers often took the form of mortgages on land. In Holland, the interest rate on these loans had decreased to 3.5–4 per cent by the middle of the eighteenth century (Baars, 1973: 118). From around the same time, short-term credit without real estate as collateral (*obligaties*) could also be obtained from family members or the urban bourgeoisie. This can be seen as a kind of alternative to social systems of solidarity within the family or groups of neighbours (Brusse, 1999).

Forms of peasant resistance

In the thirteenth and early fourteenth centuries, the south-eastern shores of the North Sea saw some of the biggest rural revolts of late medieval Europe, with large sections of the rural population of whole regions rising against their sovereign or noble rulers. In Greater Frisia, stretching from Holland in the west to far into present-day Germany in the east, revolts and armed resistance had been a recurrent phenomenon during the eleventh and twelfth centuries, but they intensified in the thirteenth and fourteenth centuries (van Bavel, 2010b). In most revolts, as in Drenthe and west Frisia, the rebels demanded respect for their self-governing powers and for their customary organization of taxation. They resisted the growing power of noblemen and comital representatives, who undermined the power of villages, and challenged their rights and customs. In 1227–40 (Drenthe), 1275 (Kennemerland) and 1345 (Friesland) for instance, the rebels were successful: the territorial lords were defeated and had to accept most of their demands.

The biggest revolt in the late medieval Low Countries, in coastal Flanders in 1323–28, was repressed. Here, a rural revolt combined with urban discontent provoked by taxation and the monopolization of power by small closed patriciates. Recent research has revealed that the duration and intensity of this revolt was caused by the progressive replacement of traditional peasant organisation by new capitalist formations, which created antagonism amongst many rural dwellers. Nobility and princes from all over Western Europe recognised the threat which this revolt posed: they set aside their individual disagreements to cooperate in its repression. In the sandy 'peasant' areas of the Netherlands, on the other hand, with the exception of the Drenthe, no major revolts are known from the Middle Ages although we do know of organised protests when common lands were privatised.

Rural revolts in the Low Countries were few and far between after the Black Death, whereas in other parts of Europe many revolts occurred in that period. The rise of the *Kaas-en broodvolk* (the cheese and bread people) in late fifteenth-century Holland was one of the few exceptions. Rural peace was also characteristic of the Dutch Republic, and the disturbances which occurred were small scale and localised. One of the revolts which lasted longest was the unrest on the island of Walcheren in 1655, sparked by a rise in the drainage taxes, but the demands of the rebels came to articulate a more general dissatisfaction about fraud by officials, maladministration of water boards, and the like ('t Hart, 1994). The agitation ended with some democratization of the water management administration, a cut in taxes and the transfer of the burden of taxes to the owners of the land.

The striking absence of rural revolts in the regions which underwent a transition towards capitalism after the fourteenth century can be explained in part by the fairly high standards of living, the widely based participation in administration and the very fragmented political structure which made revolts highly localized. In addition, social factors included the polarization of rural societies, the rise of a strong group of wealthy farmers, and the dissolution of rural communities as individuals became more autonomous. Recourse was also made to silent forms of protest – such as the collective refusal of a village community to rent the farm of a neighbour who was about to be evicted – which offered an alternative to armed revolts (Brusse, 1999).

7.3 Government and public policies

State policies towards landlords, farmers and peasants

The Low Countries were politically highly fragmented. Since the High Middle Ages, regional lords like the count of Holland and the duke of Brabant had been virtually independent. In the fifteenth and sixteenth centuries, the Burgundian dukes and Habsburg kings attempted to centralize the state, finally provoking the Dutch revolt and the rise of the federal Dutch Republic in the north. So when we speak of the 'state' in the Low Countries, we mean the government at regional level rather than a central state. It was the provinces who decided both fiscal policy and policy towards landowners and farmers.

In the coastal parts of the Low Countries, countrymen in the High Middle Ages had many opportunities for self-organization in horizontal associations. Sometimes they organized themselves into regional public bodies, as in West Frisia, where villagers were accustomed to choose delegates and send them to regional meetings, the *warven*, while all adult Westfrisians met once a year in a general assembly. It was in West Frisia and Frisia proper that the self-organization of the rural population went furthest. Through the weakness of feudal organization and the near absence of the authority of territorial lords, a tradition developed of free men, who saw themselves as placed directly under the king. These free countrymen had started to organize autonomous communities by the eleventh century, perhaps initially with a prominent role for the local elites, but the participation of free countrymen in public matters was well established by the twelfth century. In the thirteenth, the organization of communities further proceeded, with the appearance of the *redjeven/grietmannen*, judges and representatives, appointed by the community (Ehbrecht, 2003). At the same time, some 25 *terrae* or lands developed in the Frisian districts, each with its own board, consisting of the joint representatives of the area. This was the mature form of self-government among the Frisian communities, and survived into the sixteenth century.

Especially in the thirteenth century, this self-organization collided with the growing power of the territorial lords, who were extending and intensifying their administrative and fiscal power. This resulted in all kinds of tensions, leading to the revolts mentioned previously. The introduction of fiscality and a growing tax pressure was widely resisted as an infringement of the previous customary arrangements. The development of princely central administration also compromised self-government and reduced the power of local communities. Although some of the rural revolts were successful, in most regions and eventually even in Frisia, the central princely organization came to dominate.

In most of the Low Countries, the politics of the principalities were dominated by the towns, who were opposed to taxes on trade and so most taxes were levied on real estate, especially land. From the twelfth century a tax, the *bede,* was levied on villages, first intermittently, and later on an annual basis. The sum that had to be paid was divided between the villagers; nobility and clergy were exempt. In many areas it was only in the later Middle Ages, or even in the sixteenth century, that the tax due was divided according to the amount of land each person owned and an inclusive land tax (*verponding* or *schatting*) established (van der Linden, 1956: 132; Hoppenbrouwers, 1992: 628).

As the need for successive configurations of the state increased, more taxes were introduced. In the seventeenth century, the agricultural sector was subjected to a whole series of taxes: land tax, taxes on cattle, horses and cultivated arable land, and several excises (Bieleman, 1987: 173; Thoen and Soens, 2007). An improvement for the peasant population was that after the mid-fifteenth century in some districts and more generally from the mid-sixteenth, noblemen and ecclesiastical institutions were no longer exempt from the land tax. The burden of taxes became especially heavy in the decades after 1690, when the Dutch Republic was faced with huge financial obligations because of the wars against France (Bieleman, 1987: 176–77; van Cruyningen, 2000: 85). In Flanders taxes were also increased considerably in the seventeenth and eighteenth centuries and fell heavily on the smaller peasants. It forced them to have cash to pay the taxes and is therefore often seen as a factor which encouraged protoindustrialisation. It has been estimated that the average tax burden was three times higher in that period than in the later Middle Ages (Thoen and Soens, 2004).

Increasing taxation, especially when combined with depressed economic conditions as in the late seventeenth century, hit farmers and peasants hard, but the effects were not always the same. An important factor was whether landlords were able to pass their increased taxes on to their tenants (Hoppenbrouwers, 1992: 657). When the lease market was slack, for instance during an economic downturn, they were often unable to do so, because it would make it impossible for them to find tenants. So landlords were confronted with both rising taxes and stagnating (or even falling) rents. This prompted many of them to sell their land and thus we can observe in a number of areas the paradoxical development that owner-occupation increased during the agricultural depression of 1650–1750 (Baars, 1973: 108; Brusse, 1999: 126; van Cruyningen, 2000: 106–08).

The public regulation of the countryside

In the western provinces of the northern Low Countries, public authority had regulated reclamations and drainage projects since the Middle Ages. The counts of Holland and Zeeland and the bishop of Utrecht were empowered to do this because they possessed the regalian power over all uncultivated lands within their territories. From the eleventh century the peat areas in Holland and Utrecht were reclaimed. The groups or individuals who wanted to reclaim peat land made agreements with the count or the bishop, often via entrepreneurs who acted as intermediaries. These contracts were called *cope* (buying) agreements (van der Linden, 1956: 79). The buyers received property and jurisdictional rights over the land in exchange for payment of a yearly recognition. In this way count and bishop regulated the judicial organization of the reclaimed peat lands by establishing courts in the newly-founded villages (van der Linden, 1956: 94).

During the later Middle Ages and later, agreements comparable to the *cope* called *octrooi* ('patent'), made with the provincial government or States General, were also used to regulate the drainage of the coastal marshes. These were highly sophisticated documents stipulating the rights and obligations of the patentees, defining the rights of adjoining polders and laying down the specifications for dykes and drains. Another standard clause in the *octrooi* established a water board responsible for the maintenance of the new polder, and this board was granted the right to collect taxes and to issue regulations for owners and users of land within the polder. A new court was established or the newly reclaimed land was annexed to the territory of an existing court. Thus a legal framework was created to guarantee an orderly execution of the drainage project and an enduring organization of the new territory after its completion. The *octrooien* usually contained exemptions from property taxes for landowners in the new polders for periods of from three to 27 years (van Cruyningen, 2005/06: 129–30).

The state governments may therefore be seen to be encouraging a particular form of enclosure. But in neither the Dutch Republic nor in the southern Low Countries was there any government policy towards the enclosure of the remaining open fields and commons in the early modern period. The duchy of Brabant now and then sold commons, but this was meant to generate extra income and was not the result of any considered policy of modernizing agricultural practice. In the Austrian Low Countries such a policy would be developed only from the 1750s and in the Netherlands even later, starting with the constitution of 1798.

Government encouragement of trade and markets

During the Middle Ages, the rise of an efficient land market was made possible by the protection of property rights and the registration of land transfers. Since taxes on land were an important source of income for the principalities, the state was concerned that property rights should be both defined and registered. Voluntary registration of land transfers had been possible since the fourteenth century: from the fifteenth some principalities made registration obligatory (van Bavel, 2010a: 169–71). A positive side-effect for the state was that this made it possible to levy a tax on land transfers. In the so-called Generality Lands, the parts of Flanders, Brabant and Limburg controlled by the States-General, a tax of 2.5 per cent was levied on land transfers from 1669. The most important effect, however, was that registration offered security for people operating in the land market, a prerequisite for the functioning of such a market. Likewise the operation of the capital market was improved by the practice of registering mortgages and other forms of credit relationship from the fourteenth century.

Government interference in the grain market had been important in the late Middle Ages. Urban governments aimed at ensuring a stable supply of grain and dampening price fluctuations. In order to achieve this, they imposed maximum prices and prohibited forestalling. In some regions, urban governments went a step further by acquiring staple rights to force farmers and traders to their market. This can mainly be observed with the oldest towns who show tendencies towards the creation of a kind of city-state, like Groningen in the north, but particularly Flemish towns like Ghent from the twelfth century onwards. The territorial lords were often forced to confirm or grant these privileges in order to secure the political support of these towns.

In the early modern period the public authorities in the north of the Low Countries shifted towards advocating a free trade in grain, but again in order to ensure a steady supply. The Baltic grain trade formed the basis of the economic success of Holland from the late Middle Ages and the free, unrestricted import of grain was increasingly seen as a prerequisite for continued economic development. Since Holland was the most powerful province, free trade became the basis of the economic policy of the Dutch Republic. This could lead to tensions between Holland and the more agrarian provinces. In 1671, when agriculture was depressed, the province of Zeeland asked the States-General to impose tariffs to protect domestic agricultural production, since Zeeland was dependent upon cereal farming. The States-General, dominated by Holland, refused because tariffs would damage trade. An exception to this rule remained the province of Groningen, where the town of Groningen maintained its medieval staple rights for grain, cattle and dairy into the seventeenth and eighteenth centuries, although they were progressively eroded.

The social standing of the peasant

Little work has been done to ascertain the attitude of the elite to the peasantry before 1750. However, literature and paintings show two opposed views. The more negative of the pair is found particularly in Brabant and Flanders, where urban elites from the fourteenth century had peasants portrayed as bumpkins, more interested in drinking than farming. This view is also found in sixteenth-century paintings, such as those by Breughel, which seem realistic but at the same time convey feelings about the lack of control and insobriety of the peasants, as contrasted with the civilized manners of the urban elites. On the other hand, there is also a feeling that peasants possessed more joy in life and a simple wisdom. In the northern parts of the Low Countries, and especially in Holland, these stereotypes are found less clearly. Dutch paintings of the sixteenth and seventeenth centuries often depict rural scenes in a realistic fashion, and peasants or farmers on their way to the market. Perhaps it is no coincidence that this was a part of the Low Countries where the formal boundaries between town and countryside were less clear-cut and the dominance of urban elites over the countryside was mainly economic in nature and secured without coercion.

Bibliography

Abbeele, H. Van Den (1985) *De penningkohieren als sociaal-economische en demografische bron. Het land van Waes omstreeks 1671,* (Unpublished thesis, Ghent University).

Baars, C. (1973) *Geschiedenis van de landbouw in de Beijerlanden,* Wageningen.

Bavel, B. J. P. van (1993) *Goederenverwerving en goederenbeheer van de abdij Mariënweerd (1129–1592),* Hilversum.

Bavel, B. J. P. van (1999) *Transitie en continuïteit. De bezitsverhoudingen en de plattelandseconomie in het westelijke gedeelte van het Gelderse rivierengebied, ca. 1300-ca. 1570,* Hilversum.

Bavel, B. J. P. van (2001) 'Elements in the transition of the rural economy. Factors contributing to the emergence of large farms in the Dutch river area (15th-16th centuries)' in P. Hoppenbrouwers and J. L. van Zanden (eds.), *Peasants into farmers?,* pp. 179–201.

Bavel, B. J. P. van (2003) 'Early proto-industrialization in the Low Countries? The importance and nature of market-oriented non-agricultural activities in Flanders and Holland, *c.* 1250–1570', *Revue Belge de Philologie et d'Histoire,* 81, pp. 181–237.

Bavel, B. J. P. van (2009) 'Rural development and landownership in Holland, c.1400–1650', in O. Gelderblom (ed.), *The political economy of the Dutch Republic,* Farnham, pp. 167–96.

Bavel, B. J. P. van (2010a) *Manors and markets. Economy and society in the Low Countries, 500–1600,* Oxford.

Bavel, B. J. P (2010b), 'Rural revolts and structural change in the Low Countries, thirteenth-early fourteenth centuries', in R. Goddard et al., (eds), *Survival and discord in medieval society. Essays in honour of Christopher Dyer*, Turnhout, pp. 249-67.

Bieleman, J. (1987) *Boeren op het Drentse zand. Een nieuwe visie op de 'oude' landbouw,* Wageningen.

Billen, C. (1983) *Propriété et exploitation paysanne dans le tournaisis du XIVe au XVIe siècle*, 2 vols. Unpublished PhD thesis, University of Brussels (ULB).

Brusse, P. (1999) *Overleven door ondernemen. De agrarische geschiedenis van de Over-Betuwe, 1650–1850,* Wageningen.

Cruyningen, P. J. van (2000) *Behoudend maar buigzaam. Boeren in West-Zeeuws-Vlaanderen, 1650–1850,* Wageningen.

Cruyningen, P. J. van (2005–06) 'Profits and risks in drainage projects in Staats-Vlaanderen, c. 1590–1665', *Jaarboek voor Ecologische Geschiedenis,* pp. 123–142.

Dekker, C. (1983) *Het Kromme Rijngebied in de Middeleeuwen. Een institiutioneel-geografische studie,* Zutphen.

Delatte, I. (1945) *Les classes rurales dans la Principauté de Liège au XVIIIe siècle,* Liège.

Dewald, J. (1996) *The European nobility, 1400–1800,* Cambridge.

Ehbrecht, W. (2003) 'Gemeinschaft, Land und Bund im Friesland des 12. bis 14. Jahrhunderts', in H. van Lengen (ed.), *Die Friesische Freiheit des Mittelalters: Leben und Legende,* Aurich, pp. 135–193.

Formsma, W. J. (1981) 'Beklemrecht en landbouw. Een agronomisch-historische studie over het beklemrecht in Groningen, in vergelijking met ontwikkelingen elders', *Historia Agriculturae,* 13, pp. 1–135.

Genicot, L. (1982) *L'économie rurale namuroise au bas moyen âge, 1199–1429,* 3 vols, 1943–82, III, *Les Hommes, Le Commun.*

Hart, M. 't. (1994) 'Een boerenopstand op Walcheren. De strijd om het waterschap 1655–1671', *Tijdschrift voor Sociale Geschiedenis,* 20, pp. 265–281.

Hoppenbrouwers, P. (1992) *Een middeleeuwse samenleving. Het Land van Heusden (ca. 1360-ca. 1515),* Wageningen.

Hoppenbrouwers, P. (1996) 'Op zoek naar de "kerels". De dorpsgemeente in de dagen van graaf Floris V', in D. E. H. de Boer, E. H. P. Cordfunke and H. Sarfatij (eds.), *Wi Florens… De Hollandse graaf Floris V in de samenleving van de dertiende eeuw,* Utrecht, pp. 224–242.

Hoppenbrouwers, P. and J. L. van Zanden (eds) (2001) *Peasants into farmers? The transformation of rural economy and society in the Low Countries (Middle Ages-19th century) in light of the Brenner debate* (CORN Publication Series 4), Turnhout.

Kezel, L. De (1988) 'Grondbezit in Vlaanderen 1750–1850. Bijdrage tot de discussie over de sociaal-economische ontwikkeling op het Vlaamse platteland', *Tijdschrift voor Sociale Geschiedenis,* 14, pp. 61–102.

Limberger, M. (2008) *Sixteenth-century Antwerp and its rural surroundings. Social and economic change in the hinterland of a commercial metropolis (c.1450-c.1570),* Turnhout.

Linden, H. van der (1956) *De cope. Bijdrage tot de rechtsgeschiedenis van de openlegging der Hollands-Utrechtse laagvlakte,* Assen.

Linden, H. van der (1972) *Recht en territoir,* Assen.

Moor, T. De (2002) 'Common land and common rights in Flanders', in M. de Moor, L. Shaw-Taylor and P. Warde (eds), *The management of common land in north-west Europe, c.1500–1850* (CORN 8), Turnhout, pp. 113–42.

Pirotte, F. (1974) *La terre de Durbuy aux XVIIe et XVIIIe siecles. Les institutions, l'économie et les hommes,* Liege and Louvain.

Priester, P. R. (1998) *Geschiedenis van de Zeeuwse landbouw, ca. 1600–1910,* Wageningen.

Ruwet, J. (1943) *L'agriculture et les classes rurales au Pays de Herve sous l'Ancien Régime,* Liège.

Scheelings, F. (1990) *De heren en het heerlijk regime in Brabant in de 18de eeuw* (PhD thesis, VUB).

Soens, T. (2009) *De spade in de dijk? Waterbeheer en rurale samenleving in de Vlaamse kustvlakte (1280–1580),* Ghent.

Soens, T, and Thoen, E. (2008) 'The origins of leasehold in the former county of Flanders', in B. J. P. van Bavel and P. R. Schofield (eds), *The development of leasehold in north-western Europe, c.1200–1600* (CORN 10), Turnhout, pp. 31–55.

Steurs, W. (1993) *Naissance d'une region. Aux origines de la Mairie de Bois-le-Duc. Recherches sur le Brabant septentrional aux 12e et 13e siècles,* Brussels.

Thoen, E. (1988) *Landbouwekonomie en bevolking in Vlaanderen gedurende de late middeleeuwen en het begin van de moderne tijden. Testregio: de kasselrijen van Oudenaarde en Aalst, eind 13de - eerste helft van de 16de eeuw,* Ghent.

Thoen, E. (1993) 'The count, the countryside and the economic development of the towns in Flanders from the eleventh to the thirteenth century. Some provisional remarks and hypotheses', in: Erik Aerts, B. Henau et al. (eds) *Studia Historica Oeconomica, Liber Amicorum Herman Van der Wee,* pp. 259–278.

Thoen, E. (2001) 'A "commercial survival economy" in evolution: The Flemish countryside and the transition to capitalism (Middle Ages-19th century)', in P. Hoppenbrouwers and J. L. van Zanden (eds.), *Peasants into farmers?,* pp. 102–49.

Thoen, E., and Soens, T. (2001) 'Van landschapsgeschiedenis naar ecologische geschiedenis. Waterbeheer in de Vlaamse kustvlakte in de Late Middeleeuwen en het Ancien Régime', *Jaarboek voor Ecologische Geschiedenis,* pp. 1–23.

Thoen, E. and Soens, T. (2004) 'Appauvrissement et endettement dans le monde rural. Etude comparative du credit dans les différents systemes agraires en Flandre au bas Moyen Age et au début de l'Epoque Moderne', in *Il mercato delle terra. Secc. XIII–XVIII,* Prato, pp. 703–20.

Thoen, E., and Soens, T. (2008) 'The Social and Economic Impact of Central Governement Taxation on the Flemish Countryside (end 13th–18th centuries)' in: *La fiscalità nell'economia europea secc. XIII–XVII, Fondazione Istituto Internazionale di Storia « F. Datini»* Prato, Firenze University Press, pp. 957–971.

Vandewalle, P. (1986) *De geschiedenis van de landbouw in de Kasselrij Veurne (1550–1645),* Gemeentekrediet, historische uitgaven in 8°, n°66, Brussels.

Vries, J. de (1974) *The Dutch rural economy in the Golden Age,* New Haven and London.

Vries, J. de (2001) 'The transition to capitalism in a land without feudalism', in P. Hoppenbrouwers and J. L. van Zanden (eds.), *Peasants into farmers?,* pp. 67–84.

Zanden, J. L. van (1993) *The rise and decline of Holland's economy,* Manchester.

Zanden, J. L. van (1999) 'The paradox of the marks. The exploitation of commons in the eastern Netherlands, 1250–1850', *Agricultural History Review,* 47, pp. 125–44.

Zuijderduijn, C. J. (2009) *Medieval capital markets. Markets for renten between state formation and private investment in Holland, 1330–1550,* Leiden and Boston.

Demonstration against the Mansholt plan, Brussels, 1971
(Source: KADOC, Leuven)

8 The Low Countries, 1750–2000*

Paul BRUSSE, Anton SCHUURMAN, Leen VAN MOLLE
and Eric VANHAUTE

8.1 Ownership, power relations and the distribution of property

Types of landowners

After 1750 four main types of non-farmer landowners can be distinguished in the Low Countries: ecclesiastical institutions; investors in land (those who buy, own and sell land for profit); (noble) landowners who inherited land and aimed to pass it on to their offspring; and finally government bodies, both regional and local, and other public institutions. Farmers with full property rights (owner-occupiers) also controlled substantial areas of the countryside although the proportion varied regionally.

The importance of the church as a landowner between the Reformation and the French Revolution differed between the northern and southern Netherlands because of their Reformation experiences. The confiscation of the lands of the church in the northern Netherlands in the Reformation led to the emergence of provincial governments as important landowners. For instance, until the 1760s, the provincial government of Groningen was the owner of about 25,000 hectares in the province, but during the later eighteenth and nineteenth century, several provinces sold parts of their land. Many Catholic charities, like orphanages, were allowed to retain their land at the Reformation.

In the western provinces of the northern Netherlands many large landowners belonged to the urban elite. Rich inhabitants of the capital of Zeeland, Middelburg, owned a great deal of land on the Isle of Walcheren, but they also invested heavily in reclamation projects in other parts of the province. These urban landowners viewed their land in a more business-like fashion than the noble landowners in the east of the country, regarding it as an investment which could be liquidated when necessary. In the nineteenth century many investors from Belgium and France bought land in Zeeland, but in the twentieth century, especially in the second half, the investor in agricultural land diminished in importance.

Much land in the provinces of Friesland, Overijssel and Gelderland was in the hands of members of the old rural nobility. Some families had possessed their land for centuries. In the delta area of the Rhine, Meuse and Waal rivers in Gelderland nobles owned almost half of the land in the eighteenth century, but rarely as contiguous landholdings. In the Graafschap, situated in the eastern and sandy part of the province of Gelderland, some noble families did own ring-fenced estates of more than 1,000 hectares, but most estates were no larger than 300 hectares. Some rural estates

* In this chapter, the Netherlands refers to the modern Dutch state and southern Netherlands to the Austrian Netherlands, from 1830 Belgium.

Map 8.1 The Low Countries, 1750–2000

remain today, but it has been difficult for them to survive the late twentieth century because rent yields were relatively low.

Having lost so much land, the role of the government as landowner was reinvented in the twentieth century, but its main task became the protection of nature. In this context a new type of landowner also came to the fore: (private) nature and landscape conservancy organizations, who now own a great deal of agricultural land (Priester, 1991; Brusse, 1999; Van Cruyningen, 2005; Van Cruyningen, 2006). As a result, the national, provincial and the local authorities, the Dutch Forestry Commission (*Staatsbosbeheer*), nature, water and landscape conservancy organizations now own 25–30 per cent of the land in the Netherlands. In addition, the central government owns agricultural land reclaimed in the twentieth century in the large polders of the IJsselmeer area (in the new province of Flevoland). In some important and environmentally sensitive areas, the authorities and conservancy organizations own a high proportion of the land, for instance in the small coastal dune areas where they have more than 65 per cent. In some districts conservancy organizations are buying agricultural land with the intention of turning it over to nature (source: www.ruimtemonitor.nl).

In the pre-Revolutionary southern Netherlands, the ecclesiastical institutions and the nobility owned about 25 to 50 per cent of the land. Most big domains were in hands of the Church. Urban investors controlled about 10 to 15 per cent of the land, with highest proportions in the more densely populated regions of Flanders. Fifty to 65 per cent of the land was owned by its occupiers or was common land controlled locally. This ratio was higher in the south and the east of the country. The sale of the *biens nationaux* in the 1790s affected mainly the ecclesiastical lands, most of whose land was acquired by members of the old and new (industrial) bourgeoisie. Local farmers only managed to secure between 10 and 23 per cent of the land depending on the region (Vandenbroeke, 1979). These sales promoted the subdivision of the large ecclesiastical estates and the concentration of property into the hands of bourgeois owners.

In mid-nineteenth century Belgium more than 80 per cent of all landed property was in private hands with public institutions controlling most of the balance. After 1850, the share of public property diminished because of the sale of communal property, especially common land. The property in private hands was extremely subdivided. On average, a cadastral property title measured only three ha. in mid-century, shrinking by the end of the century to two ha. In 1845 almost six out of ten households had at least one property title in the Cadastre. By 1910 the proportion had fallen to only 41 per cent, but had risen slightly to 43 per cent by 1930. From this time onwards the number of households with landed property rose again. The number of large estates was largely stable in the nineteenth century, with about 1750 landowners holding more than 100 ha each. Around 1900 only 146 families owned more than 1000 hectares, the two biggest ones having in total 12,800 hectares. However, proprietors with more than 50 hectares, no more than one per cent of the total number, controlled half the land. In 1900 69 per cent of all proprietors had less than one hectare of land, owning in total only 5 per cent of the land. Ninty-five per cent of proprietors held less than five hectares. Until at least the inter-war years, the number and proportion of large properties diminished significantly, a consequence of the equality of inheritance, demographic growth and taxation.

Changing social property distribution

A snapshot around 1900 shows significant regional differences in the position of landholding in the Low Countries. In the south (Belgium), leaseholding was dominant. Almost three quarters of the cultivated land and more than half of all agricultural holdings were held and cultivated on lease (Vanhaute, 2001). The highest proportion of land held on lease was found in inner Flanders and between Antwerp and Brussels (up to 80 or 90 per cent of farms and farmland). Low proportions of leasehold characterised the Campine region in the provinces of Antwerp and Limburg and the Ardennes (at most 40 per cent of farms and farmland). In the Netherlands, owner-occupiers held about 53 per cent of agricultural land at the beginning of the twentieth century. High proportions of owner-occupation were found in the north-east (Groningen, Overijssel) where up to 70 per cent of the land used for arable, grazing or horticultural purposes was owned the farmers who cultivated it. Elsewhere in the country, the percentage of land held by owner-occupiers was much lower, 26 or 27 per cent in Zeeland and Friesland.

The balance between owner-occupation and tenancy changed considerably in the centuries before 1900, and continued to change thereafter. In the former Duchy of Flanders in the sixteenth century for example, half of the land and the farms were owned by the farmers themselves. This ratio was reduced to a third in the eighteenth century and less than 20 per cent (and locally often less than 10 per cent) after the mid-nineteenth century. Between 1846 and 1895, the number of smallholdings of less than one hectare mainly or completely held by lease doubled. This trend was accompanied by a process of proletarianization. In 1850 almost six out of ten families in Belgium owned land. In 1910, this was only four in ten (Vanhaute, 2001). In regions with high proportions of leasehold, the beginning of the twentieth century marked a turn in the secular trend of decline of peasant land. This was most pronounced in the case of small family plots of less than an hectare. In 1950 55 per cent of them were held in owner-occupation where farms of more than an hectare were still exploited mainly or completely on lease. That is why in Belgium the overall share of leasehold remained high at 65 per cent. Around 1950 the regional differences still reflected the historic distribution of owner-occupation: a predominance of leasehold in the Polders, the sandy and sandy-loam regions up to the Condroz (75 per cent and more), against less than 50 per cent in the Campine and the Ardennes regions. Leases were normally limited to terms of three or at most nine years, but in densely populated areas of Flanders, annual verbal agreements for potato plots, pasture and even for arable land were not exceptional. The distinction between owner-occupation and tenancy narrowed with the improved statutory protection of leasehold. A statute of 1929 established a minimum leasehold term of at least nine years for arable land and the protection of the tenant was further extended by legislation of 1951, 1969 and 1988 (Segers and Van Molle, 2004).

Eighteenth-century regional patterns of landownership among farmers in the northern Netherlands were different. In contrast with the southern regions, individual property holding increased. In Over-Betuwe, in the river region of the province of Gelderland, this development began shortly after 1700. Comparable developments were underway in Zeeland by 1740. In the Salland region of Overijssel, it seems that the only purchasers of farm estates after 1750 were farmers, which meant that the proportion of leased land fell whilst that of owner-occupied land increased. The same process can be observed in Friesland and Groningen. In the nineteenth century, the trend towards increased owner-occupation was reversed, although developments in this period are less well documented. It seems that after 1817 developments in all parts of the modern Netherlands ran in parallel. Between 1884 and 1910, the numbers of landowning farmers grew less rapidly than those of leaseholders. In 1910, 53 per cent of the land was being farmed by its owners. Thereafter, the proportion of the land owned by farmers decreased in most provinces and by 1950, only 44 per cent of Dutch agricultural land was in owner-occupation as land seems to have been acquired by investors. In the second half of the twentieth century, ownership by farmers in the Netherlands increased again as a result of the Agricultural Holdings Act of 1958 which made the leasing of land much less profitable. In 1959 more than half of agricultural land was rented by farmers: by 2004 this had fallen to 29 per cent (Priester, 1991; Priester, 1998; Van Zanden, 1984; Brusse, 1999).

Systems of tenure

Systems of tenure also varied regionally and can be directly related to the prevailing regional agro-system. In the clay and more market-oriented areas, relations between leaseholders and landowners were businesslike. Rent was usually paid in cash. Leasehold relations in these areas were flexible and both parties saw the continuation of the lease as being in their interest. At times of falling rentals, for example between 1650 and 1750, landowners made many concessions to assist their leaseholders. In more favourable times, like the period between 1750 and 1817, it was the other way around. In depressed times many farmers and smallholders preferred to rent their farms because this way the risks of agriculture could be shared. On the other hand, in times of economic upswing, it was advantageous for farmers to buy their land because landlords did not hesitate to raise rents. However renting a farm was accepted as normal in market-oriented regions. Some tenants on the clay land of Zeeland and Gelderland were renting huge farms but still counted amongst the leading figures in their villages. In some commercialized regions the tenure system retained some traditional features. The government was the largest landowner in the clay area in Groningen, but completely failed to exploit its rights over its tenants. Here farmers were able to strengthen their hold over the land they rented through the so-called *beklemrecht,* a form of hereditary leasehold which gave them a perpetual tenancy (Priester, 1991; Brusse, 1999).

On the sandy soils landlord-tenant relationships were often more paternalistic. In some regions the landlord expected to be the godfather of the tenants' children. The sons of tenants in Overijssel were expected to introduce their brides to their father's landlord for his approval (Van Cruyningen, 2005). In other regions tenure systems were part of village-based credit networks. The bigger farms exchanged their capital surplus (horses, equipment) for labour surpluses on the smaller, often rented holdings. In many peasant-like regions, this dense system of credit and exchange served to keep rents low. Rents themselves were part of the credit relations and could be reduced or postponed in depressed conditions.

Nonetheless, land prices rose sharply in both Belgium and the Netherlands in the eighteenth and nineteenth centuries. In densely populated regions with a high proportion of smallholdings, the competition for land was intense. In Inner Flanders between the middle of the eighteenth century and the third quarter of the nineteenth, the real price (expressed in days' labour) of one ha of arable land increased three-fold (to more than 90 days' wages). This rise also reflected a changing balance of power between farmers, landholders and the state. While in Flanders, the nominal value of land taxes hardly changed in the eighteenth and nineteenth centuries, we notice a sharp increase in the value of rents (Vanhaute, 2001). In other words, the productivity gains which were made in eighteenth- and nineteenth-century Flemish agriculture were entirely expropriated by private landowners. The income transferred from agriculture towards private owners via rents can be estimated at 10–15 per cent of the capital invested in the third quarter of the eighteenth century and 20–25 per cent in the nineteenth. Net yearly profits of landowners can be estimated at a return of 3.5 per cent of the total income of the land before 1880 and 4.5 per cent after 1895.

In some sandy-soil regions such as Gelderland and Overijssel, *métayage* remained common until the early nineteenth century. Until then more than 90 per cent of the arable land of the Veluwe was leased under this system (Roessingh, 1969). Leaseholders had to pay rent in kind, up to half of the harvest. The landowner sold this in urban markets. In this system the landowners often contributed to the variable costs, by supplying seed and manure.

The balance of power in the relationship between lessor and leaseholder helped shape these regional differences. In the river-clay regions such as Gelderland, rents were largely determined by the market and the market in tenancies was free and open. Every six years, farms were re-leased and farmers had to compete to secure a tenancy for a further term. The relationship between lessor and lessee was purely a business one. That is why rents increased around three times on average between the second half of the eighteenth century and the beginning of the nineteenth century, in some cases as much as five times. On the clay soils of Overijssel, where leasing arrangements were equally business-like, rents also rocketed (Van Zanden, 1984; Brusse, 1999). In such eastern sandy areas as Overijssel, Gelderland and the Campine region, the position of leaseholders was stronger. Over time landowners in these district, whose attitude was, as was explained before, more paternalistic, had conceded excessive privileges to their leaseholders who usually managed to retain their agricultural surpluses. As a result, rents only rose by an average of 50 per cent between 1770 and 1810. This was, as we noticed, very different to the densely populated proto-industrial region of Inner Flanders, where the competition for land pushed prices upwards between 1750 and 1870.

In the eighteenth century, those who farmed the clay soils of Groningen had increased their hold on the land because of the *beklemrecht*. When, around 1770, investors bought this land hoping to profit from the rising agricultural prices, the rights of the leaseholders were confirmed by litigation. As a result, investors did not make much profit on their investment. By contrast, farmers profited from the agricultural boom, strengthening their social position in the nineteenth century. In the second half of the twentieth century the position of all farmers in the Netherlands and Belgium who rented their land and farm was strengthened by successive Agricultural Holdings Acts, of which the first ones were brought into force in 1929 (Belgium) and 1938 (The Netherlands).

The economic value of land

In general, the economic value of farming land in the Low Countries was determined by market forces and by the mechanism of supply and demand. The level of rents and sale prices started to fall in the middle of the seventeenth century and continued at depressed levels until around 1750. By then land prices had started to rise, sharply so after 1800. A peak was reached shortly after 1815, followed by a sharp but temporary fall in rent levels. They subsequently rose again from 1825 until around 1875. The second half of the 1870s marked a new turning point because the rent started to drop again and continued to do so for about two decades. Between 1895 and about 1925, rent levels rose, but in the second half of the 1920s and especially in the first half of the 1930s, they took a turn for the worse. Prices began to rise again from around 1935. In the second half of the twentieth century the price of land was rising in response to its increased scarcity. However, throughout that period, all leases and property transactions were regulated by the *Grondkamer* (Land Tenure Control Board) established in 1941 which held sale prices and rents at below market rates (Van Zanden, 1985; Brusse, 1999; Priester, 1998; Van der Bie and Smits, 2001; Knibbe, 2006).

So, after 1750, the value of land was increasing because demand was growing in response to rising demands for agricultural products. In the delta of the rivers Rhine, Waal and Meuse in Gelderland, the increase in the amount of land owned by farmers at the end of the eighteenth and beginning of the nineteenth centuries was regarded by contemporaries as being the outcome of favourable economic developments. Many farmers borrowed large sums to purchase their farms. Whether farmers preferred to buy their lands or to remain tenants varied between regions and period. In the Dutch river region in the late eighteenth and early nineteenth century, many farmers chose to purchase land because rents rose faster than wheat prices, the main crop in this area. It is likely that farmers in Zeeland could buy land for relatively low prices, at a time when urban landowners were in a desperate need for money as a result of the collapse of the urban economy after 1795. In the sandy area of the province of Overijssel, the farmers became landowners for the opposite reason: that the rise of rents lagged behind farmers' income. It was therefore a logical step for the landowners to sell their land because farmers (in anticipation of future profits) were prepared to pay high prices for the freehold. When the land prices started to fall after 1817, some of them were forced to resell because of accumulated arrears of mortgage payments. The same upswing in sale and resale activity can be seen in other commercial regions such as Friesland and in Zeeland after 1878. In the twentieth century, especially in the second half, the economic value of land was determined by factors other than the profitability of agriculture. Land became increasingly scarce because of population growth and urban development (Van Zanden, 1984; Wintle, 1986; Priester, 1998; Brusse, 1999, Brusse 2009).

The cultural and political value of land

The cultural and political value of land differed between social groups and regions. Until the end of the eighteenth century, political power in the Dutch province of Friesland was directly connected to the possession of certain parcels of land. This was not the case in other provinces, but the ownership of land conferred social prestige and therefore political power everywhere in the Netherlands. Until 1795 the most important administrator in the district of Over-Betuwe (eastern river clay area), the *ambtman,* was always a noble man and large landowner. On the isle of Walcheren, urban owners of rural land wielded the most political power in the countryside, although their power was in fact based on the possession of so-called *ambachten.* In Holland the administration of the water board districts was in the hands of large landowners (Brusse, 1999; Faber, 1972; Stol, 2002).

In the nineteenth century, in both Belgium and the Netherlands, the right to vote for and to be elected to a public administrative body was to a large extent based on the amount of land tax that one paid (the so-called 'census suffrage'). The nineteenth-century Belgian Senate reflected the enduring power of noble and bourgeois landowners. Only the 400 to 600 highest tax payers (mostly those paying the most tax, predominantly land taxes) were eligible to be nominated for, and allowed to vote for, members of the upper chamber. Forty-three per cent of its seats were held by the 'new' bourgeoisie in 1842 and 92 per cent in 1892. Many industrial families, such as the Ghent textile manufacturers, invested heavily in land, both for financial security but also for prestige and as summer residences (De Belder, 1977). In the Netherlands between 1848 and 1887, only a very small group of male tax payers were eligible for Parliament. In Gelderland for example, although one of the most populated province of the country, only 144 were eligible in 1875, most of whom were large landowners.

At the local level, most mayors (elected in Belgium, appointed in the Netherlands) had an additional income from land. Although farmers were not without political influence in the eighteenth century, they had to wait until after the administrative reforms of the nineteenth century before their possession of land gave them the opportunity to hold the more important local administrative positions. With the institution of universal male suffrage in 1887 in the Netherlands and in 1893 in Belgium, other social groups were able to secure political power. That said, throughout the first half of the twentieth century, farmers are found running the local administration in the countryside. They were disproportionally represented in municipal councils and many served as alderman. However from the 1960s onwards, as agriculture became a marginal economic sector, farmers lost their political power (Munters, 1989).

8.2 The occupiers of land

Peasant ownership of land and the changing size of holdings

About 1900, the English sociologist avant-la-lettre B. H. Seebohm Rowntree described Belgium as '*un pays de petites exploitations*'.[1] This fragmentation of agricultural land into many small holdings was the outcome of an age-old process which only culminated in the first part of the twentieth century. Around 1850 55 per cent of all farms in Belgium were smaller than one hectare. In 1900 this had increased to 66 per cent and by 1950 75 per cent. Most of these smallholdings were transformed into vegetable gardens for working families living in the countryside but who worked in nearby towns. It was only in the 1960s that the average area of the farm started to rise significantly. The mixed, market-oriented family holding, exploiting on average 7 to 10 ha became the standard farm in the 1960s and 1970s. The typical farm consisted of three ha in 1950, 11.5 ha in 1980 and 22 ha in 2000 (Segers and Van Molle, 2004). Again, there were substantial regional differences. In the nineteenth century, in the sandy and sandy-loam regions of inner Flanders and Hainault, more than three quarters of the holdings were smaller than one hectare against less than 40 per cent in Limburg Campine and the Luxembourg Ardennes. The typical region of small peasant farming was the old Duchy of Flanders (the provinces of East and West Flanders), until the early nineteenth century the most prosperous and heavily populated region of the southern Netherlands. These very small leaseholds of less than one or two ha, which were mostly too small to sustain a family for a whole year, were the outcome of a very long-term, secular process. The fragmentation and expropriation of the Flemish farm started in the 'long thirteenth century', accelerated in the 'long sixteenth century' and culminated in the 'long nineteenth century'. About 30 to 40 per cent of all farms in Inner Flanders in the second half of the sixteenth century were smaller than a hectare, a ratio that had doubled by the nineteenth century. Commercial farms of 10 ha and more were characteristic of the clay regions in the sea and river polders (coast and the Schelde river district) and in the loamy region south of Brussels. However even the smallest village had its *coqs du village,* bigger farmers who had a pivotal role in the local rural economy. Over time, their number remained surprisingly stable, a legacy of the old, village-based agro-system (Thoen, 2001).

The available information about farm size in the northern Netherlands between 1750 and 1880 is more impressionistic, but it seems that in the eighteenth century and perhaps in the first half of the nineteenth too the average size of farms was increasing in the alluvial parts of the Netherlands, a continuation of much earlier trends. However, in the north-eastern sandy regions, especially in Drenthe, the smallholding definitely won ground, although in Salland (Overijssel), also situated in the east, the number of large farms grew relatively quickly. In the eastern part of the river clay area, the growth of employment in agriculture was determined by the rise of smallholders, many of them farming tobacco.

1 B. H. Seebohm Rowntree, *Comment diminuer la misère en Belgique* (Paris, 1910), p. 535.

The period from about 1850 or perhaps 1880 at the latest through to around 1930 can be considered to be the golden age of the Dutch smallholder. Throughout the Netherlands, the number of farms of one to five ha grew rapidly. Between 1878 and 1910 their number rose 64 per cent, while the total number of farms increased only by 39 per cent. In the province of Drenthe the number of smallholders doubled. In 1910 more than half of the farmers there had less than five ha each and almost 90 per cent had less than 20 ha (Van Zanden, 1984, 1985; Bieleman, 1987; Priester, 1998; Brusse, 1999).

In contrast, until the second half of the twentieth century, Belgium remained predominantly a land of small family farms, many of whom adopted horticulture. Between the middle of the nineteenth and the middle of the twentieth century the total number of farms more than doubled. Nevertheless the contribution of agriculture to average household income started to decline in this period. In the middle of the nineteenth century, the number of farms was 65 per cent of the number of families. This fell to about 50 per cent around 1900 and to a mere 35 per cent in 1950. If we take one ha as a lower limit, in 1850 29 per cent of all Belgian families exploited a family farm. In 1900 this had fallen to 18 per cent and in 1950 less than 10 per cent were agricultural households.

Large holdings of more than 10 ha lost ground between 1850 and 1950, from 16 to 9 per cent of the agricultural land, although the numbers of these farms remained remarkably stable at around 45–46,000. After 1950, the distribution of land changed quickly: in 2000 75 per cent of the remaining farms were bigger than 10 ha, against only 28 per cent half a century earlier.

From 1930 onwards small farmers in the Netherlands increasingly ran into difficulties and after 1950 their numbers quickly decreased, while the number of farmers with more than 20 ha in cultivation rose. Between 1950 and 2000 the total number of farms fell from 338,500 to 97,500. In 2000 less than a quarter of the farmers had only one to five ha in use. The increase in scale in Dutch agriculture is also shown by the considerable rise of the number of dairy cattle per farm. In the early 1950s, about seven cows were kept on a medium-sized dairy farm, but by 1995 a medium-sized dairy farm had a herd of 45 or more (Bieleman, 2010). In Belgium, the number of farms producing primarily for the market fell by 75 per cent between 1950 and 2000. The biggest part of Belgium's farmland – roughly 80 to 85 per cent – is now held by farms of between 10 and 50 hectares.

The disappearance of communal land use systems

Communal land use systems existed in the eighteenth- and nineteenth-century Low Countries only in its eastern (sandy) and southern (forest) parts. Common land and common use rights were regulated and protected by village institutions, as a rule through a strict set of ordinances. Access and use were restricted to villagers. In forested areas in the south, the usage of a yearly rotating system of de- and re-forestation often survived well in the twentieth century. In Belgium, French law confirmed these public property rights by appointing the local authorities as sole proprietor of these lands. In the eastern provinces of the Netherlands, the so-called *markegenootschappen* – which that laid down rules for the use of uncultivated ground – were entrusted with the management of this land. The main aim was to keep it for grazing cattle and for peat cutting. All landowners (including smallholders, farmers and noble landowners) in the villages in the neighbourhood of the *marken* were represented in these organizations, but the largest landowners had more votes than the smallholders.

The first publicly-sponsored attempts at a general privatisation and division of common lands in Belgium in the second half of the eighteenth century were unsuccessful. At that time about 40 per cent – perhaps 400,000 ha – of agricultural land was either waste or forest, the larger part exploited as common land. Local resistance to division weakened in the nineteenth century, and after the general law for the reclamation of uncultivated lands of 1847, village authorities sold their common lands with increasing speed. In 1910 only 100,000 hectares of 'vague' lands were left. The main instigators behind this process were the larger (often, but not always, urban) landowners, who wanted their share of this land. At the beginning of the nineteenth century, the Dutch government took the first steps towards making enclosure possible, but there was still much popular resistance to partition. It was only when it was considered to have become economically advantageous that farmers cooperated. In the period 1820–60 the country, especially the province of Overijssel experienced a boom in enclosure and the land was rapidly divided. The enclosure act of 1886, which ordained that any member of a *markgenootschap* could demand its division, stimulated further enclosure. In general, the large landowners and larger farmers profited the most from these enclosures. It had the effect of increasing social polarisation within the rural society. The last communal land in the Low Countries disappeared in the first half of the twentieth century, except for some forested areas in the Ardennes (Van Zanden, 1984, 1985; Demoed, 1987, Van Cruyningen, 2005).

Power in the villages

During the nineteenth century and to a lesser degree in the twentieth, it was the owners of large landed properties who exercised power in the countryside of both the northern and the southern Netherlands. Their ownership of property was also acknowledged because payment of the land tax was linked to the franchise until the late nineteenth century. At this date in Belgium, the most influential people in rural villages were often the local nobility, *nouveau riches* from the new industrial bourgeoisie who had built chateaux in the countryside, the educated elite of the village, including the parish priest, the superior of a convent or monastery, the notary (should there be one) and the schoolmaster, and, of course, the biggest farmers. The polder villages and the *markgenootschappen* of the northern Netherlands were both dominated by the established farmers and larger landowners. In both countries it was not unusual for members of the same family to retain dominant positions in village politics and administration over several decades. The political opinion of the most influential villagers often determined the political 'colour' of the village as a whole: Catholic, Liberal or indefinable in nineteenth-century Belgium, with a clear preference for the Catholic party in Flanders and the Liberal party in Wallonia (de Smaele, 2009). In a number of small Belgian villages this meant that municipal elections were never held because there was only one list of candidates, those of the mayor and his followers. The relatively immobile status of remote villages made them immune from the sometimes heated political discussions at the national level, such as the attempt to introduce a 'monastery bill' in Belgium in 1856, which would have facilitated gifts and legacies for poor relief to religious institutions, and the 'school war' between Liberals and Catholics of 1878–84. The attempts of the Belgian socialist party before the First World War to gain support in the countryside remained unfruitful (Van Molle, 1989).

Rural municipalities were self-governing within a framework of provincial and national regulations and laws. The powers of the local administrations extended to matters such as the organization of poor relief through a public *Bureau de Bienfaisance* (charity office, compulsory since the French Revolution), the provision of a public school (at least one public primary school per municipality was compulsory in Belgium from 1879 onwards), the maintenance of public order (the rural policeman), safety and health (including the fight against contagious cattle diseases) and the construction and maintenance of local roads. The rural elites worked hard – both for ease of personal travel but also for access to agricultural markets – to secure their own railway station or at least a tramway connection. In 1890 Belgium had the densest railway network in Europe: 15.9 km per 100 km^2, followed by another 12.4 km per 100 km^2 of tramways by 1910. This efficient transport infrastructure curbed the so-called 'rural exodus' and encouraged commuting. But because of the frequent contacts between the rural and the urban world, expectations of the standard of living changed rapidly. After World War I, local politicians felt the need to provide new public services, often through the foundation of municipal enterprises shared between several communes: water supply, a sewer system, electricity, gas distribution, telephone etc., followed after the Second World War by public transport, sports centres, public libraries and cultural centres. Local authorities competed with each other to increase their prestige and become the most modern and (beautiful) village of the region. This modernization process was encouraged by the Belgian government, for instance through the *Commission nationale pour l'embellissement de la vie rurale* (National Committee for the betterment of the countryside), that functioned from 1905 to the 1950s.

Meanwhile power relations in the countryside had started to change in both Belgium and the Netherlands. The introduction of universal male suffrage at the end of the nineteenth century and the women's vote (in the Netherlands in 1922, in Belgium first at municipal level in 1921 and then at national level in 1948), the increasing literacy of the masses and the rising degree of organization among farmers and workers in unions and other forms of association, all were factors which contributed to a heightened self-awareness. Leaders of the local branches of the farmers' unions at village level soon became an influential part of the local social and political elite (Bax and Nieuwenhuis, 1981). Power relations changed once again after the Second World War when sprawling suburbs and the construction of new residential areas in the countryside multiplied the influence of newcomers. In Belgium this process was fuelled by the so-called De Taeye act of 1948 (named after the minister who sponsored the legislation) which subsidised new housebuilding. Numerous rural municipalities seized the opportunity to attract new inhabitants by putting building land at the disposal of social housing companies and private builders. By doing so, they reversed the pattern of migration from the countryside: it was urban centres in densely populated Flanders which in the 1950s and 1960s witnessed a net loss of inhabitants, whereas villages saw their population grow. The expansion of villages with new housing provoked hostility and tensions between 'natives' and newcomers. In combination with the diminishing number of farming people, the countryside became a zone of mixed 'cohabitation'. The process of 'counter urbanisation' also meant that cities had to cope with shrinking tax incomes, the degradation of their housing stock and a decreasing appeal for retailers who preferred to settle in new shopping centres in the vicinity of the new housing areas in the countryside. It is in this context that the successive mergers of Belgian municipalities, whose numbers fell from 2670 in 1964 to 589 in 1983 must be understood: it was a way to reduce costs and increase tax revenues from a larger population base. Comparable developments took place in the Netherlands where the number of municipalities decreased from 1250 in 1819 to 537 in 2000, declining steadily from 1900 (when there were 1121 municipalities) but accelerating after 1965 (when 994 municipalities remained) (van der Meer, 2006). The loss of local autonomy was unwelcome to the majority of the villages.

Peasant organizations

From the second half of the eighteenth century, and in parallel with demographic growth and pressure on the food supply, the interest of the elites in farming increased. The first agricultural societies, founded earlier in the northern than southern Netherlands, sought to bring about progress by experiment, through publications and lectures. Their sphere of action was local or regional and their membership limited to well-to-do aristocrats and large landowners, politicians and scientists. The Low Countries, in the same way as Britain and France, became gripped by a real 'agromania'. The number of prestigious agricultural and horticultural societies grew through the period of French rule, during the United Kingdom of the Netherlands (1815–30) and continued after the division of the kingdom. Some had a semi-public status as royal or provincial agricultural associations or regional *comices agricoles*. But a wide gap remained between these rather elitist initiatives and the day-to-day practice of the mass of smallholders.

The organization of these smallholders started in earnest only in the later nineteenth century and was prompted by the agrarian crisis. The existing agricultural societies were unable to meet the needs of farmers who struggled with falling market prices. New types of farmers' organizations succeeded in filling the gap: firstly small-scale cooperatives for the purchase of fertilizers and livestock feed, savings and loan cooperatives and cooperative dairy farms, and mutual insurance societies; secondly farmers' unions on the model of the German *Bauernvereine*. The farmers' unions presented themselves as the political representatives of the farmers, secured the support of much of the cooperative and mutual insurance movements, and efficiently supported their members in the process of modernization. It was not by accident that the foundation of the farmers' unions coincided with the introduction of universal (male) suffrage. On the eve of the First World War, there was already a branch of a farmers' union and a mutual cattle insurance association in every other Belgian municipality, and a *Raiffeisenkas* (a cooperative savings and loan fund) in one in four. By uniting rural women and youth during the inter-war period, the unions gradually created a strong identity as a 'second home' for the whole farming family (Van Molle, 1990).

In the Netherlands the unions quickly acquired an anti-liberal character, either strongly Catholic in the provinces of North Brabant and Limburg or strongly Protestant, particularly in Gelderland and the east of the country. Thus Dutch farmers' organizations became involved in the process of ideological pillarization (*verzuiling*). Locally, the competition between Catholic, Protestant and more liberal associations reinforced the degree of organization (Smits, 1996). In Belgium, the establishment of farmers' unions formed a part of the Catholic offensive against liberalism and socialism. The Catholic party's unbroken political ascendency from 1884 to 1914 contributed further to the identification of agriculture and countryside with the Catholic establishment. In this respect the First World War was not a turning point.

The membership of the farmers' unions reached record highs in the 1920s. The *Belgische Boerenbond* (Belgian Farmers' Union), founded in 1890 and the largest union before the war, tended to a virtual monopoly position after the war, but soon lost ground to new, ideologically neutral, organizations, especially in Wallonia where the dominance of Flemish and explicitly Catholic organizations was no longer accepted. During the crisis of the 1930s, a small number of discontented farmers turned to extreme right-wing politics and formed their own *Parti Agraire Belge* and *Boerenfront* in Belgium, and the *Nationale Bond Landbouw en Maatschappij* in the Netherlands. But in both countries the remarkably extensive network of traditional farmer's unions remained in place, strengthened its position through mergers and continued to put pressure on the national agricultural policy. Moreover, from the late nineteenth century onwards, private and state initiatives towards agriculture (in the field of education for instance) became tightly interwoven, forming together a solid 'agricultural institutional matrix', which remains in place today notwithstanding the decimation of the agricultural population (Schuurman, 2010).

From the 1960s the well-oiled agricultural lobby itself came under pressure. First from outside, because of the negative effects of the agricultural policy of the EEC which produced surpluses at a high cost and caused environmental damage (Kooij, 1999), but secondly, from internal dissent. Increasingly some rejected the productivist path, formed alternative farmers' organizations, and turned towards organic farming, agricultural tourism and social care farms, traditional regional products and direct sale from the farm to consumers (Van der Ploeg, 1999; Segers and Van Molle, 2004). But all this happened gradually without major shocks or social dramas. In order to understand this smooth evolution, it is necessary to point once again to the powerful driving and protective role of the farmers' unions. After a long period of stability in the organizational landscape, at the end of the twentieth century they entered a new round of mergers in both the Netherlands and Belgium (for instance the foundation in Wallonia in 2001 of the *Fédération Wallonne de l'Agriculture*). The result is that farmers are less clearly organized according to the ideological 'pillars' but in large regional associations or by agricultural specialism.

Peasant resistance

The modern rural Low Countries are not known for either rebellion or disorder. The fact that small ownership and tenancy were both widespread, and that large properties were relatively rare, made for a social hierarchy in the countryside which was less questioned than that of Britain. Instead of conflicts within the farming population – between proprietors and tenants, or between employers and agricultural workers – Belgium experienced repeated hunger crises in the first half of the nineteenth century which provoked conflicts between those who were able to afford food and those who could not. The last food riot took place as late as 1861. It is true that there were periodic complaints about high rents, violations of the hunting rights of landowners and problems with poaching, all as described in well-known late nineteenth-century novels of the Flemish naturalist and writer Cyriel Buysse. After lengthy discussions in the Belgian Parliament from 1894, a law of 1900 gave tenants the right to take vermin on their farms, including rabbits.

The absence of serious class conflicts within rural society can also be explained by the fact that, at least in Belgium, the number of agricultural labourers diminished drastically from the 1860s onwards. New job opportunities with higher wages in expanding industries drained the countryside of manpower. In 1880 Belgium counted *c.* 180,000 agricultural workers, in 1910 about 160,000, but by 2008 barely 20,000 were left. Although their living and working conditions fell far short of those of urban and industrial wage earners, the socialist party failed to mobilize them and lost interest in rural affairs.

In the Netherlands, the farm labourers' strike of 1929 in the Oldambt, a region in the province of Groningen where the polarization between farmers and their labourers had grown since the second half of the nineteenth century, is seen as a turning point. Groningen in the north-east and Zeeland in the south-west of the Netherlands were both arable farming regions with relatively many labourers. Against the background of high unemployment amongst them, their union, the *Nederlands Verbond van Vakverenigingen* (NVV) called for a strike for higher wages at the beginning of the harvest season. In the end a compromise was reached, but it was a pyrrhic victory for the labours' union because the farmers responded by quickening their adoption of labour-saving machinery (Jansma and Schroor, 1987).

If collective protests were seldom made in the nineteenth century about either scarcity or high rents, they sometimes burst out in the twentieth-century context of overproduction and falling market prices, and of the growing importance of politics. Farmers learned from the example of the industrial trade unions how to put pressure on the government. Spontaneous demonstrations of Belgian farmers took place in 1936 because of the low prices for milk and potatoes. In the 1960s and 1970s hundreds of demonstrations were held complaining of low prices and low demand, with or without the approval and support of the farmers' union. The violent demonstration in Brussels

and markets turned out to be harder to achieve than had been hoped, and the farmers themselves were not prepared to have theoretically ideal models of rationalization such as the Mansholt plan (launched in December 1968 by the European Agricultural Commissioner Sicco Mansholt, formerly Dutch agricultural minister) imposed on them. Hence the massive protests of 1971.

Changing government attitudes towards consolidation and enclosure, public regulation of the countryside and landscape change

In the eighteenth and the first decades of the nineteenth century, land reclamation was organized primarily at local or regional level, with or without the encouragement of higher authorities. The growing anxiety about possible food shortages encouraged the Austrian government of the southern Netherlands to introduce compulsory land reclamation. King William I encouraged attempts at internal colonization in less densely populated sandy regions – in particular the reclamation projects at Veenhuizen, Wortel and Merksplas – although none of these were successful. To increase domestic food supply, in 1847 the Belgian government launched the obligatory reclamation of wasteland and the drainage of waterlogged areas using public funding, both measures achieving fairly respectable results. Through the systematic improvement of the road network, efforts were also made to ease the conveyance of fertiliser and the transportation of crops. In the Netherlands, the role of the central government was noticeable in the legislation for the enclosure of common land (cf. *markenwetten* of 1809 and 1837). Most remaining common land was divided in the middle years of the century.

Rural landscapes altered in other ways too: increasing rural housing, industrial expansion and land consolidation. The fear, current since the late nineteenth century, of a rural exodus and social unrest in urban and industrial areas inspired the Belgian government to subsidize the building of new housing in the countryside. In 1935 the *Nationale Maatschappij voor de Kleine Landeigendom* (National Society for the Small Property) was founded for that purpose (Dejongh and Van Windekens, 2002). This move of housing into rural areas was advanced further by the De Taeye Act (1948). A decade later, measures were taken to facilitate the establishment of industrial parks in the economically-less developed areas of Belgium, with the intention of attracting American and other foreign companies, but at the expense of arable land.

In the Netherlands additional land was reclaimed in the nineteenth century, notably the Haarlemmermeer in 1840–52. Reclamation continued into the twentieth century with the winning of part of the Southern Sea, which became the Ijsselmeer. Land policy was one of the cornerstones of twentieth-century agricultural policy (Van den Bergh, 2004; Karel, 2005). Especially in the 1950s and 1960s, the countryside was deliberately reorganised for the improvement of agricultural production (Groeneveld, 1985). This was the highpoint of agricultural modernisation. Landholdings were re-arranged, and farmers trained by officials from the state advisory service in new business models, technical innovations, accounting methods and the running of efficient farm households.

Since the 1960s public opinion has became more and more aware that attempts to modernize agriculture were in conflict with developing environmental concerns. In 1973 Belgium passed a law on nature conservation, while in 1974 the Dutch government published a document (*Relatienota*) which explicitly championed the importance of landscape and nature (Kooij, 1999). Public interest shifted towards nature conservation, animal welfare, food quality and food security with the result that agriculture and the countryside were no longer synonymous. Today the countryside is mainly perceived as a residential and recreational space for non-farmers, while agriculture itself is reduced to a small link in the global agro-industrial food chain.

Government and markets

Before the mid-eighteenth century the Low Countries had no real agricultural policy: at most, there was an urban food policy, a mercantilist trade policy and a physiocratic reclamation policy. The southern Netherlands produced small grain surpluses and the Dutch Republic acted as grain broker for the European markets. Because of rising food prices and inspired by Enlightenment ideas about the promotion of the general interest, the Austrian government of the southern Netherlands started to collect descriptive statistics (grain stocks, market prices and import and export flows), and introduced import and export duties. In doing so, they strove to achieve a proper balance between food production and consumption requirements and a fair price for producers, traders and consumers (Van Dijck, 2008: 305–11). For flax, a crucial source of income for smallholders in Flanders, a thoroughly protectionist approach was taken.

Government concerns about maintaining the food supply to both the population and the French armies became more acute after 1806 because of the Napoleonic 'continental system'. The United Kingdom of the Netherlands sought to safeguard both the lucrative grain trade and food security. Grain exports slackened and from 1816 imports were permitted, subject to payment of a very low import duty. Following the British and French example, Belgium and the Netherlands introduced sliding scales for duties on the import of bread grains in 1834 and 1835 respectively (Van Dijck, 2008: 341–93).

But because of rising tensions in the food market, both countries abruptly abandoned this semi-protectionism in 1845–46. During the crisis of the 1840s, caused both by failed harvests and the collapse of the linen weaving industry, the Belgian government did not confine itself to lifting duties from imports, but also imposed export restrictions. The structural deficit in domestic grain production made minds in both the Netherlands and Belgium receptive, from the 1850s onwards, to the cause of free trade in an open, competitive market in line with the ideas of classical political economy. The young Belgian state, with its fast-growing group of wage-dependent workers in coal mining and the iron and textile industries, could not afford food shortages and high food prices, both because it needed to maintain its competitiveness with British industry but also because it feared popular disorder. By the 1870s, the liberalisation of the market in both countries was complete.

In Belgium, the *laissez-faire* principle was not an obstacle to government intervention in the fields of research, agricultural education, public works, cattle breeding and efforts to combat cattle diseases. Belgian faith in progress through science and education was particularly striking. The Belgian state launched a veterinary school in 1836, 15 secondary-level agricultural schools in the 1840s, and the *Institut agricole de l'Etat* (Institute for higher agricultural education) at Gembloux in 1860. The state subsidised cattle competitions, agricultural and horticultural exhibitions, demonstrations of agricultural machines, and several hundred lectures and courses every year. With manuals in both French and Dutch, medals, diplomas and prizes, it encouraged farmers to modernize. Private initiative produced books, farming almanacs and journals. But this was not yet enough to produce effects on a macro-scale (Segers and Hermans, 2009). In the Netherlands however, the role of the central government remained limited.

Large-scale grain imports from the 1870s onwards, mainly from North America, and the resulting fall in market prices, quickly gave agricultural policy in both states a new direction. Despite fierce international competition and pressure from interest groups for the introduction of far-reaching protectionism, both countries broadly maintained an open market policy: Belgium in order to safeguard its industrial interests, and the Netherlands to preserve its position as a food exporter.

Belgium's governments before the First World War went no further than highly selective market intervention. Only a few products were subject to (limited) import duties: oats, livestock and meat, flour and pasta, canned food, dairy products and confectionery. The intention was clear: the government wanted to keep bread as cheap as possible whilst seeking to reorient agriculture towards more lucrative market segments and encouraging the food-processing industry. The economic recovery from the 1890s increased the purchasing power of the working classes, which contributed to growing domestic demand for meat, butter, vegetables and fruit. The Netherlands made the same policy choice, eschewing protection and opting for a reorientation of mixed farms towards cattle farming, dairy and market gardening. More than in Belgium, there was a strong export focus. The Netherlands established a prominent position in the international market for butter, cheese and horticultural products. Increasing use was made of artificial fertiliser on farms, and the Netherlands became one of the biggest importers of maize, which was used as a concentrated cattle food. Government inspection of finished products was intended to generate confidence in Dutch foods.

The remarkable expansion in both Belgium and the Netherlands of agricultural research and education from the late nineteenth century onwards should primarily be seen as a response to the agrarian crisis. In the Netherlands, the agricultural school at Wageningen was converted in 1876 into a national institution which became the pivot of Dutch agricultural research and education. Both countries established agricultural research stations which played an important role in the struggle against the adulteration of fertilizers, cattle feeds and foodstuffs.

Paradoxically, the strength of the post-war recovery was the cause of the next crisis. As a result of overproduction and sharp price decreases on a worldwide scale, both agriculture and industry again found themselves in difficulties in the 1930s. Agricultural policy was reactivated in both countries in a particularly difficult context of governmental crises, monetary instability, budget problems and right-wing extremism. There were again calls for protectionism, but neither of these small, export-oriented countries was inclined to take this approach very far. What followed in both was a complex set of measures such as import licences, import quotas, low import duties and a crisis law to reduce the financial pressure on leaseholders. These measures were intended to have a price-stabilising effect, but met with only limited success. Moreover, the Netherlands and Belgium were working against one another. The Convention of Ouchy, which was held in the summer of 1932 and sought to abolish the tariff barriers between the two countries, remained unratified.

In 1933, the Dutch parliament passed the Agricultural Crisis Act, which gave the government the power to intervene in production, processing and sales. A special small farmers' committee was established by the Dutch government in 1936. Support for these farmers was coupled with measures to rationalize their farming activities. In Belgium too, a number of people spoke out in favour of a corporate reorganization of the agricultural sector, but they found few supporters. The Belgian Ministry of Agriculture sought to reactivate the sector in the 1930s by creating government bodies to raise agricultural productivity, improve product quality and promote sales.

The objectives of post-war Dutch agricultural policy were essentially similar: the encouragement of higher productivity to ensure domestic supply and a strong export position, plus an adequate income for farmers. A strong framework for cooperation between the agricultural industries and the Department of Agriculture was forged with the establishment of an Agricultural Council in 1945, which became the Agricultural Board in 1954. It was charged with regulating and stimulating activities in the sector, improving the quality of production, animal health, advising the government and representing and generally promoting the interests of the sector. Farmers' and workers' organizations were represented. To fund its activities, the Board was empowered to raise taxes. Commodity and sectoral boards were founded; and these were given powers to regulate economic relations between the production chains. The sectoral boards were given responsibility for wage control, quality control and structural policy. In practice, the Agricultural Board exerted most influence on official government policy through intensive consultation rather than through exercising its capacity to regulate (Krajenbrink, 2005).

The government's involvement increased yet further. In the late 1950s, mechanization, rationalization and economies of scale were recommended as the way to give Dutch family farming a new future. But at the same time, the government abandoned the ideal of maintaining large numbers of less profitable farms. Many small farmers were forced into leaving agriculture. Measured by its own economic targets, this policy was highly successful. Both productivity and incomes rose rapidly, but agrarian employment dropped in both absolute and relative terms (Bieleman, 2010).

Belgian agriculture had a hard time after the Second World War contending with the competitive advantage of the Dutch farmers, particularly in the dairy sector and horticulture. For agricultural products the Benelux Customs Agreement of 1944 proved problematic. The trade agreement of the BLEU (Belgo-Luxembourg Economic Union) with the Dutch, concluded in 1947, served as a manoeuvre to slow down price harmonization. Yet due to a shortage of export markets, Belgian agriculture was faced with new problems. With the prospect being able to access an extensive foreign market within the union, Belgium became an important supporter of the EEC. Economies of scale, mechanization, intensification and specialization became the watchwords in Belgium too, in combination with the policy of closing down of unprofitable farms (*Landbouwsaneringsfonds*) which was subsidized by the government from 1965 onwards.

With the Stresa conference of 1958, the EEC Common Agricultural Policy (CAP) was properly launched. The EEC gave both countries' agriculture an important boost, as new markets became available. The firm policy of Mansholt as Agricultural Commissioner reinforced the policy of subsidising and stimulating competitive sectors (Merriënboer, 2006). The EEC developed the market and price policy, with guaranteed minimum prices for the farmers, whereas the member states assumed responsibility for structural policy such as land consolidation.

The disadvantages of the CAP became apparent in the 1970s. It was very expensive, due in part to monetary instability which involved huge expenditure on MCAs (Monetary Compensatory Amounts). Belgian and Dutch farming faced overproduction, and farmers' incomes often lagged behind those of wage earners in industry and the service sector. The McSharry reform of 1992 launched all aspects of EC agricultural policy in a new direction. Environmental and animal welfare issues have also been taken more seriously since the 1990s (Silvis, 2008).

Peasants and farmers as political force in national politics and their social standing

Belgian historical imagination ascribed farmers a hero's part. The so-called *Boerenkrijg* (peasants' battle) of 1798 – the revolt of the rural population of the southern Netherlands against French conscription, high taxes and persecution of priests – became the symbol of Belgian romantic nationalism. But whether and to what extent Belgian farmers were already politized and considered to be real 'citizens', in the perception of the elites before the introduction of universal male suffrage in 1893 remains unclear. The truth is that the connection between the right to vote and taxes before 1893 favoured farmers because the ownership of even small parcels of land entitled them to the vote, at least at municipal level. This was also the case for tenants who paid one third of the taxes on the land they leased. In the parliamentary elections of 1884, 27 per cent of the voters were farmers. The democratic reforms of 1893 favoured farmers in a further way. The plural voting system established then (which continued until 1921) gave the owners of real estate and heads of households an extra vote.

Hence the increasing electoral propaganda aimed at the farming population, as much by Catholics as Liberals. The countryside became more and more the province of the Catholic electoral campaigns, what has been labelled by de Smaele (2009) as 'ruralisation' of Belgian Catholicism, whereas the Liberals and later also the Socialists developed their support chiefly in the urban and industrial parts of Belgium. The Catholics portrayed farmers as intrinsically religious and faithful to church and throne, the countryside as the healthiest part of the country and agriculture as the necessary basis of the national economy, despite the increasing import of bread grains. Social unrest in industrial cities in the 1880s, the socialist threat, the electoral reforms of 1893 (universal suffrage) and 1899 (proportional representation) and the inadequate food supply during World War I, all gave this emotional discourse and the political efforts in favour of farmers extra boosts. It is important to underline again that the Catholic farmers' unions played a pivotal role in the political 'housing' of the peasantry, especially in Flanders and with the *Boerenbond* in front. They succeeded in being recognized as their political representatives and spokesmen. Farmers themselves made a rational choice when renewing their membership, often from generation to generation, because of the advantages (financial and other) it offered (Van Molle, 1990). The Ministry of Agriculture was headed from 1884 until its abolition as a federal ministry in 2002, with only minor interruptions, by a Catholic (later Christian Democrat) Minister of Agriculture. In the Netherlands the countryside voted mainly conservative-liberal (in Groningen and Zeeland) or Christian Democrat (on the sandy soils). With the changing social structure of the countryside since the 1960s, this pattern became less solid, but remained dominant until the 1990s. The most famous Dutch minister of agriculture, Sicco Mansholt, however, was a social democrat from Groningen. As in Belgium, after the introduction of the universal suffrage in 1918 and, more especially since the 1930s, there were strong links between religious and liberal parties on the one hand, and the farmers' societies on the other hand. During the whole of the second half of the twentieth century the spokesmen for the major political parties in Dutch parliament, whatever their ideological colour, were almost invariably either farmers by profession or connected to agricultural organizations.

Political weight does not necessarily equal social respect. Public discourse and collective representations of farmers, agriculture and countryside were often paradoxical, oscillating between distaste for their backwardness, superstitiousness and conservatism, as in the biting naturalist poetry of Emile Verhaeren around 1900, and praise for their innate moral virtues, cultural values and contribution to wealth and welfare. The growing identification of Flemish Catholicism with an anti-urban and anti-industrial discourse formed the breeding-ground for the cultural representation of Flanders as rural and conservative, despite its high degree of urbanization since the Middle Ages and the progressive industrialization from the late nineteenth century onwards. In the Netherlands similar developments can be seen, with, as a highpoint, the *Vaderlandsch Historisch Volksfeest* (The National Historical Peoples' Celebration) of 1919 in Arnhem which attracted some 400,000 visitors. The parade started from the recently opened (1918) Dutch open air museum. In the 1950s and 1960s, when Flanders started to develop its own television programmes, it presented itself to the public with films which were based on the rural novels of Stijn Streuvels, Ernest Claes and Felix Timmermans. These were filmed at the open-air museum of Bokrijk which presented itself as a true representation of the Flemish rural past. The Dutch chose for their national symbols tulips and wooden shoes. Since the 1960s, the effects of the CAP and the single-minded pursuit of higher income via higher productivity have once more set a negative tone, blaming farmers and agriculture for exorbitant expenses, overproduction, environmental damage and questionable food quality. The sector took a long time to come to terms with this criticism. Next to niche markets for biological products, mainstream agriculture also started to pay more attention to landscape preservation, animal welfare, and the environmental effects of farming. Recent problems with industrially processed food, for instance the dioxin crisis in 1999, even won new public respect for farmers and a recognition of them as hard working professionals who were themselves victims of the complex agro-food chain. Traditional production methods and authentic 'produits du terroir' have come into vogue again. The imagined re-invention of farmers and countryside, whether it be in the positive or the negative sense, appears to be fruitful and usable at different times and circumstances.

Bibliography

Bax, M. and Nieuwenhuis, A. (1980) 'Boerenemancipatie in Brabant: vergruizeling van een beeld', *Tijdschrift voor Sociale Geschiedenis,* 6, pp. 163–181.

Belder, J., de (1977) 'Adel en burgerij 1840–1914', *Algemene Geschiedenis der Nederlanden,* 12, Haarlem, pp. 78–98.

Bergh, S. van der (2004) *Verdeeld land. De geschiedenis van de ruilverkaveling in Nederland vanuit een lokaal perspectief, 1890–1985,* Groningen and Wageningen.

Bie, R. van der and Smits, P. J. (2001) *Tweehonderd jaar statistiek in tijdreeksen 1800–1999,* Voorburg and Heerlen.

Bieleman, J. (1987) *Boeren op het Drentse zand, 1600–1910. Een nieuwe visie op de 'oude' landbouw,* Wageningen.

Bieleman, J. (2010) *Five centuries of farming. A short history of Dutch agriculture, 1500–2000,* Wageningen.

Brusse, P. (1999) *Overleven door ondernemen. De agrarische geschiedenis van de Over-Betuwe,* Wageningen.

Brusse, P. (2009) 'The connection between rural rise and urban decline in Zeeland, 1750–1850', paper presented at the symposium 'The countryside contested', 26 June 2009, at Wageningen University.

Cruyningen, P. J. van (2005) *Landgoederen en landschap in de Graafschap,* Utrecht.

Cruyningen, P. J. van (2006) 'Profits and risks in drainage projects in Staats-Vlaanderen, *c.*1590–1665', *Jaarboek voor Ecologische Geschiedenis 2005/06,* pp. 135–37.

Dejongh, G. and Van Windekens, P. (2002) *Van Kleine Landeigendom tot Vlaamse Landmaatschappij. Vijfenzestig jaar werking op het Vlaamse platteland, 1935/2001,* Brussels.

Demoed, H. B. (1987) *Mandegoed schandegoed. De markeverdeling in Oost-Nederland in de 19e eeuw*, Zutphen.

Dijck, M. van (2008) *De wetenschap van de wetgever. De klassieke politieke economie en het Belgische landbouwbeleid, 1830–1884,* Leuven.

Faber, J. A. (1972) *Drie eeuwen Friesland. Economische en sociale ontwikkelingen van 1500 tot 1800,* Wageningen.

Groeneveld, J. (1985) *Veranderend Nederland. Een halve eeuw ontwikkeling op het platteland,* Maastricht and Brussels.

Jansma, K. and Schroor, M. (1987) *Tweehonderd jaar geschiedenis van de Nederlandse landbouw,* Leeuwarden.

Karel, E. H. (2005) *De maakbare boer. Streekverbetering als instrument van het Nederlandse landbouwbeleid, 1953–1970,* Groningen and Wageningen.

Knibbe, M. (2006) *Lokkich Fryslân. Landpacht, arbeidsloon en landbouwproductiviteit in het Friese kleigebied, 1505–1830,* Groningen and Wageningen.

Kooij, P. (1999) *Mythen van de groene ruimte,* Wageningen.

Krajenbrink, E. J. (2005) *Het Landbouwschap. Zelfgedragen verantwoordelijkheid in de land- en tuinbouw, 1945–2001,* Den Haag.

Meer, A. van der and Boonstra, O. (2006) *Repertorium van Nederlandse gemeenten, 1812–2006* (Dans Data Guide 2), Den Haag.

Merrienboer, J. (2006) *Mansholt. Een biografie,* Assen.

Molle, L. Van (1989) *Katholieken en Landbouw. Landbouwpolitiek in België, 1884–1914,* Leuven.

Molle, L. Van (1990) *Chacun pour tous. Le Boerenbond belge, 1890–1990,* Leuven.

Munters, O. J. (1989) *De stille revolutie op het agrarische platteland. Boeren en openbaar bestuur, 1917–1986,* Assen and Maastricht.

Ploeg, J. D. van der (1999) *De virtuele boer,* Assen.

Priester, P. (1991) *De economische ontwikkeling van de landbouw in Groningen, 1800–1910. Een kwalitatieve en kwantitatieve analyse,* Wageningen.

Priester, P. (1998) *Geschiedenis van de Zeeuwse landbouw, c.1600–1910,* 't Goy-Houten.

Roessingh, H. K. (1969) 'Garfpacht, zaadpacht en geldpacht in Gelderland in de 17e en 18e eeuw', *Bijdragen en Mededelingen Vereniging 'Gelre',* 63, pp. 72–97.

Schuurman, A. (2010) 'Agricultural policy and the Dutch agricultural institutional matrix during the transition from organized to disorganized capitalism', in P. Moser and T. Varley (eds), *Integration through subordination. Agriculture and the rural population in European industrial societies,* Turnhout.

Segers, Y. and Hermans, H. (2009) 'Between ideology and science: higher agricultural education in Belgium and the development of a Catholic agricultural network, 1850–1814', *Agricultural History Rev.,* 57, pp. 236–256.

Segers, Y. and Van Molle, L. (eds) (2004) *Leven op het land. Boeren in België, 1750–2000,* Leuven.

Silvis, H. (2008) *Agrarische structuur, trends en beleid. Ontwikkelingen in Nederland vanaf 1950,* Den Haag.

Smaele de, H. (2009) *Rechts Vlaanderen. Religie en stemgedrag in negentiende-eeuws België,* Leuven.

Smits, M. G. M. (1996) *Boeren met beleid. Honderd jaar Katholieke Nederlandse Boeren- en Tuindersbond, 1896–1996,* Nijmegen.

Stol, T. (2002) 'De Leeuw en zijn longen. Waterbeheersing, landaanwinning en landverlies', in T. de Nijs and E. Beukers (eds), *Geschiedenis van Holland, 1572–1795,* Hilversum, pp. 109–135.

Thoen, E. (2001) 'A "commercial survival economy," in evolution. The Flemish countryside and the transition to capitalism (Middle Ages - nineteenth century)', in P. Hoppenbrouwers and J. L. Van Zanden (eds), *Peasants into farmers? The transformation of rural economy and society in the Low Countries (Middle Ages - nineteenth century) in light of the Brenner debate* (CORN Publication Series 4), Turnhout, pp. 102–157.

Vandenbroeke, C. (1979) 'De landbouw in de Zuidelijke Nederlanden 1650–1815', *Algemene Geschiedenis der Nederlanden,* 8, Haarlem, pp. 73–101.

Vanhaute, E. (2001) 'Rich agriculture and poor farmers. Land, landlords and farmers in Flanders in the eighteenth and nineteenth centuries', *Rural History,* 1, pp. 19–40.

Wintle, M. (1986) '"Dearly won and cheaply sold". The purchase and sale of agricultural land in Zeeland in the nineteenth century', *Economisch- en social-historisch jaarboek,* 49, pp. 44–99.

Zanden, J. L. van (1984) 'De opkomst van een eigenerfde boerenklasse in Overijssel, 1750–1850', in *A.A.G. Bijdragen,* Wageningen, pp. 105–131.

Zanden, J. L. van (1985) *De economische ontwikkeling van de Nederlandse landbouw in de negentiende eeuw, 1800–1914,* Utrecht.

NORTH-WEST GERMANY

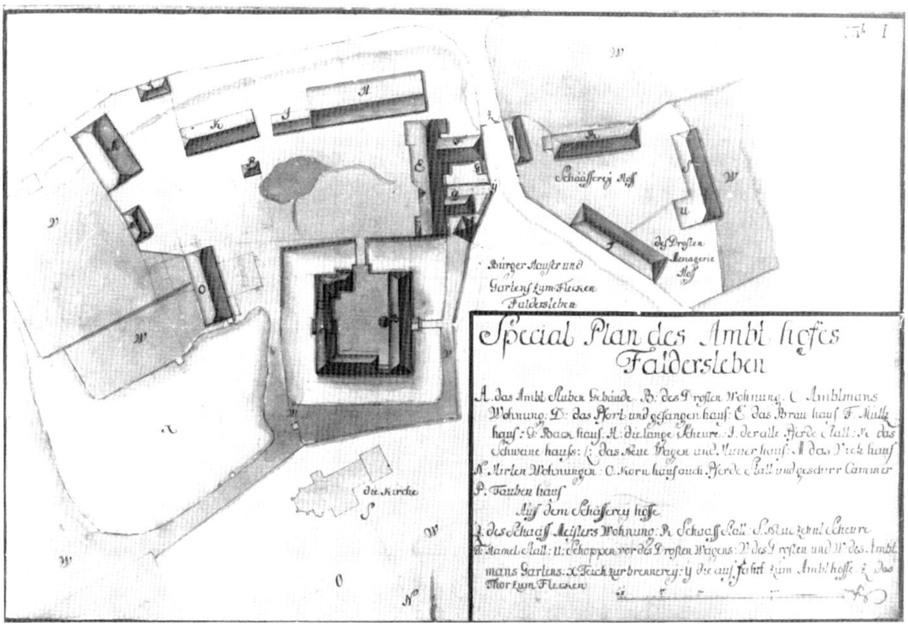

The Hanoverian demesne farm at Fallersleben about 1765.
Such demesnes were important collecting points of peasant dues to the princely states. (Source: NLA, Hauptstaatsarchiv Hannover, Mappe 785, Blatt 1)

9 North-west Germany, 1000–1750

Stefan BRAKENSIEK

North-west Germany includes the lowlands adjoining the North Sea, stretching from the Dutch border in the west to the Baltic Sea in the east, and from the Danish border in the north to a number of low mountain ranges in the south. Today the region covers the German Federal 'Länder' of Schleswig-Holstein, Niedersachsen, Hamburg, Bremen, and the Westphalian part of Nordrhein-Westfalen.

In early medieval times this area was settled by Saxon, Frisian, and Slavonic tribes. In the early ninth century Charlemagne conquered Saxony and incorporated it into the Frankish Empire. The region north of river Elbe, the future duchies of Schleswig and Holstein, remained contested between Frisian, Saxon and Slavonian settlers until it was seized by Henry the Lion (1154–64). After his fall in 1180, this northernmost region, with its hybrid population, was gradually absorbed by the Danish crown, but it continued to be enmeshed in the politics, economy and culture of northern Germany.

Due to its late conversion to Christianity, north-west Germany only gradually gained access to European culture. In the time of the Ottonian and Salian dynasties (919–1024 and 1024–1125 respectively), Saxony became one of the central territories of the German Empire. Only the coastal areas of Frisia and Schleswig-Holstein kept their distance from Imperial politics.

From the twelfth century until the great plague of around 1350, this late-developing region was remarkably dynamic. With the encouragement of steep population growth, soils in the remoter parts were cultivated for the first time, new farmsteads were established and the marshes on the North Sea coast and along the rivers Elbe and Weser were reclaimed by domestic, Frisian and Dutch settlers. Regionally, but mainly in the small loess basins with very fertile soils, scattered hamlets developed into nucleated villages, and a growing number of towns were founded which came to be affiliated to the Hanseatic League. Subsequently the colonisation of the Slavonic north-east was undertaken by noble entrepreneurs and their peasant followers, in large part drawn from the north-west of Germany. As a result, the region was integrated into a new system of political dependencies and economic exchange, acting as a channel of communication between Western and Eastern Europe. But compared with western Europe as a whole, the north-west of Germany stayed weakly urbanised, leaving the countryside as the predominant social sector.

9.1 Ownership, power relations and the distribution of property

Types of landowners

From medieval times until today, north-western Germany has been dominated by peasant agriculture. But until the nineteenth century, peasants did not usually own

Map 9.1 North-west Germany, 1000–1750

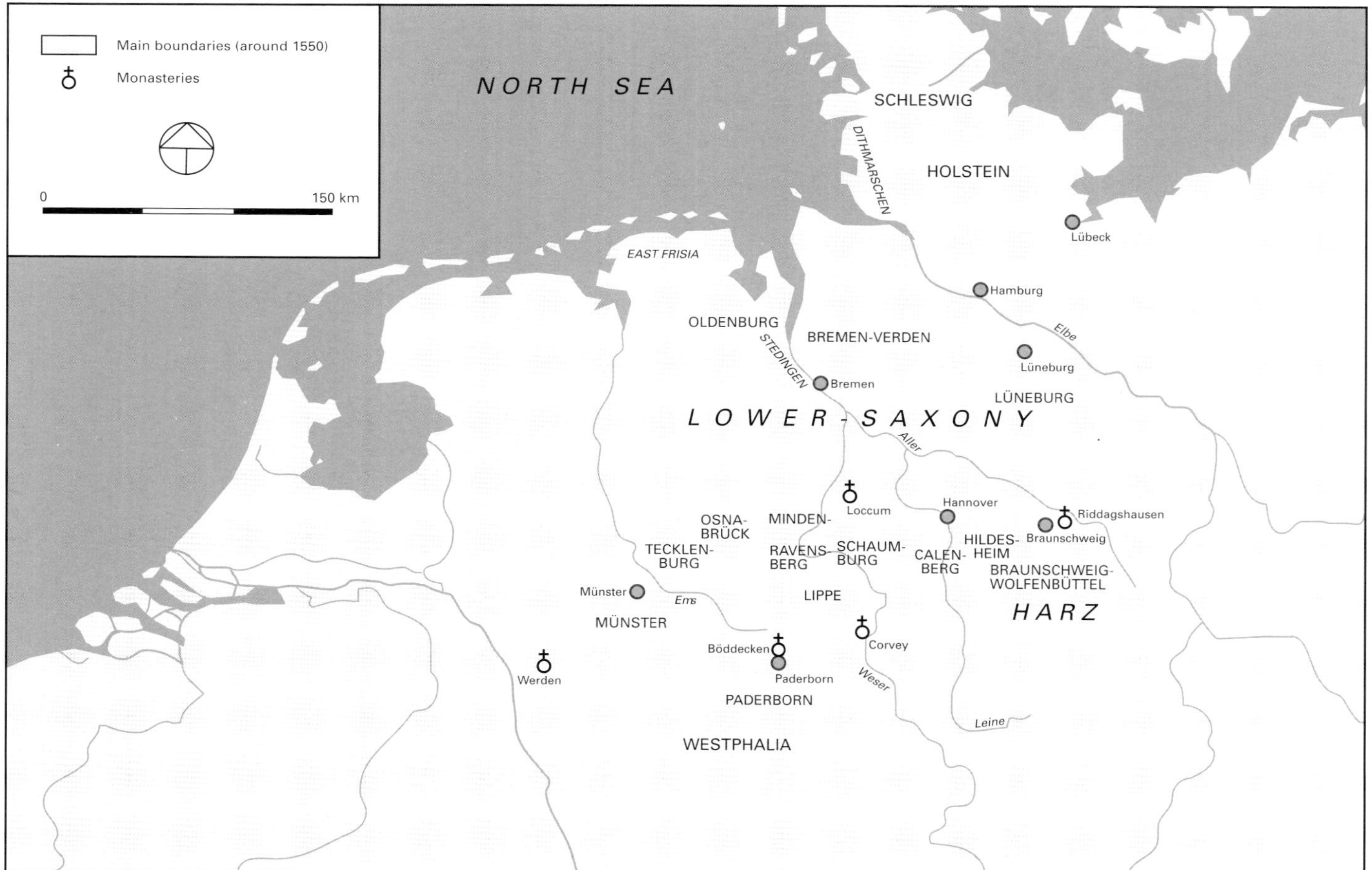

the soil they tilled: typically, freeholders were found only in the coastal regions close by the North Sea, and in the marshes of the rivers Elbe and Weser. In all other parts of this region, peasants were characteristically dependent upon manorial lords.

The ownership of landed property about 1000 is hard to assess due to the lack of sources. Apart from the extensive manors of the churches and abbeys, the demesnes of the Emperor and the noble dynasties were of great importance (Rösener, 1985). The imperial patrimony originated in that of the Ottonian dynasty, but over time, large parts of it had been transferred to ecclesiastical institutions. From the high Middle Ages, the importance of the royal demesnes also diminished, as they were annexed by the emerging princely territories. We know little about the economies of the palace demesnes and the system of villein tenures connected to them. But obviously these royal manors were managed to supply the king and his entourage with sufficient provisions and goods during their visits. In the middle of the twelfth century the *Tafelgüterverzeichnis* lists the royal manors, 20 of them lying in Saxony, most of them concentrated around the *Harz* mountains (Rösener, 1996: 294–96).

We know even less about the properties of the nobility in the high Middle Ages. Many high-ranking native nobles had acquired estates through holding office as counts after the incorporation of Saxony into the Frankish realm, and thus were able to expand their possessions. This so-called *Amtsgut* became treated as inheritable family property, but at the same time, the nobility made many donations to churches and abbeys (Hauptmeyer, 1997: 1056).

Therefore, a large proportion of the cultivated land and its servile peasantry belonged to ecclesiastical institutions. Since the church – especially the monasteries – were the guardians of literacy in a predominant illiterate environment, we are particularly well-informed about their possessions. Obviously the large churches and abbeys disseminated the system of the *villicatio*, a combination of servile tenant farming on local demesnes integrated into a hierarchy of manors, which originated in the Franconian heartland and was adopted to some extent in the north-west. The Benedictine abbeys of Corvey and Werden, both founded in the early ninth century, offer the best examples of manors organized in this way. Generous grants endowed them with estates all over Saxony. Their enormous holdings of land and bondsmen gave them a power that could easily compare with that of bishops and secular lords. At the beginning of the twelfth century, Corvey possessed about 100 manors and 3,000 tenant holdings (Rösener, 1980: 131). Where these monasteries had received donations of widely scattered land, they were satisfied with rents in kind produced by their villeins. In Frisia and much of Westphalia, manors functioned solely as collection centres for peasant dues. But, wherever possible, the Benedictines established consolidated demesnes managed by bailiffs (*villici*) who received an allocation of land or an allowance of produce for their service. For the Corvey demesnes in the Ems-Hunte area, the ratio between demesne land (*Salland*) and the land let to the peasantry has been calculated at about 1:4 (Last, 1983).

The economy of self-sufficient demesnes may have played an important role when market relations were poorly developed in the Ottonian and Salian period. But one should not imagine that demesnes cultivated by unfree servants in husbandry and by the corvées of villein tenants were so very extensive. All in all, the land in the possession of dependent peasants was three or four times greater than the acreage of the demesnes. Where fertile soils prevailed, we are more likely to find an agrarian system characterised by nucleated villages and villein tenancies providing labour for a demesne. In less fertile districts, lords of the manor were more likely to be consuming dues in kind from peasants settled in single farmsteads or hamlets.

Changing social property distribution

From the twelfth century, the increase in population, the expansion of the area of land under cultivation, the emergence of towns and of a market-based society generated new types of landed property. The disintegration of the *villicatio* and the transition to new types of manorial organisation should be emphasised. The dissolution of the old manorial system resulted from different factors, of which the new monetised economy, peasant resistance against labour service, and the struggle of the stewards for greater independence stand out (Hauptmeyer, 1997: 1084–87). The stewards (*Meier, villici*) originated from amongst the villein tenantry and functioned as administrative heads of imperial, noble or ecclesiastical demesnes. In the twelfth and thirteenth centuries they strove for independence and a better legal status. From their ranks the new social group of knightly *Ministerialen* emerged. In many cases they succeeded in transforming their traditional administrative function into hereditary offices. Their descendants acquired the tenancy of the demesnes and became members of the gentry. Typically, the possessions of this lower nobility (*Ritteradel*) remained modest when compared to the considerable holdings of the ecclesiastical institutions.

Parallel to the dissolution of the old manorial system, the newly founded collegiate churches and reformed abbeys, most notably those of the Cistercians, developed a novel organisation of their manors. Unlike the Benedictine abbeys, the Cistercians managed their demesnes to a great extent as granges (*grangiae*) operating with the help of lay brothers and wage labourers (Wiswe, 1953). The produce of these monastic farms was sold in the flourishing cities, and the profits were used for improvement of the demesnes and for the acquisition of further farmland (Rösener, 1990). The economic success of the Cistercian abbeys like Loccum and Riddagshausen rested less upon agricultural innovations or clearings, and more upon their efficient manorial organisation (Boetticher, 1990). So, in late medieval times, a great variety of types of landed property and manorial systems existed side by side. Unfortunately, we have no reliable figures for the distribution of acreage or income among territorial princes, ecclesiastical institutions, nobility, townsmen, and freeholding peasants. But a number of local and regional studies show that a general process of consolidation took place because most lords were eager to sell the more remote parts of their estates in order to buy property close to their main demesnes.

Whilst the Emperors had lost all their possessions since the high Middle Ages, the territorial princes had gained crucial influence over the countryside, partly as estate-owners, partly as beneficiaries of tithes, rents and services, and overall as

Table 9.1: Number and percentage of bondsmen of the territorial lords, of the nobility and of ecclesiastical institutions before and after the Reformation in the duchies of Schleswig and Holstein

		Duke		Nobility		Church		Total	
		n	%	n	%	n	%		%
Schleswig	1523	10,431	71.1	2300	15.6	1950	13.3	14,681	100.0
	1592	11,511	78.4	2527	17.2	643	4.4	14,681	100.0
Holstein	1523	2122	29.1	2358	32.2	2815	38.6	7295	99.9
	1592	3343	45.8	2641	36.2	1311	18.0	7295	100.0

Source: Prange, 1983: 80, 89.

the recipients of taxes. Even the imperial taxation to finance war against the Turks turned out to be means of expanding princely revenues. As much of the German north-west followed the Lutheran Reformation, most monasteries were dissolved in the sixteenth century. We are particularly well informed about the effects of the Reformation on lordship over the peasantry in Schleswig-Holstein. Table 9.1 demonstrates that the prince took over monastic demesnes and the dues owed by peasants to ecclesiastical institutions, and although plenty of them were granted to noble followers or Protestant collegiate churches, he remained in possession of a high proportion of the land and income. Similar developments occurred all over Lower Saxony and in the secular principalities of Westphalia. For example, in 1550 in the Lutheran county of Ravensberg, 1,172 (43.1 per cent) of the serfs belonged to the prince, 1,213 (44.7 per cent) to members of the squirearchy, 299 (11.0 per cent) to ecclesiastical institutions, and 31 (1.1 per cent) to burghers and town magistrates (Schreiber, 1907: 19). Only in the vicinity of important towns, i.e. Braunschweig, Bremen, Lübeck and Hamburg, did burghers and city magistrates acquire former ecclesiastical possessions.

During the agricultural booms of the sixteenth and the eighteenth centuries, the regional nobilities tried to enlarge their estates and to increase the rent payments of their dependents, but – with the exception of Holstein – these efforts were restrained by the territorial princes, who in most parts of the north-west of Germany, succeeded in the preservation of the peasantry (*Bauernschutz*) in order to safeguard their tax revenues. Therefore, most noblemen lived on the basis of peasant rent, and had second incomes as courtiers, officers and civil servants of the princely states. Since the Reformation failed in most of Westphalia, there bishoprics, chapters and abbeys remained the main beneficiaries of peasant dues.

Systems of tenure

In the early Middle Ages, the manorial system of the *villicatio* with its tendency towards self-sufficiency was an aspect of an economy characterised by poorly developed exchange relations, the compulsory labour of serfs and very limited surpluses. The high medieval upswing of the urban sector and the intensification in the exchange of goods caused long term changes in the system of rural surplus extraction. Two types of development can be distinguished. Firstly, the traditional main demesne (*Fronhof*) might be leased to a single peasant who operated it with the aid of some corvée, but mainly with wage labour. In this circumstance, the demesne retained its closed character and remained the collection point for manorial dues. In the second scenario, the arable land of the demesne could be completely subdivided into farmsteads, and the corvée reduced to a few days a year, being mostly converted into fixed rents in kind or money. Both strategies did not result in the dissolution of the manorial system but in its monetarization. Although the peasants obtained more secure use rights and could farm more independently, their burdens may actually have increased.

In the fourteenth century, climate change caused crop failures and devastating erosion, which, coupled with the great plague, brought to an end the long expansion of the rural economy and led to an agrarian depression which affected all the different regions of the German north-west to varying degrees. Overall, approximately a quarter of all rural settlements were deserted (Abel, 1976). Permanent abandonment occurred mainly in the barren and remote regions, whereas temporary desertion of farmland and settlement prevailed elsewhere. The open fields of abandoned settlements were often added to the cultivated land of neighbouring villages and their common lands used as sheep pastures by the lords of the manor. Sheep farming was one possible response of the lords to the dramatic decrease in their income, caused by decline in rents, dues in kind and agricultural prices. Other strategies included increasing the output of their demesnes through an expansion in the compulsory labour required from its tenants, or its reverse, the reduction of labour services to promote the recovery of the peasant economy (Hauptmeyer, 1997: 1111–31).

The classic work of Werner Wittich provides us with basic information about developments in Lower Saxony and the eastern parts of Westphalia (Wittich, 1896). In the thirteenth century secular and ecclesiastical landlords began to lease the main grange of their *villicatio* to a personally free tenant, on short-term contracts of three, six or nine years. Initially the majority of the peasants remained in an unfree condition as *Laten*, but following the great plague (which reached north-western Germany in 1349–50), lease contracts spread amongst them, too. All attempts to coerce peasants to stay in their traditional state of bondage proved to be futile. A study of the village of Tudorf, situated in the prince-bishopric of Paderborn (Lienen, 1991), shows the implications of the dissolution of a *villicatio*. After the great plague, most surviving peasants left the barren grounds of Tudorf for more fertile regions in the neighbourhood. To retain those who remained, the abbey of Böddeken, as the local lord, had to abandon serfdom completely. Thereafter, peasants could lease land on short lets and at reasonable prices, according to the needs of their households and market conditions.

Leasehold did not establish any hereditary right nor a relationship of dependence. In the fifteenth century, the situation gradually changed. Initially peasant families tried to accumulate farms and property. From about 1480 they strove for longer leasehold contracts in order not to be exposed to the worsening terms of trade, and over the course of the sixteenth century, they had to accept new forms of dependence in exchange for security of tenure. A new feudal stability arose which was characterised by legal certainty for both sides: higher rents for the lord, hereditary use-rights for the peasant. Peasants though were required to preserve the unity of their farms and could only entail them to a single heir, leaving the other surviving children with much smaller legacies. Nor was the tenant allowed to sell parts of his farm or to secure a loan without seigneurial permission. In most cases corvée played only a minor role. Peasants usually had to pay a mixture of rents in cash and grain or livestock. This relationship between lords and peasants was called *Meierrecht*, and it left peasants personally free (Achilles, 1998; Saalfeld 1998).

In the seventeenth and eighteenth centuries *Meierrecht* was the dominant legal form of the relationship between lords and peasants in nearly all the territories of Lower Saxony. In Braunschweig-Wolfenbüttel, Hildesheim and Paderborn, *Meierrecht* was accompanied by more advantageous leasehold contracts (*Erbzins*) for those peasants with the most sizable farms. For instance, in Braunschweig-Wolfenbüttel in 1685, three quarters of all peasants held their farms according to *Meierrecht*, one fifth as leaseholds, and 5 per cent as freeholds (Saalfeld, 1998: 646). Leasehold was even more usual in the south-east, in Göttingen-Grubenhagen.

By contrast, in most parts of Westphalia, an attenuated form of medieval bondage – *Eigenbehörigkeit* – was preserved until about 1800. The opportunity for peasants to move in the later middle ages to nearby regions with better terms of tenure forced lords to moderate services and rents. The numerous smallholders created since the sixteenth century had never been subject to bondage, with the result that the wealthiest peasants were bondsmen, whereas their poorer neighbours were personally free (Mooser, 1984). Table 9.2 shows the percentage of freeholders and bondsmen of the respective prince, noblemen, ecclesiastical institutions and townsfolk in several Westphalian principalities at the end of the eighteenth century. It demonstrates the continuing significance of servitude in a small secular principality like the County of Lippe and shows the continuing importance of the clergy as feudal lords, both in bishoprics like Osnabrück, Paderborn and Münster, but also in Protestant territories like the Prussian province of Minden-Ravensberg and Lippe.

Westphalian bondsmen had to deliver a heriot (*Sterbfall*) and a recognition fee (*Weinkauf*) on their inheritance and marriage fines (*Auffahrt)* for a spouse who married into a farmstead. From the sixteenth century onwards, these dues lost some of their oppressive nature because they were monetarized, with the amounts being determined by the territorial courts. When grain prices recovered in the eighteenth century, lords tried to profit by increasing regular rents and casual dues. These attempts were only partly successful because the princely states were eager to protect peasants against this 'réaction seigneuriale' (Scharpwinkel, 1965). All in all they guaranteed stable feudal dues, and ensured that peasants retained an adequate

TABLE 9.2: Bondsmen and freeholders in some Westphalian regions in the eighteenth century (per cent)

	Bondsmen (*Eigenbehörige*) of				Freeholders	%
	Territorial Lord	Nobility	Ecclesiastical Institutions	Burghers/ Magistrates		
Osnabrück (Artland)	4.4	14.0	11.8	1.3	68.5	100.0
Osnabrück (centre)	9.2	24.9	7.6	22.5	35.9	99.9
Paderborn	19.9	7.1	2.3	-	70.7	100.0
Münster	6.0	33.8	34.7	9.0	16.5	100.0
Lippe	66.7	7.6	8.7	-	17.0	100.0
Minden-Ravensberg	29.0	22.3	7.2	-	41.4	99.9

Sources: Prince bishopric of Osnabrücker: Artland 1772, Reinders-Düselder, 2000: 203; Prince bishopric of Osnabrück: Central region 1723, Hirschfelder, 1971: 52; Prince bishopric of Paderborn: 1750–1800, Mooser, 1984: 97; Prince bishopric of Münster: Oberstift in the late eighteenth century, Feldmann, 1994; County of Lippe: late eighteenth century, Krawinkel, 1935: 146–48; Prussian province of Minden-Ravensberg, 1795, Mooser, 1984: 97).

income. Stability did not imply stagnation. Recent local studies (Schlumbohm, 1994; Rüffer, 2008) have shown that an apparently rigid rule, for example, impartible inheritance by a single male heir, was actually administered in quite a flexible fashion. The rules established only a framework, within which members of peasant families and landlords pursued their respective strategies. It must be pointed out that in most parts of the north-west Germany, these contests produced no definite winners or losers because most lords of the manor were prevented from securing complete jurisdiction over their peasants.

Where however feudal dependency and jurisdiction were held by a single lord, regions or at least islands of manorialism emerged. Grain-producing demesnes using corvée on a large scale came into existence in the sixteenth and seventeenth centuries. Until recently, the impact of this flourishing manorial economy in the west of Germany has been underestimated by a historiography which has been preoccupied with the dualism between western *Grundherrschaft* and eastern *Gutsherrschaft*. The dominance of peasant agriculture supporting a rent-consuming nobility in the west of Germany should not be denied, but the territories of some petty princes, e.g. in the Counties of Lippe (Linde *et al.*, 2004), and Schaumburg-Lippe (Schneider, 1983), the Duchy of Braunschweig-Wolfenbüttel (Saalfeld, 1960; Lutterloh, 1969), and the liberties of the Gottorf side lines in Holstein (Rasmussen, 2005), bear a striking resemblance to the domains of the Prussian or Bohemian aristocracy. For example, the County of Schaumburg-Lippe – one of the small territories of the Holy Roman Empire and in the ninteenth century a sovereign state – 'strikes the retrospective observer as a huge domain with a patriarchal prince at its top' (Rothe, 1998: 140). Corvée was used on a large scale there: the peasantry not only had to till the fields of ten state demesnes, but were also obliged to maintain the road and path network, to build the princely fortress and palace, and to carry grain from the Count's domains, timber from the Count's forests, and coal from the Count's pits. So, the obligatory services of tenants holding substantial farms (*Vollmeier*) could be as many as 200 days per year, forcing tenants to maintain an additional team of draft animals and a hired labourer with which to undertake their service (Schneider, 1983: 73–85).

Although on a smaller scale, similar developments can be found in the eastern swathe of Lower Saxony where manors of noblemen (*Rittergüter*) exercising civil and criminal jurisdiction over single villages or a number of villages were quite common. The rise of big grain producers in the sixteenth century did not happen by chance, since these regions had easy access to the expanding markets of west Europe via the rivers Elbe and Weser. Recent studies (Linnemeier, 1992a; Bei der Wieden, 1993; Rappe-Weber, 2005) have shown the relevance of these manors for the economy and culture of their local environments. What is more, in most territories in the seventeenth and eighteenth centuries state demesnes were leased to bailiffs (*Amtleute*), who administered the law, and collected taxes and dues in their district (Linnemeier, 1992b). Some of these officials ran the domains as gentlemen farmers, while others sublet them. This practice constituted a starting point for the emergence of a small but prosperous middle-class elite whose members acquired estates whenever opportunities arose in the eighteenth and nineteenth centuries, whether on the failure of a noble family, the privatisation of state demesnes, or the secularisation of ecclesiastical foundations. Again, these were important developments on a local level, but they did not change the fundamental character of the social structure of the region.

In the Duchies of Schleswig and Holstein, the situation of the peasantry developed in divergent ways. Freeholdings were characteristic of the western marshlands and customary tenants in the central region. In the eastern parts of Holstein bordering the Baltic Sea, heavily burdened servile peasants were commonly treated as mere accessories to estates from the fifteenth century (Steinborn, 1982; Prange, 2008). In 1524, at a moment of financial and political weakness, the Danish crown had to enact the so-called 'Great Privilege' (*Großes Privileg*) which assigned the exercise of high jurisdiction to prelates and knights. It resulted in a bifurcation of rural development in the sixteenth century, which only ended in the eighteenth. In the eastern parts of Holstein, favoured by fertile soils and easy access to the Baltic Sea ports, the privileged lords used their unrestricted local power to erect an extreme form of manorialism, based on the corvée of serfs (Prange, 1971: 592–93). On these manors the famous *Holsteiner Koppelwirtschaft*, a productive convertible husbandry evolved. The more infertile and distant inland regions of Schleswig developed in a completely different way, along the same lines as neighbouring Lower Saxony, and state and noble estates both remained small. As everywhere else in the north-west, noble landowners tried to extend their holdings in the course of the sixteenth century, but they made no great progress and with the crisis of the seventeenth century, they realised that *Dienstablösungen*, the conversion of corvée into rents, produced better profits (Rasmussen, 2005). In the eighteenth century this policy was adopted by a minority of the Holstein nobility who granted their peasants manumission for humanitarian and commercial considerations (Cord, 1997).

Several regional studies provide us with sophisticated data on the impact of feudal and public burdens on the peasant economy in the eighteenth century, particularly for Lower Saxony, whereas details of the situation in Westphalia remain unsatisfactory. Table 9.3 demonstrates that the territorial princes received the lion's share of taxes, dues and services of the rural population.

To start with the Duchy of Braunschweig-Wolfenbüttel in 1760, two-fifths of the state revenues stemming from the countryside consisted of taxes (mainly *Kontributionen* i.e. real-estate taxes), another fifth in services, a quarter in tithes, and only 13.7 per cent in rents. Traditionally the tithes weighed heavily on the rural population, but the overall burden had been much aggravated by increases in taxation in the course of the seventeenth century. The rural tax incomes of the Duke increased from 5,700 Taler in 1636 to 39,000 Taler in 1659, reaching 149,900 Taler in 1698 (Achilles, 1998: 695). This demonstrates the striking ability of the princely administrations to access peasant surpluses, a necessary precondition for the survival of petty principalities until 1800 (Achilles, 1991: 35–41). By 1760, feudal and fiscal burdens had risen to a very high level indeed, ranging from a third to a half of the gross proceeds of the peasant economy. The smallest share of income was paid by leaseholders, whereas peasants with *Meier*-contracts were the most heavily burdened (Saalfeld, 1960: 39–46). Until rising grain prices in the late eighteenth century improved their economic situation, peasants owning substantial farms do not

Table 9.3: Percentage of peasant taxes, tithes, rents and services paid to the princely states, noble lords of the manor, ecclesiastical institutions and townsfolk in the eighteenth century

	Territorial Lord	Nobility	Ecclesiastical Institutions	Burghers/Magistrates	%
Hanover (Altes Land)	44.5	34.2	11.2	9.6	99.5
Hanover (Scharmbecker Geest)	73.0	21.5	0.5	5.0	100.0
Hanover (Suderburg parish)	69.5	26.3	4.2	-	100.0
Braunschweig-Wolfenbüttel	68.3	16.6	8.0	7.1	100.0
Paderborn	60.0	30.0	10.0	-	100.0

Sources: Hanover: Altes Land 1760–1780, Brümmel, 1975: 89–91; Hanover: Scharmbecker Geest, 1760–1780, Brümmel, 1975: 89–91; Hanover: Suderburg parish, 1743, Wendler, 1999: 175; Duchy of Braunschweig-Wolfenbüttel, 1760, Lutterloh, 1969: 171–73; Paderborn: 1750–1800, Henning, 1969: 80.

appear greatly better off than smallholders because taxes, dues, and services creamed off so much of their income (Achilles, 1982). These findings should warn us not to have too great an admiration of the princely *Bauernschutz*-policy. To some degree, the situation of the peasantry in the smaller German principalities can be characterized as a form of state slavery.

In the larger territories, the position of peasants was more advantagous. For example, in three northern districts of the Hanoverian principality of Lüneburg in the middle of the eighteenth century, substantial farmers had to deliver labour services for not more than 54 days per year (Risto, 1964: 9–14). In the Duchy of Bremen-Verden, situated in the west of Lower Saxony, services were negligible, and tithes normally were leased to the peasant communities. Taxes, dues and services amounted to at least 14.7 per cent and at most 30.7 per cent, all in all a modest proportion of the gross proceeds of peasant economies (Brümmel, 1975: 136–37). Peasants were better off in the periphery of the Hanoverian territorial complex. In the district of Wildeshausen owners of substantial farmsteads (*Vollmeier*) had to deliver 11.1 per cent of their gross product. In the district of Diepenau the corresponding value is estimated at 16.0 per cent. The owners of smaller farms were burdened with a smaller level of obligation (von Bremen, 1971: 79–83).

As one would expect, the situation of peasants in the Duchy of Holstein depended on their rights of ownership. A comparison of various regions shows that freeholders had to deliver about 25 per cent of their gross product, mainly in the form of taxes and public services, to church and commune. The subordinates of three state demesnes were charged with 37 per cent on average, the bondsmen of three noble estates with about 48 per cent (Steinborn, 1982: 61).

In the ecclesiastical principalities of Westphalia, the peasants' situation was relatively advantagous in general, though varying widely in detail, and dependant on whether a farmstead belonged to the bishop, to a monastery, or to a secular lord of the manor. In the bishopric of Osnabrück substantial farms belonging to manors were burdened with obligations ranging from 23.2 per cent up to 33.7 per cent of their gross product, whereas the dependants of the bishop had to deliver between 19.5 to 28.5 per cent and those of abbeys between 17.0 and 24.3 per cent. In the northern part of the bishopric of Münster the ecclesiastical prince received only very small percentages (2.8 up to 11.8 per cent) of the gross product of his *Eigenbehörigen*, whilst the peasants on the noble estate of Daren paid 25.0 per cent (von Bremen, 1971: 79–83). All in all, these findings affirm the contemporary opinion that it was 'best to live under the crook'.

Finally, an attempt should be made to summarize these complicated variations. The total obligations of a peasant depended – as we might expect – on his legal status in relation to the lord. In each given region, a bondsman owed higher dues than a free tenant or a leaseholder. Even if the occasional financial penalties of serfdom, namely payments on marriage or inheritance, did not pile up insurmountably, they were dreaded by peasants because they normally coincided and could cause heavy debt (Henning, 1964). Therefore, during a period of high grain prices in the late eighteenth century, bondsmen were willing to pay astonishingly high redemptions to their lords in order to be rid of these aggravating personal obligations (von Bremen, 1971: 114–18). Nevertheless, in all regions, a trend towards standardization can be detected. As a rule, peasants situated far from the lord's administrative centre had to cope with much lower obligations than their unlucky companions farming close to the princely demesne or the manor to which they were attached.

In case of emergency (as a result of war, fire, hail, crop failure or epidemic), peasants under feudal obedience enjoyed a general right of remission of their obligations. As this entitlement was nowhere precisely formulated, the peasants concerned had to hope that the ideal of magnanimity and generosity would operate in practice. The example of the district of Wildeshausen (a part of the Hanoverian Duchy of Bremen and Verden) shows that this hope could be realised. There, remissions accounted for an average of 2.4 per cent of the expected annual income in the eighteenth century with a range of between 0.2 per cent and 10.8 per cent (von Bremen, 1971: 125–28). Remissions were a matter of constant bargaining between lords and peasants. The peasants often refused to deliver all dues on time, and called for a respite or a full remission. In case of official refusal, they nevertheless sometimes did not pay the full amount. Surprisingly, the disobedient were normally not evicted from their farmsteads although the law allowed for that to happen.

In the eighteenth century most peasants were inclined to convert their dues and services to money rents, whilst lords adopted different attitudes according to their manorial regime. In fact, the lease of arable in small parcels to the growing rural population proved to be the most profitable option and a majority of the lords of manors adopted this strategy. But where corvée was owed by peasants and their teams in abundance it was possible to run an estate successfully. The question of whether it was wise to preserve corvée was increasingly a matter of debate in the eighteenth century. In the Prussian provinces of the West, state demesnes were parcelled out and let for rent as early as the 1720s, whereas in the Hanoverian territories this was not done before the 1830s.

The trend towards cash rents involved not only services, but also those dues that peasants traditionally had to deliver in kind. In the eighteenth century the proportion of rents paid in kind ranges from nothing to more than half. Again, in times of rising prices, peasants were eager to commute payment in kind into cash. Where such a commutation had been agreed upon 'since time immemorial' (usually since the seventeenth century), the inflation of the eighteenth was to the peasants' advantage. But most lords were aware of changing prices, so that the terms of commutation were often the subject of annual negotiation. Sometimes the manager of an estate agreed upon a rate of commutation tied to the *Kammertaxe*, an official price table published by the government which was regularly adjusted in line with market prices. As monetarised dues became more and more usual, the integration of the peasant economy into markets proceeded.

The economic and the cultural value of land

The economic value of land should be determined by examining its price, but this is not as easy as we might suppose because markets in land were subject to restrictions and peculiarities. In the early modern period, in most parts of the north-west of Germany, state authorities prohibited the buying and selling of peasant farmsteads and even single parcels of farmland. The price of estates also differed according to whether or not they conveyed political rights as well as land or permitted the exercise of manorial jurisdiction or other forms of local power. All these factors influenced the attitudes of owners who could look upon their estates as profitable investments, but for the most part mainly valued their lands as sources of social and cultural status.

The few studies available demonstrate that, except for the coastal marshes where market transactions were quite common due to the lack of feudal ties, commercial land transfers among villagers were of little importance (Brakensiek, 2004). For instance, in the district of Schöningen in the Duchy of Braunschweig, the official registers recorded just a small number of sales at low prices between 1661 and 1808. Single plots were primarily sold to pay off debts; arable land that had been mortgaged only passed to a new owner if the debtor had lost all hope of repayment. On the buyers' side there were relatively large numbers of non-peasants, often rural craftsmen eager to invest their surplus money in land. Even during the last decade of the eighteenth century, when the local land market was at its height, there was a turn-over of less than 0.1 per cent of the total acreage per year (Achilles, 1965: 11). This marginality of transactions was due to legal restrictions and does not indicate the economic or cultural insignificance of landed property. The value and prestige of land can be demonstrated by the demand for allotments (*Zuschlag*), plots which had been part of the village commons and which were rented out to the landless poor by the administrations of most territorial states in the eighteenth century as part of a policy of encouraging population increase. Although the cultivation of these meagre heaths and moorlands proved to be very arduous, the initiative was quite successful, especially in those regions where a linen industry had emerged. The demand for these allotments shows how indispensable landed property was, both as a means of feeding a family, but also as an indication that its holder would become a full member of the rural community (Brakensiek, 1991: 204–07, 261–63).

9.2 The occupiers of the land

Peasant ownership of land

Before the Frankish conquest the Saxon population was divided into serfs (*servi)*, semi-dependent peasants (*Laten* or *liti*) and freemen (*liberi*). But the sources are silent about the proportion of the different categories. The consolidation of the manorial system in the high Middle Ages resulted in a decrease in the number of free peasants, whereas the numbers of serfs and semi-dependent peasants rose. The latter, the so-called *Laten,* were the most numerous group in the rural population and their servile status came to predominate. From the eleventh century onwards, the sources increasingly name the people cultivating the land as simply peasants (*rustici*), and terms which record the degree of their servility gradually disappear (Hauptmeyer; 1997: 1058).

By the end of the Middle Ages only a few freeholders can be found in Westphalia and Lower Saxony. By contrast a greater number of free peasants could be found in the wetlands. Wealthy freeholders are mentioned in Frisian records from the eleventh century and they were not totally displaced by the expansion of manors in the twelfth and thirteenth centuries (Schmidt, 1973; Hauptmeyer, 1997: 1095–1100). The free peasants here were a wealthy minority who in turn had dependent smallholders, wage labourers and servants. Rural society took similar forms along the coast of Schleswig-Holstein and at the banks of river Weser and Elbe, where in the eleventh century, a series of new settlements were founded which joined together to form strong associations. All these freeholding communities were reliant on the construction and maintenance of dykes. They benefited from their easy access to supra-regional markets with the result that stratified societies emerged at an early date. But none of them were immune to threats from their nearby feudal lords. In the Weser marshes attempts by neighbouring lords to extend lordship over freeholding peasants were successful as early as the twelfth century (Deike, 1959). The most striking example of the erosion of economic and political freedom of freeholders is provided by the Stedinger-Crusade of the thirteenth century, which ended with the defeat of the peasant cohorts against the cavalry of the Bishop of Bremen in 1234 (Schmidt, 1982–83). North of the mouth of the river Elbe, the freeholders of Dithmarschen succeeded in building a territorial state in the fifteenth century, with an army that was able to defeat the knightly contingent of the Danish crown in 1500 at the battle of Hemmingstedt. Even when this was overwhelmed by in 1559, the peasant *Regenten* negotiated a peace with the Danish king which conferred regional self-administration and secure property rights (Stoob, 1959; Witt, 1975).

Everywhere else dependent peasants dominated agriculture, but that does not mean that there was social equality amongst the rural population. In the eleventh century every tenant family cultivated a *Hufe* (*mansus*) which varied in size from about 5 to 10 ha according to the conditions of the soil. However, in the high Middle Ages numerous cottage holdings (*Kate, Kotten*) came into existence which consisted of only a few hectares. By the later Middle Ages, stratification was far advanced throughout north-west Germany. In most villages peasants running substantial farms lived side by side with smallholders and lodgers who made their living as stockbreeders, day labourers, craftsmen, and pedlars.

During the economic revival of the sixteenth century, social differences among the rural population intensified. Table 9.4 shows the social stratification of the rural population of Lower Saxony in about 1600.

Certainly, the losses of the Thirty Years' War offered possibilities for smallholders to acquire larger farms. But in the course of the eighteenth century, social conditions deteriorated again as the rural population increased and agricultural prices rose sharply. The villages were crowded with labouring poor who tried to acquire a garden plot or a small allotment enclosed out of the commons. In Lower Saxony the eighteenth-century increase in population pushed up the numbers of medium-sized farms (*Köter*) and smallholdings (*Brinksitzer*), whilst the numbers of substantial farms (*Meier*) stagnated or were even reduced in number (Achilles, 1991: 58). In Westphalia too, the holders of substantial farmsteads, called *Meier*, *Hufener* or *Wehrfester,* represented only a minority of the rural population. In the Prince bishopric of Paderborn for example, smallholders and crofters already constituted the majority in the early eighteenth century (Henning, 1970: 30). At the same time in the county of Schaumburg-Lippe, peasants did not account for more than 39.0 per cent of the adult male population. Rural craftsmen formed 22.5 per cent, day labourers 10.5 per cent, subtenants who made their living as industrial workers or miners up to 12.0 per cent and servants in husbandry up to 16.0 per cent (Schneider,

TABLE 9.4: Peasant classes in Lower Saxony at about 1600

	Percentage of number of farms	Percentage of acreage	Mean possession (ha)	Mean variation (ha)
Vollmeier	22	61	18	15 – 30
Halbmeier	13	18	9	6 – 15
Große Köter	18	11	4	2 – 8
Kleine Köter	39	9	1.5	0 – 3
Brinksitzer	8	1	0.5	0 – 1.5
	100	100	6.5	

Source: Saalfeld, 1998: 656.

1983: 42). In Minden-Ravensberg, Tecklenburg, Lippe, and in parts of Osnabrück where the linen industry was a major employer, the landless poor were in the majority from the late eighteenth century (Mooser, 1984: 232). The land the *Heuerlinge* needed to cultivate for food and flax was sublet from the peasantry. They made their living partly from smallholding and partly as labourers for the peasant who provided them with land.

Communal land use systems, their adaptation and disappearance

German historians of the nineteenth and early twentieth centuries were fascinated by questions of origins. Following Romantic scholarship, they were confident of the great antiquity of the constitution of the commons (*Markenverfassung*), which was said to reflect the popular spirit (*Volksgeist*) in the German and even the Germanic past, characterized by general equality and community. This view cannot be verified by either archaeological or written sources. Not until population growth in the high Middle Ages was it necessary to regulate the use of heathland and moors, pastures and woods. These resources were then used in various ways by cooperatives, by whole village communes, or by privileged groups within the villages. They grazed their cattle there and gathered firewood and forage. Collective use was not limited to areas in common ownership; communal use rights could also be exercised over many fields, meadows and woods in private ownership. Common rights were of considerable significance particularly in those areas with nucleated villages and an open field system in which regular crop rotations were practiced. Domestic animals were driven on to stubble and fallow pasture. They were also allowed to graze on the meadows in spring when grass was starting to grow, and again in late summer, after the hay had been cut. Often village communities were allowed to collect fallen branches and firewood and to let cattle graze and swine feed in private forests. Private and common ownership of land was so intertwined that peasant survival could only be guaranteed if they took advantage of both (Brakensiek, 2002).

Large common woods, wastelands and pastures were owned by cooperatives known as *Marken*. The *Markgenossenschaften* were complex self-governing organisations. The first references to them are found in the twelfth century, but sources become more numerous from the fifteenth century onwards. By that time, *Marken* were particularly common in the ecclesiastical principalities of Westphalia. Local courts, known as *Höltinge* or *Markengerichte*, were held regularly and attended by lords and peasants. Peasants with full rights of usufruct on the commons were known as *Erben* ('inheritors'). The *Markenrichter* (lay judges) and *Erbexen* (persons entitled to use the commons in a privileged manner) were drawn from amongst the local nobility. The courts examined infringements of the regulations of the cooperative and controlled the use of the *Marken* according to agreed by-laws (Schütte, 2004).

In the lay principalities, on the other hand, small *Gemeinheiten* (village commons) prevailed. Here the lords of the manor or the territorial princes exercised the right of ownership, although the peasants were granted rights of use over most of the land. In Lower Saxony access to the commons was only open to members of the rural municipalities according to the size of their holdings. In Westphalia and Schleswig-Holstein, use of the commons also depended on the occupation of land. Rights of usufruct were attached to some or all peasant holdings in a hamlet, village, municipality or parish. A recent edition of village by-laws (*Dorfordnungen*) in the Duchy of Schleswig demonstrates how lords and village communes cooperated to regulate the *Marken* in line with local needs (Rheinheimer, 1999).

Wherever cultivable soils could be found in the north-west, common land was transferred to private hands as a *Zuschlag*, a form of piecemeal enclosure made from the late fifteenth to the eighteenth centuries. Allotments were made to old-established peasants as well as settlers and resulted in an increase of the arable at the expense of the commons. These newly cultivated plots of arable, scattered like an archipelago in the sea of common woods, heaths and fens, were used in severalty. Locally, such developments could result in the complete enclosure of the commons, but both in Lower Saxony and Westphalia, they normally remained largely intact until 1770. In contrast, an enclosure movement started as early as the sixteenth century in Schleswig-Holstein, gained in pace in the seventeenth and had run its course by 1800. Some Holstein regions were notably quick to enclose, mainly in the surroundings of the ports of Hamburg, Lübeck, and Schleswig. Here, peasants were eager to participate in the prosperity of manorial livestock farming, and took steps to enclose their open fields and common grazings before 1730. After a phase of stagnation in mid-century owing to cattle disease and a slump in agricultural prices, enclosure made rapid progress after 1763 with the support of the Danish crown, and it had largely been completed by 1800 (Prange, 1971: 610–39).

The exercise of power within the village

Starting in the thirteenth century, rural communes emerged which developed out of older forms of informal regulation of crop rotation and pasture between neighbours (Wunder, 1986: 26–32; Troßbach and Zimmermann, 2005: 21–45). Where an association of villeins belonging to a *villicatio* or a community of privileged settlers existed, their collective business might have been administered by an autonomous local court (*Hofrechtsverband, Meierding, Hägergericht*) (Hauptmeyer, 1991). But usually different forms of peasant communes developed as semi-autonomous corporations with varying functions in the late Middle Ages: the parish as a union of households whose members belonged to a local church, the *Bauerschaft* as the smallest entity of neighbouring farmsteads enabling peasants to solve jointly the diverse problems of everyday life, and the association of commoners (*Margenossenschaft*) which normally embraced a greater number of *Bauerschaften* and some manors. In those regions where scattered settlements prevailed, all three forms coexisted until about 1800, whereas in regions with nucleated villages the different functions were normally merged into one village commune.

In medieval times all types of communes and corporations used to administer their own local law: a lord in person or his deputy 'found' a judgement with the help of a peasant jury. From the fifteenth century, justice was increasingly administered without the involvement of peasants by powerful outsiders: sometimes by a lord of the manor or – mostly – by an *Amtmann* or *Vogt*, a high-ranking princely official residing in the next town or borough. Full juridical and political autonomy of village communes survived only in some parts of Frisia, Holstein, and Westphalia (Lange, 1988). Elsewhere, early modern communities enjoyed only partial autonomy in day-to-day economic matters. But the history of the village communes is not only marked by this loss of autonomous power. Alongside the rising power of the princely territories, the functions of the peasant communes increased, because state officials could not avoid relying upon village functionaries to implement the state's agenda. The state's agent might be the parish priest (the traditional provider of writing in the village), but normally peasant village officials were held responsible for the collection of taxes and tithes, the construction and maintenance of paths and ditches, the recruitment of soldiers, and the organisation of schools and poor relief. The last two duties were carried out by parish authorities, i.e. churchwardens and clergy. Most other tasks were in the hands of secular village authorities, headed by a mayor who was assisted by a treasurer, and sometimes by deputies. In time these communal officials were obliged to record their transactions (Ottenjann, 2005). They were usually unsalaried, but here and there they were remunerated by reductions in taxes and services or exemption from military service.

In some regions the village mayor was elected by the village assembly, but in some places, notably Westphalia, the office was tied to a specific farmstead which had been the former centre of a *villa* (*Schulte*). In large parts of north-west Germany the office of the *Bauermeister* circulated amongst the holders of the more substantial farmsteads, notwithstanding their personal status as freeholders, tenants, or bondsmen, on a customary rotation. The appointment of all communal offices was subject to confirmation by the state authorities. In Lower Saxony the state regulations of *Meierrecht* resulted in a segmented social and political structure in the villages. The peasantry was neatly subdivided into classes depending on the size of their farms (*Vollmeier, Halbmeier, Großköter, Kleinköter, Brinksitzer*). This status conferred unequal rights in their use of the commons, sharply differentiated political influence in the parish assembly, but also graduated public dues and services, with particularly heavy burdens for the substantial farms of the *Meier* (Lange, 1988). The situation in Westphalia and Schleswig-Holstein differed only slightly. Here, political rights and financial dues inside the villages were not so closely linked to a formal hierarchy. Nevertheless, the owners of substantial farms formed the backbone of the socio-political order of the countryside. Two characteristics of the early modern rural commune should be stressed. Within villages the exercise of power was neatly intertwined with peasant wealth, in particular with the extent of individual holdings. And it was integrated into the emerging territorial state as self-government at the prince's command.

Forms of peasant resistance to landlord demands

The crusade of 1234 against the *Stedinger* stands out as the most spectacular medieval conflict between peasants and lords in the north-west. It ended with the defeat of this peasant *universitas* situated in an outlying area of the archbishopric of Bremen (Schubert, 1997: 568–574; Schmidt, 1982–83). The conflict can only be understood against the background of the emergence of a number of wealthy and militant peasant federations in the marshland. In effect, the archbishop and his followers were fighting a feud against a rival power.

The strength of the peasant communities in the marshes remained a factor in regional politics until the sixteenth century. For instance, they interfered in a conflict between King Christian I of Denmark and his younger brother Gerhard, vicegerent of the Duchies of Schleswig-Holstein, in the 1460s. In order to force his sibling to divide their patrimony, Gerhard conspired with a coalition of discontented noblemen. Moreover, he visited and campaigned in those parts of the Duchies where peasants had achieved some autonomy. He negotiated alliances of mutual help with the peasant communities of the marshes near Hamburg and of northern Frisia. This coalition finally failed, but only because the Danish king was able to forge a stronger counter-coalition of nobles, the Hanseatic cities and the fierce Dithmarschen peasantry (Poulsen 1989; Hoffmann, 1990: 293–304). So it can be argued that peasant republics acted like other powers until the eve of modern times. Their last engagement in a 'normal' state-building conflict was in the wars in the first half of the sixteenth century between the Danish crown and the Dithmarschen peasant federation. The peasants' defeat in 1559 ended their role as an autonomous player in the political process. From that time peasants in arms were held to be guilty of treason against their princely lord (Stoob, 1959).

Apart from these conflicts, we are poorly informed about peasant resistance in the medieval and early modern periods. Traditionally, the north-west of Germany is regarded as a quiescent region without any major insurrections. This judgement is particularly based on the failure of the region to participate in the great German Peasants' War of 1525 (Postel, 1975). But one has to be tentative about this because detailed studies are rare. It may be no accident that all the case studies that deal with peasant resistance in the north-west examine those minor regions with stricter forms of manorialism, mainly in Holstein (Göttsch, 1991; Lorenzen-Schmidt, 1995) and in the eastern part of Lower Saxony (Fenske, 1999). Here, violent conflicts arose when lords of the manor tried to enlarge their demesnes at the expense of the peasants' land and demanded more corvée. As bondsmen were obliged by law to accept these demands, resistance was exceptionally difficult and depended on unity between peasants and manorial workers, which was often enforced by intimidation.

There are good reasons for arguing that individual conflicts between lords and peasants over dues and services were as commonplace in the north-west as anywhere else. But joint actions of whole village communities seem to have been less widespread than in other German regions, perhaps because the peasant communes of the north-west were less comprehensive in the range of the responsibilities they possessed, social stratification was more pronounced and political participation inside the villages was less egalitarian. Evidence can be found for the late eighteenth century that in some regions social segregation inside villages became so marked that wealthy peasants collaborated with the local state officials to exercise control over the populace rather than showing solidarity with the poor spinners, weavers, and migratory workers (Mooser, 1984; Frank, 1995).

Apart from these peculiarities, developments were similar to those in other regions of the Holy Roman Empire in the early modern period. Where ever rural conflicts arose, they were increasingly resolved in the courts instead of being fought out violently. The imperial courts provided a model for territorial justice. Individual peasants, and their corporations and communes appealed to these tribunals. Normally conflicts arose because peasants reacted to initiatives of lords and princely authorities infringing their 'good old law', 'vested interests' and 'traditional freedoms'. They resisted all attempts to levy new taxes, increase corvée, curtail the legal status of tenants, or abrogate contracts which peasants very often interpreted as perpetual (Troßbach and Zimmermann, 2005: 155–69).

Although village communities in dispute with their lord normally went to court, they acted violently as well, especially if they suspected that the lord would not respect the court's judgements or if their honour had been severely violated. Conflicts escalated if one of the petty princes was involved, because impartial justice was not guaranteed. Some of these rulers, in trying to keep up with more powerful and wealthier neighbours, went beyond what was bearable and encountered obstinate peasant resistance. They were therefore frequently forced to call for military help from their mighty neighbours (Hauptmeyer, 1983). Generally, peasants were well aware of the bargaining power of their adversary, since there was a difference between entering a conflict with, say, a noble officer commanding a garrison as opposed to an aristocratic widow whose property rights were challenged by rival kin. In early modern times peasant resistance in the north-west was confined to localities; it had no regional dimension and it made no attempt to alter the whole social and political order.

9.3 Government and public policies

State policies towards landlords and peasants

In the Middle Ages there is no evidence for a state policy towards landlords and peasants. Beginning in the fifteenth century, territorial princes started to interfere in the relationship between the two with decrees that provided for the fixing of peasant duties. In 1433, for instance, Duke Heinrich of Wolfenbüttel decided to abrogate some heriots (*Kurmede*), to regulate merchets (*Bedemund*) and to restrain the *Besthaupt*, a payment of cattle made on a peasant's death. As mentioned before, from the sixteenth century, the territorial states in Lower Saxony developed a consistent policy that enforced the stability of the *Meierrecht* because of its utility for tax collection and recruitment of soldiers. So, the princes pretended to be the protectors of the peasantry against aristocratic demands for their own private advantage. In Oldenburg peasant holdings were made indivisible in 1542, and in Ostfriesland in 1545. In Braunschweig-Wolfenbüttel prince and diet negotiated a settlement to make holdings indivisible in 1597 (*Salzdahlumer Landtagsabschied*) and Calenberg followed in 1601 (*Gandersheimer Landtagsabschied*). Laws protecting peasants against all-too voracious lords of the manor were made in Westphalia and Schleswig-Holstein in the eighteenth century. Lords tried to take advantage of the recovery of grain prices in the last three decades of the eighteenth century by increasing both rents and occasional dues. These attempts were only partly successful, since the princely states were eager to extend legal protection to peasants against this seigneurial reaction. The *Calenbergsche Meierordnung* of 1699 provided a model adopted by other Hanoverian territories. In Westphalia the *Osnabrücker Eigentumsordnung* of 1722 marks the beginning of the process, followed by the *Minden-Ravensbergische Eigentumsordnung* of 1741 for the western territories of Prussia, the *Paderborner Meierordnung* of 1765, and finally the *Münstersche Eigentumsordnung* of 1770 (Scharpwinkel, 1965). But it must be pointed out, that these orders also provided the legal means for the recipients of dues and services to compel peasants to meet their obligations.

The social standing of the peasant

From the high Middle Ages, onwards the peasantry had a Janus-faced image. On the one hand, most members of the privileged estates despised them as filthy, servile, stubborn, rough, ignorant, and wily persons, who could not be trusted. After Paradise was lost, God's curse 'by the sweat of your brow you shall eat your bread' seemed to have been primarily laid on them. But on the other hand, some clerics and scholars glorified the peasantry as hard-working, simple, upright, and honest. This ambivalence was never resolved until, in the second half of the eighteenth century, Justus Möser the counsellor of the Osnabrück estates, amongst others, 'discovered' the Westphalian peasant as the stronghold of social stability against all pernicious change – and launched a strand of thinking with long term political implications.

In the late medieval and early modern times it goes without saying that individual peasants suffered from their despised position in society, but nevertheless most of them enjoyed the legal capacity to make a contract not only with fellow peasants but with anyone else. What is more, peasant corporations such as village communities, and more importantly political federations like the peasant *Landschaften* might even be the contractural partners of princes and kings. But this capacity to operate on equal terms was reduced from the sixteenth century. In the memorable aphorism of Heide Wunder, in early modern times *Herrschaft mit Bauern* (ruling with peasants) turned into *Herrschaft über Bauern* (ruling over peasants).[1]

[1] The titles of successive chapters of Wunder, 1986.

Bibliography

Abel, W. (1976) *Die Wüstungen des ausgehenden Mittelalters*, third edn, Stuttgart.

Achilles, W. (1965) *Vermögensverhältnisse braunschweigischer Bauernhöfe im 17. und 18. Jahrhundert*, Stuttgart.

Achilles, W. (1982) *Die Lage der hannoverschen Landbevölkerung im späten 18. Jahrhundert*, Hildesheim.

Achilles, W. (1991) *Landwirtschaft in der Frühen Neuzeit*, München.

Achilles, W. (1998) 'Ländliche Wirtschafts- und Sozialgeschichte von der Mitte des 17. bis zum Beginn des 19. Jahrhunderts', in C. van den Heuvel and M. von Boetticher (eds.) *Geschichte Niedersachsens,* 3/1, Hannover, pp. 691–727.

Bei der Wieden, B. (1993) *Außenwelt und Anschauungen Ludolf von Münchhausens (1570–1640)*, Hannover.

Boetticher, A. von (1990) *Gütererwerb und Wirtschaftsführung des Zisterzienserklosters Riddagshausen bei Braunschweig im Mittelalter*, Braunschweig.

Brakensiek, S. (1991) *Agrarreform und ländliche Gesellschaft. Die Privatisierung der Marken in Nordwestdeutschland, 1750–1850*, Paderborn.

Brakensiek, S. (2002) 'The management of common land in north-western Germany', in M. de Moor, L. Shaw-Taylor and P. Warde (eds.), *The management of common land in north-west Europe, c. 1500–1850* (CORN 8), Turnhout, pp. 225–45.

Brakensiek, S. (2004) 'Farms and land – a commodity? Land markets, family strategies and manorial control in Germany (18th-19th centuries)', in B. J. P. van Bavel and P. Hoppenbrouwers (eds.), *Landholding and land transfer in the North Sea area (late Middle Ages – 19th century)* (CORN 5), Turnhout, pp. 218–34.

Bremen, L. von (1971) 'Abgaben und Dienste der Bauern im westlichen Niedersachsen im 18. Jahrhundert', *Jahresheft der Albrecht-Thaer-Gesellschaft*, 15, pp. 73–159.

Brümmel, P. (1975) 'Die Dienste und Abgaben bäuerlicher Betriebe im ehemaligen Herzogtum Bremen-Verden während des 18. Jahrhunderts', *Jahresheft der Albrecht-Thaer-Gesellschaft*, 17, pp. 51–184.

Cord, A. J. (1997) *Der Strukturwandel in der ostholsteinischen Gutswirtschaft um 1800 dargestellt am Beispiel der adligen Güter Rixdorf und Salzau*, Neumünster.

Deike, L. (1959) *Die Entstehung der Grundherrschaft in den Hollerkolonien an der Niederweser*, Bremen.

Feldmann, B. (1994) 'Die Höfe des Münsterlandes und ihre grundherrlichen Verhältnisse', *Beiträge zur Westfälischen Familienforschung*, 52.

Fenske, M. (1999) *Ein Dorf in Unruhe. Waake im 18. Jahrhundert*, Bielefeld.

Frank, M. (1995) *Dörfliche Gesellschaft und Kriminalität. Das Fallbeispiel Lippe, 1650–1800*, Paderborn.

Göttsch, S. (1991) *"Alle für einen Mann ..." Leibeigene und Widerständigkeit in Schleswig-Holstein im 18. Jahrhundert*, Neumünster.

Hauptmeyer, C.-H. (1983) 'Bäuerlicher Widerstand in den Grafschaften Schaumburg-Lippe, im Fürstentum Calenberg und im Hochstift Hildesheim: Zur Frage der qualitativen Veränderung bäuerlicher Opposition am Ende des 18. Jahrhunderts', in W. Schulze (ed.), *Aufstände, Revolten, Prozesse: Beiträge zu bäuerlichen Widerstandsbewegungen im frühneuzeitlichen Europa*, Stuttgart, pp. 217–32.

Hauptmeyer, C.-H. (1991) 'Die Landgemeinde in Norddeutschland', in P. Blickle (ed.), *Landgemeinde und Stadtgemeinde in Mitteleuropa*, München, pp. 359–81.

Hauptmeyer, C.-H. (1997) 'Niedersächsische Wirtschafts- und Sozialgeschichte im hohen und späten Mittelalter (1000–1500)', in E. Schubert (ed.), *Geschichte Niedersachsens*, 2/1, Hannover, pp. 1041–1279.

Henning, F.-W. (1964) *Herrschaft und Bauernuntertänigkeit: Beiträge zur Geschichte der Herrschaftsverhältnisse in den ländlichen Bereichen Ostpreußens und des Fürstentums Paderborn vor 1800*, Würzburg.

Henning, F.-W. (1969) *Dienste und Abgaben der Bauern im 18. Jahrhundert*, Stuttgart.

Henning, F.-W. (1970) *Bauernwirtschaft und Bauerneinkommen im Fürstentum Paderborn im 18. Jahrhundert*, Berlin.

Hirschfelder, H. (1971) *Herrschaftsordnung und Bauerntum im Hochstift Osnabrück im 16. und 17. Jahrhundert*, Osnabrück.

Hoffmann, E. (1990) *Spätmittelalter und Reformationszeit* (Geschichte Schleswig-Holsteins, 4/2), Neumünster.

Krawinkel, H. A. (1935) 'Die Grundherrschaft in Lippe', *Mitteilungen aus der lippischen Geschichte und Landeskunde*, 15, pp. 82–162.

Lange, U. (ed.) (1988) *Landgemeinde und frühmoderner Staat: Beiträge zum Problem der gemeindlichen Selbstverwaltung in Dänemark, Schleswig-Holstein und Niedersachsen in der frühen Neuzeit*, Sigmaringen.

Last, M. (1983) 'Villikationen geistlicher Grundherren in Nordwestdeutschland in der Zeit vom 12. bis zum 14. Jahrhundert (Diözesen Osnabrück, Bremen, Verden, Minden, Hildesheim)', in H. Patze (ed.), *Die Grundherrschaft im späten Mittelalter*, 1, Sigmaringen, pp. 369–450.

Lienen, B. H. (1991) 'Aspekte des Wandels bäuerlicher Betriebe zwischen dem 14. und 17. Jahrhundert an Beispielen aus Tudorf (Kr. Paderborn)', *Westfälische Forschungen*, 41, pp. 288–315.

Linde, R., Rügge, N. and Stiewe, H. (2004) 'Adelsgüter und Domänen in Lippe: Anmerkungen und Fragen zu einem brach liegenden Forschungsfeld', *Lippische Mitteilungen*, 73, pp. 13–107.

Linnemeier, B. W. (1992a) *Ein Gut und sein Alltag. Neuhof an der Weser*, Münster.

Linnemeier, B. W. (1992b) 'Die landesherrliche Domänenwirtschaft und die Amtshäuser des Fürstentums Minden', *Mitteilungen des Mindener Geschichtsvereins*, 64, pp. 49–80.

Lorenzen-Schmidt, K.-J. (1995) 'Gutsherrschaft über reiche Bauern. Übersicht über bäuerliche Widerständigkeit in den Marschgütern an der Westküste Schleswig-Holsteins und Jütlands', in J. Peters (ed.), *Gutsherrschaft als soziales Modell: Vergleichende Betrachtungen zur Funktionsweise frühneuzeitlicher Agrargesellschaften*, München, pp. 261–78.

Lutterloh, E.-O. (1969) *Dienste und Abgaben der Bauern des Herzogtums Braunschweig-Wolfenbüttel in der Mitte des 18. Jahrhunderts*, Göttingen.

Mooser, J. (1984) *Ländliche Klassengesellschaft, 1770–1848: Bauern und Unterschichten, Landwirtschaft und Gewerbe im östlichen Westfalen*, Göttingen.

Ottenjann, H. (2005) 'Der Identifikationsraum Kirchspielbauerschaften und dessen Artikulationen als Kult-, Kommunal- und Sozialverband', in M. Hirschfeld (ed.), *Die Gemeinde zwischen Territorialherrschaft und Selbstverwaltung*, Cloppenburg, pp. 31–58.

Postel, R. (1975) 'Zur Sozialgeschichte Niedersachsens in der Zeit des Bauernkrieges' in R. Wohlfeil (ed.), *Der Bauernkrieg, 1524–26*, München, pp. 79–104

Poulsen, B. (1989) 'Schleswigsche Bauern und europäischer Markt. Ein Aufstand aus dem Jahre 1472', *Demokratische Geschichte*, 4, pp. 9–26.

Prange, W. (1971) *Die Anfänge der großen Agrarreformen in Schleswig-Holstein bis um 1771*, Neumünster.

Prange, W. (1983) 'Landesherrschaft, Adel und Kirche in Schleswig-Holstein 1523 und 1581. Die Zahl der Bauern am Ende des Mittelalters und nach der Reformation', *Zeitschrift der Gesellschaft für Schleswig-Holsteinische Geschichte*, 108, pp. 51–90.

Prange, W. (2008) 'Die Wurzeln der Leibeigenschaft in Holstein', *Zeitschrift der Gesellschaft für Schleswig-Holsteinische Geschichte*, 133, pp. 7–56.

Rappe-Weber, S. (2005) 'Neuerungen in der Gutswirtschaft um 1770: Zwei niedersächsische Rittergüter im Vergleich', in J. Ebert, C. Baierl and I. Marschall (eds.), *Landwirtschaftliche Großbetriebe und Landschaft im Wandel: Die hessische Domäne Frankenhausen im regionalen Vergleich (16. bis 20. Jahrhundert)*, Bielefeld, pp. 104–19.

Rasmussen, C. P. (2005) 'Domänenwirtschaft im Herzogtum Schleswig von 1530 bis 1770', in J. Ebert, C. Baierl and I. Marschall (eds.), *Landwirtschaftliche Großbetriebe und Landschaft im Wandel: Die hessische Domäne Frankenhausen im regionalen Vergleich (16. bis 20. Jahrhundert)*, Bielefeld, pp. 81–103.

Risto, U. (1964) *Abgaben und Dienste bäuerlicher Betriebe in drei niedersächsischen Vogteien im 18. Jahrhundert*, Göttingen.

Reinders-Düselder, C. (2000) *Das Artland: Demographische, soziale und politisch-herrschaftliche Entwicklungen zwischen 1650 und 1850*, Cloppenburg.

Rheinheimer, M. (1999) *Die Dorfordnungen im Herzogtum Schleswig. Dorf und Obrigkeit in der Frühen Neuzeit*, 2 vols, Stuttgart.

Rösener, W. (1980) 'Strukturformen der älteren Agrarverfassung im sächsischen Raum', *Niedersächsisches Jahrbuch für Landesgeschichte*, 52, pp. 107–43.

Rösener, W. (1985) 'Zur Struktur und Entwicklung der Grundherrschaft in Sachsen in karolingischer und ottonischer Zeit', in A. Verhulst (ed.), *Le grand domaine aux époques mérovingienne et carolingienne*, Gent, pp. 173–207.

Rösener, W. (1990) 'Die Wirtschaftsstruktur der niedersächsischen Zisterzienserklöster im Mittelalter', *Jahrbuch der Gesellschaft für niedersächsische Kirchengeschichte*, 88, pp. 41–60.

Rösener, W. (1996) 'Sächsische Königshöfe im Spiegel des Tafelgüterverzeichnisses', in L. Fenske (ed.), *Deutsche Königspfalzen,* 4, Göttingen, pp. 288–307.

Rothe, H.W. (1998) *Zur Geschichte der ländlichen Gesellschaft im Schaumburger Land: Lindhorst*, Melle.

Rüffer, J. (2008) *Vererbungsstrategien im frühneuzeitlichen Westfalen*, Stuttgart.

Saalfeld, D. (1960) *Bauernwirtschaft und Gutsbetrieb in der vorindustriellen Zeit*, Stuttgart.

Saalfeld, D. (1998) 'Ländliche Wirtschafts- und Sozialgeschichte vom Beginn des 16. bis zur Mitte des 17. Jahrhunderts', in C. van den Heuvel and M. von Boetticher (eds.), *Geschichte Niedersachsens*, 3/1, Hannover, pp. 637–88.

Scharpwinkel, K. (1965) *Die westfälische Eigentumsordnungen des 17. und 18. Jahrhunderts*, Göttingen.

Schlumbohm, J. (1994) *Lebensläufe, Familien, Höfe. Die Bauern und Heuerleute des Osnabrückischen Kirchspiels Belm in proto-industrieller Zeit, 1650–1860*, Göttingen.

Schmidt, H. (1973) 'Adel und Bauern im friesischen Mittelalter', *Niedersächsisches Jahrbuch für Landesgeschichte*, 45, pp. 45–95.

Schmidt, H. (1982/83) 'Zur Geschichte der Stedinger', *Bremer Jahrbuch*, 60/61, pp. 27–94.

Schneider, K. H. (1983) *Die landwirtschaftlichen Verhältnisse und die Agrarreformen in Schaumburg-Lippe im 18. und 19. Jahrhundert*, Rinteln.

Schreiber, K. (1907) 'Das Urbar der Grafschaft Ravensberg vom Jahr 1550', *Jahresbericht des Historischen Vereins für die Grafschaft Ravensberg*, 21, pp. 1–107.

Schubert, E. (1997) 'Geschichte Niedersachsens vom 9. bis zum ausgehenden 15. Jahrhunder', in E. Schubert (ed.), *Geschichte Niedersachsens*, 2/1, Hannover, pp. 15–904.

Schütte, L. (2004) 'Markenrecht und Markengerichtsbarkeit in Nordwestdeutschland', in U. Meiners and W. Rösener (eds.), *Allmenden und Marken vom Mittelalter bis zur Neuzeit*, Cloppenburg, pp. 31–45.

Steinborn, H.-C. (1982) *Abgaben und Dienste holsteinischer Bauern im 18. Jahrhundert*, Neumünster.

Stoob, H. (1959) *Geschichte Dithmarschens im Regentenzeitalter*, Heide.

Troßbach, W. and Zimmermann, C. (2005) *Die Geschichte des Dorfes*, Stuttgart.

Wendler, U. (1999) *Ländliche Gesellschaft zwischen Kirche und Staat: Das Kirchspiel Suderburg in der Lüneburger Heide, 1600–1830*, Suderburg-Hösseringen.

Wiswe, H. (1953) 'Grangien niedersächsischer Zisterzienserklöster. Entstehung und Bewirtschaftung spätmittelalterlich-frühneuzeitlicher landwirtschaftlicher Großbetriebe', *Braunschweigisches Jahrbuch*, 34, pp. 5–134.

Witt, R. (1975) *Die Privilegien des Landschaft Norderdithmarschen in gottorfischer Zeit 1559 bis 1773*, Neumünster.

Wittich, W. (1896) *Die Grundherrschaft in Nordwestdeutschland*, Leipzig.

Wunder, H. (1986) *Die bäuerliche Gemeinde in Deutschland*, Göttingen.

Postcard from Badbergen about 1900.
The dairy of the local cooperative and the railway station are shown as typical signs of rural modernity. (Source: Stadtmuseum Quakenbrück)

10 North-west Germany, 1750–2000

Stefan BRAKENSIEK and Gunter MAHLERWEIN

10.1 Ownership, power relations and the distribution of property

Types of landowners

Beginning in the 1770s and continuing through the nineteenth century, liberal reforms freed the rural population from serfdom (*Bauernbefreiung*), and abolished all feudal dues and services (*Lastenablösung*). Concurrently, the partition of common lands (*Gemeinheitsteilungen*), enclosures (*Verkoppelungen*), and the abolition of rights of usufruct (*Servitutaufhebungen*) terminated all cooperative claims over the soil. Taken together, these reforms established a system of unconditional landownership. From 1850 and perhaps earlier, agriculture in the north-west of Germany has been dominated by farmers, who owned and occupied their holdings in severalty, whilst forestry has become an enterprise of the state. Only in some regions (mainly Holstein and the east of Lower Saxony and Westphalia) have great estates owned by noble or middle class entrepreneurs remained of significance. In contrast to other parts of western Europe, urban capital never dominated the rural economy. Throughout the nineteenth century, the countryside in the north-west of Germany was overwhelmingly in the possession of peasants who were progressively turning into farmers.

Changing social property distribution

The demise of the Holy Roman Empire in 1803/06 led to a second wave of secularisation under Napoleonic rule. In the end, Prussia incorporated the forests, and some ecclesiastical demesnes, into its state demesnes, but the properties of the dissolved ecclesiastical institutions were mostly sold at auction to a range of new proprietors. It depended on the local situation whether an industrial investor or aristocrat acquired a whole estate or whether peasants and smallholders bought it in parcels. In some regions, mainly in the south and east of Westphalia, manorialism was strengthened. One can plausibly argue that the liberal reforms not only put in place the legal foundation for a rural society of owner-occupiers, but also completed social developments which had been underway since the later Middle Ages.

Table 10.1 is suggestive of the distribution of arable and forest in the Kingdom of Hanover in 1831 between the state, the royal *Klosterkammer* (an endowment established in the course of secularization to provide for the support of schools and the University of Göttingen), privileged estates which gave their noble owner the right to vote for the diet, communes, Protestant churches and schools, and private landowners. The table demonstrates the economic and social predominance of the peasantry, because the

Map 10.1 North-west Germany, 1750–2000

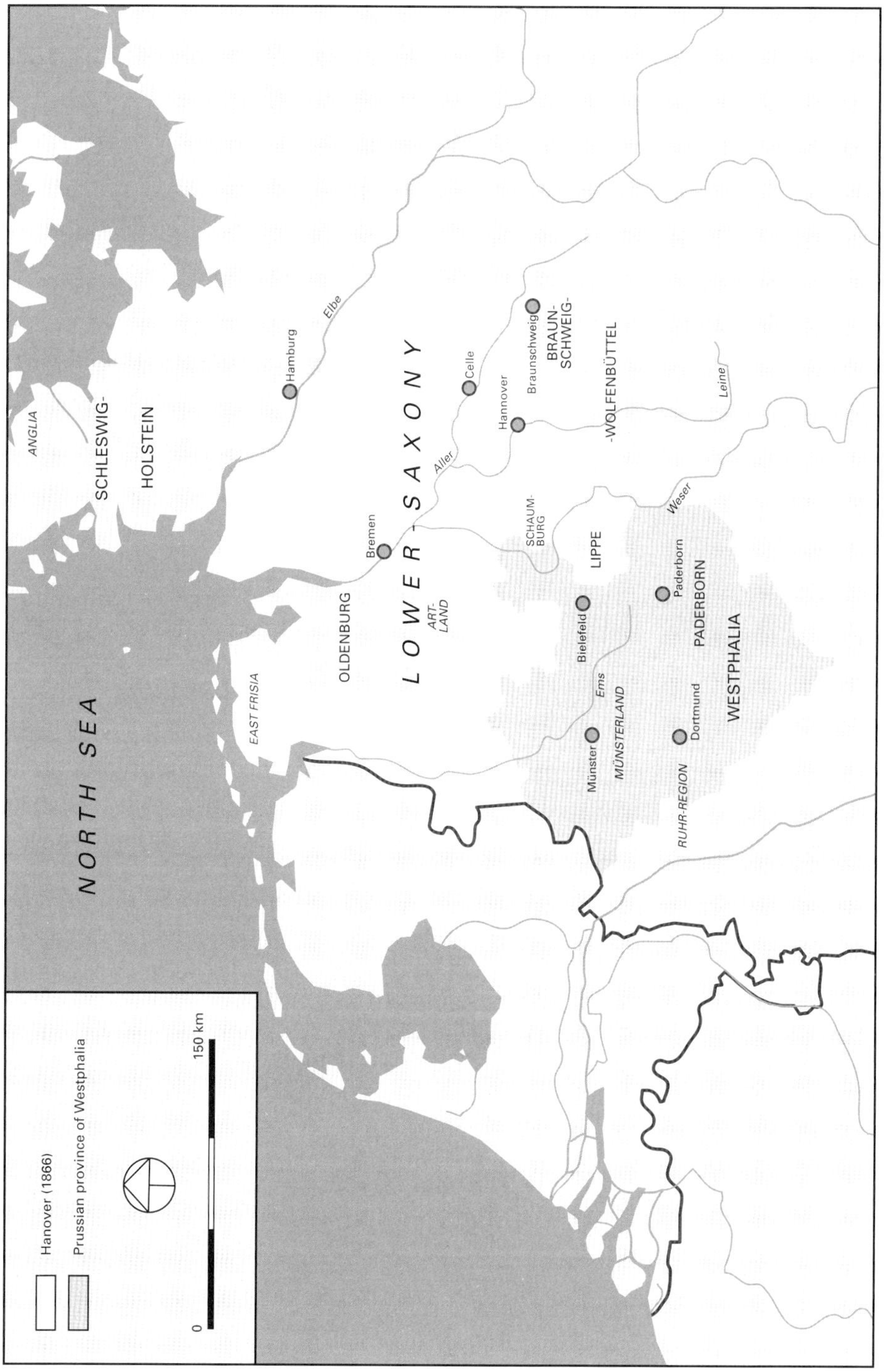

TABLE 10.1: The distribution of landownership in the Kingdom of Hanover, 1831

	Gardens, Arable, Meadows		Forests	
	ha	%	ha	%
State domain	52,685	3.6	302,379	53.9
Royal *Klosterkammer*	10,624	0.7	7,674	1.4
Noble Estates	80,404	5.5	42,813	7.0
Communes	18,517	1.3	181,436	32.4
Churches and schools	35,369	2.4	2,607	0.5
Private landowners	1,261,277	86.5	23,739	4.8
Total	1,458,876	100.0	560,648	100.0

Source: Hindersmann, 2001: 88

peasant owners of substantial farms held the larger part of the arable, meadows and gardens in the possession of private landowners. Noble estates were quite common but were normally relatively small. It is possible to identify 956 manors, but they had a medium size of only 128 ha. The arable of these comparably small estates was often located in scattered parcels alongside those of peasants, so that leasing it to villagers was the most profitable way to exploit the land. The table also shows the dominant role of the state in forest economy, particularly as communal woods were increasingly controlled by the government's forest administration.

The rise of the peasant owner-occupier was equally characteristic of those regions which had been dominated by manors since the sixteenth century. In Schleswig-Holstein for instance, from about 1750 onwards the so-called *Bauernfreunde* (friends of the peasantry) dominated public opinion, so that the Danish authorities, who had traditionally favoured the path of English agrarian capitalism, performed a dramatic about-turn. Between 1761 and 1798 Danish state demesnes were dissolved completely, leaving the peasantry with only moderate obligations. In 1797 the nobility decided to manumit the remaining bondsmen on its estates within eight years. In the end, the Danish government terminated all forms of peasant dependence in 1805, stipulating that the former bondsmen could buy or lease the land they had tilled since time immemorial on easy terms. In the district of Anglia 75 per cent of the land belonging to the estates of the nobility was placed in the hands of the peasantry, so that the social structure of a district which had been characterised by manorialism for 300 years rapidly became dominated by a substantial peasantry. This was typical of the German north-west (Dipper, 1980: 71–74).

Throughout the nineteenth century, the owners of medium to large farms formed the backbone of the socio-political order of the countryside in north-west Germany.

Due to the prevailing custom of impartible inheritance, the number of substantial farms remained stable. With a drastic rise in rural population, the number of smallholdings increased rapidly, so that in most villages the majority were not able to live solely by husbandry. The question arises of from where the new smallholders acquired their land. There is no single answer because conditions varied from village to village. In the second half of the eighteenth century state authorities pursued a policy of facilitating new settlements on heathland and moors (the so-called *Peuplierung*) which had a considerable impact on some parts of Lower Saxony and Westphalia. During the Napoleonic era the secularisation of ecclesiastical institutions and the dissolution of state demesnes also boosted the number of new smallholdings. In some localities the agricultural crises of the 1820s and 1870s resulted in the bankruptcy of the owners of manors which were subsequently sold in parcels. The privatisation of the commons, mainly accomplished in the first half of the nineteenth century, offered opportunities for the acquisition of small parcels of heathland, because farmers and estate owners were inclined to sell the remoter parts of their allotments. Finally, time and again individual heirs of a farmstead leased a small parcel of their patrimony to a younger sibling in order to meet their obligations to kin. All these phenomena resulted in an impressive process of internal colonization which by 1850 had deeply altered the social order of the countryside and the landscape itself. One can plausibly argue that the growth of smallholdings provided the basis for the dramatic agrarian intensification which took place between 1780 and 1880, and which was mainly based upon increased employment of labour (Kopsidis, 1996).

This expansionary period ended between the 1840s and the 1870s according to region. The limited opportunities for rural paupers to earn their living by day labour, by spinning and weaving flax, hemp or wool, peat-cutting, or undertaking migratory labour, all proved to be insufficient to support an ever-growing population. Therefore sections of the rural population migrated to either America or to the booming industrial regions and commercial centres within Germany. But although population stagnated in most villages of the German north-west after the middle of the nineteenth century, farmers remained a minority.

Table 10.2 provides a review of the rural structure in the early twentieth century in a number of different districts within north-west Germany. It is based upon statistical data that the Prussian authorities collected in 1907. The manorial tradition in the eastern parts of Holstein and Lower Saxony can be easily identified, as a greater number of large holdings continued to exist in the districts of Schleswig and Hildesheim. But here, much as everywhere else, peasant farms covering from 5 to 100 ha owned between two-thirds and four-fifths of the acreage.

In the twentieth century an accelerating process of consolidation occurred. From 1900 until 1930, the number of small farms decreased rapidly. Their acreage was predominantly acquired by middle-sized farms of 5–20 ha. For example, in the south of Oldenburg, the share of these farms rose by 7 per cent from 1925 to 1933. The agrarian crisis of the late 1920s and the early 1930s slowed the consolidation process because it mainly affected larger farms (50–100 ha) whose numbers declined by 16 per cent in Oldenburg between 1925 and 1933 (in the whole of Germany by 5 per cent) (Böckmann,

2000: 34–38). The pre-war years showed a rise of the peasant farms holding an acreage from 10 to 50 ha, as intended by the Nazi regime (Münkel, 1996: 34). Generally, for the first half of the twentieth century, one can discern a strong decline in the number of smallholdings (with an acreage of less than 5 ha), a moderate decline in small farms (5–10 ha), a strong rise in the number of substantial peasant farms (10–100 ha), some increase of large farms (100–200 ha) and a decline of agricultural establishments comprising more than 200 ha (Wilde/Barnstedt, 1964: 191).

The most striking structural change in German agriculture did not commence until the 1950s. The increasing ease with which smaller farmers could find well-paid jobs encouraged them to give up unprofitable farms. The land of those farms was generally not sold but leased to neighbouring farmers. At the same time, the outflow of the agricultural workforce into urban occupations made mechanization necessary, but to operate a mechanized farm effectively required increasingly larger acreages. What is more, since the 1960s, the establishment of 'profitable' farms was the aim of both domestic and European agrarian policies (Vock, 1991: 45–46). Accordingly, by 1960, an acreage of 20 to 30 ha was regarded as the threshold for a profitable farm in Schleswig-Holstein, whilst in 2005 the corresponding figure was more than 100 ha. The number of farms decreased from 54,226 in 1949 to 17,664 in 2005. During the second half of the twentieth century the average farm size there rose from 20.8 ha to 57.0 ha (Agrarbericht Schleswig-Holstein). Similarly in Lower Saxony the number of farms was reduced by two-thirds between 1960 and 2001, whilst their average size increased from 13 to 44 ha. Since 2003 only farms with more than 100 ha of arable are continuing to increase in number (Agrarstatistik Niedersachsen).

Systems of tenure

Tenancy has been neglected by German agrarian historians who have been preoccupied with the social figure of the peasant. In fact, in the nineteenth century leasehold contracts for medium sized farms were rare. Nevertheless, leasehold gained a growing importance in the rural society of the German north-west as a flexible instrument by which land, capital and workforce could be allocated. Column c in Table 10.3 provides an impression of how frequently all social strata of rural society supplemented their possessions with some leaseland. Leases had traditionally been used by aristocratic and bourgeois owners when letting entire manors to middle class tenants. This remained the case throughout the nineteenth century. Accordingly, Table 10.3 indicates that at the end of the nineteenth century larger properties were still commonly held on lease. It remained unusual for peasant farms, but was frequently used for smallholdings where the rural proletariat rented a parcel of land from an estate or a farmer. As estates had dismantled their traditional peasant corvée, their owners often tried to pay their farmhands in kind (with housing, garden plots and payment in natural produce).

A similar sort of leasehold relationship can be identified in the rural industrial areas of Minden-Ravensberg, Tecklenburg, Lippe, and in parts of Osnabrück where the rural linen industry was a notable employer. Here the landless took leases from peasants, some as contract workers (*Heuerlinge*) who paid a considerable part of their rent

Table 10.2: Rural landholdings in the Prussian provinces of north-west Germany, 1907

	Smallholdings <2 ha		Small Farms 2–5 ha		Farms 5–20 ha		Large Farms 20–100 ha		Establishments >100 ha	
	N	%	N	%	N	%	N	%	N	%
Reg.Bez. Schleswig	97,069	2.8	14,994	3.7	25,004	20.0	21,021	**57.8**	922	15.7
Reg.Bez. Hanover	41,408	5.9	11,500	11.6	12,664	**44.8**	2,820	30.8	107	6.9
Reg.Bez. Hildesheim	60,222	11.0	9,391	14.0	9,568	33.5	2,132	24.9	214	16.6
Reg.Bez. Lüneburg	38,509	4.0	14,274	7.9	14,219	27.6	6,276	**54.3**	143	6.2
Reg.Bez. Stade	31,475	4.2	11,108	11.2	11,894	**41.1**	3,573	**40.7**	89	2.8
Reg.Bez. Osnabrück	25,846	4.9	14,762	15.7	11,365	**55.2**	1,521	23.4	11	0.8
Reg.Bez. Aurich	21,725	6.7	5,948	10.9	4,885	26.6	2,786	**52.4**	50	3.4
Reg.Bez. Münster	62,743	5.7	16,026	11.7	14,010	**37.0**	4,818	**40.6**	46	5.0
Reg.Bez. Minden	62,199	10.4	16,995	15.8	13,016	**41.0**	2,609	25.3	107	7.5
Reg.Bez. Arnsberg	161,188	11.4	14,471	13.7	12,638	**35.4**	3,123	**31.8**	85	7.7

in labour, or as leaseholders (*Zeitpächter*) who paid in cash. In the districts of Halle, Herford, and Bielefeld in the 1820s, leases of the *Heuerlinge* accounted for at least 7.3 per cent of the total acreage, *Zeitpachten* for another 7.4 per cent (Mooser, 1984). Despite public criticism from the early twentieth century onwards, the *Heuerling* system survived and in 1952 was even sanctioned by a *Landpachtgesetz,* albeit after lively political discussion. But in the middle of the twentieth century the area cultivated as *Heuerland* was very small. In 1949 it formed only 0.6 per cent of the farmland in Lower Saxony, in 1960 a mere 0.2 per cent in Westphalia. *Heuerlinge* disappeared in the 1960s because of the superior employment prospects offered by industry (Theine, 1991: 314–26; Böckmann, 2000: 163–70).

Today, the situation has completely changed, and leasing is the most important way to acquire agricultural land. Already in the 1970s it played the most important role in changing the occupation of property in Schleswig-Holstein, accounting for 40–45 per cent of the total turnover. Between 1971 and 2005 the share of leased arable increased from 30 to 51 per cent. In Lower Saxony, as much as 55 per cent of the agricultural land was leased in 2005. The acreage of the additional parcels leased by farmers from their neighbours in order to extend their holdings is definitely larger than the total acreage of entirely leased farms. As a rule the proportion of leasehold is significantly smaller in regions where impartible inheritance is practiced than in those regions with a tradition of partible inheritance. And it is widely used in the vicinity of towns. A further increase in the amount of leasehold can be expected given the tendency for farmers to leave agriculture (Wehner, 1987: 17–30; Wilde/Barnstedt, 1964: 191–93; Thissen, 1988: 172, 267–69). Hence, structural change in agriculture has generated a new category of landowners: former farmers or farmers' heirs who lease their land. But these lessors do not form a new rural leisure class because their income from rent is normally insufficient to make a living.

Note: Reg. Bez. Schleswig, i.e. the southern part of the former duchies of Schleswig-Holstein and the duchy of Lauenburg; Reg. Bez. Hanover, i.e. the former counties of Hoya and Diepholz and the principality Calenberg; Reg. Bez. Hildesheim, i.e. the former prince bishopric of Hildesheim, the principality of Göttingen-Grubenhagen and the Eichsfeld, a part of the former prince bishopric of Mainz; Reg. Bez. Lüneburg, i.e. the former principality of Lüneburg; Reg. Bez. Stade, i.e the former principality of Bremen-Verden and the Land Hadeln; Reg. Bez. Osnabrück, i.e. the former prince bishopric of Osnabrück, the counties of Bentheim and Lingen and the northern part of the prince bishopric of Münster (so-called Niederstift); Reg. Bez. Aurich, i.e. the former principality Ostfriesland; Reg. Bez. Münster, i.e the southern part of the former prince bishopric of Münster (so-called Oberstift), the counties of Tecklenburg and Steinfurt and the Vest Recklinghausen which had belonged to the archbishopric of Cologne; Reg. Bez. Minden, i.e. the former principality of Minden, the county of Ravensberg, the sovereignty of Rheda, the county of Rietberg and the prince bishopric of Paderborn; Reg. Bez. Arnsberg, i.e. the former duchy of Westfalen, the county of Mark and the Imperial City Dortmund.

Source: *Zeitschrift des Königlich Preussischen Statistischen Landesamts* 52 (1912): 93–174.

TABLE 10.3: Percentage of owner occupiers, tenants and farmers cultivating mixed holdings in various Prussian provinces, 1895

Prussian Province	Smallholdings <2 ha			Small Farms 2–5 ha			Farms 5–20 ha			Large Farms 20–100 ha			Establishments >100 ha		
a	a	b	c	a	b	c	a	b	c	a	b	c	a	b	c
Schleswig-Holstein	31	42	27	58	13	28	64	5	31	70	7	23	59	21	20
Hanover	20	49	31	28	22	50	51	5	44	67	6	27	35	34	31
Westphalia	20	55	25	42	11	47	57	5	38	70	5	25	45	29	26

a = owner-occupiers, i.e. farmers cultivating property exclusively
b = tenants, i.e. farmers cultivating leasehold exclusively
c = farmers cultivating a mixture of owned and leasehold land.

Source: *Preußische Statistik*, 142 II: *Berufs- und Gewerbszählung vom 14. Juni 1895*, (Berlin 1902): 19–21.

The economic and cultural value of land

Whereas the second half of the eighteenth century saw a continuous rise in price of land, in the early nineteenth century, the liberalization of land markets, the supply of secularized estates for purchase, and the pan-European agricultural depression caused a significant decline. But even then, the high demand for land on the part of smallholders and landless prevented a deep fall in prices. Because of the scarcity of land for sale in the crowded industrial regions, leaseholds were very expensive there. For instance in the County of Ravensberg in the 1820s the landless poor had to find annual rents ranging from an extortionate 18.0 to 23.6 Taler per ha in its most fertile parts, and even 5.2 to 8.8 Taler per ha in the sandy districts (Mooser, 1984: 477).

During the 'golden years' of German agriculture, which lasted from about 1830 to 1870, the value of smallholdings, farmsteads and estates rose steeply. But peculiarities of land markets continued even in these years of economic liberalism. A recent study based on the careful investigation of three differently structured Westphalian villages (Löhne, Oberkirchen and Borgeln) comes to the conclusion that until World War I, village land markets remained seller's markets. Between 1830 and 1866, sales of land affected 2.5 per cent of the total acreage of Löhne per year, in Oberkirchen 1.6 per cent, and in Borgeln a mere 0.8 per cent (Fertig, 2007: 79). The supply of plots available for sale was so tiny that the price they obtained did not follow normal economic rules. Social relationships often determined who had the opportunity to buy land.

Because tenancy agreements react more quickly to the price movements of agricultural products than the price of land, the number of leases reflects changes in agricultural profitability. Thus, following the terms of trade, a rise in the number of leases is found until 1870 after which it slows down, to rise again after 1900. Between the World Wars it reacted to the rapidly changing economic cycles. From 1956 to 1964 an exceptional rise of leasing rates by 12 per cent could be detected (Abel, 1967: 181–96). Land prices rose from the middle of the 1970s to 1980 and stagnated or even dropped afterwards until 2006. Prices in Lower Saxony and Schleswig-Holstein stayed below the national average, but this is influenced by the prevailing high prices in southern Germany (Kindler, 1993: 70). Currently the rising prices of agricultural commodities and the appearance of crops dedicated to make biofuels has led to a rise in both lease and land prices (Bruns, 2008).

From the 1870s until today investment in farmland could not compete against other strategies of capital investment because the rates of return have always been disappointing. Thus, the purchase of agricultural land was, and is, deeply linked to the social rationalities of a specific rural way of life. Farms and estates were normally not purchased but inherited by their proprietors, who increasingly sought to enlarge the lands they owned with additional leasehold land. This trend depended on a multitude of socio-political and economic factors, amongst which state intervention proves to be crucial. In recent decades the prices of farmland and leases were determined by the demand and price for agricultural products on the one hand and by the level of agricultural subsidy subventions on the other (Möhl, 2006).

Traditionally, social status within the village was conferred by the possession of property. This allowed fine distinctions to be drawn through, for instance, lifestyle, attitudes to leisure, or conspicuous consumption at family feasts (Troßbach and Zimmermann, 2006: 212). If there was little interest in the acquisition of farmland by outsiders, there was nonetheless a belief in the cultural superiority of the peasantry and country life which can be traced from around 1870 to the middle of the twentieth century. Above all, political conservatism was associated with an agrarian romanticism which valued the peasantry as a bulwark against modernity. Industrialisation and urbanisation were held to uproot modern man. To counter this, the preservation of a politically reliable and economically solid peasantry was vital. This ideology justified governmental initiatives which supported the peasantry, e.g. prohibitive corn-tariffs, settlement policies, cheap rural credit, and at a later date agricultural subsidies. The collective experience of hunger in World War I and again in the post-war crisis from 1945 to 1948 fostered the esteem with which the peasantry were viewed well outside conservative, nationalist or racist circles. So it comes as no surprise that this positive attitude towards the peasantry as a stabilizing societal element continued into the early years of the Federal Republic of (West) Germany. In opposition to the collectivisation of agriculture in East Germany, in the West landed property, mainly the peasant family farm, received an extraordinary degree of support from the state.

This was insufficient though to halt the slow decline in the esteem which rural property holding attracted. As we mentioned, landed property had traditionally established social reputation within the village. The farmers' standing evaporated with the progressive loss of economic significance for agriculture, the shrinking incomes of farmers, and the dependence of agriculture on state subsidy. This started in the 1960s, and accelerated during the 1970s. A survey of a number of Westphalian villages demonstrates how the owners of substantial farms had dominated the municipal councils up to the 1970s, but then quickly lost their purchase (Exner, 1997: 231, 260–64). Today, even in the smallest villages, the possession of landed property no longer carries any social cachet.

10.2 The occupiers of the land

Peasant ownership of land

In north-west Germany between 1770 and 1850, the traditional rural order was completely overturned. Liberal reforms released the peasantry from its dependency on lordship. The so-called *Bauernbefreiung* (peasant liberation) terminated personal subjection but in order to become full owners of their farms, peasants were obliged to make redemption payments to their lords. In the course of this *Lastenablösung* (commutation of obligations) it was possible to make a single payment but this was rarely done; instead, payment in instalments prevailed. It must be emphasised that, in contrast to the eastern provinces of Prussia where peasants had to cede valuable parts of the farmland to their former lords, the peasants in north-west Germany normally kept the whole acreage of their farms.

The agrarian reforms were part and parcel of a comprehensive reorganisation of both state and society driven by bureaucrats who saw reform as an answer to the challenge posed by the French Revolution. In essence, they aimed for an enhancement of productivity by eliminating 'feudal' obstacles to agricultural innovation, so that in the long run tax revenues could be raised. But apart from these financial objectives, agrarian reforms advanced the project of transforming traditional corporate society into a modern society of property owners. Furthermore, the intermediate power of privileged persons and corporations was abolished, so that a legally egalitarian union of subjects could arise. Locally laws were unified, manorial courts were abolished, and rural municipalities were integrated into the hierarchy of the state administration.

The German states implemented these reforms at different rates according to the differing political preferences of princes and governmental elites. In general, three phases can be distinguished. First, in the second half of the eighteenth century the 'agrarian movement' emerged. This set an agenda for liberal reform which was implemented in some, but not all, regions. Then, in the period from 1794 until 1815 reforms were broadly implemented as a reaction to the revolutionary impetus, partly as a result of French occupation, partly because a comparison of the traditional and the revolutionary order proved the fiscal and military superiority of the latter. Third, in the reactionary political atmosphere of the 1820s and again from the late 1830s to 1848, reform stagnated, but the reform agenda was finally implemented as a concession to the revolutionary movements of 1830 and 1848.

In north-west Germany three regionally distinct patterns of development can be discerned. First, in Schleswig-Holstein the traditional rural order was abolished by the Danish crown extremely early in 1805, on very advantageous terms to the peasantry. Feudal bondage was eliminated without compensation. Peasant dues and services were purchased by a single payment of only 50 per cent of their value: this sum was lent to the peasants by the royal credit institute. As a result, a class society rapidly emerged, with a stable group of wealthy estate owners and farmers on the one hand, and a growing number of landless rural workers.

Second, in Lower Saxony liberal agrarian reforms had been launched by the French empire in the first decade of the nineteenth century, but these were only sporadically implemented, partly because of legal difficulties, partly because in 1815, following its restoration, the Kingdom of Hanover rescinded all these measures. It was only in 1831, under the pressure of widespread peasant unrest and violent riots in nearby Braunschweig, that the second chamber of the diet passed a redemption law despite the resistance of the conservatives in the upper house and the state bureaucracy. Here, as in the neighbouring princedom of Oldenburg and Braunschweig, the commutation of obligations started in the 1830s. All in all, peasants had to redeem their obligations at 25 years' purchase, but payments were divided into small amounts which continued to be paid until the new bouyancy in the agricultural economy of the 1850s and 1860s made their redemption easier. Again, public credit institutes were established which functioned as a buffer between peasants and the mainly aristocratic recipients of redemptions (Kulhawy, 2008).

Third, in Westphalia, the Napoleonic 'model-state' of the Kingdom of Westphalia, at the moment of its creation in 1808, decreed the abolition of peasant servitude which was regarded as a vestige of feudal barbarity. But strong words were followed by half-hearted legislation, because peasant rents and services, as the most valuable part of the state's property, were needed to support the Napoleonic elite. The only obligations which were abolished were those which were perceived to be a sign of personal obedience, such as the obligatory services owed by adolescent bondsmen, heriots in case of succession and marriage fines for the spouse who married into a farmstead. The bulk of peasant dues remained unaltered as they could only be discharged by a lump sum payment of 25 times their value. So, until 1813, redemption laws remained of little effect because of the insecure political situation, the deteriorating terms of trade for agricultural products, and difficulties peasants faced in securing a loan. When Prussia secured Westphalia after the Treaty of Vienna, it decided to accept the Napoleonic legislation because Westphalia had been amongst the transitory states which had been recognised by the Treaty of Tilsit in 1807. The Prussian agrarian legislation of the 1820s and 1830s followed the same lines which made it of little value to the peasants. In the Prussian province of Westphalia during the 1830s and 1840s, peasant redemption payments started mainly when the former lords of the manor sought payment. Instead, the Prussian agrarian authorities urged the commutation of tithes, tithes, rents and services to perpetual rents. Therefore, the redemption of feudal obligations was not a burning issue for either the landlords or their peasants. In the former prince-bishopric of Paderborn, the payment of redemptions was made easier by the creation of a public lending institution in 1836.

But the majority of the Westphalian peasants waited until the middle of the nineteenth century to apply for redemption. Although the revolution of 1848 failed in a political sense, it resulted in a reduction of peasant redemption payments to 18 years' value. Whilst it has traditionally been argued that peasants were unable to make their redemption payments without the help of a public bank, it has recently been pointed out that by continuing to pay permanent annual rents, peasants acted rationally so long as they were less expensive than their redemption payments. Even in the second half of the nineteenth century, only a minority of the peasants harkened back to the amortisation schedules offered by the newly founded public *Provinzialrentenbank*, but preferred to obtain private credits which were no costlier and at the same time offered more flexible conditions of repayment. As peasants in the Prussian province of Westphalia had been able to borrow on mortgage since 1820, they could have easily raised sufficient credit privately. As for the nobles, they continued the practice of living off their rents except these now took the form of a secure if modest income from the *Provinzialrentenbank*. When seen in this perspective, the public credit institution, allegedly founded to support the peasantry, actually served the needs of the nobility (Bracht, 2006).

The repercussions of the reforms varied enormously between the different classes in rural society. In the long run, the rent-receiving members of the aristocracy lost more than they gained. The abolition of serfdom, as well as the gradual commutation of peasant dues and services, must be seen in the context of the upheaval which took place in the early nineteenth century, e.g. the secularisation of ecclesiastical principalities, the dissolution of the monasteries and other religious establishments, and the privatisation of the commons. Although redemption payments, together with the indemnities for the division of common lands, enabled a minority of estate owners to enlarge and modernise their manors, this was not compensation for their loss of authority over land and people.

There can be no doubt that the peasants gained most from the reforms. While the abolition of personal bondage meant that the peasant became a full member of civil society, the acquisition of full property rights in his land provided him with the material means to use his newly-acquired freedom. Within a short time, from 1770 to 1848, the peasants advanced from being regimented and often despised subjects to being respected members of an order which, as we noticed, many contemporaries considered to be guarantor of social stability at a time of widespread upheaval (Gagliardo, 1969).

The dominance of peasant land ownership which was the outcome of the reforms of the nineteenth century has endured until today. Nowadays, the largest share of the agriculturally used acreage is in the possession of 'natural persons', either individuals or couples. In Westphalia 93 per cent of the acreage belonged to individuals in 1979, whereas only 7 per cent of the arable was owned by the state, the church, cooperatives and enterprises (Thissen, 1988). The share of large estates owned by aristocratic families has been estimated to have been about 5 per cent in Westphalia in the 1970s, while about 12 per cent of the arable was possessed by city dwellers. These shares vary by region: in peripheral areas noble families and peasant farmers hold significantly more property. But one has to point out, that throughout the nineteenth and twentieth centuries, agriculture in the German north-west was mainly a family business conducted by peasant farmers.

Communal land use systems, their adaptation and disappearance

From the late eighteenth century onwards, most state authorities promoted the privatisation of common land (Prange, 1971; Brakensiek, 1994). Taken together, *Gemeinheitsteilungen* (partition of common lands), *Verkoppelungen* (enclosure) and *Servitutaufhebungen* (the abolition of rights of usufruct on specific plots of land or forest) should have terminated all communal claims over the soil. The first legal regulations designed to encourage privatisation, to standardise the procedure to be employed and provide guidelines, were enacted in the last three decades of the eighteenth century. In many regions a few partitions took place at this time, but the reforms did not gain pace before the 1820s. The initiative of the state authorities had to be backed by local actors if it was to be implemented. Due to the varying degrees of willingness to cooperate on the part of the local communities affected, the reform process lasted from 1750 to 1890. Different regional patterns of development can be traced; these run across borders and indicate patterns of change other than those initiated by the legislators.

The reform saw early success in those regions where agrarian individualism was of long standing and where market access was readily available, as in Holstein and northern Westphalia, comprising the principalities of Tecklenburg, Osnabrück, Ravensberg, and Lippe. In Holstein, the governmental elite (the educated state officials and courtiers, Protestant pastors, professors and teachers, and so on) who advocated the dissolution of the traditional rural order in the late eighteenth century could count on sections of the nobility and the whole of the peasantry for support, for both were eager to expand their export-oriented agriculture. Here, government reforms were completing an enclosure movement which had been underway since the sixteenth century (Prange, 1971).

In the northern quarter of Westphalia, the partition of common lands was achieved early on account of the coincidence of several favourable factors. The common wastes and grazings were fertile enough to make cultivation worthwhile: scattered settlement patterns and the individualised organisation of the fields did not pose any insuperable impediments, as communal crop rotations and compulsory collective farming were unknown. The domestic linen industry offered an alternative source of income to the agrarian sector. At the same time agriculture and the linen industry were so closely intertwined that the agrarian sector benefited from the growth in population: the labouring poor demanded flax and food, and simultaneously provided the workforce to cultivate the privatised heathlands.

But in other parts of Lower Saxony and Westphalia, the attempts of reform-inclined bureaucracies to privatise the commons faced serious difficulties. In the area of nucleated village settlement covering the south-eastern part of the region, open-field farming was usual in the eighteenth century and incremental agricultural reorganisation the norm. The order of the fields and the use of common lands were an important material foundation for the political and social unity of the village community. If any individuals sought to disrupt this unity, then conflict was inevitable. Besides, lords of the manor were usually entitled to graze their flocks of sheep on commons and open fields. They therefore sought to impede enclosure until overwhelmed by the peasant upheavals during the revolution of 1848 (Prass, 1997).

In the wide coastal plains and the Westphalian *Münsterland,* the partition of common heathlands did not commence until the beginning of the nineteenth century and was generally completed by 1850. Actually, the extensive moorlands were not privatised or transferred into state ownership until the 1880s: the cultivation of this land had not been worthwhile at an earlier date. Here, a conversion of the peasant holdings to a more profitable agricultural system was impeded not so much by the existing field system, but the severe limits which the nature of the terrain and the climate set on all attempts to increase yields. In large parts of north-western Germany, cultivation of the moors could not be undertaken until modern technology – steam ploughs, drainage and artificial fertilizers – made it possible.

The privatisation of the commons both fostered and cushioned social and political change. Certainly, the local power of aristocratic estate owners was weakened by the abolition of their sovereignty over the local courts that had traditionally administered the complex commons called *Marken*. And certainly, the economic, social, and political position of the wealthier peasants was strengthened because the largest part of the privatised common lands fell into the hands of this group. But after the revolution of 1848, the struggle between nobility and peasantry was definitely at an end. Exceptionally profitable market conditions enabled the commutation of peasant obligations and, together with the partition of common lands, provided the material basis for the truly 'historic compromise' between peasants and their former manorial lords. The compensation the lords received took the heat out of the struggle for land between nobility and peasants.

The losers in the division of common land were the rural proletariat. Although their use of common pastures and woods had never been a legal right, it was ultimately impossible to exclude the small man from grazing some animals. The privatisation of the commons terminated this aspect of their household economy. So, it was the landless people who felt the full force of the reforms, which aggravated the social differences between peasants and the rural proletariat. That this did not erupt into open conflict reflects the particular form that enclosure took. As it was required by the state, to all intents and purposes the common lands, an essential element of the 'moral economy' of the proletariat, were destroyed – whether allegedly or genuinely – by powerful outsiders.

The exercise of power within the village

The local power of the peasant elite culminated in the nineteenth century. Liberal reforms weakened the traditional influence of the lords of the manor, but the states did not rush to establish the local bureaucracies which in the twentieth century would increasingly permeate the rural society. Until about 1890 the state authorities preferred to operate by the long-established system of 'indirect rule' by central legislation, through strict budgetary controls, and powers delegated to local village courts which were normally dominated by the proprietors of substantial farms. Landed property and the exercise of local power were neatly connected. In those regions where Ultramontane piety or Lutheran revivalism were well entrenched, the Catholic and Protestant clergy were able to exert moral authority over village affairs by controlling the schools, charities and relief institutions which elsewhere were organised by the secular authorities.

From the the late nineteenth century, the emergence of rural cooperatives and the growing self-confidence of workers living in villages close to industrial centres led to the appearance of a new balance of power within the village in which farmers lost some of their control over the allocation of resources. But it was the Third Reich which thoroughly undermined the power base of the landowners inside the villages, despite posturing as being strongly sympathetic to the peasantry. Communal autonomy was sharply reduced. Instead of landed property, membership of the Nazi party, or at least conformity with the national socialist system, became essential in order to secure local power. As a consequence, many people from the lower strata of rural society were appointed to local offices.

After World War II those members of the landowning groups who had not cooperated too closely with the Nazi party reclaimed their traditional authority for a short period. But in the 1960s landed property finally lost its claim to local influence. Global economic and social change, the rapid improvement of the infrastructure, migration and better education made landed property and kinship ties redundant as criteria for appointing people to offices. Instead, other criteria prevailed, such as membership of political parties and cooperatives, professional standing and personal character (Exner, 1997: 141–301). Furthermore, the communal reforms of the 1970s established centralised and considerably enlarged councils, administered by professionals instead of the voluntary officeholders of the past.

Peasant organisations

Agricultural organisations are found at the point where agricultural producers, commercial interests, government influence, power relations among different social actors, and scientific expertise all come together. The first agricultural societies (*Landwirtschaftsgesellschaften*) were founded in the eighteenth century as a form of enlightened sociability committed to the development of the public weal. The first one in Germany was the *Königliche Landwirtschaftsgesellschaft* in Celle which was founded in 1764 by a circle of dignitaries, namely district administrators, scholars, and public officers of the Hanoverian regime. They aimed to advance agricultural improvement by maintaining a library, organising competitions on agricultural theory and practice, publishing leaflets which would inform the 'simple' peasant about the cultivation of new fodder-crops, and sending members to England to investigate which agricultural innovations could be adapted to conditions in north-west Germany. The *Landwirtschaftsgesellschaft* in Celle came to play a role advising the Hanoverian government, notably in the very late eighteenth century when its chairman, Albrecht Daniel Thaer, distinguished himself as the leading agricultural expert in Germany. Members of this association wrote the basic ordinance of 1802 laying down the procedure for enclosure and they participated in its implementation. Nevertheless, their impact was limited, since it was an elitist association which failed to make much impact on the peasantry (Ulbricht, 1980).

By the early nineteenth century agricultural experts were well aware of the peasantry's disinterest in their innovative ideas. This they interpreted as a reflection of their educational shortcomings. Perhaps this was so, but very often the peasants declined to follow the advice they received because of its impracticality. However, experts and governments established regional institutes to assist the local farmers' associations which were founded in numerous villages from the 1830s onwards. The main objective of such a local *Landwirtschaftsverein* was the promotion of peasant education. There is only one detailed study of the work of a farmers' association, that of Badbergen, founded in 1839 situated in the *Osnabrücker Artland* (Pelzer, 2002). The survey shows that the membership of the association consisted of the owners of farms, local craftsmen and manufacturers of agricultural machinery. They quickly shed the influence of the bailiff and the pastor who initiated its foundation. Indeed, peasant education through reading and lectures was an important objective, but it was completed by entertainment and the circulation of news. The *Landwirtschaftsverein* of Badbergen showed its utility in the 1870s and '80s when the cultivation of grain ceased to be profitable. It engaged an expert to advise on the improvement of meadows and its members instructed each other in how to improve stock breeding. Their machinery was improved by local manufacturers who copied British, Belgian and German examples from images in the agricultural journals to which the association subscribed or machines displayed in regional exhibitions. In 1889 members of the Badbergen peasants' association founded a dairy cooperative. One can assume that *Landwirtschaftsvereine* generally supported the change in peasant attitudes, from the traditional subsistence orientation, to contributing to the regional grain trade in the eighteenth and early nineteenth centuries and then to full integration into national and international agricultural markets after the middle of the nineteenth century.

The long-established agricultural associations had a reputation for being under the surveillance of the authorities. From the 1860s onwards they were viewed sceptically by both peasants and aristocrats, especially in those parts of Westphalia with a majority of Catholics. Hence it was a Catholic nobleman, Burghard Freiherr von Schorlemer-Alst, who founded the first independent peasant association (*Bauernverein*) in 1862. In his judgement the rural population was given insufficient attention by either the public at large or the state, both of whom were preoccupied with rapid urbanisation. He argued for a strong and autonomous association to represent the professional interests of agriculture and the welfare of rural society in a world undergoing rapid urbanisation and industrialisation. His initiative was overwhelmingly successful. In 1871 the *Westfälischer Bauernverein* was founded which quickly embraced hundreds of local associations and tens of thousands of individual members. Along the way, the peasant associations and other forms of rural sociability formed a public platform for the enhancement of the image of the aristocracy, turning it from a privileged order into a social elite (Reif, 1979).

Although it was originally rooted in Ultramontane Catholicism, the movement found adherents among Lutheran peasants. Prima facie, the *Bauernvereine* eschewed party politics (a condition of their tolerance by the state). They organised winter schools for the education of adolescent as well as agriculturalists, and provided mutual insurance against hail, fire and cattle disease. Their members founded thousands of local and regional cooperatives with different functions: purchasing fertilizer, machines and feeding stuff, operating dairies, securing financial investment and credit and establishing cooperatives for the sale of agricultural products. But apart from these progressive self-help activities and its lobbying, the *Westfälischer Bauernverein* was instinctively hostile to urban modernity. This was true of most rural organisations from 1870 to 1933. They were modern in respect of their organisational structure, their encouragement of agricultural progress, and their use of mass media, but were politically and socially retrogressive, and mostly anti-Semitic. The traditional rural elites and the 'simple' farmers were deeply angered by the worsening terms of trade for grain and cattle from the 1870s, the migration of rural labourers into the growing urban centres which offered better wages, and declining relevance of the rural sector to German society. Whenever taxes, prices for fertilizers or railway-tariffs were on the verge of being raised, rural unrest arose.

In the late nineteenth century this was perceived as a serious threat to the social and political order by the government of the *Reich*. In response, the authorities founded

Landwirtschaftskammern (Chambers of Agriculture), inclusive institutions which all agricultural producers were compelled to join. These institutions inherited the functions of the old-established agricultural societies. They were channels of communication between state and farmers, they promoted improvements in agricultural practice, and they enhanced agricultural education. Unlike their colleagues in Schleswig-Holstein and the provinces in the east of Prussia where chambers of agriculture had been founded in the late nineteenth century, farmers in the western provinces of Westphalia and Hanover were initially opposed to these government initiatives. They suspected that they would be a tool in the hands of the Prussian *Junker* who dominated the powerful pressure-group, *Bund der Landwirte*. It was only in 1899–1900 that *Landwirtschaftskammern* were created in the western provinces. Peasant fears proved to be baseless: the chambers complemented the autonomous institutions of peasant self-help by publishing agronomic literature, establishing experimental stations, and after 1920, taking over the agricultural schools. Even if it were not the *Junker* who dominated the chambers, the owners of larger farms were over-proportionally represented on their executive boards because they were elected by the *Kreistag* (county council), whose composition depended on the Prussian three-class system which favoured the wealthier voters. Not until the Weimar Republic could lessees and smallholders participate in the chamber elections and agricultural workers only after 1949. Until their abolition in 1933 the chambers commented on agrarian politics; after 1949 the re-created *Landwirtschaftskammern* were obliged to be non-political (Albers, 1999; Hohenstein, 1990).

As mentioned before, after the late nineteenth century agricultural cooperatives became a driving force in agricultural developments, but their contributions differed according to regional structures. In south-west Germany, the owners of small and middle-sized farms founded credit unions to avoid extortion and over-indebtedness. In northern and eastern Germany, the owners of more substantial farms and estates primarily used cooperatives to try and solve their supply and marketing problems with the help of cooperatives. They drew on credit unions to obtain loans and to make investments until the inflation of the 1920s. After that time the connection between cooperative activities and local sociability lost its significance, with the consequence that the distinctions between cooperative and private banking have almost vanished.

With the foundation of the national socialist *Reichsnährstand* in September 1933 all existing agricultural organisations, associations and cooperatives were abolished. When re-established after World War II, strongly centralized cooperatives dominated the marketing of cattle and dairy products (Böckmann, 2000: 132–35; Albers, 1999: 117, 169). Due to the progressive deagrarianization of post-war society, the re-founded peasants' associations lost their significance, although they did maintain their influence over agrarian politics (Henning, 1988: 141–43, 160–69, 208–20; Lohmann, 1964: 15–44).

Forms of peasant resistance

In the late eighteenth century the traditionally 'quiet' north-west of Germany experienced a number of local peasant uprisings. Even if some of these incidents were encouraged by news from France, they should not be interpreted as revolutionary actions but viewed as a continuation of traditional conflicts. The long phase of extraordinarily favourable prices for grain, flax and other agricultural products in the last third of the eighteenth century prompted some lords of the manor to raise peasant dues. Peasants reacted as they had always done: with litigation and, if that should fail, with violent forms of resistance (Hauptmeyer, 1983).

Things changed thoroughly during the early nineteenth century. Whereever lords of the manor attempted to maintain their traditional privileges, they were confronted with fierce peasant opposition in the revolutionary years of 1830 and 1848. This was especially the case where manor courts had survived the sea change in landlord-tenant relations around 1800 and were still used to punish insubordinate peasants. Such behaviour was considered to be anachronistic and provoked considerable resentment. In central and south-west Germany these quarrels between lords and peasants were a crucial stimulus for the rural revolutionary movement, but in the north-west of Germany this was only the case in the south-eastern periphery of the region. Elsewhere something completely different occurred: peasant owner-occupiers and aristocratic estate-owners found themselves allied against the rural proletariat. In 1830, and again in 1848, those who had lost badly in the liberal reforms demanded affordable leaseholds and the right to participate in local politics. Initially, the authorities and local peasant leaders made tactical concessions, but when the revolutionary movements lost their impetus, local power relations were restored. So, the political calculations of liberal reformers were proved to be correct: peasants acted as a pillar of the social and political order in the countryside. They saw themselves as the owners of their farms and as the legitimate masters of the labourers and poor, and wholly rejected egalitarian ideas (Düwel, 1996). This attitude remained until at least 1914. Even widespread discontent among peasants in the Wilhelmian era never resulted in them adopting left wing positions.

The prosperity of the peasantry

A tour through north-west Germany shows the informed observer the built legacy of the economic cycles of agriculture during the last 250 years. The impressive great and comfortable farmhouses built during the last decades of the eighteenth century demonstrate that this must have been a time of considerable peasant prosperity. Indeed, a rural consumer society emerged during this boom time in a number of market-orientated regions (Ottenjann, 1990). This period of prosperity was followed by severe difficulties caused by the Napoleonic wars and the agrarian depression of the 1820s. The decades from 1830 to 1870 – the 'golden years' – were characterised by low wages, high prices and increasing incomes. During this phase the peasantry was able to extend cultivation over large parts of the former common wastelands, to intensify its husbandry in order to meet the growing demands of the urban markets, to erect numerous brick stables and barns, and simultaneously shoulder the redemption payments to the lords of the manor (Kopsidis, 1996; Bracht, 2006). In contrast, as all over Europe, the last decades of the nineteenth century were very difficult. German agriculture was increasingly integrated into the globalising market-economy and proved to be unprepared to compete with overseas grain production. But this crisis was weathered more easily by peasants than estate owners. Farmers could rely on family labour when they intensified their agriculture by increased livestock breeding, by the cultivation of potatoes and beets, or in the vicinity of urban centres, by dairy farming and market gardening. Traditional peasant caution was replaced by a growing readiness to alter production to meet changing markets.

From World War I until about 1950, agriculture could remain detached from a society in a more or less permanent state of emergency. During wartime, most adult males were in the army, the supply of foreign animal feed collapsed, and chemical fertilizers were in short supply, with disastrous effects on agricultural production and farm income. On the other hand, there were advantages to being in an agricultural profession. In times of war, post-war dislocation or inflation, farmland provided an insurance against being either hungry or homeless.

In both post-war periods, state-regulation stifled initiative and peasants were forced to exploit the flourishing black market in ways that poisoned the relationship between them and urban consumers. Even the deinflationary effects of the depreciations of currency in 1923 and 1948 did not last for long. In the late 1920s and again in the late 1950s, farmers and estate-owners carried a heavy burden of debt because investment was necessary after long periods of underinvestment in wartime (Theine, 1991: 28, 60; Bergmann/Megerle, 1989: 208–211).

The crisis of the inter-war period had regionally different impacts. Agriculture in northern Germany suffered most whilst Westphalia was least affected. In the *Münsterland* the income of farmers with 20–50 hectares was comparable to the salaries of employees and even small farmers did better than workers (Theine, 1991: 50–67). In the south of *Oldenburg* smallholders with a farm of up to five hectares achieved the average income of worker's households, whereas a farm amounting from 20 to 50 hectares guaranteed an income at the level of an artisan, salesman or mid-ranking civil servant. The owners of substantial farms of 50 hectares and had incomes comparable to those of high ranking civil servants (Böckmann, 2000: 144–156). Schleswig-Holstein was affected by the crisis most severely: indebtedness caused massive protests in the late 1920s; agricultural incomes reached their nadir in 1932.

The attractive promises the Nazi regime made to the peasantry were only partly implemented. At first, until 1935, agricultural incomes increased by about 20 per cent, but as the price of purchased inputs (seeds, fertilizers, pesticides and machinery) were not regulated, the increase did not continue beyond 1936. The higher prices for agricultural goods during World War II allowed peasant incomes to increase again, at least until 1942 when the control of the economic activity was tightened. Over the whole Nazi period, agricultural revenues stagnated (Münkel, 1996: 111, 128).

After 1948 the dissociation of peasant revenues from the general development of incomes strengthened, resulting in a massive abandonment of small and medium-sized farms. For instance, from 1950 to 1975 the income of all people working in agriculture increased nine-fold, whereas workers' income rose fifteen-fold (Henning, 1988: 278). Over the whole period from 1914 until today, the improvement in farmers' income and hence the increase in their standard of living has fallen short of that of industrial workers and professionals.

10.3 Government and public policies

State policies towards farmers and rural society

From 1820 onwards legal and social tutelage for the peasantry was a characteristic trait of state policy in Germany. This might sound curious in the light of the 'liberal' reforms which freed peasants from seigneurial bonds. But on closer inspection it may be seen how the state tried to replace traditional lordship with supervision by the state authorities. This was surely the case under the restored regimes in Hanover, Oldenburg and Brunswick, although the Prussian government initially followed a course of economic liberalism. But in the Prussian province of Westphalia, the regional authorities took the opposite approach. Ludwig von Vincke, governor from 1816 to 1844, held that the 'inexperienced' peasants were not mature enough to withstand the seductions of their new freedom. He was backed by a conservative public discourse which feared that peasants who were free to sell parcels of land, mortgage their properties, and to share their holdings amongst their children would inevitably bring about the atomisation of their farms and the decay of the 'sound order of peasants'. Above all the free saleability of the soil would benefit the Jews who, allegedly, were keen to exploit peasants. Recent research has proved what sober contemporaries always knew, that all these ideas were fantasies, but of enduring impact (Rouette, 2003).

After Prussia annexed Hanover in 1866, the old debate was renewed. Should peasants be allowed to sell, lease, divide and mortgage their property? Plans to abolish the traditional Hanoverian *Anerbenrecht* which enforced the impartible inheritance of farms came under fire. As a compromise, the *Höfegesetz* of 1874 allowed any farmer to voluntarily register his farmstead in a so-called *Höferolle*, after which it had to be bequeathed to a single heir. The German Civil Code (*Bürgerliches Gesetzbuch*) of 1900, which decreed egalitarian inheritance to be the norm, specifically excluded peasants so they could maintain their practice of impartible inheritance. But an obligatory *Anerbenrecht* for all peasants, as sought by an agrarian lobby in the 1920s, could not be realized (Henrici, 1964: 121; Thissen, 1988: 27–28; Hohenstein, 1990: 146–50).

Elements of the peasant *Anerbenrecht* and the aristocratic *Fideikommiss* (estates entailed in the male line) were incorporated into the Nazi *Erbhofgesetz*, which drastically curbed the owner's rights of disposal. Farms of between 7.5 and 125 ha, which had to be listed in the register or *Erbhöferolle*, were not to be sold, burdened with debt or divided. Women's rights of inheritance were greatly reduced. Poor husbandry or an lifestyle incompatible with National Socialist moral precepts could be punished, even by the seizure of the peasant's estate. In the traditional areas of impartible inheritance in north-western Germany, many more estates were subject to the *Erbhofgesetz* than in other parts of the *Reich*. For instance, in 1939 in the district of Stade (near Hamburg) 38.0 per cent of the peasant holdings were *Erbhöfe*, whereas the average for the *Reich* as a whole was only 21.6 per cent (Münkel, 1996: 112–20, 192–260).

Even in the post-war years in the British zone of occupation, the *Landbewirtschaftungsordnung* (law of land use) provided for the enforced transfer of a peasant holding to a trustee in the event of the owner's mismanagement. Even today in the federal states of Nordrhein-Westfalen, Schleswig-Holstein and Niedersachsen farmers can still opt to register their holdings to subject them to impartible inheritance (Hohenstein, 1990: 146–63).

Traditionally agriculture had been more heavily taxed than other occupations. This inequality was overcome during the second half of the nineteenth century at a time when public debate was concerned with protective tariffs. Not until the era of the Weimar Republic was the taxation of agriculture once more a matter for discussion. The trigger was the increased tax burden caused by the *Steuernotverordnung* (emergency decree on taxation) of 1923 that aimed to re-establish the liquidity of the state but at the same time drove many farmers into debt because their tax burden was raised to levels 3.5 to 7.0 times higher than pre-First World War levels. But with the tax reform of 1925, the agrarian sector became fiscally privileged. Exemptions and a favourable system of assessment reduced the total tax burden on agriculture by a third, whereas national tax revenue rose because other economic sectors were charged with higher taxes. As a result, from 1931 onwards, most farmers in Oldenburg, for instance, were tax-free. Subsequently their income improved, and by 1936 a proportion of farmers were again liable to pay tax after their tax allowances were halved. Again, after World War II, taxes were reduced for farmers by cutting income tax and by establishing a number of tax exemptions for agricultural producers. In 1971 only 15 per cent of the farmer's income was liable to income tax and 75 per cent of the farmers paid no income tax at all (Theine, 1991: 75–83; Böckmann, 2000: 121–25; Bundesministerium der Finanzen, 1988: 611–24; Becker, 1990: 210–45; Abel, 1967: 322–33).

Another area of state intervention was the Kaiserreich's land settlement policy which was given a new impetus in 1917 by Hindenburg's promise of plots of land for returning soldiers. This was consciously an attempt to strengthen the peasantry as a bulwark against socialism. (In addition, new settlements in the eastern provinces of Prussia were also directed against the growing demographic weight of the Polish population and thus had ethnopolitical aims.) (Henning, 1988: 145, 200; Dix, 2005: 71). These policies had little agricultural impact, and were even less important in the north-west of Germany where no large vacant areas remained which might be settled. In Schleswig-Holstein between 1919 and 1933, 5,000 farmsteads were founded, mostly on land parcelled out of former estates and another 3,700 in the province of Hanover, mainly in the marshlands (Theine, 1991: 349–50; Böckmann, 2000: 49).

There is continuity of conservative conceptions of the peasantry which saw them as protecting the German people from the destructive and malign effects of modernity. This reached its highest elaboration in the National Socialist *Blut-und-Boden* ('blood and soil') ideology which proclaimed the 'elevation' of the peasantry as part and parcel of their racist mission. In this perspective, the aim of policy was to guarantee the succession of generations of 'Aryan' peasant families. The individual peasant was of no great interest except that 'honest' behaviour as defined by Nazi ideology was a prerequisite for the disposal of property rights (Münkel, 1996: 115). These ideas had been circulated before 1933 by eugenicist and social-Darwinist authors, who agreed that the conservation of the peasantry was the main task of a 'renewed nation' (Henning, 1988: 212).

Public regulation of the countryside

In general, the process of agricultural intensification had a profound impact on the landscape. In the late nineteenth century and particularly since the 1930s, drainage and improvement of wetlands allowed the cultivation of large areas of wasteland, so that moors and heaths rapidly vanished. At the same time, the layout of holdings was radically altered by the so-called *Flurbereinigung* (consolidation) which established larger parcels of land and provided a better network of field paths. Since the new *Flurbereinigungsgesetz* of 1953, a rapid consolidation of fields has taken place. Between 1945 and 1961 18 per cent of the agricultural area of West Germany was reorganised. Whereas before 1950 these activities aimed to increase agricultural production by the improvement of farmland, the *Flurbereinigung* in the second half of the twentieth century has been aimed at enabling mechanized agriculture by enlarging fields in regular shapes, levelling land, straightening of rivers and brooks, and by hedge clearance. This has resulted not only in a desolate landscape, but also one which is ecologically impoverished. Consolidation was promoted not only by administrative means, but also by the subsidies which encouraged mass production. As a reaction to the ecological awareness which has emerged since the 1970s and to the fiscal problems posed by over-production, plans to 'renaturalize' parts of the landscape have been put into effect: wet meadows have been created, land set aside, and grassland used in a more extensive manner. Even though these measures have been successful, they only affect a small percentage of the landscape and, in view of the current boom in biofuels and the rising prices of agricultural products, the tendency to reduce the area used by agriculture might soon be reversed (Ditt, 2001: 85, 95–96, 113–14; Becks, 2001; Ipsen, 2005: 129, 134).

Government encouragement of trade and markets

In the nineteenth century, farmers had no problem selling their produce into rising markets. In the late 1870s this long-term trend came to an end, as international competition led to a decline of prices (Theine, 1991: 12). A debate on protection resulted in the implementation of grain tariffs in 1880. This marked the beginning of an era of agrarian protectionism, which can be differentiated into three periods. In all three the problems political forces faced in establishing a consumer-orientated policy can be discerned (Langthaler, 2005: 11–15). In the first period, 1880–1914, the agrarian sector was still strong enough to resist the new conditions caused by globalisation (Mai, 2007: 478). So, in the 1880s and from 1902 to 1914, consumers were put at a disadvantage by high tariffs which guaranteed farm-gate prices above the global market level (Theine, 1991: 12). During the First World War, agrarian markets were regulated: between 1919 and 1925 all tariffs were cancelled by allied decrees (Böckmann, 2000: 177). The second period of agrarian protectionism, which lasted from the later 1920s to 1936, was prompted by the double crisis in the late 1920s. Strict tariff protection was reckoned to be an inefficient way of dealing with this crisis, which had its origins in overproduction and underconsumption.

After a period of low taxes, a policy of high tariffs followed in 1929, which caused domestic grain prices to rise to double world market levels. This stimulated renewed overproduction and a decline of consumption, especially of animal products and, as a consequence, declining prices which could not be stabilized by state intervention in the market. The tariff policy of the Weimar Republic was characterized by the conflicts of interest between the estate owners in eastern Germany, who demanded high grain tariffs, and the farmers, especially in north-western Germany, who sought low prices for imported animal feed (Langthaler, 2005: 11–12; Theine, 1991: 113–15, 133; Böckmann, 2000: 177–215).

With fixed prices, the National Socialist market regime attempted to guarantee a stable income to the farmers and steady prices to the consumers. Interventions such as the prohibition of direct marketing and on-farm food processing, the increasing reliance on quotas and delivery obligations, diminished the farmers' autonomy to an unprecedented degree after 1934. After 1936 agriculture was integrated into the four year plan and subordinated to the interests of the arms industry, and from 1939 onwards war economics totally controlled all sectors of the economy and especially agriculture (Münkel, 1996: 94, 106–20, 326–37).

In the post-war period the conflict between agriculture and industry was almost resolved. Nevertheless agriculture remained subject to state planning (Langthaler, 2005: 14; Mai, 2007: 475). The controlled economy of the first post-war years was followed by a third period of protectionism starting in the 1950s which sought to satisfy demand for food by stabilizing the structure of agricultural holdings. Because of the socio-political objective of maintaining a solid class of farmers and the economic task of supplying non-rural consumers, the government did not want to apply free market principles to agriculture. In the early 1950s a system of market regulations was again erected. Production was stimulated by guaranteed minimum prices and by avoiding international competition. As a consequence, the basic food supply was guaranteed, but it was only achieved by increasing the funds allocated for its support. The agricultural law of 1955, the Grüner Plan (Green Plan), connected the objective of stimulating productivity with that of stabilizing the standard of living of people working in agriculture at a level compatible with those working in other sectors. This was only possible though permanently fixed prices and – in the long run – by reducing the agricultural labour force. The economic union of West Germany, France, Italy and the Benelux countries in 1957 and the establishment of the single European market exposed German agriculture to competition, but guaranteed standard prices and product sales by transferring German market regulations to the other European countries. By the 1970s, the consequence of this policy was structural overproduction. The 'Mansholt Plan' (1968), named after the Dutch agrarian politician, introduced the principle of 'growing or vanishing': the removal of small farmers and consolidation of big agricultural holdings. At the same time the policy of price intervention in which high prices were supported by subsidies delayed a more thorough-going structural change (Ditt, 2001; Kluge, 2005a: 36–67; Kluge, 2005b).

By the end of the 1970s, the disadvantages of European agrarian policy could be seen very clearly. The guaranteed sales and prices and the protection against imports caused a massive surplus of products which brought increasing costs. Nicknames such as 'butter mountain' or 'milk lake' demonstrate how critical public opinion was of this policy. The first attempts to reduce the costs provoked massive protests by farmers. Hence agricultural policy had to solve the task of reducing overproduction and subsidies, which took an increasing share of the European budget, whilst still maintaining the comparability of agricultural and industrial incomes. Increasing intensification by high-output farms was seen as the answer to these problems. New subsidies aimed to encourage small farmers to leave agriculture and big farmers to increase mass production. But this policy succeeded in neither reducing overproduction nor levelling of income between sectors. On the contrary, production grew from 1973 to 1988 at 2 per cent per annum, whereas consumption was growing only by 0.5 per cent. In addition, the subsidy policy provoked trade conflicts, especially with the US and Canada, and led to problems of pricing agricultural products in the developing countries. Since the 1980s the reduction of prices, more extensive agricultural methods, the use of set-aside land and the early retirement of farmers have aimed at stabilizing the cost of the common agricultural policy. The objective to equalise incomes was abandoned (Kluge, 2005a: 40–45).

In the late 1980s overproduction, the inability to compete in global markets, continuing technical progress, the expense of agrarian policy, the ecological problems caused by agriculture and the loss of the next generation of farmers, all indicated the inherent necessity for structural change. These problems led to a paradigm shift in agrarian policy. Already in the 1990s, pressured by the GATT negotiations, the price of grain and beef was cut, and direct payments to the producers to compensate for the loss in income were introduced. From 1999 the cutting of prices continued without compensation. In spite of more extensive methods, yields continued to increase because of progress in breeding and technology. In 2003, faced with the WTO-negotiations and the planned expansion of the EU into eastern Europe, the European ministers of agriculture decided abandon the agrarian policy which had formed the basis of the Community since its foundation: they broke the link between production and payment, but related the payments to aspects of environment and animal welfare. The consequences of this reform of agrarian policy and the Community's expansion will be seen in the future (Mahlerwein, 2008: 47).

Peasants and farmers as a political force in national politics

From the late nineteenth century, the process of deagrarianization was impeded by the demands of the agrarian sector for involvement in decision making, especially in the 'Caprivi years' (named after the Leo von Caprivi, Chancellor 1890–94, who pursued a low tariff policy after 1891), and again in the agrarian crisis of the late 1920s. Debates about the cutting of grain tariffs led to a rapid increase in the number of agrarian associations. In 1893 the *Bund der Landwirte* (BdL) was founded, which demanded high tariffs. Because this association was suspected to represent only the interests of the big east-Elbian Protestant landowners, competing associations were formed: in Catholic regions *Christliche Bauernvereine* (Christian Peasant

Associations), in others the *Deutsche Bauernbund*. Influence over agrarian policy was guaranteed by the prominence of a number of its leading members in parliament and by the enormous interest the public took in the association's affairs (Henning, 1988: 163–66). Because of economic and confessional differences, the development of the agrarian associations differed regionally. The *Bund der Landwirte* was established only in the old-Prussian Protestant regions including the (later) Lower Saxony, but in largely Catholic Westphalia, the *Westfälischer Bauernverein* was predominant, and this was linked to the *Zentrum* (Catholic Centre Party). Where the BdL pressed the interests of the east-German big landowners, the Westphalian *Bauernverein* sought low prices for animal feed and grain (Lohmann, 1964: 26, Albers, 1999: 15–16; Hohenstein, 1990: 10).

In the Weimar Republic, the agrarian associations could continue much as in the era of the German Empire and try to influence legislation, not least through their influence over the Chambers of Agriculture, but until the late 1920s their impact on agrarian policy remained limited. In 1921 *Reichslandbund* was founded as a union of the BdL and the *Landbünde*. This continued the lobbying policy of the BdL, but it was also politically connected to the right-wing *Deutschnationale Volkspartei* (German National People's Party) and opposed the democratic system. The *Bauernvereine* remained allied to the *Zentrumspartei*. Even though the demands of the associations for the abolition of the post-war controlled economy and the reintroduction of protective tariffs after 1924 were fulfilled, their influence over these developments was small (Theine, 1991: 141). In 1929, in response to the developing crisis, the associations united at a national level to form the *Grüne Front* (Green Front), but they remained separate competing entities at the regional level.

The associations were placed under pressure by an agrarian protest movement which first emerged in 1925, grew stronger in 1928 and which tried to influence agrarian policy by militant action, including the bombing of finance offices and the homes of civil servants. Significantly, no association was established at a regional level in Schleswig-Holstein, which was a centre of the radical opposition, so the barely organised *Landvolkbewegung* (Land's people movement) became entrenched in this crisis-ridden region (Bergmann/Megerle, 1989). From the very beginning, the *Landvolkbewegung* was influenced by the radical right. Whereas the *Reichslandbund* and also the chambers of agriculture were infiltrated by national socialists (or its members became national socialists), the *Bauernvereine* remained allied to the *Zentrum*. It was only in 1931–2 that the new president of the Westphalian *Bauernverein* began to cooperate with the Nazi-controlled *Landbund*, which shows how the policy of the *Zentrum* and its agrarian faction was now shifting to the right. The failure of the last Weimar government was caused not least by its unsuccessful agrarian policies and the radical opposition of the agrarian sector, which was deeply influenced by the Nazi party (Kluge, 2005a: 23–26, 82–8; Henning, 1988: 208–12; Bergmann/Megerle, 1989; Lohmann, 1964: 29; Theine, 1991: 141–42; Böckmann, 2000: 224–30; Albers, 1999: 44–47).

From 1930 the policies of the agrarian associations became subordinate to the National Socialist agrarian agenda. From 1931 agrarian representatives were active in the *agrarpolitischer Apparat* (agrarian political apparatus) of the NSDAP and, from

1933, in the National Socialist agrarian organisation *Reichsnährstand*, into which all the existing associations were merged. Nevertheless, soon after the seizure of power in 1933, the influence of the agrarian sector on Nazi policy was diminished and agrarian policy was subordinated to the power-political interests of the regime (Münkel, 1996: 88–98).

During the war and the first post-war years, the *Reichsnährstand* continued as an executive organ of the managed economy. From 1947 the re-established chambers of agriculture took over the representation of agrarian interests. The influence of the chambers over agrarian legislation was guaranteed by their institutional role and by the fact that many lobbyists of the associations were also members of the chambers. From 1948 the *Deutscher Bauernverband* exercised great influence over agrarian policy: in 1955 it insisted that the equalisation of the living conditions between agricultural and non-agricultural sectors should be one of the main aims of the new agricultural legislation. The *Bauernverband* remains one of the most influential lobby groups in Germany despite competing groups and the increasing Europeanization of agrarian policy.

The social standing of the peasant

The diminished economic significance of agriculture has changed the social standing of the peasantry since the late nineteenth century. Debates about the future development of Germany as an agrarian or as an industrial society were prominent in public discourse around 1900. Whereas statistical evidence of the increasing urban and the diminishing rural population encouraged politicians like Chancellor Caprivi to align their policy with the interests of urban-industrial consumers, the spokesmen for agrarian society continued to have great influence over public opinion. In the tradition of the nineteenth-century agrarian romanticism, they emphasised three functions of agriculture and rural society, firstly as being fundamental to all economies, secondly as a provider to the whole nation and thirdly as a guarantor of continued population growth (Weipert, 96–103; Wehler, 1995: 617–19). As shown above, the Nazi 'blood and soil' ideology adopted these arguments, but the rural world continued to decline in importance during the Nazi ascendancy. After World War II the agricultural population was still considered to be a socially stabilizing element within society. But from the 1950s onwards, even in small villages, farmers became a social minority and since that time industrial society has set the cultural norms and values. Paradoxically, the income of workers and wage earners, who in the past had been considered as dependent lower classes by the peasantry, now became the benchmark to which farmers aspired (Hagedorn, 1996: 401). During the last decades the public perception of agriculture has been formed by the debates about subsidies and their consequences for the national budget, about overproduction and its problems for international trade, by the negative ecological effects of an 'industrialized' agriculture, and by crises like BSE (Kluge, 2005a: 47–56). Farmers increasingly suffered from their poor image (Becker, 1995: 170–186). But recent surveys show that the reputation of agriculture is changing for the better, mostly because of the more positive image of organic farming (Das Image, 2007).

Bibliography

Abel, W. (1967) *Agrarpolitik*, Göttingen.

Agrarbericht des Landes Schleswig-Holstein, http://www.agrarbericht-sh.de/

Agrarstatistik Niedersachsen, http://www1.nls.niedersachsen.de/statistik/

Albers, H. (1999) *Die stille Revolution auf dem Lande. Landwirtschaft und Landwirtschaftskammer in Westfalen-Lippe, 1899–1999*, Münster.

Barnstedt, K. (1964) 'Der Agrarkredit' in Albrecht-Thaer-Gesellschaft (ed.), *Die Landwirtschaft Niedersachsens*, Hanover, pp. 200–07.

Becker, H. (1990) *Handlungsspielräume der Agrarpolitik in der Weimarer Republik zwischen 1923 und 1929*, Stuttgart.

Becker, H. (1995) *Dörfer heute. Ländliche Lebensverhältnisse im Wandel, 1952, 1972 und 1993/95*, Bonn.

Becks, F. (2001) 'Die räumliche Entwicklung der Landwirtschaft in Westfalen seit den siebziger Jahren des 20. Jahrhunderts – Gründe und ökologische Folgen', in K. Ditt, R. Gudermann, and N. Rüße (eds.), *Agrarmodernisierung und ökologische Folgen. Westfalen vom 18. bis zum 20. Jahrhundert*, Paderborn, München and Wien, pp. 451–477.

Bergmann, J. and Megerle, K. (1989) 'Protest und Aufruhr der Landwirtschaft in der Weimarer Republik (1924–1933). Formen und Typen der politischen Agrarbewegung im regionalen Vergleich', in J. Bergmann *et al.* (eds.), *Regionen im historischen Vergleich. Studien zu Deutschland im 19. und 20. Jahrhundert*, Opladen, pp. 200–87.

Böckmann, O. (2000) *Landwirtschaft im Oldenburger Münsterland, 1919–1933. Untersuchungen zur wirtschaftlichen, sozialen und politischen Situation*, Vechta.

Bracht, J. (2006) 'Reform auf Kredit: Grundlastenablösungen in Westfalen und ihre Finanzierung durch Rentenbank, Sparkasse und privaten Kredit (1830–1866)', *Zeitschrift für Agrargeschichte und Agrarsoziologie*, 54/2, pp. 55–76.

Brakensiek, S. (1994) 'Agrarian Individualism in north-western Germany, 1770–1870', *German History*, 12, pp. 137–79.

Bruns, V. (2008) 'Woraus resultieren steigende Bodenpreise?', www.bodenmarkt.info.

Bundesministerium der Finanzen (ed.) (1988) *Der wissenschaftliche Beirat beim Bundesministerium der Finanzen, Gutachten und Stellungnahmen, 1974–87*, Tübingen.

Das Image der deutschen Landwirtschaft. Ergebnisse einer Repräsentativumfrage in Deutschland (2007), http://www.ima-agrar.de/images/DasImagederdeutschenLandwirtschaft-2007.

Dipper, C. (1980) *Die Bauernbefreiung in Deutschland*, Stuttgart.

Ditt, K. (2001) 'Zwischen Markt, Agrarpolitik und Umweltschutz: Die deutsche Landwirtschaft und ihre Einflüsse auf Natur und Landschaft im 20. Jahrhundert', in K. Ditt, R. Gudermann and N. Rüße (eds.), *Agrarmodernisierung und ökologische Folgen. Westfalen vom 18. bis zum 20. Jahrhundert*, Paderborn, München and Wien, pp. 85–125.

Dix, A. (2005) 'Ländliche Siedlung als Strukturpolitik. Die Entwicklung in Deutschland im Ost-West-Vergleich von 1945 bis zum Ende der Fünfzigerjahre', in E. Langthaler and J. Redl (eds.), *Reguliertes Land. Agrarpolitik in Deutschland, Österreich und der Schweiz, 1930–1960*, Innsbruck, pp. 71–82.

Düwel, A. (1996) *Sozialrevolutionärer Protest und konservative Gesinnung. Die Landbevölkerung des Königreichs Hannover und des Herzogtums Braunschweig in der Revolution von 1848/49*, Frankfurt am Main.

Exner, P. (1997) *Ländliche Gesellschaft und Landwirtschaft in Westfalen, 1919–1969*, Paderborn.

Fertig, G. (2007) *Äcker, Wirte, Gaben. Ländlicher Bodenmarkt und liberale Eigentumsordnung im Westfalen des 19. Jahrhunderts*, Berlin.

Gagliardo, J. G. (1969) *From pariah to patriot. The changing image of the German peasant, 1770–1840*, Lexington.

Hagedorn, K. (1996) *Das Institutionenproblem in der Agrarökonomischen Politikforschung*, Tübingen.

Hauptmeyer, C.-H. (1983) 'Bäuerlicher Widerstand in den Grafschaften Schaumburg-Lippe, im Fürstentum Calenberg und im Hochstift Hildesheim. Zur Frage der qualitativen Veränderung bäuerlicher Opposition am Ende des 18. Jahrhunderts', in W. Schulze (ed.) *Aufstände, Revolten, Prozesse. Beiträge zu bäuerlichen Widerstandsbewegungen im frühneuzeitlichen Europa*, Stuttgart, pp. 217–232.

Henning, F. W. (1988) *Landwirtschaft und ländliche Gesellschaft in Deutschland,* II, *1750 bis 1986*, (sec. edn), Paderborn.

Henrici, E. (1964) 'Das bäuerliche Recht' in Albrecht-Thaer-Gesellschaft (ed.) *Die Landwirtschaft Niedersachsens*, Hanover, pp. 171–76.

Hindersmann, U. (2001) *Der ritterschaftliche Adel im Königreich Hannover, 1814–1866*, Hannover.

Hohenstein, A. (1990) *Bauernverbände und Landwirtschaftskammern in Niedersachsen, 1945–1954*, Hildesheim.

Ipsen, D. (2005) 'Landschaft' in S. Beetz, K. Brauer and C. Neu (eds.), *Handwörterbuch zur ländlichen Gesellschaft in Deutschland*, Wiesbaden, pp. 129–35.

Kannewurf, T. (2004) *Die Höfeordnung vom 24. April 1947*, Frankfurt am Main.

Kindler, R. (1993) *Landwirtschaftliche Boden- und Pachtpreise im Ost-West-Vergleich*, St. Augustin.

Kluge, U. (2005a) *Agrarwirtschaft und ländliche Gesellschaft im 20. Jahrhundert*, München.

Kluge, U. (2005b) '"Veredlungswerkstatt" oder "Rohstofffabrik"? Westdeutsche Agrar- und Ernährungspolitik zwischen wirtschaftlicher Rekonstruktion und Römischen Verträgen', in E. Langthaler and J. Redl (eds.), *Reguliertes Land. Agrarpolitik in Deutschland, Österreich und der Schweiz 1930–1960*, Innsbruck, pp. 46–58.

Kopsidis, M. (1996) *Marktintegration und Entwicklung der westfälischen Landwirtschaft 1780–1880. Marktorientierte ökonomische Entwicklung eines bäuerlich strukturierten Agrarsektors*, Münster.

Kulhawy, A. (2008) 'Financing the agrarian reforms and promoting the modernisation of farming in nineteenth-century Germany. The Example of the Duchy of Brunswick', in N. Vivier (ed.), *The state and rural societies. Policy and education in Europe, 1750–2000*, Turnhout, pp. 77–94.

Langthaler, E. (2005) 'Reguliertes Land. Agrarpolitik in Deutschland, Österreich und der Schweiz 1930–1960', in E. Langthaler and J. Redl (eds.), *Reguliertes Land. Agrarpolitik in Deutschland, Österreich und der Schweiz 1930–1960*, Innsbruck, pp. 8–18.

Lohmann, D. (1964) 'Die landwirtschaftliche Organisation in Niedersachsen von 1764 bis 1964', in Albrecht-Thaer-Gesellschaft (ed.), *Die Landwirtschaft Niedersachsens*, Hanover, pp. 15–44.

Mahlerwein, G. (2008) *Aufbruch im Dorf. Strukturwandel im ländlichen Raum Baden-Württembergs nach 1950*, Stuttgart.

Mai, G. (2007) 'Die Agrarische Transition. Agrarische Gesellschaften in Europa und die Herausforderungen der industriellen Moderne im 19. und 20. Jahrhundert', *Geschichte und Gesellschaft*, 33, pp. 471–521.

Möhl, J. (2006) 'Auswirkung der Reform der Gemeinsamen Agrarpolitik auf die Preise von Agrarland', in www.geobasis-bb.de.

Mooser, J. (1984) *Ländliche Klassengesellschaft 1770–1848. Bauern und Unterschichten, Landwirtschaft und Gewerbe im östlichen Westfalen*, Göttingen.

Münkel, D. (1996) *Nationalsozialistische Agrarpolitik und Bauernalltag*, Frankfurt am Main.

Ottenjann, H. (1990) 'Kultur-Leitbilder der bäuerlichen Oberschicht in Nordwestniedersachsen', in W. Jacobeit, J. Mooser and B. Stråth (eds.), *Idylle oder Aufbruch? Das Dorf im bürgerlichen 19. Jahrhundert*, Berlin, pp. 97–111.

Pelzer, M. (2002) *Landwirtschaftliche Vereine in Nordwestdeutschland. Das Beispiel Badbergen. Eine Mikrostudie zur Vereins- und Agrargeschichte im 19. und frühen 20. Jahrhundert*, Cloppenburg.

Prange, W. (1971) *Die Anfänge der großen Agrarreformen in Schleswig-Holstein bis um 1771*, Neumünster.

Prass, R. (1997) *Reformprogramm und bäuerliche Interessen. Die Auflösung der traditionellen Gemeindeökonomie im südlichen Niedersachsen, 1750–1883*, Göttingen.

Reif, H. (1979) *Westfälischer Adel 1770–1860. Vom Herrschaftsstand zur regionalen Elite*, Göttingen.

Rouette, S. (2003) 'Erbrecht und Besitzweitergabe: Praktiken in der ländlichen Gesellschaft Deutschlands, Diskurse in Politik und Wissenschaft', in R. Prass et al. (eds.), *Ländliche Gesellschaften in Deutschland und Frankreich, 18.-19. Jahrhundert*, Göttingen, pp. 145–66.

Schapper, T. (1964) 'Siedlung, Strukturverbesserung und die Eingliederung Vertriebener', in Albrecht-Thaer-Gesellschaft (ed.), *Die Landwirtschaft Niedersachsens*, Hanover, pp. 114–16.

Theine, B. (1991) *Westfälische Landwirtschaft in der Weimarer Republik*, Paderborn.

Thissen, G. (1988) *Die Entwicklung des landwirtschaftlichen Grundeigentums und Grundbesitzes in Nordrhein-Westfalen unter dem Einfluß von Urbanisierung und Industrialisierung*, Gießen.

Trossbach, W. and Zimmermann, C. (2006) *Die Geschichte des Dorfes*, Stuttgart.

Ulbricht, O. (1980) *Englische Landwirtschaft in Kurhannover in der zweiten Hälfte des 18. Jahrhunderts. Ansätze zu historischer Diffusionsforschung*, Berlin.

Vascik, G. (1991) 'The German Peasant League and the limits of rural liberalism in Wilhelmian Germany', *Central European History*, 24, pp. 147–75.

Vock, H. J. (1991) *Der agrarstrukturelle Wandel im mittleren Niedersachsen*, Göttingen.

Wehler, H. U. (1995) *Deutsche Gesellschaftsgeschichte*, III, *Von der "Deutschen Doppelrevolution" bis zum Beginn des Ersten Weltkrieges, 1849–1914*, München.

Wehner, B. (1987) *Die Bestimmungsgründe der Entwicklung der Landpacht unter besonderer Berücksichtigung der die Pacht beeinflussenden agrarpolitischen Maßnahmen*, Bonn.

Weipert, M. (2005) 'Siedlung und innere Kolonisation' in R. Mackensen and J. Reulecke (eds), *Das Konstrukt "Bevölkerung" vor, im und nach dem "Dritten Reich"*, Wiesbaden, pp. 95–107.

Wilde, S. and Barnstedt, K. (1964) 'Die Pacht', in Albrecht-Thaer-Gesellschaft (ed.), *Die Landwirtschaft Niedersachsens*, Hanover, pp. 191–93.

SCANDINAVIA

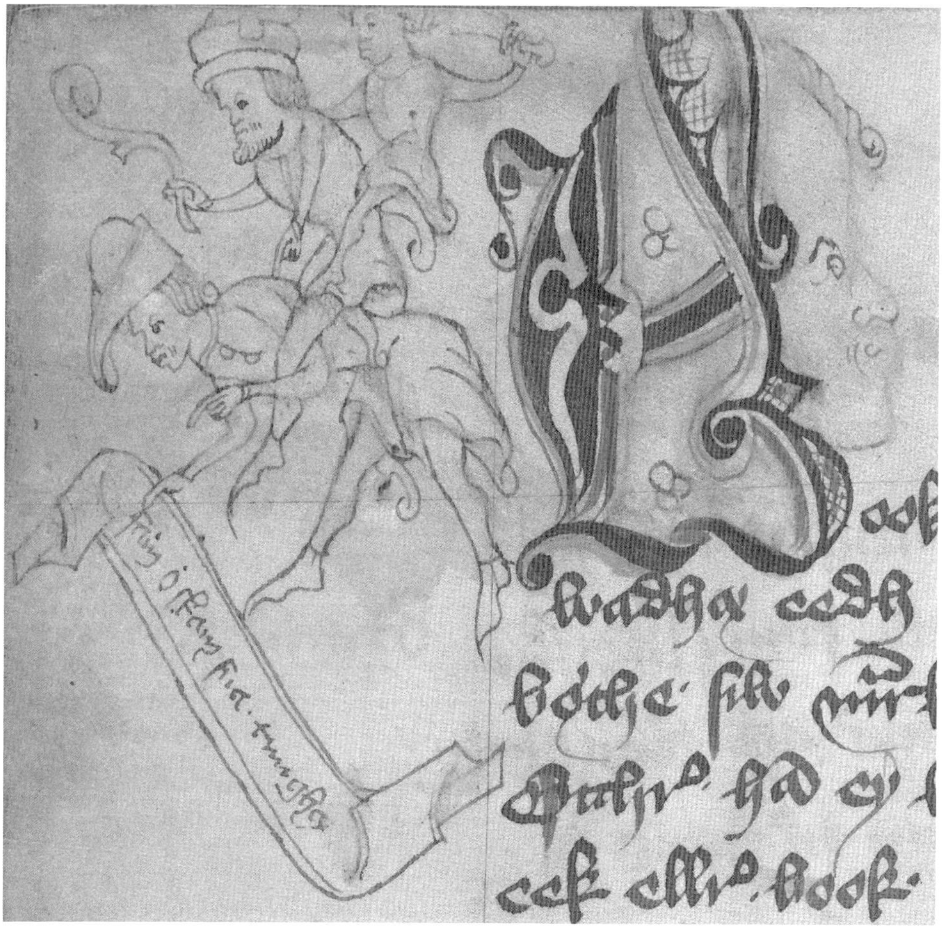

Illuminated manuscript from 1436–7 in which the social hierarchy is shown. The peasant is ridden by the sheriff of the county and on the top sits the king. This manuscript was made just after a rebellion in Sweden, when peasants fighting against taxes made an alliance with sections of the nobility against the king. It is a manuscript of the Swedish Law, and made for Bengt Jönsson, one of the higher nobility who joined the rebellion. In the scroll held by the peasant he says 'Shame on you, laying such heavy burden on me'. (Source: National Library of Sweden, MS B172, fol. 70v.)

On this manuscript see Janken Myrdal, *Den predikande räven*, Lund 2006.

11 Scandinavia, 1000–1750

John Ragnar MYKING and Carsten Porskrog RASMUSSEN

11.1 Ownership, power relations and the distribution of property

Landowners

Earlier commentators saw the old Norse communities as kin-based societies (*ættesamfunn*) where either the family (*ætt*) or individual and personally free peasant households owned the great majority of the land. During the high Middle Ages most peasants were turned into tenants.

Against this, a more recent view stresses the importance of big men or chiefs controlling substantial areas either in the form of large farms or networks of personal bonds built up over surrounding peasant households. In Norway this view has been substantiated by studies of royal estates in western Norway, while studies of inland eastern Norway indicate that owner occupiers of medium sized farms were possibly more frequent in that part of the country. In Denmark the existence of large aristocratic estates is certain from the twelfth century, but other sources seem to indicate the widespread existence of owner occupiers (Iversen and Myking, 2005: 8–13; 133–42; Myhre and Øye, 2002: 59, 87; Hybel and Poulsen, 2007: 165, 308–09).

Whatever the balance was around 1000, ownership structures changed substantially between 1000 and 1350. Firstly, after christianization, the church emerged as a new category of owner, which acquired substantial landed property in all Scandinavian countries. Secondly, a formal distinction between nobility and peasant freeholders emerged, defined by the relationship of the two groups to the crown with nobles performing military service and freehold peasants paying regular taxes. The system seems to have been established around 1200. In the beginning movement from one group to the other seems to have been common, but gradually the distinction between the two became firmer, leaving nobles and freehold peasants as distinctly different categories of landowners. Finally a division between the possessions of the 'realm' and those of the royal family, visible in Denmark and Sweden in the thirteenth century, disappeared.

As a result, there are four distinct categories of owner by the end of the fourteenth century: crown, church, nobles and peasant freeholders. In weakly urbanised Scandinavia, townspeople were insignificant as landowners before the middle of the seventeenth century, and those who did hold land were either regarded on a par with nobles or with freehold peasants. Most, but not all, farms owned by 'freeholders' were farmed by owner occupiers, but it was possible for a peasant to own farms leased out to others and yet remain socially and legally a tax-paying peasant.

Map 11.1 Scandinavia, 1000–1750

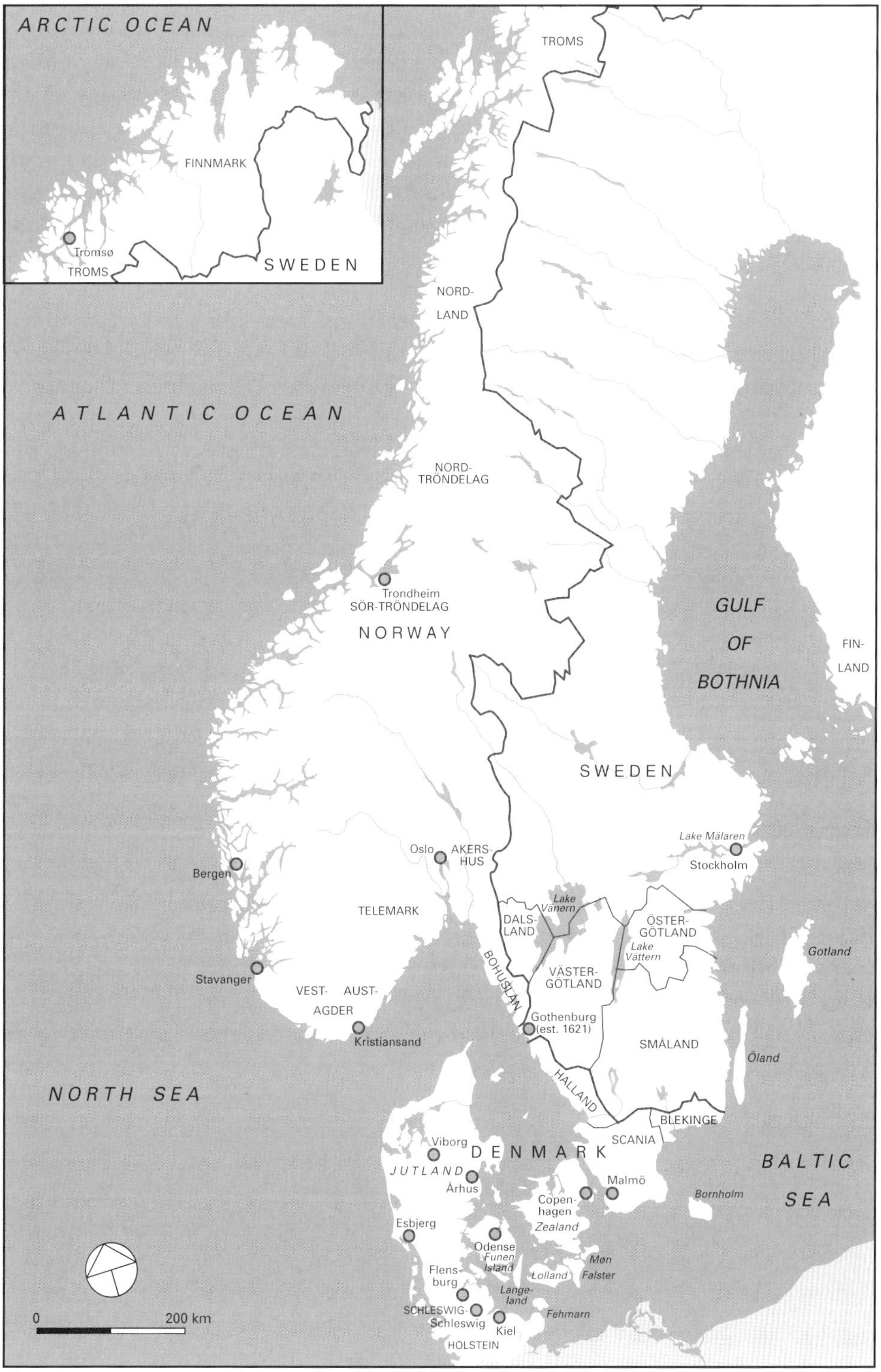

In Denmark and Sweden, not only were 'freehold' peasants defined as a special group of landowners, but 'freehold land' or 'tax land' emerged as a specific kind of property. By about 1400 the privileges of lay and ecclesiastical lords had expanded so far that the crown received no regular income from land held by these groups. Kings had, for a long time, unsuccessfully tried to prevent the movement of tax-paying peasant land into the hands of the church and nobles, but in 1396, Queen Margrete I, then ruler of the whole of Scandinavia, was able to ban the acquisition of 'freehold land' by the privileged groups and at the same time strengthen crown control over the land the freeholders held. Henceforth 'freehold land' in Denmark and Sweden became a category of its own, where members of the peasant estate were immediate landowners, but the crown had an overlordship which included the right to regular taxes and dues. In Norway the crown retained the right to levy taxes and other dues from tenants of nobles and ecclesiastical institutions as well as from freeholders. Therefore the king had no interest in claiming any special overlordship of freehold land (Iversen and Myking, 2005: 15–18, 29–37, 133–42, 153–65, 260–65; Myhre and Øye, 2002: 221–30; Lunden, 2002: 95–103; Porsmose, 1988: 255–65 and 380–90; Myrdal, 2000: 97–100; Poulsen, 2003: 424–33, 588–91).

Finally, Scandinavia contained areas which differed greatly in socio-economic terms from the mainstream, of which the Frisian marshlands in western Schleswig and the islands of Fehmarn and Gotland were the most important. Whilst there were enormous gulfs between rich and poor, there was no legal distinction between estates.

The distribution of property at the end of the Middle Ages

Not only were the categories of owners and land defined in the high Middle Ages, but also the property unit. In areas of village settlement, the alienation of single fields was apparently quite common in the high Middle Ages, but largely ceased thereafter. Henceforth property rights were attached to the farm as a unit and to a defined share of the total resources of the village. In the fifteenth and sixteenth centuries, both single farms and farms in villages could be subdivided into two halves or other shares, but after that time, such splitting of holdings largely ceased in Denmark, although it continued in the other countries. In the early modern period subdivision of farms was banned by monarchs who wanted solid taxpaying units, and on private manors in Denmark and parts of Sweden by landlords who wanted farms big enough to provide horses and people for labour service (Porsmose, 1988: 266–72; Poulsen, 2003, 658–64; Lunden, 2002, 95–100).

While farms normally only had one owner at any one time in Denmark and Sweden (apart from the overlordship of the crown over 'freehold' farms), a somewhat different development took place in Norway, which kept the farm as a production unit, but allowed a sort of shared ownership. In the Middle Ages property rights over many farms were divided among several owners, generally as a result of partible inheritance. From 1514 the owner of the largest share had the right to farm the farm or to find a tenant and collect certain dues from him, while minority owners only had a right to a share of the regular rent (Dørum, 1996: 33). A wholly different property system existed in the

TABLE 11.1: Distribution of landownership in Scandinavia, *c*.1525–1750 (per cent)

	Crown	Freehold	Lay landlords	Church
Denmark				
1525	10	15	38	37
1651	54	6	44	0
1683	35	2	63	0
1765	28	2	70	0
Norway				
1525	7.5	32[a]	13	47.5
1660	60	30[a]	10	0
Sweden				
1523	6	52	21	21
1560	29	50	21	0
1655[b]	35		65	0
1700	36	32	33	0
1765	20	47	33	0

Notes:

[a] Including land owned by peasants but farmed by other peasants as tenants

[b] In traditional statistics freeholds were divided according to overlordship between the crown and those nobles to whom the crown had alienated its rights to rents and taxes from the majority of freeholders.

Sources: Norway: Bjørkvik and Holmsen; Sweden: Hecksher, 1936: 132–33, 302–4, 337–38; Denmark: Porsmose, 1988, 132–3, 337–8, 389–90; Frandsen and Dombernowski (1988): 192, 248–57.

Schleswig marshes, where each plot was freely alienable and no regular farm structure existed (Iversen and Myking, 2005: 263).

Estimates of property distribution among the main groups can be made for the early sixteenth century (Table 11.1). As the only major changes in the balance between owner categories since 1400 were acquisitions of land by the church from the nobility, the picture is fairly representative for the whole period 1400–1525. At national level, aristocratic and ecclesiastical landlords seen together had the largest share of land in Denmark, and the least in Sweden. These national patterns had political consequences.

Ownership may, however, also be divided into three main regional patterns, crossing national borders. Most of Denmark, most of eastern Schleswig, most of the central plains and some forest regions in southern Sweden and some areas in south-eastern Norway were dominated by noble and ecclesiastical landownership. Many local differences in the property pattern (i.e. the balance between noble and church properties) existed within each of such regions, but not between them. Most of coastal Norway, including the fishing district, was so different that it can be seen as representing a second pattern. The proportion of the land owned by peasants was small, but as the bulk of the property was owned by the church, there were few aristocratic seats or demesnes.

The strongest contrast to both these groups of regions were those dominated by land owned by 'freehold' peasants. They comprised the whole of northern Sweden, certain other forest regions in that country, large parts of inland Norway, large parts of western Schleswig, and a couple of minor provinces in eastern Denmark. In most of Denmark freehold domination could only be found at parish level, rather than the provincial. In Sweden and Denmark the bulk of freehold farms were held by owner occupiers. In Norway about a third of freehold land was farmed by tenants, but owned by other 'peasants' (Porsmose, 1988: 380–90; Holmsen and Bjørkvik, 1972; Porskrog Rasmussen, 2003: I, 74–102; Hecksher, 1936: 129–34 and App. IV).

The distribution of property, 1530–1750

The Reformation of the 1530s meant that most church lands were seized by the crown. This had important consequences in all three countries, turning the crown from a relatively minor into a major landowner. In Sweden the church completely disappeared as a landlord, while local churches, cathedral chapters, and schools retained some property in Denmark and Norway.

In the latter half of the sixteenth century, the Danish king started a process of massive property exchanges with the nobility through which he became sole proprietor in certain districts in Denmark, mostly in parts of Sjælland and adjoining islands, while the nobility increased its share in Skåne, Fyn and certain Jylland regions. In this way the distribution of property changed considerably at the regional level, but stayed much the same when viewed in national perspective. The Danish crown also alienated its right over many freeholders and gave the new overlords the right to purchase full property over such farms from the peasants. The consequence was the almost total disappearance of freehold land in Denmark, while it remained a substantial category in Norway and Sweden.

This left Denmark from the early seventeenth century as a country with only two substantial owner categories: the crown and nobility, holding almost equal shares. The share of the politically strong Danish nobility was generated between 1482 and 1660 by laws prohibiting both the crown and non-nobles from taking over noble land (apart from exchanging property of equal value with the crown). Bourgeois creditors could take over land from an indebted noble, but were compelled to sell it to another noble within a year (Frandsen and Dombernowsky, 1988: 100–10; Feldbæk,1993: 8–10, 30–1).

In Norway most regions were dominated by tenancy, but contained few resident landlords as most farms belonged to the crown or to church institutions. Some regions remained dominated by freehold property. Sweden had three almost equally important owner categories: the crown, the nobility and freeholders, whose relative distribution differed greatly from region to region (Lunden, 2002: 284–85; Myrdal, 2000: 334–35; Gadd, 2002: 42–5).

Massive changes in the distribution of property took place in the seventeenth century, but due to different national political situations they took different forms in each country. Between *c.*1620 and 1660 the Swedish crown granted or sold a large proportion of its land to nobles and the newly-ennobled civil and military servants who were influential in the period of Swedish foreign expansion. The grants and sales comprised both crown land in the proper sense and the crown's rights over freeholders. By 1655 Sweden had become the most aristocratic of Scandinavian countries, surpassing Denmark, as seen in Table 11.1. This situation did not last long. Following the Danish-Swedish war 1675–79, the Swedish parliament, in an alliance of king, freehold peasants, burghers, and the lesser nobles against noble magnates passed laws of resumption which in principle meant the confiscation of all crown land donated to nobles over the previous couple of generations.

After the resumption, the distribution of land in Sweden was roughly a third share each to the crown, the freeholders and the nobles, close to what it had been in 1600. Each farm officially belonged to one of these categories, and only members of the relevant social group could acquire land assigned to each category. If a townsman wanted to become a landlord, he had to seek ennoblement. Ennoblement took place on a large scale in Sweden, though the applicants for nobility were normally either military officers or civil servants who sought to establish their family as country squires. In that way the formal social order supported by the Swedish parliamentary system with estates of nobles, burghers, clergy, and freehold peasants was maintained, but *de facto* social dynamics were possible (Heckscher, 1936: 299–359; Magnusson, 1985).

Even if only one major wave of change occurred in Denmark, it had more lasting consequences. The wars with Sweden of 1643–45 and 1657–60 not only led to the ceding of a number of provinces to Sweden, but also left the Danish-Norwegian state heavily indebted. The crown, after the establishment of absolutism in 1660–61, chose to pay its creditors with land. Between 1661 and 1664 roughly a quarter of all land in the remaining parts of Denmark was transferred from the crown to its creditors. The strengthened royal government chose to alienate land but increased land taxation, which it could now do largely at will.

In 1683 the crown owned a quarter of the land in Denmark, churches and schools 10 per cent, freeholders less than 2 per cent, and private landlords 63 per cent. Denmark had become a country dominated by private lay landlords. Over the next 80 years this picture was further sharpened as the crown's share fell and that of private landlords rose. Denmark became a country of private manors, but unlike Sweden, Danish landlords, following the establishment of absolutism in 1660 were no longer necessarily noble. The main beneficiaries of the transfer of the crown lands were great merchants, both Danish and foreign, and the absolutist government gave burghers the right to acquire land previously held by old noble families, many of whom were forced into sales due to hard times. In 1683 new landowning families owned as much land as the old noble families did, a dramatic change over one generation. Sales to merchants, civil servants, and bourgeois estate managers continued throughout the period, but frequently these new landowning families sought and achieved noble titles, and even if they came from cities, they generally transformed themselves into country landlords within a generation or two. Land ownership was not only an important source of social prestige, but also the most important long term investment option in a country which was still overwhelmingly rural (Frandsen and Dombernowsky, 1988: 173–94; Feldbæk, 1993: 61–6).

The precise distribution of property in Norway after 1661 is not known, but the share of private landlords was dramatically increased in relation to the 10 per cent held by the nobility in 1661, as the Danish-Norwegian crown also transferred much of its Norwegian properties to its creditors in the 1660s. Most of the property quickly passed into the ownership of persons of a bourgeois background, mainly merchants and civil servants. Old nobles mattered very little and new landowners – again, unlike Denmark and Sweden – were rarely ennobled, making bourgeois landlords a prominent landowning group around 1700. Not only did members of this new landowning elite formally remain bourgeoise or civil cervants, they tended to keep their principal residences in towns.

Over the course of the next century, they gradually sold many of their farms to their tenants as they found more rewarding investment opportunities than land. This led to an unprecedented increase in the number of freeholders. The proportion of land measured in *landskyld* (rent value) owned by owner-occupier peasants rose from 20 per cent in 1660 to 40 per cent in 1750, thus reaching levels like those in Sweden. Bourgeois landlords on the other hand retained much land in areas of iron and timber production, where land was especially valuable. The cultural status of country gentleman for these merchants was maintained through the ownership of smaller summer residences close to the towns (Dyrvik, 1977; Lunden, 2002: 291–99, 304–17).

Manorial structures and forms of tenancy

Our knowledge of the organisation of the property of major landlords before the thirteenth century is far from incomplete. Certainly large farms were important, farmed by *thralls* (slaves) or dependant peasants in the neighbourhood. In charge of these farms in both Denmark and Sweden was the *bryde* (Latin *villicus)*, a trusted but unfree person. In most cases, the individual manor seems to have consisted of one major farm with dependencies in the same village or surrounding dispersed farms and hamlets.

From the twelfth to the fourteenth centuries both ecclesiastical and lay estates in Denmark and Sweden usually consisted of manors or large farms in the charge of a *bryde*. The organisation of such farms was, however, changing. The status of the *bryde* changed from a bailiff to a sharecropper and often changed again to a tenant paying a fixed rent as manors were gradually farmed out. As *thralls* disappeared, some of the labour seems to have been provided by either cottagers, the so-called *inquillinii (gårdsæder)*, who were mainly found in Sjaelland, or by *coloni*. The *colonus (landbo)* was a new group which emerged in the eleventh and twelfth centuries and who usually occupied medium or smaller holdings, originally held on very short leases. The relative numbers of *villici* and *coloni* and their share of the land are known only from a few ecclesiastical estates, where *villici* held a high proportion. Even less is known about proportions in Sweden. In Norway the categories of *villicus* and *landbo* are unknown. Any manor-like estates depending on the personal bonds of peasant households had vanished by the twelfth century (Iversen and Myking, 2005: 8–13; Hybel and Poulsen, 2007: 166–75; Porsmose, 1988: 255–65; Myrdal, 2000: 97–100; Myhre and Øye, 2002: 257–76).

As in many other parts of Europe, the fourteenth century saw a major drop in population in Scandinavia. In Norway, with its small and dispersed settlements, the obvious consequence was the desertion of farms, especially the more marginal ones. In more densely populated Denmark, only a few settlements were totally deserted, but the structure of villages and farms altered in response to population decline. Manors were farmed out and often split up and small farms joined together. In Sweden the observable effects of population decline are generally small.

The outcome of the crisis was the amalgamation of various forms of tenant farms into one, the medium-sized family farm, run by the peasant family and with possibly a few servants. In most of Scandinavia rents were hereafter mainly paid in kind, of which one product usually made up the greater part. These basic rents became fixed at a lower level than earlier, and then largely remained unaltered until the eighteenth century. Lifelong tenure seems to have emerged as the *de facto* norm, and around 1500 entry fines were introduced both in Denmark and Norway. They were negotiable and have some similarity to the purchase of a life lease.

Fifteenth-century Scandinavian landlords, spiritual as temporal, lived from rents and other dues paid by tenants. Demesnes were few and small and primarily functioned as residences and administrative centres, and estates were scattered and volatile. The inheritance system tended to favour the splitting up of estates, as land was divided among all children. As both spouses inherited land, each marriage could create new estate structures. In Denmark, as well as in Norway and Sweden, we have examples of lords trying to concentrate their estates through the purchase of tenant farms close to their demesnes, but the rather volatile land market did not necessarily aid consolidation. At least some Danish lords bought farms rather indiscriminately, and in Norway and Sweden it has been suggested that some of them deliberately gathered property in several districts in order to seek rents of different kinds. Church estates tended to be more coherent, as property once brought together remained together (Gissel *et al.* 1981: 79–114 and 159–68; Iversen and Myking, 2005: 19–23 and 34; Hybel and Poulsen, 2007: 175–87; Porsmose, 1988: 341–43; Myrdal, 1999: 125–27; Lunden, 2002: 44–94).

The rise of early modern manorialism

In the early modern period many Scandinavian landlords, like their fellow estate owners south of the Baltic, increased demesne farming and corvée, thus making areas of Scandinavia part of the 'refeudalisation' of east-central Europe. The rise of demesnes was partly triggered by the western European demand for Baltic grain, partly by a legal regime defending fixed rents but allowing landlords to increase corvée largely at will. A moderate increase in corvée may at first have been seen as a 'costless' increase in the efficiency of the use of labour and draught force of peasant farms, but gradually it rose to levels which made it a substantial cost for peasants, but also a central resource for landlords. The development towards demesne farming and labour services was most evident in regions where private landlords were dominant – i.e. most of Denmark and the central Swedish regions.

A precondition for increased demesne farming was more geographically consolidated estates. By 1550 this had only been fulfilled in south-eastern Schleswig. In Denmark the policy of concentrating royal lands in the latter half of the sixteenth century facilitated a concentration of noble estates as well, and similarly the later alienation of crown lands in Sweden facilitated estate concentration around demesnes. In Denmark the nobility also started a process of internal land exchanges with the purpose of consolidating their estates. The process continued through much of the seventeenth century, and by the latter half of the century, most nobles had a clear majority of their tenant farms in close proximity to their demesnes. In Sweden landlords at the time of the resumption were largely allowed to keep demesnes and tenants close to them. In Norway a process of concentration can also be seen in the seventeenth century on the few noble estates.

The effects of concentration were strengthened by a gradual change in the way estates were inherited. Danish nobles from the end of the sixteenth century tended to give their heirs complete manorial complexes where ever that was possible. If division was necessary, one heir tended to get the nucleus of the estate. Later it became usual throughout Scandinavia for one heir to receive the whole estate and other heirs to receive legacies of money or other valuables. The introduction of forms of indivisible estates tended to advance further the consolidation of manors. This development started in Sweden in 1562 with the creation of counts and barons who were given crown lands as hereditary fiefs. These fiefs were removed by the resumption of 1680, but other forms of entailed estates were introduced in all countries. Entailed estates still only covered a minority of private manors in both Denmark and Sweden in 1750, but the number was growing. Norway was the exception and only a handful of entailed estates emerged here.

The first initiative in the direction of increased demesne farming was undertaken by King Gustav Vasa of Sweden (ruled 1523–60) who established an extensive network of crown demesnes in the 1550s. However the crown started to reduce its demesne farming in the 1570s. In the later decades of the sixteenth century the Danish king also started establishing demesnes, but here too the initiative was partly reversed after 1600. At least in Denmark the efficiency of crown estates was low, probably due to the long distances from manager to owner, and besides the monarchs had other ways of increasing income from their domains, notably new taxes.

Demesne farming became considerably more important on private estates. The development was most dramatic in south-eastern Schleswig, where demesnes grew continuously from the middle of the sixteenth century till the beginning of the eighteenth, by which time they included half the arable land of these estates. This region thus displayed an extreme form of manorialism only matched by the areas along the southern coast of the Baltic.

In Denmark development was less extreme, but a continuous process of increasing the extent of demesne lands can be seen from the second half of the sixteenth century. Existing demesnes were enlarged and new ones were established. The overall number of demesnes did not grow as small demesnes were converted into tenant farms, but the average size of those which remained grew considerably. Such an enlargement of demesnes was most evident in the most fertile areas, and came at the expense of peasant farms. In Sweden an increase in demesnes seems to have started slightly later and taken a somewhat different form. The number of private demesnes has been estimated at 3–400 at the end of the sixteenth century, but a century later it had risen almost tenfold. This enormous increase had to do with the alienation of crown lands and the creation of a great number of new nobles, who sought a manor and a demesne for the status it conveyed. However, as many as a third of the formally existing demesnes were, in reality, ordinary peasant farms freed from taxes, and most of the remainder were small.

In 1682 there were 700 demesnes in Denmark with an average size close to 100 ha of arable. They covered 9 per cent of the land in Denmark. It is a fair estimate that the total amount of demesne land had doubled since the end of the middle ages. For the next half century the extent of demesne land increased only moderately. By 1679 demesnes and dependant tenants in the home village covered only 6 per cent of Swedish land, varying from 16–17 per cent in the central plains to none in the north. The number of demesnes was over 3,000 but their average size was less than 30 ha. The relative importance of private manors grew after 1680, as the reduction largely left demesnes untouched. As private manors made up only a small part of Norwegian landholding, the role of demesnes in the national picture was negligible.

Demesnes made up 15–20 per cent of the arable land on most private estates in Denmark in both 1683 and later, and in Sweden a proportion of 15 per cent demesne land was found on a sample of 18 estates in the eighteenth century. In both countries the proportion of demesne land varied from estate to estate, but tended to be higher on smaller estates. Most of the private estates of Denmark and the 'noble' estates of Sweden were private manors centred around demesnes. Estates of this sort encompassed up to two-thirds of all land in Denmark, but less than one-third in Sweden. They were the dominant form of landownership in most Danish regions largely irrespective of natural conditions, but were limited to certain parts of Sweden, mainly the central plains. On these manors rents were mixed, comprising taxes in money, rents in money and kind, but also a substantial element of labour rent. Only in Schleswig did labour rent become all-dominant (Myrdal, 1999: 218, 334–39; Heckscher, 1936: 318–30; Weidling, 1998: 176–84, 253–79; Porskrog Rasmussen, 2003; Porskrog Rasmussen, 2004: 56–9; Feldbæk, 1993: 32–5, 66–68).

Alongside this demesne-centred estate system two other patterns of landownership continued to exist. One comprised estates consisting of rent-paying tenant farms where rents and taxes in money and kind were the only form of rent. The other comprised the 'freehold' peasants, who similarly paid taxes in money or kind to the crown. The former system covered perhaps well over a third of peasants in Denmark, Schleswig, and Sweden and a large majority of peasants in Norway by the end of the seventeenth century. The latter system encompassed an increasing number of peasants in both

Norway and Sweden in the eighteenth century and close to half the peasantry in Schleswig, but very few Danish peasants before 1750. In practical terms, the conditions of peasants under these two systems was broadly similar. The important distinction was between those peasant households who paid rents and taxes in money or kind, and those under the demesne-centred systems whose rent was largely paid as corvée.

The value of land

Around 1300, at the end of the high medieval expansion, the level of rent of land in Denmark and Norway reached a peak which remained unsurpassed for centuries. The medieval peak arose out of the technical advances of previous centuries, the growth in population (which itself peaked about this time), and an advantageous climate. Other signs of the demand for land are the clearance of more marginal areas, particularly in Norway and Sweden, and the existence of a large class of more or less landless cottagers in Denmark.

After the population crisis of the fourteenth century, rents collapsed, most dramatically in Norway. At the national level, rents in Norway fell to between a fifth and a quarter of their pre-crisis level by the beginning of the sixteenth century, after having been even lower during the trough of the demographic crisis in the middle of the fifteenth century.

Rents on tenant land in Sweden and Denmark also decreased during the late Middle Ages. Developments in land rent in Sweden are difficult to trace due to the lack of sources, but there are indications of considerable reductions by the middle of the fifteenth century, to approximately half the pre-crisis land rent in the plains of southern Sweden and possibly even further in the woodlands of Småland. In Denmark the fall began around 1370, and the rent level reached its nadir in the early fifteenth century. Here the fall in rents seems to have differed widely by region. In the Århus area on the eastern coast of Jylland, rents were down to one third, whereas rents in the south-western parts of Jylland and on the island of Sjælland stabilized at about two thirds of the pre-crisis level. The purchase price of land also decreased markedly, but not as much as rents (Gissel *et al.,* 1981: 143–71; Lunden, 2002: 44–53; Myrdal, 2000: 144–45; Poulsen, 2003: 529).

Resources other than agricultural land became much more important from the fourteenth century. One was fishing, particularly along the coasts of northern Norway where the church owned much of the land and benefited from its development. In Norway and Sweden timber and tar became important export commodities in the early modern period, generating wealth for freeholders who had access to timber, and even more so for landlords owning farms and estates which included large tracts of forest. In north-central Sweden, iron production was important. In the sixteenth century, ironworks were run by the crown, but in the seventeenth century they were sold to an emerging class of bourgeois ironworks owners, many of which were ennobled. In many cases taxes or rents from peasants near the iron works were leased to the work's owners so they receive these rents in the form of either charcoal or carrying services (Lunden, 2002: 304–17; Hecksher, 1936: 427–506).

A moderate increase in rents and thus land value started in the late fifteenth century in Denmark. The basic rent remained frozen throughout all of Scandinavia, but Danish landlords succeeded in introducing new minor dues in addition to it. In both Denmark and Norway a negotiable entry fine (*indfæstning, førstebygsel*) was introduced around 1500. As agrarian prices and the demand for land rose in the sixteenth century, it became an important source of income. The price of land rose considerably due to a fall in the average interest rate from about 10 per cent *c*. 1400 to 5 or 6 per cent in the early sixteenth century.

A more marked increase in land value started at the middle of the sixteenth century and lasted for about a century, partly due to increasing grain prices which made the value of rents paid in kind higher. On top of that, Danish and Swedish landlords expanded their demesnes and made greater demands for corvée from their peasants. As the other rents were not reduced, the recourse to corvée meant an increase in the total rent of the land. In Denmark, the prices of land reached a peak around 1640. The price rose more than the return as the land market became increasingly speculative.

From the middle of the seventeenth century, a new crisis brought marked decreases in the price of land throughout Scandinavia. Falling commodity prices reduced the value of both rents paid in kind and demesne production, and a dramatic increase in the taxation levied on tenant land owned by private landlords in Denmark and Norway further reduced both the income from and the value of privately-owned landed property (Lunden, 2002: 291–99; Weidling, 1998: 158–63; 193–96: Feldbæk, 1993: 31–2, 75–7, 99–100).

In the late Middle Ages as well as in the early modern period, investment in land throughout Scandinavia mainly had the character of rent seeking. Landlords made hardly any investments in the 80 per cent and more of their property held by tenants. The establishment of demesnes with new buildings and herds of cattle required investment, but the demesne land was largely farmed by the same people using the same implements as the neighbouring peasant farms. Demesnes were therefore rarely more productive than ordinary farms and often less so, and they show few signs of agricultural innovation, the adoption of large scale dairy farming on Danish demesnes in the early eighteenth century being a modest exception. Investments were made in the establishment of sawmills in Norway and even more so in ironworks in Sweden and Norway, but these were not investments in farming as such.

11.2 The occupiers of the land

In contrast to many of their European counterparts, Scandinavian peasants as early as *c*.1000 were considered to be free men in law. What remained of personal bonds between big men or chiefs and peasant households were turned into impersonal tenancy contracts by the twelfth century. Later restrictions on the right to leave a farm or obligations to do corvée labour were formally laid upon the farm, not upon individual persons.

Before *c*.1350 the legal and social status of those who worked the land in Scandinavia varied a great deal. At the top of the peasant society stood the ordinary *bonde* ('peasant').

A *bonde* was a free person who was working a farm or a holding as a tenant or a freeholder. He had the right to represent himself and his family in court and was entitled to the full penalties under the law. Until the thirteenth century (and in Sweden probably well into the fourteenth), these free peasants were contrasted with a workforce of slaves called *thralls (trælar)*. Central to the upholding of this system of forced labour was access to slaves acquired through Viking raids and slave markets in the British Isles and Ireland in the west and across the Baltic Sea to the east. An estimate of the number of slaves has proved difficult to give, although most scholars agree that it must have been substantial. Slaves were used in individual peasant households as well as by chiefs and big men on their demesnes. Over time these slaves and their descendants were given, or were allowed to buy, their freedom, including by being given grants of land to clear, although a transition from slaves to totally free men took generations. Slavery in the Nordic countries came to an end during the thirteenth century, or in the case of Sweden, the early fourteenth. This may have been due to the drying up of the slave markets as well as an increase in domestic population which made more servants and labour available.

In between the slave population and free peasantry there existed a mixed group of semi-dependent status. Some of them were slaves or descendants of slaves who had managed to buy their freedom but who were still bound by personal bonds to their former owners or their descendants. By the thirteenth century such personal bonds were rapidly waning, giving way to formalized impersonal relations between landlord and tenant (Iversen, 2004; Iversen and Myking, 2005: 8–13).

Tenancy conditions

A majority of Scandinavian medieval peasants were tenants with a legal status equal to freeholders. In thirteenth-century Denmark and Sweden, however, the legal status of tenants differed. The so-called *bryder* or *villici*, originally high status servile persons, were parts of the *familia* of the landlord, while the *landboer* or *coloni* were not. The *bryder* were no longer servile persons, nor had they generally a lower status than *landboer*. They paid some of their fines to the landlord who probably also exercised a kind of police authority over them, but their status was not one of bondage. Both *bryder* and *landboer* were free to leave the estate having given notice of their intention to do so. In the course of the fourteenth and fifteenth centuries the categories of *bryde* and *landbo* were amalgamated into one. The category of *bryde*, it might be added, was unknown in Norway.

According to the regional and national laws of the region, tenancies were formally very short, ranging from a minimum contract of a year in the oldest regional law, the twelfth-century Gulating law of western Norway, to six to eight years in the regional Swedish laws dating from the end of the high Middle Ages. As these laws referred to minimum terms, they did not limit the length of tenure a landlord might offer his tenants. The surviving contracts have only been studied in Norway where they were found to vary from a few years in duration to lifelong and even hereditary tenures, with a preference for longer tenancies on royal land and church estates. As Norwegian medieval laws do not mention lifelong or hereditary contracts, the absence of such clauses in Swedish and Danish law codes does not rule out the existence of similar arrangements in these countries.

The demographic crises from the middle of the fourteenth century weakened the landlords' position. Until the first half of the sixteenth century, potential tenants in all Scandinavian countries could choose from a wide variety of deserted farms and vacant holdings. Landlords had to be content with drastically reduced rents if they were to keep their tenants or attract new ones to occupy abandoned holdings. In this climate two different strategies were open to landlords: either to offer favourable terms for tenants or constrain their opportunity to migrate. The last option seems only to have been available to some Danish landlords.

In Norway, with scattered landholdings, a relatively weak aristocracy and a crumbling late medieval state, landlords only had the option of the first strategy, and rents fell dramatically. In addition to favourable rents, tenants were also offered long term and hereditary contracts to induce them to stay on their holdings. As tenant contracts have not been studied in detail in either Sweden or Denmark, it is not yet possible to say whether reduced rents were followed by longer and more favourable contracts as in Norway (Myhre and Øye, 2002: 106–07; Iversen and Myking, 2005: 20).

By the middle of the sixteenth century, the length of contracts in Sweden differed according to who owned the land. Tenants on *frälsejord* (land belonging to the nobility) seem to have enjoyed short contract periods, while tenants on land belonging to the crown were given relatively long leases. In Denmark and Norway life tenures were the general norm. They could only by cancelled if tenants were found guilty of violating the terms of their contract, for instance for non-payment of rent. Otherwise a tenancy could only be given up by the tenant or his widow.

In Norway this resulted in tenants being able to sell or transfer their right to the holding. The landlord was entitled to sanction their choice of successor, but could not appoint a new tenant of his own choosing. Peasants on crown lands in Schleswig seem to have acquired much the same rights, but here inheritance seems to have predominated strongly over sales. On the Swedish crown estates, which were widely dispersed within the country, tenure became hereditary but the right of sale was not conceded.

The existence of this tenant entitlement to transfer tenures in Norway and on crown land in Sweden and Schleswig shows a divided property right that gave tenants a *dominium utile* with considerable amount of control over their holdings. In Denmark tendencies to the development of similar peasant rights can be found in areas where tenants owned the buildings, as in south-western Jylland and on some minor islands, but in the greater part of Denmark and on private manors of Sweden and Schleswig, landlords controlled the succession to farms. This can most likely be ascribed to the widespread use of labour service and the extensive control Danish landlords in general exercised over their tenants, powers that they shared with their fellow landlords on *frälsejord* (noble land) in Sweden (Myking, 2005: 128–47; Olsson, 2005: 147–50; Porskrog Rasmussen, 2003: 527–35).

Non-economic landlord power

Restricting tenants' ability to move to other estates does not seem to have been an option for Norwegian and Swedish landlords. The Swedish aristocracy tried to introduce such rules on a number of occasions in the fifteenth century but failed at each attempt. Danish landlords were more successful. The prevention of tenant migration became one of their main strategies. In 1377 the Danish Council of the Realm curbed attempts by landlords to restrict tenants' free movement, and their interference with the wedding of their daughters. But, from the last decade of fifteenth century, tenants on the island of Sjælland and some neighbouring islands were forbidden to depart from the estates on which they had been born, thus precluding any attempt to bargain for better conditions by threatening to move to the estates of another landlord. Camouflaged as an opportunity to be protected (Danish: *værnet*) by their landlord, this *vornedskab* on the eastern islands became a major instrument by which landlords could control their tenants.

In Denmark, landlords' non-economic power over their peasants was further strengthened by some of them obtaining extensive judicial powers. In the early fourteenth century Danish noble and ecclesiastical landlords progressively acquired the right to collect almost all fines from their peasants, and from 1523 they definitively also held the so-called 'right of neck and hand' *(hals- og håndsret)*, i.e. the right to prosecute their tenants for crimes and to execute capital punishment. The 'right of neck and hand' did not, however, include the right to act as judge. A few estates had manorial courts, but generally public courts prevailed. In the sixteenth and seventeenth centuries the number of manorial courts grew, but without ever becoming the dominant legal forum. The Danish example was, for a long time, the ideal that Swedish lords strove to secure for themselves. Throughout the sixteenth century, the Swedish nobility failed in these efforts (Myrdal, 2000: 153; Iversen and Myking, 2005: 34–5; Iversen, Myking and Thoma (eds), 2007: 214 and 230–31; Feldbæk, 1993, 10).

The introduction of absolutism in 1660 meant a dramatic loss of national political power for Danish nobles, but they largely retained their local authority. New, non-noble, landlords were not given the right of neck and hand, but did get access to the other forms of landlord authority. Furthermore, in the years after 1660, the king gave landlords the responsibility for levying taxes and conscripting soldiers on their estates. Taxation was levied according to a national cadastre, and the landlord was made responsible for meeting state demands. In this way Danish society was built upon a feudal system of authority without, however, limiting the power of the state in any substantial way. As for the landlords, the delegation of state authority gave them substantial power over their tenants, although peasants could appeal to royal district governors (Løgstrup, 1985).

Though Norway was under the same king as Denmark from 1380, Norwegian landlords never secured the same authority over their tenants as their Danish counterparts. Judicial authority and the right to collect fines in non-ecclesiastical litigation remained in the hands of the crown throughout the Middle Ages. In 1646 Norwegian nobles were given the right of neck and hand and the right to all fines, but this was of little consequence as much of the scarce noble land shortly after passed into the hands of non-nobles. In addition tax collection and conscription was kept in the hands of the king's officers (Weidling, 1998, 196–200).

The creation of comital and baronial fiefs meant an important increase in privately-held judicial and administrative authority over peasants in Sweden in the seventeenth century. Like other feudal developments in this country, it was, however, short-lived. As part of the resumption of crown lands of the late seventeenth century, the crown recovered its alienated judicial authority, which remained its hands for the latter part of the period.

Communal land use systems

A striking feature of Norwegian and Swedish agriculture outside the rich grain-growing districts of Scania and mid-Sweden was the abundance of grazing land, upland pastures and other outfield resources. In such regions the fenced and intensively utilized farmland proper, consisting mostly of arable land and meadows, was clearly distinguished from the more extensively utilized outfields, wastes and commons.

In the richer grain-growing districts of the Danish isles, parts of Jylland, Scania and a region stretching almost across central Sweden from the lake of Vänaren to the Baltic Sea (Västergötland, Östergötland and the regions close to lake Mälaren), arable land expanded at the expense of wastes, woods and commons. In these regions, the distinction between infield and outfield areas gradually became less important than the distinction between fields lying fallow and fields that were utilized for grain growing.

The need to prevent cattle from destroying crops was a problem that had to be solved by collective effort, either by erecting fences or by herding cattle. In parts of Jylland a system with flexible arable fields without fences required cattle to be herded or tied. In most of Scandinavia, however, fences kept cattle out of fields and meadows during the growing season. The task of building and repairing fences between the infield and the outfield area, as well as between fallow and fields with different crops, was an important communal effort for peasant households in the open field areas in both Denmark and southern Sweden, as well as for areas with an infield-outfield system in Norway and parts of Sweden.

In both systems gates to allow grazing were opened after the crops and hay had been harvested in the autumn and closed again when fields and meadows needed to be protected against cattle in the spring. In areas practising arable rotations, fences were in addition opened and closed according to the rotation of sown fields and fallow, creating a common grazing ground for cattle on fallows and resting outfield areas. In this system, the rotation of crops and fallow was in many cases synchronised between several villages to create a continuous pasture for their cattle on fallows and wastes (*vanglag*).

Individual peasant households held exclusive rights to the use of their own strips or plots of infield arable land and meadows, while pastures were used communally, even on infield land. Wastes, woods and pastures, resources abundantly found in the infield-outfield areas of Norway and Sweden, could sometimes be shared by several hamlets, villages or single farms. Although unenclosed areas were normally considered to be common pastures for a village or a hamlet, individual households could nevertheless enjoy separate rights to some resources, like collecting firewood or felling timber in designated parts of woods or forests, or taking turf or heath in specified parts of common moors. Exploitation of separate meadows on commons or upland pastures might also be granted to individual households or farms.

The number of cattle which each household could graze was determined communally, in village assemblies where they existed, or by formal or informal agreements in other gatherings. As single farms were found in most parts of Norway as well as in parts of Sweden with an infield-outfield system, some peasants were not in any way involved with the communal use of infield resources. Outfield grazing and upland pastures might still be utilized communally with peasants from neighbouring farms.

In mountainous fiord- and inland regions, farms or hamlets, collectively or separately, could enjoy spring pasture in a designated area close to their farms, summer pasture on upland pastures in higher altitudes and then autumn grazing near their farm. Peasant households also found valuable pastures in the mountainous and uninhabited regions of Norway and Sweden, although these could be far from the permanent settlements. From the outset these pastures were considered to be seasonal commons in which every household could let their cattle graze, mow grass and sometimes take timber: their utilisation was regulated in the early medieval regional laws. These granted the king ownership of any permanent settlements made in these commons, thus indicating a kind of royal superior ownership of the wastes, and in the early modern period peasant households in some areas are known to have bought grazing and harvesting rights in the king's commons.

While individual farms in the southern Scandinavian open field region were allocated plots of village infield meadow to mow, this was not true for east midland Sweden. In this region hay was mowed communally, and then shared according to the size of the holding. In parts of northern Norway, communal use of infield resources went even further. Ploughing, sowing and harvesting might be done collectively and the crops shared according to the size of the holding. It has been suggested that this usage might be linked to the importance of fisheries in this part of Norway. As fisheries were vital to obtain a viable livelihood, available labour for farming was scarce and had to be intensely utilized during harvest seasons (Myhre and Øye, 2002: 230, 291–313, 361–95; Frandsen and Dombernowsky, 1988: 11–37, 61–78; Myrdal, 2000: 36–8, 223–24, 261–70, 300; Gadd, 2000: 137–41).

Village assemblies and other conflict handling institutions

In areas where settlements were concentrated in villages, strong institutions developed to cope with the complex system of land cultivation and need to fence arable land and meadows. The classical area for Scandinavian village assemblies was that of the open field area in parts of Jylland, the Danish isles and Scania, but also in a region stretching across mid-Sweden. Village assemblies in dispersed villages and hamlets are also known from other areas of Scandinavia where cultivation systems were quite different.

The regular meetings of the village assembly were composed of the head of every peasant household. It was therefore largely a meeting of male peasants, although widows might represent their households. Each village had its own laws which regulated agricultural proceedings, access to common resources, and aspects of village life. Many village laws were written down from the late Middle Ages onwards. In Denmark, from the mid-seventeenth century, such by-laws were usually approved by the manorial lord, a development that may be seen as a strengthening the village assembly's authority as well as giving the manorial lord an opportunity to look after his own interests. In Sweden, a formalized, centrally written set of village by-laws, which to a degree could be modified to meet local needs, was circulated in the mid-eighteenth century.

Decisions in the village assemblies were made by vote and were binding on its members. Cottars and other persons living in the village might attend meetings, but had no vote. An elected *oldermand* summoned the assembly, led the proceedings and had the responsibility to make sure that the meeting's decisions were implemented. Householders not complying with the village regulations or the assembly's decisions could be fined, often by being compelled to deliver a barrel of beer for common consumption. As early as the late Middle Ages, village assemblies exercised the power of arbitration and dealt with minor criminal cases and disputes between neighbours, thus fulfilling the important function of resolving conflicts in the local community. To cope with the complicated questions arising from cooperation between several villages in the so-called *vanglag,* members of several village assemblies assembled from time to time to decide the rotation of crops and grazing and to elect an official from one of the villages who was to ensure that their agreement was not violated (Frandsen and Dombernowsky, 1988: 27–9 and 34–7; Iversen, Myking and Thoma (eds), 2007: 206–07; Myrdal, 2000: 100–03 and 291; Gadd, 2000: 69–71, 128, 267–69).

Outside the zone of the classic nucleated village, Scandinavian agriculture displayed a variety of cultivation systems and settlement structures. Some of these systems also required a high degree of cooperation between individual peasant holdings as witnessed by the complicated divisions of arable fields and meadows in nucleated settlements along the coast and fiords of Norway where village assemblies were also found. On the many smaller farms and hamlets in Norway and Sweden, the need for cooperation and formal institutions was less urgent. Nevertheless, Norwegian law from the end of the thirteenth century presupposes an annual meeting of neighbours (*gardting*) to resolve questions regarding fencing.

Although not usually resulting in identifiable formal institutions, the utilization of wastes, woods, and upland pastures also called for peasant regulation of access. This included regulating the period of summer when different upland pastures and meadows could be utilized and setting a limit to the number of cattle a household, farm or hamlet might graze on to the common pasture (Myhre and Øye, 2002: 308–11, 367–68; Lunden, 2002: 177–85).

In the absence of, or in addition to, formal peasant institutions, several fora could be used for settling disputes in Scandinavia. In Sweden outside Scania and some of the western plains of Sweden, villages were often small. The parish community (*sockenstemna*) often became an arena for solving conflicts. The institution of the *sockenstemna* was also found in Denmark in Middle Ages, but seemingly vanished later. In the Middle Ages two other institutions were frequently used to solve conflicts. One was the ad hoc commission (*nemnd*), frequently administered by an elite of peasants, that dealt with conflicts over borders, grazing and forests, in addition to resolving a wide variety of other conflicts within peasant society. The other instrument was the local *ting* where an elite of peasants passed sentences and helped solve conflicts within the framework of national (Norway) or regional (Denmark, Sweden) law, at times assisted by the authority of royal officials.

With the development of stronger national states in the early modern period, ad hoc commissions were replaced by proceedings within the frame of the *ting*. The influence of the peasant elite was gradually reduced in the seventeenth century as professional judges were introduced, appointed in most of Scandinavia by the government, but in some manors in Denmark and Sweden by landlords. Besides, landlords more often informally functioned as settlers of disputes in these areas. Some peasant influence, especially when it came to conflicts relating to peasant use of resources, can still be found in the eighteenth century, even on Danish manors (Gadd, 2000: 208; Iversen, Myking and Thoma (eds), 2007: 187–203).

Peasant resistance

Throughout, Scandinavian peasants resented what they deemed to be excessive claims from landlords, the church and the crown to their agricultural surplus. This was especially true when demands for taxes, tithe and fees were held not to conform to old customs and practice. For the most part, peasants expressed their resentment in complaints and petitions to the king or by being reluctant to fulfil their obligations, but from time to time their resentment flared into open rebellion.

Open resistance could be directed against royal demands for taxes and the abuses of royal officials as well as against demands for rent and other dues from landlords. In their fight against the crown, peasants could sometimes ally themselves with their landlords who had an interest in minimising royal claims in order to maintain their tenants' capacity to pay rent. More often they could gain the support of aristocratic factions, in which case their movements were sometimes were led by members of the aristocracy, or they could align themselves with merchants.

Peasant revolts in Denmark, Sweden and Norway are sparsely recorded before the middle of the fourteenth century, with the exception of Denmark which, in the hundred years after the mid-thirteenth century, experienced a series of peasant risings against both royal taxation and seigneurial demands. Except for a rising against taxes in Sweden in 1371, conditions in Norway and Sweden were relatively peaceful until some decades into the next century.

By the mid-fifteenth century, all three countries had experienced serious peasant risings, in Denmark against royal taxes and demands from landlords, in Sweden in well-organized open rebellions, supported by members of the aristocracy and the clergy and led by members of the lower aristocracy. Peasant risings on a much smaller scale were at the same time recorded in eastern Norway in protest against taxes and abuses by foreign bailiffs. In contrast to Sweden, the Norwegian rebellions were usually led by members of the local peasant elites.

From the turn of the late Middle Ages to the early modern period, overt peasant rebellion in Scandinavia, with some exceptions in Denmark, was mostly directed against the crown and their representatives rather than against landlords. They were used by factions of the aristocracy and merchants in their conflicts with kings and by pretenders to the crown. This is evident in the Danish peasant risings, in Scania (1525) and in north and west Jutland (1534), and in the prolonged internal struggles in Sweden in the fifteenth and sixteenth centuries. The many local riots in Norway against taxes and bailiffs in the period 1490–1520 were purely peasant risings, although peasants from large parts of the country were involved in a revolt by a native Norwegian aristocrat against the king in 1501–02.

Serious peasant risings are not recorded in Denmark after 1534 and Sweden after 1543. Norwegian peasant unrest lasted longer, but was usually very localised and not greatly violent before the second half of the seventeenth century. This relatively tranquil period was interrupted by two major and more violent regional peasant risings, in western Norway in 1765 and again in south-eastern Norway in 1786–87. The first rising was triggered by what peasants saw as excessive taxation and was directed against royal officials. The second revolt was, in addition to complaints against royal officials, also directed against sawmill privileges given to the citizens of the coastal towns of southern Norway (Porsmose, 1988: 405; Myrdal, 2000: 177, 180–98; Katajala, 2004: 32–49, 90–117).

11.3 Government and power relations

King, lords and peasants: power relations and political regulation

The three Scandinavian kingdoms emerged as states between the ninth and eleventh centuries. From 1319 to the Reformation, sometimes all three, at other times two, of the kingdoms were united under one monarch. Even so, they still remained separate kingdoms with political institutions of their own. After the Reformation two states emerged: Sweden and Denmark-Norway. The internal political development of the two monarchies differed greatly. Though Copenhagen was the political and administrative centre of the Danish-Norwegian state, its decisions took into account the obvious differences in agrarian structure and natural conditions. As state intervention grew in the early modern period, differences at the national level between the three kingdoms increased.

Taxation and conscription

From the High Middle Ages we have evidence of a military system where large parts of the population had military obligations, being attached to ships, which they were to crew, bringing their weapons. When that system came into existence remains disputed. It seems to have been in decline over the course of the thirteenth century and was replaced by a system in which a minority performed fully armed military service while the military obligations of the greater part of the population were largely replaced by taxes. As noted before, this gradually developed into a clear division between nobles on the one hand and peasants on the other. In the late Middle Ages the military contribution of peasants to state warfare was generally modest. Kings looked to the peasantry for taxes, not soldiers.

The first regular taxes seem to have been introduced in Denmark in the twelfth century. As early as the thirteenth century, noble and ecclesiastical tenants in Denmark and Sweden were exempt from these, which were henceforth only levied on freeholders. *Bryder* (*villici*) were exempt first, *landboer* (*coloni*) somewhat later. The same did not happen in Norway, where the power of the aristocracy was weaker.

As the value of the 'ordinary' taxes declined, so-called 'extraordinary' taxes were introduced, levied by kings from time to time. These tax demands often triggered unrest or even revolt. During the fifteenth century, it was generally acknowledged that 'extraordinary' taxes could only be levied with the consent of either a regional *ting*, a national diet, or an aristocratic council, one of which emerged in all three countries in the fourteenth century. After the Reformation, the Danish council assumed this role for Norway as well. This facilitated the levying of quite frequent extraordinary taxes in Denmark in the late Middle Ages, making taxes one of the main sources of royal revenue paid in cash, much rent from the crown domains being paid in grain (Myrdal, 2000: 103–05, 150–51, 175–76; Porsmose, 1988: 309–11, 392–94; Hybel and Poulsen, 2007: 299–322; Lunden, 2002: 100–03).

In Denmark-Norway the military system remained largely unaltered until the early seventeenth century and taxation remained low in periods of peace. Taxation became less necessary as the crown lands grew in extent, and the influential aristocratic council of the realm favoured peace and low taxation. The first steps towards a military-fiscal state were made in Sweden during the period when the country was involved in protracted wars against Russia and Poland on its eastern fronts. A system of peasants performing military service instead of paying rent was introduced in the 1550s, and in times of warfare more general conscription was used. In addition, extraordinary taxes were more common in Sweden in the sixteenth century than in Denmark and Norway.

The military ambitions of Sweden's leaders rose in the seventeenth century. Before 1630 a great deal of effort was put into the creation of a conscripted army, which, for a period, was one of the most successful in Europe. At the height of Swedish power in the middle decades of the century, however, its armies increasingly came to rely on mercenaries while the homeland saw a dramatic rise in taxation rather than conscription. In the long run it proved impossible for Sweden to maintain sizeable professional armies in peacetime. In 1671 the diet froze taxes, and in 1680–82 the army was reformed to make it once again mainly based upon a sort of conscription by which a major part of the Swedish landholding peasantry was obliged to provide, pay, feed, and equip soldiers. Those who were charged with the provision of cavalrymen, including their horses, were exempt from taxes and rents liable to the crown. Those who were required to provide foot soldiers continued to pay their other dues, but were regarded as compensated by their release from personal military service. Both these systems – *indelningsverket* – and the frozen taxes survived virtually unaltered until the nineteenth century.

The growing strength of Sweden put pressure upon the Danish-Norwegian government. Between 1614 and 1660 a standing army emerged and taxation rose, but the council of the realm, as well as occasional diets, limited the scale of development. Following the military and political disaster of 1660, absolutism was introduced. The king used his new powers to increase the size of the army and level of taxation. The backbone of the army in the kingdom of Denmark was a professional cadre. Conscription weighed more heavily in Norway, and provided not only soldiers for the Norwegian army but also much of the rank and file of the Danish-Norwegian navy. For peasants in Denmark the military burden was primarily felt in the form of dramatically increasing taxation, but also a gradual rise in conscription.

In Denmark as well as in Sweden, conscription and taxation were originally levied more heavily on crown and freehold peasants than on noble peasants. Danish nobles in 1525 obtained full tax exemption for tenants in the home parish of their demesnes who performed regular labour service. Swedish nobles received a similar privilege, but only covering the home village of the demesne. In Norway noble privileges of this sort were insignificant.

From the late seventeenth century, tax and conscription burdens on private estates in Denmark and Sweden developed in opposite directions. In Denmark, where the crown alienated land to private landowners, the absolutist government removed the privileges of private estates with the exception of the demesnes. From 1682 tenants on private estates were subject to the same taxation and conscription levels as tenants on crown lands. In Sweden the resumption of 1680 reversed the extension of private estates which had taken place over the century but permitted landlords to keep their privileges over the land they retained. Noble estates were taxed much more lightly than crown or freehold land and bore only a small share of the burden of conscription. This may be seen as a part of a compromise in parliament enabling the resumption of noble estates in 1680 and, for the next century, the political balance of power in Sweden ensured that these privileges went unchallenged (Myrdal, 2000: 326–38, 346–54; Olsson, 2005: 23–100; Frandsen and Dombernowsky, 1988: 179–83, 188–94, 289–83; Lunden, 2002: 279–90, 300–34).

From the late seventeenth century the crown in Denmark and Norway owned only a minor part of the countryside and so, instead of receiving its surplus as rent, it received it as taxation. The burden of taxation (including conscription) placed on the peasant was at least as great as that of rents and labour service to the landlord. In Sweden the crown continued to control a major part of the countryside through its ownership of estates, and taxed freehold land, and the income from those sources largely sufficed for its purposes.

The regulation of farm structure and tenure

In as far as government regulations affected rural structure in Scandinavia before 1750, they were generally focused upon the fiscal-military interests of state power and tended to strengthen the medium-sized peasant farm, which was the basic tax paying unit. Under Queen Margrethe in the years around 1400, there were various initiatives aimed at securing freehold land as a tax base. Particularly in Sweden, the nobility had to restore the freehold land they had acquired, and in all three countries the further acquisition of freehold land by church and nobility was banned. As population grew after the end of the Middle Ages, both the Danish-Norwegian and Swedish crowns also wanted freehold land to remain divided into farms large enough to pay taxes and forbad further subdivision.

Before 1660 nobles could convert tenant holdings into demesne lands at will in one of two ways. Either a single peasant holding could change status to a small demesne or several peasant farms could be dissolved to create a larger demesne. In Denmark the change of tenant land into demesne land was prohibited from 1682. Such regulations were necessary as peasant farms under private landlords after 1664 provided the bulk of taxes as well as conscript soldiers in Denmark and to some degree in Norway (Frandsen and Dombernowsky, 1988: 179–94; Feldbæk, 1993: 67–8).

Things were very different in Sweden. After 1680 the crown largely lost interest in peasants belonging to private manors as they contributed so little to taxation and conscription, and the noble interest in parliament fought to keep it so. Interestingly, the Danish crown similarly gave the landlords of Schleswig a free hand over their manors, which can be explained partly by the fact that they made up only a minority of the Duchy.

The political and social status of peasants

The old Scandinavian word for peasant, *bonde*, originally signified a free man with full authority over his household. In the later Middle Ages in Denmark, this was both the technical word for a freeholder and a common word for a peasant, and it became the usual usage for the latter in the early modern period. The declining status of the word may be associated with the declining status of (a group of) peasants.

National and provincial assemblies that, among other things, elected kings or made laws, were common in the high Middle Ages. They were often dominated by aristocrats, but still seem to have comprised large groups of the population. Such provincial *ting* assemblies continued to exist throughout the Middle Ages, even though aristocratic *rigsråd* (councils of the realm) of bishops and nobles became the strongest national political institution in all three countries from *c.*1400. The *ting* assemblies were loosely organised and without any division into estates. They remained important until the early sixteenth century, but were weakest in Denmark and strongest in Sweden where freeholding peasants dominating the northern provinces were a particularly strong political force (Myrdal, 1999: 197–99; Lunden, 2002: 103–15).

After the civil war of 1533–36, peasants almost completely disappeared as a political force in Denmark for more than 200 years. Provincial and local *ting* were reduced to law courts and ceased to have any political function. Peasants could appeal to the crown, protest, or resist orders, but generally only at a local level. In Norway no official political role remained for peasants either, but here more organised peasant resistance to taxes still occurred. A rudimentary peasant organisation survived at a provincial level to which the government found it prudent to defer (Lunden, 2002: 339–58).

Swedish developments are more ambiguous. The Vasa kings set out to establish a strong monarchy, but integrated peasants into it. The independent peasants of the north had been their strong supporters in the fight for a national kingdom, but were also seen as a constant threat to royal power which needed to be brought under control. The provincial assemblies, which had so often been the centre of uprisings, disappeared, and a national estate assembly, the *Riksdag*, established, in which, unlike similar assemblies in Europe, freeholding peasants were included as one of four estates, first in 1527 and then continuously from 1544. With minor exceptions this remained the case throughout the period. It proved a satisfactory solution for both peasants, who had their interests represented directly, and the crown, which largely ended the rebellious tradition of the Swedish peasantry as well as gaining a counterweight to the aristocracy. Only freeholders and tenants of the crown – who were given a more active role than in Denmark – were represented in the diet and in the parish assemblies that held some authority. The village assemblies included all kinds of tenants (Gadd, 2000: 81–2, 195, 208).

While the political status of peasants differed from country to country as early as the early sixteenth century, there is little evidence of differences in social standing. For the period from the middle sixteenth century to the middle of the seventeenth, peasants prospered in most of Scandinavia, not the least in Denmark, and many had a lively economic and social interaction with townspeople and clergy.

An important change took place over the period 1650–1750. In Denmark the prosperity as well as the social standing of peasants deteriorated, but the same did not happen in Norway. By 1750 other social groups in Denmark generally held peasants in very low esteem and tried to distance themselves from them. At the same time their appreciation of Norwegian peasants was far higher. Danish peasants were conceived of as idle, stupid, and either stubborn or creeping, while Norwegian peasants were held to be proud, independent, and striving. Peasants on the crown estates and freehold lands of Schleswig also had a higher social standing than Danish peasants. In Sweden the freehold peasants of the forest districts were held in higher esteem than the peasants of the plains. This may partly have to do with the fact that many of the latter were under private manors.

Bibliography

Almås, R. (ed.) (2004) *Norwegian Agricultural History*, Trondheim.

Bjørkvik, H. and Holmsen, A. (1972) *Kven åtte jorda i den gamle leiglendingstida? Fordeling av jordeigedomen i Noreg i 1661*, Trondheim, previously printed in *Heimen* 9 (1952–54).

Dyrvik, S. (1977) 'Overgangen til sjølveige i Norge. Nokre nye data for 1700-talet', *Historisk tidsskrift*, 56.

Dørum, K. (1996) *Oppløsningen av skyldeiesystemet. En studie av eiendomsformer og eierinteresser knyttet til jord i Norge, ca. 1600–1800*, Oslo.

Feldbæk, O. (1993) *Danmarks Økonomiske Historie, 1500–1840*, Viborg.

Frandsen, K.-E. and Dombernowsky, L. (1988) 'Det danske landbrug før landboreformerne' in C. Bjørn (ed.), *Det danske landbrugs historie*, II, *1536–1810*, Copenhagen.

Gadd, C.-J. (2000) *Den agrara revolutionen, 1700–1870, Det svenska jordbrukets historia*, III, Stockholm.

Gissel, S. *et al.* (1981) *Desertion and land colonization in the Nordic countries, c.1300–1600. Comparative report from the Scandinavian research project on deserted farms and villages*, Stockholm.

Heckscher, E. F. (1936) *Sveriges ekonomiska historia fran Gustav Vasa*, vols 1–2.

Hybel, N. and Poulsen, B. (2007) *The Danish resources*, c.*1000–1550. Growth and recession*, Leiden.

Iversen, T. (2004) *Knechtschaft im mittelalterlichen Norwegen* (Abhandlungen zur rechtswissenschaftlichen Grundlagenforschung 94), Elsbach.

Iversen, T. and J. R. Myking (eds.) (2005) *Land, lords and peasants. Peasants' right to control land in the Middle Ages and the early modern period – Norway, Scandinavia and the Alpine region* (Trondheim Studies in History 52).

Iversen, T., J. R. Myking and G. Thoma (eds.) (2007) *Bauern zwischen Herrschaft und Genossenschaft. Peasant relations to Lords and Government. Scandinavia and the Alpine region, 1000–1750*, Trondheim.

Katajala, K. (2004) 'Against tithes and taxes, for king and province. Peasant unrest and medieval Scandinavian political culture', in K. Katajala (ed.), *Northern revolts. Medieval and early modern peasant unrest in the Nordic Countries* (Studia Fennica Historica 8), Helsinki.

Lunden, K. (2002) 'Frå svartedauden til 17. mai. 1350–1814'. *Norges landbrukshistorie*, II, Oslo.

Løgstrup, B. (1985) 'Den bortforpagtede statsmagt. Godsejeren som offentlig administrator i det 18. århundrede', *Bol og by. Landbohistorisk Tidsskrift*, 1, pp. 21–58.

Magnusson, L. (1985) *Reduktionen under 1600-talet, debatt och forskning.*

Myrdal, J. (2002) *Jordbruket under feodalismen, 1000–1700, Det svenska jordbrukets historia*, II, Stockholm.

Myhre, B. and Øye, I. (2002) 'Jorda blir levevei. 4000 f.Kr. – 1350 e.kr., *Norges landbrukshistorie*, I, Oslo.

Myking, J. R. (2005) *Herre over andre si jord? Norske leiglendingar i europeisk lys, 1500–1800* (Studia Humanitatis Bergensia 21), Kristiansand (Høyskoleforlaget).

Olsson, M. (2005) *Skatta dig lycklig. Jordränta och jordbruk i Skåne, 1660–1900*, Lund.

Porskrog Rasmussen, C. (2003) *Rentegods og hovedgårdsdrift. Godsstrukturer og godsøkonomi i hertugdømmet Slesvig, 1524–1770*, 2 vols, Aabenraa.

Porskrog Rasmussen, C. (2004) 'Modern manors? The character of some manors in Denmark and Schleswig-Holstein', in K. Sundberg, T. Germundsson and K. Hansen (eds.), *Modernisation and Tradition. European local and manorial societies, 1500–1900,* Lund, pp. 48–77.

Porsmose, E. (1988) 'Middelalder O. 1000–1536', in Claus Bjørn *et al* (eds), *Det danske landbrugs historie* I, *Oldtid og middelalder*, Odense.

Poulsen, B,. (2003) 'Middelalderens landbrug' in L. S. Madsen and O. Madsen (eds.) *Det sønderjyske landbrugs historie. Jernalder, vikingetid og middelalder.* Aabenraa, pp. 375–433 and 458–715

Weidling, T. (1998) *Adelsøkonomi i Norge fra reformasjonstiden og fram mot 1660* (Acta Humaniora 43), Oslo.

'Turn here!' a propagandist advertisment for *Svenska Mejeriernas Centralorganisation* (the Swedish central association of co-operative dairies) in the professional journal *Lantmannen*, 1935.
The farmer with the milk wagon can either choose to bring his milk to the consumer milk market in the city (Staden), where many small producers tended to force down prices through competition, or to deliver it to the cooperative dairy (Mejeri). The national cooperative associations wanted to restrict competition in order to maintain prices, and this required discipline from producers – i. e. that they delivered all their milk to the cooperatives.

12 Scandinavia, 1750–2000

Mats Olsson and Mats Morell

12.1 Ownership, power relations and the distribution of property

Types of landowners and changes in property distribution

Before the middle of the eighteenth century, either the crown or freeholding peasants owned most of the land in Norway, Schleswig and large parts of Sweden. In Denmark and in south and east-central Sweden, aristocratic and other private landowners predominated. In all three countries, the share of the land owned by freeholders gradually increased over the eighteenth and nineteenth centuries. This process started earliest in Norway. Here the land purchases that had started in the early eighteenth century accelerated, and by the end of that century a majority of peasants were freeholders. It has been debated whether this process was initially driven by peasants' calculations of the costs and benefits of land purchase, or the threat of other purchasers taking over their farms (Myking, 2005: 182–202). In the following century, the shift to owner-occupation was completed. Whilst one in five Norwegian peasants was a freeholder in the mid-seventeenth century, two hundred years later, four out of five were, and by 1929 88 per cent of holdings were owned by the occupier (Dyrvik 1979: 185–86; Historical Statistics for Norway).

In Sweden defensive tenant purchases of crown land occurred in 1701–18, when wealthy speculators took advantage of the earliest law permitting the sale of crown land. Subsequently purchases were banned, but when the law allowing sales was reintroduced in 1789, the possibility of outsiders securing a farmstead by outbidding the tenant was removed (Heckscher, 1944: 113–14). The price was fixed at six years' crown taxes. This offer became increasingly attractive because of inflation and rise of peasant production. By 1870 most crown land had been turned into freehold.

Manorial (tax exempt) land was, after the seventeenth century, never subject to state supervision in Sweden. Particularly around Lake Mälaren and in Scania, landlords maintained their position. By the 1870s the old nobility still held more than half of the tax exempt land in the country. A further quarter had been voluntarily sold to peasants, particularly in western Sweden, and another quarter to other private landowners (Carlsson, 1949: 168). Counting both tax exempt and taxed land, freeholding peasants held 70 per cent by 1870, the nobility held 15 per cent and other private owners (urban capital, tradesmen etc.) 7 per cent. The state and other public bodies owned around 8 per cent of the land (Table 12.1).

Denmark underwent a radical process of peasant emancipation in the second half of the eighteenth century which had a huge impact on land ownership. A series of statutes from 1769 to 1792 encouraged peasants' land purchase, and made it possible by means of new forms of credit. Landowners were encouraged to sell parts of their

Map 12.1 Scandinavia, 1750–2000

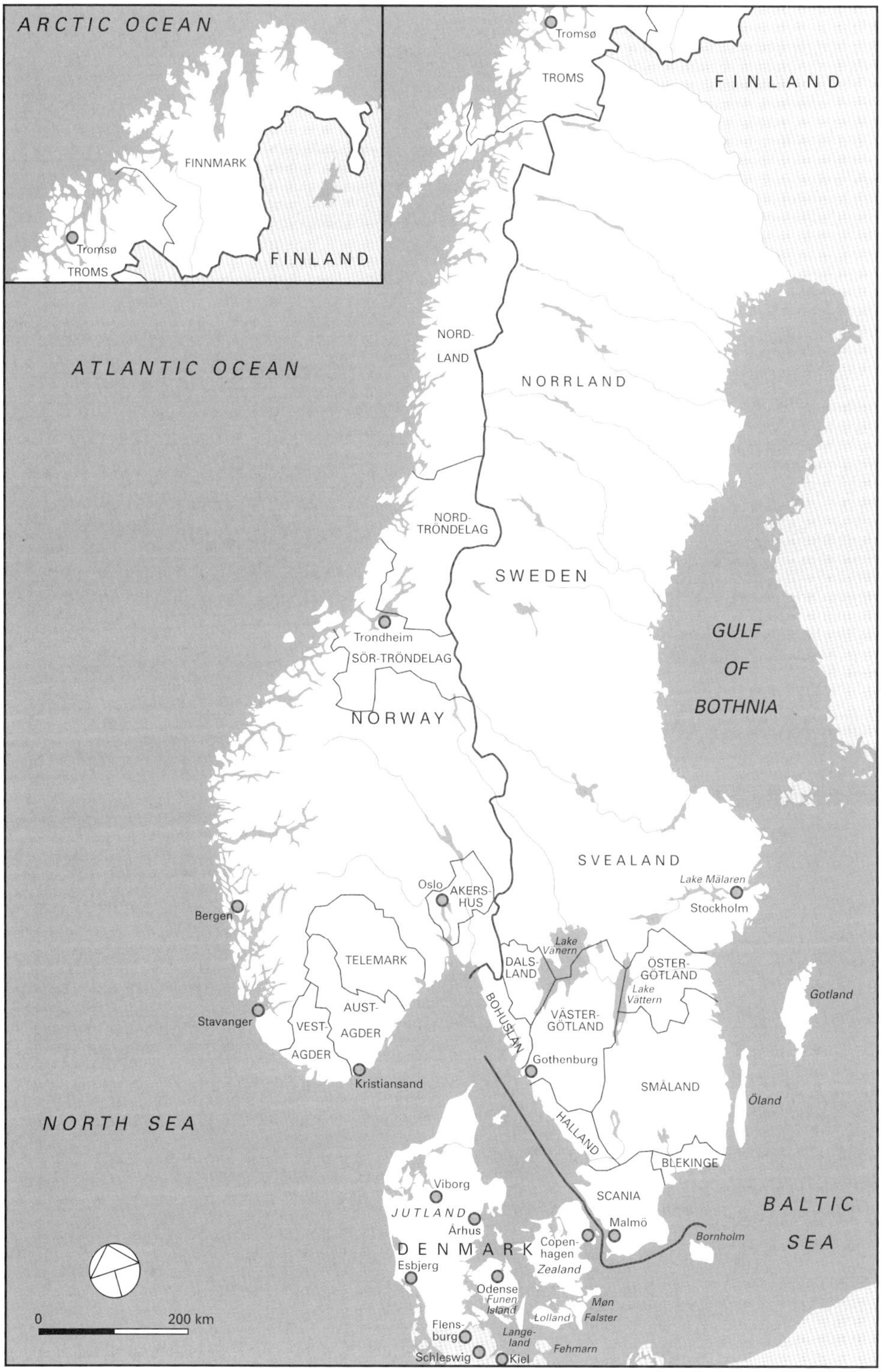

TABLE 12.1: Distribution of landed property in Sweden, 1772–1878, per cent

Year	Lay Landlords	Crown	Freeholders
1772	33	20	47
1825	33	13	54
1878	32	8	60

Sources : Heckscher 1935, Appendix IV, p. 14.

land to tenants in exchange for retaining their traditional exemption from crown taxes for their demesnes.

In contrast to their Swedish counterparts, Danish landlords were prevented from both raising rents and expanding demesne production by the eviction of tenants. Landlords were placed in a position in which they had no alternative but to sell, and, from the 1830s onwards, there were more freeholders than tenants in Denmark. In the 1850s, legislation gave the tenants of farms owned by the state or public bodies a right of purchase and new laws in the 1860s and 1870s made sales more attractive to private estate owners. The spread of the freeholding system was quicker in Jutland than on the islands, particularly Zealand, where the manorial structure remained intact longer. By 1885 only 5,436 tenanted farms – out of 75,000 peasant farms – remained. Owner occupancy was already dominant when a law of 1919 granted the remaining tenants the unconditional right to buy their land (Jensen, 1936: 76–81; Skrubbeltrang, 1978: 322–23, 416–18; Dombernovsky, 1988: 354–59; Dieckmann Rasmussen *et al.*, 1988: 219–22).

Owner occupiers continued to dominate land ownership in Scandinavia throughout the twentieth century, although subletting and partial leases became commoner after 1950.

Systems of tenancy

Despite the tendency towards owner-occupation, tenancy was important in Denmark and Sweden up to the early twentieth century. Except for those Swedish tenants holding from the nobility, most peasants in Scandinavia had achieved a basic security of tenancy by the end of the eighteenth century. This meant the establishment of tenant control over farm succession and a right of possession which continued as long as rents and taxes were paid, the land was managed to an adequate standard, and buildings were kept in good condition.

In Denmark secure tenancies were introduced in the reform era (from the 1760s to the early nineteenth century). Tenants in Jutland and Funned Island had accomplished secure tenancies by the late eighteenth century, and in the following decades the process spread to the eastern Islands (Skrubbeltrang, 1978: 329–32, 339–40).

Nineteenth-century Danish legislation aimed largely at protecting peasant farms. There were ways in which landlords could extend their demesnes – they were allowed to close down one tenant farm in exchange for setting up two crofts with arable land (1791), or in exchange for abolishing all boon work on the estate (1813) – but these loopholes played a marginal role (Bjørn, 1988: 26). The position of tenants was further improved by a law of 1861. This ensured the return to the tenant of any investment he had made in land and buildings at the end of his tenancy and protected new tenants from having to refurbish derelict buildings (Dieckmann Rasmussen *et al.*, 1988: 220, 222).

Tenants in Norway had achieved the most secure tenancies in Scandinavia by the end of the seventeenth century. Tenancy was both lifelong and hereditary. The only circumstances in which a landowner could legally evict his tenant, except in instances of the obvious mismanagement of the farm or failure to pay rents, was if the owner could prove that he was without house and farm, the so-called *buslirett*. This was seldom a real threat, unless another smallholder outbid the tenant in cases of land sales (Myking, 2005).

In Sweden – but not in Denmark or Norway – there was a sharp distinction between crown tenants and tenants of the nobility. Crown tenancies in Sweden were in practice secure and inheritable from the eighteenth century onwards. This was the case from 1684 for tenants charged with the supply of a furnished cavalry soldier, and from 1789 for other crown tenants. On manorial land, contracts could be from six years to the tenant's life, but the only legislation on security of tenure was the legal day of notice (Jonsson, 1983; Gadd, 2000: 105–06). Evictions would normally take place on 15 March in the year after the notice of termination had been given. In eighteenth-century Sweden, evictions were rare, but, in Scania in particular, the nineteenth century was characterised by the expansion of demesnes at the expense of tenants and here every second peasant holding from the nobility was evicted over the course of the nineteenth century. The counties surrounding Stockholm were also strongly affected (Olsson, 2005: 147–49).

A croft (Norwegian *husmansplass,* Danish *hus,* Swedish *torp*) was a sublet piece of land subordinated to a peasant holding or a larger estate. Crofters normally performed labour duties to the mother farm. While the corvée labour of tenants was generally abolished in the early nineteenth century in Denmark, a law of 1807 stipulated labour duties for crofters (*husmen*). By 1848 these duties were abolished and it was stipulated that crofters should pay their rent in either money or kind. However this rule could be circumvented by making a crofter two contracts which were not formally connected (Banggaard, 2006). Crofters had to wait until 1902 to attain rights similar to those achieved by other tenants in 1861. The number of *hus* increased from the reform period onwards, but crofters, as well as other tenants, tended to buy their plots free (Dieckmann Rasmussen *et al.,* 1988).

Norwegian crofters or cottars normally had lifelong leases, but shorter leases and even hereditary tenancies developed in some regions. A law of 1851 made written formal contracts a requirement. In eastern Norway and Trøndelag, most cottars were obliged to do labour service on the mother farm, while in western Norway they mostly paid their

TABLE 12.2: Percentage of farms with at least some land leased and percentage of total area leased in Sweden, Denmark and Norway, certain years, 1956–1999

	Farms (%)			Area (%)		
	Sweden	Denmark	Norway	Sweden	Denmark	Norway
Year						
1956	23.6			26.8		
1966	34.5	8.7		30.6	3.2	
1979	49.9		31.0	41.4		20.3
1981	50.9			41.8		
1982		30.4			17.2	
1989		35.2	39.0		19.3	23.4
1991	50.9			43.9		
1999	52.0	48.0	54.8	46.7	25.2	31.2

Sources : Sweden, *Jordbruksstatistisk årsbok 1970, 1980, 1992, 2002* ; Denmark, Pedersen 1988: 17, Statistics Denmark; Norway, Statistics Norway. Total leased area in Sweden 1991 and 1999 is estimated.

rent in money. The number of crofts in Norway increased up to the mid-nineteenth century but decreased rapidly from then on. They were either incorporated into the mother farm or they were sold to freehold (Lunden, 2002: 376–80; Gjerdåker, 2002; Hasund, 1936: 337).

Crofters in Sweden held by unsecure tenancies from which they could be evicted after a period of notice. The labour duties of crofts belonging to large estates were heavy (Jonsson, 1983). As in Norway, the number of crofts increased until the mid-nineteenth century, but later decreased. Some crofters were evicted following enclosures, and in the late nineteenth century many left for other occupations, while other crofts were bought free. After 1907, a tenancy law regulated the terms of contracts and the laws governing for crofts were made the same as those governing any leasehold land. Henceforth, written contracts were required. By 1943 a new leasing law prohibited labour rents and the croft as an institution disappeared (Morell, 2001).

The rise of owner occupancy mirrored the decline of tenancy in Sweden until the mid-twentieth century when the trend was reversed. Leasing has, throughout the twentieth century, been more prevalent in Sweden than either Denmark or Norway. In 1927 20 per cent of *entire* farm units were leased in Sweden (crofts included). The proportion continued to fall and has remained at about 14 per cent since the mid-1950s. The total leased acreage started to rise in the 1950s, and while leasing had previously normally involved entire farms, it is partial leasing that has emerged strongly, particularly in plain land districts in southern and central Sweden but in the other countries too (Table 12.2).

Partial leases have become common because the market in land is sticky and has not responded to signals for structural change from technical development, market factors, government policy and lately European Union subsidies. Small landowners tend to lease rather than to sell their land. Thus recent structural developments have created large numbers of nominal (mostly small) landowners, leasing out all their land except for the farm house. While the number of commercially viable farms requiring the full-time labour of their owners has dwindled, the number of *nominal* agricultural properties has remained more stable.

Whilst the market in leaseholds has been used to form very large farming enterprises out of scattered units of ownership, some large estate owners, particularly in Scania have, since the 1970s, enlarged their farming enterprises by incorporating leased out holdings into their own 'demesnes' (to use an anachronistic term). In the plain land districts of Sweden, it has also become common since the 1990s for several landowning farmers to form a production cooperative or a limited company, pool the land they own, lease more land and invest in very large scale machinery. With the emergence of partial leasing and the trend towards companies managing several holdings, the dominance of the family farm – the backbone of the twentieth-century farm structure – has been challenged.

Land rents and taxes

Major parts of the land rent and tax systems in the Scandinavian countries were unchanged throughout the eighteenth and nineteenth centuries. In Sweden a tax system – the military and civil allotment system (*Indelningsverket*) – was implemented in 1683 and lasted for the following 217 years. By this system, civil servants and military officers were granted the taxes from specified peasant farms. The allocations were to appointments, not persons, the system aimed at stability and the crown was disinterested in authorising local tax collectors to increase taxes. Therefore, throughout this time, no possessor of public rent could impose new burdens on any peasant, and, after the hardships of the Great Nordic War (1700–1720), no monarch either. After the death of Charles XII in 1718, all new tax proposals had to be approved by the diet, in which the peasantry was represented. The principal programme of the peasantry in the Swedish parliament was to protect the existing tax system and this helped to ossify the late seventeenth-century arrangements (Thomson, 1923: 47–48).

The rents of Swedish crown tenants were identical with their taxes. Thus, they too were fixed after 1683 and diminished in real value over time through inflation (Herlitz, 1974; Olsson, 2005). Tenants of the nobility, on the other hand, paid insignificant taxes to the crown, but variable rents to their landlords. The most striking development took

FIGURE 12.3: Land rent burden, including taxes, for peasants in Scania, Sweden 1660– 1900, total rent value as percentage of farm gross production output

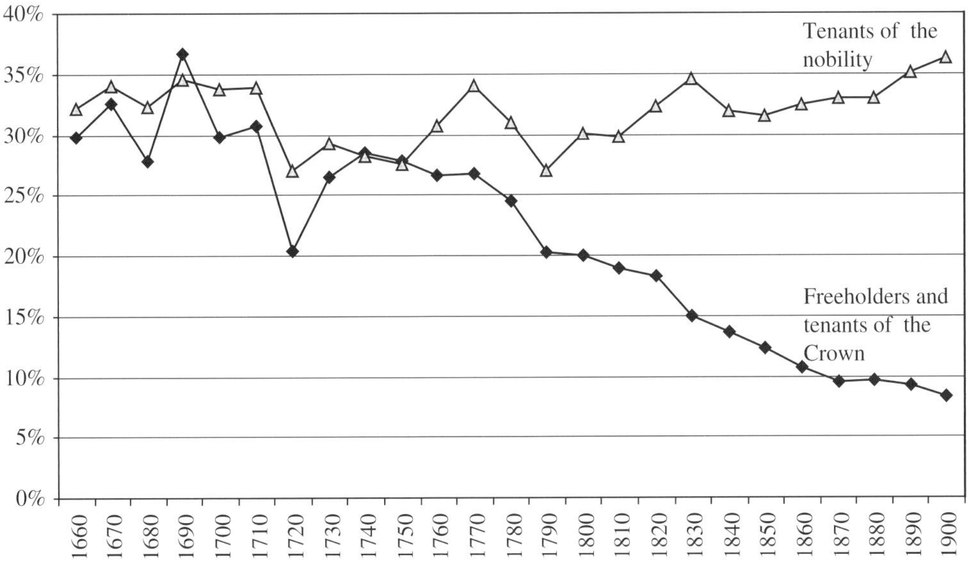

Source : Olsson 2005:173. By the late nineteenth century the corvée obligations of tenants on noble land were normally transformed into money rents.

place in the former Danish provinces of Scania and Halland, where corvée obligations were not checked by custom. In the early nineteenth century a typical Scanian corvée tenant worked 80–120 days a year for his landlord. By 1850 he performed more than 300 days of service a year (Olsson, 2002: 262).

The way in which the burden of rent on the two groups of peasants grew apart is illustrated in Figure 12.1. After 1740 the freeholder or tenant of the crown enjoyed a progressive decline in the share of farm production paid in rent, from 25–30 per cent to less than 10 per cent. This fall was due to the regime of fixed taxes, inflation and the rise in farm output in the course of the agrarian revolution. The corvée tenant's rise in production was shared with his landlord in the form of additional boon works on the demesne and, eventually, as cash rents.

The development of the burden of taxes placed on the peasantry in the other Scandinavian countries was complex and varied for different groups, but for many peasants, the overall development in real terms was similar to that for Scanian freeholders and crown tenants. In Norway the taxes on tenants were fixed from 1672 to 1802, although other taxes could fluctuate, and the view that Norway was a 'low tax country' in the late eighteenth century has recently been questioned (Lunden, 2002: 300–04). The estimates that have been done for Denmark indicate that the tax burden (in real terms) for a normal peasant farm fell continuously after 1720. After 1760 some new taxes were imposed, but peasants benefitted from tenant reforms and better market conditions (Rafner, 1986: 92; Dombernovsky, 1988: 280–82). In the Danish case, the effects of an increased burden of corvée up to the 1770s levied on some tenants has not yet been integrated into the calculations.

By end of the nineteenth century taxes levied on specifically peasant land had been renounced in all the Scandinavian countries, as general property taxes, income taxes and indirect taxes were introduced (Morell, 2001: 113–14; Dieckmann Rasmussen *et al.*, 1988: 236).

Land market and the value of land

In both Norway and Sweden the wider kinship retained an interest in family land. If an owner sold his land to a non-relative, a proven relative could purchase the land from the non-family purchaser at the price he or she paid for it. In Sweden the right of *bördsrätt* was weakened from the late eighteenth century, but remained until 1863 (Herlitz 1974: 284–87; Rosén 1994: 38–9). In Norway the *odelsrett* was guaranteed in the Eidswoll constitution of 1814 and still remains in force (Gjerdåker 2002: 96–97). It prioritized men over women and older siblings over younger ones, but in 1974 women were given the right to *odel* on the same conditions as men (Almås 2002: 292–94). These customs should have impeded the land market but a recent Norwegian study shows that even in the early nineteenth century, more farms were sold outside the kin than were transferred within families (Gjerdåker 2002: 283).

The entitlement of kin was combined with a right among male siblings to inherit equal shares of the parental property. Daughters inherited only half shares until 1845 in Sweden and 1854 in Norway. There was, however, a right for a single sibling to buy out the shares of the others and keep the holding undivided (*åsetesrett* in Norway). Prices were set at customary low levels in these cases, but rising market prices in non-kin transactions tended to force kinship prices upwards over time. Up to the 1890s a male heir in Sweden enjoyed a preferential right to purchase his sisters' portion. The outcome of gender-equalized inheritance was largely to increase the burden of debt carried by a new farmer (Sjöberg, 2006). In Norway however, a law of 1863 formalized the payment for siblings' shares – *åsetestakst* – at customary levels (Gjerdåker, 2002: 99).

The selling of crown land and the widespread practice after the late eighteenth century of Norwegian and Danish tenants buying their farms did little to open up the land market (Rydeberg, 1985; Myking, 2005). The selling of noble land to non-nobles in Sweden had a different outcome. Most of these holdings were *not* bought by their tenants but by other freeholders. Many holdings were frequently re-sold (Gadd, 2000: 202–04).

It has been shown there was an increase in the non-kin land trade in the second part of the eighteenth century and a more obvious upturn in the early nineteenth century. Volumes of land traded continued to rise throughout the nineteenth century (Martinius, 1970). Much of the demand for land in the early nineteenth century came from well-to-do freeholders who tried to acquire land with which to endow more than one of their heirs so the social and economic standing of younger children could be preserved (Holmlund, 2007). In the late nineteenth century on the other hand, demand for smallholdings grew immensely. The loans for smallholdings offered by government from the turn of the century encouraged the demand for small plots and created opportunities for large estates to sell marginal land (Morell, 2001).

The sale price of tenant farms stagnated in comparison to freeholders' land in Denmark from the late eighteenth century. Similarly in Sweden, from the mid-eighteenth century, the price of freeholders' land rose due to falling tax pressure, while the price of tax exempt tenant holdings was stagnating (Herlitz, 1974: 311, 333–34).

In the nineteenth century at least, there was strong correlation between land price and grain price movements, although the sale price of larger farms was more sensitive to trade cycle fluctuations than those of smallholdings (Martinius, 1970:107–115). In the post-war era, land prices have increased. In both Denmark and Sweden, it reached very high levels following entry into the EC/EU (in 1973 and 1995 respectively) as community membership was seen to promise a new buoyancy in agriculture.

The cultural value of land and the leisure sector

The pan-European enthusiasm for the country estate in the second half of the eighteenth century was reflected in Scandinavia as well. Aristocratic landowners, Norwegian and Swedish sawmill and ironworks owners of bourgeois origin acquired mansions and invested in farming. Hunting was reserved for the landowning class in manorial areas and was a way of distinguishing status, whereas peasants' hunting in freeholding districts formed part of their survival strategies. The gulf between hunting as a sport and hunting as an economically important activity remains in northern Scandinavia.

In Norway the first – mostly English – mountain walkers appeared in the early nineteenth century. Tourism and recreational activities related to landscape and rural areas had expanded considerably by the end of the century and is reflected in the foundation of national tourist associations (Norway in 1868, Sweden 1885, Denmark 1899). Although the Swedish association in the inter-war years focused on 'ordinary' rural landscapes rather than the mountain ranges, access to rural recreational sites was for a long time restricted to the wealthier classes for both ideological and practical reasons. Field sports continued to be practiced mainly by large estate owners and their guests.

The rising standard of living in the post-war era made rural recreation accessible to the broader masses and a recreational industry emerged. Claims on land for leisure services – golf courses, ski slopes, hunting, fishing, walking, horse riding and guest house services – grew.

The growing consumption of leisure service was accompanied by a growing interest in rural housing. In the environs of towns, people leaving farming and switching to urban employment tended to continue to live in their farm houses. It was equally common for urban people to move out to the nearby countryside, buy a farm and nominally (for tax reasons) establish themselves as landowners/ farmers, only to lease out the bulk of the arable, whilst keeping the house, some stabling and pasture for grazing leisure horses. This trend was encouraged by images of traditional rural life. Recent studies have shown that this does not necessarily imply gentrification. Both manual workers and self-employed craftsmen and tradesmen are well represented amongst new migrants to the countryside, along with people running stables as a business to meet the demand for recreational riding (Hedenborg and Morell, 2008).

12.2 The occupiers of the land

Manorial farming

In late eighteenth-century Scandinavia, manorial demesne production was still found in Denmark and parts of Sweden and Schleswig. The typical demesne in the old Swedish realm was small, only 20–50 ha of arable land, and less than 10 peasants or crofters with work obligations. In Scania and in Denmark the demesnes were generally larger; often between 50 and 200 ha of arable, employing 20–100 corvée tenants each (Olsson, 2002). South-eastern Schleswig was characterized by even larger demesnes and heavier labour service dues.

However, developments in the country-specific legal conditions for manorialism changed the scene in the nineteenth century. In both Denmark and Schleswig, peasant subjugation under the nobility was regarded as a national problem and an obstacle to progress. In 1788 *stavnsbandet,* introduced in Denmark in 1733 in order to guarantee the supply of labour for the estates and soldiers for the army, which had prohibited young men from leaving their home estate, was abolished. In the wake of peasant emancipation, legislation against the enlargement of demesnes through the eviction of tenants was implemented, in Denmark in 1789 and in Schleswig in 1804 (Hvidtfeldt, 1963: 430). Furthermore, when landlords were encouraged to sell land to their tenants, the demesnes, fully or partly, were usually parcelled out and sold. Those remaining were often held to be pioneers of modern agricultural practice. By the middle of the nineteenth century, many manors had separated their tenant estates from their demesnes, whereby the former were transferred to freeholders or leaseholders, and the latter transformed into modern large-scale farming units using wage labour (Bjørn, 1988: 95–98).

In Sweden freeholders and crown tenants already held a strong position by the end of the eighteenth century. They were represented in parliament but they did not use their position there to promote the cause of the tenants of the nobility. Accordingly, no obstacles were placed in the way of the enlargement of noble demesnes in the nineteenth century. In Scania demesnes were continuously expanded and by 1865 they often covered more than half of the acreage of manorial parishes (Olsson, 2002). Similar trends may be seen in the other manorial regions of Sweden. This late wave of manorialism, in parallel with the rise of the freeholder, lasted into the twentieth century and left its mark on both the landscape and the economy of the manorial districts.

In these areas, much of the demesne work was still, in the mid-nineteenth century, performed by tenants, but the tendency was to discharge them, incorporate their holdings into the demesnes and run the demesnes with the labour of crofters. In Denmark too, crofters continued to pay labour rent (Bjørn, 1988; Dieckman Rasmussen *et al.*, 1988). The next phase was to replace crofters with wage labourers, in Sweden by labourers and their families, *statare*, who were contracted for a year at a time and paid largely in kind (including their housing). This system reached its peak in the early twentieth century and survived until 1944 (Morell, 2001; Lundh and Olsson, 2006; Olsson, 2006). Similar arrangements are found in Denmark, but were not as general or enduring (Banggard, 2006).

The persistence of large estates in certain areas of Sweden was reinforced by the use of entails (*fideikommiss*). The entail had developed to counteract the fissile tendencies of the inheritance system and to keep large estates unified under a single family head. By the early nineteenth century the right to entail estates had been abolished in most countries, including Sweden. But whereas laws requiring the dissolution of existing entails had been introduced quite early in most countries, such a law was only passed in 1963 in Sweden. At that time some 200 entailed estates still existed, a few of which still remain exempt from the legislation, amongst them some of the largest agricultural enterprises in Scandinavia. In Denmark, baronies and entailments disposed of considerable acreages in the nineteenth century, but in 1919 they were dissolved and transformed into regular private property (Pedersen, 1988: 82). In Norway entailed agricultural estates were of little importance, but some survived into the early twentieth century (Hasund, 1926).

Farm structures – size of farms

State prohibitions against farm division were first liberalized in Sweden in 1747 and Norway in 1769, and then successively in the nineteenth century. Furthermore in Sweden, the selling to freehold of crown tenancies in the eighteenth and nineteenth centuries, particularly after 1789, increased the number of farms that could be subdivided. Similarly in Denmark the rapid transformation from tenancy to owner occupancy led to smaller units, for whilst landowners had resisted the division of their leased holdings, there were no restraints placed on owner-occupied farms. The number of small units also increased when demesnes were parcelled out. As a result of all these factors, the number of farms increased. It doubled between 1750 and 1855 in Norway; it grew by 30 per cent between 1805 and 1860 in Denmark and by 17 per cent between 1750 and 1870 in south and mid-Sweden (Dyrvik, 1979: 185–86; Jensen, 1945: 160–61; Bjørn, 1988: 28; Dieckmann Rasmussen *et al.*, 1988: 223; Morell, 2001: 122; Wohlin, 1909).

Sweden experienced a mixed pattern of consolidation and partition. In many manorial parishes in the south there were strong tendencies towards consolidation into large demesne farms, and whole peasant villages were destroyed. In adjacent freehold parishes the tendency towards partition prevailed, but particularly in mid-Sweden it was common for expanding peasant farmers to combine several holdings into larger units on either a temporary or permanent basis.

Except for the remaining manorial areas, medium-sized family farms – using family labour augmented by farm hands – and smallholdings dominated in Scandinavia by the turn of the nineteenth century. In Denmark and Sweden, most *land* belonged to medium-sized farms – and has continued to do so – while smallholdings made up most of the *farms*. Norway was – and remains – the paramount smallholding country. While in Denmark and south and mid-Sweden, around 70 per cent of the farm land was held by farms of 50 ha or more in the year 2000, the corresponding figure for Norway was still only 11 per cent.

The growth of independent smallholdings (rather than crofts) had several causes. Subdivision of farms was one. But the background to the growing demand for small farms in the late nineteenth century was the strong growth in the number of landless workers in rural areas, itself an aspect of a substantial increase in population (particularly in Norway) in the earlier part of the century (Historical statistics for Sweden, I; Johansen, 1985: 107–08; Gjerdåker, 2002: 169–72). Furthermore, although many rural municipalities industrialised, industrial employment was often seasonal and insecure and supplemented by small farm plots. In coastal Norway dual economies of fishing and farming were important, while combinations of forestry work and smallholding were important in Austlandet in Norway as well as in northern Sweden. The demand for such small plots remained until 'full employment' policies and state welfare insurance became established after the Second World War. Market developments, which favoured animal husbandry and dairy farming with marginal economies of scale, emerging cooperatives and government support, also stimulated growth in the number of smallholdings.

In Norway a trend towards the formation of new small farms is discernible after 1850 (Gjerdåker, 2001: 116–17, 170–71). The number of smallholdings grew until the Second World War (Table 12.4). A reduction in farm numbers and a moderate increase in farm size started in the 1950s, but remained almost insignificant before the 1990s. The average farm size remained around 4 ha up to 1959. In 1989 it was still only 6.6 ha but by the turn of the century it had reached about 15 ha. The largest farms (averaging 10 ha in 1949 and 30–35 ha by end of the century) were found in the south-eastern counties, Oslo-Akershus and Østfold. Historically the smallest farms existed in Finnmark, Troms and Nordland in the far north and in Vest and Austagder in the far south. The southern districts, together with most of western Norway, still have comparatively small farms (Historical statistics for Norway; Almås 2001: 210).

In Denmark in 1905 there were 76,610 farms (*gårdar*) and in addition about 183,000 crofts (*hus*) with at least some taxed land. However the *hus* accounted for no more than about 10 per cent of the agricultural area. All these *hus* and the 57,425 peasant farms taxed up to 4 tdr. hartkorn[1] could be considered smallholdings, whereas the large estates which held more than 20 tdr hartkorn were about 900 in number (Dieckmann Rasmussen *et al.*, 1988: 223–25; Jensen, 1988: 272). Restructuring started in the 1950s and gained pace in the 1960s (Table 12.5). The average farm size was about 15 ha up

[1] tdr. Hartkorn was an assessed land value approximating to the value of ½ ha of top quality arable land.

Table 12.4: Number of farms by size of agricultural area (ha), Norway, 1907–99

Year	0.5–5.0 ha	5.1–10.0 ha	10.1–20.0 ha	20.1–50.0 ha	> 50 ha	All farms
1907	124,563	21,494	11,129	4761	371	162,654
1929	150,652	36,968	15,762	4844	324	208,842
1939	144,759	45,013	18,782	5432	392	214,378
1949	150,130	42,526	15,597	4809	379	213,441
1959	135,830	42,126	15,074	4870	415	198,315
1969	88,481	42,240	17,938	5822	496	154,977
1979	62,017	32,716	21,632	8228	709	125,302
1989	37,031	24,969	25,330	11,194	858	99,382
1999	14,517	16,720	22,286	15,640	1577	70,740

Sources: Hasund, 1926: 336; Historical statistics for Norway, Table 14.1; Statistics Norway, Farming

Table 12.5: Number of farms by size of agricultural area (ha), Denmark, 1919–99

Year	0.55–5.0 ha	5.1–10.0 ha	10.1–30.0 ha	30.1–60.0 ha	60.1–120.0 ha	> 120 ha	All farms
1919	67,256	41,889	68,858	22,552	4039	1335	205,929
1933	55,623	50,054	72,352	21,406	3769	1027	204,231
1951	42,922	55,165	82,019	21,401	3390	938	205,835
1959	37,584	54,405	81,116	19,649	2891	861	196,506
1969	16,309	31,396	71,390	21,856	4199	1061	146,211
1980	15,693	20,503	51,688	19,506	9616	2149	119,155
1982[a]	2952	18,501	47,605	23,697	6989	1359	101,103
1989[a]	1364	12,517	33,800	21,661	9101	1956	80,399
2000[a]	946	8457	17,719	12,295	10,158	4166	53,741

Note: [a] Smallest units are 0.1–5 ha, second largest is 60–125 ha, largest >125 ha.
Sources: Johansen, 1985: 129–130; Statistics Denmark, Agriculture and fisheries.

TABLE 12.6: Number of farms by size of agricultural area (ha), South and central Sweden, 1919–2000.

Year	2.1–10.0 ha	10.1–20.0 ha	20.1–10.0 ha	30.1–50.0 ha	50.1–100.0 ha	>100 ha	All farms
1919	160,639	54,181	17,320	11,270	5265	2543	251,218
1932	155,814	52,825	16,515	10,643	5027	2371	243,195
1951	125,662	51,673	17,058	11,040	5356	2306	213,095
1961	91,544	45,141	17,231	11,719	5346	2169	173,150
1969	54,859	32,288	16,284	13,538	7198	2516	126,683
1981	32,297	22,210	13,345	14,003	9552	3187	94,594
1989	25,981	17,343	10,721	12,687	10,335	3753	80,820
2000	20,632	12,926	7491	9295	9730	5150	65,224

Sources: Historical Statistics of Sweden II: *Jordbruksstatistisk årsbok 1970*; Statistics Sweden, Agriculture, forestry and fisheries.

to 1960, but grew successively to 49 ha by the turn of the century. There has been little regional variation in farm sizes in Denmark. In 2000 the largest farms, averaging over 60 ha, were found in Storstrøm county and South Jutland and the smallest in the counties of Copenhagen and Viborg in north-west Jutland (around 40 ha).

In Sweden excluding the north (Norrland), 340,000 farm units (including 60,000 crofts) existed around 1900. Apart from the crofts, 65,000 farms held less than 2 ha of arable, 181,000 held 2–20 ha, and 3,175 held more than 100 ha. There was little change in the farm structure between 1900 and 1919, but the structural change began in Sweden earlier than in the other countries. In south and west it started in the inter-war period, but generally it gained pace in the early post-war period (Table 12.6). The average farm size remained at 13–14 ha around 1950, but rose to 21 in 1969 and 37 ha in 2000. Farms were, and remain comparatively large in the plains around Lake Mälaren (averaging 17 ha in 1919 and 55 in 2000), the plains of Östergötland and Scania. They have remained smaller in marginal woodland areas like in Småland and southern Västergötland (6 ha in 1919, 19 ha in 2000).

Agricultural organisations: top down societies and farmers' unions

In all three countries the governing elite formed semi-official organisations to advance agricultural progress and increase production. In Denmark the Royal Danish Agricultural Society (*Kongelige Danske landhusholdningsselskabet*) was founded in 1769. In Norway a National Patriotic Society (*Selskabet for Norges Vel*) was founded in 1809 quickly followed by the Royal Academy of Agriculture (*Kungliga Lantbruksakademien*) in Sweden (1811). All three societies worked through publications, prizes and premiums, helped to introduce new tools and machinery and promoted agricultural education. For periods they functioned as the branch of government responsible for agriculture.

Regional agricultural societies were formed in close connection to the national societies. The Danish and Swedish societies took initiatives to develop regular agricultural meetings – modelled on the German *Wandersversammlungen* – combining exhibitions, trade fairs and colloquiums for discussion of agronomic matters. In Sweden they initiated savings banks, mortgage societies, insurance cooperatives and cooperative dairies. From around 1840 they founded agricultural schools (under the supervision of the Academy) and from the 1860s they collected agricultural statistics.

While the Swedish regional societies remained elitist and became the regional administrative tools of the government Board of Agriculture (founded in 1890), the Danish societies had developed by the mid-nineteenth century into independent professional interest groups of well-to-do farmers. They were then transformed into local farmers' unions (*landboforeninger*) with a broad membership. By 1860 almost 40 existed and by 1914 there were 120 unions, organizing 99,000 farmers. Gradually as more local societies were founded, they started to cooperate regionally and in 1893 a loose national federation of local societies was founded. In time the central board achieved considerable lobbying power and emerged as a centralised farmers' union (Bjørn, 1988: 351, 354–59).

By the end of the nineteenth century, smallholders – in Denmark *husmen* – started to organize themselves into separate local associations and by 1910 they had a functional national leadership. From the outset they sought their emancipation from their landlords. In Norway too, strong but opposed farmers' unions developed. In 1896 the Norwegian Farmers Union (*Landmansforbundet,* later *Norges Bondelag*) was founded. It agitated for grain tariffs to protect arable farmers. However, smallholders did not benefit from tariffs as they normally had to buy grain. Consequently in 1913 they formed their own association, the Norwegian Farmers' and Smallholders' union (*Norsk Småbrukerforbund* later *Norsk Bonde- og Småbrukarlag)* and adopted a free trade policy in line with that of the liberal government of the day (Just, 2009).

In Sweden, farmers were less well organised. Members of the local elites formed local farmers clubs which engaged in informal discussions and supported the spread of cooperative ideals. In 1917 the General Swedish Agricultural Society, *Sveriges Allmänna Lantbrukssällskap* (*SAL*) was formed as a pressure group of estate owners and large farmers. It lacked local roots, had few members and failed to play any significant role before the end of the 1920s. In sharp contrast to it, a number of smallholders' associations were founded in various regions in the early twentieth century. In south Sweden they mostly aimed at providing consultative and commercial services for smaller farmers. In the north, the associations organized not only smallholders but also forestry workers and farmhands and took on more of a trades union role. As they lacked shared concerns, the regional associations failed to unite under a single programme. Their failure to form a national association of smallholders paved the way for the creation in 1929, following the desperate market conditions of the late

1920s, of the Farmers' Union, *Riksförbundet Landsbygdens Folk* (*RLF*) which aimed to organize *all* farmers. Tensions remained, but after it had started to collaborate with the cooperative movement, the *RLF* emerged as a powerful mass organisation of farmers (Morell, 2009; Just, 2009).

The founding of cooperative organisations

The breakthrough of the cooperative movement in the final decades of the nineteenth century was connected to the market-led development which made animal husbandry and milk processing more profitable than grain production. Denmark was transformed into a butter, livestock and pork exporting country within a few decades. Sweden and Norway also developed dairy exports, but domestic markets remained more important there. In Denmark, but not in the two other countries, agricultural products constituted the most important source of export income. Therefore the organisation of the food processing sector was vital for the Danish economy.

In Denmark the development of the cooperative movement was part of a second wave of emancipation of the middle-sized farmers, another dimension of which was the rapid spread of rural folk high schools.[2] Cooperative dairies were formed from 1882 onwards and soon spread all over the country. By 1890 they numbered over 700 and 30 per cent of milk producers delivered to them. Cooperative slaughterhouses were established from 1887 onwards. By the turn of the century, their market share had reached 50 per cent. In the mid-1890s many cooperatives merged into larger associations and in 1899 a central board was founded. The dairy cooperatives further merged into a central dairy cooperative organisation in 1912. By 1919 cooperatives produced 80–90 per cent of the processed milk and meat output in Denmark, but the export trade remained in private hands (Bjørn, 1988: 368–81; Pedersen, 1988: 54; Just, 2009).

Dairy cooperatives were founded earlier in Sweden, and Norway. In Norway, the first one was started in Rausjødalen as early as in 1856, but the great expansion of numbers took place around 1870. They quickly outnumbered private dairies and by the turn of the century over 85 per cent of the 800 or so dairies were run as cooperatives. In addition, cooperative slaughterhouses were founded after the turn of the century. Cooperatives tended to be locally based until the 1930s and they often competed with each other. By 1920 however, the Norwegian Dairy Association, existing since 1881, was taken over by the producer cooperatives and transformed into their central organisation (Gjerdåker, 1988: 254–62; Just, 2009; Espeli, 2006: 21–27).

In Sweden exporting dairies were formed foremost in the south, but the dairy sector expanded over all the whole country and increasingly milk was processed by

[2] The idea behind the original folk high schools, which originated in Denmark in the 1840s, was to ensure that the peasantry and others on the lower rungs of society had access to secondary education within a Christian framework. General topics such as history and languages were mixed with a theoretical farm education. Early schools were attended by the sons of civil servants and wealthy peasants and teaching was restricted to the winter months when the labour demand from farms was low.

cooperatives. In 1920 they accounted for little more than half of the processed milk, but afterwards their market share grew quickly, and had reached 80 per cent by 1930. Export cooperative slaughterhouses were formed in Scania after the turn of the century, but apart from the dairies, cooperatives supplying farmers with inputs – seed, fertilizers and feeding stuff – were more important. By 1920 the central organisation of farmers' supply cooperatives, founded in 1905, embraced 1,353 local cooperatives with 85,000 members. Other than that, Swedish cooperatives did not form any national organisation before 1930 (Morell, 2001).

Cooperative credit associations, insurance associations and cooperatives for bull-keeping and milk control also developed, as did cooperative associations for the distribution of electricity in Norway and Sweden. The cooperative movement came to be all inclusive, but by 1920 it was in a much more developed state, with the key central organisations in place, in Denmark than in the two other countries.

This was the beginning of a fundamental change in the structure of the agricultural sector. Farming continued to be carried out in small units, while processing and distribution was concentrated in units and organisations that were to become ever larger over the twentieth century.

12.3 Government and public policies

Peasants and farmers as a national political force

Whilst different peasant groups had their own political objectives, all agreed on resistance to rises in taxes and other levies. Few however had any access to political power. The exception was the Swedish freeholders and crown tenants through their unique position in the Swedish parliament. By the mid-eighteenth century they had managed to make alliances in support of their sectional interests, i.e. concerning ground taxes, the right to sublet land and to subdivide farms. Their political influence increased with the transformation of wealthy freeholders into fully fledged landed proprietors. But, as we noticed before, they did nothing to advance the cause of the peasant tenants of the nobility.

The entry of the peasantry into Danish politics was a consequence of their emancipation and transformation into freeholders. It allowed the appearance of a wealthy middle peasant stratum which was freed from manorial jurisdiction. Peasant politics in Denmark was encouraged by the introduction of regional advisory assemblies in 1834, in which both tenants and freeholders were represented. Peasant representatives demanded relief from corvée and other dues, equitable taxation and the right for the remaining tenants to buy the land they tilled. The focus of the peasants' political action was thus, unlike in Sweden, aimed at advancing the remaining tenants' interest. The movement culminated in 1848, when the bureaucratic absolute monarchy was overthrown in a peaceful revolution. A new constitution was created with universal male suffrage and a bi-cameral parliament (Bjørn, 1988: 116–23).

Simultaneously, Danish grain exports, which were mainly in the hands of large landowners, developed strongly. This stratum remained for some decades the politically and economically dominant group in the countryside. During the emergence of local farmers' unions and the shift towards an export-led animal economy, starting in the 1870s, the middle-sized farmers rose to challenge their position. In these processes the conservative party of the large landowners, *Höyre,* and the Liberal party, *Venstre,* representing the middle peasants, took shape. By the turn of the century the Liberals were the dominating force, but the party split in 1905 and the Social Liberal party, *Radikale Venstre* was formed, mainly with support from smallholders.

The democratic evolution was quicker in Norway where all 'active, independent and autonomous men' were granted voting rights by the Eidswoll constitution of 1814 (Gjerdåker, 2002: 16). By the 1830s freeholders were exercising the power the franchise gave them. They dominated the parliament, but remained in opposition. Their programme – as was usual amongst parliamentary representatives from peasantries – stressed restraint in public expenditures, the abolishment of burdens resting solely on the peasantry and increased local self-government. By the 1850s a more radical opposition, uniting the urban middle classes and rural freeholders, had emerged, but it only achieved political power after 1882 when its demand that the government needed to command a majority in parliament was conceded. It was in these political battles that the conservative party, *Höyre* which defended the old bureaucracy and *Venstre,* the Liberal party backed by the peasantry, were both established. *Venstre* came to be associated with the Smallholders' Union who argued for free trade, while the protectionist, corn-producing peasants active in the Farmers' Union formed the Agrarian party (*Bondepartiet*) in 1921. Many smallholders also supported the Social Democratic party.

The parliamentary reforms of the 1860s accentuated the powerful position of landowning peasants in Sweden. National voting and eligibility rights were determined by income *or* real estate ownership and this worked in their favour. Consequently their representatives became conservative and accepted universal male suffrage with reluctance in 1909 having secured arrangements that perpetuated their influence in the wake of the numerical and political growth of the rural landless and the urban working classes. Until then, they had dominated the second chamber of the reformed parliament and acted in a similar fashion to their Norwegian counterparts. They were, for example, reluctant to increase military spending – but only so long as the burden fell solely on the peasantry. They split on the greatest issue of the day: the reintroduction of grain tariffs in the 1880s. Representatives from the mid-Swedish plains, where rye was still the most important commercial product, voted for tariffs, whereas farmers from the forest areas, which imported grain, and from Scania, where a switch towards dairy production was already under way, voted for continued free trade. When the modern party system emerged around the turn of the century many larger farmers and estate owners followed the conservatives or liberals, while many smallholders turned towards the Social Democrats. A modern agrarian party, *Bondeförbundet,* was formed in 1921. From the outset it acted as a lobby group for farmers.

In all three countries, alliances between farmers' organisations and the labour movement were manifested in the political compromises of the 1930s made between the Social Democrats (and in Denmark the Social Liberal party) on the one side and those parties more directly connected to farmers' interest on the other. The alliance was strongest in Sweden where the Social Democrats were supported by the Agrarians up to the 1950s, whereas the Norwegian Social Democrats achieved a majority after the war. From the 1960s, Agrarians in Norway and Sweden, and Social Liberals in Denmark have (with some exceptions) shifted to the right. In the very long perspective, peasants' political involvement – disregarding varying interests among different strata – has moved from being a force for emancipation and radical change, sometimes in alliance with the labour movement, towards a more unambiguously non-socialist, conservative standpoint.

When the question of affiliation to the EC was debated in the 1960s and 1970s, farmers in Sweden and Norway, where agriculture was directed towards the domestic market and heavily subsidized, were opposed to membership. In Denmark, farmers had long been strongly export-oriented and it was important for them to secure access to the open and growing European market especially after British entry to the European Union. In Norway, farmers' opposition and strong regional interests managed to defeat proposals for entry in referendums held in 1972 and 1994. In Sweden, membership of the EU only became a serious option with the decline of Social Democratic opposition after 1989. Simultaneously, the deregulation of the farming sector that started in the late 1980s left Swedish farmers with the prospect of competing in a more global market without the intervention prices, regional support and border protection that existed within the union. Therefore farmers' organisations lobbied for EU membership and promoted the successful vote for entry in 1994.

Peasant involvement in local government rose in parallel with their influence at the national level. Enclosure made the village assembly obsolete, and larger entities became important. In all three countries the hundred, where the landowning peasants were represented, retained their juridical relevance, but lost most other functions although hundred commons remained in many cases. In Sweden, more than in any of the other countries, the parish was from the outset a relatively independent entity and grew in administrative importance in the seventeenth and eighteenth centuries. In 1817 this was recognised and it was decided that landowners and tenants (authorized by the landowner) should have the right to vote for the church assembly, although votes were graded by size of landholding. By 1862 the church assembly and the communal assembly were formally separated.

Voting rights for the communal assembly, which was responsible for poor relief and primary schools, were still weighted according to income and value of property, in a way which tended to favour the landholding peasantry (and, in the north, the large forestry companies). This system remained right up to 1918, when equal communal voting rights were stipulated. In Denmark, the peasantry had been much more strongly subordinate to the nobility up to the late eighteenth century, and in Norway the dioceses had dominated the parishes throughout. Therefore, in both instances, the local government reforms of the nineteenth century inherited nothing from the earlier parish institution which had been much less powerful than in Sweden. On the other hand, voting rights for the modern local governments in Norway and Denmark were more universal and equal than in Sweden. In Norway peasants had the right to stand and vote in local elections after 1837. The same was true in Denmark from 1841.

In all three countries poor relief was a matter for the home parish/commune. In Sweden the poor relief decree of 1871 released local government from its unconditional responsibility to support the destitute and gave the authorities a degree of discretion instead. Poor relief in the countryside could take several forms: cash allowances, boarding out (providing cheap labour for the care giver), auctioning out (to lowest bidder), ambulatory care and institutional care in poorhouses. Local government expenditures rose strongly in the late nineteenth and early twentieth century, mostly because of rising costs for schools but also because of increasing poor relief costs as populations became increasingly dominated by elderly. These costs were met by local taxes and the secular trend of falling tax quotas for the landed peasants was broken. Generally – in all three countries – peasant representatives in local government were mindful of the taxpayers and acted with frugality in school and welfare matters. In Sweden some of the pressure on local governments was released when an universal old age pension reform was introduced in 1913 (Morell 2001).

Farmers' dominance in rural local government persisted up to the 1950s. In many localities however, they lost power as they became increasingly outnumbered. In the post-war period local municipalities were – particularly in Sweden – progressively merged and many rural areas were combined under the same local authorities as towns, and so the influence of the agricultural interest in local politics dwindled.

Government support for agriculture in the eighteenth and nineteenth centuries

The eighteenth century saw an increased interest in agricultural progress amongst state officials and enlightened landowners. Debates were lively, official reports were initiated and changes in land management were suggested. Besides emancipation in Denmark and the enclosure legislation, the supply of grain was often a matter of government concern and debate. Sweden, in contrast to Denmark, imported grain throughout the eighteenth century and up to about 1820. The Swedish government tried to balance the supply in good and bad years by manipulating tariffs and employing export and import prohibitions, and in poor years by banning distilling and organising the inter-regional transfer of grain. The main instrument of this policy was the General Grain Storage (*Allmänna Magasinsinrättningen*) which maintained granaries in all counties. It stored and transported grain paid as tax and was responsible for provisioning the army. From 1810 it was also responsible for delivering relief to deficit areas in bad years and for buying up surpluses in good years to maintain farm gate prices. The institution managed the first task well, but not the latter: surpluses were exported at huge losses in 1820 and 1821. The state granaries were abolished by parliament in 1824.

From the 1820s Sweden and Denmark produced grain surpluses. Both countries took advantage of the British free trade policy from the 1840s to build up a substantial corn export trade. In Norway, which still needed large imports of grain, grain tariffs supporting domestic production were cut sharply in 1850. Sweden similarly signed a multilateral free trade treaty in 1865. However, following the influx of American and Russian grain, Sweden reintroduced – after a bitter political fight – grain tariffs in 1888, but Denmark (and for a long time Norway too) stuck to free trade. Norway imported grain throughout, Denmark went from exporting to importing grain and both countries came to concentrate on animal husbandry and dairy farming. Tariffs impeded this shift in Sweden. In Norway the farmers' union, formed in 1896, and which largely represented grain-growing districts in Austlandet and Trøndeleg, consistently argued for increased corn tariffs, but the Liberal government, supported by the Smallholders' union (mostly representing peasants in parts of Sørlandet, Vestlandet and Nord-Noreg, who normally had to buy grain themselves), resisted their arguments (Bjørn, 1988; Morell, 2001; Gjerdåker, 2002).

The governments also supported agricultural education. Apart from abortive small scale undertakings, regional agricultural schools were established in the 1830s (Denmark) and 1840s (Norway and Sweden). In all three countries conflicts emerged over the content of the teaching which reflected the contested social goals of the schools. The first schools focused on the practical training of foremen and supervisors for large estates and were unattractive to aspiring peasant farmers' sons. Later on, the county schools in Norway and a new form of school in Sweden offered shorter courses with a more theoretical and general curriculum. Sometimes in Sweden these schools functioned together with folk high schools, a concept imported from Denmark (Kile, 1997; Christensen, 1988; Morell, 2001).

In Denmark folk high schools directed towards the peasantry were established from the 1840s. They offered a general education with more specialized agricultural training. This was an important element in a second wave of emancipation of the well-to-do peasants, the *gårdmen* (Christensen, 1988). In Norway, tensions remained throughout the nineteenth century between local and regional initiatives focusing on regional and adapted needs and national generalised education. There was also a lobby in Norway for special courses/schools for smallholders and this was implemented in 1915–32 (Kile, 1997).

Government-financed and approved higher institutes for agricultural studies, which later developed into agricultural universities with integrated veterinary and forestry education, were founded in all three countries in the mid-nineteenth century (Morell, 2001; Bjørn, 1988; Kile, 1997).

Enclosure and the demise of communal land use

Legislation to bring about enclosure is the outstanding example of government intervention in agriculture in the eighteenth and nineteenth centuries. The plain lands of Denmark, Schleswig and south and mid-Sweden were, until the late eighteenth century, characterized by villages and manorial demesnes. In forested parts of Sweden, and in most of Norway, solitary farmsteads or hamlets dominated. The village communities, with their open field systems, scattered strips, and mixture of private and communal ownership, were regarded as obstacles to a major breakthrough in grain production.

The first legislation to promote enclosures (*Storskifte* – 'large field') originated in Sweden in 1749 and laid down how exchanges of land among villagers should be conducted in order to create larger consolidated fields for each individual farmer. Later acts from 1757 onwards introduced the rule that enclosure had to be undertaken at the request of a single villager. Thus it became possible for one landowner to impose re-distribution of land on his fellow villagers. Within a few decades, large numbers of plain land villages had been enclosed (Gadd, 2000: 277–82). The eighteenth-century Swedish legislation was however vague about how thorough the consolidations should be. Many peasants were left with a number of parcels and village communities remained intact. The outcomes of these early reallocations were often depreciated by both contemporary writers and twentieth-century historians, but later research has upgraded their significance (Olsson, 2005).

Denmark never had a widespread movement of land reallocation *within* the village communities. Instead, it was the forerunner in the radical enclosure movement. State committee reports and proposals in the 1750s and 1760s advocated the complete abandonment of the open field system. Despite some earlier privately-sponsored enclosures, the general take off of the Danish enclosure movement occurred in the 1780s following a statute of 1781, which more or less ordered the dissolution of village communities, and gave any landholder in the village the right to demand the redistribution of its land. Thirty years later almost every peasant village in Denmark had been enclosed into solitary farmsteads (Skrubbeltrang, 1978: 276–303; Dombernovsky, 1988: 311–31).

The same drastic legislation was introduced in Scania in 1803 and into the rest of Sweden in 1804–07, and a first wave of radical enclosures lasted until 1820, mainly in the southern plains. The requirement that the peasant's entire land had to be combined into a single plot hampered the spread of the movement into areas with more varied topography. Eventually an act of 1827 moderated this condition, and the rest of the Swedish countryside was enclosed over the following half-century (Utterström, 1957, I). It was typical of the Swedish – and Norwegian – enclosure movement that once the permissive legislation was enacted, enclosure was, to a great extent, driven by the peasants themselves. It was only in Sweden where the crown tenants (but not tenants of the nobility) were seen as equal to landowners when it came to demanding enclosure (Svensson, 2001: 101–02).

In Norway the open field system was prevalent in the south-western and central part of the country, Vestlandet and Trøndelag (Lunden, 2002: 176). Inspired by the Danish example, parliament passed an enclosure act in 1821. Most villages in Norway were small. Hence, the arable strips were not so scattered that the peasants regarded it as a major problem (Tønnesson, 1981: 197). Initially, the landowners were deterred by the threat of a 25 per cent rise in crown taxes if enclosure was not implemented within eight years of the initial application. In spite of this penalty being moderated in 1827, it was not until the implementation of new legislation in 1859, which required the involvement of professional officials and introduced stricter requirements for allotting peasant's entire land into one consolidated plot, that enclosure was adopted on a large scale. Over the next 60 years most villages with open field systems were enclosed (Gjerdåker, 2002: 198–209).

Due to natural and institutional differences, the extent and timing of enclosure diverged between the three countries. The aim and result was however the same: radical redistributions of land, the abandonment of collective property rights and the creation of unitary single farmsteads. But while the farmhouses in Denmark often remained in the village by means of creating fan-shaped land holdings, farmhouses were much more frequently moved out to desolate locations in the southern plains of Sweden and Norway. In much of Norway, in inland southern Sweden and in east-central Sweden, where small villages or hamlets had dominated, the effects on settlement structure were milder (Utterström, 1957, I: 566).

Radical enclosures meant the dissolution of village communities. Village and parish commons and the intricate systems for keeping cattle out of arable fields were dissolved (Gadd, 2000). However many district commons, *bygdeallmenningar* in Norway, *häradsallmänningar* (hundred commons) in Sweden, the ownership of which was from time to time claimed by the crown, have remained. The right of the part owners of the Swedish hundred commons – cadastral farm owners within the hundred – to collective self-governance was enforced as late as 1934 (Lovén, 2003). In both countries the commons still extend over of considerable acreages of forest which are now run as commercial enterprises, some placing an emphasis on recreation and tourism.

Government policy and the expansion of the smallholdings

In the last decades of the nineteenth century smallholdings were seen as a panacea to solve a range of rural problems. Late nineteenth-century liberal reformers promoted the creation of freeholding smallholders with sufficiently large plots to guarantee an independent existence for the smallholder and his family. For conservatives smallholding was a way of vaccinating the growing labouring masses against the lure of socialist ideas. Large estate owners often wished to recreate a crofters system of small farmers, tied to the land, who would form a pool of wage labour for larger farms while much of their living costs would be borne by the smallholding workers themselves. Even Scandinavian Social Democracy (with the brief exception of Norway) from the 1910s promoted small scale independent land ownership and smallholdings and abandoned notions of the nationalisation of land (Morell, 2001: 127–28; Banggaard, 2006; Just, 2009). Another reason for the promotion of smallholdings was found in contemporary agronomic discourse which stressed the intensive land use found amongst smallholders. Economists and politicians assumed that national agricultural production would be enhanced if small farms were promoted. Finally, particularly in Norway and Sweden, a substantial emigration developed in the last quarter of the nineteenth century. National romantic anti-emigration propagandists claimed that the prime reason for young people leaving Scandinavia was the impossibility of acquiring land. The proposed remedy was state support for the creation of new smallholdings (Gjerdåker, 2002: 263–70; Morell, 2001: 77–8, 127–28).

In Denmark the smallholders' movement lobbied for the allocation of land to agricultural workers and for the emancipation and free-sale of crofts (*hus*) (Dieckmann Rasmussen *et al.*, 1988: 224–25). Large landowners complained about the impending lack of agricultural labour and favoured a law of 1899 which aimed at helping landless workers buy marginal parcels of land but stopped short of creating independent smallholdings. Young male applicants who wanted to establish a smallholding could borrow 90 per cent of the value of a small land parcel on favourable terms from a special government fund (Dieckmann Rasmussen *et al.*, 1988: 226–31; Banggaard, 2006: 303–04). From 1906 the Treasury started to grant loans to associations which bought up large estates and divided them into smallholdings. The local smallholders' unions created several associations (*udstykningsforeningar*) which helped form somewhat larger smallholdings than was usual (Dieckmann Rasmussen *et al.*, 1988: 232).

The 1919 law which ordered the sale of the remaining tenancies in Denmark included in its terms the remaining leased *hus*. Publicly-owned land was parcelled out as 'rent smallholdings' which smallholders did not buy, but paid the interest on their capital value. The original 1899 law was revised in 1921, 1947 and finally 1971. Parcels formed under the later laws tended to be larger than the early ones. The practice in Denmark was to allow the creation of somewhat larger smallholdings which allowed for peasant independence instead of simply supporting agricultural workers' demands for holdings to supplement their wage labour (Banggaard, 2006: 304).

In Norway and Sweden similar government loan funds for smallholdings were created in 1903 and 1904 respectively. The Norwegian Smallholders Union urged the enforced sale of cottages to their tenants and in 1928 such a law was formulated. The land law also placed a duty on local government to provide land to local dwellers in need. On certain conditions (misuse of land, ownership of several holdings) land could be expropriated to be parcelled out to presumptive smallholders (Almås, 2002: 60–62).

In Sweden the smallholding enactment of 1904, with certain amendments, remained in force until the 1946. In the late 1930s it had been concluded that smallholdings were no longer desirable, since industrial expansion required labour which smallholdings tended to lock into the countryside. With the emergence of an agricultural surplus, production had ceased to be a problem, and smallholdings were now seen to be inefficient and capable only of supporting a low standard of living. Therefore, in the 1940s, government support for the creation of smallholdings was withdrawn (Morell, 2001). In Denmark and Norway, support for smallholdings was not reversed quite so abruptly. In these countries strong smallholders' unions – absent in Sweden – existed and they fought with some success to retain a policy of keeping land accessible to smallholders (Almås, 2002; Pedersen, 1988: 256, 259, 264).

Farmers' organisations and governmental trade policy from the inter-war years

The depressed market conditions of the 1920s forced the agricultural associations of all three countries into collaboration. The crisis around 1930 led them to demand substantial state support for the market regulation they considered necessary.

In Sweden the General Agricultural Society, *SAL*, managed to unite the cooperative movement in 1929–30. National cooperative associations were formed for all major branches of agriculture and when the prospect of serious crisis loomed, *SAL* and the newly-founded National Dairy Association (*Svenska Mejeriernas Riksförening*) came together to urge the government to support regulation of the milk market. The association of dairy cooperatives were allowed to levy a duty on all milk sold from all producers, whether they were members or not, and to use the revenues to subsidise butter exports. Thus the organisation was granted the power of public taxation while the obligatory duty lured the remaining independent producers into cooperatives. By 1938 the proportion of dairy milk passing through dairy cooperatives had reached 91 per cent (Morell, 2009). The milk market was regulated along similar lines in Norway. A government-sanctioned trade board composed of the agricultural associations was allowed to regulate all trade in dairy and meat products and to collect fees from producers. The industry levy was then used to stabilize prices and finance exports. Similar arrangements were developed for most branches of agriculture in both countries (Just, 2009).

In Denmark the importance of agricultural exports had cemented the belief in free trade and non-interventionist policies. But the imposition of import quotas by Germany and development of British 'Empire preference' ended the resistance to state intervention. A bacon board, a butter export board and boards for the other agricultural industries were established in 1932. Their purpose was the regulation of supplies, distribution of export quotas, collection of duties on domestic consumption and the redistribution of this income among producers to stabilise farm gate prices. The administration of the boards, the regulations and the collection of fees was handled by the cooperatives, sometimes in collaboration with the Farmers Union (Just, 2009; Pedersen, 1988).

A series of political agreements between the ruling Social Liberals (dominated by smallholders), the Social Democrats and the Liberal party (dominated by well-to-do farmers) culminating in that of January 1933 guaranteed stable political support for the Danish regulation. Likewise in Sweden. Here the Agrarian Party (*Bondeförbundet*) had consistently urged agricultural support where the Social Democrats had supported free trade and income-distribution. After the Social Democratic victory in the 1933 election, a concordat was struck whereby the Agrarians agreed to support Social Democratic labour market policies (based on large scale public works paid for at market wages), and in return for Social Democrats' support for agricultural regulation. This proved to be more than a short term crisis management. The emerging farmers' movement and the trade unions strove to control their principal commodity, food and labour respectively. The agreement therefore sanctioned the vital role of interest groups in the economy, but also secured consumer support for a regulated agricultural sector and it formed the basis of the long term rule of the Social Democrats, supported by the Agrarians, which continued to the 1950s. Similar results followed from an agreement along the same lines between Agrarians (*Bondepartiet*) and the Social Democrats in Norway in 1935.

A further reaction to the crisis of the 1930s was the appearance of extremist right wing organisations (*Landbrugernes Sammenslutning* in Denmark, *Bygdefolkens krisehjelp* in Norway and elements within the *Riksförbundet Landsbygdens folk* in Sweden) which – intermingled with pure Fascist tendencies – argued for much more radical support for farmers and tried to set farmers against other sectors of society. In all three countries the established organisations and parties managed to articulate the discontent of the majority of farmers and the extremist organisations in the Scandinavian countryside remained marginal (Just, 2009).

In Norway and Sweden the regulations formulated in the early 1930s committed the government (in principle) to the purchase of all output at fixed prices. The regulation was made permanent and the agricultural lobbies were given a role in determining the level of support in annual price negotiations with the government from 1940 in Sweden and 1950 in Norway. These arrangements, with certain adjustments, governed the economy of the agricultural sector – and food prices – until the late 1980s (Morell, 2009; Flygare and Isacson, 2003; Just, 2009; Almås, 2003).

In Denmark the government market boards had been dissolved by 1950, but the agricultural organisations established new export boards and these took over the huge capital reserves of their predecessors. During the following decades the cooperative export organisations managed to outcompete the private ones and achieve a virtual monopoly of both processing and sales. Regulation of home market prices and farm gate prices by negotiation between the government and the agricultural organisations continued. Direct annual support in various forms was also paid to producers. This continued until Denmark entered the Common Market in 1973.

In Sweden the costs of the agricultural regulation became exceedingly high in the 1980s as growing surpluses had to be exported at a loss. A programme for inducing farmers to leave land fallow and take marginal fields out of use was inaugurated. It was decided that internal price regulation should be dismantled. Before the effects of these measures was fully felt, Sweden joined the European Union in 1995 (Flygare and Isacson, 2003).

Norway stayed out of the European Union. Strong regulation of the agricultural sector with considerable state support has remained, together with a very active regional policy. This has preserved a huge agricultural sector and supported scattered settlements in Norway, but it has also meant high consumer prices. From the mid-1990s, government in both the EU and Norway has forced the agricultural sector to pursue new goals, normally the maintenance of bio-diversity and landscape and cultural heritage (Almås, 2002).

Land policy and structural transformation in the post war era

The profound restructuring of agriculture in the post war era (Tables 12.4–12.6) was a reaction to technical change and labour market factors. However social structure and government policy certainly played a role as well. On the one hand, government support for farming through negotiated farm gate prices or direct subsidies tended to maintain the profitability of farming and so mitigate market influence and preserve the existing structure of agriculture. On the other hand, there was a shift in focus of land policy from promoting smallholdings towards encouraging larger family farms. The general idea was that labour and capital resources should be transferred from low productivity agriculture towards industry in order to maximise economic growth, while farming should be modernized and production made more efficient to keep costs down.

In Sweden government land policy answered the needs of industrial expansion. The demand for labour attracted people from agriculture in the early post-war years and stimulated the mechanisation of agriculture. A law of 1945 made agricultural education and skill a precondition for the acquisition of land (although inheritance legislation overruled this law). Following a 1947 parliamentary decision, regional farming boards (*lantbruksnämnder*) were authorised to negotiate the merger of small farms to achieve a structure of family farms of 10–20 (later 20–30) ha, of a size thought able to produce efficiently. Negotiated, government-guaranteed prices were to give these farmers incomes comparable to those of industrial workers. When a farmer left farming and a farm's lands were offered for sale, the boards could determine who should acquire its land. Loans could be offered: the Boards had a reserve power to expropriate land. The closure of 'sub-optimal' units was further promoted by an 'active' labour market policy involving severance payments, resettlement allowances and re-schooling schemes for smallholders. Whereas the intention from 1947 was to preserve viable family farms, the policy became more radical in the 1960s when it was used to promote – via price pressure – efficiency in production without any reference to the type of farm: large corporations were allowed and might be preferred if they proved to be more efficient. This radical turn in policy caused massive unrest amongst farmers. From the 1970s onwards, the structural-dirigist element in Swedish agricultural policy has vanished (Flygare and Isacson 2003).

In Norway too, an income equity goal for farmers was often referred to as the objective of policy. But it proved impossible to stipulate any precise normative farm size because of the powerful smallholders' union and the ruling Social Democratic party's strong smallholders' faction (Almås, 2002: 125, 221–22). A new land law of 1955 stated that the government should help presumptive farmers to attain land and that the farms created should have sufficient land to support a household. Moreover the government secured powers to buy land to form larger units. Land could be expropriated if misused but also to create more viable unities (Almås 2002: 124, 185–87).

This legislation, which was similar to that in Sweden, hardly had any effect before the 1960s. Moreover, by 1964 the tide was turning: it was claimed that farming – together with development of local industries – was essential to maintain settlement in rural areas. Such statements argued in favour of keeping a larger number of small units in business than would be defendable on solely economic grounds (Almås, 2002: 225). Following discontent led by smallholders from Hitra Island in Sør Trøndelag in 1975, who threatened a tax strike and further direct action, the policy became one of tempering structural change. Domestic production should be increased through reclamation, the income security of farmers was stressed and investment in farms larger than was needed to support a household was discouraged. Like the fall of the dirigist policy in Sweden in the 1970s, this policy shift was justified by rising world market prices and (alleged) universal food shortages (Almås, 2002: 260–82).

Market reforms, internationalisation and increasing oil-related wealth of Norway however led to the practical abandonment of the equity principle in the early 1990s and since then structural change has accelerated. One outcome is that many Norwegian farmers have become part-time agriculturalists. Only 27 per cent of farm households draw their main incomes from farming. In that way farm support has been 'privatised' and relies on at least one of the farming spouses working off the farm (Almås, 2002: 329–46, 371–75, 378–79).

In Denmark the government offered premium loans as a means to encourage the enlargement of small farms in 1971. Here too the income equity principle was sometimes referred to, but as in Norway there was no clear-cut ideal farm size. Liberal and Social Democratic politicians wanted to repeal the remaining laws designed to preserve agrarian structures, which hindered the flow of capital and labour from agriculture to other sectors, and in doing so promote the creation of a more viable structure by way of market forces. The smallholders' union was understandably hostile to these measures. From 1973 onwards agricultural policy in Denmark has followed EC lines.

Peasant unrest and labour relations in agriculture

As freeholders – and in Denmark and Norway tenants as well – gradually achieved improved civil rights and access to government, open unrest came to be confined to crofters, landless labourers and in Sweden the tenants of the nobility. The only major protest action against crown taxes in this period occurred in Norway. This has been explained by the assumption that the tax pressure was higher in the poorer Norwegian districts than in other parts of Scandinavia, but also by the distance – geographically, socially and culturally – between the rulers and the peasantry (Lunden, 2002: 352). When the regime in Copenhagen imposed an individual extra tax in 1762, the rebellion known as *Strilekrigen* (the war of *Strils),* started in the Strileland, the rural area around the town of Bergen. Eventually Danish troops were sent in and the rebellion was crushed in 1765. Despite this outcome, the extra tax was first reduced and then abandoned in 1772.

In Denmark the reform period was preceded in the 1760s and 1770s by scattered examples of peasant resistance directed towards corvée duties. Contemporaneous peasant disturbances in Sweden were restricted to Scania and Halland, and were aimed at securing agreements limiting the number of work days. The tenants in southern Halland in 1773–76 managed to coordinate their actions between villages under different estates, and take their cause all the way to the Swedish supreme administrative court. However, the peasants lost at all levels (Smedberg, 1972: 150). Another anti-corvée uprising originating in protests against military enlistments emerged in Scania in 1811 but was violently crushed with severe casualities and hundreds of peasants arrested. The last major outburst of tenant unrest in Scandinavia was the 'Tullberg movement' in 1867–69 which involved around a thousand Scanian manorial tenants who demanded an end to corvée labour and the right to buy their farmsteads from the nobility. Again the tenants lost the struggle. Their objective of securing the abolition of corvée was not achieved until the twentieth century and their quest for the right to purchase their land from their landlords remains unsatisfied.

With the increasing dominance of owner occupiers, unrest involving landless groups and tensions between farmers and labourers became more important than disputes between landlords and tenants. An early example is the Thrane movement which emerged in 1849 in Norway. It started amongst destitute labourers in towns, but soon rural people in Austlandet and Agder and in Trøndelag, came to participate.

Amongst its demands were the repeal of the corn tariffs and the public distribution of land. Larger plain land peasants did not approve of these goals and the movement mostly consisted of smallholders, crofters and landless. It was crushed by police action in 1851 (Gjerdåker, 2002: 140–42).

Farm workers' trade unions were founded in the early twentieth century, but grew more slowly than other trade unions. Paternalistic relations between master and servant in agriculture and the large number of small workplaces inhibited organisation. In the early years the emerging unions – for example in Scania 1907 – were involved in bitter strikes which employers met by evicting workers' families from the housing they provided, a method still in use in the 1930s. The unions strived for higher wages, the right of association and for collective agreements, while employers insisted on individual annual contracts which guaranteed the workers' labour over the harvest season. It was only in the 1930s and after the compromise between the Agrarians and Social Democracts that the situation eased and the level of organisation increased. However, this was the very moment when mechanisation left fewer and fewer farm workers to be organized (Morell, 2001).

Visions of the peasantry

Perceptions of the peasantry have been transformed several times over the last 250 years. In the mid-eighteenth century and later, the cultural and landed elite and the emerging agro-scientific community regarded peasants as conservative brakes on development, illiterate, traditional and reluctant to try out new methods. Still, it was acknowledged that future progress demanded their involvement and paternalistic educational projects developed in all three countries, manifested in the top-down agricultural societies described earlier. Gradually the social and political status of peasants was raised as freeholders were increasingly viewed in the nineteenth century as independent and respected property owners. Political action and, in Denmark, the continued strong educational and cultural emancipation of the well-to-do peasantry, the *gårdmen*, later combined with their commercial success under the wings of cooperation, favoured the emergence of a view of the peasantry as responsible, bourgeois members of society. The cooperative and sectional organisations of farmers in the early twentieth century were eager to portray themselves as modern, rational entrepreneurs on a par with industrialists (Morell, 2001; Björn, 1988; Christensen, 1988; Gjerdåker, 2001).

However by the end of the nineteenth century, nationalist romantic views of the peasantry had also emerged. As industrialisation and urbanisation unfolded, peasants were idealised. The landed peasantry, which had not produced any uprising since the mid-eighteenth century, was now viewed as a bulwark against proletarian unrest and socialism and as the basis of the national army. In Sweden the independent peasantry was favourably contrasted with landless and rural dwellers holding by lease and there was public hostility to their dispossession by timber companies buying their land. The peasantry was deified in certain governmental committees in almost racial-biological terms. In this mindset, it was only the influx of fresh blood from the peasantry that saved the urban masses from degeneration. At the same time, amongst some authors (for example Strindberg) and scientists in the new urban elites, an anthropological perception of the almost exotic 'otherness' of the peasantry – a population group that had to be deliberately *studied* in order to be understood – was evident (Morell, 2001: 26–29).

Whereas the peasant (or farmer) and the countryside was idealised from around the turn of the previous century, rurality and the farm sector was, from the 1930s (and even more so in the early post-war era), once again regarded as obsolete, archaic and regressive. This was particularly true in Sweden where the industrial expansion was strongest. However, with the emergence of environmentalism and trends of contra-migration from towns to countryside in the 1970s, this view was challenged. And while farmers by then came under attack for their productivist practices and the emergence of a strongly chemical-driven way of farming, they managed from the 1980s to turn the tide. With massive lobbying on the part of their lobby groups, farmers managed to create a perception of themselves as 'green' enterprisers who were at the same time efficient and rational as well as environmentally concerned and anti-capitalist. And they were preoccupied with creating and protecting cultural and natural heritages and popular idyllic rural images – foremost the almost mythical 'open landscape' – against the both symbolic and real plantation of dark, evergreen forests.

Bibliography

Almås, R. (2002) *Norges landbrukshistorie,* IV, *1920–2000: Frå bondesamfunn til bioindustri,* Oslo.

Banggaard, G. (2006) 'Lantarbetare i Danmark, 1800–1919', in C. Lundh and M. Olsson (eds.), *Statarliv – i myt och verklighet.* Hedemora/Möklinta, pp. 287–310.

Bjørn, C. (1988) '1810–1860' in C. Bjørn, *et al.* (eds.), *Det danske landbrugs historie,* III, *1810–1914,* Odense, pp. 7–192.

Carlsson, S. (1949) *Ståndssamhälle och ståndspersoner, 1700–1865. Studier rörande det svenska ståndssamhällets upplösning,* Lund.

Dieckmann Rasmussen, J., Jensen, S. P., Bjørn, C. and Christensen, J. (1988) '1860–1914' in C. Bjørn, *et al.* (eds.), *Det danske landbrugs historie,* III, *1810–1914,* Odense, pp. 193–431.

Dombernowsky, L. (1988) 'Ca. 1720–1810', in C. Bjørn, *et al.* (eds.), *Det danske landbrugs historie,* II, *1536–1810,* Odense, pp. 211–394.

Dyrvik, S. (1979) *Norsk økonomisk historie, 1500–1970,* I, *1500–1850,* Bergen.

Espeli, H. (2006) 'Gjennombrudd og konsolidering', in T. Bergh, H. Espeli, and A. Rønning, (eds.), *Melkens pris – perspektiver på meierisamvirkets historie,* Oslo, pp. 20–39.

Flygare, I. A. and Isacson, M. (2003) *Jordbruket i välfärdssamhället, 1945–2000: Det svenska jordbrukets historia,* V, Stockholm.

Gadd, C.-J. (2000) *Det svenska jordbrukets historia,* III, *Den agrara revolutionen, 1700–1870,* Stockholm.

Gjerdåker, B. (2002) *Norges landbrukshistorie,* III, *1814–1920: kontinuitet og modernitet,* Oslo.

Hasund, S. (1926) 'Norges landbruk, 1875–1925' in *Lantbruket i Norden, 1875–1925,* Göteborg, pp. 329–49.

Heckscher, E. F. (1935) *Sveriges ekonomiska historia från Gustav Vasa,* I,1, Stockholm.

Heckscher, E. F. (1944) 'Ett kapitel ur den svenska jordbesittningens historia. Skatteköpen under 1700-talet', *Ekonomisk tidskrift,* 2, pp. 103–23.

Heckscher, E. F. (1949) *Sveriges ekonomiska historia från Gustav Vasa,* II:1, Stockholm.

Hedenborg, S. and Morell, M. (2008) 'Hästar och hästarbete: Ett klass-, genus- och generationsperspektiv på förändringarna under 1900-talet', in A. Houltz, *et al.*, *Arbete pågår – i tankens mönster och kroppens miljöer,* Acta Universitatis Upsaliensis (Uppsala Studies in Economic History 86), Uppsala.

Herlitz, L. (1974) *Jordegendom och ränta. Omfördelningen av jordbrukets merprodukt i Skaraborgs län under frihetstiden,* Gothenburg.

Hvidtfeldt, J. (1963) *Kampen om ophævelsen af livegenskabet i Slesvig og Holsten, 1795–1805,* Aarhus.

Jensen, H. (1936) *Dansk jordpolitik, 1757–1919,* I, *Udviklingen af statsregulering og bondebeskyttelse indtil 1810,* Copenhagen.

Jensen, H. (1945) *Dansk jordpolitik, 1757–1919,* II, *Fæstevæsendets afvikling og jordlovgivningen i perioden 1810–1919,* Copenhagen.

Johansen H. C. (1985) *Dansk økonomisk statistik, 1814–1980* (Danmarks historie Bind 9), Copenhagen.

Jonssson, U. (1980) *Jordmagnater. Landbönder och torpare i sydöstra Södermanland, 1800–1880,* Stockholm.

Jordbruksstatistisk årsbok (1970). Stockholm.

Just, F. (2009) 'The Scandinavian food system between organization and state', in S. O. Olsson (ed.), *Managing crises and de-globalisation: Nordic foreign trade and exchange, 1919–1939,* Abingdon and New York, pp. 121–36.

Kile, E. (1997) *Landvruksskulen, 1825–1990. Mål, innhald, arbeidsmåtar,* Oslo.

Lovén, U. and Lovén, H. (2003) *Häradsallmänningarna: från medeltida kulturarv till modern samverkan,* Björklinge.

Lunden, K. (2002) *Norges landbrukshistorie,* II, *1350–1814: Frå svartedauden til 17. mai,* Oslo.

Lundh, C. and Olsson, M. (2006) 'Statare och statarsystem – en introduktion', in C. Lundh and M. Olsson (eds.), *Statarliv – i myt och verklighet.* Hedemora/Möklinta, pp. 9–40.

Martinius, S. (1970) *Agrar kapitalbildning och finansiering, 1833–1892,* Gothenburg.

Morell, M. (2001) *Det svenska jordbrukets historia,* IV, *Jordbruket i industrisamhället, 1870–1945,* Stockholm.

Morell, M. (2009) 'Trade crisis and regulation of the farm sector: Sweden in the interwar years', in S. O. Olsson (ed.), *Managing crises and de-globalisation: Nordic foreign trade and exchange, 1919–1939,* London and New York, pp. 137–57.

Myking, J. R. (2005) *Herre over andre si jord? Norske leiglendingsvilkår i europeisk lys, 1500–1800,* Kristiansand.

Olsson, M. (2002) *Storgodsdrift. Godsekonomi och arbetsorganisation i Skåne från dansk tid til mitten av 1800-talet,* Lund and Stockholm.

Olsson, M. (2005) *Skatta dig lycklig. Jordränta och jordbruk i Skåne, 1660–1900,* Hedemora.

Olsson, M. (2006) 'Storjordbruk, statare och andra', in C. Lundh and M. Olsson (eds.), *Statarliv – i myt och verklighet.* Hedemora/Möklinta, pp. 41–86.

Pedersen, E. H. (1988) *Det danske landbrugs historie,* IV, *1914–1988,* Odense.

Rafner, C. (1986) 'Fæstegårdmændenes skattebyrder, 1660–1802', *Fortid og Nutid,* 33, pp. 81–94.

Skrubbeltrang, F. (1978) *Det danske landbosamfund, 1500–1800,* Copenhagen.

Rosén, U. (1994) *Himlajord och handelsvara: Ägobyten av egendom i Kumla socken, 1780–1880,* Lund.

Rydeberg, G. (1985) *Skatteköpen i Örebro län, 1701–1809* (Acta Universitatis Upsaliensis, Studia Historica Upsaliensia 141), Uppsala.

Sjöberg, M. (2006) 'Agrara förhållanden, 1500–1850', in S. Hedenborg and M. Morell (eds.), *Sverige: en ekonomisk och social historia,* Lund, pp. 173–95.

Smedberg, S. (1972) *Frälsebonderörelser i Halland och Skåne, 1772–76,* Stockholm.

Statistics Denmark, www.statbank.dk

Statistics Norway, www.ssb.no.

Statistics Sweden, www.scb.se

Svensson, P. (2001) *Agrara entreprenörer. Böndernas roll i omvandlingen av jordbruket i Skåne, 1800–1870,* Lund and Stockholm.

Thomson, A. (1923) *Grundskatterna i den politiska diskussionen, 1809–1866: ett bidrag till lantmannapartiets förhistoria,* Lund.

Tønnesson, K. (1981) 'Tenancy, freehold and enclosure in Scandinavia from the seventeenth to the nineteenth century', *Scandinavian Journal of History,* 6, pp. 191–206.

Utterström, G. (1957) *Jordbrukets arbetare. Levnadsvillkor och arbetsliv på landsbygden från frihetstiden till mitten av 1800-talet,* 2 vols, Stockholm.

Weibull, C. G. (1923) *Skånska jordbrukets historia intill 1800-talets början,* Lund.

Wohlin, N. (1909), 'Den jordbruksidkande befolkningen i Sverige, 1751–1900: statistisk-demografisk studie på grundval af de svenska yrkesräkningarna' *Emigrationsutredningen,* 9, Stockholm.

13 Conclusion: reflections on property and power over the last millennium*

Richard HOYLE

Our study of power and property in the rural societies of the countries bordering on the North Sea offers us the opportunity to define changes in the region as a whole, but also to make comparisons between different parts of the territory, and to explain change in terms of the various dynamic elements.

At the present time, setting aside social difficulties, looming environmental problems and much angst amongst intellectuals, the people of the North Sea countries must rank among the most successful, prosperous and fortunate in the world. They face no imminent prospect of war or social conflict, and have high incomes and a comfortable standard of living, protected by high quality health care and social welfare systems. The present wealth and stability of the North Sea countries is widely recognised, as is shown by the constant flow of migrants into the region.

The North Sea countries enjoyed a reputation for economic achievement in earlier periods, having experienced periods of urban expansion in the period between 950 and 1300, and again in the fifteenth, sixteenth and seventeenth centuries. The great ports became hubs of regional trade in the Middle Ages, which was extended to commodities from the whole world with the advent of the seaborne empires. The farming systems of Flanders, the coastal regions of the Low Countries, Norfolk and Kent, all were known as innovative and productive from at least the thirteenth century.

There is a danger in adopting an approach which embarks from the present state of the North Sea countries, and sees the last 1500 years as a period in which its society moved forwards in a linear and progressive fashion towards the modern situation. We are not however dealing with a story of continuous progress over the whole North Sea littoral, and the various contributors in their chapters on different parts of the region have shown that there were periods of recession and setback, even in the intensively farmed districts, and that in some parts, such as the woodlands and uplands of Scandinavia, or the sandy plains of north-west Germany, populations were always thin and agricultural methods could never be intensive.

As this volume is focussed on social relations, property and power, we will naturally consider whether we can identify developments in lordship, communal structures, and town and country relations, as well as in the involvement of the state. These developments can display dynamism, but more apparent is perhaps the stability and continuity in these fields, and the path-dependency of processes, with differences between the various parts of the North Sea area enduring over long periods. Structures of power and

* I am grateful to members of the editorial board for many conversations which are reflected here. Some of the text is based on drafts by them. I am especially grateful to Bas van Bavel and Mats Morell for their comments on an earlier version of this essay.

property can change, and indeed they did, but generally incrementally, over long periods of time. And because of their stability, they often acted as a cause or even determinant of the development of the countryside in general. This occurred in interaction with dynamic forces such as the rise and fall of population, the development of markets, shifts in the volume and character of trade, and technological change. This concluding chapter will investigate these interactions and speculate to what extent the structure of power and property contributed to the intermittent and discontinuous development of the North Sea area towards the prosperous situation we know now.

13.1 Ownership

Seen over a perspective of 1,500 years, we can perhaps detect two phases in the development of ownership, the first the development of seigneurial ownership and the second the development of universal full-property or freehold rights in land. Wherever we look, we can see a phase in which allodial land was brought into legal frameworks and made dependent upon lords. Such peasant organisations as existed were suppressed. In north-western Europe this phase had ended by 1000: it took rather longer to bring it about in some regions of Scandinavia. This was perhaps the period in which feudalism was at its most coercive and arbitrary, in which independent peasants needed (or were compelled) to attach themselves to a lord for protection. It is true that there remained some bodies of free peasants, notably those of the Elbian marshes, who remained as independent players until late in the Middle Ages; but within most of the North Sea area, the age of the autonomous independent peasant had passed. This was a society in which lords cultivated demesne land with the labour of slaves and then, with the disappearance of slavery, serfs (above: 25–43).

The second phase extended over much of the last millennium. Over the very long term all European countries saw a reduction in the land owned by seigneurial lords (who held judicial or other powers over their tenants and the inhabitants of their estates) or big landowners who held multiple holdings, sometimes totalling hundreds of hectares. Private jurisdictions disappeared or were annexed to the state. Over the period there were very different patterns of landholding. There were some areas with extensive areas of state, noble or ecclesiastical landholding, but state landholding tended to disappear with time. In those countries which experienced a Protestant Reformation, the lands of the church came into the hands of the state and reinforced its landholdings: but the long term tendency was for these too to be granted away for patronage reasons or sold to cover deficits on the state's current account. In France the lands of the church were seized and sold with revolutionary fervour after 1790. The manumission of serfs in Germany in the decades following the French Revolution reduced the landowning aristocracies of those areas to the owners of demesnes and annuitants, and created an owner-occupying peasantry (above: 54, 141, 255, 263–65).

This extended period was also marked by a bifurcation in property ownership. Legally property belonged to a lord. But the lord's rights over *his* land was compromised by the emergence of customary rights which gave the tenants use rights in the land from which they could not readily be dislodged. Hence tenants often had a rival system of landownership which buttressed their conviction that they land they farmed was essentially theirs' to sell, mortgage, bequeath, subject to the payment of quit rents and (sometimes) the registration of their title in the lord's court. Hence 'tenant' in this period covered a wide range of conditions, from an almost complete lack of rights on the part of the occupiers of the land to their almost complete ownership.

The norm became the owner-occupier who owned and cultivated his own land. The speed at which this happened differed enormously from country to country. The North Sea area of 1900 contained areas in which the possession of land was widely dispersed amongst the population (France, Flanders, Scandinavia generally), some where it was largely possessed by farmers (much of north-west Germany) and others where big estates still predominated (England, Scotland, some parts of Sweden) and where the owner-occupation of land was relatively rare.

The relations between lords and tenants within the feudal system had its own internal dynamics. These are best described as political as they were not simply determined by economic circumstances. Tenants looked for, and found, ways of diminishing their duties and payments, by negotiation and petitioning but also by appeals to higher authority, refusals to cooperate, and withdrawal of rent. They undertook work services with reluctance and perhaps put less effort into them than into their own farming. They often appealed to custom which they believed gave them enduring rights in matters of tenancy and access to common assets. Lords sought ways of winning influence among the tenants, by enlisting allies and using persuasion, and by invoking their own versions of custom, which gave them rights which the tenants had hoped to forget and sometimes disputed. They also brought more direct pressure to bear, enlisting help from the state to compel tenants to comply, and making threats using their own coercive and judicial power as well as that of the state. Most of these tensions were resolved by negotiation within the individual manor. Some were taken to the state's judicial authorities. Occasionally they broke forth into armed insurrection and what emerged was a critique – even a rejection – of the feudal system as a whole.

And yet what is surprising is how quickly feudalism disappeared as a real force in some of the core areas of the North Sea area. It dissolved from within (above: 172). It was not destroyed by force or rebellion although insurrection made some aspects of it untenable. Some sections of the feudal elite were willing participants in its disappearance because they saw advantage in other forms of property holding. One characteristic feature of its decline in northern France and the Low Countries is the grant of charters to rural vills during the twelfth century (above: 115, 126, 187–8). These served to limit the arbitrary characteristics of feudalism, but even if no charter was granted, relations between lords and tenants came to be governed by custom. Rents diminished in value through inflation. At much the same time lords withdrew from demesne farming and commuted labour services to rent (above: 118, 172, 186–8). In these circumstances the seigneurial interest rapidly became unimportant. Both political power and income came to rest with the occupiers of the land. Here manorialism disappeared at a time of population pressure: it had largely gone by the disastrous decade of the 1310s and certainly by the arrival of the Black Death. In addition, we might notice that the expansion of cultivation into new areas in the eleventh to thirteenth centuries, especially into the marshes and peat lands of the Low Countries, produced societies which were only lightly feudal in character (above: 171–2, 186). The promise of personal freedom was needed to encourage peasant settlers into the uncultivated forests and marshes.

Arguably the early decline of feudalism in northern France and the southern Low Countries came about because of the expansion of the urban economy within this area and the wish of lords to access both urban products and urban lifestyles. In this analysis money was more important to them than labour rent: grain did not need to be produced within the estate but could be bought (above: 172–3). But it is also plain that the disintegration of feudalism was assisted by divisions within the feudal elite, with the superior lords wishing to undermine lords of lower status by granting charters which undermined their standing or promoting ideas of personal freedom (above: 188). In this the towns themselves were players, making alliances with the Counts of Flanders. We may speculate that the towns too were competing for the peasant surplus: it was in their interest to have peasants spending their money locally rather than lords sending it abroad. Moreover, we have to acknowledge that the interest of urban patriciates in acquiring land may well have brought about changes in the definition of the rights inherent in that land. What urban investors were interested in was full property in land, not an impermanent interest, nor one which compelled them to undertake servile duties or attend on a lord. At a later date the need of the state to identify who was liable for land taxation may also have encouraged a view that the occupier was, in a modern sense, the owner (above: 179).

In other of both north-eastern France and the Low Countries, forms of manorialism remained an organising force in the countryside into the eighteenth century, especially in those districts where the influence of towns was less marked (above: 116, 173).

Whilst south-eastern England and East Anglia are seen as having broadly similar economies to those of the Low Countries, the trajectory of ownership was completely different. Full property rights did emerge, but much later and only incompletely, in conditions of population decline. At the end of the twelfth century the English state buttressed serfdom by withdrawing from disputes between lord and tenant and making the lord's own court the forum in which disputes over serfdom were rightly tried. Lords continued to maintain their demesnes – indeed, the English lords' response to late twelfth-century inflation was to take land in hand (above: 56, 60). Many lords continued to cultivate demesnes using servile labour for at least a generation after the population collapse of 1348–9. Indeed, their attempts to maintain feudalism in the classic form of manorial serfs undertaking corvée and paying fines marking their personal disability was one of the factors which emerged as the subject of peasant anger in the rising of 1381. There are no instances of the English crown granting civic rights to peasant communities: in fact, the grant of corporate rights to towns was jealously guarded and little used before the later Middle Ages.

By the end of the fifteenth century serfdom had almost entirely disappeared in England. Where it survived, servile tenures had been transformed into copyhold which conferred an inheritable right on the tenant, together with rights of sale and increasingly the right to sublet. The latter allowed investors to acquire land and let it to tenants who paid an economic rent whilst the formal tenant paid a customary rent to the lord. But some medieval landlords – notably monastic houses – had often protected their position by making leases of land, especially demesnes.

The breakthrough in England was therefore incomplete. It is true that there were substantial numbers of customary tenants in England *c.*1640, but this marks a high water, after which their numbers diminished. By the time we have detailed figures for the number of owner-occupiers at the end of the nineteenth century, they owned no more than 10 or 15 per cent of the land area, perhaps the exact reverse of the situation in the Low Countries at about the same time.

A mix of customary tenant and leasehold properties also seems to have been characteristic of areas of northern France at the end of the middle ages. Where customary tenancies in England diminished in both number and the proportion of the land they held, in France customary tenants secured effective control over the land, reducing the lord to the passive recipient of annual rents and transfer taxes on the sale or inheritance of land. Seigneurial attempts to revive lost customary rents and duties in the pre-revolutionary decades are largely held to have failed although they did provoke tenant discontent (above: 119–20). By the time of the Revolution, the peasant conviction that the land was their own was all pervasive: the seigneur of customary land was an irrelevance. His interest, was, of course, swept away in the Revolution (above: 113, 139).

The experience of parts of Scandinavia and northern Germany was quite different. Here seigneurial controls over land strengthened after the end of the Middle Ages and demesnes were extended. In Sweden the resumption by the crown in 1680 of land granted to the nobility over the previous half century restricted the future expansion of aristocratic landowners. Freeholders, some of whom had bought their land from the crown, increasingly dominated rural society from the late eighteenth century onwards. On the other hand, after 1680, noble landowners were allowed to increase rents and enlarge their demesnes, and a belated form of quasi-feudal manorialism continued to develop well into the nineteenth century, particularly in Scania. In Denmark and Schleswig Holstein similar forms of extreme manoralism – in this case combined with a form of serfdom – appeared, and practically no freeholders remained. Normally these extended demesnes in Scania, Denmark and Schleswig Holstein were farmed using the corvée labour of tenants (or rather servants employed primarily to work on the lord's demesnes). In the latest phases of Scanian manorialism, tenants were displaced, their lands added to noble demesnes and farmed with servant labour (above: 324).

However there emerged in Denmark a strong movement for agrarian reform in the later eighteenth century which identified the prevalent social relations of the countryside as an impediment to economic development. The idea that giving the peasantry full property rights in land would release their full potential was a popular one: it was, of course, an application of the 'English model' to societies whose recent history had taken them away from free markets in tenancies and land. The government legislated against serfdom, seigneurial jurisdiction and corvée labour in Denmark and Schleswig-Holstein in 1789 and 1804 respectively and increasingly put pressure on landowners to sell farms to their tenants (above: 255, 315–7).

The reform of the countryside was also given a new urgency by the French Revolution which served as a warning to other European states of the violence which could be unleashed at moments of political breakdown. In most areas where the 're-feudalisation' of the countryside had taken place, it was dismantled by a mixture of private and state initiative in the last years of the eighteenth century and the first years of the nineteenth. In those states which became satellites of the French in the Napoleonic wars, the manumission of serfs and abolition of corvée was arranged as part of the implementation of Revolutionary ideas. Where remnants of manorialism survived through to mid-century, they were frequently abolished in the heady days which followed the risings and agitation of 1848 (in Germany for instance, above: 262–4). The result of these reforms was to give the peasantry the full ownership of their land subject to the servicing of mortgages granted by state credit institutions. The interest of the former lords was cut back to their core estates, houses and demesnes. For income, they received what was in effect an annuity paid them by the state credit agency (above: 263–4). The result was that large swathes of north-west Germany and most of Denmark at this late date passed into the hands of owner-occupying peasantries. In Sweden this situation was largely achieved by the purchase of crown land by its tenants (above: 315).

If the North Sea area is now predominantly one of owner-occupying farmers (less so in England and Scotland), it may be appreciated that the individual areas within the whole have arrived at that end by different and sometimes circuitous routes. It may be suggested however that owner-occupation is, by its character, inherently unstable. Free land markets allowed successful peasants to buy out the interests of their less successful neighbours, producing a concentration of land in fewer hands. As much mortgage capital and many of the buyers of land come from towns, rural landholding is always liable to be undermined by urban capital seeking investment opportunities. Urban investors have a variety of reasons for wanting land, but their acquisition of land from freeholding farmers inevitably means the appearance of a new underclass of tenant occupiers paying rents to an 'owner'.

This, it may be suggested, is a universal fact of life. Where there are towns, there is urban capital seeking a rural outlet. It may be seen in the medieval Low Countries for instance, in the predatory behaviour of ecclesiastical institutions and townspeople buying up the freeholds forfeited after flooding (above: 173, 180). At a much later date, after the emancipation of serfs in Westphalia, and in what might be a continuation of seigneurial rules, the new freeholding peasantry was seen as too immature to be allowed a right of free sale of its property precisely because it would leave them exposed to the dangers of urban (and Jewish) money lending. There was also a tendency here to encourage peasants to place their property outside the reach of the land market by employing entails. These restraints reached a peak with National Socialist idea of *Erbhofgesetz* which placed farmers under state surveillance and limited the owner's right of disposal, as well as allowing the state to confiscate the farm if the owner did not meet approved standards of personal probity and farming efficiency (above: 273–4). These fears show an acute recognition of the capacity of freeholding peasantries to be transformed into tenant societies.

That freeholders were not undermined to a greater extent in the twentieth century perhaps reflects the determination of north European governments to ensure that the leasing of land did not pay. The *Erbhofgesetz* lies at an extreme, but the establishment of tax systems to place landlords at a disadvantage has been part and parcel of the fiscal regimes under which they have labourered throughout the twentieth century (above: 81–2, 97, 203). Ultimately the rise of a new form of tenancy could not be resisted. As the size of holdings grew after the Second World War, it became imperative for successful farmers to absorb the holdings of their neighbours whether by purchase or the establishment of new tenancy arrangements which protected the ownership but transferred the right to cultivate the land into the hands of others (above: 259, 320).

13.2 Tenure

All landowners had to confront the tendency for the real value of rents specified in currency to fall over the long term. This was simply a consequence of inflation. As prices rose and rents remained fixed, the purchasing power of a fixed rent fell: likewise the proportion of the tenant's income he needed to pay his landlord (for an example, above: 172). Of course, there might be countervailing tendencies at times when the demand for land was high and some forms of rent, including entry fines, could be raised. The rents of the tenants of new land could be market-related and for this reason the level of rent over a community could vary enormously according to the time and circumstances in which a tenancy was initially contracted. The problem of the diminishing real value of rent became particularly acute when the coinage was deliberately debased, as in England in the 1540s and early 1550s.

To this problem we must also add the implications of the rule of supply and demand. We have already mentioned one aspect of this in the tendency for rents to be fixed according to demand at the time when a tenancy was first created. There is a further dimension of this however. After the demographic collapse of the fourteenth century – whether dated from the famine years of the second decade or the sharp contraction in numbers produced by plague in mid-century and later – it was inevitable that a shortage of tenants and a reduction in demand would be met by falling rents (for instance, above: 60, 297–8). If we add to this the destruction of property and the localised depopulation of the countryside in some areas of the North Sea area over the same period, it follows that rents were generally much lower by the mid-fifteenth century than they were a hundred years before. Whilst the rural economy was often running at a low ebb at this time, it is likely that the share of the tenant's income taken by lords was also at an all-time low.

The revival of population and the increase in demand in the later fifteenth and early sixteenth centuries which seems to have been fairly general over the North Sea area therefore offered lords a challenge as well as an opportunity. We have already suggested that tenants regarded the land as theirs and not their lords' (or, at the least, they saw their use-right in the land as taking precedence over the lord's interest). In the same way, where rents were paid, tenants tended to regard them as fixed by custom. Of course, it was part of the peasant character that these rents could be reduced in times of adversity: it was much harder to have tenants accept increases in their rent to reflect a shifting balance of demand.

The challenge that this posed to landlords has often been discussed in the Marxist debate over the Transition from Feudalism to Capitalism. In effect, landlords had four options. One was to accept the existing levels of rent, which were probably tied to the hereditary possession of land by the tenants; the second to find ways of loading additional rent onto the tenants which might entail the third, the entire reformulation of the tenurial relationship, which normally involved the introduction of the lease. The fourth possibility was to dispossess the tenants and for the lord to take the land into demesne to be cultivated by the lord himself (although this land could be subsequently let by lease). Of course, tenants could be expected to resist the growth of the lord's powers over their land. The lord's freedom of manoeuvre could be restricted by the capacity of the tenants to organise in defence of their old rights and customs and the attitude of the state and its judicial wings to what could all too easily be characterised as landlord oppression.

There were then a variety of ways in which the lord could try and recoup some of his losses in the more favourable economic conditions of the sixteenth century. Which option was chosen depended on a range of factors. It is clear that in some parts of northern Europe, especially areas within the Low Countries, the seigneurial interest was so atrophied by the end of the Middle Ages that for many purposes it had ceased to exist. In France and England we see the continued existence of mixed polities of customary tenancy and leasehold. Whilst customary tenancies are seen with hindsight as a low yielding asset in England (after all, extensive areas of it survived into the twentieth century), it may not have been so disadvantageous to lords in the sixteenth century when they could charge entry fines at market rates. It was later judicial rulings which had the effect of ensuring that fines were limited to a small part of the capital value of the property to ensure that an inheriting tenant's right of inheritance could not be denied by a lord asking for too high a fine. It was this, and the customary tenants' assumption that fines were notional, that ensured that customary tenancies were wasting assets. Over the longer term, the tendency was for the customary tenant to pay only a small fixed rent and the occasional fine to his lord, and to collect for himself the profits of farming from (sub-) tenants (above: 58–9).

In retrospect, the right choice for lords was to adopt the lease. (For recent work on the lease, van Bavel and Schofield, 2009). The lease, by being time limited, allowed rents to be readjusted periodically. It also allowed lords to create competition between potential tenants by having them bid against each other. That said, the force of the lease could be blunted where the tenants were able to maintain solidarity against their lords and ostracise interloping tenants. Where seigneurial supervision was inattentive, they could try and erect customs which gave them rights of sale of their lease and the right to the first option on the releasing of the property. Customs whereby a departing tenant was allowed to sell some forms of asset onto his successor also emerged. Hence customary claims were not wholly incompatible with leasehold (above: 178, 203, 204–5).

Landlords within some areas of the eastern North Sea area adopted a different strategy marked by the extension of the landed area directly cultivated by the lord. Taking land in hand to farm directly was also associated with the extension of labour rents or corvée. This made the tenants of the remaining peasant farms responsible for the supply of both the labour to cultivate their lord's lands as well as the supply of animals and capital equipment. Whilst the lord forewent the advantages of money rents, he also passed on to his tenants many of the costs of farming, including the cost of labour itself. Here the character of the contract between landlord and tenant mattered less than the form in which rent was paid (above: 235–36, 294–97). Exactly why this 'refeudalisation' should have been attractive to landlords is far from certain. In some areas it may be a response to legislative controls over money rent; in others it reflects the seigneurial interest in profiting from the Baltic grain trade. As 'Second serfdom' grew incrementally over time, there was also a degree of path dependency about it: that every extension in practice grew naturally from what had gone before. We discuss this at greater length below.

13.3 The form of rent

The form of rent needs to be seen as distinct matter from the form of tenancy. A survey of the rural history of the North Sea area produces a whole range of forms of rent, some of them historically specific. Again, there is a general evolution towards a simple form of rent, the payment of cash, in those areas where some form of tenancy survived. Historically we can identify a range of forms of payment, including the payment of a fixed quantity of produce (although this might be paid as a money equivalent), the payment of a proportion of the produce in sharecropping, payment of rent in the form of labour or payment in cash. Landowners might also farm themselves, in which case their return from the land was a varying quantity of produce which they could use to victual their houses or sell into the open market.

We may suppose that there was a preference for the payment of specie as being the easiest to manage but also the one which transferred the greatest risk to the tenant. The value of the produce from a farm varies from year to year according to both the quantity and the value of the crop. Whilst it is often supposed that poor years with high prices produce high incomes for farmers, this is not necessarily so (Overton, 1996: 21). In theory the farmer pays a fixed rent for his farm, making (after the payment of his rent) a surplus in some years and a loss in others. In reality, in years of both high prices and low prices, farmers might have to carry arrears of rent from one year to the next. Ultimately a debt relationship between a farmer and his landlord might be settled by the seizure of his goods and his eviction. But, the point is that until it was paid or forgiven, the farmer carried a personal debt for unpaid rent.

By contrast, the payment of rent in crops in sharecropping involves the landlord in accepting some of the risk of outputs and prices varying from year to year. Where rent is paid in labour, the lord has the difficulty of disposing of the crop and so again accepts some of the risk. In the Scottish system, where rents were paid in crops, but valued against a local price index, some of the risk was avoided but the landlord could not predict what quantity of produce he would receive in any one year, for its quantity would rise and fall whilst its notional value would remain fixed. In some districts of north-west Germany in the eighteenth century, the value at which labour services were commutated was measured annually against a state-produced price index (above: 239).

Risk then offers an additional explanation of why landlords might prefer money rents although it was never possible for them to avoid all of the risk inherent in agriculture. Tenants might go bankrupt, indebted tenants might flee before their goods could be confiscated and, as in north-west Germany, customs could arise which compelled the landlord to accept a shortfall in rents in a poor year (above: 239). But the acceptance of produce or labour rents could be a necessity. It solved problems of coin shortage and monetary instability. It made it easier for tenants to pay rents in areas of low urbanisation where the classic model of the farmer taking his grain to market week by week simply could not operate. These are all reasons why landlords should involuntarily be compelled to accept produce or labour rents. It needs to be asked whether in some circumstances landlords deliberately sought produce rents in much the same way as they sought to increase the extent of their demesnes, because they saw profit in being involved in the grain trade. There is some evidence which suggests that they did (above: 236, 294–5). Moreover, as we observed before, the use of labour rents could be seen as being 'free', being in addition to existing money rents. They also brought with them the use of tenant's equipment, so allowing the lord to avoid the real costs of capitalising his farm operation. Seen in this light, the use of corvée labour seems less a ideological and more a pragmatic response to a particular conjunction of opportunities – or problems. The difficulty, we suggested earlier, is that once a particular course has been embarked upon, it tended to determine future developments. Landowners could be locked into decisions taken by their predecessors. Hence, if manorial demesne farming ceased to pay, then landlords could resort to a half-way house of leasing the demesne to a bailiff – often a peasant entrepreneur – rather than dismantling a system which had served them well and might do so again in the future. Any form of institution could outlive its original purpose because once established, it was difficult to unpick, especially where it had come to form a species of property which had its own value, and which its owners saw as requiring compensation on its abolition. In this light it is easy to see how neo-serfdom might be an answer to one set of circumstances but survive into greatly altered conditions as an anachronism.

13.4 Changes in farm structure

At the end of the twentieth century, farm sizes throughout the North Sea area were much larger than had ever been the case in the past. This was a stage in a process which began in the Middle Ages and has continued, though not consistently, nor at the same speed in all countries, through to the present day and which will doubtless continue into the future. It marks the transition from peasants, who had only small landholdings, cultivated primarily by their family group, and who ate a high proportion of the produce of their holding, to farmers, capitalists with extensive landholdings, who often had large numbers of labourers in their employment in the nineteenth century and substantial capital machinery at their disposal in the twentieth, and who ate little or none of their produce of their farm. Instead they sold their production to middlemen and factors operating in capitalist markets for processing and resale.

There has not been a linear transition from peasant to farmer in all areas. The English transition is still taken as the usual although in many respects a market-led growth in farm size is far from characteristic of northern Europe as a whole. In Scotland, the growth in farm size in the eighteenth century seems to have been much more an aspect of the landlords' reorganisation of the landscape (above: 91). In some regions, particularly the Netherlands and Belgium, there has been a strong tendency to fragmentation and morcellization. By the early twentieth century, this had resulted in a mass of holdings of only 1–4 ha, and it was only after the end of the Second World War that this trend was reversed and a process of consolidation begun (above: 207–08). Some districts in medieval East Anglia reveal a similar fragmentation before the Black Death but a consolidation of holdings subsequently. In the Low Countries this did not happen because smallholders from the late Middle Ages onwards often combined farming with proto-industrial activities and market-oriented services. The agriculture practised here was highly labour-intensive and market-oriented, including dairy farming and the production of fruit, vegetables, flax and other cash crops. This type of agriculture was well-suited to the structure of smallholdings and at the same time perpetuated it. The resulting population growth caused further fragmentation of holdings (above: 174, 181). The viability of these smallholdings was assisted by the appearance of a new food crop, the potato, in the eighteenth century.

Historically rural societies have contained a diversity of farm sizes. Demesne farms have tended to be large units, often increasing in size as tenant farms were folded into them. Tenant farms have also often shown a tendency to increase in size over time. These same communities often also contained cottagers or smallholders, sometimes with land, sometimes without, sometimes independent figures living off their land, access to commons and dual economies, sometimes almost entirely the dependent workers of larger farmers and the proprietors of demesnes. Large holdings had to co-exist with smaller farms and smallholdings because of the need for labour to be transferred within the village from smaller farms which could not support a full-time farmer to those properties which were labour-deficient.

Large farms and smallholdings and cottages were therefore linked in a symbiotic relationship: the one normally needed the other. From the earliest evidence in the estate surveys towards the end of the first millennium, the peasantry was already stratified. The original divide in the ninth to eleventh centuries between the substantial tenants with 6–12 ha and the smallholders and cottagers with less than 2 ha or less, a gap which widened until by the early modern period a substantial minority of tenants and farmers had 20–100 ha, and many labourers had no more than a cottage, or were farm servants entirely dependent on their employers for bed and board. Hence, there was always a section of village society which employed labour, and another section that needed to earn wages, but by the eighteenth century many countrysides possessed a group of landless workers had become entirely dependent on their earnings. Such a group were the by-product of the clearances of the Scottish lowlands where the abolition of the cottar (smallholder) as a class led to the appearance of the labourer who was entirely dependent on his employer and might receive some of his wage in potato ground and manure. Similar dependent relationships are found in Germany and Sweden (above: 91, 257, 318–19, 325).

The growth of the landless populations produced social problems which might be solved, to a degree, through the development of rural industries. Farmers could take advantage of this by creating smallholdings or offering cottages for extremely high rents. But where rural industry did not take root, the answer to rural landlessness and unemployment might well be out-migration, occasionally abroad, more often, by the mid-nineteenth century, to the growing urban centres. The result might well be rural depopulation, which posed problems for farmers when they required casual labour at the seasonal peaks.

The answer to the twin problems of a landless element in rural society as well as rural depopulation, adopted in a number of European countries, was the government-sponsored creation of smallholdings in the late nineteenth and early twentieth century. The fall in grain prices following the inflow of cheap extra-European corn led, in the 1880s, to a crisis foremost for large scale commercial grain growers. In most countries there was a switch over to dairy farming and animal husbandry, and to horticulture, in general to the production of those commodities for which demand was increasing due to rising incomes in industrial urban areas (in which we would include the British market). This opened possibilities for smallholders. At the same time, economies of scale were achieved through the development of cooperative processing and distribution. Large farmers who were afraid to lose their labour supply through emigration favoured workers who were bound to the land and who, by their own labour, made up much of the reproduction cost of labour. Nationalists used the smallholders movement to fight emigration and radical liberal reformers idealized a society made up of independent small property owners.

The creation of smallholders therefore solved a number of problems and could serve the needs of a number of differing groups. More or less simultaneously, a number of governments created credit funds from which smallholders could borrow to finance the purchase of land and obtain working capital. They also took steps to obtain land from estates, if necessary by compulsory purchase. Smallholdings were also favoured in a number of nations as the solution to the resettlement of servicemen returning from the First World War (above: 89, 274, 326, 337–8). For a period, smallholding seemed a win-win solution to a number of rural problems. Retarded industrial expansion in the inter-war period tended to preserve many of the smallholders, as there was little demand for labour from other sectors, and the great wave of farm mechanisation and motorization which started in the 1920s in the United States did not spread to Europe at that time because land-labour ratios were very different. That said, by the mid-twentieth century much of the logic which had underpinned the creation of smallholdings had become anachronistic. The idea that a livelihood could be made from labour-intensive, peasant-style forms of spade cultivation, fruit production or pigs and poultry was rightly seen to be a dead end. Government policy universally swung from the defence of the smallholder and the small farmer to viewing them both as a problem.

Where free markets in land existed, or where the estates remained able to direct the shape of farming, farm size had increased over time. Certainly in seventeenth- and eighteenth-century England, the small farmers of one generation tend to be the medium-sized farmers of the previous generation, as income pressures forced farmers to strive for the advantage of scale. The agricultural depression of the late nineteenth century made many existing farms unviable even where domestic prices were maintained by the imposition of tariff barriers or the development of export trades. Given the inability of European producers to match the price of American and Russian grain in European markets, there was a flight into dairying, especially butter and cheese-making, but the market for farm butter and cheese was diminishing in an age which valued the consistency of factory-produced products. Cooperative dairies emerged in a number of countries as a means to maintain the family farm in adverse conditions. It gave them an outlet for their raw milk, reduced the costs of processing, produced a uniform quality product and undertook its marketing into national and international markets (above: 267, 270, 330–1). It may be suggested that the adoption of cooperation allowed the family farm to survive for a couple of generations, and deferred the need for it to grow in size. Likewise the adoption of mechanisation, especially after the Second World War, gave the farm a further period of grace as capital investment allowed it to shed labour.

On the other hand, the adoption of machinery changed the optimum size of the farm and it became rational to merge farms. Government increasingly no longer saw advantage – merely cost – in the survival of smaller farms, and most European governments introduced programmes for the state-sponsored amalgamation of farms. This has often involved the surviving farmers buying or taking on lease the land of their less successful neighbours (above: 21, 89, 143, 146–47, 219, 257, 341–2). The second half of the twentieth century therefore saw substantial increases in mean farm size throughout northern Europe. The threshold for profitability of a farm in Schleswig Holstein, as we saw earlier, was judged to be 20–30 ha in about 1960 but by 2005 it had reached 100 ha. Mean farm size grew from 20.8 ha to 57.0 ha. Changes of this scale can be found in most other countries.

Although farm size has increased, governments have remained strongly committed to the idea of the family farm in the sense of the farm owned by its cultivator. With the replacement of farm labour by machinery, this has increasingly become the farm on which the sole employees were the farmer and his close family. The seasonal need for labour has often been replaced by the agricultural contractor who supplies harvesting machinery – and the specialist labour to use it – for a few days each year.

It is true that there are advantages inherent in the family farm. The cost of supervising workers tends to make very large scale farm enterprises inefficient. In many ways family labour is easier to motivate and control (there are sanctions for ill-discipline which do not exist if labour is hired) and a potential heir can be motivated to work hard as he has a long term interest in the success of the enterprise. But perhaps one of the overwhelming reasons for the survival of the family farm is that farming has, increasingly over the past half century, been unable to offer reasonable wages to its workers or an adequate return on capital. The ambition of the post-war generation of agricultural trade unions to secure for their members a household income comparable to those of industrial society failed. Rather than a business, farming has often become a vocation, perhaps even an hereditary vocation into which the farmer is born and for which he suffers a life of low income. Intensive seasonal farm enterprises – for instance fruit picking or vegetable harvesting – and many round the year enterprises (say poultry slaughter, processing and packing) are now the preserve of migrant labour throughout the North Sea area as the wages offered are unattractive to native workers. Where farm enterprises are currently profitable, one often sees either farming on a considerable scale (in arable production) or the adoption of value-added processing on the farm itself, be in farm cheese, yoghurt or ice cream, or preserved meats.

13.5 Commercialisation and urbanisation

Whilst we can say that the North Sea area was one of the most commercialised and urbanised areas of Europe, it encompassed a wide range of societies, some highly and precociously developed and others much more lightly so. A clear core can be distinguished in a triangular zone which includes the western Low Countries, north-eastern France and south-east England. Goods – and people – flowed towards this core area. Even by the end of the Middle Ages, the influence of this zone extended throughout the North Sea area: increasingly it extended well beyond it.

The impact of the urban economies can be seen to operate at a variety of levels, all of them influenced or even skewed by towns and urban elites. There is firstly the impact in the immediate vicinity from which goods can be supplied by men and women walking to urban markets, or taking goods by horse, carts and latterly motor vehicles, perhaps on a daily basis or to a weekly market. Characteristically these are perishable products – vegetables, milk, poultry – but also bulky products including firewood. Secondly, there are then those products which can be conveyed over the medium distance because their value will stand the cost of transport. Especially notable here is grain and cattle (although the latter are often fattened and brought to prime on pastures on the fringes of towns) but also preserved dairy products. As we observed in the introduction, the distance that grain can be carried in pre-industrial societies is determined by distance, but that access to the sea or inland waterways foreshortens distance. Marketing is often highly regulated and sometimes influenced by all kinds of urban privileges or even outright market coercion, as most clearly exercised by the Flemish towns in the late Middle Ages. Finally, we have those products which are brought long distances, barrelled fish or wine for instance. The impact of a town may therefore be felt over a much greater area than its immediate market hinterland; that of a great city might extend over several hundred miles. In this way the growing Dutch urban economy stimulated the production of grain in north Germany and Poland at the end of the Middle Ages. Three hundred years later, the industrial markets of Britain stimulated grain growing in such improbable areas as Hanover, Scandinavia, Scotland and Ireland and later still, drew butter and cheese from Denmark and Sweden (as well, of course, from its colonies).

However, in order to compete in distant markets with more local grain producers, distant producers needed to have two advantages. The first was volume and the second low labour costs, the latter necessary to counter what were inevitably higher transport costs than those which local producers would face. This tended to produce a particular configuration of distant producers: extensive manorial or estate demesnes, using corvée labour or at later date, labour paid in kind, whether housing, liveries of grain or potato ground. We would not suggest that this is the only reason for corvée labour being resorted to – we have offered others – but the preference for labour rent over money rent suggests societies in which the prime income for landlords came from the sale of grain into international markets rather than the cash rents of tenants. In fact the efficiency of low cost but distant producers, whether the East Elbian producers in the early sixteenth century or the Americans after the 1870s, was such that they not only matched local producers, but undercut them. Hence, as is well known, grain growing largely disappeared from parts of northern Europe after the 1880s and continued on a much diminished scale elsewhere. In its place there was a recourse to dairying and meat production. East Elbian grain had had much the same impact on the early sixteenth-century Dutch rural economy, displacing the districts from which the Dutch had traditionally drawn their grain, discouraging grain production in areas of high risk or high cost, and encouraging the Dutch farmer to move into horticulture, dairying and industrial crops. This is not to say that grain growing disappeared entirely, far from it, for the Dutch had a different asset available to them in the form of copious urban night soil and, through the system of internal canals, a cheap and efficient means to bringing it from town to countryside. What we see in reaction to the penetration of the grain market is the development of intensive systems of farming, one element of which was a bread grain, in short a recourse to the production of higher value goods (de Vries and Van der Woude, 1997: 198–204). The recourse to dairying in the later nineteenth century was a similar response to a similar problem.

This allows us to identify one of the reasons for the precocious escape from the Malthusian trap: not merely intensive agriculture but also the wealth to access foodstuffs from well outside the urban zone. The Amsterdam grain market supplied East-Elbian grain to its regular customers whilst maintaining a reserve which could be sent where it was required (de Vries and Van der Woude, 1997: 414–19). This was the pull of high prices, and so we have reports of 'Danzig' (Gdansk) grain being imported to alleviate poor harvests into England in the later 1590s and again in the early 1620s, years in which it was also imported into Wales and Scotland too (for Scotland see Flinn, 1977: 122, 124).

Of course, these changes also involved the dismantlement of traditional views of how the market should operate. The medieval notion, well evidenced in England, that grain should be brought to market by its producers and sold under regulated conditions – which often favoured townspeople – and the common prejudice against reselling were inappropriate when grain was being collected by factors to be conveyed over long distances or was being supplied by merchants who were themselves at the end of long supply chains. Moreover, urban purchasers increasingly bought flour rather than grain. Nonetheless, urban grain markets continued to be closely regulated until there was confidence that supplies were robust enough for the government to stand back and allow free markets to operate. The date at which this situation was achieved varied markedly from nation to nation: compare, for instance, the indifference of government to the English grain market after 1650 with the debates over the regulation of the French grain market in the revolutionary years of the 1790s. In Sweden, public granaries survived until their abolition in 1824 (above: 72, 97, 157–58, 334; Persson, 1999).

The varying ease with which towns could be accessed, as well as environmental considerations, means that we should expect quite large variations in agricultural practice but also wealth over short distances. It is not even certain that proximity to a town offered a greater stimulus to the countryside, rather it may well have offered a *different* stimulus. In an uncomplicated world one might assume that the further from a town one went, the less intensive and the more extensive the prevailing farming regime would become.

Farmers bought foodstuffs and unmanufactured commodities to the town. In return they bought manufactured goods, exotic foodstuffs including wines and spirits, they bought leisure, legal services and in Protestant Europe they probably came to hear sermons too. In years of distress, they doubtless came in search of charity. They also went to town to pay rents, borrow money and settle debts. There can be no doubt that there were many bourgeois, at all periods, who had money which they wished to invest. They had many reasons for wanting to do so. For one there was the safety of investments in land and the return they offered. This allowed a means of diversifying out of trade: conversely, land could underpin trading activities by offering a capital reserve which could be accessed at time of illiquidity or even failure. For a minority of the most wealthy, the acquisition of land involved the purchase of an estate, with a house, park and perhaps sporting rights, and jurisdiction over tenants. Successful bourgeois were always willing to prey on the misfortunes of unsuccessful gentry and to acquire their estates. At times when the crown (England, Sweden) or revolutionary regimes (France in the 1790s) were willing to sell land, they might also take the opportunity to invest. Urban capital was active in the consortia who drained polders in the late sixteenth- and seventeenth-century Netherlands. Much urban money was also lent to peasants and farmers. This might ultimately result in the acquisition of their land; but in most cases the principal was surely repaid.

The sale of land by peasants was particularly marked in years of high prices and near or actual famine. It is a familiar phenomena from late thirteenth and early fourteenth century England, but sixteenth-century harvest failure there had no obvious impact on the land market and it may be hazarded that with the growth of holding size, a moment of vulnerability had passed. It remains a marked feature of French peasant society in the eighteenth century although it is suggested that much of this land returned into the hands of the peasantry in the years after a crisis and that its bourgeois purchasers were disinterested in holding small parcels of land for long periods (above: 116–17).

The degree of urban penetration of rural land markets varied from country to country. In England it has barely been considered as a phenomenon because of the assumption that lawyers or merchants amassing estates would, in the second generation, emerge as landholding gentry. The urban ownership of the single farm has barely been considered. The French, Belgian and Dutch countrysides were, from an early date, well penetrated by urban landowners but selectively, for land near towns was preferred. In Germany, after the enfranchisement of the serfs, steps were taken in some territories to stop the acquisition of land by townspeople whilst it was not a significant feature of the Scandinavian countryside, perhaps because their urban sector was weakly developed and for those with money, better opportunities were available (above: 114, 116–17, 173–74, 273, 287). The interest urban society had in the acquisition of rural land varied over time: when returns were high it was an attractive investment, but as in the Netherlands, at times of agricultural crisis, individuals and even endowed charities sought to divest themselves of land and move their capital into better performing investments (above: 203; de Vries and van der Woude, 1997; 218 for other examples). This allowed farmers to reacquire land which they, or their ancestors, had sold (above: 203).

The essential pre-condition which underpins urban intervention in the land market has to be the existence of secure and specified property rights. This simple requirement surely limited the circulation of credit in feudal society. From the point of view of the lender or mortgagor, looking for secure investments, lending on the security of goods if these could be confiscated by a lord on the death of a debtor, or on life tenancies of uncertain duration, was plainly dangerous. Likewise, long term investments in land required that the investor should have full ownership of the land or something akin to it: it also needed to be free from arbitrary impositions and any danger that the urban investor would be treated as a serf or his urban possessions might become liable to being seized by a lord. Urban investors may have had no outlet for their capital if full property rights did not exist; nor could peasants or farmers borrow from urban lenders unless the latter were convinced that their investment was secure. Hence it may be seen how under some seigneurial regimes, capital for investment could be in short supply. There might be little activity in a land market where borrowing was difficult because ownership was insecure. Conversely, urban capital must have been a major force in establishing full property rights.

It is therefore not too hard to see why there should have been a degree of correlation between the freehold possession of land and urban ownership, nor why urban ownership should have been an active force in the disintegration of feudalism. In the Low Countries, urban capital could have a further transformative effect on rural societies dominated by small freeholding peasants as in the surroundings of Ghent, Antwerp and particularly in Holland. The latter region in the sixteenth century saw the rapid extension of burgher landownership, as a result of the continuing purchase of small plots of land from peasants, and their consolidation into large tenant farms. This is but an aspect of a much larger phenomenon, the buying up of independent freeholding peasants by urban capital and the long term transformation of societies of freeholders into societies in which tenancy was the norm (above: 177).

13.6 Government

In the introduction we argued that the state needs to be seen as an independent player, concerned to achieve its own objectives. These may be relatively simple: its own preservation from internal and external enemies, the maintenance of established property rights and public peace, in the twentieth century the improvement of the living standards of its citizens through economic growth, redistributionist public policies or a mixture of the two. Beyond this it may be useful to see the state as being at the centre of a range of competing power groups which sought to determine its policies. There are obviously enough landowners and peasantries. Whilst we may see them as being opposed and in a form of balance (the influence of one rises as the other falls), in fact the purchase that either of them exercised over government diminished progressively over the nineteenth and twentieth centuries. In many respects the power of both has been superseded by that of urban populations who, of course, numerically predominate in parliamentary democracies. We should also assign weight to public intellectuals with a vision for agriculture, whether medieval lawyers concerned to confer corporate status on the village in France and the Low Countries, physiocrats and other reformers in the eighteenth century or the architects of the European Community in the mid-twentieth. Finally, late twentieth-century government has been subjected to the lobbying of recreational and amenity groups, environmental and conservation groups, all with their own agendas, but which may often be seen as anti-farming. In combination with low prices and the farmers' loss of esteem, they have provoked debate over how the countryside should be used, over the responsibility of government to the farmer, and the responsibility of the farmer to both the larger public community which pays him through subsidies and to the landscape itself.

In order to survive the state needed to ensure its own financial survival. The long term tendency was for states to shed their landed base. Admittedly, most medieval monarchies seem to have been poor stewards of their lands, perhaps because they were, by definition, forced to work through intermediaries, and the local management of the lands often became a dimension of the exercise of monarchial patronage. There were irresistible temptations to grant land to reward political supporters or, in medieval Europe, to endow monastic houses in the hope of purchasing an easy passage into the world beyond. The sale of land also funded wars, and so in a strange way, the loss of landed endowments was all part and parcel of the early modern state building. Hence it was perhaps not a question of whether a monarchy would run out of lands, but how quickly. The Holy Roman Empire was merely an early example of a tendency to disendowment (above: 230).

At some moments the state could re-endow itself by the confiscation of land, either from those to whom the land had been granted (a strategy with a high political cost attached, but used in Sweden in 1680) (above: 292) or by the seizure of the lands of the church, but this was a trick which could only be played once. In England the re-endowment of the Tudor monarchy with the estates of the church only really lasted for a generation: the temptation to use the capital value of the endowment to pursue aggressive wars was all too great (above: 54, 231, 292). In these circumstances states were forced into switching from being 'domain states' into 'taxation states'. If states became taxation states however, they were then in a competition with landowners for the peasant surplus. In this respect states may be broadly categorised as being pro-landowner – in an alliance with them against the peasantry – or pro-peasant, in which case they tended to see the landowning aristocracy as opponents. The long term tendency in all European states was to be pro-peasant in that they sought to being about the dissolution of aristocratic landholding. Whilst this might be overtly a way of striking against the nobility, it may at some times be justified in terms of personal freedom or as a means of releasing the economic potential of the peasantry. Pro-peasant policies may be seen in the actions of the Counts of Flanders against their subordinate landowners in the twelfth century, granting charters to peasant communities, in the support of copyhold by English courts in the sixteenth century, the enfrancisement of serfs in Denmark and the German states in the late eighteenth and early nineteenth century and in the taxation policies of those twentieth-century states which set out to favour the owner-occupier over the landowner (above: 187, 59, 262–65, 97, 203).

States also needed to ensure their own political survival. This takes us out of the countryside. Brenner saw agrarian class structure as being something determined in the countryside: but over time, this is increasingly not so. Government had always to balance the needs of countryside with those of towns. European history is littered with examples of states which lost the ready compliance of their subjects. Faced with insubordination or even revolt on a large scale, there was little that medieval or early modern states could do; and for that reason it was better to appease rather than incite. This was especially the case with urban populations and for that reason governments attempted to configure the supply of food to towns to suit urban demands at the cost of rural needs. To this end, medieval marketing arrangements were often designed to give advantage to urban purchasers over rural suppliers.

But, as we have mentioned before, the growth of urban and industrial sectors within the countryside shifted the equation further away from the peasantry to the point where government was more attentive to urban that rural needs. From around 1875 or 1880, have a situation in which some – not all – European governments favoured the import of foodstuffs at prices which undercut domestic production. Hence in industrial, nascent democracies, a calculation was made that cheap food policies were more important than policies which protected the domestic farming community. From this calculation, which was perhaps the only one that governments could make, a great deal followed.

First, where landowners remained important in the countryside, falling farm incomes naturally fed into diminished rents, and that in turn encouraged the sale of land to their occupiers.

Second, at the same time, low prices provoked the establishment of peasant organisations which came to supersede the more genteel farmer's clubs of the early and mid-nineteenth century with their interest in technical innovation and the development of farming standards. Peasant unions, born out of a reaction to free trade and low prices, offered a new challenge to government. Almost universally governments coped with them by incorporating these organisations into the fabric of the state, delegating state roles to them (and even allowing them to tax and involving them in commodity price setting). At an extreme this resulted in the amalgamation of all agricultural organisations into a single state-sponsored organisation, the National Socialist *Reichsnährstand* (above: 270). The high point of the involvement of corporate government in agriculture came with the reversal of free trade policies, a development of the 1930s which reached its apogee during and after the Second World War, and the corresponding development of productivist policies. Ministries of agriculture became ministries for farmers, especially in the pro-productivist conditions of the forty years or so years after the war. They shared personnel with the farming community and the farmer's organisations, not least in the Netherlands (above: 221). Faced with determined lobbying from farmer's organisations, governments could also accede to their demands for greater legal rights against their landlords, including longer terms of tenancy, compensation on eviction, the right to take game or vermin (above: 85, 144, 202, 205, 213). So it may be seen how low prices and agricultural depression after the 1890s contained nuggets of advantage for the farming community.

Third, faced with an urban working class that was numerically in the majority, government could also seek to strengthen its hand against them by developing the peasantry into a conservative, landholding bulwark against socialism. This partially explains the popularity of government-sponsored smallholding movements in some European nations at the end of the nineteenth century and later (above: 89, 274, 337–8). This aspect of the politicisation of the peasantry in some countries, seen at an extreme in Germany during the 1930s, produced a strong identification of the peasantry with the national spirit or ethos and a hostility to the urban masses which became associated with eugenic ideas of national degeneration (above: 163, 279, 343–4).

A fourth response to low prices was to make government much more active in regulating the quality of produce, especially when this was to enter export markets (making quality a matter of national repute), but ultimately to ensure that domestic produce matched imported produce in quality. This also necessitated improving farm standards and it was to this end that government-sponsored education emerged as a positive factor at the end of the nineteenth century, to be progressively elaborated by the establishment of specialist higher education institutions and state advisory services in the twentieth.

In truth though, it is impossible to see the engagement of farmer's organisations with government in agrarian corporatism as doing much more than making the weather.

The climate, the broad environment in which farmers operated, was determined by external considerations and larger political calculations. All the responses of government to low prices we have just mentioned were conditioned by a determination to maintain elements of free trade and cheap food. And whilst the farmers might be seen as being hand in glove with government after 1945, the abrupt way in which policy turned against them after the 1980s shows just how far their power was a chimera, conditional on other factors favouring them.

It should not be supposed that states were invariably pro-peasant. It is also possible to find instances in which states acted to strengthen the hand of landowners, notably during periods of population shortage when they tried to maintain landlord incomes through tying tenants to the land. This may be seen as a dimension of a larger tendency to configure labour markets so that they served the interests of elite social groups – farmers in other circumstances – and placed the employed at a disadvantage against the employers in the institutions of employment (above: 71, 73, 301, 324–25). Some states could also go further than this, and assign some of the roles of the state, especially judicial powers, to landowners (above: 301).

13.7 Government, enclosure and landscape change

One particular area of government engagement with the countryside – in driving forwards enclosure, consolidation and landscape change – requires particular consideration. Enclosure is a matter which historians – and their students – often find confusing. It is generally seen to involve two things: the conversion of land subject to common rights into land held in severalty (where an individual owner has the sole right of use) and the reorganisation of the countryside so that individual owners have their land in a single parcel within a ring fence. Within that fence they have an exclusive right to exploit that land for their sole advantage without communal restraints.

This dual definition is appropriate when we are discussing the enclosure of open fields or sub-divided arable, a situation in which the cultivators of the land (who may also be its owners) have land scattered within an arable field or fields or commons in the sense of common grazing. The second part of the definition is less appropriate if we look at enclosure over a longer time span. The dual definition applies only to enclosure in the eighteenth and nineteenth centuries and so describes a specific process applied to certain types of land in certain conditions. But the eighteenth- and nineteenth-century enclosure movement is only part of a much longer process. We might suggest that it is actually the second of three phases of enclosure.

Although the Bible does not tell us, one assumes that the Garden of Eden was unenclosed. The point to be made here is that every act of making an arable open field out of waste, every assart from the coastal wastelands of the Low Countries, the British Pennines, the wastes of Brittany or the Scandinavian mountains, is an act of enclosure. Even the making of *marken* out of the heathlands of Drenthe and north-west Germany is an act of enclosure in the sense that the common and the rights over it were defined and limited even if the land itself remained open. Initially enclosure is a process whereby land was taken from the waste, its use was changed and intensified, and it became subject to new forms of property rights (which may, or may not, be rights in severalty). In this perspective, the enclosure of an open field or common in the eighteenth or nineteenth century is the second enclosure of that tract of land, the first perhaps having been six or seven centuries earlier.

Dyer has recently written of the 'enclosure movement in England, 1220–1349' and this is surely right (Dyer, 2006). The great age of expansion in the rural economy in the eleventh and twelfth centuries saw the enclosure of enormous areas of land through the creation and extension of open fields, individual farms and the definition of the remaining commons. This was a process in which some governments had a hand, the Counts of Holland and Zeeland and the bishops of Utrecht, for instance, authorising the drainage of the coastal marshes of Flanders (above: 171, 192–93). Elsewhere government could have a negative effect on enclosure by defining areas of wood and forest which were not to be enclosed but which, were reserved for elite sport (although the deer often shared with commoners' cattle) (above: 73–4, 130, 156). In the late medieval depression, the forms enclosure took altered. In place of the incorporation of more land into intensive farming systems, rural depopulation forced the abandonment of arable cultivation in some areas and the adoption of extensive pastoral cultivation in its place. This typically resulted in the depopulation of villages and individual farms although it remains a vexed question how far this was a reaction to changed conditions and how far lords sought deliver the final coup to settlements which were already weakened. Warfare and the destruction of property in civil strife also brought about rural depopulation in some limited areas.

With the renewal of population growth in the later fifteenth and early sixteenth century, enclosure started again: but it is at this point that we see a distinction arising between England and its continental neighbours. Population growth in England did not bring about any cessation in the enclosure of open field arable. This continued throughout the sixteenth, seventeenth and eighteenth centuries, often bringing about the conversion of arable to pasture and the localised depopulation of the countryside. At the same time there was a movement to enclose commons and wastes. It has been estimated that by the end of the seventeenth century 75 per cent of the land area of England had been enclosed. This was not the result of any government-sponsored movement (although government did encourage the enclosure of former crown forests after about 1610). On the contrary: depopulating enclosure was illegal for much of the sixteenth century and intermittent prosecutions of enclosers continued into the 1630s. It was only after the Restoration that the English government ceased to take any interest in enclosure.

The early modern enclosure of England was therefore the result of individual initiatives, sometimes made possible because a single landowner owned the whole extent of a manor, sometimes because he had bought out the other landowners. In other cases enclosure was made by an agreement struck between the landowners, some of whom may have been owner-occupying farmers. In this event the state provided a judicial process to bind the parties to their agreement, but it did not encourage enclosure, nor did it provide any process to facilitate the making of agreements. It was therefore the pursuit of private profit which drove the enclosure of England, and this remained the case into the eighteenth century. Neither was there any government initiative underlying the classic period of parliamentary enclosure in the later eighteenth century. This was also true in Scotland where government was largely agnostic about the landlord-driven enclosure and depopulation of the Lowlands which began in the mid-eighteenth century. This is not wholly without continental parallels, for instance the early enclosure of open fields and commons in parts of Schleswig, largely undertaken by peasant initiative and which had largely been completed by the end of the eighteenth century (above: 71, 89–91, 243).

Seen in this light, the government-driven initiatives which brought about enclosure in much of northern Europe after the mid-eighteenth century were emulating something which had been achieved in Britain and one or two other locations *without* government involvement. This is a reflection of the relative weakness of peasant property rights in Britain and their corresponding strength in much of northern Europe. But it also reflects the *fragmentation* of property rights, with the ownership of land, whether freehold or customary, being divided between many individuals. There was no possibility of enclosure being driven forwards on the English model by a landowning elite or relatively small numbers of large farmers in much of northwest Europe.

Moreover, whilst European governments and their advisors plainly saw the abolition of common rights over arable lands, the reorganisation of arable and the enclosure of wastes as a necessary stage in improvement, the ways in which they were forced to bring the process about suggests all too clearly that the drive to enclosure often lacked public support and had to be imposed on the farming community. Hence the French law of 10 June 1793 which followed the rural code of 1791 had only a very limited impact since many farmers preferred to enjoy the manure of the community's animals. Inspired by the French example, the legislation of 1809–10 in the Kingdom of Holland sought to encourage the partition of the *marken* and offered tax incentives to do so. It obliged the governors of the *marken* to ballot on the desirability of dividing the commons, but only a minority did so, there were very few votes in favour of partition and only one *marken* was divided at that time. The appearance is that the proprietors with a share in the *marken* did not, at that time, see advantage in their partition: when the legislation was revived in changed circumstances in 1837, partition quickly followed (Hoppenbrouwers, 2002: 106–07).

Whilst much of the legislation was merely permissive, laying down processes which allowed peasant aspirations to be achieved, we can also see in some respects a determination to configure the process to ensure the right outcome. One of the ways in which this was done was through legislation which obliged a community to enclose at the request of a single landowner. Legislation to this end was adopted in Sweden in 1757, Denmark in 1781 and in the Netherlands, to bring about the partition of the remaining *Marken,* in 1886. In Norway legislation of 1821 threatened a penal tax on unenclosed lands although this was moderated by later legislation (above: 335–37, 209). The desire of government to bring about enclosure – and in doing so the complete restructuring of village government and society – is plain enough.

By the end of the nineteenth century there was virtually no unenclosed land left in northern Europe, lightly grazed coastal or mountain wastes excepted. Now there is a debate to be had over whether this outcome would have come about anyhow, being driven by market need, or whether the hand of government was needed to ensure that land in severalty became the universal norm. Here we may quickly refer to another debate, that over 'The tragedy of the commons' provoked by Hardin's classic article of 1968. Hardin saw the commons as essentially unregulated spaces upon which all the inhabitants of a place could draw: the long term tendency was therefore for commons to be overgrazed. It would now be accepted that Hardin misunderstood the degree to which commons were actually managed spaces. Subsequent work by Ostrom, and a great deal of work inspired by her, has described just how sophisticated the management of commons might be. Importantly, access to commons was usually limited to propertyholders and closed to the poor and itinerant. Moreover, those with the right to graze were often subjected to stints which limited their use. The exercise of common rights was policed and trespassers fined or expelled. Hence, it is much more likely than Hardin supposed that 'common pool resources' might be sustainable through achieving an equilibrium between the use of the common and its carrying capacity (de Moor *et al.* (eds), 2002 is key here). In a sense this leaves the historian with the problem of weighing some recent accounts which stress the institutional and agricultural viability of commons with the eyewitness reports of contemporaries who drew an unflattering, perhaps hyperbolic view of their (mis-)management. The possibility that commons were usually well managed must not be neglected. We cannot argue that enclosure was a solution to an institution which was beyond reform: on the contrary, some commons seem to have been vigorously managed right up to the moment of their dissolution (de Moor, 2009, offers an example from Belgium and others can be found in de Moor *et al.* (eds), 2002). We also need to appreciate that modernising movement was highly ideological and was probably not inclined to see merit in institutions which it characterised as backward. We can speculate that even with permissive legislation, the timing of enclosure to some degree lay with the community being enclosed. On the other hand, the legislation probably allowed communities with elements who wanted to enclose to break the institutional blockage which might have indefinitely deferred enclosure if a consensus was needed to bring it to fruition.

It remains a somewhat open question whether government action was needed to bring about enclosure, redistribution and partition or whether the same outcomes would have resulted from the operation of market forces. Those who advocated legislation identified open fields and commons as a problem which needed to be resolved: neither the fact of the problem nor its solution might have been accepted by those who drew their living from open fields and commons. It is surely the case that legislation, by establishing procedures by which property rights could be amended and reallocated, speeded enclosure, but the existence of the procedures did not oblige landowners to use them and in many cases they plainly resisted the opportunities which legislation offered until satisfied that the time was right. This was clearly the case in France: while north-western communities seized the opportunity of dividing commons, other regions waited decades or even rejected the possibility.

If we identify the eighteenth- and nineteenth-century movement as the second age of enclosure, then the third quarter of the twentieth century saw the third age of enclosure, with the government sponsored reorganisation of the countryside, taken to an extreme in the Netherlands and Germany with the wholesale reallocation of land (above 145, 216, 275). All countries saw some element of reshaping, with government-sponsored hedge clearance and landscape reorganisation, undertaken within a context of attempting to increase farm size and assist mechanisation. Again, this may be taken as an example of government initiative speeding what may have been inevitable changes, but ones which the market alone might have taken decades to bring about.

13.8 Speculations masquerading as a conclusion

In an English work on farming of 1853, the chapter on the purchase and tenure of land is headed by a little vignette of a farm. In front of a barn and buildings, a number of cows mill about. The buildings are plainly old: there are holes in the thatch. It is a scene of rural decrepitude. At the end of the chapter we have the parallel illustration. We see 12 oxen tethered on straw in a covered yard being fed – perhaps with chopped roots – by a farmer from a bucket. The building is modern, the beasts fat. It is a scene of well-managed industry. The contrast between these two vignettes is unavoidable. But the lesson is not one of ancient and modern, or loss and profit. The first illustration is captioned 'yearly tenancy', the second 'the long lease'. Give the tenant a long lease it says, and exploit his energy, his willingness to invest (although buildings may well have been supplied by the landlord). Deny him an interest in the future and he will not even repair the holes in the roof of his barn. The point was so obvious it was never referred to in the intervening text.[1]

And so we have to ask whether the denial of property rights in land produced farming regimes which were as backward, inefficient and unproductive as these pictures might suggest. Would one have been able to travel round the Europe of the eighteenth century and associate different agricultural regimes with different forms of tenancy? Arthur Young evidently thought so in his tours of France and condemned sharecropping in particular for dragging down agricultural practice. Yet it has been suggested that the hard facts collected by Young were overlain by Young's ideological preferences: he was an advocate of a tripartite system (of landlords, tenants and labourers) of agrarian relations, of big farms, enclosure and turnips, and so what seems like informed and impartial observation turns out to be somewhat less than that (Allen and O'Grada, 1988). Any modern attempt to relate productivity to tenure is beset with difficulties. Tenure and landholding can only be one of a number of factors which influence farming – soil, location, access to markets and the strength of market demand are plainly others. And then we have to distinguish between the desirability of different forms of productivity. The Flemish agriculture of the seventeenth and eighteenth centuries was plainly well

[1] G. H. Andrews, *Modern husbandry: a practical and scientific treatise on agriculture* (London, 1853), pp. 22, 42.

regarded at the time, but might also be condemned for its high labour inputs. If we measure the success of agriculture by the standard of living it offered its farmers, then neo-serfdom was not a failure, but there was equally a very clear belief on the part of the late eighteenth-century public intellectuals of Denmark and Germany that yet higher levels of productivity could be unleashed by enfranchisement. In exactly the same way, Young and his contemporaries thought that enclosure would handsomely repay (and how difficult economic historians have found it to demonstrate that empirically!). In our own time, the family farm has been seen to be the most efficient form of agricultural enterprise. These are matters of ideological preference as well as economic efficiency, and so in our own times the taste for big firms over small firms, for private industry over nationalised industry, free markets over tariff protection.

This may seem to suggest that the nature of property holding and tenure in the countryside did not matter in terms of productivity. Contemporaries clearly thought that it did, even if their thinking was coloured by ideology. (Their thinking might also be intensely pragmatic, perhaps seeing certain forms of property-owning tenancy as a matter of political calculation, or as a device to avoid civil unrest). Ultimately we might treat ownership and tenancy alongside the soil, the weather and the price of crops as a factor with which farmers had to cope: but it was also one which they could hope to influence through all the ways we have discussed: by negotiation, petitioning, the exercise of mutual solidarity or collective truculence, migration or abandonment, even, *in extremis*, demonstrations or rebellion. Questions of ownership and tenancy were naturally power relationships, and so political, dynamic and flexible.

The human relationships described in this book *do* matter. Peasants and farmers rarely acquiesced in the ownership of their property by others. When their interest stopped short of a full property right, they developed use rights which allowed them to buy and sell their property regardless. Their capacity to maintain these rights through their internal solidarities materially effected the wealth of the landowning class but also the state, and where lords or, at a later date, landowners, failed to maintain their ability to seize the peasant surplus or share in the farmer's profit, they disappeared as a class. It is certainly possible to argue that with the globalisation of food markets after the 1870s, the rise of industrial society, the adoption of democracy in place of government by landed elites and the appearance of many other forms of investment, power relations in the countryside have become of secondary importance. But debates over the ownership, use and access to land have far from ended and the history of farming has not come to a full stop. Indeed, the present neo-colonial race to secure farming land in such parts of the world as the Ukraine, sub-Saharan Africa and Australia suggests not that these are dead issues so much as ones of which we are ignorant. So long as we eat, there will be farming, and so long as there is farming, the issues discussed in this book, of ownership, capital, employment, labour and power will attract the attention of policy makers – and historians.

Bibliography

Allen R. C. and O'Grada, C. (1988) 'On the road again with Arthur Young: English, Irish, and French agriculture during the Industrial Revolution', *J. Economic History*, 48, pp. 93–116.

Bavel, B. J. P. van and P. R. Schofield (eds) (2009) *The development of leasehold in north-western Europe,* c. *1200–1600* (CORN Publication Series 10), Turnhout.

Dyer, C. (2006) 'Conflict in the landscape: the enclosure movement in England, 1220–1349', *Landscape History,* 28, pp. 21–33.

Flinn, M. *et al.* (1979) *Scottish population history from the seventeenth century to the 1930s*, Cambridge.

Hoppenbrouwers, P. (2002) 'The management and use of commons in the Netherlands: an overview', in M. de Moor, L. Shaw-Taylor and P. Warde (eds), *The management of common land in north-west Europe,* c.*1500–1850* (CORN Publication Series 8), Turnhout.

Moor, M. de, L. Shaw-Taylor and P. Warde (eds) (2002) *The management of common land in north-west Europe,* c.*1500–1850* (CORN Publication Series 8), Turnhout.

Moor, M. de (2009) 'Avoiding tragedies: a Flemish common and its commoners under the pressure of social and economic change during the eighteenth century', *Economic History Review*, 61, pp. 1–22.

Overton, M. (1996) *Agricultural revolution in England: the transformation of the agrarian economy, 1500–1850*, Cambridge.

Persson, K. G. (1999) *Grain markets in Europe, 1500–1900: integration and deregulation*, Cambridge.

Vries, J. de and Woude, A. Van der (1997) *The first modern economy: success, failure, and perseverance of the Dutch economy, 1500–1815*, Cambridge.